The Occult
Establishment

The Occult Establishment

James Webb

Open Court
La Salle, Illinois

OPEN COURT and the above logo are registered in the U.S. Patent & Trademark Office.

© 1976 by James Webb

First printing 1976
First paperback edition 1985
Second printing 1988
Third printing 1991

All rights reserved. No part of this publication may be reproduced, stored in a retrieval system, or transmitted, in any form or by any means, electronic, mechanical, photocopying, recording, or otherwise, without the prior written permission of the publisher, Open Court Publishing Company, La Salle, Illinois 61301.

Printed and bound in the United States of America.

Library of Congress Cataloging in Publication Data

Webb, James, 1946-1980
    The occult establishment.

    "A Library Press book."
    1. Occult sciences—History. I. Title
BF1429.W4   133'.09   75-22157
ISBN 0-87548-434-4

Contents

Preface   1

Introduction
  The Struggle for the Irrational   7

Chapter 1
  Ginungagapp   21

Chapter 2
  Eden's Folk   81

Chapter 3
    Wise Men from the East   145

Chapter 4
    The Conspiracy against the World   213

Chapter 5
    The Magi of the North   275

Chapter 6
    The Hermetic Academy   345

Chapter 7
    The Great Liberation   417

Chapter 8
    A Grammar of Unreason   489

Index   519

Preface

I HAD already begun to write this book when I discovered that I had first to come to terms with another completely neglected historical development. My starting point had been an attempt to verify or disprove some of the claims made about a relationship between Nazism and the occult. My puzzlement grew with every advance in knowledge. Some relationship obviously existed, but it was not that of popular superstition. An acquaintanceship with occult habits of thought began to reveal esoteric lore in the most unlikely places. What did this mean? I soon discovered that despite the immense amount of material on the subject, no one had bothered to discover *what "the occult" in fact is*. So my first step toward understanding the problems discussed in this book was a preliminary quest for the meaning of the "occult" and its extraordinary revival at the end of the last century.

The result of this first investigation was *The Occult Under-*

ground.* *The Occult Establishment* is less a sequel than a companion volume, and it is not necessary to have read *The Occult Underground* in order to follow the argument of the present book; the introduction and the first chapter contain all the information needed to show the role of the occult in the developments with which it is concerned. Neither will those who have read *The Occult Underground* find more than a few pages of inevitable repetition. The author believes that the arguments of either book will be greatly illuminated by those of the other.

The Occult Underground was concerned with a general crisis of 19th-century thought, of which the most important aspect was the specifically occult revival. *The Occult Establishment* is also concerned with the occult—but the occult in politics and society, and in supposedly "scientific" or "rationalist" theories of man and the universe which appear to have nothing to do with the irrational at all. In one sense, the influence of the "occult" or mystical is only one part of a process that has many other aspects; it might be argued, for example, that Albert Einstein was as much the father of the Yippies as the grand old men of the Occult Revival. In this there would be some truth—as indeed there is in the statement that Metternich or Messaens or Mickey Mouse has a direct relationship to Adolf Hitler. But for the purpose of coherent narrative, it is necessary to use a tangible key to unlock the door of huge and intangible changes; and the understanding of the occult Underground has proved such a tangible key.

The book itself will show the relevance of this Underground to mainstream history. But apart from numerous specific examples, the occult has as a category one great advantage over other "keys" to broad historical developments. It is more comprehensive. That is, the obsessive quality of occult beliefs results almost invariably in their domination of their possessor's mind Even the most circumspect analyses of *homo economicus* or man the political animal must often ignore the fact that all human beings have other sides to their natures than that specifically under discussion. Economic man may also be a lay preacher, a collector of sculpture, or a Ping-Pong

*First published in the U.K. as *The Flight from Reason* (Macdonald, 1971) and in the U.S.A. as *The Occult Underground* (Library Press/Open Court, 1974).

champion; and just conceivably these other aspects of his life may one day be treated in histories of religion, art, or table tennis. The whole man escapes. While it is obvious that to write the history of "the whole man" is impossible—particularly in the fragmented modern world—the occultist considered *as occultist* has considerable advantages over other such partial constructs of the historical imagination. He is no less likely to be involved in activities that have little to do with his occultism. But in aspects of his life that concern any philosophical or ideological alignment, his occult ideas are liable to play a leading part. If influential people are discovered to harbor occult ideas, it is quite reasonable to take these ideas as an index of a wider attitude to the broader questions of life and thus to arrive at an approximate "history of some men seen whole." For, fundamentally, occult beliefs often imply an all-embracing world-view of the sort that was once associated with religious faith and is today demanded by totalitarian politics.

It may be difficult to believe that ideas of the sort discussed in this book ever take active form. This is the result of modern orthodoxy, by which metaphysics is rigorously separated from the affairs of everyday life, and also of the sort of "history of ideas" that considers ideas in some limbo divorced from the human possessors of the minds that conceive them. I have attempted to avoid this brand of "intellectual history" and to show that unorthodox ideas are powerful forces to move men: indeed particularly powerful the more unorthodox they are, because of the increased effort that is demanded to present them favorably to others.

In no sense can *The Occult Establishment* claim to be anything more than a partial study of the developments with which it is concerned. A complete examination of what I have called "illuminated politics" would occupy more space than this book itself, while the chronological limits of the study are frequently overstepped in order to relate developments to the earlier occult revival. The reader may, of course, read as he chooses, but a large part of the argument is cumulative—for example, it will be difficult to appreciate the relationship of psychoanalysis and the occult, if the pervasiveness of occult theory in the backyards of the European mind has not been fully appreciated. The author would be grateful for readers whose judgment is passed on the argument as a whole.

It should hardly be necessary to add this last caution, but in self-defense I must do so. *Nowhere* do I maintain that secret societies or hidden hands direct the course of history. That is a pastime I leave to those often delightful, sometimes terrifying, always dedicated men, the High Irrationalists.

I owe thanks to the librarians and staffs of the University Library, Cambridge; the British Museum; the London Library; the Institute of Contemporary History, Wiener Library; the Welcome Library for the History of Medicine; the Bundesarchiv, Koblenz; the Bayerische Staatsbibliothek, Munich; the Warburg Institute, University of London; and to Mr. Wesencraft of the Harry Price Library, the Senate House, University of London.

I am particularly indebted to Dr. Michael Weaver and the American Documentation Centre of the University of Exeter.

So many people may find their ideas in the distorting mirror of these pages, that I shall content myself with generally expressing my gratitude to all those who have answered my queries with remarkable patience. Of firsthand informants, several have asked to remain anonymous. But I am very grateful to John Hargrave for answering a barrage of questions on the little-known developments outlined in Chapter III and to Liz Cowgill who provided me with an invaluable translation of the document known as "The Secret of the Jews."

Two particular debts remain to be acknowledged. Largely in response to the suggestion of Francis King, I began to consider the developments of English illuminated politics discussed in Chapter III; and his generous handing over of his discovery of the pamphlet *The Hebrew Talisman* enabled me to complete my argument about the nature of *The Protocols of Zion*.

Ellic Howe not only encouraged the enterprise from beginning to end but allowed me to trample over the fields he has so expertly tilled. He has helped me with the names of informants and with the loan of books, information, and unique documentary material. The passages in this book dealing with Germany could not have been written without the help of material laboriously gathered for his forthcoming *Lunatic Fringe in Germany 1890-1925*. The fact that we differed on the interpretation of evidence has nowhere hampered his generosity.

For all eccentricities and downright mistakes I alone am responsible.

J.W.
London
June 1973

Introduction
The Struggle
for the Irrational

The Flight from Reason—The Occult as Rejected Knowledge —Secular Religions—The First World War and the Failure of Rationalism—The Occult and "Illuminated Politics"—The Consistency of the Irrational

THE present century has both physical and intellectual conflicts that rival those of past ages in terms of blood shed or ink spilled. Historians of the future will have to decide whether the more obvious eruptions are significant in themselves or whether they represent aspects of a greater process that relates them all. This book attempts to anticipate the verdict of history by suggesting that one of the greatest battles fought in the 20th century has been that between the forces of rationalism and those of unreason. The battlefield is undefined, the weapons unhandy, and the outcome uncertain.

The struggle toward an irrational interpretation of life can be noticed at certain points in history. It remains largely unremarked by many of those who engage in it. This is because the human function of which it is the result—the attempt to impose meaning on the self and its environment—most often remains unconscious, much as vital bodily processes like the heartbeat or the cleansing of the bloodstream by the liver remain unnoticed until they start to go wrong. Man's efforts to put himself in some sort of secure relationship with the universe seem to be as indispensable to him as the action of the liver or the circulation of the blood. When large numbers of people together are afflicted with doubt, angst, ennui, loss of purpose, or whatever term is to be applied to a condition of mental insecurity, their attempts to provide satisfactory explanations of the human condition take on a frantic aspect. It is in such a situation of crisis that the struggle for the irrational begins. The more support that can be obtained for any point of view, the more the chance of convincing others that it is "true" or "real."[1] And so the struggle is carried on with a peculiar desperation. The visions of reality that the irrationalists would have us accept can be wildly divergent—and there are several which should not be rejected out of hand—but they share a common fear or mistrust of what they see as the prevailing wisdom. Their ideas of exactly what constitutes the prevailing wisdom are often completely out of date, for the struggle for the irrational in this century has its roots in the crisis of consciousness of the last.

Our present predicament is partly the outcome of a historical development that I have called "the flight from reason" and which manifested itself during the 19th century as a reaction to patterns of thought and society that were emerging as a product of 18th-century rationalism. Social and economic change engendered fear both in classes that were liable to profit and those that were liable to lose by far-reaching alterations in society. Scientific and philosophical developments deprived man of his divine image and replaced it with that of an ape. Security of political ordering or religious faith became increasingly tenuous, and the burden of responsibility on the individual grew more difficult to bear with every access of personal freedom.[2] The resulting crisis of human consciousness produced a revulsion from the methods of thought and action that were responsible for the insecurity of Western man. Because these were seen as *rationalism and materialism,* the reaction from what was unpalatable and new took the form of a rejection of Reason, a resurrection of faith and the spontaneous generation of causes of an exalted or mystical nature, whose concepts might be no less religious for being clothed in the vocabulary of politics.

The flight from reason cannot be accurately dated. But it is possible to say that from the time of Napoleon's defeat until the vast eruption of 1848, the new irrationalism achieved its first successes, and that the latter half of the last century saw the progressive advance of the irrational to a position which, by the 1890s, was one of perceptible hysteria. It is certain that the process had occurred before and that it is still going on. What psychologists have referred to simply as "anxiety" is now known as "future shock," a condition defined by its discoverer as "the dizzying sensation brought on by the premature arrival of the future." This expression of contemporary anxiety might stand as well for the 19th-century crisis of consciousness as for that of today.

> By changing our relationship to the resources that surround us, by violently expanding the scope of change, and, most crucially, by accelerating its pace, we have broken irretrievably with the past. We have cut ourselves off from the old ways of thinking, of feeling, of adapting. We have set the stage for a completely new society and we are now racing towards it.[3]

Although it might well be argued that the dangers of a hypothetical future carry less weight with the mass of humanity than the perceptible discomforts of the present, it is important that this condition has received contemporary expression. It remains impossible to understand this modern dilemma fully without realizing that it is only one symptom of a disease that was contracted over a hundred years ago.

The rejection of Reason as a category of thought involved the rejection of the society whose weapon Reason was. The Establishment culture of late 19th-century Europe—based on capitalism, individualism, and the pursuit of profit—was confronted with a selection of idealisms whose kingdoms were not of this world, whose categories of thought were apocalyptic, were based on visions of absolute values and drew sustenance from traditions of thinking that have, through historical accident, remained rejected throughout the course of European history. This Underground of rejected knowledge, comprising heretical religious positions, defeated social schemes, abandoned sciences, and neglected modes of speculation, has as its core the varied collection of doctrines that can be combined in a bewildering variety of ways and that is known as the occult. The occult is diametrically opposed to the type of society and the ways of thought that were represented by the Establishment culture of the late European industrial revolution. It was only natural that those who revolted against the direction in which that society appeared to be heading would turn for support and philosophical justification to a perennial Underground of rejected knowledge, which had traditionally furnished an armory for thinkers of an idealistic stamp. It was natural, too, for those elements of society that found themselves excluded by the Established social order to make alliances with the protagonists of anti-Establishment methods of thought. It therefore came about—of course this scheme, like all such schemes, is not rigid—that the Establishment, whose collapse produced such a widespread feeling of anxiety, was challenged ever more strongly by the emergent Underground of Europe.[4]

The importance of this Underground of rejected knowledge can scarcely be overestimated. Its inmates, and their philosophies, can tell us more about ourselves and our Established civilizations than many direct studies of such societies themselves. Often the analysis may amount to no more than a combing of the trash cans of society—but it is well-known that garbage men are often connoisseurs of human nature. Not infrequently, however, an examination of the Underground may leave the inquirer thoughtful as to the precise reasons why a particular power of the occult conflation has found no place in the society that rejected it. He may come to the conclusion that sometimes such products of human endeavor are branded anathema because they have offended against our most jealously guarded inheritance—those implicit assumptions of our living, which are not criticized simply because they are not perceived. The occult is the mirror image of society: an inevitable mirror image.

In the 19th century, the crisis of consciousness presented itself to many people chiefly in a religious form. For this there were two reasons. The first was the inherited tendency—which can still be easily perceived—for mankind to think in religious terms. The second was the historical fact that the certainties most obviously threatened by the new methods of thought were those of the Christian religion, which had itself been for centuries the established interpretation of life in Europe. During the period that saw the emergence of the rationalist-materialist-industrialist society against which the 19th-century irrationalists reacted, the Christian religion had continued to be used by the European Establishment as a convenient means of maintaining the social ordering. But with the *de facto* appearance of a new sort of society in which power came to depend more and more upon negotiable capital, the social sanctions of the Christian religion were nullified at the same time as the literal truth of Holy Writ was subjected to scientific scrutiny. It was, therefore, often to the more obviously religious aspects of the Underground of rejected knowledge that the 19th-century rebels turned, to reinforce a solid edifice turned unexpectedly to flux. Not only were the early irrationalists preeminently concerned with saving their souls, but their attempts to repair or reform the tottering social fabric bear the stamp of the religious approach. In the non-Christian religious attitudes which form the nucleus of occult tradition, they discovered philosophical approaches that could be turned to good use against the monster of materialist society. As the concern of opponents of the Established order turned increasingly away from individual salvation and sought the conditions of collective security, the fundamentally religious approach did not alter, although inevitably it became transformed.

One turn-of-the-century observer who noticed this tendency was Gustave Le Bon, whose book *The Crowd* furnished several Fascist leaders with a remarkably effective source of inspiration. Although not impressive to modern sociologists or valid for all periods of history, the principles of Le Bon proved themselves capable of an appallingly direct application, which says much for the acuteness of his observation of his own time. "Many people," wrote Le Bon in the middle of the First World War, "used to consider our period as a positivist age which obeyed only reason. Experience came to show that the world had remained governed by the most chimerical Utopias." Mystical power was the force to move men. "The most certain truths of reason only acquire popular prestige after having disguised themselves in a mystical form."[5] As early as 1896, he had proclaimed: "A person is not religious solely when he worships a divinity but when he puts all the resources of his mind, the complete submission of his will, and the whole-souled ardor of fanaticism at the service of a cause or an individual who becomes the goal and guide of his thoughts and actions."[6] Nihilists, Freemasons, socialists, and other "adepts of political sects" he characterized as "religious beings having lost old beliefs, but unable to do without a creed to orient their thoughts."[7] The chief disadvantage of socialism was that its gods were abstract: "If it possessed some precise divinity to worship, its success would be very much more rapid." It requires only the most rudimentary knowledge of subsequent history to see how his opinions might be regarded as amply confirmed.

Among the various attempts to provide a coherent and comforting interpretation of the human situation during the 19th century, there were thus several varieties of secular religion, whose devotees were implacably opposed to the Establishment version of reality, and who, from the point of view of the proverbial man in the street were idealistic, impractical, and frequently more religious than political. Often the actions of the socially rejected, identifying themselves with the sustaining Underground of rejected knowledge, provide evidence for the theories of Le Bon about mass manipulation. The struggle between rationalist and irrationalist interpretations of the universe may be hottest where it is unperceived.

The crisis that had slowly been developing during the 19th century was precipitated by the carnage of 1914-18. The pragmatic method was seen by many observers to be irreparably damaged: the war was the culmination of *Realpolitik*, the mutual destruction of the ironclads of rationalism and materialism. Toward the end of the war occurred a shattering event: the revolution in Russia, which presented to Europe a new form of society, which had previously only existed briefly in France. This was theocracy—the God-orientated state—but with the People made divine. In the escape from an unpalatable social ordering, as in the escape from the order of the Christian God, freedom was too dangerous a commodity to play with.

Disillusionment provoked by the war combined with the political

Introduction   *13*

situation provoked by the Treaty of Versailles to augment the crisis of consciousness of prewar days. Uncertainty as to man's position in the universe was made more palpable by specific uncertainty as to his political and social future. What modus vivendi might be reached, what structure placed on the human components of state or nation? The justification of political procedures had been called into question by the war, and demands for a new society from "Left" and "Right"—such labels have little meaning in our present context —implied more often than not the vision of a new philosophical basis for that society: new morals, new values, new men. Laissez-faire and ad hoc measures were no longer effective in creating the necessary illusion of stability. Events demanded ideological programs to support the political. To the providing of bread and circuses, governments had once more to join the ancient responsibility of providing a belief.

Because the method that was seen as having failed was pragmatic, materialist, and rational, the systems projected to repair its record of failure were often of a preconceived, idealistic, and irrational character. That such systems had earlier attracted to themselves the Underground of rejected knowledge, I have already shown. That they did so again after the First World War is the contention of this book. As in the 19th century the revival of occult beliefs and practices formed a major part of the flight from reason, so the occult plays a leading part in our consideration of the later period. But, whereas in the earlier period the occult seemed to provide solutions to a crisis of consciousness that was fundamentally religious in character, after the First World War the problems with which rejected knowledge became entangled were the more imminent concerns of ethics and social order. It is important that the use made of the occult in this book should be clear at the outset. When occult ideas are found tangled up with political and social projects, they indicate a sort of thinking which it is convenient to call "illuminated," a definition of reality that transcends the materialist point of view, and the emergence of the rejected—both in terms of ideas and of men—into unaccustomed positions of prominence. In the period under discussion, the sort of elements that had in the 19th century formed an Underground of opposition to a materialist Establishment penetrated dominant positions in society with astonishing success.

The justification for paying so much attention to the occult is not only that it crops up again and again demanding to be assessed. Of its nature it frequently entails matters that come under the headings of faith and religion. The occult, therefore, embodies basic attitudes toward both universal questions and historical conditions. In the "occult" response to historical stimuli is found a factor common to many more sharply defined responses articulated in fields as diverse as the writing of history, theories of aesthetics, political manifestos, or the healing of the mind. A "religious" position may represent a primary and relatively undefined impulse, which can either become codified into theology or allow its drive to become transformed into specific areas of human activity—politics, society, the realms of material possibilities. In the historical conditions of the past hundred years, the prominent place occupied by specifically "occult" forms of religious response is a basic indicator to the nature of other attitudes with which the occult has become entwined. Because the fundamentally "occult" is so often found tangled up with what will be called "illuminated" politics, scholarship, or social theory, such positions can best be understood by a preliminary understanding of their common occult denominator.

For Gustave Le Bon, mystical logic formed a state of mental functioning inferior to rational thought. The advance of science he considered as having slowly but surely driven back the frontiers of the mystical, which had been forced to take refuge in areas outside scientific jurisdiction. But he never tired of reiterating the dangers of human susceptibility to the mysterious. One of his examples was the "unlimited credulity of certain *savants*" in occult matters generally and Spiritualism in particular. Le Bon himself had helped on one occasion to expose the medium Eusapia Palladino, and he had a poor opinion of Spiritualism. But in order to explain the credulity of other distinguished academics, he was forced to admit that their gullibility was a mental state to which anyone might fall prey. They must not forget, he warned his readers, that the rational and the mystical temperaments often coexist, operating within their separate forms of logic. The academics who became converted to Spiritualism made the mental change of gear involuntarily; but once entered into the "cycle of belief" there they became anchored.[8] This description of the conversion experience can apply equally well to adepts of the less religious forms of rejected knowledge. The universe they inhabit

Introduction

obeys a logic that is unlike that of the rationalist universe of mutually agreed discourse and cannot be understood as logical in its terms. It is, nevertheless, crucial to realize that its own laws are as consistent as those more commonly accepted as "logical"; for to call an Irrationalist "mad" is to prevent any possibility of understanding his universe.

The crisis that gave power to the Irrationalists was intimately connected with the occult revival of the 19th century. In the battle to define reality, to impose an often transcendental vision on the immanently real, the viewpoints of what were once tiny minorities have played an extraordinary part. Because the weapons and the state of mind of the combatants are unfamiliar, it is necessary first to introduce some specific examples and general considerations, which apply to the world of the irrational in the period after the First World War. This will necessarily appear impressionistic; but there is no other way of making sure that the reader is equipped with the background necessary to understand—to take a few examples—the components of early Nazism, some directions of psychoanalysis, the rebellion of the hippies, or the urgencies of flying saucers."The occult" has been defined as "rejected knowledge." This means that knowledge of a potentially valuable kind may be classified as "occult" just as easily as knowledge once accepted but now discarded as primitive, facile, or simply mistaken. The term is so loose and all-embracing that it can be made to cover Spiritualism, Theosophy, countless Eastern (and not so Eastern) cults; varieties of Christian sectarianism and the esoteric pursuits of magic, alchemy and astrology; also the pseudo-sciences such as Baron Reichenbach's Odic Force or the screens invented by Dr. Walter Kilner for seeing the human aura. All these subdivisions of the occult will recur in the following pages. In the battle to define reality, to impose an often transcendental vision on the immanently real, the viewpoints of what were once tiny minorities have played an extraordinary part.

Although such bodies of opinion are frequently in direct conflict with one another, very often they share one common belief: the idea of "spiritual development." This concept has assumed great significance in the ideological struggles of this century; for in the crisis of consciousness from which this argument takes its starting-point the governing factor is *anxiety induced by change.* This means that people thinking about—or even unconsciously, reacting against—what seemed intolerable social conditions were faced by a confrontation with *time*.

Put in the abstract this may seem a concern of little relevance to any but philosophers. But in concrete terms it means that a man has to decide at the simplest level whether things are going to get better or not, and what he can do about his life's situation. Presented with a society of which he disapproves, he must decide in what manner this may in its turn be altered to produce a better life. Does the best hope lie in creating new institutions to regulate society? or in the gradual inculcation of a new sort of ethics? or in a struggle to improve the nature of man itself—a suppression of the old Adam by the new superman? Of course, this problem is always faced by those dissatisfied with their present conditions. But because the crisis of consciousness was occasioned so greatly by the conscious or unconscious perception of *change,* the ultimate possible *change* began to appear to many reformers the only fruitful method of attack. This was the changing of man himself—the perfection of the human being, so palpably imperfect and self-destructive.

This possibility presented itself forcefully because the 19th-century crisis had as one of its catalysts the Darwinian theory of evolution. If man had evolved from the ape he might be improved progressively until *homo superior* was as far removed from the puny creature of the present day as *homo sapiens* from his ignoble ancestor. Most commonly this idea was expressed in one or another form of "Social Darwinianism" which visualized a selective improvement of the "best" strains in humanity by a breeding program or by encouraging the "survival of the fittest." What is almost always ignored is that at the same time as theorists began to seek for ways to improve the human animal, others began to apply Darwin to traditional notions of the human *being*—a creature with an immortal soul or a divine destiny.

It is commonly held that the idea of "progress" was born in the 16th century, when Europeans were proud to think that they were recovering some of the lost knowledge of antiquity and were rapidly improving civilization from the static position it had maintained during the Middle Ages.[9] This may be true as far as man's view of society as a whole is concerned. But the idea of individual progress is considerably older. It is found as the cardinal point in all mystical texts of the Middle Ages and relates to the successive stages of the mystical ascent toward God.[10] The doctrine of "spiritual progress" was resurrected by the prophets of the 19th-century occult revival. Theosophists, magicians, and mystics of all sorts eagerly affirmed that in following their various systems they were emulating the saints of all religions and cultures in approaching Divinity. One influential writer on occult subjects was Baron Carl Du Prel, and he was merely codifying a widespread body of opinion when he decided that:

> As a further development of physical organisation beyond the human is highly improbable, it is to psychical indications in man that we have to look for the field of future evolution. Darwinism has thus dealt with but one half of the task prescribed by the doctrine of evolution; to solve the other the abnormal functions of the human psyche must be drawn into consideration.[11]

On one level the immense popularity of Spiritualism was hailed as heralding a new age in which man would concentrate on the neglected "spiritual" aspects of existence—although most supporters of this theory declined to state how sitting around in dimly lit rooms listening to the travels of uncles and grandmothers in the realms beyond would greatly assist the dawn of the new era. On another level entirely were the vitalists of various descriptions, most of whom followed the theories of Henri Bergson. His *L'Evolution créatrice* appeared in 1907, but his ideas had begun to influence French intellectuals as early as 1897.[12] Like Bergson himself, his most notable followers were interested in psychical research. Hans Driesch presided over international conferences on the subject, while William McDougall followed the originator of vitalism in becoming president of the London Society for Psychical Research. From a specifically religious viewpoint Bergson's doctrine of evolution (perpetuated by a mysterious *élan vital*) gave strength to the Catholic revival while at the same time acting as the point of departure for the unorthodox speculations of Teilhard de Chardin.[13] The appeal of Bergson to those shaken by the loss of their status as the privileged of God was immense. Evolution did not stop with man as he was then known, and such a continuing process might even grant the qualified immortality of Bergson's assurance that "the whole of humanity, the space and time, is one immense army galloping beside and before and behind each of us in an overwhelming charge able to beat down every resistance and clear the most formidable obstacles, perhaps even death."[14]

This element of hope was shared by the occultists. They often made great use of Bergson to support their extension of the idea of "spiritual progress" to cover more than the traditional ascent of the soul toward God. Magicians, mystics, and alchemists needed to do no more than apply their traditional terminology to the body of mankind. Theosophists elaborated a complex doctrine of man's spiritual evolution through successive races. There were countless personal syntheses of occult doctrine and Darwinian science. One such was that of W. E. Evans-Wentz, who in his travels in search of fairy lore constructed his "Celtic esoteric theory of evolution" which embodied the belief that "the gods are beings which once were men, and the actual race of men will in time become gods."[15] The importance of the various concepts of supernatural evolution which circulated at the same time as more materialist applications of Darwin's theory, is that the area in which they were current was that of the Progressive Underground where occultists and idealistic social reformers met and mingled. The esoteric idea of the "spiritual development" of the individual man could be extended by social theorists to all humanity—or, as often happened, to a particular *race*. As will be seen, such notions of altering the very stuff of man—performing, as it were, an alchemical transmutation upon whole peoples—could quite easily accompany the most rationalist ideas of eugenicists concerned to "breed a better human animal."

This solution was an optimistic answer to the problem of time. It combined the appeal of the idea that "all things will be made new" with the conception of "world without end." From this root sprang many ideas of the advent of a new age—or, if one preferred, like Yeats, to adopt an alternative occult view of cyclic time, the beginning of a new cycle.[16]

One of the most notable of such apocalyptic ideas was that of the Thousand Year Reich. With similar optimistic assertions men strove to counter the sort of pessimism of which the most famous philosopher was Oswald Spengler. Spengler saw the war of 1914-18 as "the type of a historical change of phase occurring within a great historical organism of definable compass at the point preordained for it hundreds of years ago."[17] The death of the old world had been inevitable. But so, even Spengler conceded, was an eventual resurrection.

For those who fled in horror from both the failures and the successes of rationalism, the irrational Underground provided not only a welcome personal relief but a hopeful theory of history. Perhaps nothing is more important in an era of constant change than to demonstrate an inevitable continuity.

1. Peter L. Berger and Thomas Luckman, *The Social Construction of Reality* (London, 1967).
2. See my introduction to *The Occult Underground*. The concept of "the fear of freedom" is, of course, that of Erich Fromm.
3. Alvin Toffler, *Future Shock* (London, 1970), pp. 13, 19.
4. Cf. Friedrich Heer, *The Intellectual History of Europe* (London, 1966).
5. Gustave Le Bon, *Enseignements psychologiques de la guerre européene* (Paris, 1916), pp. 7, 15, 78.
6. Le Bon, *The Crowd* (London, 1896), p. 64.
7. Le Bon, *Enseignements,* p. 164.
8. Le Bon, *Les opinions et les croyances* (Paris, 1911), pp. 276, 92 ff., 326-27.
9. E.g., J. B. Bury, *The Idea of Progress* (London, 1920).
10. See Joseph E. Milosh, *The Scale of Perfection and the English Mystical Tradition* (London, 1966), pp. 51 ff.; Evelyn Underhill, *Mysticism* (12th ed., London, 1930), pp. 168-69.
11. Carl Du Prel, *The Philosophy of Mysticism* (tr. C. C. Massey, London, 1899), vol. II, p. 119.
12. On the influence of Bergson, see Richard Griffiths, *The Reactionary Revolution* (London, 1966), pp. 35-37; Julien Benda, *Sur le succès du bergsonisme* (Paris, 1924); G. Turgnet-Milnes, *Some Modern French Writers* (London, 1921).
13. Of the vast vitalist literature, see for some idea of the possible applications, Hans Driesch, *History of Vitalism* (London, 1914); William McDougall, *Modern Materialism and Emergent Evolution* (London, 1929); Pierre Teilhard de Chardin, *The Future of Man* (London, 1964).
14. Henri Bergson, *Creative Evolution* (London, tr. A. Mitchell, 1911), p. 286.
15. W. E. Evans-Wentz, *The Fairy-Faith in Celtic Countries,* (London, 1911), p. 514. For other syntheses, see the theories of Rudolf Steiner, Owen Barfield, P. D. Ouspensky, and those unattached to any school, like L. E. Eeman, *Self and Superman* (London, 1929); Charles Walston, *Harmonism*

and Conscious Evolution (London, 1922); Lancelot Law Whyte, *The Next Development in Man* (London, 1944).
16. On cyclic theories generally, see Grace Cairns, *Philosophies of History* (London, 1963), and for Yeats, Giorgio Melchiori, *The Whole Mystery of Art* (London, 1960), pp. 140-43, 158-61.
17. Oswald Spengler, *The Decline of the West,* vol. I (London, 1926), pp. 47-48.

Chapter 1
Ginungagapp

A Neurasthenic Society—Occultism in the Twenties—Irrationalist Currents in Central Europe—The Progressive Underground and Occultism—The Occultism of Prague and Vienna—The Munich Cosmics—Communes and Colonies—Rudolf Steiner's Anthroposophy

IN Norse mythology Ginungagapp is the void before the creation of the world. It is the unformed chaos in which the necessary elements are present, but not yet fashioned into recognizable patterns or infused with the breath of life. Such a chaos, or vacancy, existed politically and ideologically through much of Western Europe after 1918. The war had merely presented in a drastic form problems that had been obvious to those of a reforming temper during the previous century. The quest for political solutions, which led many into the Communist party or one of the various forms of Fascism, is linked indissolubly to the seeking for a new spiritual standpoint that had been so prominent a feature of European society in the period immediately preceding the great catastrophe.

In that time a strange illness had struck the educated classes of society, and the epidemic continued after the war. Its effects can be seen in the novels of Thomas Mann or Aldous Huxley. It was called "neurasthenia" or "nerves." Frequently it manifested itself in "an appalling boredom, a lassitude of soul and body."[1] This fashionable disability had been epitomized by Kierkegaard some half a century before.

> If a melancholy man is asked what ground he has for it, what it is that weighs upon him, he will reply, "I know not, I cannot explain it!" Herein lies the infinity of melancholy. This reply is perfectly correct, for as soon as a man knows the cause, the melancholy is done away with, whereas, on the contrary in the case of the sorrowful, the sorrow is not done away with when a man knows why he sorrows. But melancholy is a sin, really it is a sin *instar omnium,* for not to will deeply and sincerely is a sin, and this is the mother of sins. This sickness, or rather this sin, is very common in our age, and so it is under this all young Germany and France now sighs.[2]

So spoke an agonized sufferer from the early days of the epidemic. A modern medical historian has diagnosed the later stages as proceeding partly from boredom, and he adds a catalogue of circumstances that furthered the spread of the condition.

> The fact that at about 1900 an illness became fashionable has however other reasons. Although at this time civilization guarantees a pleasant and ordered life, its promised security is really only a facade behind which doubts conceal themselves ill enough. The churches have lost a great part of their power over mankind. Freedom of belief rules; it is permissible to believe in nothing. Humanistic ideals no more possess the same significance that they did a century before. Society is constricted in its inherited structures. Even these have declined into an arid observance of custom, behind which all corruptions can conceal themselves. A new art is to replace religion and animate the human mind. But it grows rigid in its dead ornamentation. Man feels himself without an anchorage. His natural inclination to venerate a higher, di-

recting Power, can no longer be fulfilled. He has materialized his soul. No more is it for him the arcane power of the Romantics, penetrating all bodies, but merely a complicated reflex mechanism of organic matter. He supposes he will achieve his well-being and his happiness through civilization, through science, but not through an invisible God.

This expectation science amply fulfills: it discovers an illness which justifies melancholy, spiritual and bodily exhaustion, irritation, all the small cares of humanity.[3]

The neurasthenic is the extreme example of someone trapped by an inability to overcome the historical pressures operating on him. The sense of insecurity has its active as well as its passive results, and a feverish searching for a creed is as characteristic of the rootless as the vegetable agonies of the neurasthenic. The years just before the First World War witnessed just such a searching, and the impact of the war itself reinforced the determination of the seekers to discover a solution. On the one hand, consciousness of change merely augmented the crop of those who took refuge in disorders of the nerves and a cozy impotence;[4] on the other, the void was troubled by the birth pangs of a new Creation.

On the most basic level, for example: in 1914 there were 320 Spiritualist Societies in Britain, of which fewer than half were affiliated to the National Union of Spiritualists. By 1919, 309 societies had become affiliated, and there were many more unattached groups. The Depression of the Thirties saw a further increase in the numbers of Spiritualist devotees. By one estimate there were over 2,000 British churches in existence with a total of 250,000 members.[5]

The Great War reintroduced to Western Europe the entire repertoire of the supernatural. If the British particularly favored Spiritualism, the French retired upon their native tradition of High Catholic prophecy: and during the fighting, omens and apparitions confirmed the various armies in the belief that the hosts of heaven fought with them. The British reported the intervention of St. George and the Angel of Mons, the French went into battle under the standard of Joan of Arc, and the Russian armies were encouraged by visions of the Madonna and a fiery cross. And the years of stress bequeathed a legacy of neo-Spiritualist philosophizing. It was remarkable how often the speculations of those who had lost friends or family in the conflict ended by establishing personal religious syntheses. Sir Oliver Lodge, whose book, *Raymond, or Life and Death,* ran through twelve editions between its first appearance in 1916 and the revised version of 1922, took his argument on to a galactic plane, reasoning that the war was part of a divine evolutionary plan, which would eventually justify all the sorrow and the wastage of human life.[6] Another example is Sir Arthur Conan Doyle, who was also converted to Spiritualism during the war. Instead of following his fellow-knight's lead into metaphysics, he became involved with an investigation carried out by certain members of the Theosophical Society who were convinced that fairies had been photographed in the Yorkshire dale of Cottingley. It was not until 1935 that the Cottingley fairies were conclusively exposed, but the photographs met with severe criticism from the day they were published. Despite this, Doyle's books attracted a widespread public, and his readers from different parts of the world sent their own "supernormal" photographs to be inspected by the creator of Sherlock Holmes.[7]

Few incidents demonstrate better than the extravagant affair of Doyle and the fairies the crucial points for understanding the place of the occult in the inter-war period. It was related to the 19th-century revival—Doyle's conversion to Spiritualism and his association with Theosophists have both demanded mention. It was related to the shock of World War I—for it is difficult to believe that such unbridled fantasy would have attracted the support which it did attract had there not been pressing reasons for belief. It is accordingly very significant that the more traditional occult "teachers" who had been so prominent during the thirty years immediately preceding the war, were afterwards somewhat in eclipse.

Gurus in plenty, there were of course—a few extremely successful. Some like the Sufi Inayat Khan and the "perfect master" Sri Meher Baba, were in the traditional mold of wise men from the East. Scholarly Theosophists—following the lead of those mystical pioneers H. P. Blavatsky and Colonel Olcott—still made their way to the Orient and returned with mysterious wares. One of the most prominent was Evans-Wentz, who had started his spiritual quest where Conan Doyle left off—with the fairies—but graduated to become the respected interpreter of Buddhist texts such as *The Tibetan Book of the Dead*. It was after the war that Aleister Crowley attained his greatest notoriety—although it should never be forgotten that he emerged from the very *fin de siècle* atmosphere of the Hermetic Order of the Golden Dawn, and that he was a supreme example of the type of Symbolist magus who had flourished in Paris during the 1890s. The Theosophical Society itself—the very pillar of the late 19th-century revival—had entered a new and potentially very successful phase. Under the leadership of Annie Besant, it sought to combine social reform with its more occult principles. Around the shrines dedicated to the Himalayan Masters clustered many smaller tabernacles dedicated to anti-vivisection, vegetarianism, and a new social order. The Society was an accepted part of that body of progressive thought which formed the mainstream of opposition to the materialism and rationalism of the powers which were: a circumstance which did not prevent its giving birth to a Messiah. In 1911 the Society founded the Order of the Star in the East to propagate the cult of Jiddu Krishnamurti, a young Hindu born about 1897 in South India, whom Mrs. Besant and her colleague, Bishop C. W. Leadbeater, had decided was to be the vehicle for the coming of a new World-Teacher.

In 1929 Krishnamurti dissolved all the organizations which had been established to support him, and the Theosophical Society dwindled in numbers through defections, disillusionment, and secession.[8] It was sheer coincidence that this event coincided with the beginnings of the economic depression; but it is true that during the Thirties people's minds were turned to other things. The gurus who had been so successful during the Twenties—even the most prominent, such as Gurdjieff—vanished from sight, at least temporarily. Politics and economics absorbed men's conscious minds and animated the anxieties of their unconscious. It is significant that the most influential religious movement in the Protestant countries during the period between the wars altered its complexion to suit the times. This was Moral Re-armament (MRA) founded by the Swiss-American pastor Frank Buchman about 1921-22. Buchman's initial recruits were almost all British ex-officer undergraduates, who had been disoriented by the experience of the war and jumped eagerly at the fundamentalist approach of the new movement. By the late Thirties the movement was being accused of pro-Fascist sympathies, and the texts of Buchman's speeches confirm that such charges were not wholly without foundation.[9]

It is important to note that even in the nebulous form of MRA, the impulse of ill-defined idealism which originated in the trenches found itself turned from an exclusively religious orientation to an implicitly political point of view. The needs and aspirations which during the Twenties had driven men to religion or the occult were transmuted during the decade which followed. As objects of devotion the gurus gave way to the political masters. But the vocabulary and the modes of thought employed by some of the idealistic politicians were profoundly influenced by their previous experience of the occult underground. In certain cases, whole ideological positions were taken over from occultism, and the underground became an underground no longer.

The political movements which resulted were of a peculiar nature, and can only be understood if it is realized that their roots were in the progressive movements of pre-war years: the very movements where occultism and social reform rubbed shoulders. By 1920 the world was presented with a solid revolutionary achievement, an indication that an alternative to the despised Establishment system was at least possible. However, the Communist example had drawbacks for many would-be reformers. Before 1914 progressive opinion had been virtually unanimous about the primary evil afflicting society. This was rampant materialism; and the solutions proposed for remedying social abuses were idealistic in the extreme, ranging from the establishment of small Utopian colonies through the education of a ruling elite to the wholesale application of economic panaceas which savored more than a little of Holy Writ. To this predominantly idealistic opposition the Marxists were the exception, proclaiming at least in theory a materialism of their own completely opposed to the kingdom of the ideal.

In Germany the publication of books officially classified as "occult" rose to peak in the middle of the 1920s, when a slight decline began in the fortunes of occult publishing, but the steady flow of occult and mystical works continued through the next decade, and was not entirely stifled by strong official discouragement, and ultimately by the persecution of the later Nazi era. If victorious England had been affected by the irrationalism resulting from the Great War, how much more so were the defeated countries! It is scarcely surprising that their political solutions smacked also of the religious. For the moment it is with the more specifically religious aspects that we are concerned: the opting for the knowledge of other realities which reveals at its lowest common denominator the response underlying the illuminated approach.

Into this category come the symbolic and allegorical journeys described by Hermann Hesse to exotic territories of the spirit. These he collectively characterized under the heading of *The Journey to the East,* a mysterious pilgrimage undertaken by the members of a secret League whose veiled objectives are founded in the quests of 19th-century occultism: the knowledge of the Tao, or the True Way of Chinese philosophy, the awakening of Kundalini, or the Serpent Power of Yoga. This "Journey to the East" might easily be confused with other voyages of the same period.

> At the time that I had the good fortune to join the League —that is immediately after the end of the World War— our country was full of saviors, prophets and disciples, of presentiments about the end of the world or hopes of the dawn of a Third Empire. Shattered by the War, in despair as a result of deprivation and hunger, greatly disillusioned by the seeming futility of all the sacrifices in blood and goods, our people at that time were lured by many phantoms, but there were also many real spiritual advances. There were Bacchanalian dance societies and Anabaptist groups, there was one thing after another that seemed to point to what was wonderful and beyond the veil. There was also at that time a widespread leaning towards Indian, ancient Persian and other Eastern mysteries and religions, and all this gave most people the impression that our ancient League was one of the newly-blossomed cults.[10]

Thus, although the most obvious effect of the Bolshevik revolution was to send large numbers of European seekers for security into the arms of the Communist parties, for many, who were equally sincere in the search for a creed, the Communist alternative was merely old Mammon in a different guise. These were the rebels with their roots in the idealistic opposition of pre-war days. They saw the war as the final confirmation of their thesis that not just a change in the social order, but transformation of the very nature of man was necessary to cure the evils of Established society. The condition of anxiety or boredom which had turned the attention of Europeans in the direction of the magi and prophets of an earlier period, was transformed into a more altruistic idealism, and the post-war magi were as likely to speak of the necessary constitution of the social order as they had earlier been to indicate the route to eternal life.

The term "magus" is no figure of speech—it refers to occultists proper. Because the idealistic Underground of prewar years had included both proselytes of new religions and seekers of social creeds, the various groups intermingled and used one another's terms. The often-repeated calling for a "New Age," heard both before and after the war, can refer either to a practically conceived plan for social betterment, or to a religious revelation like that preached by the Swedenborgian New Church. After the war the mystics of the occult revival did not vanish—far from it. In some cases they remained religious prophets, but in others they changed their spots, responding to the pressure of a social gospel by emphasizing the parts of their teachings which seemed relevant to their country and their time. This phenomenon was particularly remarkable in Germany where they multiplied extraordinarily, and with remarkable results.

An exalted mood, arising out of a sense of deep despair, a knowledge that the old realities of physical well-being or military might had been annihilated, the pressure of economic hardship and political uncertainty, turned the minds of men to things of another world.

> It was shortly after the World War [Hermann Hesse wrote] and the beliefs of the conquered nations were in an extraordinary state of unreality. There was a readiness to believe in things beyond reality even though only a few barriers were actually overcome and few advances made into the realm of a future psychiatry. Our journey at that time across the Moon Ocean to Famagusta under the leadership of Albert the Great, or say, the discovery of the Butterfly Island, twelve leagues beyond Zipangu, or the inspiring League ceremony at Rudiger's grave—those were deeds and experiences which were allotted once only to people of our time and zone.[11]

Like the rest of Europe, Germany had been affected by the prewar crisis of consciousness, but the occult revival and the penetration of the country by exotic sects took place in general later than in France and England. Although the more eccentric groups on the fringes of Freemasonry kept alive the occult teachings of 18th-century Masons, it was from the Paris of the Symbolists and the Theosophical centers at London and Adyar that the German-speaking irrationalists derived the greater part of their inspiration. There was also a certain revival of native pietism; and the growth of interest in mysticism and the occult naturally stimulated a search in German traditions for Teutonic prophets and seers.

All the familiar components of the occult mélange were present at the turn of the century, and when Eberhard Buchner walked round Berlin in 1904 investigating outlandish sects he found a fair variety.[12]

There were the "Apostolic Congregation," which stemmed from the movement begun by the Scottish evangelist Edward Irving; the "Dissident Christians," led by a former blacksmith called Brother Kammerling; and a branch of the American John Alexander Dowie's Catholic Apostolic Church in Zion.[13] There were also the eccentrics, the more "occult" groups. Buchner discovered a remarkable commune of mystics calling themselves the Lodge of "Oschm-Rahmah-Johjihjah," which derived from the Swedenborgian New Church. Buchner also sought out a meeting of Christian Theosophists in a vegetarian restaurant where he was most put out by having to abandon beer for barley-water. The lecturer extolled the virtues of Jacob Lorber, prophet of the new age.

> Now I want at once to make it clear that Jacob Lorber has had the bad luck not to have found a place in any encyclopaedia.... I suppose that no one has taken notice of his career except this tiny roomful of Christian Theosophists which has dispersed through the land, held together throughout the decades, and now sets foot in Berlin. With horror, I see that Jacob Lorber has a quite colossal quantity of literature on his conscience, including works which extend to 1600 pages.[14]

The influence of Lorber was in fact considerably more widespread that Eberhard Buchner suspected; his words had a significant circulation in mystical circles, and were promoted by an organization called the New Salem Church which had its headquarters in Württemberg. In the search for German prophets of the ideal, Lorber's name figures beside those of more celebrated mystics like Meister Eckhart and Angelus Silesius.

Spiritualists abounded, as they did throughout Europe. Another investigator, who was a keen protagonist of scientifically-conducted psychical research, registered his disgust with both the small spiritualist circles and the larger organizations.

> Whether you visit spiritualist organizations in Berlin, or pursue investigations in the Dresden societies, whether you go to meetings in the South German capital or take part in séances of the Budapest or Zurich associations, it's always the same story: an inferior mass, thrust into Spiritualism for one reason or another, who stick to this point of view through their own stubborn laziness, avid for "phenomena," unscrupulous in creating mediums and in experimentation and fanatically investigating everything that doesn't chime with their tune; and standing apart from this crowd some few brighter intellects who—if they don't push off rapidly—either support an undiscriminating idealism or combine Spiritualism with other interests.[15]

The Theosophical Society had established itself in Germany in 1884. The branch was founded in the "Occult Room" of the house in Eberfeld belonging to the husband of Marie Gebhard, a friend of H. P. Blavatsky and a former pupil of the French magician Eliphas Levi. The president was Dr. Wilhelm Hübbe-Schleiden, who had held diplomatic and civil service posts. After lengthy journeys in Equatorial Africa he had produced a series of works on foreign policy and the need for German colonial expansion; now he turned his energies to editing a Theosophical magazine. The next year saw the return to Europe (with the ailing Madame Blavatsky) of Franz Hartmann, a Theosophist of unsavory reputation. Hartmann had been born in 1838, served as a volunteer in the Bavarian artillery, then emigrated on impulse to America, where he qualified medically and took out American citizenship. Until 1883 he remained in the United States, becoming a coroner in Georgetown, Colorado, and a Spiritualist in New Orleans, where one of his patients developed mediumistic gifts which Hartmann was later to claim she had passed on to him. That year he sailed for India and joined the Theosophical Society at Adyar, where he was left alone to face the investigator of the Society for Psychical Research. His return to Europe was at first intended to be temporary, but on what was intended as a brief visit home he met Dr. Karl Kellner, the discoverer of a manufacturing process for cellulose. Hartmann adapted Kellner's idea to compound a drug to be inhaled against tuberculosis; and he established himself as director of an Inhalation Center in Hallein, near Salzburg. His prolific writing won his brand of Theosophy a substantial public, and he too began to publish a periodical.[16]

By the turn of the century, most of the elements of the Occult Underground which were known outside Germany had secured some sort of foothold inside the country. Masters of all sorts found a ready following. In the period between the two World Wars, when the occult and the mystical emerged from their residence below ground, the choice of cults was large. Eastern and dubiously Eastern religions rubbed shoulders with movements for Christian revival. Prophets illuminated by God Himself contended with creeds constructed from every religious dogma known at any period in history.

There were Pentecostalists, Jehovah's Witnesses, offshoots of the Plymouth Brethren, Adventists—in 1930 Germany boasted 10 percent of the world Adventist membership—and various Christian sects of native derivation. One such was that called "Sheep and Shepherd," founded by the Saxon handloom weaver Friedrich Hain (1847-1927) who about 1885 gathered round him a group which eventually left the Church in 1921. To a pantheistic creed they coupled beer-swilling, belief in the miraculous family of *"Vater Hain"*—who was himself the word made flesh, boasted the Christ-child as one of his own and whose first wife had been a devil—and a conviction that it was evil to bury the dead, whom they deposited in the street. Further up the social level came the *Bund der Kämpfer für Glaube and Wahrheit* which also had its seat in Saxony, appealing chiefly to the lower strata of the intelligentsia in the larger Saxon towns. It had been founded about 1900 in response to Spiritualistic prompting by Max Däbritz and Emil Bergmann, the directors of a factory they called the Bombastus Works. They manufactured cosmetics and herbal medicines according to Paracelsian prescriptions, and employed some two hundred people. From advertising *"Medicines—mouthwashes—toothpaste, prepared according to the recipes of Paracelsus Bombastus von Hohenheim"* the two entrepreneurs graduated to the status of occult chiefs. Their organization was arranged in a sequence of seven grades of which women members were allowed only to penetrate the third. The names of their degrees were derived from the spirits, who had revealed the original language of mankind through the mediumship of one of the directors of the Bombastus Works. During the 1920s this previously secretive cult underwent a period of expansion. Another intriguing growth of the decade after the First World War was the *Gottesbund Tanatra*. This was founded in 1923 in Görlitz—the home of the 17th-century mystic Jacob Böhme—by Feder Mühle, a businessman who became involved in Spiritualism after the war and promptly discovered mediumistic gifts. It was prophesied that by 1927 the altar of the Tanatra Lodge would be set up in the Peterskirche at Görlitz; but while in 1929 this had still not come to pass, there were 37 congregations in various places with 1500 members in Görlitz alone. Members wore the God's Eye badge and cultivated the writings of Jacob Lorber. They maintained a curious doctrine that homosexuals were vocationally mediums and that heterosexual intercourse impaired the mediumistic talent. A report of a meeting which took place in 1929 describes 1800 people as present. There were songs and trance sermons. On view were the symbols of the Lodge; the God's Eye, the seven veils of wisdom, a naked boy, and two towers.[17]

These are a few examples out of many. There were more sophisticated prophets at large, such as Bô Yin Râ—alias the painter Joseph Schneiderfranken (1876-1943)—whose saccharine spirituality apparently satisfied a large number of readers[18]—or the eccentric Ottoman Zar-Adusht Ha'nish, whose cult of Mazdaznan established a "university" at Herrliberg, ten miles from Zurich, and exercised a powerful influence over mystically inclined German intellectuals. Its founder's real name was Otto Hanisch, and he was born in 1854, the son of a music teacher in Posen. Mazdaznan was a peculiar religion, claiming to be derived from the Zoroastrian faith but combining insistence on a vegetarian diet with Theosophical doctrine and an obsession with the appalling spiritual results of constipation.[19] The university was known as Aryana, and only the fair-skinned "Aryan" races were permitted to become bearers of the new ideal.[20]

Mazdazdan shares this insistence on "Aryanism" with other occult groups, whose influence on racialist theories has been (as we shall see) extremely important. For the moment it is necessary only to notice that theories which were later to achieve notoriety might easily form part of the fundamental move toward the irrational. And if within the fringe groups of the German irrationalists are discovered what can subsequently be seen as tenets of *political* significance, these should not be ignored. The interpretation must wait for the accumulation of more evidence.

Expectations of political apocalypse are never very far from hopes of the Coming of God's Kingdom, and it is interesting that several of the miscellaneous sects born of Germany's time of trouble display preoccupations which the hindsight of history can immediately detect as significant.

The *Gottesbund Tanatra* expected the advent of the Thousand Year Reich. Another Saxon sect, the Laurentians, shared this belief and made preparation for its imminent arrival. The world was to last 6,000 years, of which the last two thousand—from the coming of Christ to the establishment of the Thousand Year Reich—had almost elapsed. The elect (in Saxony some 5,000 of the Biblical total of 144,000) were to take the necessary clothes and food into the Erzgebirge, from which vantage-point they would contemplate Armageddon. Hermann Lorenz, the prophet who led the sect from 1914, involved himself and his followers in nationalist politics which the Laurentians found not at all incompatable with spiritualism, mystical speculation, and an admixture of peasant superstition. Most intriguing of all is the sect of the Weissenberger, which by the 1930s numbered over 100,000. The founder, Joseph Weissenberg (1855-1941) left his Silesian home sometime after the turn of the century in response to a vision of Christ and traveled to Berlin where he began practicing magnetic cures. In 1908 he left his wife, in whom he saw the embodiment of the Serpent, to live with a spirit medium called Gretchen Müller who was discovered to be the reincarnation of the Virgin Mary. (Frieda Müller—perhaps a daughter?—reestablished the cult in 1946.)

It is not so much such familiar trappings of the Weissenberger that are significant as the unequivocally political character of their tenets. They venerated Bismarck as the appointed savior of the state, and saw his fall as engineered by Freemasons and Jesuits. In the spiritualist sessions which confirmed Weissenberg's authority, prominent apparitions included Martin Luther, the *Geistfreund* Bismarck and the famous air ace Baron von Richthofen.[21] The prophecies of Weissenberg referred specifically to things of this world and particularly to the fate of those who had opposed Germany in the Great War.

England, of course, was doomed to utter perdition. On the 29th of May, 1929, at 11 P.M. it was destined to be obliterated from the face of the earth. When this did not happen Weissenberg decided that the truth of his prophecy remained unaffected. The divine chastisement was to come "like a thief in the night" and it was dangerous to predict exactly when. Nor was Italy to be spared. Italy had betrayed Germany in the Great War and was to be punished through a Bismarckian intervention. In the spring of 1929 the great struggle to free Germany would take place with little loss to the German side. The combat would be chiefly fought on the spiritual plane, with "Prince Michael, the Holy Spirit in Joseph Weissenberg" leading on the German forces, enlisted on the side of God under the holy banner of black, white and red. The introduction of the colors of fallen imperial Germany carries emotional overtones quite other than those of religious apocalypse and takes the inquirer directly into the territory of the illuminated predecessors of Nazism known as the *völkisch* movement. Paul Scheurlen, the indefatigable historian of German cults between the wars, noticed the tenor of the Weissenberger, and he made a more explicit connection. The weekly paper of the sect, he recorded—it went by the name of *Der Weisse Berg*—was printed on the presses of the *Deutsche Zeitung,* the organ of the ultranationalist Pan-German Association; and it was probable that members of the former Potsdam headquarters of that society were followers of the Weissenberger.[22] It becomes evident that something more is at work than the antics of eccentric sectaries.

Precisely what, it is our intention to uncover. It has already been indicated that the elements which had formed part of the flight from reason before 1914 were present generally in European society after the Great War; that the seeking for realities of another world was to be found outside the boundaries of defeated Germany, but that the effects of the War were naturally most severe within the territory of the former Hohenzollern Empire. It is, however, important to make a distinction between two groups of irrationalist movements. One group is formed by ill-defined or traditionally orientated sects, generated by anxiety and change. Such were the numerous Christian sects—whether imported, like the Adventists and the Apostles, or of native origin, such as Sheep and Shepherd of *Vater* Hain and the Laurentians. These represent the most basic responses to anxiety. The challenge of a forbidding future was countered by a compendium of Christian tradition, millennarian expectation, and the adoption of spiritual comforts temporarily in vogue. Of these, the most easily adaptable was spiritualism, which itself forms part of the first group of fundamentalist answers to the crisis. The second group is composed of those cults which took the trouble to present a more original theology and had their roots in the occultism of the pre-1914 Progressive Underground. The *Gottesbund Tanatra,* with its grade structure reminiscent of a magical temple, comes under this classification, as do the teaching about self-realization put about by Bô Yin Râ and the emphasis upon restoring the Aryan race to its pristine condition through nuts and colonic irrigation purveyed by Mazdaznan. This latter group naturally appealed to higher social levels and rather more educated classes than the more fundamentalist movements.

If the religious response is taken as a "basic response" to the crisis in human affairs, it should not surprise us to find similar transcendental, or "illuminated" approaches to politics, art, or society, attaching themselves to one or other of the essentially religious groups. It is a perfectly natural situation to find the Weissenberger attached to the Pan-Germans, or Mazdaznan advocating theories of Aryan supremacy. The illuminated approach to the basic problem of man's relationship with the universe does not necessarily entail an illuminated approach to politics; but such an approach is very likely indeed. In the historical period under review material reality represented for many people hardship, injustice, and lack of hope. They turned naturally to immaterial realities in all fields of human action. Put another way, they abandoned the present, induced by a rationalist, capitalist Establishment, in favor of possible futures entertained by the Irrationalist Underground. The "religious" response was the most basic—*but it did not have to be.* In Germany, the "Establishment" represented not only the Weimar government, but also the occupying powers and the whole Western commercial system which had reduced the Empire to defeat. We shall see how the Irrationalist Underground came to the surface in Nazi Germany in a political form: this is a symptom not of a particular, but a general crisis, involving all areas of human activity.

The irrational then, was abroad in 20th-century Germany. But so far we have examined only the secondary figures. The most influential occultists were a different caliber altogether. They can be divided into four main groups: (1) the Theosophy and Rosicrucianism of Prague and Vienna; (2) the Cosmic Circle of Munich; (3) the various colonies set up by the Progressive Underground to prepare for the coming new age; and (4) the Anthroposophy of Rudolph Steiner.

Central Europe had been affected by the 19th-century crisis of consciousness as much as areas on the periphery of the Continent. The difference was that the circles in which mystical viewpoints could be successfully maintained were smaller, the sources of occult lore in Paris, Adyar, or London dauntingly inaccessible, and the means of expressing such convictions more limited than in France or England. Within such groups as did exist, and for these very reasons, the dedicated attitude of the members made up for their lack of numbers.

In 1891, for example, the Theosophical Lodge of the Blue Star was established in Prague and it consisted of only ten members, meeting at the flat of the novelist Gustav Meyrink and presided over by Karel Weinfurter. This small group of persons imposed on themselves considerable austerities. For two-and-a half years they became vegetarians, gave up alcohol, and resigned all worldly pleasures in the hopes of attaining to some higher state of consciousness; but all these sacrifices produced no effects, and were abandoned. Their first hero in matters occult was the Freemason J. B. Kerning—in fact Johann Baptist Krebs (1774-1851)—whose writings they perused assiduously.

At the beginning of the 1890s Kerning had suddenly come back into fashion, rather like the weighty Jacob Lorber. In 1893, Dr. Hübbe-Schleiden of the Theosophical Society decided to republish his works with Franz Hartmann as editor. But the Prague occultists found ultimately as little to satisfy them in the murky symbolism of Kerning as in their regime of austerity.[23]

They tried breathing exercises and other occult disciplines. They wrote enthusiastically to any publisher of occult literature in the hopes that he might have something to offer them. They made contact with a magician who lived in the north of England, was over eighty years old, and published a journal called *The Magic Mirror.* "From the contents of the journal it was manifest that he had attained certain results in ceremonial Magic. In particular he was able to evoke the different forces dwelling in old trees." Some of the members of the Lodge of the Blue Star began to practice the old Englishman's concentration exercises, one of which seemed to produce results: it concerned the evocation of "a certain spiritual Brotherhood, of which the Pole Star was both the symbol and the force-giving center." Those who carried out the instructions obtained identical visions, but the distant and ever-watchful Theosophical Society of Vienna warned them to proceed no further. The Lodge of the Blue Star turned sadly back to the Tantric exercises contained in Rama Prasad's *Nature's Finer Forces,* a Theosophical publication which did little or nothing for the Prague Theosophists although it probably assured those of Vienna that the Blue Star was not liable to slip from their control.[24]

The translator of *Nature's Finer Forces*—and of other Theosophical books[25] was Gustav Meyrink, whose celebrity as a novelist during and after the First World War is matched only by his rapid eclipse thereafter. Gustav Meyrink was born Gustav Meyer in Vienna in 1886. His father was Karl von Varnbüler von und zu Hemmingen, minister of state for Württemberg; his mother the Bavarian actress Maria Meyer. After a cheerless upbringing, Meyrink entered a bank belonging to his mother's family and settled in Prague, where he led a life to all appearances extravagant, snobbish, and shocking. He made an unsuccessful first marriage, and his second was nearly prevented by his future brother-in-law, whose brother-officers fought a long succession of duels with the unfortunate Meyrink. In the middle of a scandal, surrounded by allegations that he ran his bank with aid of spiritualist prognostications, Meyrink was thrown into jail, and underwent a physical crisis—he was thought to have broken his spine, and he temporarily lost the use of both of his legs. While in a sanatorium recovering from these and other ailments, Meyrink met the writer Oskar A. H. Schmitz, who encouraged him to write. Immediately Meyrink wrote a short story, which he had accepted by *Simplicissimus*. In 1903 he had his first collection published; and in 1905 he married for a second time in Dover.[26]

From the inception of the Lodge of the Blue Star, Meyrink played host to its members. His own interest in the occult began in the year of the lodge's foundation. Meyrink had been contemplating suicide as the result of an unhappy love affair, when his gloomy deliberations were interrupted by a magazine pushed under his door. It turned out to be an occult magazine, and the young man "put to sea," as he expressed it, into a boundless ocean of occult books. He then set out to look for a Master, in company with the other seekers of the Lodge of the Blue Star. Meyrink tried Orientals, clairvoyants, prophets, and ecstatics of all sorts; but to no avail. In the laboratory of the Munich psychical researcher Baron Schrenk-Notzing he snipped a fragment of "ectoplasm" for chemical analysis off the baron's famous medium "Eva C" and thus began the exposure of poor Eva. Through the Blue Star and the Theosophists of Vienna, he came into contact with Annie Besant, and he began a correspondence with a pupil of Ramakrishna who lived in the Himalayas. He read much Theosophical literature, and through taking up Yoga he claimed to have achieved a telepathic contact with an Indian Maharishi who also became the guru of Paul Brunton. According to an unidentified friend of Meyrink writing to his biographer, Meyrink had undergone unpleasant experiences with exercises recommended by Kerning and with others advocated by "Sebottendorff" (presumably the Rudolf Freiherr von Sebottendorff of whom there will be more to say). Meyrink apparently succeeded in provoking certain paranormal experiences. One attempt to transport himself psychically to the home of a painter friend resulted in his producing a perceptible effect on a table, and he seems to have managed to appear visibly to his first wife. During the period of his strictest regimen—which probably coincided with his contact with the headquarters of the Theosophists—he took only three hours sleep a night, observed a strict vegetarian diet, performed arduous exercises, and drank gum-arabic twice a day to induce clairvoyance. At the end of these privations he had a vision like that of the Emperor Constantine (*in hoc signo vinces*") and of abstract geómetrical designs.[27]

Meyrink was sadly disillusioned by many of his occult investigations. In 1921 he was writing that, although there were indeed occult orders, it was an error to imagine that their members had any special powers. He had tried everything—even the most practical alchemy. All the necessary conditions for the alchemical "first matter," as he thought, were fulfilled by an element called "*Struvit*" or "*Ulex*" which had only been discovered in Germany (in Hamburg, Dresden, and Braunschweig) and always in ancient sewers. It therefore arose, argued Meyrink, in human excrement; and this substance fulfilled all the conditions laid down in alchemical texts. It was yellow in color, conductive, and crystallized. So from a "primaeval cess-pit" in Prague, he took a lump of excrement about the size of a nut and followed the instructions of his textbooks. The necessary color-changes took place, but at a crucial point of the process his retort burst and the half-transformed *prima materia* hit the aspiring alchemist in the face. It should not be thought from this that Meyrink's credulity was unbounded. The story is told of a visit paid to the novelist's house on the Starnbergersee by a wandering prophet known as the *Wunderapostel* Hauser, who hammered on the door in the middle of the night and announced portentously, "I AM." Meyrink asked him to complete the sentence: "I am Christ," decided Hauser. The novelist led him down to the shores of the lake and commanded, "Walk!" The *Wunderapostel* considered his declaration again and rephrased the sentence: "I am hungry." Whereupon Meyrink led him back to the house for a meal.[28]

The outcome of Meyrink's occult experiments was a series of remarkable novels and short stories, almost all dealing with some aspect of the occult quest for perfection. His most popular novel, *The Golem,* was published during the Great War, and sold over 200,000 copies. It concerns mysterious doings in the ghetto of Prague and—as in *The Greater Trumps* of Charles Williams—a leading role is played by the symbolism of the Tarot pack. In Meyrink's novels the quest is perpetually in the foreground; the object of the hero is to be, as one of his characters phrases it, "both on this side and on that side of the veil a living being." This is perhaps most easily seen in a short tale, *Master Leonhard.* The hero is involved in a gruesome tragedy, is disillusioned with the world, but finds no consolation in the Church. In response to an obscure inner prompting, Master Leonhard sets off in search of the long-dead master of the Order of the Templars, Jacob de Vitriaco. On the way he falls in with a quack doctor, Dr. Schrepfer, a worker of miracles. Everything Schrepfer does is two-edged—"he lies and his speech contains the highest truth: he speaks the truth and lies smirk out from it."[29] Eventually Master Leonhard sees through the magician and pursues his quest to a vision of the one, eternal "I," learning the lesson that all his fantastic adventures are merely "the wandering of the soul in circles through mists of existence towards death." This story even in bald outline bears interesting hints of a psychology like that of C. G. Jung, himself an admirer of Meyrink. It is important to notice that its author sprang from occultist groups of the 1890s to literary celebrity, and that the final message was a refusal to accept the problems of the present as insurmountable. The tortured soul of Master Leonhard "comes home at last": and this insistence on the "return home," the *Heimkehr,* is by no means confined to Meyrink in German literature of the period. In some cases it sprang from an occult basis and referred to the return of the weary human soul into the bosom of Deity; in others, it took root merely in the general condition of anxiety and represented a despairing hope that the anguish would one day be over. The myth of the "Return Home" was pervasive and significant.

By the time that Meyrink himself returned to whatever awaited him, in December 1932 in the "House of the Last Lamp" on the Starnbergersee, his friends of the Blue Star had themselves advanced from their frantic searchings of the 1890s. Several had committed themselves to a particular school, a particular vision of reality. This commitment was reached only after searchings as devious as those of Meyrink himself. Their asceticism had little result, although their friends of the Theosophical Society in Vienna contrived to prevent the Prague circle from coming to much physical harm. But they themselves were in an equally barren state, despite the fact that one of their number "had been fasting for fourteen years, being emaciated to the bones. At the same time he was sleeping on a ladder, carrying out different ascetic practices." Three members of the Prague group went to London and joined the Esoteric Section of Annie Besant's Theosophical Society; but they decided that the practices carried out in that organization were as ineffectual as any they had previously tried. Eventually, one of the most dedicated of the

Blue Star occultists achieved some spectacular results with magical experiments in concentration. These are described as "an imagination practice"; and the imagination of an unnamed "Mr. R." was so powerful as to enable him to cut his hand on an imaginary knife and to burn his finger in the flame of a visualized candle. Full of his success, Mr. R. left for Vienna to tell the Theosophists there of what he had achieved: they only poured cold water on his aspirations. A few days after his disconsolate return to Prague, he received a cable from Vienna: "Come at once, the way is open." The Prague occultists hastened to Vienna to sit at the feet of the Master whom the Viennese had found after so much searching.[30]

It was a severe comedown after their exotic experiments to find that the new leader taught a doctrine that was almost entirely Christian. He was evidently a weaver by trade and quite elderly when they made contact with him. He claimed to have been initiated by a "true Rosicrucian" and was definite about forbidding all practical magic. Among his disciples was Franz Hartmann, the Theosophist, and obviously some adherents of great wealth, as the weaver was presented with a country house by an admirer the day after he resigned from the factory where he had worked. In his circle great stress was laid on Kerning; on Bô Yin Râ (whose writings were thought to be the continuation of Kerning's work); and on other German mystics like von Eckartshausen and Angelus Silesius, together with texts of the occult revival like the *Oupnek'hat* and the American mystic Prentice Mulford. It seems also that the group around the weaver was either connected through him or afterward became aligned with the Anthroposophy and "Rosicrucianism" preached by the influential Rudolf Steiner. The Second Coming of Christ was confidently expected: "His word will penetrate the world like fire."[31]

Of the Lodge of the Blue Star and the group around the enigmatic weaver, nothing further can be said. But the Viennese Theosophists who kept such vigilant watch over their younger brothers in mysticism and who directed them to their chosen guru merit closer attention. Their leading spirit was Friedrich Eckstein, a gray eminence of Viennese cultural life, who published almost none of his occult work but whose private lectures seem to have exercised considerable influence on those—like Gustav Meyrink—who heard them.[32]

Friedrich Eckstein was born about 1860, the son of a paper manufacturer near Vienna. His interest in mysticism and the occult began almost as early as was possible for Central Europe. At the age of twenty he met Dr. Oscar Simony, a *Dozent* at Vienna University, whose speciality was number theory.

Simony was concerned with the possibility of further mathematical dimensions and, accordingly, followed with interest the experiments of Professor Zöllner of Leipzig, who postulated a fourth dimension of space. Zöllner became ensnared by spiritualism through his keenness to prove the existence of his fourth dimension and interpreted the feats performed by the Spiritualist medium Henry Slade on the basis of spirits operating in this hypothetical area. In 1879 Zöllner published the third part of his *Scientific Essays* embodying his experiments with Slade. The consequent furor naturally concerned Simony, who persuaded his old friend Lazar, Baron Hellenbach (a speculative metaphysician and the leading Austrian spiritualist) to bring Slade to Vienna so that he could test Professor Zöllner's conclusions for himself. Hellenbach's protégés were notoriously unsuccessful: the baron had once had to undergo the ignominy of seeing the Archduke Johann unmask the medium Harry Bastian.[33] Simony had no luck with Bastian and little with Slade, who broke control during the séance, although apparently he succeeded temporarily in making a table vanish.

The mathematician—who was chiefly interested in refuting Zöllner's theory of the fourth dimension—concocted a theory that mediums possessed abnormal muscular development and that the electrical energy in their peculiar muscular contractions could produce the phenomena attributed to the spirits.[34] According to their original project, Slade was to have stayed with Friedrich Eckstein during the period of Simony's experiments, but he refused to come unaccompanied, and as the object of the plan had been to prevent any possibility of confederacy, the scheme was dropped. Eckstein's first encounter with the miraculous was unfortunate. Shortly afterwards he and Simony visited the distinguished British scientist Lord Rayleigh, who was at that time living in Vienna, and recounted their experiences. Rayleigh claimed to have seen Indian ascetics move objects from a distance, and Simony asked how he explained this. Rayleigh answered that it was obviously the work of the spirits, and to the astonished query of his visitors he replied that he believed in spirits because he *saw* them.[35]

Eckstein determined that he would discover whether there were grounds for such belief and decided to join the newly founded Theosophical Society. He corresponded with Theosophists everywhere and traveled to England, where he met H. P. Blavatsky, Colonel Olcott, A. P. Sinnett, and the retinue of Indian members who accompanied the leading Theosophists to Europe on their visit of 1884. He brought back with him a whole library of occult works. Meanwhile, it became clear to him and Simony that in order to test mediums satisfactorily they would have to become experts in sleight-of-hand rather than in esoteric philosophy. The mathematician's interest in the spirits waned after a substantial rebuff dealt his career when he had rashly expressed his misgivings about mediums at the dinner table of an influential *Excellenz*. Eckstein, on the other hand, although always circumspect in his occult dealings, progressed from primitive spiritualist phenomena to an abiding interest in occult philosophy. He visited H. P. Blavatsky at Ostend not long before her death, and in the early 1890s he went to live for a few months in London to carry out some business in connection with his profession as a chemist. He had a laboratory in the Victoria Docks, was appalled by the British habit of commuting—he lived in South Kensington—and was disgusted by bank holidays. At the same time he was closely in contact with Annie Besant and the "esoteric Christian" Edward Maitland; he became particularly friendly with Herbert Burrows and was able to soothe his disturbed nerves with a Theosophical vegetarian picnic near Maidenhead, at which Mohini M. Chaterji gave a talk on the *Bhagavad Gita*. It was largely through Eckstein's agency that the Vienna Theosophical Society came into existence and it was probably his directing hand that hovered over the Prague Lodge of the Blue Star.[36]

It is of great importance to understand the sort of circles in which Eckstein moved and in which his Theosophy found a ready welcome. With the alteration of time and place, these were very like the artistic coteries of Symbolist Paris, or the similar groups on the fringes of the English Decadence in which the occult revival found its earliest supporters. Instead of Baudelaire, however, the Grand Master of the idealistic Underground in the German-speaking countries was quite naturally Richard Wagner. The composer-playwright's handling of myth coincided with "esoteric" interpretations favored by the occultists.[37] His early setting of the occultist Bulwer Lytton's novel *Rienzi* gave an obvious clue to budding mystics. In 1880, just at the time when Eckstein became interested in spiritualism and belonged to the central clique of the Viennese idealists, the Bayreuth Master wrote an essay entitled *Religion and Art* which had the profoundest effect on the Progressive youth which sat at his feet, and particularly on Eckstein's immediate circle.[38]

Religion and Art is in many ways the synthesis of all the goals of the Progressive Underground in the period before the First World War. Wagner called for Art's return to its high vocation of symbolically expressing divine truth, and he announced his program to redeem the world from materialism by the practice of symbolically conceived music. He also praised the ecstatic rites of the American Shakers and gave expression to the underlying anxiety which afflicted many of his readers. "The deepest basis of every true religion we see now in the knowledge of the transitoriness of the world, and arising from this, the positive instruction to free oneself from it." The composer's vegetarianism and his opposition to vivisection place him directly in the category of the Progressive Underground, and his vision of the coming regeneration of man matched the apocalypses of the greatest enthusiasts. He castigated the hypocrisy rampant among his fellow vegetarians. There were those who "set the basic precondition of the problem of regenerating the human race firmly in view." But "from a few superior members is heard the complaint that their comrades have taken up abstaining from flesh merely from personal consideration of diet, and in no way coupled with it the great ideals of regeneration which they must approach if the organization wants to win power."[39] There was to be a league of noble spirits pledged to redeem mankind from its fall through the achievement of individual salvation. Of such spirits, Friedrich Eckstein was among the most possessed. For the first performance of *Parsifal* he made the journey to Bayreuth on foot; and there was a legend—which was not in fact true—that he had gone in sandals, like Tannhäuser.[40]

At the end of the 1870s a favorite rendezvous of Eckstein's group of young Viennese idealists was a vegetarian restaurant on the corner of Wallnerstrasse and Fahnengasse. Here they met in a gas-lit cellar to talk of Pythagoras, the Essenes, the Neo-Platonists, therapeutics, and the evils of flesh eating. "Ever and again there swam before us the vision of Empedocles of a golden age in which the greatest sacrilege for men would be 'To take life and stuff oneself with noble elements.' " The group consisted of a typical collection of Bohemians. Eckstein's description of the scene gives substance to the rumors of his Wagnerian pilgrimage. "It was mostly young people who met there and took part in the collective exchange of views: students, teachers, artists and followers of the most diverse professions. While I myself, like several of my closest friends went summer and winter almost completely clad in linen, according to the theories of Pythagoras, others appeared clothed in hairy garments of natural coloring. And if you add to this that most of us had shoulder-length hair and full beards, our lunch-table might have reminded an unselfconscious spectator not a little of Leonardo's Last Supper." The spiritual descendants of this lunch-table are everywhere. To this circle belonged two later *Staatspräsidenten* as well as the young Hermann Bahr and the Polish poet Siegfried Lipiner, who was in correspondence with Nietzsche. Victor Adler, the founder of the Social Democratic Party, occasionally came. Gustav Mahler turned up, and Eckstein's future roommate, the composer Hugo Wolf, met the Pythagorean Theosophist at his vegetarian *Stammtisch*. For the first performance of *Parsifal* in the summer of 1882, the group met at Bayreuth. In Vienna, another rendezvous was the Café Griensteidl on the Michaelerplatz, known locally because of its clientele as Megalomania Café. The crowning success of these young irrationalists was their summer colony of the year 1888, when they took the Schloss Bellevue at Grinzing and filled it even fuller with eccentricity than the Café Griensteidl.[41]

To the Schloss came the feminist Marie Lang and her husband Edmund (both at the center of Theosophical gatherings and the protectors of Hugo Wolf). Friedrich Eckstein's friend from student days, Rosa Mayreder, who was to become another leading protagonist of women's rights, developed during the summer a friendship with Hugo Wolf that led to their collaboration on the opera *Der Corregidor*. Other visitors were Carl, Graf zu Leiningen-Billigheim, a young diplomat who had attached himself to Eckstein because of his acquaintance with H. P. Blavatsky, and the dubious Theosophist Franz Hartmann, who received unusual visitors from all parts of the world and had already presumed on Eckstein's hospitality for a whole year immediately after his return from India. Marie Lang cooked vegetarian meals. Wolf composed *Lieder*. Theosophy was the main topic of conversation.[42]

In Vienna, as in the rest of the world, the more occult aspects of Theosophy—the elaborate cosmology, the miracles, the letters from Mahatmas—went hand in hand with the "progressive" in social thought. Indeed, there was a necessary association between all idealistic forms of opposition to that which existed. As Leiningen-Billigheim saw it: "In the middle of the chaotic pattern of pleasure-seeking and covetousness, error, arrogance, self-deception, and cowardice, the idealistic point of view once more arises as a helpful and ultimately victorious force."[43] It is symptomatic of the climate in which he spoke that the title of the essay from which these general observations are taken is "What is Mysticism?" and that it was published in a Theosophical series. Against the common enemy all idealists united; and, some of those bent on restructuring the world would adopt some portion of Theosophy as a concession to their religious impulses. Theosophy was Progressively respectable; often Christianity was not.

It is worth examining some of these associates of Eckstein. Hugo Wolf was a composer of the Wagnerian school; Eckstein, who had private means and musical interests—he was the continual companion and unofficial private secretary to the aging Brückner—offered to finance the publication of Wolf's *Lieder*. This proved not to be necessary; but the Theosophist and the composer lived together for a period. Wolf's biographer has described their friendship: "Eckstein's knowledge was encyclopaedic: his rooms were lined from floor to ceiling with books and scores. They discussed *Parsifal* together in relation to German and Spanish mysticism, Palestrina's masses, freemasonry, vegetarianism, and various oriental subjects." After the summer colony at Grinzing, Wolf and Eckstein left once more for *Parsifal* at Bayreuth on the *Wagner-Verein's* special train. Together they hunted all the way through Swedenborg's *Arcana Coelestia* for the sources of Berlioz's Hellish language in the *Damnation of Faust*.

With Hermann Bahr, the leading critical exponent of Expressionist theories, Eckstein maintained a relationship through discussions on metaphysics—often in a three-handed commerce with Hugo von Hoffmansthal. Bahr had arrived in Vienna in 1887 direct from a Paris in which the mystical was rampant and Rosicrucian Orders revived. As he wrote, "every student made himself out a Paracelsus in front of his *grisette;* seriously or half in fun there was everywhere an anxious yearning *vers les au-delà-mystiques.*" He found a home from home in the Café Griensteidl. Bahr gave thanks that he had gone to Paris when he did; for there, he thought, the spirit of the 18th century was finally being overturned. In the Socialist Victor Adler, whom he had known from Berlin, he saw something of the same process of "spiritualization"—the Marxist was becoming an idealist.[44] Even the feminist Rosa Mayreder displayed what has seemed to at least one commentator her own sort of mysticism in which theories of the respective roles of the sexes can be compared to the alchemical fusion of opposites.[45]

This milieu will become of crucial importance when we come to consider the origins of psychoanalysis and the early work of Freud.

If in Prague and Vienna there were hints that the philosophical substrata of everyday were crumbling, Munich at the turn of the century might have displayed, to those with eyes to see it, a similar instability. It must be emphasized that this condition was not specifically a German condition, but European; and it is a wrong use of historical hindsight which discovers in German culture alone the necessary ingredients for political irrationalism. At the turn of the 19th and 20th centuries it was not at all certain—unless one believed in the gloomy prophecies of a Marxist determinism—what was to emerge from the rubble when the materialist bastion had fallen. A restructured logic? a pre-Adamite humanity? At any rate a new world, imagined in its variegated and terrifying colors in the artists' quarters and Bohemian resorts of the great cities. In Munich, this meant Schwabing.

> Schwabing!—the suburb not only of Munich, oh no: "the suburb of a new world!" . . . I have contrived simply to exist there as a mere man: a simple man of his time amidst all these abnormalities and enormities, an insignigicant creature amongst all these strident super-men, under-men, new men

and nonmen. Whole crowds of these prodigies surrounded me: partly intellects of exceptional talent, partly only unusually foolish poseurs and confidence tricksters![46]

There were the "Cosmics" who assembled "in incense-laden, hieratically-gloomy studios high up in the attics of working-class suburban houses"; protagonists of all forms of nationality; and occultists:

> The occult fashion of the time after the first world war had its origin here in Schwabing! Theosophists, of course feuding among themselves to the extent of the most fanatical hatred, and splintered into different schools of thought; mystics, Gnostics, Taoists, Mazdaists, Buddhists, Neo-Buddhists, Zionists crowded together with Nihilists, Collectivists, Syndicalists, Bolshevists, Pacifists (these mostly women, here known as "Peace-furies") and other world-reforming fanatics of all races. Here everything impossible to man was jumbled together with all human possibilities. All types of humanity came together, from the tragic inner circle around the Most High, from those who were never tired of themselves, from those bitten by heroism to sacrifice themselves for an idea, for a great matter, for a divine Leader, for a woman.[47]

This was the atmosphere of the age which even then the astrologers were heralding as the Age of Aquarius. The most original contribution that Munich made to the new irrationalism came from a group which formed, at first, part of the charmed "George Circle" around Stefan George and his magazine, *Blätter für die Kunst;* it subsequently broke off, becoming known in Schwabing as the "Cosmic Circle." Apart from George himself, the most influential figures were Alfred Schuler, Ludwig Klages, Karl Wolfskehl, and Ludwig Derleth. There also presided over the posturings and proclamations the spirit of the romantic Swiss anthropologist J. J. Bachofen (1815-87), whose ideas were enthusiastically adopted by the Munich Cosmics.

In 1890 Michael Georg Conrad founded in Schwabing the Society for Modern Life, around which had gathered George, Wolfskehl, Schuler, and Countess Fanny von Reventlow. Two years later the first issue of *Blätter für die Kunst* appeared, with its proclamation of a new "spiritual art" and the obvious overtones of French Symbolism which its perpetrators at once denied. It would get no one anywhere, they maintained, to call them "symbolists," "decadents," or "occultists." Yet in 1895 Wolfskehl is found announcing that "A new priesthood has arisen to found a new Empire of the spirit," and it was for his "spiritual" qualities that Stefan George was prized by subsequent generations of German youth. George remained resolutely attached to his poetry and could not be dislodged from his isolated and aesthetic stance to take part with the others in attempts to hammer out a plan for a new society. As Alfred Schuler said: "George has the power! But what does he create with it?—Art!" On the other hand, Klages, Schuler, and to some extent Wolfskehl tried to envisage a real future from their initially aesthetic positions. Their visions were symbolic, transcendental, and "illuminated," possessing little coherence outside the context of the self-contained world which engendered them.[48]

In 1899 Schuler, Klages, and Wolfskehl first came together. All three were influenced by Nietzsche and the spirit of *Blätter für die Kunst,* but the presiding influence on the group was Bachofen. The appeal of the Swiss anthropologist rested on his romantic approach to evidence, supported by a cult of ancient Rome (which became widespread around the turn of the century, not only among the Cosmics) and, most importantly, by his theory of human evolution. This postulated five stages from the most primitive society till that of the present day. The original condition of man, however, was expressed by the term "Mother-Right," for Bachofen considered that the state of nature had been a condition of complete sexual promiscuity in which the mother's name was the only recognized basis of establishing kinship and hence of social relations. He argued this through the interpretation of color-symbolism and funeral ornaments, as well as from well-known facts such as that in some primitive tribes no connection is yet made between copulation and conception. To the appeal of his symbolic method, therefore, Bachofen added the vision of a Golden Age, free from repression, in which all might discover their ideal.[49]

It was a vision peculiarly adapted to the times, and it harmonized well with the irrationalist opposition to the society which was. Wolfskehl was intrigued by hermaphroditic Oriental gods and so found food for thought in Bachofen; Klages saw in his symbols the designs of a sinless humanity. Schuler took over the cult of the Great Mother and combined it with his personal mysticism and reverence for ancient Rome.[50]

Ludwig Klages (1872-1956) began his unorthodox inquiries into the nature of humanity in the field of graphology. He had become interested in the scientific study of handwriting at the age of sixteen. In 1896 he and the criminologist Hans Heinrich Busse founded the German Graphological Society and began to issue a journal for their rapidly expanding membership. One of Klages's graphological colleagues introduced him to Schuler as "an interesting paranoid." Alfred Schuler (1865-1923) lived with his mother until she died in 1912, and cultivated mystical theories and a reverence for Rome; for some time he had studied archaeology in the seminar of the Munich archaeologist Furtwängler. At the time he met Klages, Schuler was contemplating an exposition of his theories in the form of a novel dealing with life in the Rome of the Emperor Nero. Schuler impressed the graphologist by deducing from one of his poems a sexual experience which Klages had had at the age of eight or nine and had kept firmly secret.

The two circumspectly approached Wolfskehl—who, as a Jew, was immediately suspect to Schuler, a great part of whose theories turned on the importance of "pure" blood.[51] The climax of this association, which led to the beginning of the breach between the Cosmics and their earlier hero, Stefan George, came in April 1899, when Schuler gave a "Roman feast" to which George and the Cosmic Circle were invited. As Schuler took the floor and began to declaim, George increasingly showed signs of impatience while the others lapsed more and more under the speaker's spell. Eventually George succeeded in persuading Klages to leave with him and demanded to be taken from the house of madmen to the nearest and most ordinary beer house where good, solid, ordinary citizens swilled beer and smoked cigars.[52] The prophet of spiritual art balked at the prophet of an irrationalist civilization. The breach was smoothed over until 1904, when the combination of Schuler's and Klages's anti-Semitism and Wolfskehl's divided loyalties caused the secession of the latter from the Cosmics and their final rupture with George. After the quarrel with George, Schuler went about claiming that George had bewitched him into impotence, and Klages took some twenty years to recover.[53]

George's opinion of Schuler seems to have fluctuated. In 1901 he dedicated a poem to "the genius of Alfred Schuler"; and Wolfskehl's wife reported a remark made by George to a mutual friend: "When I saw Schuler for the first time, I had the feeling that I stood before a Potency." But George could not stomach the events of the years 1900-04 in which the Cosmics attempted to make Munich the center of a new, "Cosmic" consciousness. They were to overturn the established order and return to the *Urheimat* of the soul, the primeval realm of freedom displayed by Bachofen; or, as it has also been put, to liberate the forces of the unconscious. Thus Schuler, reproached by Stefan George for his disregard for Art, replied that he preferred to live—he might almost say, *to be lived*.[54]

The liberation of the new consciousness involved some recourse to the old magic. Schuler at one point projected a resurrection of an ancient Greek dance of healing to cure the sick Nietzsche, in which the dancers would wear copper armor. Klages met in the Cosmic Circle a "Jewish Egyptologist, a member of a secret order" who told him that he had an astral body, but had not yet traveled in it. Even in the less extravagant society of Stefan George, the occult had always had some place, for all the coy disclaimers; and it is entirely appropriate that George's circle after the breach with Klages and Schuler should include the writer on occultism Maz Dessoir, as well as the young English musician Cyril Scott, who was later to become a devoted Theosophist.[55]

For Klages and Schuler, the return to primeval consciousness signified different, and almost equally indefinite, ideals. Klages set Bachofen on his head. Whereas the anthropologist had seen in the overthrow of Mother-Right the triumph of Apollo over the demonic forces of the old world, Klages saw this as a sin against the spirit and yearned for a return to the times of antiquity. He came to preach the triumph of "Eros"—which signified for him cosmic ecstasy.

> Eros means elemental or cosmic, inasmuch as the individual possessed by it, experiences himself as penetrated and flowed through by an instantaneous electrical current.

Originally, however, Eros had signified blood-brotherhood, and this "racial self-consciousness" would lead all its bearers back into the secret of the sinless world.[56] Schuler's theories, even more than those of Klages, emphasized the racial doctrine. He found his reverence for Rome supported in Bachofen, seeing the Roman Empire as the stalwart defense of the West against the debilitating influences of the Orient. Jews and Christians together contrived the fall of the Empire; but the Aryan race alone had preserved a pure bloodline. Along both Rhine and Danube Klages discovered what he called the "illumination of the blood."[57]

It is becoming clearer that certain notorious theories which became bound up with Nazism are part and parcel of the search for "immaterial reality"; but this is not at the moment the important point. We have not moved far away from occultism pure and simple. We are still in the sociological territory of the Underground, and the undifferentiated yearning for an ideal state of human nature is to be found in many hearts during the decade 1890-1910. The insistence of Schuler that Judeo-Christian civilization suppressed the true German virtues is naturally seen in the context of later political history. But his theme, that the true religion—or culture, or science—has been concealed by an Establishment conspiracy is a staple of occult literature. We have seen it already in the works of the Freemason Kerning, and it finds a notable expression in Madame Blavatsky's *Isis Unveiled*. The precise definition of Underground and Establishment is always up to the definer. Time and place always worked upon the basic impulse, and ideas like Schuler's were resurrected after the Great War in very specific form.

Ludwig Derleth was another prophet who lived in Schwabing, that suburb of the new world, at the time of the Cosmic Circle's crusade to alter the consciousness of their contemporaries. He was peripherally a "Cosmic" himself, but of a different stamp. Ludwig Derleth (1870-1948) forms an important link between the illuminates of Munich and the major figures of the occult revival. In 1889-92 he was at Munich University studying a wide range of subjects. After a wretched period of schoolmastering and some small success with his poetry, Derleth left his job and entered a monastery near Munich in 1896. Next year he journeyed to Rome, with the intent of studying for the priesthood and founding a new religious order. The German College refused to admit him, and he was enrolled in the Polish Community of the Resurrectionists. Three months after his admittance he was dismissed for lack of vocation, and he made for Paris, threatening to make himself the leader of "such a movement as has not yet been seen in the history of the world."

He lived for a while on the Isle Saint-Louis but failed to find any candidates for the projected Order. Four years earlier, Derleth had visited the Catholic magus Joséphin Péladan, and it seems that on this second visit to Paris he renewed his occult friendships which included Papus (Gérard Encausse) and his disciple, Paul Sédir. The inspiration behind Derleth's scheme for a new order was George Oppenheimer, whom Derleth had met in the Munich monastery. Oppenheimer dubbed the group of friends a "Company" and ordered Derleth to call him "His Majesty." Derleth announced that he would resign from the Company when he had converted three worthy men. By 1899 he had lost hope in his artistic and esoteric connections and again began to teach in Munich. His inspirer Oppenheimer dropped out completely: he appeared briefly in Munich as a musician in 1900, in 1913 he left Montmartre for Tibet to return as a Buddhist lama, and he was later noticed by the Paris literati in the Café du Dôme. In 1924 he surfaced once more in Munich as an irrecoverable degenerate.[58]

Ludwig Derleth was a deeply committed member of the idealistic and occultist Underground, and the fate of Oppenheimer might well have been his. He had met Alfred Schuler in the middle of the 1890s, and remained respectful although cool toward him. Derleth saw the séances, in which Schwabing believed Schuler to indulge, as black magic. When the Cosmic circle broke up in 1904, he issued invitations to three readings of his *Proclamations* which held forth the promise of a new world as irrationalist as that of Schuler but based on principles entirely his own. To one of these readings came the novelist Thomas Mann.

> There were sermons, comparisons, theses, laws, visions, prophecies and exhortations like Orders of the Day, which followed each other in gaudy and unpredictable series in a mixture of styles drawn from the tones of the Psalms or Revelations together with technical terms from military strategy as well as philosophical criticism. A feverish and terribly waspish Ego elevated itself in lonely megalomania, and threatened the world with a flood of powerful words. *Christus Imperator Maximus* was his name, and he was recruiting death-hardened troops for the conquest of the globe; he appointed embassies, stipulated his pitiless conditions; he demanded poverty and chastity, and repeated

> again and again in unbounded tumult with a sort of unnatural sensuality the order for implicit obedience. Buddha, Alexander, Napoleon and Jesus were named as his humble predecessors, unworthy to clean the shoes of the spiritual emperor....
>
> Calumnies and Hosannahs—incense and the reek of blood mingled. In thunderous battles the world was conquered and set free.[59]

The Proclamations were a nine-day wonder and remained in the minds of their hearers for very much longer. The concluding sentence became notorious: *"Soldiers, I deliver unto you for plundering—the world!"* The second *Schwabinger Beobachter,* the newspaper of the Bohemians, which was edited by Countess Reventlow and Oskar Schmitz, appeared after the readings with a motto describing the advent in Schwabing of *"Jesus Bonaparte."*[60] With Schuler and Klages, Derleth shared an admiration for Napoleon; but the coming Reich of Christ the King was his alone. He had not given up all hopes of founding an Order. The flat he shared with his devoted sister in Munich remained until 1924 a place of pilgrimage for the idealistic intelligentsia, and Derleth became occupied with the thought of translating his concepts into practice.

Under the stress of the Great War, and in mounting distaste for the civilization which had produced it, many of the denizens of Schwabing were moving to the country to found colonies where the true life could be lived away from the collective mistakes of humanity. In 1916 Derleth's friend Christine Ulrich moved to Kassel to look for the good life on the land. The Schwabing prophet wrote a new version of the *Proclamations* and dreamed of the establishment of his ideal city, the *Rosenburg.*

In the *Rosenburg,* the inmates would have the freedom to work under the direction of the master of the order toward the alchemical transmutation. Their task would also be to train the younger generation as an élite.

> Through fasting, prayer and ascetic exercises, through the washing of the body and the purification of the soul, through the natural music of the sacred trees, when there is a storm and the metallic beeches crash their branches together, prepare yourselves . . . and grow in the temple-garden of the

Order; young eagles, who when you are fledged, may fly over the walls of Paradise.

Derleth's biographer compares the project of the Order to other attempted Utopias founded at this time, and specifically to the Order of the New Templars of Lanz von Liebenfels and the mythical Castalian Order of Hermann Hesse. Hesse's creation—a secluded order where elite spirits take part in the "Glass Bead Game," the supreme synthesis of human achievement, somewhere between mysticism, mathematics, and music—is a sort of distillation of all the Utopian plans in the air between the wars. (We shall take up later the specifically political and German aspects of Lanz's orders.)

Derleth's *Rosenburg,* although itself never realized, did bear tangible fruit. Utopian conceptions were all of a piece with the temper of the times, and it will be useful to survey here some of the more nebulous of such achievements, which embodied the idealistic impulse without more specific goals than the establishment of a small enclave in the city of Mammon. For, as Derleth put it: "Over the whole world asylums of inner freedom are multiplying themselves," and the search for another reality to be found within a closed circle was in Germany before and after the First World War a part—as it always had been—of the search to realize the good on earth.

If Derleth's vision of a healthy soul in a purified body seems reminiscent of the less poetic Utopia of Mazdaznan, the similarity of some of his aims to those of the followers of Otto Hanisch should not be glossed over. The retreat from material reality took place with a few basic ideas—the evilness of society as at the time constituted, the evilness of sacrificing animal life to live oneself, the necessity for "spiritual" development, and the training of the better men who were to follow. But the precise combination of social theory, vegetarianism, mysticism, and sense of mission varied from colony to colony. Once more, the unspecifically mystical and the definitely occult can furnish the inquirer with a useful index of the illuminated pattern of thought.

Leaving out for a moment the more political colonies, the spectrum ranged from the alchemical conception of Derleth through the eccentricities of Mazdaznan to the colony called *Friedenstadt* established by Joseph Weissenberg and his followers in 1926 at Trebbin in der Mark. Undoubtedly the chief motive for almost all—even the political colonies—was the urge to escape the pressure of life in the industrial towns. To one observer most of the colonies seemed at first to have been founded "as rendezvous for vegetarians hungry for light and air."[62]

The same observer described several Utopias. There was *"Jungborn"* in the Harz mountains, which was really a sanatorium run on Theosophical principles. There was the *"Graalhohe"* near Schmiedeberg, based on the precepts of the German-American occultist Dr. Philipp Braun, who was concerned with developing "the individuality" of his pupils.[63] There were the relatively famous colonies directed by Johannes Müller, first at Schloss Mainberg and latterly at Schloss Elmau in Bavaria. Müller (born 1864) had left the University of Leipzig in 1892, convinced that Christianity had become a fraud. He felt that a fresh spontaneity was necessary and could be found in a reinterpretation of the commandment *"become as little children."* Müller became secretary of the Mission to the Jews and traveled in the Balkans and South Russia, where he met his future colleague, Heinrich Lhotzky. In 1903 Schloss Mainberg was opened as a "center for organic life"; but the venture almost foundered, first because Müller had differences with Lhotzky, to whom he had entrusted the administration of Schloss Mainberg. Müller's vision was of the coming reign of God—whereas Lhotzky's interpretation of the universe was distinctly magical. Indeed, some time later Lhotzky resigned his office as a Lutheran pastor and finally decided that Christianity was a great misinterpretation of Jesus.[64]

After the departure of the Lhotzkys, Müller developed his personal plans but refused constantly to define what he was trying to do.[65] It could be that this very indefiniteness resulted in success. In 1911 he had to leave Mainberg for Elmau, where in the middle of the Great War his establishment became a place of refuge for the Munich intelligentsia. Müller asserted the primacy of the Sermon on the Mount, the importance of a sympathetic education for a child, and he attacked contemporary "intellectualism." When the National Socialists came to power in 1933, he thought that he saw in the movement the possibility of realizing his hopes of an "organic society" and gave support to the regime in his publications. Müller himself received official praise for his views. Indefinite as they were in their hostility to the intellect and insistence on developing a more "spiritual" form of society, they might easily have been seen as analogous to Nazi thought. In 1943, however, he fell afoul of the *SS*, and only the personal intervention of Alfred Rosenberg saved him from the concentration camp.[66]

The ease with which a harmless idealism might be converted to an illuminated approach of a very different nature is significant.* When Schloss Elmau was in its prime, it was described as "a hydropathic for better-off people ... at the same time a holiday haven for poor students and badly paid women—conditions being made to suit all classes." The simple existence advocated by Müller undoubtedly appealed to the world-weary of all ages. His prescription for daily life began with getting up immediately on waking and the devotion of the morning to perceiving the "hidden motions of the soul." The day's work should be done without haste, which was the root of the anxiety blighting people's lives, and the evening was for sociable activities. The day ended with an examination of its events.

The most famous of all the colonies was Monte Verita. To this Utopia at Ascona in Switzerland came, at one time or another, most members of the Progressive Underground. It had close connections both with occultism springing from Theosophy and with the Munich of the Cosmics. The idea originated in the summer of 1899 at a nature cure at Veldes in Austria, when the twenty-four-year-old Henri Oedenkoven (the son of a rich Antwerp industrialist) met a pretty music teacher called Ida Hoffmann in whom he discovered a kindred spirit. Oedenkoven's illness and that of Ida Hoffmann were classic cases of neurasthenia. The young Belgian had discovered the swindle of civilization; and when nature therapy accomplished his cure, he determined to apply the remedy to all the ills of mankind. In October, 1900, in Ida Hoffmann's house in Munich, seven freedom seekers gathered under the leadership of Oedenkoven and Ida. They

---

*A similar progress can be seen in Hermann Bahr, whose initial rebellion against rationalism and realism in art turned increasingly to Roman Catholicism and at the same time, to the Christian Socialist revival of Carl Ritter von Schönerer and Carl Luger. Bahr met Johannes Müller for a two-day conference in Berchtesgaden and Salzburg in 1911 or 1912. It was considered surprising that the meeting had not occurred before. Bahr wrote of Müller: "He opened up my heart to me."[68]

included a Theosophist and an *Oberleutnant* Karl Gräser, whose military experiences had converted him to pacifist opinions and an idealistic anarchism. The group discovered and bought a small hill above Ascona, an area already populated with artists, philosophers, Theosophists, vegetarians, and political refugees. The hill was christened Monte Verita, and the colonists started to build.

Their troubles began early. One disturbing influence was the brother of the *Oberleutnant,* who arrived in a toga, reciting vegetarian poems. He was sent away and he teamed up with a clairvoyant with eight children whom he disposed of progressively by the simple procedure of leaving them "for a while" with some friendly passerby in the street and not coming back.[67]

Within the colony dissension arose as to the *type* of new world they were building. Oedenkoven wanted to preserve private property, Karl Gräser held out for a phalanstery on the principles of Fourier; and an artisan called Fritz Rohl, whom the leaders had imported out of a sense of duty, lectured on phrenology and spiritualism while loudly demanding *complete* communism. Members of the Underground arrived unheralded, to "help" in the construction of the colony; most proved to be ill either physically or mentally. In the winter of 1902 the severe snow drove most of the new arrivals to warmer climates, and a party left to establish a colony on Samoa. Fritz Rohl tried to emigrate to America but died in a police cell at Naples.[69]

Henri Oedenkoven, who had the money, of course won in the end. From 1902 onward Ascona became a center for the Progressive Underground. Among the celebrated visitors to Monte Verita were Bakunin, Kropotkin, Lenin, Trotsky, Hermann Hesse, Countess Reventlow, Erich Mühsam, Karl Wolfskehl, Martin Buber, Hans Arp, Stefan George, Paul Klee, Boris Jawlensky, Isadora Duncan, Emmy Hennings, and Hugo Ball. The locals grew suspicious of the motley collection. There were arrests for such crimes as wearing shorts. Politicians like Dr. Raphael Friedenberg (publisher of the *Sozialistische Monatshefte* and a pioneer of the idea of the General Strike) mingled with eccentrics like the Baltic baron known as "mad Rechenberg" because his Theosophy—he belonged to Franz Hartmann's persuasion—forbade him excessive physical movement and led him to consider that it was a holy act to kill a woman.

Rechenberg's creed competed with that of the leading Ascona occultist Frau Dr. Paulus (a friend of Annie Besant) who at the age of ninety-two considered herself the reincarnation of Giordano Bruno. Meanwhile, as the reputation of Ascona grew (and journalists wrote absurd articles on how the "natural men" of Monte Verita lived in holes in the ground), Oedenkoven and Ida Hoffmann kept in touch with other centers of idealistic experiment. They toured similar colonies, visited Johannes Müller, and attended Bayreuth. The "cure" offered by Monte Verita for a time prospered. It was not an ordinary cure, wrote Ida Hoffmann, "but much more a school for higher life, a place for arousing of expanded knowledge and expanded consciousness (these places will multiply) made fruitful by the sunbeams of the Universal Will."

Thus, to Oedenkoven's original project of redeeming the world by expanding centers of vegetarian socialism, there was added a substantial dose of the mystical. It had been present from the first in the Monte Veritaner and was fertilized by contact with existing Ascona occultism. *Oberleutnant* Gräser developed the conviction that he could personally drive back the cold; and another member of the colony retired into the hills where she improved her soul by contemplating nature and earned the reverence of some of the pious. Ascona became a place of pilgrimage for small sects. Ida Hoffmann became ever more Theosophical; and in the town of Ascona the reincarnated Giordano Bruno ceded precedence to a spiritualist Frau Steindamm, whose daughter married a convinced follower of Rudolf Steiner and kept an Anthroposophical salon. In this circle there appeared one Hermann Schutz, conversing with Zarathustra, Christ, Lao-tse, and Socrates. He bought some land near Monte Verita and decided to found a male order toward which object he issued a newspaper called *Hastinapura, a journal for the propagation of a more elevated viewpoint.*[70]

The most significant occult organization to be associated with Monte Verita was the magical society known as the *Ordens Tempel der Ostens,* otherwise, the Order of the Templars of the Orient. This society originated in a charter given by an English masonic entrepreneur called John Yarker to three German occultists: Joshua Klein, Franz Hartmann, and Theodore Reuss. This charter licensed them to set up in Berlin a Grand Lodge of the masonic rite called "Mizraim and Memphis" which Yarker had concocted from two moribund organizations. (By 1904 a fourth name and a new title were being mentioned in the magazine of the Order: Karl Kellner and the O.T.O.)[71]

Joshua Klein had been one of the earliest visitors at Monte Verita. He had arrived somewhat in the manner of the *Wunderapostel* Hauser at house of Meyrink, striking himself on the chest and exclaiming, "I am that I am." In 1902 Oedenkoven and Ida Hoffmann had returned the call by traveling to Klein's own colony, *Erdsegen,* in Upper Bavaria, which Klein had established after inheriting some half-million marks, and whose basis was that the spiritual state of the human being affected his state of physical health.[72] In occult circles Klein enjoyed an unsavory reputation. We have already met his friend, Franz Hartmann, whose own standing was equally disputed, as an associate of Madame Blavatsky and a leading figure in the circle of Viennese Theosophists around Friedrich Eckstein. Hartmann had himself lived for some time around Locarno and Ascona.[73] His colleague, Karl Kellner, was the originator of the process which Hartmann had developed into the cure he practiced at his "Inhalation Center"; he is described by one authority as "a wealthy iron-master."[74] Kellner died in 1905, and Theodore Reuss took over the organization of the O.T.O. Reuss was half-German and half-English. Francis King has discovered that his talents included singing in the music halls and spying for the Prussian political police on the Social Democratic Federation in Britain.[75] He had lived in London and Paris before moving to Basel, where he worked as a newspaper correspondent and a teacher of English at the Berlitz school. By 1919 he was announcing himself on his visiting card as an "Honorary Professor at the College for Applied Medicine (Université de France)."[76] Two or three years earlier, Ida Hoffmann had met Reuss in Spiritualist circles, and introduced him to Oedenkoven and Monte Verita.

At first, Reuss presented himself to Oedenkoven as a disciple of his vegetarian socialism. According to Robert Ackermann (who tried to revive the colony at Monte Verita in the 1920s and afterwards became the historian of the group) Oedenkoven was doubtful of the sincerity of the new colonist. But he allowed him to stay for a year, because the fortunes of Monte Verita had run low as a result of the war and a tax on foreigners levied by the neutral Swiss. Eventually, Reuss with the support of Ida Hoffmann, introduced the O.T.O. to Monte Verita. The peculiarity of this magical society was that it used "sexual rites." Precisely what this meant in fact, is a difficult problem. In 1912 Theodore Reuss chartered Aleister Crowley to run a branch of the O.T.O., and it was from this source that Crowley developed his theories of the magical power of sex. It is said that the order owed its sexual teachings to the researches of Karl Kellner in the lore of Bengali Tantricism.[77] But the charge of using, or abusing, sex has so often been levied unjustifiably at occultists, that it is as well to be wary of all insinuations of "horrible goings-on" and to record the fact that—whether the O.T.O. at Monte Verita attempted to produce magical effects through sexual intercourse, or whether its members tried to sublimate their sexual energy and turn it to magical purpose—the reputation of the colony worsened. Rumors of midnight orgies persisted into the 1930s. Several children were said to have been born with "no father but God."

Oedenkoven at last threw Reuss out—but not before the magician had called a fortnight's congress at Monte Verita from 15 to 25 August 1917. This "A-national Congress" was designed to appeal to the pacifists, anti-vivisectionalists, and the Progressive Underground generally. It was said to be organized by the "Ordo Templi Orientis, and Hermetic Brotherhood of Light, the A-national Grand Lodge and Mystic Temple, 'Verita Mystica'." To reactionary politicians and supporters everywhere of conspiracy theories, it seemed that their worst forebodings were confirmed—the forces of subversion had joined hands under the supervision of a black magician!

A revival of interest engendered by the Congress sustained Monte Verita for three more years. But in 1920 Oedenkoven, who had become disillusioned with his Utopia, left with his wife and Ida Hoffmann for Brazil, where they established a second colony; in 1934 it was still in existence.[78] Ascona remained a town of philosophers, artists, and Theosophists, a center of the Underground. Its traditions were to be resurrected. And at Dornach, not so far away, was the headquarters of a more highly organized occult group than any Ascona had boasted: Rudolf Steiner's Anthroposophical Society.

Rudolf Steiner (1861-1925) was born in Kraljevec in what was then part of the Hungarian jurisdiction of the Dual Monarchy and is now in Yugoslavia. His father was a railway official, and Steiner spent his childhood at various villages on the Austrian Southern Region. His parents moved near Vienna so the boy could visit the Technische Hochschule in 1879.

Soon after the family's move to Vienna, Steiner met a rustic herbalist called Felix Kogutzki, whom he greatly revered as a natural mystic and repository of traditional wisdom. Theosophical followers were afterward to assert that he met a Himalayan master at the same time.[79] However, his first influential acquaintance who can be designated with any certainty was Professor Karl Julius Schröer, a teacher of German language and literature who specialized in the collection of folklore. In the circle of Schröer he met that concealed influence on so many of the mystically inclined, Friedrich Eckstein; and he soon became a regular member of the group who gathered in the "Megalomania Café" on the Michaelerplatz, where Steiner's old-fashioned frock coat and top hat gave his friends the impression of an "undernourished seminarian," and he distinguished himself by endless disagreements with Hermann Bahr. His approach to Eckstein was made on account of the latter's contact with H. P. Blavatsky; and Eckstein records Steiner's request for an introduction into the problems of *The Secret Doctrine*. Their acquaintanceship lasted for an appreciable time, and it was Eckstein who introduced Steiner to Rosa Mayreder and the Theosophical circle of Marie and Edmund Lang. Under their influence Rudolf Steiner studied Oriental thought, medieval mysticism, Neo-Platonism, and the Cabala, by much of which he later claimed to be repelled. But he was close enough to Theosophical circles to obtain a copy of A. P. Sinnet's *Esoteric Buddhism* soon after its appearance.[80]

At the same time as Steiner was penetrating esoteric circles, he had some success with the established authorities of literature and learning. His own philosophical development was influenced by a reaction against the system of Eduard von Hartmann, whose insistence on the dominating force of the "Unconscious" he found abhorrent—nothing, thought Steiner, should be unconscious. Through his reading of Schiller he later claimed to have attained a spiritual perception as exact as mathematics; but the chief influence on his life was Goethe. In 1883 he was invited to edit Goethe's scientific writings for the projected standard edition; and his first publications dating from 1886, are on Goethe. In 1890 Steiner left Vienna to work for six years at the Goethe Archive at Weimar, bearing with him not only the orthodox training which was to gain him a Ph.D. the next year at Rostock, but a wide-ranging body of general knowledge culled from every discipline under the sun; for he had had to support himself in Vienna by tutoring and had achieved one remarkable success in "bringing on" a hydrocephalic boy. Thus, by the time he moved to Weimar, most of the preoccupations of his later life had taken root: his interest in Theosophy, his bent for education, and a philosophical allegiance to German idealism. In Weimar, apart from his work at the Goethe Archive, he visited the ailing Nietzsche and published several philosophical books. In 1897 Steiner moved to Berlin and became editor of the *Magazin für Literatur*. Always he was searching, in the manner of his contemporaries, for the universal palliative to anxiety.

> Always the thought hovered before me that the turn of the century must bring a new spiritual light to humanity. It seemed to me that the exclusion of human thinking and willing from the spirit had reached a climax. A revolutionary change in the process of human evolution seemed to me a matter of necessity.
>
> Many were talking in this way. But they did not see that a man will seek to direct his eyes towards a world of real spirit as he directs them through the senses towards nature. They only supposed that the subjective spiritual temper of the soul would undergo a revolution. That a real, new objective world could be revealed, such a thought lay behond the range of vision of that time.[81]

Despite his later assertions, it seems that he did not at the time rule out the possibility of a reformation of human nature in terms less occult, and more related to the social goals of the opponents of materialist society. He became involved in the Free Literary Society, taught at the Berlin Workers' School, and generally behaved himself as a member of the Progressive Underground—more respectable, more established than most; but he undoubtedly belonged to this milieu. He formed a friendship with John Henry Mackay, a half-Scot, half-German anarchist of some fame who was the editor of Max Stirner and who had admired Steiner's book *The Philosophy of Freedom*. At Steiner's marriage to the widow Anna Eunicke (on 31 October 1899), Mackay was the witness.[82]

This first marriage of Steiner has given rise to conflicting reports, and as Steiner himself always refused categorically to discuss his private life, it is difficult to know just where to place the emphasis. Sources favorable to Steiner note only that after a separation of several years, Anna Steiner died in March 1911 after confessing her former happiness with Rudolf Steiner to her daughter Wilhelmine.[83] On the other hand, information from another daughter, Emmy, tells a different tale. Steiner had first come to the Eunicke family as a lodger in his early days in Weimar, when Emmy Eunicke was a girl of sixteen. It is plain that she resented the intrusion of the young academic into a family consisting of her widowed mother and her sisters. Emmy considered that Steiner was excluding the Eunicke children from their rightful inheritance both in terms of affection and of material goods. Her dislike of the newcomer became increasingly acute after he became her stepfather and the family moved to Berlin. For Steiner returned to Theosophical company, and accumulated the gaggle of adoring women invariably attracted to "occult" masters. One of his new disciples—she is not named in the published account for fear of a libel action—became Steiner's inseparable companion. According to the jealous daughter, a door was knocked in the wall between the flat of the Steiners and the parts of the Theosophical headquarters inhabited by the lesser lights, so that Steiner could visit his paramour. One summer about the year 1904 Steiner took a furnished Schlachtensee cottage divided into two flats—one for his wife and another for his lover. Eventually, Emmy Eunicke claimed to have found her stepfather and his disciple in bed together. At all events, Anna Steiner seems to have become tired of waiting on her husband and his disciples, and after the marriage of her daughter Emmy in 1906 she left Steiner to live near her. The sudden death of Steiner's wife in 1911 sent rumors fluttering around the occult press, that Steiner had "strangled her astrally."[84]

It must immediately be said that the source of this story is a two-headed Gorgon: a jealous daughter and a highly eccentric Nazi polemicist. It was made great play with by Steiner's opponents, who grew in geometrical progression, and the details should not be insisted upon. The charge most often brought against Steiner—excluding those of lunatics concerned with astral strangulation—is of opportunism, and the possibility of his having married a rich widow for her money cannot be ruled out. About the same time as his marriage to Anna Eunicke, Steiner turned from his unwontedly extroverted existence toward the Theosophical interests which had earlier concerned him and accepted an invitation from Count and Countess Brockdorff, the leaders of the Theosophical Society in Berlin, to lecture to their members. He lectured first on Nietzsche; then on the esoteric interpretation of Goethe's fairy tale, "The Green Snake and the Beautiful Lily." In the winter of 1900 he further committed himself to a mystical approach by lecturing to the Theosophists on "Christianity as Mystical Fact." In the audience was his future second wife—who, if there is any truth in Emmy Eunicke's story, was almost certainly the woman whom Steiner introduced into the strange *ménage à trois* at Schlachtensee. Marie von Sivers (1867-1948), a Baltic Russian and a frustrated actress, was a keen Theosophist. She married Steiner secretly in 1914. After her initial encounter with him in Berlin, she went to Bologna to organize a Theosophical group there but returned to Germany in time to travel with Steiner to the London conference of the Theosophical Society in July 1902. At this point, Steiner was induced by the Brockdorff group to apply to Colonel Olcott at Adyar for a charter inaugurating a new German section of Theosophists.[85]

This transition from liberal academic to mystical lecturer is at first sight baffling. Steiner was not as inconsistent as it might appear. Since Vienna he had carried with him a large body of Theosophical knowledge, and such a combination of interests was not unusual among the Progressive Underground. Steiner's academic speciality was Goethe; and he had to digest Goethe's own interest in matters symbolic and esoteric in order to carry out his task of editing and criticizing. His meeting with Häckel (the popularizer of Darwinianism in Germany and the protagonist of the theory of philosophical monism) had also given direction to his thought. Häckel's monism was very influential during the early part of this century—and not only in Germany. The scientist proposed to abolish the conventional distinction between matter and spirit and to return to the conception of a unified organism—a proposition which he himself defined explicitly as religious, and which gave rise to innumerable theories of political organization disguised under the term "organic state." For the propagation of this viewpoint—which carried overtones of reassurance, the restoration of order, and the feeling of "belonging"—were formed a number of societies.[86] At one of these, the Giordano Bruno Bund, Steiner delivered what he was later to regard as the basic lecture on his emerging "spiritual science," Anthroposophy. This lecture on "Monism and Theosophy" took place on 8 October 1902, around the time when the German section of the Theosophical Society was reorganized with Steiner as general secretary. Steiner's own explanation of why he joined the society was that, at the time, "this was the sole institution worthy of serious consideration in which there was present a real spiritual life."[87] It is obvious that from the start Steiner carried into Theosophy a rigorous academic training and a philosophical inheritance completely different from the mixture of Eastern religion and 18th-century occultism which had gone into the making of Theosophy of the Blavatsky brand. If we allow Steiner a consistency of aim and purpose he cannot be acquitted of the charge of joining the Theosophists with the intention of taking them over. Perhaps he had mentally returned to the preoccupations of his Vienna days, and merely proposed rather indefinitely to apply to these the conclusions of later years.

There was, in any case, bound to be friction between Steiner and the old guard of the German Theosophists. Of this group Steiner had later little good to say. Even Madame Blavatsky had found it difficult to stomach Franz Hartmann. "The magnetism of that man is sickening; his *lying* beastly; his slander of Hübbe-Schleiden, his intrigues unaccountable but on the ground that he is either a maniac—utterly irresponsible for the most part, or allowed to be possessed by his own *dugpa* Spirit." Steiner claimed that Hartmann had once told a story of how William Quan Judge had complained to him that *he* never received any letters from the mysterious Himalayan masters. Judge refused Hartmann's suggestion that he write some to himself with the stricture that he must be able to say that his letters arrived out of the blue in the known fashion of Mahatma letters. Hartmann's solution was simple: he volunteered to climb on a chair and drop the letters on Judge's head. Hübbe-Schleiden's sincerity was never in doubt. The trouble was that he cultivated an illusion that could explain the metaphysical universe on a chemical analogy. He kept his attic crammed with models of spiritual atoms and maintained that reincarnations must be connected by a single "Permanent Atom" (according to Steiner, "an appalling thing").[88]

An uneasy alliance persisted, however, until 1912, when two factors contributed to a split between Steiner's group and the Theosophists proper. The first was the expulsion by Steiner from the German Society of Hugo Vollrath, a disciple of Franz Hartmann and a known opportunist. The second was the growing power in Theosophical circles of Mrs. Besant's Order of the Star in the East, the vehicle of Krishnamurti and the coming World-Teacher. This Steiner could not stomach. Eventually in 1913 his followers—most of the German Theosophists—broke away and founded their rival Anthroposophical Society. Hübbe-Schleiden was left with orthodox Theosophists and the adherents of Krishnamurti.[89]

But between 1902 and 1913 much had happened in the development of Steiner's thought. He steadily built up a personal following, and first really established himself with a series of lectures that he was asked to give at the Theosophical conference in Paris in 1906. These attracted more attention than the official events. His search led him and Marie von Sivers into strange adventures, the most unlikely of which was Steiner's installation at the head of a lodge of the O.T.O. called the *Mysteria Mystica Aeterna*. The most probable date for his entry is January 1906. Steiner later maintained that his official position with regard to the O.T.O. was like that of a candidate for apostolic succession. He wanted, he said, to take over the historical authority to perform the "ancient symbolic and cultural ceremonies that embody the ancient wisdom. I never thought in the remotest degree of working in the spirit of such a society." It seems, nonetheless, that he may at one time have had the idea of creating a large international occult federation based on the structure of the O.T.O., but that, whatever use he made of the ceremonies handed over to him by Theodore Reuss, it is unlikely that he used "sex-magic" in the sense in which it was meant by his opponents.[90] What is important to notice is that Steiner could find in such diverse quarters as Theosophy, philosophical idealism, and the possibly Tantric magic of the O.T.O., material for his hoped-for revolution in consciousness.

If his sources were varied, his applications were equally so. For he intended Anthroposophy to be an all-embracing science that would provide answers both spiritually and materially satisfying in every branch of life. Agriculture, architecture, education, or politics—all were areas in which he felt qualified to operate. By the time of his death in 1925, his society had become astonishingly influential and had attracted great hostility. The reasons for this hostility were various. One of the most obvious is that the Anthroposophical Society embodied so many different aspects of the Progressive Underground and represented in itself a collection of people who compounded the felonies of Marxists, Social Democrats, and other destroyers of the social order by deliberately advocating change. Nor was the sort of change which they advocated entirely understood.

This is unsurprising. Steiner's ideas form less a "system" than an accumulation of sometimes apparently disconnected items. Thus, from Theosophy he took the ideas of *karma* and reincarnation; from his mystical studies and possibly the O.T.O., a personal "Rosicrucianism." He discovered an entirely new idiosyncratic and poetic interpretation of Christianity, and somehow contrived a seeming coherence with these teachings for theories of the social and artistic life of man. The underlying unity which he and his followers found in these elements of Anthroposophy lies in their source in Steiner's "spiritual perception." This faculty of "clairvoyance"—of insight into what might be called *real* reality—Steiner claimed to have developed early in his Vienna period; but he later connected it with Goethe's technique for immersing himself in the essence of things. He thought that "a deep chasm had opened between Reason and its allied Thought Method on the one hand, and supersensual Truth on the other."[91] In accordance with Theosophical theory, he maintained that "man is not obliged to remain stationary at the point of view he occupies today and it is possible for organs—spiritual eyes—to develop after a similar fashion to that in which those physical sense-organs of the body, the eyes and ears have been developed; and once these new organs are developed, higher faculties will make themselves apparent."[92] As man advanced in this development, the beings of higher worlds would make themselves known to him and he would advance in knowledge. Steiner does not seem to have been above using his clairvoyant faculties gratuitously in the manner of a medium. Thus he informed the Protestant clergyman Friedrich Rittelmeyer—who afterward became one of his firmest supporters—that he had seen "a beautiful ether-form" after one of his sermons and that "an individuality" whom he took to be Rittelmeyer's mother attended his lectures.[93]

The chief uses Steiner made of his faculty were enunciating moral doctrine, describing the structure of the universe, and elucidating the history of man. Human history could be surveyed as far distantly as the seer might wish—because of its impress on the "Akashic Record." This mysterious and convenient chronicle is a legacy from Madame Blavatsky; and like her, Steiner made great play with the doings of man on the lost continents of Atlantis and Lemuria. In Atlantis, for example, the inhabitants had thought in pictures, possessed extraordinary memories, and used the energy latent in plants to drive airships. The most evolved among them were gathered together by a great leader in Central Asia and subjected to a refining process with the object of making them understand the divine powers. From this group were descended the early priest-kings of the Aryans.[94] The entire course of human development followed a scheme similar to that worked out by H. P. Blavatsky with the difference that man was seen as evolving back toward a lost divine condition. Man's effort toward a renewed perfection was impeded by two malevolent powers to which Steiner gave the names of Ahriman and Lucifer. Ahriman represents materialism and the world of matter, in which he seeks to imprison man's spirit. Lucifer is the demon of pride and self-sufficiency. This conception of the universe probably stems from Gnostic and Zoroastrian sources, on which Steiner is said to have worked around the year 1906.[95]

His Rosicrucianism seems first to have blossomed in 1907 (the year after he accepted the charter from the O.T.O). Steiner proclaimed the way of the Rosicrucians as an esoteric version of Christianity, and he decided that Christian Rosenkreuz, the great master of this concealed brotherhood, had sent his favorite pupil, Buddha, to Mars, where he had regenerated the planet as Christ had redeemed Earth. In the year before he died Steiner claimed to have been in contact with a small group of Rosicrucians in Central Europe—but this happened in the early years of the 19th century before he had entered this current incarnation. Gradually the figure of Christ emerged as central to his vision of the cosmos. He saw the coming of Christ as equivalent on a cosmic scale to the effect produced on the individual by initiation in the mystery-religions: to return man to a consciousness of his divine origins. A strange and complex process was then envisaged in the universe which Steiner termed "the etherization of the blood." In the individual human being this affected the bloodstream around the region of the heart, turning it into "etherized blood." When a correct understanding of Christ had been obtained, the etherized blood of the individual mingled with the etherized blood of Christ, present in the cosmos.[96] Whether there is more meaning in this doctrine than a singular elaboration of the old idea of mystical participation in the body of Christ it is not the present task of this book to decide.

From Steiner's Christology sprang a subdivision of the Anthroposophical Society called the Christian Community. In 1921 several of Steiner's disciples approached him with a request that he construct for them a rite to be used in Christian worship for those who followed his teaching. Steiner produced such a service, "The Act of the Consecration of Man," and the group was placed under the leadership of Friedrich Rittelmeyer, who had come to Anthroposophy via several years of allegiance to Johannes Müller.[97]

Steiner's writings are verbose, diffuse, and difficult to decode. In part this is because so many thousands of pages represent published expansions of lecture notes. But there is frequently an absence of basic content—by which is meant no attempt to evaluate the material, only a statement of quantitative fact. They have been taken seriously by large numbers of people, and particularly in the period just after the Great War they represented a force to be reckoned with. Not least was this so because the founder of Anthroposophy extended his spiritual perceptions to cover the most diverse areas of human activity, and in the general reaction toward the idealistic approach his theories appeared to many of those who were in search of a secure ideological crutch to provide more of a system than in fact they did. We shall briefly return to Steiner's influence on education and the arts; and there is good reason to examine in their context his plans for political reconstruction. We can only note in passing that Anthroposophical medicine seems to be based partly on magical theories of correspondence—for example cholera is a punishment for insufficient self-confidence and the pox for lack of affection. Today the Anthroposophists run clinics, a mental hospital, and a factory for medicines which has marketed a cancer cure.[98] Anthroposophical farming is carried out on a "Bio-Dynamic" basis which forbids exhaustion of the soil through the abuse of chemical ferilizers and advocates planting of crops in accordance with the phases of the moon.[99] Some of these agricultural methods at least seem to have borne literal fruit.

The campaign against Steiner and his society grew with the anxiety of the post-war years. As early as 1917 the magazine *Psychische Studien* had carried a series of articles denouncing Anthroposophy for causing mental and physical illness and in some cases suicide. Erich Bamler, a Munich artist, claimed that he had become dissociated through using exercises recommended by Steiner and was only prevented from suicide by his Christian convictions. A young schoolmistress became convinced that she had had an astral child. Steiner's opponents made much of such reports; and it should be firmly insisted that, whatever the effects of Steiner's exercises, they are not alone in having such accusations made against them. It is an unfortunate fact that every occult or esoteric group attracts its quota of just those people who seem to be worst affected by the practices they are supposed to carry out—the hyper-suggestible, the sexually maladjusted, and those on the edge of desperation. The worst or oddest case connected with Anthroposophy concerned one Wilhelm Krieger, who claimed that he had been given occult exercises which involved the transferring of his ego outside his body. Krieger became convinced that he could not recover his "I," that it had been stolen from him, that he had been the victim of "occult vampirism." As his delusion progressed he began to issue a newsletter directed against the Anthroposophists, and eventually sued Steiner, his colleague Carl Unger, and another Anthroposophist for the return of his soul. The tragi-comedy did not end there. Denied legal redress, Krieger bided his time, and on 4 January 1929 murdered Dr. Unger at an Anthroposophical meeting in Stuttgart.[100]

Steiner and his followers were refused permission to build a center at Munich. After having naturally considered Ascona as a possible site, they erected their headquarters at Dornach. The building was designed by Steiner according to his architectural principles and embodied the same combination of woods as is used in the making of a violin. It consisted of two domed structures of which the larger slightly exceeded the size of the dome of St. Peter's. This remarkable building was known as the Goetheanum, and it was highly inflammable. On New Year's Eve 1922/3, as the Goetheanum was nearing completion, it was set on fire. It was rumored that the pastor of the neighboring village of Reinach had watched the blaze through binoculars exclaiming his approval. An outraged Anthroposophist sent him (and two other clergymen who had directed the local opposition against Steiner) a postcard bearing the words, "Where is the arsonist?" The clerics replied that their questioner should go to Dr. Steiner, who was after all the clairvoyant. They accused the Anthroposophists of burning down their own headquarters for the insurance money. They even found sinister proof of their allegations in the humdrum fact that Steiner attended the funeral of a clockmaker called Ott whose body was found in the ashes of the building.[101]

Such hostility goes far beyond the local opposition of a band of bigots. There was extraordinary vehemence in the hate directed against Steiner, who was seen as part of the Jewish-Freemasonic conspiracy to subvert the world. It will soon be necessary to discuss the meaning of this aberration, and the specific causes which involved Steiner in the "plot." These were bound up with the peculiar character of German politics in the period after the defeat of 1918. The search for realities transcending those of the material world was not confined to those who hoped for Heaven after life on earth. Throughout this survey of the German Underground of irrationalist and occultist opinion, one thing stands out: that the illuminated approach very often entailed an application of the transcendental ethic to social problems. Steiner and the Progressive thinkers of Vienna and Ascona, in all their extravagance, are examples of this tendency.

1. Andreas Steiner, "Das Nervöse Zeitalter" in *Zürcher Medizingeschichtlicher Abhandlungen*, Neue Reihe Nr 21 (Zurich, 1964), p. 116.
2. Søren Kierkegaard, "Equilibrium," in *Either/Or*, vol. II (tr. Walter Lawrie, London, 1944), pp. 159-60.
3. Steiner, p. 117. Cf. the remarks made in *The Occult Underground* (p. 23) about the possibility of seeing the outbreak of "spirit mediumship" in the mid-19th century as a psychologically classifiable illness.
4. Toffler, *Future Shock*, pp. 291-93. He cites Dr. Thomas H. Holmes's "Life Change Unit Scale," which seems to have established a correlation between great changes in living patterns and severe illness. The evidence is so strong that it is becoming possible to predict levels of illness in various populations.
5. G. K. Nelson, *Spiritualism and Society* (London, 1969), pp. 155-61.
6. On Oliver Lodge, see his *Raymond, or Life and Death* (London, 1916).
7. On Doyle, see John Dickson Carr, *The Life of Sir Arthur Conan Doyle* (London, 1949), who does not even mention the episode of the fairies; Arthur Conan Doyle, *The History of Spiritualism*, vol. II (London, 1926), p. 225; Doyle, *The Coming of the Fairies* (2nd ed., London, 1928), pp. 22, 90, 136 ff.; E. L. Gardner, *Fairies* (2nd ed., London, 1951), pp. 45-46; Joseph Jastrow, *Wish and Wisdom* (London, 1935), pp. 52 ff.
8. See Lilly Heber, *Krishnamurti: The Man and His Message* (London, 1931), p. 59. According to a Reuter telegram from Krishnamurti's Dutch center at Ommen, George Lansbury congratulated Krishnamurti on abandoning organizations for the claims of the individual conscience. He was at that time a member of Ramsay MacDonald's cabinet.
9. On MRA, see Tom Driberg, *The Mystery of Moral Re-armament* (London, 1964); Lynden Macassey, foreword to *Dr. Frank N. D. Buchman: An Eightieth Birthday Tribute* (undated); A. J. Russell, *For Sinners Only* (London, 1932), pp. 65-69; Marjorie Harrison, *Saints Run Mad* (London, 1934), p. 58; Ivor Thomas, *The Buchman Groups* (London, 1933), p. 5; Frank Buchman, *Remaking the World* (London, 1947), especially Buchman's speech of March 1935: "Norway Ablaze;" W. H. Auden, "The Group Movement and the Middle Classes," in R. H. S. Crossman (ed.), *Oxford and the Groups* (London, 1935), pp. 89, 94.
10. Herman Hesse, *The Journey to the East* (tr. Hilda Rosner, New York, 1969), p. 6.
11. Hesse, *Journey*, p. 10.
12. Eberhard Buchner, *Sekten und Sektierer in Berlin* (Berlin/Leipzig, 1904), pp. 19 ff; Paul Scheurlen, *Die Sekten der Gegenwart* (4th ed., Stuttgart, 1930), pp. 115-21.
13. Buchner, *Sekten*, p. 68. John Alexander Dowie (1847-1907) was born in Edinburgh, the illegitimate son of an illiterate mother. He began his career as a Congregationalist minister in Sydney, Australia, where he developed a

theory of "divine healing by the laying on of hands." In 1888 he emigrated to America and was the moving spirit in setting up the town of Zion City, where alcohol, tobacco, and conventional medicine were banned and which held 5,400 people by 1904. In 1903 the famous "visitation" of New York with meetings in the Carnegie Hall and Madison Square took place. Dowie's delusions of grandeur grew with the disillusion of his supporters, and the year before his death his chief lieutenant led the revolt that deposed him. See Rolvix Harlan, *John Alexander Dowie and the Catholic Apostolic Church* (Evansville, Wisconsin, 1906) and Edna Sheldrake (ed.), *The Personal Letters of John Alexander Dowie* (Zion City, Illinois, 1912).

14. Buchner, *Sekten,* pp. 78-90, 53-55; Scheurlen, *Sekten,* pp. 305-7. See e.g., Jacob Lorber, *Haushaltung Gottes* (Bietigheim, 1851).

15. Hans Freimark, *Moderne Geisterbeschwörer und Wahrheitssucher* (Berlin/Leipzig, n.d.), p. 18.

16. Ellic Howe, *Urania's Children* (London, 1967), pp. 78-79; see also Franz Hartmann, *Denkwürdige Errinnerungen* (Leipzig, 1898), note by Hugo Goering in Werner Friedrichsort, *Dr. Hübbe-Schleidens Weltanschauung* (Braunschweig, 1895), and Goering, *Franz Hartmann* (Braunschweig, 1895).

17. Scheurlen, *Die Sekten,* pp. 46-47 and passim, 193-96, 281 ff., 290-94. One Georg Schön, a wandering preacher of the Lorberian New Salem Church, had a close connection with the Tanatra Lodge. See pp. 305-7.

18. Rudolf Schott, *Der Maler Bô Yin Râ* (2nd ed., Zurich, 1960); Bô Yin Râ, *Warum ich meine Name Führe* (Basel, 1961); Baron R. Winspeare, *Esquisse somaire de l'enseignement de Bô Yin Râ* (Paris, 1929), pp. 9-10. The worst example is undoubtedly the sole English translation of Bô Yin Râ, *The Book of Happiness,* (tr. C. C. and H. B. Wood, London, 1931).

19. Ottoman Zar-Adusht Ha'nish, *Mazdaznan Health and Breath Culture* (London, 1913), orig. U. S. A. 1902), pp. 3, 78, 138; See also, *The British Mazdaznan Magazine* (vol. I, no. 1, Jan-March, 1914); Ha'nish, *Inner Studies* (Chicago, 1902), pp. 23-24; Ha'nish, *Mazdaznan Dietics and Cookery Book* (London, 1914). This book received the Medal of Progress at an International Cookery Exhibition of 1911 at Luxembourg.

20. Howe, *Urania's Children,* p. 85; Scheurlen, *Sekten,* pp. 419 ff.; *British Mazdaznan Magazine* (no. 5), pp. 189, 195.

21. Scheurlen, *Sekten,* pp. 258-62, 266, 290, 296-302.

22. Scheurlen, *Sekten,* pp. 269-70 and note 2. Cf. Weissenberger's vision of spiritual combat with the fantasies of Denis Wheatley.

23. Karel Weinfurter, *Man's Highest Purpose* (tr. Capleton and Unger, London, 1930), p. 43. The particular works were *The Key to the Spiritual World* and *The Way to Immortality.* See Gottfried Buchner, *J. B. Kerning* (Lorsch/Württemburg, 1902) and Franz Hartmann, *Lichtstrahlen vom Orient* (Leipzig, n.d.); Kerning, *Geschichtlicher Überblick über die Freimaurerei* (Lorsch, 1902); Kerning, *Maurerische Mitteilungen* (ed. Gottfried Buchner), in Kerning's *Leben und Schriften,* Band I (Lorsch, 1902), p. 39.

24. Weinfurter, *Man's Highest Purpose*, pp. 45-46. I have not been able to identify the old magician or discover his *Magic Mirror:* he was probably connected with the group that published *The Lamp of Thoth* from Keightley in Yorkshire.

25. See *The Vahan*, vol. II, no. 6, 1 January 1893 (London), p. 7.

26. Eduard Frank, *Gustav Meyrink* (Budingen-Gottenbach, 1957), p. 15; Herbert Fritsche, *August Strindberg, Gustav Meyrink, Kurt Aram* (Prague, 1935), pp. 18-20.

27. Frank, *Meyrink*, pp. 23-26, 40, 63 ff.

28. Gustav Meyrink, foreword to R. H. Laars (*i.e.*, Richard Hummel), *Eliphas Lévi* (Berlin, Vienna, Munich, 1922), pp. 12-13. Meyrink, foreword to his translation of *Abhandlungen über der Stein der Weisen*, attrib. Thomas Aquinas (Leipzig, Zurich, Vienna, 1925), pp. xxvi-xxxii; Frank, *Meyrink*, p. 15.

29. Meyrink, *The Golem* (tr. Madge Pemberton, London, 1928); Meyrink, *Meister Leonhard* (Munich, 1925), p. 121. For the "historical" Dr. Schrepfer, see Joseph Ennemoser, *History of Magic*.

30. Weinfurter, *Man's Highest Purpose*, pp. 47-50. One Arthur Rimay de Gidofalvia, who in 1893 was elected President of the Blue Star, may have been "Mr. R" if the initial is anything to go by. See *The Vahan*, 1 January 1893.

31. Weinfurter, *Man's Highest Purpose*, pp. 53 ff., 152-54, 174, 237. One of the translators of this book into English was the Anthroposophist Carl Unger, whose murder I deal with later in this chapter. There were probably connections between the Rosicrucian group and the O.T.O., with its by-this-time-attendant Gnostic Catholic Church—for which see this chapter, below, and Chapter VII—as there was much talk of Gnosticism, and the obscure Paul Sédir was studied. I have not been able to identify the weaver. *Vater* Hain of "Sheep and Shepherd" was a weaver, and according to Archduke Johann of Austria the 1880s had seen an epidemic of Spiritualism among the weavers of the district around Braunau. But this occult "Master" remains obscure.

32. Frank, *Meyrink*, p. 16.

33. See *The Occult Underground*, p. 34, and Hellenbach, *Mr. Slade's Aufenhalt in Wien*.

34. Oskar Simony, *Uber spiritistische Manifestationen von naturwissenschaftlichen Standpunkt* (Vienna, Pest, Leipzig, 1884).

35. Friedrich Eckstein, *Alte unnennbare Tage* (Vienna, Leipzig, Zurich, 1936), pp. 64-69.

36. Charles Blech, *Contribution à l'histoire de la Société Théosophique en France* (Paris, 1933), p. 115; Eckstein, *Alte unnennbare Tage*, pp. 69-77, 260-61. By 1891, the Vienna branch was officially in existence. Eckstein was president, and the secretary, Carl, Graf zu Leininghen-Billigheim, for whom see this chapter below. See *Lucifer* (London), vol. VIII, no. 43, 15 March 1891. In 1897 the count's place was taken by a Herr Ludwig when

Leininghen-Billigheim left for Munich. By then, the Vienna branch had a reading room and held weekly meetings. See *The Vahan,* 1 March 1897.

37. For an "esoteric" interpretation of Wagner, see Otto Julius Hartmann, *Die Esoterik im Werk Richard Wagners* (Freiburg, 1960).
38. Eckstein, *Alte unnennbare Tage,* pp. 110 ff.
39. Richard Wagner, "Religion und Kunst" in *Gesammelte Schriften und Dichtungen,* Band 10 (2nd ed., Leipzig, 1888), pp. 212, 239.
40. Frank Walker, *Hugo Wolf* (2nd ed., London, 1968), p. 134.
41. Eckstein, *Alte unnennbare Tage,* pp. 105-13; Walker, *Wolf,* p. 129.
42. Eckstein, *Alte unnennbare Tage,* pp. 185-86.
43. Carl, Graf zu Leiningen-Billigheim, *Was ist Mystik?* (Leipzig, 1898), p. 91.
44. Walker, *Wolf,* pp. 134-35, 210; Eckstein, *Alte unnennbare Tage,* p. 133; Hermann Bahr, *Selbstbildniss* (Berlin, 1923), pp. 230-32.
45. See Robert Brau, "Mystik bei Rosa Mayreder," in *Der Aufsteig der Frau* (Jena, 1925), a *Festschrift* prepared by the Verlag Eugen Diederichs. The volume also contains a tribute by Eckstein.
46. Friedell, *Cultural History,* vol. III, pp. 273, 466.
47. Georg Fuchs, *Sturm und Drang in München um die Jahrhundertwende* (Munich, 1936), pp. 79, 107.
48. Karl Wolfskehl, *"Der Priester vom Geist"* (orig. 1895) in G. P. Landmann (ed.), *Der Georg Kreis* (Cologne, Berlin, 1965), p. 23; Schuler, quoted in Friedrich Wolters, *Stefan Georg und die Blätter für die Kunst* (Berlin, 1930), p. 268.
49. See *Myth, Religion and Mother-Right: Selected Writings of J. J. Bachofen* (tr. Ralph Manheim, London, 1967), and C. A. Bernouilli, *Johan Jakob Bachofen und das Natursymbol* (Basel, 1924).
50. Wolters, *Stefan Georg,* p. 243.
51. Hans Eggert Schröder, *Ludwig Klages* (Part I; Berlin, 1966), pp. 166-84; Wolters, *Stefan Georg,* pp. 246-47; Robert Boehringer, *Mein Bild von Stefan Georg* (Munich, 1951), p. 106.
52. Schröder, *Klages,* p. 360.
53. Wolters, *Stefan Georg,* pp. 269-70; Boehringer, *Stefan Georg,* p. 106. Wolfskehl was, in any case, the least flamboyant of the group, although as interested in the mystical as the others. Besides his mythological studies and translations, he was a poet. He tells in "Gustav Meyrink aus meiner Erinnerung" of how Meyrink would hold his circle spellbound with tales of the supernatural. See Wolfskehl, *Briefe und Aufsätze* (Hamburg, 1966), pp. 202-3.
54. Edgar Salin, *Um Stefan Georg* (Münich, 2nd ed., 1954); and M. Nijlund-Verwey (ed.), *Wolfskehl und Verwey* (Heidelberg, 1968), quoting a letter of Hanna Wolfskehl of 4 April 1934; Wolters, *Stefan Georg,* p. 264.
55. Wolters, *Stefan Georg,* p. 249; Dominic Jost, *Ludwig Derleth* (Stuttgart, 1965), p. 46. The copper was presumably "sympathetic" to Nietzsche's ailment; Schröder, *Klages,* pp. 198-99; for Dessoir, see Kurt

Hildebrandt, *Errinerungen an Stefan Georg und seinen Kreis* (Bonn, 1965), p. 22 note 7. For Cyril Scott, his own autobiographies, *My Years of Indiscretion* (London, 1924) and *Bone of Contention* (London, 1969).
  56. Ludwig Klages, *Vom Kosmogonischen Eros* (6th ed., Bonn, 1963), pp. 56, 183.
  57. Alfred Schuler, "Vom Wesen der ewigen Stadt" in G. P. Landman, *Georg Kreis*, p. 51; and Wolters, *Stefan Georg*, pp. 247 ff.
  58. Jost, *Derleth*, pp. 25-29, 35-36.
  59. Thomas Mann, "Beim Propheten," in *Novellen*, Band I (Berlin, 1922), pp. 239-40.
  60. Jost, *Derleth*, p. 54; *"Warte Schwabing, Schwabing warte, Dich holt Jesus Bonaparte!"*
  61. Ludwig Derleth, "Das Buch vom Orden" in *Ludwig Derleth Gedenkbuch* (Amsterdam, 1958), p. 90; Jost, *Derleth*, p. 97; Derleth, *Buch vom Orden*, p. 74.
  62. Freimark, *Geisterbeschwörer*, p. 88.
  63. Freimark, *Geisterbeschwörer*, pp. 89-90. I have not been able to trace a copy of Braun's autobiography.
  64. Bernhard Müller-Elmau, "Führung und Fügung" in Marius Gerner Beule (ed.), *Schöpferische Leben* (Munich, Basel, 1964), pp. 19-27. On Lhotsky see Gregor Schwartz-Bostunitsch, "Der letzte Theologe" in *Ariosophie* (6 Jahrgang, Heft 3, 1931), pp. 66 ff.
  65. See the utterly meaningless passage quoted in Freimark, *Geisterbeschwörer*, p. 91.
  66. Müller-Elmau, "Fuhrung," pp. 30-52. For Johannes Müller's own views see his *Jesus as I See Him* (tr. Hilda Bell, London, 1928). *Neue Wegweiser* (Munich, 1920); and the study of Richard Grohrock *Der Kampf der Wesenkultur gegen die Bewusstseinkultur bei Johannes Müller* (thesis presented to University of Heidelberg, 1930).
  67. Müller, *Hidden Springs* (tr. Hilda Bell, London, 1925), p. 5 and passim.
  68. Robert Landmann, *Monte Verita* (3rd ed., Ascona, 1934). The author is in fact Robert Ackermann, who appears in the book. Pp. 32-50.
  69. Robert Landmann, *Monte Verita*, pp. 50-108. Mühsam wrote an anthem for the colony with a chorus which begins:
      Wir essen Salat, ja wir essen Salat,
      Und essen Gemüse früh und spät,
      Auch Frucht gehören zu unser Diät. . . .
  70. Robert Landmann, *Monte Verita*, pp. 111-13.
  71. Francis King, *Sexuality, Magic and Perversion* (London, 1971), pp. 96-97.
  72. Robert Landmann, *Monte Verita*, pp. 41, 53; Freimark, *Geisterbeschwörer*, p. 93.
  73. Landmann, *Monte Verita*, p. 41; John Symonds, *The Great Beast*, and cf. Goering, *Dr. Franz Hartmann*.

74. Symonds, *Beast*, p. 99, and cf. Goering, *Dr. Franz Hartmann*.
75. King, *Sexuality*, pp. 99 ff.
76. M. Kully, *Die Wahrheit über die Theo-Anthroposophie als eine Kulturverfallserscheinungen* (Basel, 1926), p. 261.
77. Symonds, *Beast*, pp. 99 ff.; King, *Sexuality*, pp. 106 ff.
78. Landmann, *Monte Verita*, pp. 140-49; Kully, *Wahrheit*, p. 38; Landmann, *Monte Verita*, pp. 150-53.
79. Johannes Hemleben, *Rudolf Steiner* (Hamburg, 1963) p. 134. The source of the "master" story is Edouard Schuré, so it appears that Steiner may at one time actually have made this claim.
80. Eckstein, *Alte unnennbare Tage*, pp. 130-31; Eckstein, "Ein Gruss aus längst vergangenen Tagen" in *Der Aufsteig der Frau*, pp. 102-3; cf. Steiner, *The Story of My Life* (London, New York, 1928), pp. 110 ff., 281, and Steiner, *The Anthroposophic Movement* (London, 1933); Steiner, *Occult Movements* (lectures given Dornach, October 1915), Lecture 2, p. 15.
81. Steiner, *The Story of My Life*, pp. 48-140; Hemleben, *Steiner*, pp. 27-43; Steiner, *The Story of My Life*, p. 265.
82. Hemleben, *Steiner*, p. 73, and cf. Thomas A. Riley, *L'Oeuvre littéraire de J. H. Mackay* (Paris, 1950).
83. Hemleben, *Steiner*, p. 73.
84. Gregor Schwarz-Bostunitsch, *Doktor Steiner, ein Schwindler wie keiner* (Munich, 1930), pp. 15-16. For Bostunitch himself, see below, chapter IV.
85. Steiner, *The Story of My Life*, pp. 285 ff.; Marie Savitch, *Marie Steiner-von Sivers* (tr. J. Compton-Burnett, London, 1967), pp. 41-50. The lectures are translated into English as *Mystics of the Renaissance* (London, 1911).
86. See Daniel Gasman, *The Scientific Origins of National Socialism* (London, 1971).
87. Steiner, *Story of My Life*, p. 300.
88. A. T. Barker (ed.), *The Letters of H. P. Blavatsky to A. P. Sinnet* (London, 1925), p. 121; Steiner, *The Anthroposophic Movement*, pp. 136-37, 141; cf. *Story of My Life*, pp. 303-4.
89. Howe, *Urania's Children*, pp. 80 ff. for Vollrath; see W. Hübbe-Schleiden, *Das Morgenrot der Zukunft* (Leipzig, 1912) for the atmosphere of Star in the East propaganda.
90. Günther Wachsmuth, *The Life and Work of Rudolf Steiner* (N.Y., 1955), p. 79; Kully, *Wahrheit*, p. 262. Crowley's Lodge was the *Mysteria Mystica Maxima;* Steiner, *Story of My Life*, p. 325; King, *Ritual Magic*, pp. 97 ff, 206-7.
91. Steiner, *Story of My Life*, p. 39; Steiner, *The Gates of Knowledge* (London, 1912), p. 148.
92. Steiner, "Haeckel, the Riddle of the Universe and Theosophy" in *Three Essays on Haeckel and Karma* (London, 1914), pp. 201-2 and cf. p. 206. Cf. Steiner's *Knowledge of the Higher Worlds and Its Attainment*

(London, N.Y., 1923), and *The Spiritual Beings in the Heavenly Bodies and in the Kingdoms of Nature* (London, 1951), in which a procedure similar to Edgar Dacqué's "nature somnambulism" is described. Cf. also the "perfective work" of James Morgan Pryse and A.E. described in *The Occult Underground,* pp. 323-24.

93. Karl Rittelmeyer, *Rudolf Steiner Enters My Life* (tr. D. S. Osmond, London, 1929), pp. 77, 102.

94. Steiner, *The Submerged Continents of Atlantis and Lemuria* (London, 1911).

95. See the convincing arguments of J. W. Hauer, *Werden und Wesen der Anthroposophie* (Stuttgart, 1922). For Hauer himself, see chapter VI below. Steiner's debt to H. P. Blavatsky is great. He thought that she had been put in "occult captivity" by sinister Brethren who had dealings with "really illicit arts" and prevented her from disclosing all the secrets that she possessed.

96. Steiner, *Theosophy of the Rosicrucians* (London, 1953; orig. 1907), *The Mission of Christian Rosycross* (London, 1950; orig. 1911-12) and—in same volume—"Rosicrucianism and Modern Initiation" (orig. 1924), p. 157; Steiner, *Christianity as a Mystical Fact* (London, N.Y., 1914); Steiner, *The Etherisation of the Blood* (London, N.Y., 1935).

97. Rittelmeyer, *Steiner,* passim, especially 117 ff. and cf. Peter Anson, *Bishops at Large* (London, 1964), p. 367 note 2.

98. Hemleben, *Steiner,* pp. 132-33.

99. See e.g., Landau, *God is my Adventure* (reprint London, 1964), pp. 187-91. Steiner anticipated the modern "ecologists" by nearly half a century.

100. Kully, *Wahrheit,* pp. 301 ff. and cf. Karl Heyer, *Wie man gegen Rudolf Steiner kämpft* (2nd ed., Stuttgart, 1932), pp. 45-46 for Krieger. Krieger was probably encouraged in his delusions by Steiner's opponents.

101. Kully, *Wahrheit,* pp. 67-71.

Chapter 2
Eden's Folk

The Disease of Civilization—The English Youth Movements—Back to the Land—The Merrie England of the Guilds—Christian Utopias—The Youth Movements and Social Relevance—Social Credit—The Illuminates and Fascism—The Illuminates and Anti-Semitism

No generation since the industrial revolution has lacked dreamers and destroyers, its quota of Luddites, or those in search of a Golden Age. For humanity seems to have removed itself from its true being in direct proportion to the growing number of giant factories, the increase in restrictive legislation, and the necessary alteration of its relationship to life and labor. In one form or another, this argument has always been before the public and every passing decade has provided new discontents with which to support the thesis. After the Great War reformers of every sort imagined that their chance had come. The crisis of European society that took place between the years 1914 and 1923 produced a myriad of plans for the reform or replacement of the materialist system.

Such plans had been germinating in the Progressive Underground since the middle of the previous century, and the projects advanced immediately after 1918 display traces of this origin. Generally speaking, they shared two characteristics: a revulsion against "materialism," which had caused the war, and a longing for some more cohesive society to replace the loose, anarchic "individualism" that had contributed to the crisis.

Edward Carpenter expressed both urges in his book, *Civilisation: Its Cause and Cure,* which dates from 1889 and had been reprinted fifteen times by 1921. Carpenter's Utopian society included vegetarianism and a return to the rural life. He deplored the fact that men had lost touch with their "inner and undying" selves, and he described the individual's "wretched feeling of isolation, actual or prospective, which man necessarily has when he contemplates himself as a separate atom in this immense universe—the gulf which lies below seemingly ready to swallow him, and the anxiety to find some mode of escape." The solution was for man to find that he was "absolutely indivisibly and indestructibly" a part of a great whole. Some higher cause—in the case of Carpenter, a union with the Divine—would unite him with his fellows and the universe.[1]

In Britain, anxiety and Progressive Underground were related as they were in Germany. Because of the chances of politics and economics, illuminated groups played considerably less part in society than they did in Germany between the two World Wars. But all the elements were present which across the North Sea were welded to a will to use unlimited force, although in Britain they were comparatively unorganized, and small in numbers. These reforming elements have been neglected, in part because they were extra-Parliamentary, and in part because they have left no interested offspring. In their time, however, they attracted substantial attention and have contributed ideas which have since been put into practice.

The illuminated movements can be detected by their tendency to gather round themselves mystical, occult, and religious elements, and in the first great agitation for the reform of society such ambassadors of the heavenly kingdoms bore credentials from precisely those realms from which help was most expected.

The means which were to establish the better world were a matter of dispute. Very often differing rationales could lead to what seems identical practice. Such different aims and methods are to be found in the postwar youth movements which arose from a combination of social Darwinianism, a reaction against urban society, and new educational ideas. They shared a reliance on the works of Ernest Thompson Seton, the American educationalist G. Stanley Hall, and the fearsomely named "Biogenetic Law" of Ernst Häckel. This latter concept was filtered through the works of Hall, who expressed it thus:

> The child from nine to twelve is well adjusted to his environment and proportionately developed; he represents probably an old and relatively perfected state of race-maturity. . . . At dawning adolescence this old unity and harmony with nature is broken up; the child is driven from his paradise and must enter upon a long viaticum of ascent, must conquer a higher kingdom of man for himself, break out a new sphere, and evolve a more modern story to his psycho-physical nature. . . . It is the most critical stage of life, because failure to mount almost always means retrogression, degeneracy and fall.[2]

Acceptance of the literal truth of Häckel's Law meant for educationalists becoming practicing Darwinians. Their charges must be induced to progress from one supposed stage in the evolution of past humanity to the next and higher. The founders of one of the organizations which took Häckel and Hall as their starting point made plain the methods they proposed to adopt.

> A complete education means the living over again by the individual of the experiences passed through by his ancestors.
> As man's progenitors inhabited fruit-producing regions along with other animals, so his children should begin life in an orchard-garden along with pet animals, whether wild or domesticated,—the ensemble being as like as may be to the traditional Garden of Eden, and to the reconciliation with the animal world as described in Isaiah XI. When the time comes for them to break out of this garden, they will proceed to lay a solid foundation of palaeolithic culture by betaking themselves under adult guidance to some suitable cave or

rock-shelter, whence issuing forth they will hunt for wild foods, get to know the ways of the wild creatures of the woods, and otherwise reproduce the life of that period. To this will succeed the more advanced and varied avocations of the neolithic cultures, marked by the domestications of animals and plants—the pastoral and the simple agricultural stages—together with such arts and crafts as can be carried on with the aid of metals. Lastly, with the use of metals and of books the adolescent passes into the modern world.[3]

The framework within which all this theorizing was placed came from the artist and naturalist Ernest Thompson Seton. In 1900, he wrote, he bought a tract of land near New York which he planned to turn into a nature reserve. Local boys started tearing down his fences, and Seton decided to win them over rather than indulge in a course of ineffective terrorism. He invited the boys to spend a weekend on his ground, and, to entertain them, he used his knowledge of the countryside and of the Red Indians. Soon he had organized a full-scale tribe, appealing to "the master-power of the savage, the love of glory."[4] The Indian model and the healthy life in the open air remained for Seton the cardinal points of his scheme. The Redskin "was the great prophet of the outdoor life," a "master of woodcraft," "taught the sacred duty of reverencing, beautifying and perfecting the body," "sought for the beautiful in everything," by nationalizing all natural resources put a stop to poverty and great wealth, and "he was the world's great historic protest against avarice."[5] From Seton's first experiment arose scattered tribes of "Woodcraft Indians" which their founder united in 1917 into the Woodcraft League of America. This was the source of inspiration for several European movements which owed debt to Seton's *Birch Bark Roll* and cultivated his principles: the outdoor life, self-government, the skills of woodcraft, a system of honors judged according to a standard rather than in competition, and the appeal of the heroic and the picturesque typified by the romance of the campfire.[6]

In the early years of the Great War, a group of Cambridge Scout workers began to contemplate a return to the principles of Seton. The attitude of Baden-Powell's movement toward the war dissatisfied them and they saw the "broad idealism" and allegiance to woodcraft which they had earlier found attractive being eroded. In 1916 Ernest Westlake and his son, Aubrey, founded the Order of Woodcraft Chivalry, with Seton as Grand Chieftain. Ernest Westlake—who died in 1922, and was buried on a campsite of his movement—was an anthropologist who had studied biology under T. H. Huxley and was much concerned with the Biogenetic Law.

His son, Aubrey, was born in 1893 and by the end of the war was house physician at Barts Hospital, London. It is important to notice that both were Quakers and, also, that Ernest Westlake was interested in psychical research. Aubrey has since become an Anthroposophist and a theoretician of water divining.[7] The idealistic and pacifist impulse of the Quaker was also deflected into other areas of rejected and anti-Establishment thought, and the Order of Woodcraft Chivalry was in its essence an "illuminated" movement. It is typical that Aubrey Westlake first developed the principles of Woodcraft Chivalry at a London meeting of members of the Baha'i Faith. He praised Seton, deplored the militaristic and civilized character of Baden-Powell's Scouts, and advocated the development of the instinct of service as the only way "to avoid a repetition of the present awful European disaster." There was naturally a strong religious element in the plan.

> Religion in the past has been too unpractical, too unsocial, we are realizing that after all the only test of a faith is by its fruits. We are in need of a social religion, one which is carried into every detail of life, one which embraces every field of activity. This religion we seek is already in every child; we have got to recognize . . . "that rightly influenced and rightly led, a boy or girl is *never* outside the kingdom of God"; and having recognized this, it is our duty to provide this religion with ways and means of expression whereby it may blossom forth in all its beauty.

To this end Westlake established as the core of the Order of Woodcraft Chivalry what was "in a sense, the church of the movement." This was the Sun Lodge, toward which members progressed through the grades of Wood Cubs, Woodcraft Scouts, and Pathfinders. Its chief function was "to preserve, through contact with Nature, the spiritual ideals of the Order from becoming merely empty formulae."[8] Seton himself had given his doctrine a pronounced Christian twist, but the founders of Woodcraft Chivalry were in search of the primitive religion of natural man. "In order to become spiritual one must first be natural,"[9] they declared, and Ernest Westlake appealed for a return to the Dionysiac spirit, invoking pagan deities with the verses of a disciple of Crowley, Victor Neuberg.[10] In the ideal educational system, there would be a "Forest School" in which the recapitulation theory would be applied, and in which the pupils could "regain Paradise," a state of harmony with all creation.[11] This program implied a revolt against all the values of the civilized world and Established society.

> The young man's protest is that of eternal youth against the fallacy that the world is old. It is the protest of the soul of man, perpetually renewed, against the notion that social conditions are fixed, masters of life and not its servants.
>
> It is not primarily the young man, but civilization, which is on trial.[12]

The Order of Woodcraft Chivalry was the earliest of the youth movements arising out of the war, but not the most effective. Its chief influence was the field of education. It established its own Forest School in the New Forest, and its propaganda resulted in the foundation of other schools, both in Britain and abroad, run on the principles of woodcraft and recapitulation. The movement's initial connection with the Quakers proper was severed soon after it was founded and it maintained contact with the growing number of woodcraft organizations through an "International Folkmoot." Its leaders were also in communication—a relationship whose nature seems to have alternated between sympathy and frustration—with a more significant rebel against Society Established and its perversion of youth. This was John Hargrave.

John Hargrave was born in 1894 in Midhurst in Sussex, and not, as one rumor claimed, in a gypsy tent on the Essex marshes. Like the Westlakes, the Hargrave family were Quakers, and all were artists. Hargrave's artistic precocity was equaled only by his enthusiasm for the ideas of Seton-type woodcraft. He himself joined the Scouts around the year 1908 and became enthused by Seton's appearance at a meeting held by Baden-Powell in the Albert Hall. By himself he concentrated on applying Seton's instructions with great fidelity—carving chipping-flints and a stone axe, making moccasins out of birchbark. He wrote a manual, *Lonecraft,* emphasizing this side of the Scout's activities, which was published in 1913; and about the same time he met Seton himself, who was brought by his publisher to visit a one-man camp set up by Hargrave according to woodcraft principles.

According to Hargrave, the origin of Seton's Woodcraft Indians did not lie solely in the moral fable which was retailed for public edification. In the whole concept Rudyard Kipling had a hand. He had summoned Seton to one of his frequently celebrated deathbeds and given him a sacred charge: the regeneration of the Anglo-Saxon race.[13] Ideas of racial betterment certainly did play some part in the thought of Seton himself. Of the open-air life, he wrote, "I should like to lead this whole nation into the way of living outdoors for at least a month each year, reviving and expanding a custom that as far back as Moses was deemed essential to the national well-being."[14] The Westlakes' Order of Woodcraft Chivalry to some extent followed the train of thought, but their program was more directed toward the education of the individual child and hence of all humanity. Hargrave was to lay emphasis on the use of woodcraft for the betterment of the whole race. During the Great War, he served as an army stretcher bearer, and was present at the Suvla Bay landings; on his return he published in 1919 a book which had been written before the war and rewritten because of it, *The Great War Brings It Home*. It declared: "The time has now come when we can control and use that process of natural selection known as Evolution."[15]

Just before the war had broken out eugenics had become a topic of great interest in the English-speaking world. In the United States, 1914 had seen a National Conference on Race Betterment, and by the next year a dozen states had passed sterilization laws. In 1910 the Eugenics Record Office had been established to support the work of Charles Davenport, one of whose functions was to advise "concerning the eugenical fitness of proposed marriages."[16] In England Sir Francis Galton and his successor Karl Pearson pursued similar researches, while their colleagues scanned the pages of Crockford's Directory of the Church and the Public Schools Year-Book to determine theories of the transmission of ability. The Eugenics Society promoted a campaign to ensure compulsory sterilization of stocks with "bad heredity and inferior capacity."[17] Even Baden-Powell would have accepted a vision of Scouting which emphasized the importance of training and keeping fit the nation's youth.

Hargrave was in the distinguished company of Julian Huxley when he advocated the improvement of the race.[18] Race betterment meant a return to natural man. Hargrave suggested "regeneration" in "the natural way." "It is the only way we have not yet tried. Give it a chance. How can you expect the 'nature' of a man to improve by unnatural means? Our very existence is unnatural. Why not seek to understand the natural law and make use of it?" The natural law asserted the primacy of instinct, the cultivation of savage virtues. The Scouting or Woodcraft movement, which would provide the means of regeneration, could rely on primitive ceremony, for "anything primitive has within it a vital ideal, because primitive man only grapples with Big Ideas." It would be coeducational, because 'the boy so trained must sooner or later need the girl so trained, and unless he can find her, his own training is useless, for he will be forced to marry into a 'less improved' bloodline."[19] The lesson of the war was that "something" must be done quickly. In 1919, Hargrave, then scout commissioner for Woodcraft and Camping, was telling his Scouts: "We're helping to evolve a New Race of Scout Men—we're the beginning of a new off-shoot of evolution."[20]

But the Great War had also taught other lessons. Like the Westlakes, Hargrave had become disgusted with the way the Scout organization was drifting away from the principles of Baden-Powell's *Scouting for Boys* and the movement put at the service of the military and ecclesiastical Establishment. As he was later to write, "The boy had been taken into the woods by his Wicked Uncles, folded in the Union Jack, and smothered."[21] He had an interview with Baden-Powell and protested against the drift of Scouts away from the tamed movement as well as the domination of their activities by the authorities.

According to Hargrave, Baden-Powell admitted that there was much truth in his accusations, but protested that if the Scouts were more independent of authority they would not obtain finance.[22] Eventually Hargrave decided to secede, or was expelled from the Scout movement—it depends which account is accepted—with (on the Scout side) accusations of his having libeled Baden-Powell and ominous murmurings of "Socialist and Bolshevist tendencies." He took with him some 300 Scout workers, and on 18 August 1920, Hargrave founded his own organization, the Kindred of the Kibbo Kift. He had already rejected an offer made by the Westlakes to join the Order of Woodcraft Chivalry, although he had become a member of their Council of Guidance.

It is unlikely that Hargrave could ever have been at home in a movement not of his own making. All the same, the most diverse fairy godmothers presided over the birth of the new youth movement—the Pethick-Laurences (Mrs. Pethick-Laurence became a member of the Kibbo Kift), the reformer Henry Nevison, and members of the New Educational Fellowship.[23] In September 1926 the Advisory Council of the Kibbo Kift included, besides Nevinson and Mrs. Pethick-Laurence: Norman Angell, H. G. Wells, Stephen Graham, Maurice Maeterlinck, Maurice Hewlett, Patrick Geddes, Rabindranath Tagore, Havelock Ellis, and Julian Huxley.[24] Under the banner of such Progressive heroes was a ragbag of the Progressive Underground. A former member of Hargrave's group has said that there were "pacifists and humanitarians of every degree; members of unorthodox sects and of strange pseudo-occult societies who took spirit photos of 'Fairies and Red Indians,' semi-Communists who sought world brotherhood by an intensive class-war, and vegetarians who deemed it inconsistent with the 'cannibalistic' eating of animals."[25]

Hargrave's reply to this was to picture his movement as a whale pestered by minnows—"They said, 'Folk Dancing'—and 'Rhythms'; they said 'Fabianism' (minus GBS), Gymnosophy (they meant Nakedness, but were unable to speak plainly), Anthroposophy, Theosophy, and Food Reform. All kinds of things they said: Co-operative Societies, Robert Owen; Sunlight and sun-bathing; experimental psychology; Nu Spelin, Nu Eras. Nu everything—*except a Nu Heaven and a Nu Earth*. Well, we took them in little bits and ate the parts which might build our backbone stronger, and chucked the other parts away."[26]

In other words, there was a period of experiment, in which the grandiose ends of the founder came near to being overgrown by a preponderance of means. At the start there was difficulty in establishing a course of training: it was found that the earliest stages posited by the theory of recapitulation—the so-called "Prehistoric" and the "Primitive"—were unpopular, and the most effective work was done in schools run according to Kibbo Kift principles.[27] But the educational work and the training of youth according to Seton's principles became gradually subordinated to Hargrave's emerging vision of his group as an elite who were to be ready when the moment came to take over power. He demanded absolute obedience of his followers. They, in turn were prepared to submit to his magnetic personality. "He was the typical Scout 'hero,' " wrote one of them, "a magical, charismatic aura surrounded him."[28] The Kin, in the words of another, "made an emotional appeal to its members like that of a nation or a church." The scope of the Kibbo Kift's plans for a new heaven and a new earth was limitless.

> We stood for the vision of Mankind United, for a universal tolerance, for a world brotherhood that would exclude no race or creed or social status. Difficult as it is to express, as difficult as patriotism or religious faith, the ideal of the Kindred was very real. It meant something to us when we signed the Covenant, taught out tribes the Declaration and unfurled over our camps the flag that showed no local or class or sectarian symbol, but the universal emblem of Mercator's projection, the World Banner of the Kibbo Kift.[29]

During this period of flux, some few constants remained. Hargrave's insistence on primitivism and pageantry was enduring. The Kibbo Kift were dressed in an elaborate uniform based on Robin Hood and went armed with a sheath knife. The members took Kin names—Hargrave's was "White Fox." The words "Kibbo Kift" were said to mean "Proof of Great Strength" and for a while the revivers of folkdancing and Merrie England held sway. One of its critics wrote in 1934 that the Kindred "indulged in obscure ceremonial and mystic symbolism. . . . The chief function of its annual assembly became (and may still be) the roasting of a sheep or an ox whole."[30]

The fascination with mysticism and the occult was present at the start. In *The Great War Brings It Home* Hargrave had advocated a universal religion of the Great Spirit, expounded the law of *karma,* and written a chapter on yoga meditation with instructions for an exercise teaching that "everything is everything." In 1919 he had told his Scouts that they might never know what the Great Life Force was but they could be certain that "it *is* there—that it *does* lie 'behind it all'—and that *we are part of it*." For his closest circle he held a "Lodge of Initiation."[31] In Hargrave's novel *Harbottle* (1924) the hero is deserted by his wife and sets off on a pilgrimage to discover reality. Throughout the searching the questioning is a substantial dose of the occult. Harbottle is introduced to the writings of one "Edward Almroth Twite" by an artist who is a member of the "Ancient and Arcane Rosicrucian Order." The occultist is an amusing parody of a Crowley-like figure and the bogus philosopher Twite stands for Ralph Waldo Trine. Hargrave evidently rejected much of occult theory, while remaining open to the fascination of the mysteries. The next year Hargrave published another novel, *Young Winkle,* a parody of Kipling's *Kim,* in which the boy who is the subject of the book is taken in hand not by a learned lama, but by a "Great Doctor" who puts him through an idealized form of Hargrave's own educational system. This includes a catechism—"I believe in the Nameless God . . . who is Time-Space-Matter: and in myself . . . as an actual organic part of the One Great Nameless God. I believe in the Holy Catholic Body of Mankind."[32] Winkle is set a night vigil as a test, and has a vision of the symbol of the Kibbo Kift. After a series of instructors have dealt with him, his final trial is to resist the sexual advances of a girl member of the Great Doctor's organization. He is then initiated as a "fully conscious member of the human race." Hargrave claimed explicitly that the philosophy of the Kibbo Kift was based on a religious foundation, and in November 1926 he announced his formulation of the Great Religious Focus of the Kibbo Kift, "a simple projection of the God-concept . . . set down as a definite and understandable inspiration for all mankind." By the time of his culminating statement of the aims of the Kibbo Kift in 1927, the call was for "a new Rosicrucian Brotherhood." Hargrave belonged, he wrote, to no religious body other than the Kibbo Kift, which he hoped was "by its works . . . something of the sort."[33]

At the outset the Kibbo Kift seemed on the verge of sweeping all before it; but it never mustered more than about a thousand uniformed members. The explanation of this is found in the development of the organization from an educational body into the repository of the elite itself. Dissension between the various

Progressive groups which had battened on to Hargrave culminated in a large defection in 1924, when a Dr. Cullen—who had interested the Royal Arsenal Co-operative Society in starting up a youth group on Kibbo Kift lines—took exception to the dictatorial assumptions of Hargrave. He left the Kindred with Leslie Paul, the energetic leader of the South London groups, to establish their Woodcraft Folk as the youth movement of the Co-operative Societies. Leslie Paul's estimate of the reason behind the breach was simple. "The truth was," he wrote, "that the different wings of the movement were inspired by different social philosophies."[34] At the time he resented the fact that Hargrave had resisted pressure from the Labour Party to turn the Kibbo Kift into a Labour Scout movement. But it would be totally wrong to see the Kindred as a "fascist" group. Among the components of the "Socialist conspiracy" discovered by the British Fascists and Mrs. Nesta Webster, the Kibbo Kift occupied an honored place.[35]

The truth of the matter is that the Kibbo Kift was Hargrave's movement and no one else's, and its leader resisted any attempts to link his creation with established political causes. He disliked the socialist tenets of class war, mass voting, and the nobility of work; and he called for "Creative Play" by which he meant "the doing of anything for its own sake, such as the painting of a picture, the writing of a play, or even the organization of a factory." As circumstances gradually excluded the possibility of the Kibbo Kift developing any broader appeal, there emerged a doctrine of its status as an elite. This concept was undoubtedly influenced by the "samurai" of H. G. Wells's *A Modern Utopia* (1905), a caste of highly qualified members of society, reminiscent of Plato's Guardians, who obey a strict rule: vegetarian, teetotal, no smoking, no gambling, and a period of reflection each year in the solitude of the wilds. Indeed some part of Wells's vision of these shepherds of society may have been with Hargrave from the start. "The Active Few," Hargrave legislated, "always influence the Multitude." Universal suffrage gave the direction of government to the least educated section of the people. Whereas it should be in the hands of "experts, coordinated by an efficiency supervisor." By the end of 1925 the Kibbo Kift had definitely assumed a political role in the mind of its founder. The movement was "an incubator for the hatching out of young men and women trained to live hard and think hard." "A woman who has married a Kinsman must recognize that she has not married an ordinary citizen. She has married a man with special obligations who is to some extent 'set apart' from other men."[36]

To this vision of an elite of fully conscious human beings the concept of the 'new Rosicrucian Brotherhood' could easily be fitted. It is evident that Hargrave was aiming at a transformation which others were attempting at the same time—an alteration in the mode of being of men, which would itself bring about correct social thought. To his early adherence to the principles of the Biogenetic Law there was accommodated a doctrine of spiritual evolution. In 1927, just before the Kibbo Kift transformed itself into a political party proper, Hargrave issued *The Confession of the Kibbo Kift,* defining the status and goals of his movement. It had begun, he wrote, as "a body-impulse to get Earth contact in a mechanical age." But it had avoided, he thought, the pitfall of romanticism. Underlying the Kindred's activities was a trust in the sureness of the instinctive impulse. "Deeply-flowing in the Kindred, undefined and unanalysed, floods that dim creative chaos which the modern psychologist has termed the Unconscious. This great intuitional flow cannot be named, and cannot be brought into consciousness without creating psycho-physical disharmonies." The solution to human problems was not the creation of new systems, but the recovery of a correct relationship to nature. This principle was upheld with apocalyptic exhortations: "Up Merlin! We have need of you on Din Breon the sacred mount!" The objectives to which Kin members were expected to pledge themselves were framed in a Covenant. This envisaged "reservations" for training in woodcraft, the carrying out of such training in family groups, and a consequent honing of bodily, mental, and spiritual faculties. Handicraft training, Craft Guilds, and the establishment of regional assemblies were to be encouraged. "Regional, national, and world peace" was to be fostered by economic reforms. For his own samurai, Hargrave imagined a sanctuary and headquarters which he christened "Kin Garth" to include a "monastery, lamasery, or house of self-initiation." This could be the center of a "Noah's Ark policy" if civilization were to founder.[37]

The Confession of the Kibbo Kift already contains substantial elements of the economic preoccupations which were to alter the nature of the movement entirely. To understand these, other movements must be considered. But before doing so, two developments connected with the early phases of Hargrave's odyssey merit attention.

The first is the break-away movement led by Leslie Paul which became the Woodcraft Folk. Paul himself had been an early devotee of Hargrave. His chief disagreements with his leader were because of his conviction of the need for a Labour Scout Movement and a dislike of the ritualistic tendencies of the Kibbo Kift. By way of local Labour Parties and Co-operative Societies the Woodcraft Folk soon reached a national position that Hargrave's group never attained. But Paul preserved the principles of recapitulation and race betterment. Despite his dislike of "mysticism" he also remained convinced of the importance of ceremonial as an expression of the communal spirit and "the only possible alternative to the discipline of the 'parade-and-orders type.' " "Remember," he advised, "that these youngsters have never lived as they should live: their primal earth desires have gone unsatisfied and they are hungry for the real vital things of life...."[38] A German observer attended a camp of the Woodcraft Folk in the Wye Valley in the summer of 1933 and remarked of the Leave-Taking Ceremony he witnessed: "This evening-ceremony was in no way ridiculous but on the contrary gave each member the feeling of being a member of a great family."[39]

There is no doubt of Hargrave's illuminated approach. But even Leslie Paul's movement, with its rationalized use of ritual, betrays a preoccupation with realities other than those of rational consciousness. The disillusionment of the leader of the Woodcraft Folk became ever more acute as he witnessed the surrender of the German youth movements to the Nazi Party; but he did not discover his own transcendental ideal until the close of the Second World War. He characterized the *Wandervögel* as a religious movement, aiming at the same sort of transformation of the human spirit as had the George Circle. They had liberated the unconscious but could not direct its action. Paul himself came out for placing beside the scientific world-view "the parallel and equal rights of religion." Beliefs, he held, were supreme, and he dedicated himself to Christianity, which had after all provided what civilization Western Europe had to offer.[40] Thus did one leader of the idealistic opposition of the years between the wars find the kingdom for which he had been searching.

Rolf Gardiner was responsible for the second significant offshoot from the Kibbo Kift. He was attached more peripherally than Leslie Paul to Hargrave's movement, and his initiative was a much more loose-knit affair than the Woodcraft Folk. Until 1926 Rolf Gardiner was gleemaster of the Kibbo Kift. His preoccupations provide a general background to the concern of the woodcraft movements with ceremonial and ancient Englishry; and the general lines of thought to which Gardiner owes allegiance form a distinct feature of British idealistic politics at the time.

At Christmas, 1899, Cecil Sharp had heard, near Oxford, the Headington morris dancers dancing "Laudnum Bunches." The enthusiasm this awoke led to the concentrated collection of folk songs and dances by himself and Vaughan Williams. In 1911 there was founded the English Folk Dance Society which amalgamated with the English Folk Song Society in 1932; and by 1934 it had 49 branches throughout England.[41] Although similar developments were taking place in other parts of Europe and in other regions of the United Kingdom, this tiny "English nationalism" or English "folkish movement" has remained unrecognized for what it was.

Whereas the various movements for Celtic Nationalism based themselves on the parallel pursuit of folklore,[42] the rediscovery of England seems to have begun with morris dancing. Cecil Sharp himself saw little future in the morris dance; and shortly before his death Rolf Gardiner had an argument with him on this very point. He had told Sharp, he writes, "that the people he ought to convert *were the farmers not the schoolteachers,* the Board of Agriculture not the Board of Education. But he was incredulous and at a loss to understand me. And yet, what would have happened if in 1922-4 we had started the revival of British agriculture, then at the nadir of depression, with the resurrection of the soul of the English countryside. Would it not then, at that crucial point in time, have been just a possibility?" In 1924, the year of Sharp's death, Gardiner took a traveling team of morris dancers through the Cotswolds. The year before, he had expressed his hopes for the revival of folk tradition. "The real and vital concern of the folk dance movement is the effect it might have on the religious and psychological evolution of our humanity."[43] With much reference to Joachim of Flora and his prophecy of the coming Third Age of the Holy Spirit, Gardiner predicted a real change in consciousness, which would unite the intellect with that of the instinctive drives. In this new way of being, the folk dance would play a part.

Gardiner had been a Scout, and until his break with Hargrave he had contributed dances and songs to the Kibbo Kift. These included one called "Al Hael" and many translations from the German. It was in Germany that he found much of his inspiration, for developments among the German youth movements were hospitable to the illuminated approach and bulked much larger than any such ventures nearer home. To his family contacts, Gardiner added the fascination which was felt by many of his generation at the universities—Gardiner was educated at Bedales and Cambridge—with the idealistic attempts to reform the shattered society of Central Europe. He maintained contact with Ernst Buske of the *Deutsche Freischarr* and established a relationship with the Prussian minister of culture, Carl Heinrich Becker. The aspects of the German *Bunde* which particularly fascinated Gardiner were the centers that grew up to inculcate by one or another means the new society and the new sort of consciousness. Becker supported several of these—for example, a workman's hostel and village school maintained by the experimental educationalist Albert Reichwein, and the *Boberhaus* in Silesia which was run as a regional center for communally training students, peasants, and workers.

Gardiner found a Danish inspiration in the Folk School at Krabbesholm in Jutland, designed to foster a peasant aristocracy. But the most important souce of communication with Germany was the *Musikheim* established by Georg Goetsch (1895-1955) at Franfurt an der Oder. Gardiner described this as "a modern Aesculapian monastery" and "an initiation into the secrets of being alive through music." It was particularly with the *Musikheim* that visits were exchanged—for example, that of October 1934 when a meeting took place at Frankfurt under the auspices of Goetsch and Gardiner, in which English and German miners met and took part in sword dancing. One of Gardiner's sympathizers, Katherine Trevelyan, married Goetsch and further cemented the links which bound the English to the Germans by their common interest in "the arts as social therapy."[44]

> It was this "secret" Germany of flourishing independent centres of social experiment and artistic training which

fascinated the English visitor. Between 1925-30 there was a growing belief that in Germany important creative work was being done which would fructify the hopes of European Union and restore the shattered pattern of Christendom. The apocalyptic feeling which had swept over Central Europe immediately after the war and which found expression in Spengler's *Untergang des Abendlandes* was in abeyance. While the politicians and economists struggled with the consequences of Versailles "Peace," the cultural vitality of youth had room for play. Those were valuable and happy years. The sad thing about them was that apart from our tiny nucleus virtually no English groups actively associated with this field of endeavour in Europe. People wondered at the profusion of events and undertakings that succeeded: music tours, festivals, work-camps, exchanges. Yet they were planned mostly by Goetsche and myself in consultation with a very few others, and carried through without any formal apparatus of organisation.[45]

After leaving Hargrave in 1926 until 1931, Gardiner and his group seem to have preserved something of the old youth movement spirit of hiking. Gradually there came about a change of emphasis. The year 1930 saw the loss of gurus. Carl Heinrich Becker was forced to resign his ministry, Ernst Buske of the *Freischarr* died, and soon afterward, D. H. Lawrence (from whom Gardiner had received much support for his idea of achieving a more "natural" consciousness).[46] Gardiner drifted nearer the Westlakes and their Order of Woodcraft Chivalry. In the winter of 1932 he read a paper to his sympathizers "On the Functions of a Rural University." He wanted to reproduce in England the spirit he had found in the regional centers in Germany. He proposed to tackle what he saw as the three main problems—that of the unemployed, the work of agricultural reconstruction, and the establishment of regional government. The unemployed needed leadership and work camps. Their leaders needed centers of assembly and renewal "just as the old religious orders required both the contemplative and the itinerant ways of life." The threatened food shortage must be avoided and the self-respect of the rural population restored. And with the general aim of training "an elite responsible for the self-government of Wessex" there was inaugurated the "Wessex Centre" at Springhead, Fontwell Magna, in Dorset. Gardiner called for "a new European chivalry" and hoped for exchanges with centers abroad. He gave vent to his romantic hopes for Springhead. "The idea of Centres or monasteries has recurred at regular intervals in the cycles of civilisation.... The heart of our civilisation is rotten. The centre, the monastery is the tiny seedling rooted in the dark earth which is the womb of all forms."[47] Of the inauguration in the autumn of 1933, a German visitor enthused. "Tell me whatever you like, but I felt like being in church and no church was ever as great as that high-skied autumn heaven over us."[48] At harvest time 1934, Gardiner consolidated his small chivalry with a work-camp at which there were almost equal proportions of unemployed, students and German visitors; and he named his circle the Springhead Ring.[49]

Gardiner and his friends have always felt themselves to be engaged in a sacramental act. And with the establishment of the center at Springhead he became involved with others who regarded the task of rural reconstruction in a similar light. The date, however, coincides too neatly with the coming to power of the Nazis in Germany and the submission or suppression of the German youth movements to avoid comment; and it is necessary to examine the precise relationship of the British and German youth movements.

Gardiner's own attitude has been much criticized and was at times equivocal. In 1927-28 he edited in collaboration with Heinz Rocholl a symposium published both in England and Germany; it was an attempt to construct a dialogue between young people in Germany and Britain. The unexceptionable tone of Gardiner's article was somewhat outweighed by the nationalistic emphasis of his coeditor and a rather wild contribution from a German incorporating almost all the myths of racist propaganda.[50] In 1930 Gardiner again contributed to a symposium, which this time was published only in Berlin. His essay on "English Tradition and the Future" is intriguing. He derived the English race from Atlantis and recalled that Britain had been known as a holy island. He was scathing about the Celts, who "never became Christian, in any blue-eyed, or at least Roman sense," and denied any racial purity to the English. Old England had died in the years 1915-20, but there was still hope of an idealistic revolution.[51] By 1933 he could endorse the Nazi coming to power as "the result of organic growth," despise liberalism and "ballot-box democracy," and excuse German ill-treatment of the Jews.[52] British publishing houses refused his book on the "German Revolution" as propaganda. In 1934 Gardiner had an interview with Rudolf Hess about the possibilities of English-German exchanges.[53] When in the same year Leslie Paul of the Woodcraft Folk lamented the decline of the German movements and their abdication to the Nazi party, Gardiner attacked him for not being able to see that the core of the *Bunde* had always had political aims and that their mission had been to train an elite for leadership. He found some satisfaction in the number of Hitler's adjutants who had been *Wandervögel*.[54]

But not too much should be made of this. Gardiner was by no means alone in having his idealistic hopes of Nazism disappointed, and his approval of the German new order is best seen as a vicarious expectation of something which his native experience did not allow him or anyone else to carry out: an idealistic revolution. The quality of idealism was what both Gardiner and Leslie Paul had admired in the *Wandervögel*.

It was this quality—together with the congenial ritualism and the direct, if unorthodox, theory—that the German movements admired in their turn in John Hargrave. Hargrave became the leading influence on the *Bünde* in the 1920s and his books were translated and published by the *Weisse Ritter* publishing house, the most influential youth movement agency of the period.[55] On his side, Hargrave predicted that the German movements would be swallowed up by the new Leviathan of National Socialism, although he and Gardiner shared with the Germans a spirit of elitism which was not found in the Socialist Leslie Paul. But even Paul had responded to the appeal of the famous *Hohe Meissner* manifesto, in which the representatives of the various German organizations had summoned their members to a mountain south of Cassel in October 1913 and proclaimed their new order.

> Youth, up till now merely an appendage of the older generation shut out from public life and reduced to a passive role, is beginning to base itself *on* itself. It is trying, independent of the demands of convention, to fashion its life for itself. It is struggling for a way of life which corresponds to the essence of youth but at the same time also makes it possible to take itself and its actions seriously, and to integrate itself as a

unique element in general cultural life. It wishes to introduce as a refreshing and rejuvenating current into the spiritual life of the nation the inspiriting factor of pure dedication to the highest tasks of humanity and of unsullied faith and will to achieve a heroic existence.[56]

From the rebellion of youth against the "bourgeois" and materialist world came the idealism which inspired the postwar British movements as it had the German. At first sight it might seem that the British movements were organized by older men according to a more artificial pattern than the German model, and that their numbers were insignificant. But Hargrave, Paul, and Gardiner were all approximately of university age when they began their independent careers as youth leaders, and the fact that they accumulated a following argues for a degree of spontaneous support. As to the size of that following, it should be noticed that the largest camps of the combined German youth movements like that at the *Hohe Meissner* itself, never numbered over 3,500,[57] and the significance of the *Bünde* in German history has never been doubted. And, as social pressures changed from those under which they had developed, so the youth movements altered their direction and co-operated with other idealistic projects for reform which showed more prospects for achieving a broad reformation of life and values. In Germany, the youth movements capitulated to the greater force of a prodigious will to power. In England the transformations were less spectacular and consisted in the channeling of the idealism which had once animated camping and training in woodcraft into courses already handcarved by others.

In the case of Rolf Gardiner, his tiny Springhead Ring turned its energies toward the task of "rural reconstruction," a phrase which had been formulated in the middle of the Great War in response to many of the same stimuli which had given birth to the youth movements. In October 1916, a number of societies concerned with the improvement of country life met to form a coordinating body to which the name was given of the Rural Organization Council. Besides various agricultural and housing associations, these included the Arts and Crafts Society, the Garden Cities and Town Planning Association, and the Peasant Arts Guild. The Order of Woodcraft Chivalry was also affiliated. If the task of reconstruction were properly carried out, the council felt that "the life that should result will be very great, and a calm, healthy glory that our forefathers had almost driven from these islands will come home again."[58] The feeling that Industrial Man had divorced himself from his roots in the soil had in fact found practical expression much earlier. In 1907, for example, the first land clubs—agricultural cooperatives—had been started. In connection with these Montague Fordham published *Mother Earth,* advocating the restoration to the people of "their mother, the earth," proclaiming that history knew no example of a nation which had survived separated from life on the land, and advocating "much more communal gaiety and amusement, particularly in relation to the land—in honor of mother earth."[59] When Gardiner settled down at Springhead to try to encourage an improved sense of community with morris dancing and the celebration of festivals, he was merely following the policy which had been advocated by Fordham and other earlier theorists.

Behind the plethora of bodies which sprang up between the wars with humdrum-sounding names like the Soil Association, the Council for the Preservation of Rural England, and the Rural Reconstruction Association, was often an impulse which was intensely idealistic in nature. Thus Fordham, writing in 1924, appealed to "the undefined spiritual laws that lie somewhere in the background of life." Thus H. J. Massingham, one of the chief theoreticians of the return to the soil, grew lyrical and mystical in his arguments. Within the ever-widening circle of those who recognized that something must be done about the spoliation of the countryside—of which the symposium edited by Clough Williams-Ellis called *Britain and the Beast* is a good representative—the illuminated approach was prominent.[60]

An example is the still-flourishing organization of the "Men of the Trees." This has its origin in the attempts of Richard St. Barbe Baker to prevent a Bantu tribe in Kenya from destroying the forests and ruining their farming land. Baker initiated a ritual "Dance of the Trees" and a "Brotherhood of the Trees" in order to persuade the tribesmen to plant rather than destroy.[61] On his return to England he decided that the English had become almost as destructive as the Bantu and founded his Men of the Trees as a body pledged to restore the dwindling tree population of Britain. The Men of the Trees "have been inculcating a tree sense." "They regard their country as a sacred trust"; and "the unselfish care of each plantation, looking to the distant good rather than to immediate gain will teach more than actual forestry. It will develop physical, moral and spiritual qualities which are essential to the well-being of man." In 1924, John Hargrave presented Baker with a plaque and a message of friendship from the Kibbo Kift and at the Conference of "The Men of the Trees" held at Oxford in 1938 a Kibbo Kift representative was present. The conference was attended by Rolf Gardiner, who gave a lecture on dowsing, and by a certain Miss Irene Goodman who announced that she was able to contact the spirit of a tree and be in touch with it "as a living personality."[62]

In the later 1930s were published Sir George Stapledon's *The Land, Now and Tomorrow* and Lord Portsmouth's *Famine in England*. These texts were taken to the hearts of the illuminated countrymen. The latter book advocated a decentralized civilization based on small stable land units, which it supposed to be a Christian contrast to the nomadic traditions of the Asiatic or Russian hordes. This conception bore some resemblance to the ideology of Walther Darré and the Nazi peasant organization; and for a short time Rolf Gardiner saw in Darré a real prospect of reviving "yeoman, peasant values, as opposed to industrial, urban, manufacturing values."[63]

The outbreak of the Second World War was seen as a renewed opportunity for the spiritual revolution; for the old order would be swept away and the prospects of reform which the years after the First War had extended would return more definitely. Accordingly, Gardiner, Portsmouth, Massingham and others met in the rooms of Edmund Blunden in Oxford to form a "Kinship in Husbandry." They published a pamphlet called *Return to Husbandry* which circulated widely among servicemen and prisoners of war. H. J. Massingham—who met Gardiner only late in life and thought of his work as "more English than the English"—wrote in an expanded version of this pamphlet "that the term husbandry" must be related "to first principles of the natural law, which is an earthly manifestation of the eternal law." "The pattern of life worked out by preindustrial rural society was an unconscious obedience to ecological laws." His crowning statement of this creed is contained in *The Tree of Life*, which is dedicated to Sir Arthur Bryant, another member of the Kinship in Husbandry. In this book, Massingham referred to

"Man's dangerous alienation from natural law" and "the approaching dissolution of civilisation." There was to be a recovery of the English tradition, which entailed a return to Christianity. Christ, the "Rural Redeemer," was to sanctify craftsmanship and agriculture, and man would again take his place in what Massingham called "the Doctrine of Creation," the perpetual unfolding of the organic process. "When a man stooks his sheaves at the right angle of incidence, he is not only true to the Doctrine of, but part of, the Creation itself."[64]

It was quite logical for illuminated farmers to turn to the only available source of lore on esoteric farming: the Bio-Dynamic system of Rudolf Steiner. In July 1950, Gardiner and Portsmouth held an agricultural conference in southern England which was attended by English, German, and Swiss representatives, including Richard St. Barbe Baker and the president of the Bio-Dynamic Association, Dr. Ehrenfried Pfeiffer of Dornach.[65] Whether Gardiner's association with the Anthroposophists—he has had a book published by the society's press—meant anything more than approval of their farming methods is uncertain. His old colleague, Aubrey Westlake of the Order of Woodcraft Chivalry, retired in 1938 to manage his estate at Godshill in Hampshire as a holiday and health center, and a place of experiment for fertility research; he had also become a convert to Anthroposophy.[66]

It should by now be clear that the links between the youth movements, the conservationists, and the supporters of what their opponents call "Muck and Mysticism," have been both strong and consistent, and that the illuminated search for the organic society has taken place in England as well as abroad. The links have as yet been only half established, and some of the most important movements are not discussed. But before the topic of the return to the land is abandoned, mention should be made of the movement for town planning and new towns.

The Quaker Ebeneezer Howard was infected in the 1890s by the ideas of the agrarian reformer Henry George and he became a Utopian under the potent influence of Edward Bellamy's *Looking Backward*. He was impressed by the proposals being made by Thomas Davidson, the effective originator of the Fabian Society, for a cooperative settlement near London "for people of advanced ideas." In 1898, Howard published a book called *Tomorrow* from which grew the First Garden City Company. The company began to build Letchworth in Hertfordshire, on the basis that the citizens themselves should own the land in common.[67]

Letchworth soon became a center for the Progressive Underground. There were Theosophists, cooperative printers, the Alpha Union for Universal Brotherhood, and a pub with no beer built by the Quaker Edward Cadbury. Ebeneezer Howard himself was president of the Letchworth Esperanto Association, and in 1912 he managed to lecture in that language on Garden Cities in Cracow. The historian of Letchworth, and Howard's assistant in building his second new town at Welwyn, was Charles Purdom, who later edited *Everyman,* for which John Hargrave did art work. Purdom became the biographer of Meher Baba and the devotee of other gurus like F. Mathias Alexander while pursuing plans to reconstruct urban life after the Second World War. The sort of Progressive opinion represented by Purdom and the denizens of the Garden Cities was as concerned with the ideal and the maintenance of a state of nature as the agrarians. He represented the reaction of townsmen rather than countrymen. "Man," wrote Purdom in 1932, "must maintain harmony with Nature in all its forms. He should keep contact with the earth and the seasons, allow the winds and rain and sun to strengthen him, and the sun to store his body with heat. Every man shut up in the city must take care to keep in time with the rhythm of natural life by going into the country as often as he can."[68]

A secondary inspirer of town planning was Patrick Geddes, whose influence on Ebeneezer Howard seems certain. Just after the Great War he and Victor Branford, the founder of the Sociological Society—both incidentally, supporters of the Biogenetic Law[69]—began to issue a series of tracts on reconstruction. These are in some ways the epitome of idealistic reaction to the war, seen as the final outcome of the Industrial Revolution. The need for a spiritual revolution was recognized. "The central issue in the matter of war and peace is: How to effect and maintain the conversion of the hunter?" The source of the evil was artificiality and change. "Since the Industrial Revolution, there has gone on an organized sacrifice of men to things, a large-scale subordination of life to machinery."[70]

Broadly speaking, these were the starting points from which the whole idealistic opposition to the English Establishment began; youth movements, life reformers, and organicists all found their particular solutions to the problem. It is tempting to use the name of Geddes to start a new foray through the thickets of the illuminated social reformers, to indicate that the redoubtable Scotsman provides a link with the occultist origins of Scottish nationalism[71] and to hint how Geddes' half-realized theories were reformulated in a more acceptable fashion by Lewis Mumford, rather in the manner in which—as we shall see—C. G. Jung reinterpreted occult doctrine. We are here only concerned with the rediscovery of England. To this end were directed three movements with which many of the figures already encountered were also associated. These are Guild Socialism, the related Christian revival, and the final upsurge of the Underground in the face of international catastrophe with the campaign for Social Credit.

There would be some truth in representing the folk-dancing, race-improving elements of the Underground as the "pagan" idealistic movement, while the supporters of guild socialism and Social Credit might be called the "Christian" wing. But there were those like Massingham and Montague Fordham who contrived to combine both aspects of the illuminated approach. The origins of guild socialism lie in a romanticizing of the Christian Middle Ages, rather than in an ideal picture of an indefinitely located past age of "natural man." Its roots are in the teachings of William Morris and John Ruskin, and in the reaction against industrial society expressed in the Arts and Crafts movement. Shorn of their aesthetic content, the social implications of this movement were plainly put by Walter Crane:

> The movement indeed represents in some sense a revolt against the hard mechanical conventional life and its insensibility to beauty.... It is a protest against that so-called industrial progress which produces shoddy wares, the cheapness of which is paid for by the lives of their producers and the degradation of their users. It is a protest against the turning of men into machines.[72]

As early as 1888 the Guild of Handicraft had been established in response to C. R. Ashbee's lectures on Ruskin at Toynbee Hall in the East End of London. The step had been taken because, Ashbee wrote, "we found those great democratic forces to which we as reformers looked for a survival of English craftsmanship, and a responsibility in its development, the Trade Union movement and the Cooperative Movement, unintelligent and indifferent in all matters relating to aesthetic training." The guild was in essence an escapist organization, and Ashbee's enthusiasm for "the old Guild system of the Middle Ages" as a means of ensuring both security and pride in achievement became directed toward the establishment of his guild in a craftsman's Utopia. Eventually, but at the cost of financial ruin, the Guild of Handicraft moved from London to Chipping Camden in the Cotswolds, where with the aid of its own songs and regulations it attempted to establish the first of several proposed "new centers of organic life."[73]

Arthur Penty, who was responsible for introducing the Guild idea to a wider public, was born in York in 1875, and was apprenticed to his father's architectural business. In 1899 he joined the Independent Labor Party and began to study politics. Two years later his father's business went bankrupt and Penty was left to fend for himself. This shock started him thinking about economics; and a second shock determined the direction in which his thoughts would lead. In July 1902, he called at the Fabian Society's office—he had been a Fabian for some time—and was taken to see the new building erected for the London School of Economics. His guide told him that the architect had been selected "on the statistical principle": that is, he had submitted the design with the most floor space. "I did not reply—I was speechless. The gulf between me and the Fabian mind was apparent. It was the turning-point in my thought."[74] His architect's soul affronted, Penty ruminated on the more aesthetic principles of the guilds; and in 1906 he produced his book *The Restoration of the Gild System*. No one else ever followed Penty's spelling; but numerous supporters began to adopt his ideas. Penty admitted that his theories were an attempt to make John Ruskin's proposals practical, and he advised his readers to supplement his book with Edward Carpenter's *Civilisation, its Cause and Cure*. He took issue with the "collectivism" of most sorts of Socialist thought, which he saw as an attempt to combat the avarice of the few with the avarice of the many. Penty was after a spiritual reformation.

And so, without committing ourselves to the unlikely theory that the Middle Ages were in every respect an ideal age and while certain that in many respects that time suffers in comparison with our own, I think we must admit its superiority in some directions.... For pursuit of religion and art were then the serious things of life, while commerce and politics, which have today usurped our best energies were strictly subordinated to these attributes of perfection.

Being social, religious and political as well as industrial institutions, the Gilds postulated in their organisation the essential unity of life. And so, just as it is certain that the attainment of intellectual unity must precede the reorganisation of society on a Cooperative basis, it is equally certain that the same or similar forms of social organisation will be necessary again in the future.[75]

Before Penty had left Yorkshire he had fallen in with A. R. Orage, then a young schoolmaster suffering from intellectual starvation in Leeds. While *The Restoration of the Gild System* was being completed, Penty and Orage had lived together in London, and the underemployed architect discussed his scheme with the fugitive from the north, whose ambition was now to write. Both Penty and Orage tried to make some progress toward popularizing the guild theory in traditional arts-and-crafts quarters. In 1906, they induced the moribund Junior Art Workers' Guild to accept the proposals, and the next year Orage and his friend Holbrook Jackson organized an Arts Group within the Fabian Society. This soon led to friction with the Fabian establishment, and the chief agency for propagating guild theory became the magazine acquired by Orage and Jackson, *The New Age*. Just before and during the war, propaganda for guilds began to make its way into quarters where there existed a real chance of carrying out reforms.

Over its short career, guild socialism never lost the traces of its origins. Its founder, Penty—typically, he worked as an architect on Hampstead Garden Suburb—remained a romantic medievalist, and supporters from the arts-and-crafts groups (like W. R. Lethaby) were prominent. Out-and-out medievalists persisted, such as G. Stirling Taylor, who challenged modernists to *prove* that Manchester was "better" than Bruges, Chicago than Florence, and Winston Churchill a greater statesman than St. Anselm.

The illuminated approach was present from the start. Orage was a prominent Theosophist and was later to become an apostle of the extraordinary Georgian G. I. Gurdjieff. Penty saw symptoms of his expected spiritual revolution in the "restoration of belief in the immortality of the soul through the growing acceptance of the doctrines of reincarnation and *karma,* and the tendency to admit the claims of mysticism." Craft guilds had even before Penty's book been a topic of discussion in Theosophical circles, and the European Congress of the Theosophical Society in 1905 had included two papers on the role of guilds as well as one by Montague Fordham, the future author of *Mother Earth.*[76] Very many of the circle around Orage were later to vow allegiance to one or another guru; others became pledged to the Christian revival. Yet in the ten years before 1923 the Guild theory increasingly seemed to have a real chance of penetrating the Trade Unions and becoming part of Socialist orthodoxy.

The first source of strength was the *New Age* propaganda. The *New Age* increasingly exercised an influence over the intellectuals of its day; Orage secured contributions from G. K. Chesterton, Hilaire Belloc, and Bernard Shaw, published Ezra Pound and T. E. Hulme, and remained the arbiter of Progressive taste. Just before the outbreak of the Great War, S. G. Hobson (a founder member of the Independent Labour Party and yet another Quaker) had contributed articles on the Guild theory to the *New Age* at the same time as Orage was attacking "wage slavery" in its columns. In 1914 Orage issued as "editor" the book *National Guilds* which had been written chiefly by Hobson and became the first real text of practical guildsmen. Yet even here the "spiritual" aspects were considered central. "The abolition of the wage system involves not merely an economic revolution, but *ex hypothesi,* a spiritual revolution also. A spiritual revolution, indeed, will be necessary as a precedent condition of the economic revolution, for we are not so blind to the lessons of history as to imagine that an economic revolution *for the better* can be engineered by force and greed alone."[77]

S. G. Hobson's scheme did not, like Penty's, require a return to the old structure of master, journeyman, and apprentice. But it was soon given a firmer theoretical foundation by another contributor to the *New Age,* Ramiro de Maeztu. This basis—which has always appeared somewhat sinister in later perspective—was the functional principle. Of de Maeztu, Hobson wrote, "Had we met him earlier, there would have been no 'Guild Socialism'. It would have been 'Functional Socialism.'" De Maeztu (1874-1935) published his first book on corruption in Spain in 1899 and was a resolute antitraditionalist. He had once disrupted a fashionable first night by rushing on to the stage shouting "Down with the Jesuits!" During the First World War he was a correspondent for a Buenos Aires paper, and he developed an admiration for England which he realized in his friendship with Orage and T. E. Hulme. From Hulme he imbibed a conviction that there existed absolute values and that fallen humanity must submit to discipline in order to regain these. During the years 1915-16 his *New Age* articles praised the Guild structure on the grounds of "limitation" and "hierarchy": the individual self must be dissolved and resurrected again as part of the whole social organism. The principle of function was "objectively" just: "it is more just, whether they like it or not."[78]

The revolt against individualism found support in academic quarters. In 1915, G. D. H. Cole, a 25-year-old fellow of Magdalen College, Oxford, failed in a bid to turn the Fabian Society from its collectivist viewpoint. He resigned with Maurice Reckitt to help found the National Guilds League on the basis of the so-called "Storrington Document," a program to which A. J. Penty and S. G. Hobson adhered, although Orage withheld his full support. Despite conflict between Cole and Hobson on the authority of the state, the league declared as its policy the abolition of capital and the establishment of state ownership of the means of production. This was to be achieved through pressure exerted by trade unions, which were then to be resolved into a system of self-governing guilds, regulated by a Central Guilds Congress.[79] There is little point in detailing the various conflicts between sections of the guild movement: its intellectual support included Bertrand Russell, George Lansbury, Rowland Kenney (editor of the *Daily Herald*), and R. Palme Dutt, as well as the sympathy of the group around Belloc, Chesterton, and the Christian revival. Apart from corroboration derived from French syndicalism, the only addition to theory was made by R. H. Tawney, who in his famous *The Acquisitive Society* (1921) made a moving plea for the limitation of the competitive instincts of man by means of the functional principle. Meanwhile, the war and industrial unrest gave the idealists a real chance of carrying out their plans. One guildsman wrote:

> To repeat, if this war means anything, it means a revolt against modern civilisation. If the modern commercial-capitalist-machine production is right, then why, in the name of common-sense, should we crush Germany, which bids fair to be the machine nation *par excellence* of the world. If modern centralised government is a good thing, then let us shed our last drop of blood in defence of the monarchy of Potsdam. If religion and romance are evil things, then let us raise our voices in grateful praise of a Prussia that would destroy Rheims cathedral rather than lose a battery of guns. Every symptom of the "modern" world has reached its highest point in Prussia.[80]

Despite the Munitions of War Act of 1915, which practically forbade strikes, the Great War saw the growth of the strike movement in Britain. In 1915, the Clyde shipyards struck, in 1917 the mine workers; in 1918, there were shipbuilding, textile, and coal strikes. J. M. Paton, who was active in the Glasgow strike movement, started *The Guildsman,* the journal of the National Guilds League; Willy Gallacher was sympathetic to their aims, and Frank Hodges (the secretary of the Miners' Federation) was on the league's Executive. In 1921, the Union of the Post Office Workers adopted a resolution to manage its affairs as a national guild, and the National Union of Teachers followed suit. S. G. Hobson induced the Manchester Building Trades Union to bid for contracts as a Guild; A. J. Penty and others organized a London Building Guild. A House Furnishing Guild was started, a Guild of Clothiers, an Engineering Guild, and an Agricultural Guild in connection with Welwyn Garden City.[81] In America and the English-speaking dominions there was interest in the guild theory; and there was a flourishing Guilds League in Japan. But very significantly, the most fertile ground for guild propaganda was in Germany, where materialism and the enrichment of the individual were also seen as leading to the war—but of course materialism in the guise of Anglo-Saxon industry, French individualism, and American go-getting. The establishment of workers' and soldiers' councils in postwar Germany was hailed by guildsmen as presaging the establishment of German guilds.

From February to May of 1919 the *Daily News* correspondent in Germany was George Young, a guilds sympathizer. His dispatches showed great enthusiasm for the German invention of Council Government. "The councils are as essential to Germany today as the Commons were to us a century ago." He rejected the old word *moot* as too archaic to describe the councils—the very fact that it occurred to him is significant—and thought that if the spontaneous eruption of the councils could be coordinated, "it may prove the salvation not only of Germany but of Europe." Looking back on his adventurous journey, he considered "that my most useful function in Germany at one time was putting German Labour leaders in possession of the conclusions of our Guild Socialists." It is uncertain precisely to whom he did in fact pass on the guild theories. However, he managed to penetrate almost anywhere he had made up his mind to reach, and his narrative of his journey by horse and carriage to Munich to interview the short-lived Eisner government is an amusing testimony to his determination. Writing in *The Guildsman* in November 1920, with the specter of Bolshevism peering over his shoulder, he predicted that "National Guilds, as a remedy for Bolshevism, will no doubt before long come back to us under a more popular name and with a more marketable appearance—like Aspirin or Lysol.[82] This interesting prophecy was partly borne out; and German interest in Cole, Penty, and Stirling Taylor endured into the period of Nazi domination, fusing with other doctrines of native origin. G. D. H. Cole himself saw the interest in guilds taken in Germany, Austria, and Hungary, as a non-Bolshevik attempt to gain government by the people for the people. Like Young, Cole turned prophet:

> It is, of course, very possible that the Guild Socialism which is emerging in Germany and Austria will show itself hostile not only to the old political Socialism and the orthodox Trade Unionism, but also to Communism, and even that it may become the rallying-point of the much-despised "Centrist" elements. It will not be a comfortable position, or an easy one to sustain; but for all that it may be the right one.[83]

In England, however, circumstances were not propitious for the search for "the third force" which so dominated the German political conscience. The National Guilds League was handicapped by its preponderantly London membership and was racked with dissension. The working Building Guild failed because problems of liquidity and dragged down the Furnishing Guild with it. The evident success of Bolshevism provided the chief cause of theoretical differences, but a further source of trouble came from a new protégé of Orage.

Major C. H. Douglas had begun to elaborate in the *New Age* a fresh economic theory which Orage called "Social Credit." This was to provide the idealistic Underground with yet another cause. In May 1920, the league appointed a committee to inquire into the Douglas proposals; but in December of the same year the annual conference rejected the committee's favorable conclusions.[84] Two years later, A. J. Penty was still complaining that, although Douglas had no mass support, his doctrines lingered on "as a religion" and promoted "intellectual confusion." Meanwhile, the Executive of the National Guilds League refused to support the Bolshevik Revolution, and the League published a pamphlet over their leaders' heads, thus securing the resignation of Tawney, Penty, Reckitt, and others. G. D. H. Cole summed up the situation: "Our left wing is pushing us into Russianised communism: our right wing, in a panic lest something may really be going to happen, is trekking at its best speed for the land of spiritual values, in which gross material things can be forgotten."[85] By 1923, guilds had ceased to exist as a political force.

It is all too tempting to classify guild socialism as a "right wing" movement, and analogies with the Fascist corporate state are correct so far as they go. Cole wrote later that it was "predominantly a left-wing movement" but "never revolutionary in the sense of seeking the violent overthrow of the existing social order." The main body of opinion was "of left-wing, non-Communist Socialists, who were strongly critical of reformist parliamentarianism, and put their main hopes on Trade Union industrial action."[86] What Cole called "the right-wing" became Douglasites; the "left" joined the Communist party. In the view of an independent historian, "a quite disproportionate number of the intellectuals who joined the Communist Party at its foundation came from the ranks of the Guild Socialist movement." These included Palme Dutt, Page Arnott, William Mellor, the Ewers, Ellen Wilkinson, and Willy Gallacher.[87] It would never be possible to describe Orage or de Maeztu or Penty as "left wing" but it is equally doubtful that the right-wing label is correct. It is apparent that guild socialism could unite those of the most diverse convictions. The movement was idealistic, concerned with the functional or organic view of life, and could be justly called "reactionary"—in the sense that it derived its inspiration from an idealized historical example, rather than an equally idealized vision of a future society.

A common characteristic of the illuminated viewpoint—the wish to annihilate the self—found in the guild idea a particular expression. In the ranks of the guildsmen were to be found not only Theosophists but also the advocates of the return to the land. The Rural Reconstruction Association sprang from a collaboration between Penty and Montague Fordham, who wrote several books and pamphlets on agriculture and the guilds.[88] These two last-named figures were no doubt among those of whom Cole was thinking when he talked of the trek toward spiritual values. For guild socialism had in its fundamental analogy with the medieval craft guilds an implicit connection with Christianity which several of its adherents tended to make embarrassingly explicit.

The Christian Socialist revival in late 19th-century England drew strength from French rather than English socialism: that of Lamennais, Buchez, and Louis Blanc. To the inspiration of Henry George was added the specifically Christian impulse of Bishop Charles Gore, whose Community of the Resurrection at Mirfield in Yorkshire was the matrix of the Church Socialist League. In 1906, a conference was held at Mirfield which included representatitves of the Northern branches of the Social Democratic Federation and the Independent Labour Party, with the Superior of Mirfield—W. H. Frere, later bishop of Truro—in the chair. As a result the Church Socialist League was founded at Morecambe the next month by about sixty Anglican clergymen. Of guild socialists specifically connected with Mirfield the most important were Father J. N. Figgis and Father Paul Bull. Bull (1864-1942) was a disciple of Gore, had won a medal in the Boer War, and foresaw the establishment of the Kingdom of God in the British Empire.[89] Another clerical guild socialist was Conrad Noel, who resigned from the Church Socialist League in the year 1916 to found his own Catholic Crusade and edited a magazine,

The Crusader, with A. J. Penty. Noel was born in 1869, the son of the poet Roden Noel, and had been converted to Socialism at Cambridge. He joined the Social Democratic Federation and the Guild of St. Matthew but remained dissatisfied with existing Christian Socialist organizations. His Catholic Crusade was based on the tenets that "the source of authority is God expressing himself more remotely through the race and more immediately through Catholic Democracy"; and that "the present industrial system being based on the mortal sin of avarice ... any attempt to make it more tolerable ... will be exposed by the Crusade as essentially vicious."[90]

Conrad Noel added a by-now-familiar element to his socialism —morris dancing. As early as 1911 the first troupe of trained morris dancers resulting from the researches of Cecil Sharp came down to Noel's parish at Thaxted, and at the yearly festivals of the Catholic Crusade folk song and dance became part of the celebrations. Noel became notorious—and received enthusiastic support from the guildsmen—when complaints were made of his hanging the Irish tricolor and the red flag in Thaxted church. The real cause of the agitation seems to have been that he was known to have sympathized with the miners' strike of that year.[91]

The church as a whole was concerned with the state of society. A report, *Christianity and Industrial Problems,* first issued in 1918 by a committee including two members of Parliament, several bishops, and the master of Balliol, was most outspoken.

> We believe that in a "day of fire" like the present, much that has been wrong and worldly in the past will be burnt away, and that in a coming time of more equal rights and better distributed power and possessions the Christian Gospel and the Christian Church may be found to be among the strongest forces making for a sound and wholesome progress.
>
> There is no moral justification for profits which exceed the amount needed to pay for adequate salaries to the management, a fair rate of interest on the capital invested, and such reserves as are needed to ensure and maintain the highest efficiency of production and the development and growth of the industry.

The report declared industry a public function and condemned the taking of income for which no service was provided. The committee declared that "the common description of workers as 'hands' summarises aptly an aspect of their economic position which is not the less degrading because it has hitherto met with too general acquiescence."[92]

It would scarcely be possible to be more explicit. But even earlier had been heard a resounding blast of the Christian trumpet against the evils of society. This proceeded from that strange literary animal that some called "the Chesterbelloc" and initially from Hilaire Belloc's book *The Servile State* (1912), of which the guildsman Maurice Reckitt wrote that he "could not overestimate the impact" on his mind and on the minds of "thousands of others." Belloc argued that there was a clear distinction between servile and nonservile conditions of labor. The original state of society had been servile, but the Middle Ages had rectified this by instinctively creating that excellent consummation of society: the "distributive state." The distributive state was the condition in which the individual owned property—which, for Belloc, meant land—but this happy situation had been destroyed by capitalism. The alternative ways of reforming capitalist society were the return to the distributive organization of small, land-based property owners—*or* the collectivist solution of state ownership, which led directly to that "servile state" from which Christianity had rescued Europe in the Middle Ages. The application of the medieval Christian ethic naturally implied the abolition of the vice of usury. As Belloc phrased it in his economic ABC, "things will not get right again in this respect until society becomes as simple as it used to be, and we shall have to go through a pretty bad time before we get back to that."[93]

Under Belloc's inspiration, there developed the doctrine of distributism, and in 1926 the Distributist League was founded as an outgrowth of G. K. Chesterton's *G. K.'s Weekly*. With Maurice Reckitt as treasurer, it was directed toward the restoration of property and against the "juggling of finance." It claimed to derive a Christian sanction from Leo XIII's encyclical *Rerum Novarum*. The emphasis of Chesterton's propaganda was directed at "the ordinary man," whom he saw as having his sacrosanct rights gradually eroded by "the new philosophy" which "utterly distrusts a man." The distributists were from the first intimately connected with the guildsmen. Belloc had laid stress on the role of guilds in *The Servile State*, and both he and Chesterton were among the earliest and most regular contributors to Orage's *New Age*. Chesterton had met Conrad Noel of Thaxted around the turn of the century at a small heterodox religious group called the Christo-Theosophical Society in which both of them read papers, and it seems that Noel was instrumental in turning Chesterton—who thought of him at the time as "an aesthetic ratcatcher"—toward the Christian faith. The National Guilds League declared of Belloc and Chesterton that "we count them with us, because on most of the fundamental issues they are not against us," and the proponents of a return to organic country life on Christian principles, such as H. J. Massingham and Montague Fordham, owed the distributists a great debt.[94]

One of the speakers for the Distributist League was Eric Gill, who moved from Fabianism to the Catholic Church. With a group of friends, he retired to the country to lead a communal life under the rule of Dominican tertiaries. They eventually formed themselves into a guild—in this Christian revival there was always a guild around the chapel corner—dedicated to St. Dominic and St. Joseph. Gill derived inspiration from the French Thomist philosopher Jacques Maritain, but also from traditional Hindu philosophy as represented by Ananda Coomaraswamy; and it is extremely suggestive that the Indian philosopher's ideas of a return to tradition could find a place in the revival of Christian social thought and the arts and crafts. Coomaraswamy recommended the social gospel expressed by the Theosophist Bhagavan Das in a treatise on the Laws of Manu. In this context it is worth remembering that the president of the Theosophical Society, Annie Besant, had been a member of an earlier Christian Socialist organization, the Guild of St. Matthew.[95]

This complicated association is important. For the presence of Theosophy within the ranks of the illuminated socialists had already been noticed, and it is necessary to understand that Gill derived support from traditions other than those of the Catholic Church to which he had pledged allegiance.

The originator of guild socialism, A. J. Penty, moved even nearer the less specific plans of Chesterton and the Distributists. He advocated a return to the medieval concept of the just price and the abolition of usury: Christian society was for him the ideal. But in the influx of Eastern occult and mystical ideas he found an encouraging rejection of materialism. He compared Theosophists, Spiritualists, and Christian Scientists to the Gnostics, Neo-Platonists, and Manichees who flourished just before the triumph of Christianity as a religious and social system.

> Does it not look as if the same thing is about to happen, and that the spiritual movement on the one hand and the social movement on the other are preparing the way for the acceptance of Christianity, which, being both spiritual and material can alone give coherence and definiteness to the vague spiritual and social impulses of our time?[96]

The Christian Socialists and the non-Christian guildsmen were united in demanding a new ethic, a new alignment of man with regard to the material resources at his disposal. If European society was out of control, the safest examples were to be found in the past—even possibly in the East. The appeal for some set of absolute and communally accepted values was heard loudly in England in the period between the Wars, and it is important to know that there was organized political groupings which sought in good faith to realize such demands. Even in the limited field of literary criticism it is necessary to know of Penty, of the guilds, and of the general movement for a "spiritual" or an "organic" socialism to understand Ezra Pound's harping on the question of abolishing interest as more than a private eccentricity best explained by an odd taste for Italian Fascism. Similarly, figures like Richard St. Barbe Baker explain the context of T. S. Eliot's *Idea of a Christian Society,* which in its demand for a "life in conformity with Nature" gives, as an example of mankind's abuse of his environment unnecessary soil erosion.[97] But many of these ideas remained in the realms of theory; and during the 1930s such hopes as the idealistic opposition still entertained of making a dent in the armor of the Establishment concentrated on the Social Credit doctrine of Major Douglas and the uniformed movement of John Hargrave.

The youth movements, which had started off after the war with ideas of reconnecting urban man with his roots, of educating deprived children in country surroundings, and of gradually evolving an improved bloodline, had always kept open a wide field of vision on general social problems. Immediately after the war, their novel ideas of education and their eugenic principles had seemed to offer some chances of utopian achievement. But as present reality weighed more and more heavily upon them the youth leaders naturally began to turn their attention to problems other than those of youth.

If Utopia were to be attained, some powerful evils of the day must be eradicated. The shadow known today as "social relevance" cast its form across the fields and woods in which the movements lingered. Leslie Paul had felt its presence before his secession from the Kibbo Kift in 1924, and the Woodcraft Folk which he led were first and foremost the youth movement of the Co-operative Societies. Aubrey Westlake of the Order of Woodcraft Chivalry and Rolf Gardiner of the Springhead Ring were influenced in similar ways. Within the Order of Woodcraft Chivalry was founded in 1926 the Wayfarers' Circle, which approached bodies like the Quakers and the Institute of Industrial Psychology to try to work out some common policy on industrial problems. They produced a memorandum on the coal crisis and held a conference on the subject, but only Kibbo Kift promised support. Next there was formed the "Mid-Folk" or "Central Party" to formulate a political program. From this sprang the New Commerce Guild, a small group of members who attempted to put into practice an experimental banking arrangement based on credit tokens issued in exchange for services—loans, accommodation, advice—obtainable from other members.[98] They seem also to have dallied with the idea of guilds.

Most practical of the experiments were the Grith Fyrd Camps which took place from 1932-34 at Cleveland in the North of England and at the Order of Woodcraft Chivalry's center at Godshill. Of these enterprises, Westlake was the chairman and Rolf Gardiner the first director. They were carried out from a base at Toynbee Hall in the East End of London, which had been founded in 1885 as the outcome of the university extension movement and the Christian Socialist revival. In 1928 the Order of Woodcraft Chivalry had produced a report called "Peace and War" in accordance with the principles of the Biogenetic Law. This report declared that the militaristic urge was quite natural and proper to a certain stage of development and its repression did actual harm. The problem was to pass beyond this stage of evolution to a higher and more altruistic level at which the destructive urge could be sublimated for the purposes of civilization. Thus was developed the idea of the Grith Fyrd—signifying in Anglo-Saxon, "Peace Army." This body of the ethically evolved was to pass through three stages of training: work "for the sheer joy of creative activity"; "a sociological education through traveling and trekking," and civic service. Originally the scheme had nothing to do with the unemployed. But the slump in 1931 turned the thoughts of the educationalists toward improving the lot of those without work. The camps lasted for periods of six months, involved their inmates in turning barren ground into fertile allotments—and of course, as with anything where Rolf Gardiner was concerned—in communal morris dancing. Westlake hoped for a spiritual transformation through the Grith Fyrd method, which he described as being "to withdraw the young man for a period from the soul-destroying monster of industrialism and heart-breaking futility of our machine-created unemployment and to put him into a natural and simple environment where he can contact the four primary elements: earth, air, fire, and water."[99]

When John Hargrave turned the attention of Kibbo Kift from gazing on far horizons to looking more closely about them, it became a more ambitious affair. In the early days of the Kibbo Kift the chief difficulty was in finding finance to move the scattered "tribes" around the country for camps. Personal economic troubles turned Hargrave's thoughts to a more general consideration of economics, and he read several times C. H. Douglas's book, *Economic Democracy*.[100] It took some three years for Hargrave to be converted and more time for him to transform his movement into a vehicle for Social Credit. A paragraph on the doctrine is therefore scarcely generous.

C. H. Douglas (1879-1952) was a major in the Royal Flying Corps and an engineering career had taken him to India and America. His first appearance in England as an economic theorist was in 1917 in Holbrook Jackson's *The Organiser.* Jackson sent him to Orage and the *New Age* where in a series of conferences between Orage, Douglas, and A. J. Penty, the first formulation of Social Credit was reached.[101] At first the Douglas theory embodied a great deal of guild theory as well, and it was to the National Guilds League that

Douglas and Orage first submitted the scheme—to be turned down, as we have seen, in December 1920. Douglas based his proposals on the conviction that the power of society to purchase goods must equal the cost of producing such goods. This is a way of saying that because society produces it is therefore entitled to consume the products of its labors. Douglas argued that the reason why men are prevented from enjoying the full measure of the goods to which their labor gives them title is the intricacy of cost accounting, which creates costs faster than it distributes purchasing power. If technological progress increases our ability to deliver goods where and when they are needed, the state must proportionately increase the ability to pay for such goods. This it should do simply by issuing money in the form of a "national dividend" and by applying the just, or scientific price at the retail end, so that all can benefit. One of the main targets at which early Social Credit propaganda was directed was the gold standard, which had been abolished in 1914 and might at any time be reintroduced. The artificiality of measuring value against the amount of gold held in the Bank of England was ceaselessly attacked—and indeed the whole unquestioned concept of *money*. What was it? Who controlled it and in whose interest? The supporters of Douglas were apt to talk of "the international money-power," a sinister organization that was at first undefined, although there is small doubt that Douglas himself was in contact with sources which had been locating the secret agents of this money-power rather definitely for many centuries. At first, however, he contrived to give an appearance of impartiality.

> No cool observer of world movements at this time can doubt that, whether as some would have us believe, there is an active, conscious conspiracy to enslave the world, or whether, as is arguable, only blind forces are at work to the same end, is a question immaterial to the patent fact that the danger of such a tyranny is real and instant.[102]

Douglas was obviously akin to the Christian and guild reformers with their insistence on the "just price" and the abolition of usury—but he was also in the line of a number of monetary reformers who had questioned the very idea of the fiction "money." The first was John A. Hobson (1858-1940), the creator of the "underconsumption" theory of unemployment, who was publishing in the last decade of the 19th century, and to whom J. M. Keynes was later to acknowledge his debt. Hobson's Ruskin-inspired approach also recommended him to the Christian Socialists.[103] The second was Arthur Kitson (died 1937), a prolific inventor whose lamps for lighthouses were his particular pride. Kitson published in the United States in 1894 his first analysis of money, and on his return to England a revised edition of his book *The Money Problem* was issued while he busied himself with founding the Currency Reform League and lecturing to the Independent Labour Party. Kitson decided that "the end sought in exchange is . . . the acquisition of commodities, not money" and denounced usury as "impossible." He was naturally much cultivated in guild and Christian Socialist circles, and in 1921 he announced his complete adherence to the Douglas proposals.[104] The third reformer was Frederick Soddy (1877-1956), a disciple of Kitson in economics, but in his own right a considerable physicist who worked with Rutherford on atomic energy and Sir William Ramsey on radium. He contributed to *The Guildsman* in 1920 and his proposals are in some ways similar to those of Douglas.[105] He too was convinced of a conspiracy to prevent investigation of the money system.

These theorists were unfortunate in that they were never taken up by movements which could provide the drive necessary to publicize their abstruse writings. Douglas had the ear of Orage of the *New Age* when he began his theorizing, and by the time of Orage's departure for France to study at Gurdjieff's Institute at Fontainebleau he was within an ace of obtaining that of John Hargrave. Nineteen twenty-four, the year of Leslie Paul's defection with what Hargrave described as "the socialist elements" of Kibbo Kift, was also the year of Hargrave's conversion to Douglasite economics. By the end of 1925 he was discussing the *political* role of his movement. Over the next three years he succeeded remarkably in imposing his vision of the new function of the Kibbo Kift as the standard bearers of Social Credit. Many of the old youth movement figures resigned. New Social Creditors came in. Hargrave, who had always insisted on "discipline," began to appear to some of the disgruntled old guard in an unpleasant light. Disillusioned with parliamentarianism and the money power, wrote one of those who resigned, Hargrave "could see only one solution to the difficulty, to emulate the exploits of Lenin and Mussolini, and to build up his Kindred until it was able to control events and assume the government of the country."[106] By the autumn of 1928, Hargrave was writing of the possibilities of a mass uprising in the *New Age*.

> We think that a time may come when this organised Mass Pressure, to the tune of at least a quarter of a million men *and women,* will be able to move in body-bulk either on foot or by motor transport towards the seat of financial and political control.... And this body of people would have to have supplies enough to last out at least six weeks.
>
> The leaders would not go to negotiate with anyone. They would not recognise the power of either a Prime Minister or a banker or anyone else to negotiate. They would go to open an office—The National Credit Account Office—in the name of the British People and to have the Social Credit Decree proclaimed, printed and posted throughout the land.[107]

The previous year had seen *The Confession of the Kibbo Kift* embody a commitment to guilds, the just price and the national dividend, and a justification of revolutionary force in the right conditions as "a matter of biologic necessity."[108] If such expectations seem impossibly grandiose, we must note that the initiative for a link between Hargrave and the unemployed came from the unemployed themselves. In December 1931 George Hickling of Coventry wrote to Hargrave for advice on founding a "Legion of the Unemployed." Hargrave replied advising that a uniform be adopted. Because of the high cost of the Robin Hood uniforms of the Kibbo Kift, the Coventry group decided on a uniform of green shirts and berets which by the end of 1932 had been adopted by the Kibbo Kift proper. The movement changed its name to "The Green Shirt Movement for Social Credit." Hargrave found a ready hearing on Tyneside, and the Green Shirts joined the Hunger Marchers as well as putting 100 uniformed members in the Trades Union Congress May Day Demonstrations of 1932.[109] Hargrave developed what he called "unarmed military technique" which involved marches and the deployment of squads of drummers—both to attract attention and to drown any opposition—whom he had trained by instructors from the Brigade of Guards. In 1935, he published a novel, *Summertime Ends*—which has been highly praised by Ezra Pound, Louis MacNeice, and

John Steinbeck—dramatizing the state of the country as he saw it and particularly of the unemployed. The Green Shirts put up parliamentary candidates in the elections of 1935 and achieved a particular success in the face of the Communists in London, until the Public Order Act of 1937 by banning uniformed political movements silenced their most effective propaganda device. On May Day 1938, the Social Creditors took part in a demonstration with their shirts hanging on coat hangers suspended from poles. They burned Montague Norman in effigy and shot arrows at the windows of 10 Downing Street. But their days of popularity were over.[110] At his most successful, Hargrave could never claim to put more than 2,000 uniformed supporters on parade, although there were some five times that number who had signed pledges of sympathy.[111]

In July 1938, John Hargrave finally dissociated himself from Major Douglas. Douglas had turned steadily away from the Green Shirts and their uniformed methods since 1933, and his own Social Credit Secretariat concentrated on trying to secure the signatures of parliamentary candidates on a pledge to introduce the national dividend.[112] The final breach seems to have come after Hargrave's visit to Alberta in Canada, in 1936-7. In the provincial elections of 1935, the Social Credit Party of Alberta, led by the radio evangelist William Aberhart, obtained a large majority which they held until 1971. The English Social Creditors became concerned that Aberhart had, in fact, little intention of introducing Social Credit. Douglas indicated that the time was not right for full implementation of his principles. But the impatient Green Shirts disagreed, and Hargrave traveled to Canada in an attempt to urge Aberhart to carry out the policy on which he had been elected. In this he was to some extent successful. He managed to precipitate a rebellion in the ranks of the Alberta Social Credit Party that forced Aberhart to approach Major Douglas officially.[113] But the difference in policy between Douglas and Hargrave had become plain to see, and in 1938 Douglas resigned from his Secretariat to set up another organization.

Hargrave's movement endured until 1951—mostly, as its leader told me, so that he could close it down in good order. During the war years his illuminated inclinations discovered another outlet in the "Spiritual Science" of Charles Boltwood. Boltwood had been born in 1889, and in the late 1930s he and his wife were "converted" by reading Mary Baker Eddy's *Science and Life*. They established a spiritualist group specializing in spiritual healing and radiesthesia. Then Boltwood's chief spirit guide, Charles Kingsley, directed him to set about preparing for the Second Coming of Christ, which would only be achieved when there had been established "the nucleus of Resurrection power." This conception signified the transmutation of human elements into immortal elements and was to begin with Boltwood's wife.[114] Boltwood's views on medicine were peculiar. He was not convinced that sex was essential for human reproduction, and he advised the eating of air as a cure for tuberculosis. Hargrave seems to have been most interested in Boltwood's techniques of healing by means of human radiation, and he claimed, for example, to have healed the scalded hand of the wife of a member of the Social Credit Party. Boltwood himself joined the movement for Social Credit, as did Rupert Naylor, a prominent astrologer. Hargrave's enthusiasm for Boltwood was not the uncritical admiration which his critics pretend, and in his praise of Boltwood's "spiritual science" there was undoubtedly a political element. At the same time Hargrave's messages to his following took on an increasingly apocalyptic tone, in which his old fascination with symbols and mythology was coupled to a new emphasis on the power of the sun. The supporters of Social Credit became "Solar Men." They were to pronounce a prayer to the sun for the success of their efforts. Hargrave denounced those who could not see that "the Social Credit mechanism is founded on a SPIRITUAL BASIS."[115] The Green Shirt leader has since devoted much research to the writing of a book on Paracelsus.[116]

It is all too easy to raise an eyebrow at the return of Hargrave's movement into the assembly of the illuminated Underground and to fail to see its significance. Supporters of Social Credit not only included the circle of illuminates round Orage but also T. S. Eliot's mentor, Father Demant; H. J. Massingham; and Aubrey Westlake (who became in 1943 the leader of the Health Section of the Social Credit Party).[117] The people who supported all the movements described in this chapter—the youth movements, the Merry Englanders, the Back to the Landsmen, the Christian Socialists, the guildsmen, the Currency Reformers, and ultimately the Social Creditors—devoted their energies to whichever of the movements seemed at the time to have the best chance of initiating an idealistic revolution. It is easy to sense that apart from their frequently interchangeable personnel, such movements had something in common, which I have called the "illuminated viewpoint." This can often be indicated by the presence of an interest in the religious, the mystical, and the occult. In England between the wars it manifested itself in a conjunction with antimaterialist, anti-individualist politics. The logic of the situation may be reinforced by a final example. It is entirely consistent that in the single case in which a movement described in this chapter achieved and retained political power—the Social Credit government which ruled Alberta from 1935 until 1971—the leader of the movement should have been a fundamentalist preacher and the province which he governed extraordinarily subject to the influence of religious sects. The conditions of economic chaos and the consequent anxiety experienced in Alberta before the emergence of William Aberhart and his Calgary Prophetic Bible Institute has resulted in a marked increase in the appeal of cults such as the Jehovah's Witnesses. Aberhart had been able to harness radio to his own revival; favorable reception conditions gave him an audience estimated in 1935 at 350,000. His denunciations of moneylenders and unspecified East Coast financial interests united with his Christian basis to make Social Credit a natural corollary to hellfire.[118] It would be difficult to think of a simpler example of the coupling of an illuminated political doctrine to a basic transcendental message.

Two very important characteristics of the illuminated approach remain to be discussed. These are the relationship between the illuminates and Fascism and the strong connection between certain sorts of illuminated politics and a paranoid hatred of Jews.

The "illuminated" movements have obvious resemblances to more familiar movements labeled "Fascist" that grew up at the same time. The emphasis on blood and soil, the improvement of the race, and the revival of national tradition can be found in Nazism. The Christian reaction is in harmony with Mussolini's Italy and Franco's Spain. The demand for guilds and the assaults on international finance occur in German and Italian Fascism alike. The occult and the mystical indicators of the illuminated viewpoint are also present in Nazism. Does it follow that illuminated politics *is* Fascism, that I have invented in the phrase another unnecessary term to confuse the issue?

The poet Hugh McDiarmid (C. M. Grieve) is an unrepentant supporter of Social Credit and once attempted to persuade the Scottish Nationalist Party to accept the Douglas scheme. He now laments:

> A friend said to me in London when I was associated with Douglas, Orage, Mairet, Symons, Reckitt, Canon Demant, John Hargrave of the Green Shirt movement, Arthur Brenton, and other Douglasites: "What are you doing among these people? Don't you realise they will all go religious-Fascist?" I did not realise anything of the kind, but they did all go religious-Fascist, and I still do not see why that should be so. It certainly has not happened in my own case.[119]

Placing the accent on the *religious*-Fascist may help to solve the problem. From the later political stance of MacDiarmid on the ideological left very many persons might well be called "Fascist" who were never such in any strict sense of the term. It is true that several of the illuminated politicians did become out-and-out Fascist sympathizers. Rolf Gardiner has already been noted as conditionally approving the Nazi seizure of power; but with his specifically German connections he was something of a special case. Odon Por (who translated S. G. Hobson's *National Guilds*) gravitated naturally into the hierarchy of the Italian corporate state.[120] Ramiro de Maeztu returned to Spain and his support for a Catholic monarchy was soon transferred to the Falange.[121] But the only prominent member of the English illuminated group who joined a Fascist party seems to have been the originator of the guild theory, A. J. Penty. As early as 1933 he recommended an exposition of Fascism as developing principles "which coincide largely with my own." In 1937, the year of his death, he gave almost unqualified praise to Mussolini and the Italian corporate state although he quarreled with the totalitarian aspect it had assumed. He welcomed the Fascist denial that social reconstruction must come from the working class. According to S. G. Hobson, Penty joined the Fascists in 1936.[122]

It might also be argued that because former Fascists became associated with illuminated groups after the failure and suppression of Oswald Moseley's movement, this betrays the essentially

"Fascist" character of illuminated sentiments. Hargrave was said to have received the war-time allegiance of Sir A. V. Roe, Major General Fuller, and the novelist Henry Williamson, all former followers of Moseley. Of these only A. V. Roe in fact became a member of the Social Credit Party (a perfectly logical step because of his earlier well-established Social Credit views). The Fascists themselves had tried to adopt Social Credit as a part of their own program, and Hargrave felt it necessary to issue a pamphlet dissociating himself from Moseley.[123] Fuller (who, according to Hargrave, never officially joined his movement) had for some time been a follower of Aleister Crowley and had written a panegyric on that magician entitled *The Star in the West*. An undoubted Fascist, Fuller was also an undoubted illuminate, and he gravitated to illuminated circles. Henry Williamson—who, again, never joined the Social Creditors officially—belonged rather more to the blood-and-soil movement than to the black-shirted marchers.[124] Jorian Jenks, the Fascist agricultural expert, came during the war into contact with Montague Fordham and the Rural Reconstruction Association. He became part-time secretary of the Soil Association in 1945 and published a book with a preface by H. J. Massingham.[125] But even he can be discovered in an earlier association with illuminates. During the 1930s he issued a work called *Farming and Money* with J. Taylor Peddie. Peddie was an interesting eccentric who attempted, with a weight of Biblical learning, to deduce a righteous economics from Scripture. "The Old Testament is the oldest economic work extant. God's economic policy concerned itself mainly with the elimination of poverty and destitution."[126]

The soundest conclusion seems to be that Fascist movements could and did contain illuminates, but that the illuminates were by no means necessarily Fascist. For example, the Green Shirts were subject to perpetual harassment by the Blackshirts. In 1927 Hargrave declared that the "difference between a Green Shirt and a black one" was that the Green Shirts were concerned with the transformation of the individual, while the Fascists wanted to set up the supreme state. The Liverpool headquarters of the Social Creditors was broken up by Blackshirts who received prison sentences as a result.[127] Nor is it really possible to call the Green Shirts "Fascist" on account of their methods. Among the other uniformed movements that fell under the strictures of the Public Order Act were the young Communists, who marched in khaki, the red-shirted Independent Labour Party, and a Jewish anti-Fascist organization called the Blue and White League who wore white shirts. Something might be made of the tendency in British Fascist circles to see themselves as the adult continuation of the Scout movement—on the lines of the German youth movements—and the image of the "samurai" which animated the Kibbo Kift was appropriated by a writer in *Blackshirt*.[128] However, the Fascist corporate state that the British Union took over from the Italian model owed little to guild theory, and the author of the unofficial Fascist program saw his predecessors in the 19th-century French syndicalists rather than in the guildsmen.[129] The truth is probably that Moseley took over an Italian Fascism, added a few German elements, and then tried to appropriate native developments like the Scouts or Social Credit to reinforce his imported policy.

Some illuminates saw in Fascist aims the possibility of achieving their hoped-for idealistic revolution. But—with the sole obvious exception of the aging A. J. Penty—it is difficult to find examples of that interchange of personnel which is so marked a feature of the illuminated groups. If for Hugh McDiarmid's epithet "religious-Fascist" we read "illuminated" and remember that McDiarmid has since been a member of the Communist party, his condemnation becomes more explicable. It is also true that so-called German Fascism—Hitler's National Socialism—did incorporate the illuminated points of view which in Britain largely escaped co-option.

There remains the question of what interpretation to place on the tendency of some illuminates to become anti-Semitic. A full discussion of the problem of illuminated anti-Semitism must be postponed until we investigate the role of the occult in the propagation of the *Protocols of the Elders of Zion*. But some characteristics can be demonstrated from the English illuminates. Of those we have discussed, Rolf Gardiner adopted an almost Nazi anti-Semitism in his accolade to the National Socialists after the *Machtergreifung*. The Jews in Germany were being repressed, he admitted, but those Jews were different from "our Jews." "They come with the smell of Asia fresh in their beards." Yet he would probably not have countenanced persecution of English Jewry, and it is interesting that the chief reason for his dislike of Jews was entirely *religious*. "How sick Europe is of the Jewish monotheistic string."[130] It may help to make clearer the type of anti-Semitism with which illuminates are concerned if it is borne in mind that these were men searching for "other realities" and "new values." If their visions tended toward the ideal, they would also have their devils.

England was probably no less guilty of the general anti-Semitic simplification than many other countries.[131] But until the activities of Oswald Moseley and the British Union there were under half-a-dozen organized groups of anti-Semites, of which two alone are important. The first is that gathered round the newspaper, *The Patriot*, founded by the Duke of Northumberland. It began publication in February 1922 with a circulation secured in advance "for the purpose of supplying briefly striking facts and arguments relating to movements threatening the safety and welfare of the British Empire." His Grace of Northumberland contributed an article to the first issue stating that "the Bolshevist revolution was the work mainly of Russian and German Jews,"[132] and throughout its existence *The Patriot* betrayed its allegiance to the conspiracy theories propagated during the 1920s by emigrants from Soviet Russia. The British Fascists were founded through advertisements taken in this paper in 1923 by Miss Rotha Linton-Orman, an eccentric who was said to wear a sword to the meetings of her movement.[133] In 1924, there appeared *Secret Societies and Subversive Movements*, the text for all British adherents of the idea that there was a conspiracy to take over the world. The author of the book was Nesta Webster, who was convinced that there were five powers supporting a world conspiracy: "Grand Orient Masonry, Theosophy, Pan-Germanism, International Finance and Social Revolution."[134] Her conflation of French and Russian anti-Jewish propaganda was avidly seized on by *The Patriot*, and Nesta Webster—whose belief in her conspiracy latterly became so strong that she would only open her front door with a loaded revolver in hand—became a lecturer much in demand at British Fascist meetings.[135] The illuminated nature of Mrs. Webster's anti-Semitism is conspicuous. "How," she asked, "is it possible to ignore the existence of an Occult Power at work in the world? Individuals, sects or races fired with the desire for world-domination have provided the fighting-forces of destruction, but behind them are veritable powers of darkness in eternal conflict with the powers of light."[136]

The other leading group of racists was an organization called

"The Britons." It was much smaller and more obscure but very diligent in inspiring anti-Semitism. The Britons were a hard-core organization and the publishers of English translations of the German *Altmeister* of anti-Semitism, Theodor Fritsch. The founder was Henry Hamilton Beamish, who—together with another of the early members, Lieutenant Colonel A. H. Lane—acquired his anti-Semitic views in South Africa during the Boer War. This South African anti-Semitism has been much neglected. It was an important source of the prejudice in England and provided material for French propagandists as well. The origins lie in the conviction formed by Sir William Butler—who arrived in South Africa in 1898 as acting high commissioner—that pressure for war with the Boers was being exercised by an international syndicate of Jews in league with the big gold-mining companies of Johannesburg. Butler's reports to the War Office were excised from the Blue Book by Joseph Chamberlain, but they provided the basis of much anti-Semitic mythology in military society.[137] Other members of "The Britons" form a good conspectus of the anti-Semitic portion of the Underground. They included a leading homeopathic physician and the man responsible for reviving archery in England, as well as Victor Marsden, who translated the *Protocols of the Elders of Zion* into English. The group was founded by Beamish in 1918 and continued to exist and publish its propaganda until recently.

Henry Hamilton Beamish himself was the brother of a member of Parliament for Lewes and lived out his days as a member of the legislature of Rhodesia. He spent most of the period between the wars traveling the world in the service of the German organization *Weltdienst* founded by Ulrich Fleischauer and later controlled by Alfred Rosenberg. In December 1922, he became involved in a libel action against Sir Alfred Mond, the reports of which demonstrate the complete inability of the founder of "The Britons" to maintain a coherent sequence of thought. At one point he succinctly stated his philosophy: it was that "Internationalism and Bolshevism were one, and Bolshevism was Judaism." Beamish and his codefendent were fined £5,000 plus legal costs. His last communication with the courts—before the fine was paid—was to send his prosecutors a statutory declaration alleging that on medical advice he was about to take a sea voyage for the benefit of his health. Almost immediately he resurfaced at the side of Hitler in Munich.[138]

It is against this background that the anti-Semitism of the English illuminates must be categorized. The monetary reformer Arthur Kitson became a member of "The Britons" the year after their foundation. Arnold Spencer Leese, the founder of the Imperial Fascist League (and an expert on the diseases of camels) was introduced to "The Britons" and to the *Protocols* by Kitson in 1923. Kitson, he wrote, "was very nervous of the Jews because of threats and injuries received, and would never speak about them at his meetings, but he knew all about them." Kitson did in fact refer to a conspiracy of German Jews in his writings. He thought that this consortium was chiefly responsible for the industrial depression among the victorious nations after the First World War. That other economic reformer, Major Douglas, became quite extravagant during the period just before the Second World War. He announced his belief in the *Protocols* and endorsed Nesta Webster's occult anti-Semitism. "Any serious endeavor to identify the origins of world unrest and war," Douglas declared, "inevitably and invariably leads back to what is loosely called occultism." He had "little doubt that the Talmud so organized the Jews, that the Masters of the Cabala were able to use them as one unit."[139] He thought that Hitler was the grandson of an illegitimate daughter of Baron Rothschild of Vienna; he maintained that Admiral Canaris was really called Moses Meyerbeer. The conspiracy imagined by Douglas included not only the standard ingredients of Freemasonry and Judaism, but also Bolshevism, American finance, and the Nazi party. The result of Douglas's obsession was that the journals under his control became devoted to anti-Semitism rather than to Social Credit.

Nor were the guildsmen free from anti-Semitic elements. In Spain Ramiro de Maeztu decided that Jews were at the bottom of all the evils of the world: an absurd theory to apply to a country which had expelled its Jewish population in the 15th century. G. Stirling Taylor's *The Guild State* of 1919—which was later translated into German—was scathing at the expense of "Trotsky and his Jewish friends." George Young's reports from Germany at the time of the council governments contain frequent pointed reference to the number of Jewish revolutionaries—or even of Jewish members of the government the revolutionaries had toppled. Thus we hear of "Preuss, the Minister of the Interior, a Jew, a jurist and an adjuster," or of "Landsberg at Justice, a red Jew from the province of

Posen." Young saw fit to tell his readers that Levine was "a black Jew of a common and rather criminal type" while registering respect for "the personal power of the idealist Jew Kurt Eisner."[140] The mysterious, diabolical, and powerful Jew was seen everywhere.

Chesterton and Belloc were also concerned with Jewish responsibility for the wicked modern world which their Distributist state would replace. Belloc's anti-Semitism dated back to his French origins and the lingering prejudices of the Dreyfus case. That of G. K. Chesterton took root in the Marconi scandal of 1912. In that year Rufus Isaacs, Lloyd George, and the chief whip of the Liberal Party were implicated in dealing in shares in the Marconi company in the knowledge that Marconi's tender for the construction of wireless stations had been accepted by the government. For those of an anti-Semitic temperament the crux of the matter was that Rufus Isaacs's brother Geoffrey was a director of Marconi and that both were Jews; the felony was compounded by Herbert Samuel's attempt to cover up the affair in Parliament.

Hilaire Belloc and G. K. Chesterton's brother Cecil mounted an attack on the proceedings in their paper *The New Witness* and were successfully sued for libel. While Cecil Chesterton became a fanatical anti-Semite, the wrath of his brother and Belloc was directed first and foremost at the financial system which they believed was largely controlled by Jews. G. K. Chesterton's attitude was profoundly affected by the Marconi scandal, but his anti-Semitism retained a vacillating character—as if there were somewhere a clear thought struggling to get out. Belloc is a different kettle of fish: it is extremely instructive to compare some of the drawings in his *Cautionary Tales* to those in Streicher's *Stürmer* or Dietrich Eckhart's *Auf gut Deutsch*. He was suspicious of the Russian revolution and the rise of "Jewish news agencies," But like G. K. Chesterton he was too intelligent to see the Bolshevik revolt as the culmination of an immemorially ancient plot by the Semitic peoples. On the publication of Nesta Webster's *The Causes of World Unrest,* he castigated it as a "lunatic book."[141] Yet for all these qualifications, an anti-Semitism remained which although not particularly virulent, would not go away.

Similar reasons drove men in the direction of anti-Semitism as propelled them toward illuminated politics. The chief were a fear of change or an outright reaction toward an idealized past, which saw the Jew as the typical *arriviste;* a nationalist temper arising from such fear, which represented the Jew as the agent of a hideous cosmopolitanism; and a suspicion that all was not well with the economic situation, which ended by personifying financial double dealing as the Jew. These were all perfectly logical appendages of any of the illuminated movements we have surveyed. It is, therefore, somewhat surprising that few of the illuminated politicians did fall into the trap. The youth movements, the vast majority of the Guild Socialists, the Social Creditors of the period before Douglas went wild, or the followers of Hargrave—all seem to have avoided the pitfall. Illuminated politicans are by no means necessarily anti-Semites—although there is an illuminated anti-Semitism which is probably the most dangerous of all.

Of this we have seen traces in the conviction of Nesta Webster and Major Douglas that the Jewish menace included Theosophy and was controlled by a vast occult organization. It has recently been argued (by Professor Norman Cohn) that 19th- and 20th-century anti-Semitism represents the rebirth of the medieval vision of the Jew as a diabolical being.[142] There is evidently much truth in this view. But the retreat to the magical that this implies was everywhere assisted by the rise of the irrationalist movements that composed the Occult Revival. In the search for "other realities" undertaken by the irrationalists, the vision of the Satanic Jew occasionally appeared. Particularly was this so when the irrationalist movements relied to any great extent upon inherited Christian traditions. The exotic Catholicism of late 19th-century France, for example, often went hand in hand with a magico-demonic distrust of the Jews. It is quite logical to find anti-Semitism among illuminated politicians who base their idealistic vision on a predominantly Christian ethic, and in particular among those who denounce "usury" in the manner of medieval churchmen seven hundred years earlier. In this way Kitson, Chesterton, and Belloc, and to some extent Douglas, can be explained, and perhaps, also, the reaction of certain medievally minded guildsmen. It should be a truism that there has always been a strong current of political anti-Semitism flowing from the "Left" as well as from the "Right." Often what both Left and Right have in common is the illuminated factor.

The divide between the illuminated anti-Semite and his less simplistic brother illuminate cannot always be securely marked. When C. H. Douglas, driven to desperation by failure, claimed that Social Credit was Christian and therefore the Truth—as opposed to Judaism, the Incarnate Lie[143]—he was merely debasing what Hargrave and his earlier self had proclaimed: that Social Credit rested on some *spiritual* basis. Whereas the latter statement was abstract and called for a reorganization of man's relations with man, that of the later Douglas identified the powers of good and evil in a specific and very primitive fashion. This fashion was continued by later commentators like the extremist Mgr. Denis Fahey. The Monsignor edited the fifth edition of a notorious anti-Semitic work published by "The Britons" invoking Social Credit and Arthur Kitson to the aid of *The Protocols of the Elders of Zion*.[144] Another instance of the thinness of the division is provided by the English Mistery. This was a body of somewhat dilettante believers in an "organic society" organized by William Sanderson and Anthony Ludovici. Sanderson advocated a return to a feudal order and laid stress on the beneficial activity of Guilds and Freemasons. The Nietzschean Ludovici believed in the aristocratic principle and the importance of selective breeding.[145] They had obvious affinities with some of the illuminates we have examined—even organizing themselves in "Kins"—and Hargrave recommended Sanderson's book, *That Which Was Lost,* in the news sheet of the Kibbo Kift.[146] Their proposals, however, contained much anti-Semitic matter, and a schismatic group called the English Array was even supposed to have conspired to poison a number of eminent Jews.[147]

Generalizations are not very useful in indicating which illuminate might, or might not, be inclined to anti-Semitism. It can only be said that a certain person was, and another was not, a Jew-hater. For many of the illuminates their redefinitions of reality were too personal to include the diabolical Jew of popular superstition. But, on the other hand, once the illuminate had left the everyday universe of rationalist reality there was nothing to prevent him from entering that other world where the Jew sat at the right hand of Satan. Neither necessarily nor predominantly Fascist or anti-Semitic, the illuminated politicians deserve a classification of their own.

This classification comprises bodies of the Progressive Underground in search of an irrationalist interpretation of society, whose members are indicated by their occult and mystical associations. Explicitly religious were the Christian Socialists and some of the rural reformers; implicitly, some guildsmen and economists denouncing usury in terms borrowed from the Christian Middle Ages. The youth movement leaders came, with one exception, from Quaker families, and cultivated in common with the protagonists of blood and soil a symbiotic approach to the landscape and doctrine of spiritual evolution.

These movements were extra-Parliamentary—which meant, in Britain, "Underground." They were numerically small but capable of astonishing eruptions. Particularly just after the First World War their opportunities were great; and a second chance was possible in the early 1930s. In point of numbers, however, the movements were also largely Underground. A third reason for applying the description lies in the illuminated attitude, which expressed itself not only in the clustering of mystical and occult groups around the political leaders, but in the transcendental principles on which their doctrines were based. They were to effect a *spiritual* reformation—sometimes based on Christianity, sometimes not. Such a transcendental impulse is even to be found in the attempts of the monetary reformers to "see through money" and abolish the existence of the cash nexus which they abhorred. The Establishment's reality which the illuminated Underground opposed—the Britain of materialism, industrialism, and Parliamentary inertia—succeeded in keeping the Underground down. For this there is one overpowering reason. The Underground was far too elitist and intellectual. Of all the figures discussed only John Hargrave ever had the common touch, and he too remained elitist over a long period.

The common premise of the Underground groups was that something was drastically wrong with society. They would return to a Garden of Eden. For the youth movements, this involved the recovery of the physical skills and emotional stability of "natural man"; for the guildsman, his integral and directed society of function; for the economic reformers, a more rational relationship between man and the products of his labor; and for the rural revivalists, a direct return to the imperatives of the soil. The fruits of their Garden were as elusive as those of the Hesperides. But neither difficulty nor disappointment has ever halted an idealist; and he does not stop to think whether the source of the greatest good may not also be that of great evil. The idealism is enough; and in all ages those concerned for a more "spiritual" society have congregated and recognized each other.

In the period just after the First World War one group became especially prominent in illuminated circles. This was composed of fugitives from the society concerned above all others with realities not of this world: that of Tsarist Russia.

   1. Edward Carpenter, *Civilisation: Its Cause and Cure* (London, 1921), p. 72.
   2. G. Stanley Hall, *Adolescence* (N.Y., 1904), vol. II, pp. 71-72.
   3. Ernest Westlake and Aubrey Westlake, general introduction to "Woodcraft Way," series no. 1—Ernest Thompson Seton, *Woodcraft* (London, 1918).
   4. Ernest Thompson Seton, *Trail of an Artist-Naturalist* (London, 1951), pp. 291 ff.
   5. Seton, *The Book of Woodcraft and Indian Lore* (London, 1913), pp. 548-49.
   6. For the influence of Seton on Europe, see Heinz Reichling, *"Ernest Thompson Seton und die Woodcraft Bewegung in England"* (*Bonner Studien zu Englische Philologie,* Heft XXX), (Bonn, 1937).
   7. I. O. Evans, *Woodcraft and World Service* (London, 1930), pp. 49-50, 125; and see Aubrey T. Westlake, *Health Abounding* (London, 1944), *Life Threatened* (London, 1967), *Miasma* (Hindhead, Surrey, 1968), and foreword to Mary C. Fullerson's *By a New and Living Way* (London, 1963).
   8. Aubrey T. Westlake, *Woodcraft Chivalry* (2nd ed., London, 1917), pp. 4, 6.
   9. E. Westlake and A. T. Westlake, "Introduction," p. 4.
   10. See Ernest Westlake, *The Place of Dionysos* (Godshill, 1927).
   11. See Ernest Westlake and Aubrey T. Westlake, *Primitive Occupations as a Factor in Education* (London, 1918).
   12. Ernest Westlake, *The Forest School* (Godshill, 1925), p. 9.
   13. Interview with John Hargrave.
   14. Seton, *The Book of Woodcraft,* p. 3.
   15. John Hargrave, *The Great War Brings It Home* (London, 1919), p. 61.
   16. See Richard Hofstadter, *Social Darwinianism in American Thought* (N.Y., 1945), pp. 139 ff. and H. H. Laughlin, *Eugenics Record Office Report,* no. 1 (N.Y., 1913).

17. See Edgar Schuster and Ethel M. Elderton, *The Inheritance of Ability* (1902) and the Eugenics Society pamphlets, *Eugenic Sterilisation* and *Better Unborn.*
18. Huxley still maintains this view; see *Evolution, the Modern Synthesis* (2nd ed., 1963), p. 578.
19. Hargrave, *Great War,* pp. ix, 226, 295.
20. Hargrave, *The Totem Talks* (London, 1919), p. 91.
21. Hargrave, "The Origin and Development of the Kibbo Kift" in *Broadsheet,* no. 13 (August 1926), p. 1.
22. Interview with Hargrave.
23. I. O. Evans, *Woodcraft,* pp. 63-65; cf. Leslie Paul, *Angry Young Man* (London, 1951), pp. 54-55.
24. *Broadsheet,* no. 14 (September 1926). The books of Stephen Graham, such as *The Gentle Art of Tramping* (N.Y., 1926), were influential in youth movement circles. Graham's own romantic wanderings were tinged with mysticism; see his early *Priest of the Ideal* (London, 1918).
25. I. O. Evans, *Woodcraft,* p. 66.
26. Hargrave, "Origin and Development," p. 3.
27. I. O. Evans, *Woodcraft,* p. 68.
28. Paul, *Angry Young Man,* p. 54.
29. I. O. Evans, *Woodcraft,* pp. 69, 71.
30. Leslie Paul, "The Decline of the Youth Movements," in *The Adelphi,* (March 1934), p. 324.
31. Hargrave, *The Totem Talks,* p. 94; I. O. Evans, *Woodcraft,* p. 69; *Broadsheet* announcement, no. 25 (August 1927).
32. Hargrave, *Young Winkle* (London, 1925), p. 171.
33. *Broadsheet,* no. 16 (November 1926); Hargrave, *The Confession of the Kibbo Kift* (London, 1927), p. 44; Hargrave in *Broadsheet,* no. 27 (September 1927).
34. Paul, *Angry Young Man,* p. 59; cf. I. O. Evans, *Woodcraft,* pp. 76 ff.
35. E.g., Nesta Webster, *The Socialist Network* (London, 1926), p. 123.
36. See *Broadsheet,* nos. 4-6 (October-December 1925); Hargrave in *Broadsheet,* no. 28 (November 1927), p. 5.
37. Hargrave, *Confession,* pp. 49-50, 67-68, 110, 283; cf. the SS Ordensburgen, for which see Chapter V.
38. Paul, *The Folk Trail* (London, 1929), pp. 41-42, *The Green Company* (London, 1931).
39. Reichling, *Seton,* p. 34.
40. Paul, *The Annihilation of Man* (London, 1944) and see also his report for the Anglican Church, *The Deployment and Payment of the Clergy* (London, 1964).
41. Reichling, *Seton,* p. 108.
42. See *The Occult Underground,* pp. 319 ff.
43. Rolf Gardiner, "Music, Noise and the Land," in *Wessex, Letters from Springhead* (Christmas, 1950), p. 52; Gardiner, *The English Folk-Dance Tradition* (Hellerau-Dresden, 1923), p. 30.

44. See Gardiner's "Thirty Years After" in *Wessex* (Whitsun, 1955), p. 151; "On the Functions of a Rural University" in *North Sea and Baltic* (3 September 1933), pp. 6-9, and note in same, Spring 1935 by Gerald Gough on a visit to Frankfurt; see Katherine Trevelyan, *Fool in Love* (London, 1962), and the obituary of Goetsch in *Wessex* (Whitsun, 1955).
45. Gardiner, "Thirty Years After," p. 151.
46. *In Northern Europe,* 1930.
47. Gardiner, "On the Functions of a Rural University," pp. 6-15.
48. Ludwig Lienhard in *Wessex* (Christmas, 1953), p. 111.
49. *North Sea and Baltic* (Spring, 1935), p. 4.
50. Rolf Gardiner and Heinz Rocholl (eds.), *Britain and Germany* (London, 1928).
51. Gardiner, "Englische Tradition und die Zukunft" in Wilhelm Freiherr von Richthofen (ed.), *Brito-Germania, ein Weg zu Pan-Europa* (Berlin, 1930), pp. 20 ff.
52. Gardiner, "The Meaning of the German Revolution," in *North Sea and Baltic* (Whitsun, 1933), p. 5.
53. *North Sea and Baltic* (Spring, 1935).
54. See Leslie Paul, "The Decline of the Youth Movements," and Gardiner, letter to *The Adelphi* (April 1934).
55. Walter Laqueur, *Young Germany* (London, 1962), pp. 137 ff.; and cf. the interest taken by Reichling, *Seton,* in English movements.
56. From "Der zweite Aufruf" in *Freideutsche Jugend* (Jena, 1913), p. 4.
57. Laqueur, *Young Germany,* pp. 26-27.
58. *The Rural Organisation Council,* p. v.
59. Montague Fordham, *Mother Earth* (2nd ed., London, 1908), p. 164.
60. Fordham, *The Rebuilding of Rural England* (London, 1924), p. viii; for a mystical experience, see Massingham, *World without End* (London, 1932), pp. 195- 97; Clough Williams-Ellis (ed.), *Britain and the Beast* (London, 1937), with contributions by Keynes, Massingham, E. M. Forster, Joad, A. G. Street, etc.
61. Richard St. Barbe Baker, *The Brotherhood of the Trees* (London, 1930).
62. Baker, *I Planted Trees* (London, 1944), pp. 77-78; *Broadsheet,* no. 14 (September 1926); Report of the Men of the Trees (Summer School and Conference, Oxford, 1938, London, 1938), pp. 75-76.
63. Gardiner, "After Thirty Years," p. 152 and cf. his letter to *The Adelphi.*
64. See *Wessex* (Christmas, 1950, and Midwinter, 1953), "In Memory Harold John Massingham"; H. J. Massingham, *Remembrance* (London, 1942), pp. 140 ff.; Massingham, "The Natural Order" in *Essays in the Return to Husbandry* (London, 1945), pp. 7, 78; Massingham, *The Tree of Life* (London, 1943), p. 209.
65. *Wessex* (Christmas, 1950), pp. 32 ff.
66. Katherine Trevelyan, after the failure of her marriage to Goetsch, found solace in Steiner's Christian Community.

67. See C. B. Purdom, *The Letchworth Achievement* (London, 1963).
68. Purdom, *Life Over Again* (London, 1951), and cf. Dugald Macfadyen, *Sir Ebeneezer Howard and the Town Planning Movement* (Manchester, 1933).
69. See Ernest Westlake and Aubrey Westlake, *Primitive Occupations*.
70. Victor Branford and Patrick Geddes, *The Coming Polity* (London, 1919), p. v.
71. See *The Occult Underground*, pp. 326 ff. As Geddes was a supporter of the Kibbo Kift, it is worth noting a nationalist youth movement called the Scottish Watch, which was much concerned with eugenics. See Wendy Wood, *I Like Life* (Edinburgh, 1930), p. 243. On Geddes and Mumford, see Lewis Mumford, "The Disciple's Rebellion" in *Encounter* (September 1966), pp. 11 ff.; Mumford, *The Culture of Cities* (N.Y., 1938).
72. Walter Crane, "Of the Revival of Design and Handicraft," in William Morris (ed.), *Arts and Crafts Essays* (London, 1893), pp. 12-13.
73. C. R. Ashbee, *An Endeavour towards the Teaching of John Ruskin and William Morris* (London, 1901), p. 7; Ashbee, *Craftsmanship in Competitive Industry* (London, 1909), and cf. the picture of his craftsman's Utopia in *The Building of Thelema* (London, 1912).
74. Quoted in Niles Carpenter, *Guild Socialism* (N.Y., 1922); and cf. the letter from Penty printed by Karl Munkes, "Arthur Penty und der Nationalsozialismus" (thesis presented to Bonn University, 1937), pp. 19-20.
75. A. J. Penty, *The Restoration of the Gild System,* (London, 1906), pp. 46-47, 64.
76. See his "Art and the Function of Guilds," in *Architecture, Mysticism and Myth* (London, 1892); G. Stirling Taylor, *The Guild State* (London, 1919), p. 21; Penty, *Guild System,* pp. 85-86; see *Transactions of the Second Annual Congress of the Federation of European Sections of the Theosophical Society* (London, 1905).
77. A. R. Orage (ed.), *National Guilds* (London, 1914), The book carried no mention of Hobson at all.
78. S. G. Hobson, *Functional Socialism* (London, 1936), pp. 15-16; Ramiro de Maeztu, *Authority, Liberty and Function in the Light of the War* (London, 1916). For de Maeztu, see later in this chapter and Martin Nozick, "An Examination of Ramiro de Maeztu" in *Publications of the Modern Language Association of America* (September 1954), pp. 719 ff.
79. Niles Carpenter, *Guild Socialism,* p. 95; *The Guildsman,* no. 1.
80. G. Stirling Taylor, *The Psychology of the Great War* (London, 1915), p. 191.
81. Niles Carpenter, *Guild Socialism,* pp. 109-10, 117-26.
82. George Young in *The Daily News* (24 April 1919), p. 2, and (26 April 1919), p. 2; Young, *The New Germany* (London, 1920), pp. 190-91; Young, "British Guild Socialism and the German Revolution," in *The Guildsman* (November 1920), p. 3.
83. G. D. H. Cole, "Guilds at Home and Abroad," in *The Guildsman*

(November 1920), and cf. reports of a visit to Munich printed July-August, 1919, p. 11.

84. Niles Carpenter, *Guild Socialism*, p. 113, and *The Guildsman* (January 1921), p. 5.

85. Penty, "Douglasism and the Guilds," in *The Guild Socialist* (April 1922), pp. 4-5; Niles Carpenter, *Guild Socialism*, pp. 134-35; Cole, "Guilds at Home and Abroad," pp. 9-10.

86. Cole, *A History of Socialist Thought*, vol. IV, part I, *Communism and Social Democracy* (London, 1958), pp. 453-54.

87. Walter Kendal, *The Revolutionary Movement in Britain 1900-21* (London, 1969), pp. 278-83.

88. Munkes, *Arthur Penty*, p. 21. See Fordham, *Agriculture and the Guild System* (London, 1923), *Britain's Trade and Agriculture* (London, 1932), and A. J. Penty and William Wright, M.P., *Agriculture and the Unemployed* (London, 1925).

89. Peter d'A. Jones, *The Christian Socialist Revival* (Princeton, New Jersey, 1968), pp. 228-37.

90. Quoted in Reg. Groves, *Conrad Noel and the Thaxted Movement* (London, 1967), p. 206.

91. Groves, *Conrad Noel*, pp. 70 ff. See Noel, *The Battle of the Flags* (London, 1921) and *The Guildsman* for 1921.

92. *Christianity and Industrial Problems* (reissue in 1927 of original 1918 publication), pp. 83, 147, 212.

93. Maurice Reckitt, *As it Happened* (London, 1941), p. 108; Hilaire Belloc, *Economics for Helen* (2nd ed., London, 1924), p. 229. *The Servile State* (London, 1912).

94. G. K. Chesterton, *The Outline of Sanity* (London, 1926). See also Robert Speaight, *The Life of Hilaire Belloc* (London, 1957), p. 485; Maisie Ward, *Gilbert Keith Chesterton* (London, 1944), pp. 433 ff.; Christopher Hollis, *The Mind of Chesterton* (London, 1970), p. 213; Conrad Noel, *An Autobiography* (London, 1945); G. K. Chesterton, *Autobiography* (2nd ed., London, 1969), p. 163; *The Guildsman* (September 1919), p. 1.

95. On Gill, see Donald Attwater, *A Cell of Good Living* (London, 1969), and see Gill's own *Last Essays* (London, 1947), in particular "The Factory System and Christianity," pp. 103 ff. (originally 1918). For Coomaraswamy and the guild idea, see Ananda Coomaraswamy, *The Indian Craftsman* (London, 1909), pp. 7-19, 114-16. Bhagavan Das is recommended in "What has India Contributed to Human Welfare" in *The Dance of Shiva* (London, 1958). See Bhagavan Das, *The Science of Social Organisation* (London, Benares, 1910). "Manu's scheme is the nearest and only approach to a workable socialism that has been tried in our race."

96. See Penty's *Distributism: a Manifesto* (London, 1938); Penty, *Towards a Christian Sociology* (London, 1923), p. 201.

97. T. S. Eliot, *The Idea of a Christian Society* (London, 1936), p. 61. Eliot's avowed masters—Christopher Dawson and Father V. A. Demant—are Johnny-come-latelies in the field of English illuminated

socialism; Dawson's *Beyond Politics* (1939) and Demant's *God, Man and Society* (1933) betray their indebtedness to their predecessors. Demant dedicated his book to Maurice Reckitt.

98. I. O. Evans, *Woodcraft*, pp. 53-55.
99. Westlake, in *Grith Fyrd* (Spring, 1933). Cf. Reichling, *Seton*, p. 108. On Toynbee Hall, J. A. R. Pimlott, *Toynbee Hall* (London, 1935) and on the Theosophical Society, "Bow Lodge," attached to it see letter in *The Vahan* (1 December 1894), p. 8.
100. Interview with John Hargrave.
101. Philip Mairet, *A. R. Orage* (2nd ed., N.Y., 1966), pp. 74-76; see C. H. Douglas, *Credit Power and Democracy* (London, 1920).
102. Douglas, *Credit Power*, p. 145.
103. Jones, *Christian Socialist Revival*, pp. 199-200 and p. 293.
104. See Leonard Wise, *Arthur Kitson* (London, 1946); Arthur Kitson, *The Money Problem* (London, 1903), p. 118 and p. 211; Kitson, *Unemployment* (London, 1921).
105. Frederick Soddy, "Economic Science from the Standpoint of Science" in *The Guildsman* (July 1920), pp. 3-4. On Soddy, see Leonard Wise, *Frederick Soddy* (London, 1946).
106. I. O. Evans, *Woodcraft*, p. 84.
107. Hargrave in *The New Age* (18 October 1928), p. 298.
108. Hargrave, *Confession*, p. 241.
109. *Annual Report of the Green Shirt Movement for Social Credit* (1922-23).
110. Eric Estorick, "The British Social Credit Party" in *Dynamic America* (July 1940).
111. Interview with Hargrave.
112. C. B. Macpherson, *Democracy in Alberta* (Toronto, 1953), p. 140.
113. *K. K. Official Report Alberta* (London, 1937).
114. For Boltwood, see *Deathless Freedom by Charles Kingsley through Crusader* (London, 1939).
115. Tom Driberg, "A Touch of the Sun," in *The Adelphi*, vol. 161, pp. 56 ff.
116. Hargrave, *The Life and Soul of Paracelsus* (London, 1951). See chapter IX for a quotation from Hargrave on the mechanics of inspiration.
117. See Westlake, *Health Abounding*, Massingham's introduction to *The Natural Order*, and Father Demant, entry in *The New Age* (3 March 1938), p. 97.
118. W. E. Mann, *Sect, Cult and Church in Alberta* (Toronto, 1955), pp. 118-21, 153-57.
119. Hugh McDiarmid, *The Company I've Kept* (London, 1966), pp. 113-14.
120. S. G. Hobson, *Pilgrim to the Left* (London, 1938), p. 177. See also Odon Por's *Guilds and Co-operatives in Italy* (London, 1923).
121. Nozick, "de Maeztu," pp. 726 ff. Cf. Richard A. H. Robinson, *The Origins of Franco's Spain* (Newton Abbot, 1970), pp. 179, 220.

122. Penty, *Communism and the Alternative* (London, 1933), p. 110 note 1. See also Penty, *Tradition and Modernism in Politics* (London, 1927) and S. G. Hobson, *Pilgrim to the Left,* p. 176.
123. Interview with Hargrave. For A. V. Roe's views on monetary reform, see L. J. Ludovici, *The Challenging Sky* (London, 1956), pp. 110 ff.; also see Hargrave's pamphlet *Social Credit and British Fascism.*
124. In particular, see Williamson, *The Phoenix Generation* (paperback ed., London, 1967).
125. See Jorian Jenks, *The Stuff Man's Made Of* (London, 1959), and *From the Ground Up* (London, 1950).
126. J. Taylor Peddie, *The Economic Mechanism of Scripture* (London, 2 vols., 1934), vol. II, p. 274.
127. Hargrave, *Confession,* pp. 244-46 and my interview with Hargrave.
128. Robert Benewick, *Political Violence and Public Order* (London, 1969), p. 240; see H. W. Kenyon in *Blackshirt* (11 January 1935), p. 10, for an attempt to equate Baden-Powell's Rover Scout textbook with Fascism, p. 10; and G. K. Chesterton in *Blackshirt* (1 February 1935), p. 1, for the samurai.
129. Arthur Raven Thomson, *The Coming Corporate State* (London, 1937).
130. Gardiner, in *North Sea and Baltic* (Whitsun, 1933), pp. 5-6.
131. See Andrew Sharf, *The British Press and the Jews under Nazi Rule* (London, 1964), pp. 194 ff.
132. See *The Patriot,* vol. I, no. 1. (9 February 1927).
133. Colin Cross, *The Fascists in Britain* (London, 1961), pp. 57-58.
134. Nesta Webster, *Secret Societies and Subversive Movements* (London, 1924), pp. 382.
135. See the notice in *The Patriot* (27 January 1927), p. 87.
136. Webster, *Secret Societies,* p. 405.
137. *The Britons* (prospectus, London, 1952); *Sir William Butler: An Autobiography* (London, 1911), pp. 406 ff., in particular the report to the War Office of June 1899, p. 436; cf. Edward McCourt, *Remember Butler* (London, 1968), pp. 245-47.
138. On Beamish, see Louis W. Bondy, *Racketeers of Hatred* (London, 1946), pp. 131 ff.; *The Times,* 5-6 December 1922 and 13 January 1923.
139. Arnold Spencer Leese, *Out of Step: Events in the two lives of an Anti-Jewish Camel Doctor* (Guildford, 1951), p. 50; Arthur Kitson, *Unemployment,* p. 12; C. H. Douglas, *The Big Idea* (Liverpool, 1945), pp. 15, 21, and cf. *The Policy of a Philosophy* (Liverpool, 1945; orig. 1937, etc.).
140. Nozick, "de Maeztu," pp. 735 ff.; Richard A. H. Robinson, *Franco's Spain,* p. 220; G. Stirling Taylor, *The Guild State* (London, 1920); George Young, *The New Germany,* p. 32 and pp. 110-11.
141. Ward, *Chesterton,* pp. 283-309; Hollis, *Chesterton,* pp. 132 ff.; G. K. Chesterton, *The New Jerusalem* (London, 1920); Hilaire Belloc, *The Jews* (London, 1923); Belloc in a letter to Major L. H. Cohn (1923), quoted by Robert Speaight in *The Life of Hilaire Belloc,* p. 456.

142. For Professor Norman Cohn's writings, see chapter V below and notes.
143. Douglas on 7 February 1948 in *The Development of World Dominion* (London and Sydney, 1969).
144. See 5th edition of Leslie Fry, *Waters Flowing Eastward,* revised, enlarged, and subtitled *The War against the Kingdom of Christ* (London, 1965). For further lunacies, see Fahey's *The Mystical Body of Christ and the Reorganisation of Society* (Cork, 1945).
145. See William Sanderson, *That Which Was Lost* (London, 1930) and *Statecraft* (2nd ed., London, 1932); Anthony Ludovici, *A Defence of Aristocracy* (London, 1915); *Recovery* (London, 1939).
146. *Broadsheet* (March 1931).
147. George Thayer, *The British Political Fringe* (London, 1965), p. 106 note.

Chapter 3
Wise Men from the East

Slav Mysticism and the West—The Russian Religious Revival —Symbolism and Decadence—The Occult Revival in Russia— Magicians at Court—The Emigration of the Mystics—Slav Gurus in Western Europe—Their Association with the Underground— Types of Russian Illuminated Politics

*E*X *oriente lux:* Western Europe's persistent hope in time of trouble. The influx of Eastern religions to the Roman Empire, the penetration of Renaissance Europe by Greek and Byzantine thought, the search of 19th-century occultists in the farther Orient—all have been governed by this expectation. The Slav peoples, on the other hand, have been forced to look both ways and have made their synthesis as a matter of necessity. The triumph of Communism in the 1920s drove out of Russia the idealistic tradition of thought that many Russians have seen as the chief expression of their national genius. Representatives of this intellectual tradition—superficially like that of the West, but essentially different—found their way into the anxiety-ridden centers of Europe.

The remarkable hospitality of Russia to wandering saints and miscellaneous religious lunatics alike speaks more of the priorities of the East than of the West. It happened that just before the 1917 revolution, the native traditions of the Christian autocracy fused with recently imported mystical and occultist doctrines to make a cultural construction of the greatest tension. Between 1917 and 1923 this construction was destroyed and its builders suppressed or exiled. In the various Slavonic prophets who gained Western followings we can observe the struggle for the irrational in its most elemental form. In the illuminated politicians who accompanied them can be seen the search for immaterial realities in the most material of spheres of action.

Such an invasion of Slav mysticism had occurred before. In the middle of the 19th century the unending tally of Polish misfortunes had driven a horde of exiles into France. There they made contact with French mystical circles and the illuminated politicians of the day. They had brought with them a penchant for occultism and a national tradition of "Messianism" which saw the Polish nation as the redeemer of the world.[1]

An important source of this doctrine had been the presence within the ranks of Polish Catholicism of large numbers of converted Jews, followers of the prophet Jacob Frank. The mystical reputation of Jews, and particularly of Polish Jews, was long-lasting. Gustav Meyrink's *The Golem* played on the natural associations made by his readers between the Prague ghetto and doings mysterious and magical. As the time of Nazi rule drew near, Rudolf Steiner's enemies tried to prove that he was the son of a Polish Jew; the aim, of course, was to involve him in the imaginary international conspiracy of Freemasons and Jews, but the choice of supposed nationality was undoubtedly prompted by the reputation of Jewish Galicians. In the Viennese circle of Friedrich Eckstein could be found the poet Siegfried Lipiner (1856-1911) who had been born of Jewish parents in the Galician town of Jaroslav and who died as archivist to the Austrian *Reichsrat*. Lipiner was greatly influenced by Wagner, Schopenhauer, and Nietzsche; but he remained committed to the Christian religion.[2]

One important representative of Polish Messianism was active up till the outbreak of the Second World War. But his unusual preoccupations will become more intelligible if placed in the context of the exotic and almost suffocating atmosphere of the Russian religious revival. The Russian Orthodox Church has always remained a puzzle to outsiders. In the words of one of the most distinguished thinkers of the emigration:

> Orthodoxy is not *one* of the historic confessions, it is the church itself, in its verity. It may even be added that, by becoming a confession, Orthodoxy fails to manifest all its force and its universal glory; it hides, one might say, in the catacombs.

The bewildering divergence of various currents of Russian theological speculation is seen as a virtue by those accustomed to the tradition. "It may be said that in the spiritual life this variety is most useful when it is greatest." As for the result: "Orthodox theology in Russia, in the 19th century and in our day, contains a whole series of original theological individualities, which resemble each other very little and which are all equally orthodox." The various different thinkers "express each in his own way the Orthodox conscience, in a sort of theological rhapsody."[3]

At the turn of the century this metaphysical orchestration achieved, if not perfect harmony, at any rate unsurpassed volume. The Orthodox tradition of popularly acclaimed sainthood found its culminating expression in Father John Sergiev (1828-1908), the Dean of Kronstadt, who had been born the son of poor peasants in Archangel province. His charity and remarkable healing powers secured him an immense following. The *Times* correspondent reported on the celebrations at Kronstadt in January 1891, to mark the thirty-fifth anniversary of the entry of Father John into the Orthodox ministry.

> The festival in his honour at Cronstadt, an island most difficult and inconvenient of access in winter, was attended by great crowds of people, rich and poor, who made their way across the ice of the gulf to the isolated island, from St. Petersburg and other places. Thirty priests officiated at the church service on the occasion, and deputations from various benevolent and other societies, including even one of beggars,

presented the reverend Father with gifts of silver-bound Bibles and holy pictures. The most touching sight of all was the gift of a small bunch of flowers by a poor sickly woman, with a child in her arms. An eye-witness states that the crowd and Father John were moved to tears. At a banquet in the evening, at which the Governor and the Admiral of Port presided, paupers, mendicants and moujiks sat cheek by jowl with ladies, officials and naval officers to drink the health and long life of father John.[4]

The almost universal veneration of Father John did not extend to the revolutionary priest Father Gapon, whose ambiguous part in the Revolution of 1905 is well known. Gapon wrote that John was surrounded by a band of twelve female acolytes, who managed his affairs on a weekly roster and solicited fees for visits; the dean of Kronstadt did indeed give alms, he admitted, but the whole business smacked of a commercial operation.[5] Even Gapon did not accuse John of fraud. But he thought that he had become the tool of the ruling classes. Certainly Father John's position with regard to the Establishment was sufficiently plain to earn him for a time the post of imperial confessor. And if John's personal saintliness is beyond question, this was not true of all his contemporaries or successors. Nicolas Zernov, who knew personally most of the leading figures of the religious revival, has recorded that while a genuine revival of traditional Orthodoxy did take place, "Men and women of questionable moral character became prominent in religious circles. Adventurers, quack prophets and healers acquired wide popularity and some of them even became bishops."[6]

The reverse side of the coin to Father John was represented by the notorious Sergei Mikhailovitch Trufanov (1880-1958). Better known as Iliodor, he built a monastery at Tsaritsyn on the Volga out of funds given by his devotees and became the center of a popular cult characterized by hysterical female admirers. Iliodor undoubtedly believed in his mission to chastize revolutionaries and Jews. His early asceticism was rivaled only by his suggestibility. In his memoirs he tells the story of how, when he was taken into a city for the first time, his brother told him that he must kneel and kiss the statue of a woman at the city gates. Believing implicitly in this statue Iliodor knelt and kissed the empty air. A similar atmosphere of pious suggestibility produced incessant reports of miracles during the First World War—escapes from death when bullets struck ikons or crucifixes, miraculous deliverance accorded worshipping congregations. After the Russian defeat at the Masurian Lakes, the imperial command was given to send to the front line the ikon of the Mother of God from the Troitsko-Sergieva monastery. The government secured a huge propaganda success when soon afterward news was received of the Russian victory near Lvor and of the Allied successes on the Marne.[7]

Apart from the individual holy men who attracted personal devotion, the main tradition of Orthodox spirituality was preserved by monks. The inheritance of the monasteries of Athos was transmitted from one generation to the next, and the Russian monasteries themselves became places of pilgrimage. The most famous was the Optina Monastery, which was succeeded in popularity by the Zossimova Hermitage. The holy men, or *startsy,* who lived at such places in relative isolation, were famous as directors of souls—although this did not prevent the philosopher Nicolas Berdyaev from finding Ambrose of Optina "almost dreary."[8]

Again, there was another side to the coin, represented by the numberless sects which led an underground (although increasingly popular) existence. These were hallowed by tradition, although outlawed by the regime. There was the Old Believers, or *Raskolniki,* who had their origins in the attempts of some 17th-century Orthodox churchmen to resist the centralizing and hierarchical reforms of the Patriarch Nikon. The Old Believers regarded themselves as the true church, and the "Christians" as frivolous and worldly. In 1880 they possibly numbered 13,000,000 to 14,000,000, and on the outbreak of the Revolution some 25,000,000. There were the *Stranniki,* or "priestless sect," who had sprung from the Old Believers and who held that the elect must wander over the face of the earth with no permanent abode. They regarded themselves as free from moral law and discouraged marriage. Legends grew up of subterranean *strannik* sanctuaries where the wanderers hid. There were the "self-baptizers," who gave themselves the sacraments, and the "milk-drinkers," who forswore all other liquids during Lent. The Doukhobors, who practiced a sort of pacifist Gnosticism, were deported *en bloc* to the Caucasus.

The *Khlysty* attained some celebrity in fashionable society. They numbered at least 65,000 in 1880, and they cultivated poetic utterance, ecstatic dancing, and leaders of a Messianic cast. The *Khlysty* gave brith to the *Skoptsy,* a bizarre sect of self-castrators, whose founder had been one of the many impostors claiming to be Tsar Peter III; in the middle of the 19th century they were popular in court circles in St. Petersburg, and on the outbreak of the Revolution they were thought to have numbered 100,000.[9]

Within such a tradition it is unsurprising that the religious revival took on an exotic and at times a frenetic appearance. Russia was no more immune to the infection of anxiety than the countries of Western Europe. But within its boundaries the causes of anxiety were simpler. The threat of changes in the government or social structure of the country grew ever more acute, and with the revolution of 1905 they became reality. Among the Orthodox and the conservative a retreat to the state religion—for the tsar was, after all, head of the church—was a natural reaction. In contrast, there were others who interpreted the Christian gospel in a more populist light, clothing unorthodox sentiments in the garment of inherited tradition.

The intellectuals were in contact with the fashions of Western Europe, and found sympathetic ideas in French Symbolism—a school of thought saturated with occult speculation.[10] The intelligentsia was trebly attracted to the study of the religious and the mystical: through native tradition and inclination, through pan-European anxiety and artistic fashion, and through their own peculiar and frustrating inability to do anything that might affect the destinies of their countrymen. Otherworldly cities had an immense appeal for this group, which one observer described as bearing "the character of a religious body rather than that of a literary class." The same writer explained:

> Again the devotion of the intelligentsia to theory, especially to the latest philosophical and social theories of France and Germany, blunted the sense of reality and made the average Russian even more impractical than he was compelled to be through lack of opportunity for action. He saw the march of events through a haze of hypothesis and logical syllogism. In long and noisy disputes around the samovar in rooms clouded

> with cigarette-smoke he analysed political occurrences from various philosophical and sociological standpoints, estimating their significance from the point of view of a remote ideal, but very often missing their immediate impact on sensibility. . . . The intelligentsia . . . evaded nature. It theorised even when of set purpose it returned to Nature and founded Tolstoyan colonies.[11]

Vladimir Sergeivitch Soloviev (1853-1900) was the father of the peculiar sort of religious speculation that most characterized the Russian religious revival. He was the son of an eminent historian who was also an Orthodox priest. Vladimir Soloviev abandoned his early materialism for an idealistic philosophy and in 1872 underwent the first of a series of mystical experiences. This consisted in the transfiguration of a girl traveling in the Moscow-Kharkov train into the figure of a divine woman.

At once Soloviev abandoned his scientific pursuits and left Moscow University to study at the Ecclesiastical Academy. In 1874 he produced a book entitled *The Crisis of Western Philosophy*. This concluded that

> Western philosophy affirms under the form of *rational knowledge,* the same truths which under the form of *faith* and *spiritual contemplation* were affirmed by the great theological doctrines of the Orient (in part of the ancient East and particularly the Christian *East*).

Soloviev called for a "universal synthesis of science, philosophy, and religion." This peculiarly Russian expression of the conflict between the claims of inherited Eastern methods of thought and intruding Western traditions was to find an enthusiastic welcome. Soloviev himself became a lecturer at Moscow University, and was stimulated by the historical interests of his predecessor in the past to investigate Spiritualism and the 18th-century seer Swedenborg. At one time he thought that he could elaborate the revelations of the spirits into a valid system of metaphysics. In 1874 he obtained a year's sabbatical and went to London to study Hindu, Gnostic, and medieval philosophy in the British Museum, where the second of his visions overcame him. Soloviev seems to have studied most of the classics of Western occultism. It is uncertain just what he was reading when he had his vision; but it was probably Knorr von Rosenreuth's *Kabbala Denudata,* a 17th-century translation of Jewish mystical texts. Once more the figure of a divine woman appeared before him. She revealed herself as "Sophia"—wisdom—a divine participant in the Creation of the world. In response to the vision, Soloviev abandoned his Jacob Böhme and his Eliphas Lévi, and rushed off to Egypt where he received a mysterious order to go to Thebes.[12]

In 1876 Count Melchior de Vogüé was introduced to Soloviev in Cairo by Ferdinand de Lesseps.

> In high Egyptian summer, this Christ was wearing a long black overcoat and a top hat. He told us ingenuously that he had gone quite alone, dressed in this paraphernalia to the Bedouins of the Suez desert; he was looking for a tribe which preserved, someone must have told him, certain Cabalistic secrets, certain Masonic traditions directly inherited from King Solomon. The Bedouins had not enlightened him in the slightest about these matters: but they stole his watch and dented his top hat.

In fact, the Arabs thought this black-garbed apparition was the devil and abandoned him in the desert for the night. In the morning, the Russian awoke surrounded by the smell of roses, and Sophia appeared to him again. At this point Soloviev was completely absorbed by occult tradition. He appears to have believed that the legendary Emerald Tablet of Hermes Trismegistus did in fact contain all secrets, and that he could discover its custodians. But he finally decided that nothing had come of his journey to Egypt and returned to Russia. There in the next year Melchior de Vogüé met him again. He found him occupied greatly with occultism, contemplating a book which would prove the divine principle to be female, and questioning the spirits about the Turko-Russian War.[13]

Basing his ideas upon those of the occult traditions he had so diligently studied, Soloviev next began to elaborate a philosophy of an "integral life," which must first be accepted by a small brotherhood, then by all Russia. He began to lecture at St. Petersburg University, and he found support from Dostoievsky, the Archbishop of Lithuania, Sophie Tolstoy, (Leo Tolstoy's widow), and Princess Wolkonsky. His obsession with the name "Sophia" and with various women of that name, whom he saw as partial embodiments of his divine conception, is interesting and not a little erotic. The poet Andrei Bely saw many of Soloviev's manuscripts, covered with curious writing signed with the letter "S," which seemed to Bely to read like love letters.[14] Toward the end of his life, Soloviev was plagued by the attentions of one Anna Schmidt (she died in 1905) who wrote a column on mysticism in a Nizhni-Novgorod newspaper. Anna decided that she was the Divine Sophia come to earth to be reunited with Vladimir Soloviev, the reincarnate Christ. Soloviev was horrified. But after his death his family kept in touch with the Sophia from Nizhni-Novgorod, and in 1916 Sergei Bulgakov published her *Notes,* including a "Third Testament," which he described as "an amazing document."[15] Soloviev's family and disciples evidently thought her worth humoring, just in case.

Soloviev's legacy is many-faceted. Although it was added to by his disciples, it is remarkable how many of the elements of the Russian religious revival were contained in the ideas of its pioneer. First, there was the idea of the "God-man," who represented the outcome of the gradual spiritualization of humanity. As the process of physical creation had produced its crowning achievement in the human being, so the process of human *self*-creation would produce from the human being—God.[16] Soloviev's other main preoccupations toward the end of his life concerned the status of the Orthodox church and the coming of Antichrist. His faith in traditional Russian Orthodoxy—he had visited the *staretz* Ambrose of Optina Pustyn in the company of Dostoievsky—was shaken by the church's reactionary political stance over the murderer of Alexander II, and after 1881 he began to regard the Orthodox clergy as tainted by their ancient persecution of the Old Believers. He made several attempts to approach Rome, but all were failures.[17] His followers were to continue Soloviev's concern with the ecumenical role of Orthodoxy. For a large number of the intelligentsia this meant subscribing, for a time, to the doctrine of "Slavophilism" —the vision of Russia's messianic mission in Europe—a belief owing not a little to the mysticism of the Polish Messianists. More important was the pessimistic attitude which engulfed Soloviev in the last two years of his life. He revisited Egypt and began to feel that all his early hopes had been disappointed. He believed that he was pursued by demons, that the end of the world was approaching, and that his divine Sophia would be incarnate only after history as such as ceased. In a dialogue he forecast the appearance of Antichrist.

> *Politician:* And do you think the catastrophe is very near?
> *Mr Z.:* Well, there will still be a great deal of rattling and bustling on stage, but the drama has been all written long ago, and neither the audience nor the actors are allowed to alter anything in it.[18]

Soloviev's death in 1900 occurred in the same year as those of Nietzsche and Oscar Wilde, who were also heroes of the Russian intelligentsia. As some of the prophet's followers had expected his immediate resurrection, they fell back on forebodings that his gloomy predictions were to be fulfilled. The Symbolist poet Vyacheslav Ivanov and his friends computed a prophecy of Cornelius Agrippa to agree with a verdict of apocalypse in 1900,[19] and the intelligentsia turned itself over eagerly to the God-seeking movement.

The conflicting claims of Orthodox tradition, the fear of apocalypse, and the example of Soloviev's occultism formed the ingredients of a hothouse atmosphere which excited some disgust among more conservative souls. One of these wrote of Soloviev that some of the secondary and unhealthy elements of his philosophical creed were unhappily a starting-point for the eager speculations and overstrung pseudo-religious emotions of certain intellectuals of orgiastic tendencies who were eager to combine the holiest mysteries of religion, the holy of holies of the Christian faith, with the sexual excitement of the Bacchanalia.[20]

To the mushroom growth of groups of religious and philosophical speculators with names like the "Circle of Seekers of Christian Enlightenment" or the Moscow "Religious-Philosophic Society in Memory of Vladimir Soloviev" was added an eruption of French Decadent and Symbolist influence which for a time dominated the cultural life of Moscow and St. Petersburg. The convulsions experienced by contemporary French irrationalists were reproduced in Russia, but in a smaller circle and with magnified intensity. Berdyaev wrote:

> It was a time of the awakening of independent and original philosophical thought, of intense poetical imagination and aesthetic sensibility; it was a time marked by a profound

spiritual disquiet and religious searching, and by widespread interest in mysticism and even occultism. We saw the glow of a new dawn, and the end of an old age seemed to coincide with a new era which would bring about a complete transfiguration of life.

But such moods were prevalent only in comparatively restricted circles, cut off from the wide and far-reaching social changes which were taking place at the time. There were unmistakable signs of incipient decadence in the whole movement: sometimes it seemed to breathe the atmosphere of a hot-house with no door or window open to the fresh air. We were in fact witnesses not of the beginning of a new era but of the collapse of an old one, and we were troubled by a sense of the approaching collapse of old Russia. And, significantly enough, while moved and inspired by great visions, we experienced no real joy. Moreover, signs of genuine creativeness were accompanied by mere fashions and imitations. For many it became simply a matter of *comme il faut* to be an aesthete or a mystic, or a "seeker after God."[21]

The centers of the literary and artistic decadence were small coteries gathered around societies or magazines. The most important in St. Petersburg were the grandiosely titled "New Religious Consciousness" (of Dmitri Merezhkovsky, his wife Zenaida Hippius, their friend Dmitri Filosofov, and haunted by the satyrlike spirit of Vasily Rozanov) and the group of Symbolists which met at the seventh-floor flat of Vyacheslav Ivanov called "the Tower." In Moscow there was the Scorpio Press of Valery Bryussov; and the short-lived but very influential *World of Art* conducted by Diaghilev, which opened its columns not only to artists but also to religious thinkers like Merezhkovsky and Rozanov. Between these poles of attraction swung important figures like the poets Andrei Bely and Alexander Blok. An impressionistic picture of this illuminated intelligentsia will show some of the influences on emigré culture.

The Russian Decadence began with the writings of Nicolai Minsky (N. M. Vilenkin, 1855-1937) and A. L. Volynsky (A. L. Flekser, 1865-1926). In 1890 the former published a Nietzschean thesis on the liberty of the individual; and the criticism of the latter broke away from the accepted "civic" standards of literature much in the way in which the French Symbolists had rebelled against the naturalism of the French novel. In 1892 Merezhkovsky published a work heavily influenced by the French Symbolists; and in 1894 a Symbolist anthology was issued by Valery Bryussov. The Symbolist approach was defined by its chief theoretician, Vyacheslav Ivanov (1866-1949) as "from the real to the more real." It was, in other words, an attempt to see through the appearances of material objects and the ordinary occurrences of life to an Absolute reality which was assumed to lie beneath them. Symbolic art, wrote Ivanov, "enables us to become aware of the inter-relationships and the meaning of what exists not only in the sphere of earthly, empirical consciousness, but in other spheres too. Thus true symbolic art approximates to religion."[22] Ivanov held his "at homes" in his Tower on Wednesday evenings. The chaotic Bohemian life of this flat was experienced by Bernard Pares when he stayed there in 1907; he was asked not to sing in his morning bath, as that was the time that the inmates usually went to bed. The doctrines of the French Symbolists were adopted wholesale: thus the poet Konstantin Balmont recorded in his notebook that "a grain of sand can become a system of the astral world."[23] Russian Symbolism, however, was permeated with the influence of Vladimir Soloviev. Ivanov had known him as a child; Andrei Bely was brought into literature by Soloviev's youngest brother Mikhail; both Soloviev's sister and his nephew Sergei wrote Symbolist poetry.

Somewhere between those who were mystics because of their art and the religious thinkers proper came "the Merezhkovskys" —Dmitri Merezhkovsky (1865-1941), Zenaida Hippius (1868-1944), and their friend Dmitri Filosofov. Their flat was as Bohemian as Ivanov's, but centered round the poetess Hippius. "The Merezhkovskys' drawing-room," Berdyaev wrote, "was not a place where you would meet a real person, though it was frequented by a multitude of people; one felt absorbed in an impersonal whole; there was a kind of magic spell overshadowing the lives—something similar to the atmosphere prevailing at the gatherings of mystical sects."[24] Merezhkovsky's own interest in mystical sects was considerable. For his novel *Peter and Alexis* he had studied the traditions of Russian dissent, he had visited Semenov on the Volga, where the mysterious city of Kitei-grad was said to be submerged and where he spent St. John's Eve talking to wandering *stranniks* and adepts of extraordinary cults. If the novel which resulted from these researches is any indication of what he found, he held conversations with *Khlysts,* Old Believers, those who hourly expected Antichrist, and he gathered material for an unforgettable character—"Tifon the Sordid," venerated for his saintly sordidness.[24] Merezhkovsky saw the possibility of evolving a "new religious consciousness" from the two peculiarly Russian types represented by Tolstoy and Dostoievsky. Tolstoy stood for a pantheistic mysticism of the flesh, and Dostoievsky for the more ascetic spiritual virtues. "In this Russian the 'Man-God' shall be manifested to the Western world, and the 'God-man' for the first time to the Eastern, and shall be, for those whose thinking already reconciles both hemispheres the 'One in Two.'" Such mystical mathematics are somewhat alien to the Western mind, but similar speculations occupied the "Religio-Philosophical Assemblies" which Merezhkovosky and his friends held from 1901 to 1903. They secured the personal sanction of the reactionary Procurator of the Holy Synod and the Metropolitan Anthony. But official permission was withdrawn when the proceedings became too outspoken, although the participants were able to issue the results of their deliberations in a magazine called *The New Way.*[26]

These assemblies mixed together Orthodoxy, apocalypse, and some curious personal heresies. The most original viewpoint was probably that of Vasily Rozanov (1856-1919), who once caused "a confusion and explosion of fury" in the Religio-Philosophical Society when he suggested that newly married couples should begin the sacrament of married life as a monastic novice keeps his vigil. Rozanov preaches an orgiastic phallic religion which he combined with a veneration for antiquity in general. "The life of Ambrosius of the Optina Monastery is not more resplendent than the biography of a veteran of Caesar's legions." One of his books was suppressed by the Holy Synod because of obscenity. When Rozanov discussed his sexual mysticism in his family circle, one of his daughters would regularly have hysterics, but his wife used to fall asleep.[27] Although he despised Christianity for its taboo on sex, Rozanov carried on a love-hate relationship with the church and died a Christian.[28] A new age was approaching: "Probably something must have happened in the semen (and in the ovum); it is remarkable that now human beings have begun to be born quite different from those of 60 or 70 years ago." Rozanov summarized his creed in a letter of 1917:

> I am sure that the whole universe is parcelled out of "the body of Apis" . . . and strictly of his *genitalia,* and still more strictly, of his eternally gushing semen, of storms of semen, of whirls of semen. Electricity, volcanoes, light, thunder, "The hammer"—all these come from the phallus and nothing but the phallus. Cosmogony, the symbols of the world—all is phallus. The fir, the spruce, the pine tree, especially the pine-cone, the "form of a tree," the cupola of heaven, is all phalloid. Everything is "he," "he" is everywhere.[29]

Between the Symbolist poets and mystics and the traditions of the Russian holy men there was only a small gap. Alexander Dobrolyubov became a Decadent while scarcely out of school. At the age of eighteen he took opium, lived in an attic whose ceiling he had papered black, and associated with the Symbolists. His poems were less a cause of his fame than his following of women and girls who began (in the words of one authority) to "take too seriously his remarks on the beauty of death." Dobrolyubov was expelled from Moscow University after an unfortunate series of suicides. He abandoned the attic room with its collection of mysterious, ritualistic objects, encased himself in iron hoops according to the tradition of wandering holy men, and set off for the Solovetsky monastery in the far north.[30]

Dobrolyubov soon decided that a monastery was not for him and went traveling on foot throughout Russia preaching a gospel of love to all beings. After gathering two Cossack deserters among his disciples, he was imprisoned. He next escaped from a lunatic asylum where his mother had had him confined in mitigation of his sentence. His obscure wanderings, punctuated by arrests, caused distant echoes to reverberate against the mystical consciousness of the intelligentsia. Once Dobrolyubov turned up with a Moslem at Merezhkovsky's; Merezhkovsky did not doubt that he was in the presence of a saint. Nicholas Berdyaev used to frequent a Tolstoyan colony in Kharkov—it sounds rather like Monte Verita—where all sorts of progressive thinkers gather. Through this colony would pass members of Dobrolyubov's sect who were under a vow of silence and could only answer questions after a year had elapsed.[31] Valery Bryussov of the Scorpio press published Dobrolyubov's *From the Book Invisible;* and the Russian idealists relished the story of the poet who had "gone to the people."

Even the religious philosophers proper—although they naturally did not go so far in heterodoxy as the Symbolist poets and the mystics of the New Religious Consciousness—could not escape an exoticism in which a few saw some artificiality. The group of which the center was Pavel Alexandrovic Florensky (1882-1952) —Rozanov thought him a saint—was composed of Orthodox priests drawn from the ranks of the intelligentsia. Heavily influenced by Soloviev, they tried to see the world as an organic whole. Florensky himself is described as having a taste for folklore and occultism. He praised the "integral" life of the people and believed that everything was related by mysterious bonds.[32] Such assertions that nature is an organic being are common in the traditions of Western occultism. And if Russia had produced similar conclusions out of her inherited philosophy, the example of Soloviev, and the mysticism of the Symbolists, it is only natural to find that occultism of a Western pattern also penetrated both intelligentsia and fashionable society. The process of exchange between West and East was already two-way—for had not that stormy petrel of the occult world, Helena Petrovna Blavatsky, been born Helena von Hahn, the daughter of a Russian military family and cousin to the future prime minister, Count Witte?

When the Sufi Inayat Khan visited Russia he found much to commend in "that Eastern type of discipleship which is natural to the nation."[33] He was not the first guru to come knocking on the gates. Spiritualism, the basis of the Western irrationalist revival, had been introduced by the famous medium Daniel Dunglas Home. Home visited St. Petersburg in 1871, gave séances before the tsar, and married a relation of the leading Russian Spiritualist, Count Alexander Aksakov. Aksakov's efforts to have Spiritualist phenomena investigated were foiled by the guardians of religious orthodoxy, and the Count was forced to publish his periodical, *Psychische Studien,* in Leipzig. In 1874 arrived the French medium Brédif, who converted Professor N. A. Wagner of St. Petersburg, with whom

Aksakov and the chemist Butlerov reopened the campaign for an investigation into Spiritualism.[34] A committee was formed under Professor Mendeleyev, which promised to hold forty séances and examine the results. But after the negative demonstrations with which their tests began, they abandoned the project as a waste of time. Amid loud protestations from Aksakov and Butlerov about the "materialist" and "biased" method of the experiments, a petition was organized which was signed by a large number of titled personages, protesting at the closure of the commission after only eight séances.[35] However, the sole tangible evidence of organized Spiritualist activity in turn-of-the-century Russia was a small magazine called *Rebus,* which was founded in 1882 and dealt cautiously with Spiritualist topics.

During the preparations of the abortive committee, Count Aksakov had written to H. P. Blavatsky—at that period (1874-76) deeply involved in American Spiritualist circles—and asked her to choose a reliable medium to sit for the commission. Madame Blavatsky and Colonel Olcott selected Henry Slade—the same Slade who was to convert Zöllner of Leipzig and fare so badly in Vienna—who unfortunately arrived in Russia after the commission had dissolved itself.[36] In the autumn of 1875 Colonel Olcott and H.P.B. inaugurated their Theosophical Society, which four years later moved the scene of its operations to India and began to build up the reputation for miracles and supernatural masters that was to prove its earliest attraction. H. P. Blavatsky's stockpiling of anti-Christian and pagan legends in her *Isis Unveiled* endeared Theosophy to the authorities of her native land no more than Spiritualism. But it was proportionately attractive to the mystical inclinations of the Russian intelligentsia. Under the pen name "Radda Bai," Madame Blavatsky contributed to the Russian press the adventurous occult tales published in English as *From the Caves and Jungles of Hindustan* (originally a series in the *Moskovkiya Vyedomosti* in 1879). There followed several further series in Katkov's *Russkiy Vestnik.*[37] Madame Blavatsky—or at least Radda Bai—was fairly well known to the literate, and in 1892 it could be written that although *Isis Unveiled* was not sold by bookshops in Russia it was "no secret; it is easy to get on order." Vladimir Soloviev favorably reviewed *The Key to Theosophy* in August 1890, commenting that H.P.B. could not have invented her masters, because the Abbé Huc had mentioned them. This seems to have been a lapse from his normally hostile position—for Soloviev usually saw Christianity threatened by a creeping Buddhism and Theosophy as "an attempt by charlatans to adapt Buddhism to the metaphysical and mystical needs of half-cultured European society."[38]

On the other hand, Vladimir Soloviev's brother, the historical novelist Vsevolod Soloviev, dallied for several years with Theosophy and its foundress. In 1884 Vsevolod Soloviev (1849-1903) was in Paris. He was planning a series of articles on mystical subjects and carrying out absorbing occult researches at the Bibliothèque Nationale, much as his brother had studied at the British Museum. But instead of a vision of Sophia, he was granted the real presence of H. P. Blavatsky. He solicited her acquaintance through a Russian friend after having been enthralled by *From the Caves and Jungles of Hindustan*. "This American Buddhist, who had been away from Russia God knows how many years, who had dissipated her life in unknown parts, among unknown people, was an incarnation of the type of old-time Russian country lady of moderate means, grown stout in her farm-house." Throughout their friendship Soloviev never ceased to remark on her as a fellow countrywoman. It is necessary to emphasize this point, because the occultists of the West have so long regarded H.P.B. as their private property that her background remains obscured. Soloviev even recalled an occasion when she had exclaimed: "I would gladly return, I would gladly be Russian, Christian, Orthodox. I yearn for it. But there is no returning; I am in chains; I am not my own." And "in half an hour her wanderings about the 'master' had begun again."

Not until 1886 did Soloviev finally turn against her as he became disillusioned with her attempts to produce miraculous "phenomena." It is evident both from his own account and from his letters published by H. P. Blavatsky's sister, Vera Jelikovsky, that in 1885, at any rate, Vsevolod Soloviev believed in masters and was thick as thieves with Madame Jelikovsky and her two daughters. He believed he had convinced the French psychical researcher Charles Richet of Madame Blavatsky's sincerity and was promising to make propaganda for Theosophy in Russia.[39]

We shall return in another connection to the quarrels and scandals provoked by Soloviev's second thoughts; in 1892 he and Madame Jelikovsky began open battle in the press. But as early as 1887 H. P. Blavatsky could write to A. P. Sinnett from Ostend:

> The Russian papers are again full of me. It appears that "my hand" saved from a death peril a gentleman while he was occupied with abusing me and calling all my writings LIES. It is called "The Mysterious Hand"—Madame Blavatsky's *slender* materialised form was recognised, the hand likewise, the voice ditto. My aunt is in a funk and a religious tremor on this occasion. Writes to me to enquire whether it is I, or the Chozain (Master) who did it. All mystic Petersburg is in a fever; and the Holy *Synod* deliberating whether they should not send me some Holy water. A Tibetan who came back with the Prjivolsky expedition (or after it)—a "plant doctor" they call him as he produces mysterious cures with simples, told Soloviev and others it appears, that they were all fools and the SPR asses and imbeciles, since all *educated* Tibet and China know of the existence of the "Brotherhood of the Snowy Range," I am accused of having invented; and that he, himself, knows several Masters personally. And when asked by General Lvov what he knew about the London Psychic R. Society since he had never been in Europe before, he laughed and told the General "looking him straight between the eyebrows" that there was not a book of any importance *pro* or *contra* Tibet and its *wise men* that remained unknown in Tchigadze. When the General, "much struck," asked him if that Brotherhood would not help Russia against England—the "Doctor" laughed again. He said England or Russia were all one for the "Wise Men"; they left both to their respective *Karma*.[40]

Thus H. P. Blavatsky was as early as 1887 a topic of debate in "mystic Petersburg" and received the prestigious support of the Tibetan Dr. Badmaev, soon to become notorious for the favor he received at court and his friendship with Rasputin. In Odessa, H.P.B.'s aunt, Madame N. A. Fadeyev, organized a Theosophical Lodge in the early 1880s. In St. Petersburg, H.P.B.'s sister, Vera Jelikovsky, recalled various supernatural incidents of their common childhood and even claimed that the fledgling Theosophist had been taken under the ample wing of Orthodoxy. In 1860, she wrote, she and her sister had left for the Caucasus to visit their grandparents. At Zadonsk they attended Mass celebrated by Metropolitan Isidore of Kiev, whom they had known in their childhood when Isidore had been Exarch of Georgia. After Mass, Isidore recognized them and asked them to visit him. Their conversation was interrupted by a tremendous outbreak of spirit rapping and poltergeist activity. Isidore "had read a good deal about the so-called 'spiritual' manifestations, and on seeing a huge arm-chair gliding toward him laughed, and felt a good deal interested in this phenomenon." The Metropolitan had kept the sisters talking for over three hours. He dismissed them with a blessing and the admonition to Helena to use her powers with discretion, as he felt sure they were given her for some purpose. Not unexpectedly, Madame Jelikovsky was not allowed to publish in full this account which she submitted to *Rebus*.[41]

Despite her natural desire to prove the respectable status of Theosophy, there is little reason to doubt her story of Isidore's reaction. Russian Orthodoxy was able to adapt itself to innumerable spiritual standpoints and was unlikely to be baffled by a mere poltergeist. But because of the strictness of the rule maintained by Pobedonstsev and the Holy Synod, the little Theosophical groups had to depend for their contact with the outside world on travelers acting as colporteurs. Of these the chief was Madame Nina de Gernet, who smuggled books across the frontier to groups in Moscow, St. Petersburg, Kiev, Kharkov, and Vladikavkaz. In 1902 two Russian visitors to the Theosophical Convention formed a new group in St. Petersburg. Three years later further circles sprang up including a publishing organization, and in 1908 the Theosophists finally managed to register themselves legally by abandoning mention of all objects other than that of universal brotherhood. This itself gave the policemen of the *Okhrana* some qualms, but it avoided the classification of "sect" and the consequent hurdle of the Holy Synod.[42]

Theosophy thus entered into the life of the Russian intelligentsia and could be found, for example, in the concourse of musicians around the Moscow Conservatoire. Meanwhile the Symbolists adopted the magical beliefs of their French counterparts. Alexander Blok declared that he had prophetic visions. Valery Bryussov dabbled in hypnotism and seems to have played Svengali to a woman who was having an affair with Andrei Bely—this ended with the girl trying to shoot both Bely and Bryussov and eventually passing through morphine addiction to suicide. As in the West, mockery was not entirely absent. The writer Alexey Remizov noted in his diary for 28 September 1905: "At Vyacheslav Ivanov's there was Spiritualism. O. Dymov was the medium; while I took the villain's part—scratched like a cat, and tapped like an imp of Satan. It was very terrible." Nicholas Berdyaev, who had been associated both with Ivanov and Merezhkovsky, was introduced to occultism by his brother, a spirit medium controlled by Himalayan masters. Berdyaev's dislike of matters occult never saved him from their obtrusion. At the end of December 1913, he was visited by a Dr. Lubeck of the "Order of the White Brothers," who transmitted the benediction of the order and prophesied that he would become a professor at Moscow University (which happened in 1920, against all the odds, for Berdyaev had no degree). Berdyaev was present at the most famous of the musical soirées organized by the Russian intelligentsia. One evening in the house of Nicolai Minsky, a group of Symbolists met to perform a rite which tried to imitate the Mysteries of Dionysios and induce ecstasy in the participants. This gave rise to all sorts of rumors about "black masses." The occultist intelligentsia soon began to see in their traditional Russian *startsy* the "initiates" of Western occultism. There then arose a belief in the existence of "hidden *startsy*." The cult of the holy men was interpreted as "the esoteric tradition in Orthodoxy."[43]

The branch of Western occultism which made the greatest headway in Symbolist circles was the Anthroposophy of Rudolf Steiner. Steiner's second wife and earliest colleague in building up his Anthroposophical movement was herself a Balt, whose family had moved to St. Petersburg in 1877, ten years after her birth. Marie von Sivers was forbidden to study by her family, and after a period living with a brother who was dabbling in social reform, she left for Paris to learn to act. She arrived in 1895, at the high point of the occult revival, and became influenced by the Theosophist Edouard Schuré. On her return to St. Petersburg Marie von Sivers found it impossible to go on the stage because of social and family pressure. She left for

Berlin, where she gave up acting as the result of disillusionment at theatrical chicanery and turned instead to Theosophy and Steiner. She naturally transmitted her enthusiasm to her contacts in Russia. In her own words, "a stream of friends began to flow to Berlin, hoping to hear more." In 1905 a group came to hear a lecture course in Marie von Sivers's rooms, and arrangements were made for Steiner to go to Russia in June 1906 to give a cycle of talks on an estate at Kaluga. But the 1905 Revolution intervened, and many of the illuminated intelligentsia chose voluntary exile rather than face disappointment at home. The result was that the lectures were given in Paris, the exile capital, when Steiner was attending the Theosophical conference in 1906. It was this unofficial series of lectures that really established the specialist on Goethe as a prophet in his own right. Of the Russian Symbolists and mystics, there came Merezhkovsky, Zenaida Hippius, Konstantin Balmont, and Nicolai Minsky.[44]

Other devotees of Steiner at one time or another were Andrei Bely, his companion Asya Turgenev, their friend the poet Kobylinsky-Ellis, and Vyacheslav Ivanov. Ivanov used the Steinerite conception of Lucifer and Ahriman. According to Berdyaev, he was heavily under the influence of Steiner's chief Russian representative, Alexandra Mintslova, who seems to have fished successfully in the waters around the Symbolist publishing house Musaget. Berdyaev, who knew her well and disliked her, thought she looked like Madame Blavatsky and once had a strange vision of her unattractive face, which he only succeeded in banishing by the greatest effort. He has also recorded the legends which surrounded her disappearance:

> A few days after her return to Moscow from the Crimea she went to the Kuznetsky Bridge with a woman friend of hers with whom she was staying. Her friend turned away for a moment, and then found that Mintslova had disappeared. No one knew where she had gone, and she was never seen again. This contributed still more to her mysterious reputation. Some believed that she had gone into hiding in a Roman Catholic convent somewhere in Western Europe, a place which was associated with the Rosicrucians; others thought that she had committed suicide because Steiner had condemned her for failing to fulfil her mission in Russia.
>
> People like Mintslova could only exercise influence in the atmosphere which prevailed among the cultural elite of that

time impelled as it was by occult moods, and seeking as it did intimate acquaintance with the secrets of the cosmos.[45]

Andrei Bely and his companion Asya (who was a niece of Turgenev) became attracted to the occult through a journey to Egypt and the Holy Land in the winter of 1910-11. On their return to Moscow, they gravitated into Anthroposophical circles, and it seems that the turning point was a course of lectures that Steiner gave at Helsingfors in 1913 especially for the Russians. The next year the Belys left for Dornach, and although the poet himself was to return to Russia, full of disillusionment at the "half-crazy occult old maids," he never lost his interest in Anthroposophy and married another former follower of Steiner. Asya Turgenev stayed at Dornach, where she engraved the glass for the windows of the second Goetheanum. Kobylinsky-Ellis also visited Dornach, and he was probably the "Dr. Kobylinsky from Berlin" who wrote to *Psychische Studien* in 1917 complaining that Steiner's exercises had given him heart disease. He stigmatized Anthroposophy as a dangerous combination of "Manicheism and Cabalistic magic with its always attendant cynicism, cunning, avarice and sexual magic." It is interesting, also, that two more vociferous opponents of Anthroposophy—they had, of course, been at one time firmly attached to Steiner—were also Russians. *Hofrat* Max Seiling, whose brochures furnished the basis for much shouting about "sexual magic," was a Russo-German; and Grigori Schwarz-Bostunitsch was an "honorary German" who came straight from the ranks of the illuminated Russian intelligentsia. He recalled meeting the poetess Olga Forsch-Komarova in Kiev in 1919 after she had been on a course at Dornach: "She was not to be recognized, and above all, scarcely to be understood—she struggled for speech like Steiner."[46]

If the intelligentsia occupied themselves with otherworldly realities, it is notorious that fashionable society and the court did the same. Here the interest was on a much more primitive level, lacking the poetic flights of mystical logic that characterize the Decadent philosophers and concerned, rather, with the cultivation of Orthodox holy men and Spiritualistic miracles. Yet the fascination with the mystical was equally intense. The French ambassador wrote in his diary for December 1915:

> I called on Mme S—for tea rather late this evening. Her company numbered about a dozen. Conversation was general, and very lively. The subjects of discussion were spiritualism, ghosts, palmistry, divination, telepathy, the transmigration of souls and sorcery. Nearly every man and woman present told some personal anecdote or incident received from direct tradition. These agitating problems had been warmly debated for two hours already, so after smoking a cigarette I retired, as once a conversation of this kind is in full swing it may last until morning.[47]

There were two chief cliques of intermediaries between the society of "mystic Petersburg" in general and the Imperial Court. For a long time, Tsar Nicholas II lived under the influence of the Grand Duke Nicholas Nikolaievitch and consequently of the "Montenegrin princesses" who were his wife and sister-in-law. They had as their object little more than to ingratiate themselves with the imperial couple. The names of the Montenegrins were Militza—who was married to the Grand Duke Peter Nikolaievitch—and Anastasia—who from 1907 was the wife of the Grand Duke Nicholas. Both were passionately interested in the occult. To them people hoping to secure imperial favor through the presence of a particular "holy man" at court would send their protégés. The group which gathered in the "black Ignatiev salon" of whom the center was Count Alexander Pavlovitch Ignatiev, were also hawkers of mystical wares.[48]

The first guru of Nicholas and Alexandra was the orthodox John of Kronstadt, who had been summoned back to the deathbed of the previous tsar after some years in disfavor. But, like the intelligentsia, the court was attracted by the teachers which the occult revival had spawned in other lands. It was natural that political ties with France should place the nobly born as well as the intellectuals in contact with the flourishing body of Cabalists, Rosicrucians, and thaumaturges that quartered in the country. The two French magi who for a time exercised great influence at Tsarskoe Selo were Papus—the most famous popularizer of Hermetic doctrines during the Belle Epoque—and his "spiritual master," who was known as "Monsieur Phillippe."[49]

Papus was the pen name of Dr. Gérard Encausse (1865-1916), a member and often the instigator of many of the occult groups of his time. He had quarreled with the French Theosophists, with whom he had made an inauspicious debut; he was on the Supreme Council of Stanislas de Guaita's *Ordre Kabbalistique de la Rose-Croix*; and he directed the leading French occult review, *L'Initiation*. His own particular specialties were Martinism—a philosophy stemming from the speculations of two eighteenth-century occultists—and the propagation of the complicated theories of his "intellectual master," the Marquis de Saint-Yves d'Alveydre. Papus, in fact, held in his hands as many of the threads of French esotericism as he could possibly manage. When the tsar and the tsaritsa visited France in 1896, it was he who sent them a greeting on behalf of "the French Spiritualists," hoping that the tsar would "immortalize his Empire by its total union with Divine Providence." This greeting was reminiscent of the hopes of mystics at the time of Tsar Alexander I's Holy Alliance and was evidence that visions of Slav Messianism, contracted through Polish influence, continued to haunt the Occult Underground of the West. The message of Papus was acknowledged by the Russian embassy. It was probably this contact that led to his first trip to Russia in the summer of 1901, accompanied by Count Muraviev-Amursky, the Russian military agent in Paris. Papus was introduced to the tsar that year by the Grand Duke Nicholas, and it was rumored that he set up a lodge of his Martinist Order in St. Petersburg with the tsar as the president of the "Unknown Superiors" who controlled it.[50] If this is true, Papus was merely reviving devotion to a philosophy that had flourished in Russia at the turn of the 18th and 19th centuries before being suppressed.

Through Papus, the Montenegrins and then the Imperial family came to know of his "spiritual master," Philippe. It is not clear whether they traveled together to Russia in 1901 or whether Philippe's visit of that year was independent. His invitation seems to have come through the Grand Duke Vladimir, and Philippe did not meet the tsar and the tsaritsa until September 1901 in the Palace of Compiégne, where the introduction was made by the Montenegrins. Muraviev-Amursky, however, was a fervent admirer of Philippe. As Count Witte wrote: "There is no doubt but that the count was practically out of his mind. He tried to involve us in a quarrel with the republican government which he hated wholeheartedly." By Witte's account, Muraviev and the other devotees of Monsieur Philippe believed that the little *Lyonais* had not been born in ordinary fashion but had descended from heaven and would leave in the same manner. It is most likely that Papus put Muraviev-Amursky and his other Russian contacts in touch with Philippe inadvertently; for he is on record as protesting to Philippe—who was jealous of his privacy—that he had never named him specifically in Russia, although he had talked of his wonderful "unknown Master." This was quite enough for the Slav mystics. They pursued Philippe throughout 1901 and began the process of escalating his reputation which culminated in the introduction to the tsar and tsaritsa. Philippe was invited to pay a second visit to Russia, and a house was set aside for him at the imperial palace at Tsarskoe Selo.[51] During this single visit to the court in 1902, Philippe exercised an extraordinary influence over his Imperial patrons.

The real name of Monsieur Philippe is somewhat in dispute. He was born to two Savoy peasants in 1849: his father was Joseph Philippe and his mother Marie Vachod. From the age of thirteen he had shown miraculous powers of healing. It was natural that the wonder-worker of Lyon was taken up by the mystics of the capital. By 1895, Philippe was established as the head of a school of magnetism and massage at Lyon, which was linked to a similar establishment at Paris over which Papus presided; and Papus himself was pledged to the Christian mysticism of his "spiritual master." Legends grew up of Philippe's powers that far exceeded those of curing the sick. Papus claimed that he had witnessed Philippe call down the lightning; and two other Paris occultists were astonished by his sudden appearance in a locked room to carry off a bundle of proofs.

Such legends multiplied in Russia. Philippe—who had undergone ceaseless harassment in France for practicing medicine without a license—was medically qualified by express order of the tsar. The tsar appointed him president of a commission for sanitary inspection and forced the St. Petersburg Military Academy to grant him the status of an army doctor. Nicholas had already failed to persuade the French government to confer a diploma on Philippe; but in Russia, where the tsar was master, the thaumaturge was promoted from the rank he held in Lyon (captain of the fire brigade) to that of general and member of the Council of State.

Philippe's hold over the Imperial couple is easily explained. Nicholas was a weak and isolated figure, whose solace was found in mysticism. His wife fostered this taste, which corresponded to her own. And both Nicholas and Alexandra needed a son, feeling the absence of a tsarevich all the more acutely because of the mounting threat to the autocracy. Prayers to their recently canonized Saint Seraphim of Saratov had gone unanswered. The ministrations of a Dr. Schrenk from Vienna proved ineffectual. Even the holy John of Kronstadt had failed in his intercessions, but (according to one story(he had appeared to salute Philippe as an equal, greeting the little man as "brother" in preference to the notables who surrounded him. Philippe had joined some daring to this apostolic succession. He actually predicted the birth of a son. Indeed, for some time it seemed that he was at once to be proved correct; for the suggestible Alexandra imagined herself into a hysterical pseudo-pregnancy and even went through the motions of going into confinement before subjecting herself to conventional medical opinion. Such an atmosphere easily explains the stories about Philippe—such as that of the day when he made himself invisible for fear of causing the tsaritsa the embarrassment of being seen with a civilian in her carriage at a military review.[52]

To his adroit handling of a ready-made position, Philippe added political advice, which told the tsar and the tsaritsa what they wanted to hear: they must not give in to demands for a constitution. Philippe was given rank and honors and presented with an imposing automobile. He really does not seem to have solicited gifts. (He had, anyway, small need for material profits from his association with crowned heads, as he had married the daughter of a rich industrialist in 1877.) But his favored position naturally made him enemies, who forced the tsar not to recall Philippe from Lyon after his single visit of 1902. The relationship between the court and Philippe continued by correspondence until the death of the healer in 1905, and the letters of the tsar and the tsaritsa bear witness to their continuing regard for their exiled mentor. Papus, on the other hand, was able to return to Russia in 1905 and 1906, and in 1904 his *Traité élémentaire de science occulte* was published in translation in St. Petersburg. On coming home from six months in Russia, he is said to have remarked to his neighbor: "Those people over there are mad; they are at the mercy of the first rogue who knows how to pander to their obsession; they are sliding towards the abyss."[53]

After the enforced exile of Philippe, seekers for power and influence continued to try to insinuate their prophets into the palace. For a short time, Nicholas hoped for something from the fortune-telling Matronushka the Barefooted, who made predictions for Petersburg servant girls; but Matronushka died in 1908. Then the imperial couple made a pilgrimage to the irascible Pasha Sarovskaya, who lived in a monastery in the middle of the Tambov forests and was said to be 110 years old. Pasha at first wanted to beat her exalted visitors and to send them away, but in the end she made a rather grudging prediction of a son. The Grand Duke Michael discovered an illiterate soldier from Kuban called Vasily Tkachenko who strode about Russia armed with an immense silver cross. This possession so excited the envy of the countless rival holy men that he required a special safe-conduct from the tsar. After the death of Vasily in a drinking bout came the supremacy of Mitya the Blissful, (otherwise Mitya Kozelsky) who was discovered by the monks of Optina Pustyn. Mitya's inarticulate grunts and cries were interpreted "by special illumination" by the sexton of Optina. According to one story, Mitya first arrived in the Ignatiev salon and was introduced to the Montenegrins by Prince Obelensky; but possibly he was introduced by the Archimandrite Theophanes, who was soon to discover Rasputin. The clairvoyant and his interpreter frightened the tsaritsa, and Mitya was replaced by Daria Ossipova, an imbecile from the estate of General Orlov who had periodic fits of violence. When Daria arrived at Tsarskoe Selo, the tsaritsa did in fact give birth, and the reputation of the "holy fool" for a time stood high.[54]

But the two figures who exercised the greatest influence over the court and so over the minds of the tsar's enemies were the Tibetan Badmaev and the notorious Rasputin. To speak of them at all requires some apology; but just because Rasputin has become so notorious it has often been forgotten that he was part of a broad spectrum of irrationalist opinion and that his opponents shared many of the assumptions of his supporters. We have seen already how Badmaev lent his authority to the claims of Madame Blavatsky;

it is also interesting to observe how the writer and prophet of the cosmic orgasm, Vasily Rozanov, could mention—certainly not casually, but not as something completely out of the way—how he met Rasputin at a party.

> He was dancing with a married woman, with whom he "lived" and in the presence of her husband was talking of it: "See, his wife loves me, and her husband too loves me!" I came up to him and said: "Why did you leave so soon last time?" (That was in the house of Father Yaroslav with whose wife Rasputin also lived, and Father Yaroslav approved of it. Altogether it was a sort of Paradise, the Eden of a community of wives and children). And he replied: "Because I got *frightened* of you." Upon my word, I felt bewildered.[55]

Court, intelligentsia, and church came in contact with the holy man as a matter of course. Grigory Rasputin's introduction followed the manner of the other prophets. At the age of twenty-eight Rasputin had repented of his sinful existence and taken to wandering about Russia. In the course of his travels he received the benediction of John of Kronstadt. This was probably the chief factor which recommended him to the Archimandrite Theophanes, who took Rasputin to visit the Montenegrin Grand Duchess Militza and her husband at Easter 1905. From this point Rasputin's rise was rapid and need not be followed. Between his introduction to the imperial family and his murder in 1917 there was only one notable check to his career: an attempt in 1912 to have him indicted. Like Philippe, Rasputin attracted his enemies, drawn mostly from moderate supporters of the monarchy, who saw their cherished institution brought into disrepute. It is, accordingly, difficult to know how much to credit the stories of Rasputin's orgies with his high society followers. To some extent they are probably true: the Siberian peasant certainly led an interesting and active sexual life, and his devotees did include a number of high-ranking and probably psychopathic ladies. Among these were the widow of a state councillor and the strange Olga Lochtina, who for a time acted as Rasputin's interpreter and went about in a hat of camel's hair inscribed with the text: "In me lies all power. Hallelujah!" The *staretz* was commonly rumored to be a *Khlyst* and to have been photographed in the middle of his heretical congregation. Again, there is nothing inherently unlikely in this; but the allegations were used to provide a religious motive for Rasputin's satyriasis and further to discredit his circle. For the *Khlysts* were thought to indulge in unbridled sexual license; yet there is little evidence other than the accusations of their enemies that they in fact did so.[56]

In the strange world of Russian sects, nothing is quite impossible.* But it is as well not to make too much of the orgies of Rasputin and to see most of the accusations as inspired by his opponents. Their mythology extended to a theatrical plot which was supposed to involve Rasputin, the Tibetan Badmaev, and the tsaritsa's confidante, Anna Vyrubova.

Shamzaran Badmaev was one of the most striking of the mystagogues who clustered round the court. He was a Buriat Mongol who had been educated at Irkutsk and St. Petersburg; he had been converted to Orthodoxy with the Tsar Alexander III acting as godfather.

From 1875 to 1893 he had held a post in the Ministry of Foreign Affairs and lectured on Mongolian at St. Petersburg University. His considerable political expertise was said to have been used to secure the Mongol tribes in the Russo-Japanese War. Badmaev's brother, Zaltin, had set up shop as an herbalist in St. Petersburg in the 1860s, and when Shamzaran Badmaev appeared in the capital, he quickly turned this establishment into a fashionable clinic of "Oriental medicine," where he prepared mysterious herbal remedies with exotic names. It is said that he entered political information on his patients' files. His powers of survival were great, and his position was unaffected by the advent of Grigory Rasputin. It was put about that Badmaev was poisoning the tsarevich with "a yellow powder" to ensure that Rasputin's services as a healer remained in demand. Their supposed confederate was the friend of the tsaritsa, Anna Vyrubova, and the mysterious conspiracy was referred to as the "Dark Forces" influencing the throne.[57] The Dark Forces—depending on the political stance of the accuser—could also be seen as in league with another conspiracy: the alliance of Jews and Freemasons, aiming at world domination.

---

*I have it on emigré authority that some of the mystics have recently turned their devotion in the direction of the atom bomb.

Needless to say, both conspiracies existed only in the minds of their detectors. The absurdity of believing that Anna Vyrubova's simple, uncritical devotion to the tsaritsa would lend itself to such a complex deception must be obvious to anyone who has read the evidence; and the unwillingness to admit the real nature of the illness of the heir to the throne is an interesting indication of anxiety.[58] The most significant part of this theory is the light it throws on the mentality of those who devised it. Created for public consumption, it was still fostered by those who believed, and the nature of this belief in the "Dark Forces" was superstitious in the extreme. It could grow only in an atmosphere in which the activities of mystics were commonplace and the vocabulary of the supernatural mingled with that of the everyday. It also found its way into politics. My next chapter will be concerned with a specific and disastrously influential brand of illuminated politics; the rest of this chapter will survey briefly some more general aspects of the impact of Slavonic irrationalists on the outside world.

The fissures in the intellectual landscape of Western Europe through which Slav irrationalism was to fall were well defined by 1917. Tolstoy and Dostoievsky, the two great obsessions of Russian literary criticism, had found their admirers in the West. From the publication of Count Melchior de Vogüé's *The Russian Novel* in Paris in 1886, the intellectual world had not been able to ignore Russian literature. The mystical tendencies which it celebrated blended so exactly with the turn-of-the-century flight from reason that the popularity of the great Russians was assured. Tolstoyan ideas, in particular, found their way into the heart of the Progressive Underground. They engendered what Péguy called "the flock of Tolstoyizing snobs" who adopted in theory the vegetarian and pacifist mysticism of the prophet of Yasnaya Polanya. Outside Russia few active Tolstoyans were found—although they would have been quite at home at Monte Verita, where indeed one of the founder members was a Tolstoyan; and Russians took part in the affairs of Monte Verita as well as in the life of Ascona.[59]

The English Progressives made contact with Tolstoy chiefly through the novelist's propaganda on behalf of the pacifist Doukhobor sect. At the turn of the century it was suffering severe persecution because of its refusal to submit to the demands of military service. A body of English Quakers made contact with the Doukhobors. The Tolstoyan V. G. Chertkov was banished for campaigning on the sect's behalf and he chose England as his country of exile. Here he set up a rather unsuccessful colony of "Doukhobors" at Purleigh in Essex, and it seems to have been this colony which once descended on Conrad Noel in London in the middle of the night. Although these Doukhobors had abandoned the belief in money, Noel noted, London hotel keepers had not, and it was his three rooms which were selected as their London base.[60] The Doukhobors proper emigrated first to Cyprus, then to Canada, where their fundamentalist fervor still periodically explodes.

The emigration after the revolution of 1917 was of a different character from the gentle optimism that had earlier characterized the Tolstoyans. And it found the Western Underground itself less transcendental, less sanguine, and more ready to adopt solutions of an extremist and even desperate nature. The role of the emigrés was threefold: as witnesses to the national tragedy and reminders of the insecurity which also troubled the West; as bearers of an illuminated culture that was preoccupied with Apocalypse; and as carriers of the plague of conspiracy-theory politics. Excluded from the citadel of dialectical materialism, the Russian idealists brought their inheritance with them.

The capitals of the European emigration were Berlin, Munich, and Paris, although there were colonies everywhere that work could be found. The emigrants scattered to Prague, for a time to Harbin in the Far East; and then, as economic pressure forced them out of their temporary refuges, increasingly to North and South America. Zenaida Hippius wrote that modern Russian literature had been bodily expelled—"whatever names you think of, they are all here." In Paris, Berlin, Prague, Stockholm, Sofia, and even in America and China, Russian publishing houses were established. In Berlin alone there were over fifty. The German capital at one time harbored Gorky, Remizov, Bely, Minsky, and hundreds more literati. In Paris lived Merezhkovsky, Hippius, Balmont, and Bunin. The Orthodox Church was naturally well represented among the exiles, as were the religious philosophers who counted among themselves several converts from Marxism, such as Nicholas Berdyaev, Sergei Bulgakov, and Simon Frank. The exotic nature of Orthodoxy was noticed by Western Europeans. "Let us only note," wrote one Frenchman, "that Slav mysticism sometimes lends itself to such regrettable deformities that one could not reasonably subscribe to it without reservations."

The material misery of the emigrés only increased their irrationalist tendencies. In 1921 the Orthodox Church in exile held a council at Karlovtsy in Yugoslavia, which deplored the increasing sectarianism among exiled Russians. It condemned their susceptibility to "occultism, Theosophy, Spiritualism and other immoral Eastern cults, Freemasonry and its organizations, especially the YMCA . . . socialism and communism and anti-Christian sects like adventism and Anabaptism." As a link between Orthodoxy and the Anglo-Catholic wing of the Church of England, the Fellowship of St. Alban and St. Sergius was founded; and in France the Russian Brotherhood of St. Photius began translating the Orthodox liturgy into French.[61]

The attempt to create a French Orthodoxy is interesting, as it shows the sort of people attracted by the unfamiliar traditions of the Russians. The translation of the liturgy was carried out by the Viscount Serge d'Hotman de Villiers. His Russian mother was a relation of Madame Blavatsky, and her Paris salons had been the center for the French occultists gathered round Charles Melinge ("Alta"), a member of Stanislas de Guaita's *Rose-Croix*. In 1927 the first French liturgy was celebrated. Three years later the group took over a congregation at Nantes descended from the Polish Mariavite Order that had been condemned by the Papacy for heresy and sexual irregularities. The chief of this group, one Georges Verdin, was named by the Orthodox hierarchy as head of the French rite. Verdin believed that since the coming of the Holy Spirit at Whitsun 1923 the members of his sect had lived in a state of grace. The cult possessed a center known as the "Earthly Paradise" and encouraged nudism. Verdin declared that after the tree had borne fruit which each of his followers had dedicated to them in the grounds of this earthly Paradise—his own was an apricot—they might take "mystical brides."[62] This was an extreme example, but it is suggestive. What had been perfectly acceptable in Russia became in the West rejected knowledge; and the rejected situation of the emigrés drove them into the arms of the Western Underground.

The most obvious impact of the Russian emigration was on the visual arts. But in terms of general philosophical outlook there were three concepts especially cultivated by the Russians which found a particular echo in illuminated circles in the West. These were the notion of the organic nature of the universe; the expectation of imminent apocalypse; and a pervasive hatred of materialism. The organic concept stems from Vladimir Soloviev and his researches in occult tradition; it might have been taken directly from Plotinus. The idea that the world is really a vast animal of which all humans are mere corpuscles gave rise to the ideal of social good called *sobornost,* which means something like "organic unity" or even "togetherness." From Soloviev, a historian of Russian philosophy writes, "the hypnosis of this conception has entered Russian thought, bewitching and subjugating men's minds." Some Western thinkers, recoiling from the disarray around them, had reached similar conclusions, and it was logical that those bred in the Russian religious revival should find them congenial. Thus—as one unimportant example—Vyacheslav Ivanov, the high priest of Russian symbolism, ended his life as a Catholic in Italy, and as a member of the Fascist party.[63] The corporate society could be seen as an attempt to realize the natural functional order.

Much more spectacular was the tradition of apocalypse, which stemmed from Vladimir Soloviev's expectation of Antichrist and was reinforced by the terrible experiences of the Revolution: a crisis, thought the Archpriest Sergei Bulgakov, which might "be compared in importance with the fall of Byzantium and the taking of Constantinople by the Turks."[64]

Vasily Rozanov died of starvation in the early days of the Revolution at the Sergieva monastery near Moscow. In his last fragmentary publications he expressed the current feeling of apocalypse: "Do you know, Europeans," he asked, "that the Universe is already transfigured? Your cut-and-dried categories don't exist any more. Where is jurisprudence? Where are the laws? There's nothing left of them. Where is pride? Europe is quite made of pride, Europe is proud, everything it has created comes from pride. It's not necessary! It's needed no longer. Heaven! Give us heaven! But heaven. . ."[65]

In Paris, Nicholas Berdyaev tried to make the feeling of the Russians intelligible to the West.

> Contemporary history is being wound up, an unknown era is upon us, and it must be given a name. The old measures of history are no longer serviceable as we realised with a sudden shock when the World War broke out; the more perceptive minds saw at once that the peaceable bourgeois pre-war way of life would become impossible. The rhythm of history is changing: it is becoming catastrophic.

Berdyaev proclaimed the end of the old Renaissance culture of humanism and its values and the beginning of a "New Middle Ages," an age of revived faith, which would witness the struggle of Christ and Antichrist. Like Penty in England a quarter of a century earlier, he saw the popularity of mystical and occult doctrines as presaging a new and hopeful era of the spirit. He called for a "new knighthood" for the spiritual combat, and asserted the fundamental presence of *meaning* in the cosmos. "Man is not a unit in the universe, forming part of an unrational machine, but a living member of an organic hierarchy, belonging to a real and living whole." His attack on bourgeois values is probably the most cogent of any:

> Individualism, the "atomisation" of society, the inordinate acquisitiveness of the world, indefinite over-population and the endlessness of people's needs, the lack of faith, the weakening of the spiritual life, these and other are the causes which have contributed to build up that industrial capitalist system which has changed the face of human life and broken its rhythm with nature.[66]

The critique of Established society evolved by the Western Underground was practically identical. Hatred of materialism—for the emigrés saw Bolshevism as yet another instance of dog-eat-dog—was an essential part of this outlook, and again such aspirations harmonized with those of the illuminated politicians of the West. As in the West, hatred of materialism implied, though it did not compel, distaste for rationalism as the mode of thought which had erected the detested social system. One famous emigré, Simon Frank, wrote that "Russian thought is quite definitely *anti-rationalist,*" and of this trait we have seen many examples: few, however, quite so explicit as Leo Shestov (L. I. Schwarzmann), an emigré author admired by D. H. Lawrence.

Can reason be anything but lazy? Laziness is of its very essence, as is cowardice. Open any manual of philosophy and you will soon be convinced that reason even boasts of its submissiveness, its humility, its cowardice. Reason must servilely reproduce what is "given" to it and it reproaches as the greatest of crimes every attempt at free creation. As for us human beings, we in turn must servilely obey all that reason dictates to us. And this is what is called "freedom."[67]

Within the body of anti-Establishment, antirationalist emigrés, there naturally arrived in the West some of the more exotic gurus who had inhabited "mystic Petersburg" and flourished in its unusual climate. Dmitri Merezhkovsky took his new religious consciousness (and a great bitterness) to Paris. He also saw the changing of the world at hand; more specifically, the Second Coming. An unorthodox, hypersymbolical, and often downright incomprehensible version of Christianity was elaborated. Christ, thought Merezhkovsky, was "concealed in paganism and revealed in Christianity." In much of Christian symbolism Merezhkovsky detected relics of the mystery religions of Atlantis, transmitted via Crete. He maintained that the physical body of Christ was not fully human—his features, for example, must always have been in flux between his human personality and his Sacred Self.[68] It is doubtful whether this "new Christianity" ever made any converts, although it attracted a surprising amount of notice. However, there were other systems more worthy of consideration.

Of Georgei Ivanovich Gurdjieff (c. 1877-1949) it is easy to say too little or too much.* Just before the outbreak of the First World War, this enigmatic figure had appeared in Moscow and St. Petersburg and gathered around him a band of disciples drawn chiefly from the illuminated intelligentsia. It was not known where Gurdjieff had derived the singularly comprehensive system that he taught. He began from the principle that mankind was asleep and that by following a technique of "self-remembering" man could wake up.

---

*See my forthcoming study of Gurdjieff and his movement, *The Harmonious Circle.* This full-length study must excuse the disproportionate space given here to some comparatively unimportant figures.

This is not the place for an examination of the details of Gurdjieff's system, which probably originates in a combination of Western occultism and certain Oriental doctrines. The ideas seem to represent a restatement of traditional doctrine in the language of the 20th century. In this aspect the work of Gurdjieff is comparable to that of Jung. Gurdjieff himself disliked occultists and Theosophists, regarding such groups as breeding grounds of delusion. But he discovered that his ideas met with an encouraging response in such circles. When this remarkable man emerged from the débris of revolutionary Russia, by the way of an astonishing spiritual and physical obstacle course in his native Caucasus, he brought with him a small group of disciples whose way toward him had led through the tortuous mysticism of the illuminated intelligentsia.

This was particularly true of the man through whom Gurdjieff was to become most widely known: P. D. Ouspensky. Ouspensky had been intimately connected with the Theosophists, and just before he met Gurdjieff he had embarked on a tour of the world during which he had visited the Theosophical headquarters at Adyar. He was a friend of A. L. Volynsky, the Symbolist critic, and his profession as a journalist had led him to an extensive acquaintance with the intellectual underworld of Moscow. When Gurdjieff and his disciples decided to leave Russia, Ouspensky broke with his former master and went to London. Gurdjieff established himself at Fontainebleau, near Paris. By way of Ouspensky's lectures, English idealists went to work at Gurdjieff's Institute for the Harmonious Development of Man. Two already mentioned in connection with the guildsmen were A. R. Orage and Rowland Kenney. There was also Katharine Mansfield, who spent her last weeks at Fontainebleau, and Maurice Nicoll, a pupil of Jung. Later, Orage went to America, where the tantalizing theories he expounded attracted other followers, like Jane Heap and Margaret Anderson of the Chicago *Little Review.* Later still, Gurdjieff collected French disciples, such as the writer René Daumal; and through the still-increasing body of his followers, his ideas have become remarkably widespread.[69]

There was a natural link between the emigré Russian intellectual Ouspensky and the idealists who had grown up in comparable traditions in the West. Orage, with his Theosophical background, was an obvious candidate for conversion. But, in general, the idealistic Underground had inherited a sufficient quantity of 19th-century occultism to make the transition from National Guilds to Gurdjieff less of a puzzle than it might appear. Nor was it inconsistent when in 1930 Orage returned from preaching the word in the United States and immediately took up anew the cause of Social Credit. There are certain ideas which are *necessarily* part of the Underground, and the system of Gurdjieff found a hearing in the same circles that—had their attention been directed to political problems—would have felt attracted to theories of effecting a spiritual revolution or to the movement of a John Hargrave.

If Gurdjieff and Ouspensky influenced the idealists of Western Europe and America, Central Europe found a source of inspiration in the philosophy of another casualty of the Russian Revolution, the Baltic Count Keyserling.

Balts occupy a quite unusual place in the story of European irrationalism. Their mystical reputation can be substantiated but not fully explained. We have already met Marie von Sivers and Grigory Schwartz-Bostunitch in connection with Anthroposophy and "mad Baron Rechenberg" at Monte Verita. Natives of the Baltic countries will recur in the following pages. To the turn-of-the-century flight from reason, the Balts had contributed the figure of Count Eric Stenbock, whose decadent occultism had decorated the scenery of the London '90s. When Ludwig Klages and his colleagues founded their German Graphological Society in Munich, they discovered an immense body of support in lands under Russian domination, and particularly in the Baltic and Polish areas. A relation of Keyserling, Baroness Isabelle Ungern-Sternberg, became a vice-president of the society. In part the Balts—often with a dual allegiance to Russia and Germany—were the representatives of Russian culture most often seen in German-speaking lands, and consequently they had fastened on to them the mystical reputation that properly belonged more generally to the nation which found them such useful administrators. In part, the enduring primitivism of Baltic peasant culture may have provided a source of irrationalist speculation. The chief cause of Baltic mysticism was probably the upheavals of the 18th century, when a series of Jewish prophets attempted to popularize the esoteric doctrines of the Cabala and in so doing contributed to the rise of

Polish Messianism.⁷⁰ A residue of mysticism dating from these episodes is the likeliest source for the Baltic propensity to the occult.

In Hermann Keyserling (1880-1947) the Baltic lands provided the most influential guru of Central Europe between 1918 and 1933. Keyserling's readiness to investigate areas that more cautious men avoided came from his Baltic background, and the cosmopolitan irrationalism of the 1890s. The philosopher remembered that "from 1898 to 1900 I was beyond doubt the most unspiritual, the crudest type of animal among the *Korps-studenten* of Dorpat."⁷¹ In 1900 the young aristocrat nearly died from a dueling wound, and the shock turned his mind toward more philosophical pursuits. From Dorpat he went to study at Heidelberg and Vienna. On his very first day in the Austrian capital, he met Houston Stewart Chamberlain, the strange and influential son of a British admiral, whose book *The Foundations of the Nineteenth Century* was published in 1900 (and was responsible for so much later theorizing about the predestined conflict of the German and Jewish races). In 1904 Chamberlain dedicated a book on Kant to Keyserling; but the count never shared Chamberlain's racist ideas and their relationship foundered after the older man's marriage to Eva Wagner. During Keyserling's time in Vienna, he formed part of a reading circle organized by Chamberlain, of which another member was Rudolf Kassner (1873-1959). Kassner was a gifted writer of mystical inclinations whose first publication in 1900 introduced the poetry of Blake and the pre-Raphaelites to Germany. He was a confirmed Neo-Platonist—a school of thought that occupies a central position in occult Tradition—and passed his enthusiasm on to Keyserling. After 1908 Kassner traveled widely in the East and came under the spell of Indian metaphysics; in the German-speaking countries he is remembered as the rediscoverer of physiognomy, the "science" of reading the character from the face. Kassner's physiognomy was of a distinctly religious nature; he called it "rhythmical" physiognomy as opposed to "rational" physiognomy, and he contrived to press his science into the service of an ill-defined "Kingdom of ultimate unity."⁷² From this Viennese friendship with the leading theoretician of German racism and a notable adept of rejected knowledge, Keyserling passed on to Paris.

Nowhere did the count ever stray far from the paths of the occult.

About this period he met at Bayreuth a beautiful Irishwoman with whom he fell in love. Together they traveled to Scotland where Keyserling sat up all night by a lochside waiting for a kelpie. In Chartres the pair spent a "mystical Christmas" and Keyserling had a religious experience in the cathedral, which he later came to consider the origin of all his work. Of the women whom Keyserling regarded as the most important influences on his life at least one other was devoted to the occult.[73]

Apart from indulging in unworldly love affairs, Keyserling wrote several philosophical works before setting out in 1911 to travel around the world. On his return he spent six years on his estate in Estonia writing the book that was to make him famous. The rambling but impressive *Travel Diary of a Philosopher* records at length its author's attempts to capture the inner experience of the countries he visited. It ends with the conclusion that "the essential truth lives beyond the sphere of definite manifestation" and that freedom depends on the feeling of oneness with the whole of nature.

During his pilgrimage, Keyserling settled for a time in Adyar at the invitation of Annie Besant, and his musings on Theosophy and occultism in general provide a revealing insight into his attitude to life. "I have been interested for years in the secret doctrine of antiquity," he admitted. "All the more important documents which are available to non-members of occult societies, I have read.... anyone who like myself takes trouble to study them seriously, will come to the conclusion that it is not all imaginary, that the possibility of much of it is certain and the reality probable." Keyserling was inclined to believe in the gorgeous pictures painted by Bishop Leadbeater of the world beyond the senses and thought it probable that the spirit if not the letter of Theosophy would one day be accepted by "the majority of men."

> Theo- and Anthro-posophy, New Thought, Christian Science, the New Gnosis, Vivekananda's Vedanta, the Neo-Persian and Indo-Islamic Esotericism, not to mention those of the Hindus and the Buddhists, the Bahai system, the professed faith of the various spiritualistic and occult circles, and even the Freemasons all start from essentially the same basis, and their movements are certain to have a greater future than official Christianity.[74]

The basis of all religious belief, Keyserling decided, was *self-realization*. His subsequent sorties in a variety of philosophical directions were all directed toward achieving or helping others to achieve this goal. In 1918 the count lost his estates when the Baltic countries caught up with the Russian revolution, and he fled to Germany where he married a granddaughter of Bismarck.

Next year the publication of the *Travel Diary* won him an immense public in Germany. He wrote: "The vital effect of the *Travel Diary* soon showed that my personal problem had thenceforth become the problem of the whole West: that I, the outsider . . . had become a representative type." Keyserling was soon able to display his representative qualities on a stage of his own. In November 1920, the School of Wisdom at Darmstadt was opened under the patronage of the former Grand Duke Ernst Ludwig of Hesse. Keyserling's vision of his center was indefinite and ambitious. "Darmstadt in no wise represents a fixed program, for it is nothing more or less than the living center of a new manner of life which issues from the spirit." In the disturbed atmosphere of Weimar Germany, the School of Wisdom formed for many more intellectual seekers for security the chief source of irrationalist doctrine. One of Keyserling's supporters wrote in 1934:

> That bent of German intellectuals, and particularly the younger ones among them towards one or another spiritual "craze," drove them in great numbers for a certain number of years to Darmstadt. . . . The tidal wave has now found its level; Keyserling is no longer a fashion for studious and over-enthusiastic German youth.

Once or twice a year the School of Wisdom held conferences at which Keyserling and his guest speakers lectured. Rom Landau attended one of these. Although he was impressed by the quality of the speakers, he thought the atmosphere of the conference more like that of a German provincial court than a center of a new spirituality. Most of the audience were as interested in the former grand duke as they were in the author of the *Travel Diary*.[75]

Of course, it was not just the social attractions of Darmstadt that made the congresses of the School of Wisdom so popular. The very indefiniteness and eclecticism of Keyserling's approach probably enhanced the appeal of a philosopher who never "filled a chair at any university, and philosophizes much more after the manner of ancient Athens or Alexandria than of contemporary Paris, Oxford, Heidelberg or Harvard." Keyserling considered his own life as an example of how the application of will could change what most people assumed to be innate qualities in themselves. To further his objective of self-realization, he investigated every area of rejected knowledge. "I know men who can draw from horoscopes conclusions of exactly the same reliability as from handwritings. I know others again, whom the observance of cabalistic tradition has enabled to attain what seem to be miraculous insights." He was introduced to Jungian psychology and found it personally helpful. Throughout his torrential sequence of ideas he maintained a consistent distaste for the "anti-metaphysical mass-spirit" and the perspectives of materialism and rationalism. "The superstitious belief in the omnipotence of reason" he thought had even led to "the bankruptcy of reason" which "no longer rules anything, not even high finance."[76]

Keyserling is very difficult to pin down as a thinker, and his self-obsession makes him profoundly irritating to read. His enthusiasm, his anti-rationalism, and his capacity for lecturing in four or five languages greatly extended his influence. After the Nazi seizure of power, Keyserling underwent a short period of harassment and was later forbidden to publish. Undeterred, the count began to write in French. In 1944 his house in Darmstadt was destroyed in an air raid, and he spent the last years of his life in a single room in a *pension* at Kitsbühel. His relationship with the Nazis is difficult to define: in 1934 he was claiming to have been one of the prophets of the Third Reich, but he was later summarily denounced by the Nazis themselves.[77] It seems that, like other idealists such as Johannes Müller, he took the Nazi regime as symbolic of the spiritual rebirth he had long been awaiting. A common opposition—at least in theory—to Rationalism and Materialism explains the confusion.

Gurdjieff, Ouspensky, and Keyserling are the best known of the prophets whom the Russian Revolution thrust into Western Europe. There were others; but before discussing their significance it is as well to make the point that Slav mysticism was not confined to Russia proper or its Baltic appendages. The sense of being the inheritor of Byzantium, for example, was found as keenly in Bulgaria as Russia, and it was natural that Bulgaria would produce its own occult prophet.

"The Master" Petr Deunov (1864-1944) was the son of a priestly family. His followers believe that his ministry began when the physical body of Petr Deunov was possessed by the spirit of the Master Deunov at the age of thirty-three. The sources of Deunov's teachings are various. Madame Blavatsky's Theosophy obviously played a large part, and to the Theosophical doctrine of the missions of various successive races Deunov and his followers added a superstructure of Slav Messianism. According to Deunov, the culture of the previous age (transmitted by the Anglo-Saxon branch of the white race) was passing. The new era was the predestined age of the Slavs. To support this claim his disciples cited Russian supporters of Slav Messianism like Andrei Bely, Merezhkovsky, Tolstoy, and Vladimir Soloviev as well as the Polish Messianist Hoëne-Wronski.[78] Deunov, the divine master, had descended from "Alfeola, the Star of Stars" to begin his mission in Bulgaria, a country adapted to his purposes both by the inheritance of the medieval Bogomil heretics and the presence of the Rila mountain range. Masters could only operate where the mountains were high.

Deunov also placed emphasis on the significance of astrology. The new age was the astrological age of Aquarius, and in 1914 at a congress held at Tirnovo by his Brotherhood of Bulgaria the Master announced its advent. He proclaimed the birth of "a new type of man" on earth, to coincide with the Aquarian Age. God Himself had sent Deunov to instruct man how to conduct himself in the new age, according to what the Master termed the Laws of Living Rational Life. The disciple was instructed that his chief task was to harmonize himself with the rhythm of the stars, and it seems that a form of natural magic was taught for this purpose. After 1945 the "Universal White Brotherhood" of Deunov's disciple Michael Ivanov made great headway in France; and contact between Paris and Sofia probably began in the late 1930s.[79] Deunov himself was greatly disquieted by the approaching Second World War; for, according to his astrology, the First should have closed a cycle.

International affairs and politics in general have always concerned prophets of new revelations. Gurdjieff and Ouspensky steered clear of political pronouncements, while Keyserling and Deunov contented themselves with general hints of what the ideal order might be. But two of the Slav prophets who taught in the West between the world wars were as concerned with politics as with their systems of metaphysics or their moral code. The minor figures of Wincenty Lutoslawski and Dmitri Mitrinović will serve as an introduction to more important considerations.

Wincenty Lutoslawski was born in Warsaw in 1863. In 1885 he took a degree in chemistry at the University of Dorpat, two years later acquired a degree in philosophy, and in 1898 became a Ph.D. at Helsingfors. From 1890 he lectured for three years at the University of Kazan and at the turn of the century held various appointments at Cracow, Lausanne, and Geneva. The influences on Lutoslawski were his native tradition of Polish Messianism, Russian irrationalism, and the Western occult revival. His early studies were guided by the Leibnitzean Gustav Teichmüller, who directed his attention toward H. P. Blavatsky and the Theosophical Society. In 1887 Lutoslawski could recommend to his readers H.P.B.'s *Isis Unveiled,* the writings of A. P. Sinnet, and a book of Franz Hartmann. But by 1890 he had become disillusioned with Theosophy and, in particular, with its foundress. Three years later Lutoslawski, writing from Kazan, seemed to have found a starting point for his own irrationalist system. At Kazan he claimed to have converted all his students to a belief in telepathy through experiments involving the transmission of numbers between two subjects. He thought that immortality could be scientifically proved and considered the greatest division among men was between those who knew incontrovertibly that they were to survive death and those who did not.[80]

This affirmation was made in a lecture delivered to the World's Parliament of Religions in Chicago. And in 1896, in the Chicago magazine *The Monist,* Lutoslawski issued an extraordinary appeal. His article is headed, "In Search of True Beings" and in tone is possibly unique. Lutoslawski considered himself, he wrote, "a real substance, outside time and space." He did not admit that God had created him. Other philosophers were "parts, manifestations or servants of their God—I am my own Lord." One day, he thought he might meet this God whose extensions most other people were; and he expected an alliance as between equals. Meanwhile, he hoped to meet other true beings and proclaimed a faith in an immortal Lutoslawski, who would maintain his independence of God and time "with everything that makes up my personality, memory, affections, the same aims and increased power." In the years 1897-99 he published a highly thought-of study of Plato and two expositions of his idealist individualism.

In November 1900 the true being met his God. He had given a course of lectures in Polish Messianism at Cracow. Because of its nationalistic overtones the doctrine had been banned by the Russian government, but the course had been outstandingly successful. While cleansing his body in a steam bath after this *coup,* the idea came to Lutoslawski that he might also cleanse his soul. The philosopher confessed to a friendly Franciscan and then went to Communion for the first time since 1879. At the moment of communicating he was converted, and he began to synthesize his philosophy with Christian dogma.[81]

From 1903 to 1906 Lutoslawski lectured at University College, London. "To many in England he seemed totally mad."[82] An anonymous English critic found it scarcely possible to believe that Lutoslawski also applied his theories to politics. For the philosopher had founded a party called the Philaretes, with the object of liberating Poland from Germany and Russia by presenting the controlling powers with the spectacle of a nation which was their superior in virtue.

> His Philaretes form, though not in the usual sense, a secret society, a sort of Polish religion within the Catholic pale. Men and women, calling themselves "Brothers and Sisters," after a public confession of all their lives, must swear to give up gambling and drinking, smoking and all immorality.

The critic of this Messianic politician was incredulous at the support given to the Philaretes.

> Lutoslawski's adherents are mostly young students of an extraordinary turn of mind, as may be supposed. As to their number, it cannot be computed, on account of the reticence observed; but there are certainly many more than those who openly profess that they belong to the party. Many branches of it are supposed to exist in Russian and in Prussian Poland.

He affirms—the present writer has heard him—that he gets his thoughts and inspirations directly from God. His followers, as a consequence, believe in him blindly; as a consequence too, other persons think him a heretic or a madman.[83]

Not counted among these was William James of Harvard. Professor James met Lutoslawski twice, in 1893 and 1899, and kept up a long correspondence with him. On the publication of Lutoslawski's *Seelenmacht* in 1899, James wrote that "it has a value beyond its possible defects, it is a Gospel, an Act, rather than a book." Around 1900-01 the American wasted his energies in trying to persuade the Pole to stick to theory, rather than trying to put his ideas into practice with the Philaretes. But gradually he was won over, declared his faith in Lutoslawski as "knight of the holy spirit," and in 1906 withdrew all criticism of his Polish friend's attempt to make political use of his occult experiments. James's final expressions of admiration arose from his conviction that through the methods of Yoga, Lutoslawski had contrived to tap his "deeper levels."[84]

The true being would not even take a master in the tricky Yogic exercises; he bemoaned his lack of success in finding a guru. "I have called in my prayers for such a Teacher for many years in vain," Lutoslawski wrote; "but whenever I was on the track of such persons, I was deceived, as when I saw and spoke to H. P. Blavatsky in London, or some of her friends and pupils or other so-called occultists in France, Belgium and elsewhere." "I need to know everything about everything and everybody for all times and places," he announced, at the same time declaring that he had no interest whatsoever in the business aspects of existence and rested in the serene conviction that if money were required for his sacred undertakings, it would immediately be forthcoming. He abstained from alcohol, tobacco, meat, and fish, and from sexual intercourse as well, in order to acquire the powers of "an emancipated soul." All these privations kept in view the Messianic role of Poland "the nation of Yogis," trained by Providence for a special purpose to help mankind in "the great approaching crisis when everything will be questioned and ruined."[85]

Lutoslawski's investigations turned in the direction of Western occultism, in particular toward the odd sexual doctrines of John Humphrey Noyes's Oneida community, Thomas Lake Harris, and Laurence Oliphant. After various lecturing jobs the Pole received enough money to enable him to set up an institute for the achievement of an "integral psychophysics" at Tlemcen in Algeria in December 1911. The work of this "Polish Forge" was to combine Yogic techniques with Western experiments in strengthening the will and to ensure a superhumanity to future generations. But the Algerian climate proved inhospitable, and Lutoslawski's French benefactress died soon after the psychophysicists arrived at their Forge. Lutoslawski failed to secure the chair of philosophy at Melbourne University, and he resolved to resume teaching at the University of Geneva, where he planned to move his institute.[86] He then disappeared during the First World War, and was discovered in 1919 living in a castle in Savoy.

When the Treaty of Versailles reconstituted Poland and the Russians had been driven back from its northern frontier, Lutoslawski became professor of philosophy at Wilno. In the year 1930 he was still appealing for the establishment of a Forge (six years earlier he had estimated that "a trifle of some £200,000 would be sufficient to ensure permanently its existence"). He lamented that in view of the Polish world mission only one university professor—presumably himself—taught Messianism. He saw his years of struggle fulfilled. "Having devoted fifty years since the age of fifteen to the quest for truth, I claim to have found it, and to own it at least within my own thought."[87]

A witness of Lutoslawski's triumphant latter years was the historian Arnold Toynbee. Toynbee met the Polish philosopher in Wilno in 1928. Lutoslawski greeted Toynbee and his wife with the inquiry, "Is it your habit to eat?"—explaining that he himself did not and claiming that he had once made possible stringent economics in the running of mines by reducing the food intake of the miners to a single lettuce per day. (Unfortunately the miners struck and resumed eating corned beef and potatoes.) Lutoslawski was then very much the spearhead of Polish culture in Wilno, which the Poles held in defiance of Lithuanian and Russian claims. So when he took the Toynbees to the theater it was the simplest of matters for him to remove three members of the audience from the front seats of the dress circle by whispering that he was *Lutoslawski*—and that the foreigners must see the play "in the interests of the resurrected Polish people." This heroic representative of his national traditions vanished in the upheavals of the Second World War, and even his son could discover nothing of his fate.[88]

An eccentric? A late representative of the peculiar school of Polish Messianism who naturally combined politics and mysticism, and whose small number of Western disciples counted for little compared to his followers in Poland? This is probably true, but it is significant that Messianism could flourish into the 20th century. Lutoslawski's peculiar amalgam of Slav Messianism, Yoga, and sexual doctrine has many points of comparison with the theories of Dmitri Mitrinović, around whom clustered members of the underground of English illuminated politics.

Dmitri Mitrinović was born about 1884 near Monastir in Herzegovina. He was not the only Serbian to become involved in London occult circles. Chedomile Mijatović, Serbian ambassador to London, had been noted for his interest in occult phenomena, and when Mitrinović made contact with A. R. Orage and his circle, he himself was an attaché at the Serbian embassy in London. The war had found Mitrinović in Munich, where he was studying art (he was a friend of Kandinsky), and he played a part in organizing the wartime exhibition in London of his friend and countryman the sculptor Ivan Mestrović, who shared some of his visionary ideals.[89] Edwin Muir describes Mitrinović as "a tall, dark, bullet headed Serbian with the lips of a Roman soldier." Both Edwin and Willa Muir have recorded the lively and attractive personality of the seer on his first arrival in London, when his mood allowed him to expand companionably on his themes of the objective science of criticism, cosmology, astrology, and mysticism.[90] It was Mitrinović's hope to influence those in positions of authority to adopt his plan for the salvation of mankind. Just at this time, Orage was in a limbo between his earlier Theosophy and his later adherence to Gurdjieff. As always, the *New Age* was open to articles of a mystical nature. In 1918, for example, yet another Serbian, "R. A. Vran-Gavran" —alias the Orthodox priest Nicolai Velimirović—contributed a series of mystical "London Songs" featuring a character called Buck Legion, who extolled the Unknowable God as the solution to all problems.

A. R. Orage and Dmitri Mitrinović began to collaborate on a series of articles on "World Affairs" under the pseudonym "M. M. Cosmoi." These were written in the most extravagant fashion, apocalyptic, symbolical, and displaying Mitrinović's personal vision of history as the development of a giant man. Each nation or people represented some particular organ of this great world body. To Mitrinović it seemed "that the Negro is black not because he is born in the Tropics, but because only on the Negro Continent of the Earth could he find his proper abode and vehicle, the globe of the Logos itself being the body of the Universal Man, his very body." Particular roles were attributed to Russian man as mankind's "greatest historical, purely human, promethean self-realization," and to the Aryan race which was interpreted "in the Nordic and solar sense of the First truly Born." The exotic and confusing terminology applied by Mitrinović to various organs of his world body is a great handicap in understanding him. For example, he called the doings of men in Britain "Caractacus" and of women "Boadicea." Caractacus and Boadicea Clubs were formed in 1939. Behind all the verbiage and the name coining was—according to those who knew Mitrinović well—the old Slav Messianic vision of a united Christian Europe. On top of this was piled the lumber of every sort of occultism and religion. Mitrinović admitted three revelations: first, the Vedanta, of whose spirit he thought Rudolf Steiner the modern interpreter; and second, Christianity. There was also a modern revelation he called Zenithism, whose prophets were Vladimir Soloviev and Erich Gutkind (who contributed to Mitrinović's publications after his flight from Nazi Germany). Almost any belief could be incorporated into Mitrinović's system. Thus in 1927 he founded the Adler Society and was responsible for introducing the work of that psychologist to London. Such eclecticism resulted in pronouncements that combined the language of the sexual psychologist and the seer. Mitrinović decided that the Holy Ghost was sperm; and the sin against the Holy Ghost was a sin against sperm, and unforgivable.[91]

Mitrinović's New Britain movement united inhabitants of the idealistic Underground who found themselves at odds with the causes they had earlier supported, or who had seen those causes come crashing round them. The New Britain movement was founded in 1933 out of an earlier Mitrinović creation called "the 11th Hour Group." New Britain was dedicated to a spiritual revolution. Its magazine was edited by C. B. Purdom, formerly of Garden Cities and Meher Baba, now of Mitrinović and the mission of Albion. Arthur Kitson and Major Douglas were both involved. Professor John Macmurray—who was also interested in Gryth Fyrd—united with Orage's biographer, Philip Mairet, John Middleton Murray, Stephen Graham, Odon Por, and G. D. H. Cole in the pages of New Britain's publications. Guilds, Social Credit, the theories of Silvio Gesell, and the economics of Rudolf Steiner—all found a place under Mitrinović's wing. The money reformer Frederick Soddy was one of the presiding spirits, together with the guildsman S. G. Hobson, while Montague Fordham wrote on rural reconstruction. George Lansbury contributed thoughts on usury and on Christianity, Hugh McDiarmid some poems on Social Credit and the New Order, and Orage himself returned from America to assume the joint directorate of New Britain with Mitrinović. Major-General Fuller mourned the death of Virility, Gerald Heard lectured on Eugenics, and it is possible to discover that the most engaging eugenic fanatic of all—the indomitable Edward Alexander Wilson, who escaped from a lunatic asylum and published numbers of pamphlets from both inside and outside hospitals on the problem of "surplus women"—spoke in Gower Street to the members of New Britain.[92]

Mitrinović's movement was composed of all the elements of the illuminated underground put together. Thus in 1934, when the representatives of New Britain held their conference at Glastonbury—what place could be more appropriate?—the organization was pledged to a functional society, guilds, social credit, the welfare state, a European federation, Rudolf Steiner's Threefold Commonwealth, and a restored Christianity.[93] The synthesis contrived from these doctrines was a major feat of logistics. The expense of publishing various lavish magazines was heavy, and although Purdom's *New Britain* achieved a circulation of over 32,000 copies per week, internal quarreling helped to sink the venture. The only source of consistent policy was Mitrinović. His recommendation that his followers read Merezhkovsky, Berdyaev, Blake, and Jung were interspersed with strange and urgent political pronouncements like the motto decorating on a page of *The New Atlantis* which asked—apparently with no rhyme or reason—"Is it or is it not fitting and righteous that HIS MAJESTY THE KING OF THE BELGIANS as a gentleman and a patriot of Europe should take initiative for Federation of Europe?" There was more consistency than might appear from the diverse commitments of the New Britain. All at least were united in hopes for an idealistic society and a spiritual revolution, while theories of an organic society could harmonize well with Mitrinović's guiding vision of the great organism of the world. But the Serbian prophet was not strong enough to hold his supporters together. Willa Muir has described the change she and her husband saw in their former friend when they returned to England in the 1930s and discovered New Britain emanating from Gower Street. Mitrinović had become flabby and pretentious and his self-sacrificing followers appeared exploited. The last years of Mitrinović's life were spent in illness; and in 1949 he renounced control over all his groups and organizations. His disciples had no doubt that his illnesses were connected with the state of the world.[94]

The consistent attraction of Slav irrationalism for illuminated movements in the West is shown by a brief glance at a French movement with which New Britain was allied. *L'Ordre Nouveau* kept closely in contact with New Britain, published its manifestoes in the British magazines, and sent representatives to Mitrinović's conferences. New Britain's commitment to European federalism stems from this French source. *L'Ordre Nouveau* arose out of the meetings of a group of young French intellectuals around Alexandre Marc which (from about 1928) began propaganda for a "Spiritual revolution." By 1933 they had established contact with organizations of a similar complexion. In Germany these were the National Bolshevists and Otto Strasser's Black Front. Apart from the New Britain movement, *L'Ordre Nouveau* looked with contempt on most idealistic British groups, which they thought would appear "a little puerile to Frenchmen."[95] Alexandre Marc was the pseudonym for Alexander Lipiansky, who had been born in Odessa in 1904, and who at the beginning of the discussions of *L'Ordre Nouveau* had been especially concerned with religious and spiritual problems. Among the

Catholic priests, Protestant pastors, and Orthodox clergy who took part in the initial conferences, there was room for Nicholas Berdyaev.[96]

There is a little more to this coincidence of Slav prophets and illuminated Western politicians than a personal and historical affinity. We have already discussed the possibilities of illuminated anti-Semitism, and both Mitrinović and Lutoslawski are suggestive in this connection. In January, 1934, Mitrinović inserted in his magazine *The New Atlantis* an "Urgent appeal to his Excellency the Chancellor of the Reich," in which he requested Adolf Hitler to renounce the evil ways which would lead to a catastrophic war. Mitrinović asked Hitler to believe that he was not himself hostile to the "Aryan idea"; his own culture was "predominantly German"; and the Aryan mission "is an idea, even politically and racially speaking, which is not foreign to my mind, not misunderstood by my own heart." In the winter of 1914, he wrote, he had been preparing a pan-European magazine which he hoped would lead to European federation and was first to be published in Germany under the title of *Das arische Europa*. When war was declared by Austro-Hungary on Serbia, Mitrinović was in the house of a famous man who he hoped would contribute to his enterprise: the Bayreuth home of Houston Stewart Chamberlain.[97]

The idea of the Aryan mission did not seem to lead Mitrinović into the associated heresy of anti-Semitism. On the other hand, under the pressure of severe personal stress Wincenty Lutoslawski jumped from Aryanism to its more sinister companion. In 1907 he was declaring that to concern himself with the standards of economics "would be unworthy of a true Aryan," and he had also decided—as did Houston Stewart Chamberlain—that Jesus was no Jew. In 1919 Lutoslawski announced that his two younger brothers had been killed by the retreating Russian armies because they had "discovered the secret treaty by which the Germans authorized Bolshevist propaganda in Poland"—"and nobody can deny now, after the publication of the British White Book on Bolshevism, that Jews have been the chief leaders of the criminal gang."[98]

The next chapter will show how both "Aryanism" and anti-Semitism are closely allied with the occult, and in particular with the Theosophy of Madame Blavatsky. But it remains here to indicate by two examples that not only did the ideas of Slav irrationalism infiltrate the Western Underground, but that they could also influence the conduct of armies.

One of the intellectual movements associated with the Russian intelligentsia around the time of the 1905 Revolution was called "mystical anarchism." Berdyaev was associated with this body of opinion, and its most famous spokesman was the Symbolist Vyacheslav Ivanov. The doctrine entailed a refusal to accept the conditions of the world and a Dostoievskian committment to the cause of individual liberty. Naturally it was also permeated with the spirit of the religious revival. Within the context of this mystical approach to social conditions it is possible to understand the relationship of Dmitri Merezhkovsky, Zenaida Hippius, and the terrorist Boris Savinkov.

Savinkov (born 1879) was one of the heads of the terrorist organization of the Social Revolutionary party, and it was he who organized the assassination of the Grand Duke Sergius in February 1905. He made a sensational escape from prison, where he had been confined under sentence of death, and went into exile in Paris, where Merezhkovsky and his wife had also established themselves. At this time—it was only two years after the founding of the Religious-Philosophic Assemblies—Merezhkovsky and Hippius had moved temporarily to the left. In 1907 they published quite a violent pamphlet (with Dmitri Filosofov) called *The Tsar and the Revolution.* Filosofov called for the destruction of orthodoxy and autocracy and the liberation of the free spirit of man. Merezhkovsky announced that the Old Believers were the first Russian revolutionaries and that Doukhobors and *Khlysty* posed the proper social and sexual problems, respectively. Zenaida Hippius expressed the dilemma of the principled activist. "One cannot shed blood, it's impossible. But in order that this impossibility should become real, one must!" We have it on the authority of Prince Mirsky that Savinkov came heavily under the influence of Zenaida Hippius and, to a lesser extent, of her husband. In the novel Savinkov published in 1909 under the title of *The Pale Horse,* the very language of Hippius can be discovered, slightly adapted, in the mouth of one of the characters. "We have to kill in order that no one should kill after that; that men should live forever according to the divine law."[99]

In *The Pale Horse* Savinkov narrates a terrorist attempt to assassinate a provincial governor. Subsequently, he described the last phase of his adventurous career: in the provisional government Prime Minister Kerensky made Savinkov acting minister of war. After the Bolshevik coup he joined the White armies but soon became disillusioned. For a time he tried to persuade the Allied leaders to cooperate with what he termed "The Third Russia," directed by a "Union of the Resurrection of Russia" which included supporters of Kerensky—and once again, Merezhkovsky, Hippius, and Filosofov.[100] The Union of the Resurrection of Russia was based in Poland, where Savinkov formed an alliance with Marshal Pilsudski and began to raise an army of 20-30,000 men to march on Moscow. Merezhkovsky, his wife, and Filosofov arrived in Poland in January 1920, and the prophet of a new Christianity immediately began to adapt the doctrines of Polish Messianism to a political object. Merezhkovsky visited Marshal Pilsudski. At once he saw him as a true hero—"the unchanged revelation of the Godhead, the Theophany." Pilsudski was designed by God to save the world, and the Messianic mission of Poland would be fulfilled by her saving Russia. But by the middle of the year Merezhkovsky was disillusioned. Poland had signed a peace with the Bolsheviks and betrayed her mission. Merezhkovsky was reduced to applying the ideas put about by Polish exiles in the last century to the Russian emigration in the 20th. They were the dispersed tribes of Israel, and Bolshevism was Antichrist.[101]

Savinkov moved off into Russia in June 1920, with the army he had largely created, but which he claimed himself incompetent to command. At Mozyr his ill-equipped forces were routed. Savinkov took to the forests with a band of peasant insurrectionaries before resuming his old activities as a terrorist. The story of this last adventure is told in another novel, *The Black Horse,* from which it is clear that the influence of Hippius and Merezhkovsky was still potent. The same vacillation is present as in *The Pale Horse,* and it ends in the same ruthlessness. The constant companion and alter ego of the narrator is an Old Believer who sees Bolshevism as Antichrist. Savinkov was arrested in 1923 by the Bolsheviks, and he committed suicide in the Lubianka prison. His brand of idealistic politics demonstrates that illuminated ideas and a life-or-death brand of politics might go hand in hand, and it is significant that Savinkov is said to have proposed to Mussolini a plan of international Fascism.[102]

The second example of Russian mystical politics is that of an out-and-out illuminate. Roman Feodorovich von Ungern-Sternberg was born into an old Baltic family in 1885. It is possible to arrive at a sketchy early biography. About 1900 Ungern went to school in Reval and was expelled. In 1903 he entered the Corps of Cadets and accumulated large gambling debts. At the outbreak of the Russo-Japanese war he was discharged from the cadet corps for demanding to fight; and by himself he made his way to the Far East, where he arrived too late to see any action. In 1906 Ungern entered infantry college (or possibly a naval school) and three years later received a commission in a regiment of Transbaikalian Cossacks at Chita. He fought many duels, and in one he received a saber cut on the head, which several chroniclers have made responsible for his later eccentricity and sadism. After this episode Roman Ungern-Sternberg left his regiment and made his way alone across unexplored country. According to one rumor, he lived for a while as a bandit; but a more probable story is that he acted as guide to an expedition of topographers. About 1911 he traveled to France, Germany, and Austria; returned to Siberia in 1912; and during the war contrived to enlist under Rennenkampf. His bravery and ferocity earned him countless decorations. After the Revolution broke out he was seen in Reval in full uniform with medals, epaulettes, and saber. Ungern left his Baltic home in December 1917 to join the Siberian forces of Ataman Semenov, who promoted him to Major-General. There then began the brutal adventure which made the baron—yet another Balt known as "the mad baron"—more of a legend than a historical character.[103]

Ungern-Sternberg very rapidly became the property of occultists, and it is important to realize why. The West was introduced to the mad baron by the Polish engineer and scientist Ferdinand Ossendowski in his book *Men, Beasts and Gods* (1924), which had sold over 300,000 copies a year after publication. It told in a very romantic fashion of Ossendowski's escape through Central Asia from his position in the government of Admiral Koltchak's Far East Republic. Its author's struggles with the elements and his human enemies were rivaled only by the supernatural marvels he encountered at the hands of Mongolian lamas. His contact with Ungern-Sternberg—whose cruelty and mysticism were already legendary—fitted artistically into this most Slavonic of traveler's tales. Soon after the publication of Ossendowski's book, the explorer Sven Hedin challenged its truthfulness. He was able to explode Ossendowski's claim to have been in Tibet, and he eventually discovered a most revealing plagiarism. *Men, Beasts and Gods* is certainly more fiction than fact. But it tells more about Ungern-Sternberg and his milieu than might appear at first sight.

Ferdinand Ossendowski was a typical member of the Russian intelligentsia: he graduated from St. Petersburg University (c. 1900) and made his first expedition to the East. He was an expert in coal and gold mining, and for some time he held a chair in "industrial geography" in the Russian capital. His political sympathies—of a social revolutionary nature—as well as his Polish birth made him for two months president of a rebel government of the Far East in the Revolution of 1905. Ossendowski was rescued from a death sentence by the intervention of Count Witte. After the 1917 Revolution he was drafted by Admiral Koltchak into the government of Siberia. From the collapse of Koltchak's armies, Ossendowski escaped—he claimed—through Mongolia.[104]

Ossendowski was brim full of illuminated attitudes and occultism. He had met Father John of Kronstadt several times and had been involved in "occult and spiritualist circles in Paris." He once encountered Rasputin and while tutor in a noble household had been invited to an unsuccessful séance given by Papus. He speaks familiarly of the Ipatyev salon and of other occult meeting places. While in prison under sentence of death he experienced mystical illuminations and was very impressed by the works of the *startsy*.[105] When this illuminated scientist took to the forests and plains of Central Asia, he certainly did not go as far as Tibet, and no detail of his narrative can be relied on. But it remains possible that he did meet Ungern-Sternberg. The baron occupies the central section of the book—one of the "men" described after the "beasts" (the Reds from whom Ossendowski had escaped), who come before the "gods" (otherwise the Mongolian lamas with their peculiar variant of Buddhism).

Sven Hedin discovered that the source for Ossendowski's final chapter was a posthumous book by the 19th-century occultist Saint-Yves d'Alveydre, *Mission de l'Inde en Europe*. In certain parts of his narrative of the "King of the World," whom Mongolian legend has dwelling in the subterranean kingdom of Agartha, Ossendowski obviously copied from the fantasies of Saint-Yves, which in their turn had derived from Theosophy.[106] Into this occultist dream-come-true, Ossendowski inserted his portrait of Baron Ungern—a sadistic dictator of the Mongolian capital, Urga, relying on prophecies and fortune telling; a convert to Mongolian Buddhism with knowledge of the exact date when he would die. Besides the obvious desire to sell books, there was another reason behind Ossendowski's placing the portrait of the mystical baron in the midst of his fantastic pilgrim's progress. This is Ungern's place within the atmosphere of credulous mysticism which surrounded the White armies. In this tradition Ossendowski tells elsewhere of how Koltchak's court in Siberia was preoccupied with Christian mysticism, Spiritualism, and even local shamans.[107]

Hermann Keyserling was related to Roman Ungern-Sternberg. Ungern's brother had married his sister, and Keyserling himself had an Ungern grandmother. He had known the mad baron from the age of twelve, when Roman had tried to strangle Keyserling's pet owl. Keyserling thought him "one of the most metaphysically and occultly gifted men I have met," and he told Sven Hedin that Ungern used to talk in geometrical symbols. Ungern's metaphysical ideas, he wrote, "were closely related to those of the Tibetans and the Hindus," and on occasion he showed clairvoyant gifts. As for his character, it was completely erratic, and vacillated between the extremes of evil and good. Keyserling remembered Ungern-Sternberg's protesting violently at being made to think. "Thinking is cowardice," he said, "thought comes and goes like a breeze." The last time he had been in contact with Ungern was when the baron telegraphed him to send the Ungern-Sternberg coat-of-arms to Mongolia, as he wished to use it as the insignia of his Mongolian state.

Keyserling did not like to believe Ossendowski, but he thought his characterization of the baron extremely accurate. In particular he commended the Pole's insistence on Ungern-Sternberg's cult of purity.[108] This particular piece of corroboration gives us license to record, without approving, Ossendowski's claim that he talked to Ungern-Sternberg who told him that he had tried to create an "Order of Military Buddhists" that was celibate and obeyed the teachings of Mongolian Buddhism. For a time, in order that the Russian should be able to live down his physical nature, he introduced all manner of excess—alcohol, opium, hashish—but afterward hanged his men for drinking.[109] Fortunately, there are more reliable authorities for Ungern's military moves, but it is necessary to arrive at them through the unreliable Ossendowski in order to see two things—how easily the baron could become part of the myth of the Russian "idealists," and how Ungern's real mysticism assisted the process.

When Ungern-Sternberg arrived in the East he was theoretically under the command of Admiral Koltchak, then of the Ataman Semenov. In practice he maintained a highly independent line of conduct. He established himself at Bauris on the Transbaikalian railway, where he instituted a regime of ferocious cruelty. In late September, 1920, after a series of differences with Semenov, he left Dauria and retreated fighting into Outer Mongolia.[110] He ousted the Chinese general "Little Hsu," who at that time controlled Mongolia. At the third attempt Ungern took Urga, the capital, and restored the Khutuktu—the so-called "Living Buddha"—who made the Baltic baron military adviser and conferred on him lavish titles indicating that he was the reincarnate God of War. In Urga, Ungern installed electricity and a wireless station. He enrolled Mongols in his "Asiatic division of cavalry" and terrorized his army with beatings, torture, and murder. It seems that he accepted aid from the Japanese—he needed all the help he could get—but his own schemes were based on the idea of a greater Mongolia extending North as far as Lake Baikal and allied both with a monarchist Russia and with a restored Manchu dynasty in China. At the end of May 1921, Baron Ungern and his small force rode out of Urga into Soviet territory. After a series of defeats the general was abandoned by his favored Mongols to the mercy of the Communists. He was captured, tried, and shot.[111]

The convictions which sustained this strange man were entirely of an illuminated nature. He literally saw Bolshevism as evil incarnate.

Thus, on 16 February 1921, he wrote to the Chinese monarchists, who he hoped would cooperate with his plan for a greater Mongolia: "It is not without consideration that I think of the Chinese blood that has been shed, and which, no doubt would be attributed to my cruelty; on the other hand I am positive that every soldier should consider it his duty to root out every revolutionist, irrespective of his nationality, for they are no less evil spirits in human shape."[112] Before setting out to emulate Ghengis Khan's ride to Moscow, Ungern issued his notorious "Order No. 15" (he had never issued an order before but the numbering, as well as the inaccurate date, were because the lamas had told him the figures were auspicious).[113] The order forbade any mercy. "The ancient foundation of justice—truth and pity—has gone. Now there must reign truth and pitiless severity. Evil, come to earth in order to destroy the divine principle in the human soul, must be wiped out together with its rationale."[114] Ungern's vision of a united Mongolia was based on a twofold reasoning. "On the one hand, to enable all the tribes of Mongolian origin to unite round one center and on the other, military and moral defense against the rotten West which is under the influence of mad revolution and the decline of morality in all its manifestations, both physical and spiritual."[115] And so the man—Keyserling wrote that the lamas recognized him by his horoscope as Tamerlane returned—rode out of Urga believing himself the real representative of spiritual powers against the equally tangible demons of materialism. Ungern ended his Order No. 15 with a quotation from the Book of Daniel. This predicted the appearance of "Michael, the great prince"—he had just proclaimed the Grand Duke Michael, "All-Russian Emperor"—and concluded "Blessed is he that waits and fulfils the 3330 days."[116]

There is further corroboration of Ungern's mysticism. At Dauria, an Associated Press correspondent found him talking of Ghengis Khan and telling his fortune with cards.[117] Dmitri Alioshin (who later served as an interpreter to General Graves's American expeditionary force and whose account is generally accepted as authentic) acted as one of Ungern's regimental fortune tellers, and he tells how his commander paid 7,000 lamas to perform services for his final expedition. His description of Ungern just before his final defeat is horrifying:

> The baron, with his head dropped to his chest, silently rode in front of his troops. He had lost his hat and clothing. On his naked chest numerous Mongolian talismans were hanging on a bright yellow cord. He looked like a reincarnation of a prehistoric ape man. People were afraid even to look at him.[118]

Alioshin confirms Ungern's extraordinary cruelty, and he concurs with all the authorities in pointing to the objects of the mad baron's particular hate: the Jews. When they captured Urga in the first days of February 1921, Ungern's henchmen, led by a Dr. Klingenberg (whose legs Ungern later broke for some misdemeanor) instituted a pogrom, and "Order No. 15" also called for the extirpation of Jews and commissars. Under Ungern's regime in Urga the Khutuktu's minister of the interior issued what has been called the only document of anti-Semitism in Mongolian history, defining the Communists as Jews "without distinction of Russian, Mongol, American, Japanese or Chinese" and as such forbidding his subjects to help them.[119]

Once more we are confronted with the existence of an illuminated anti-Semitism, which, in the case of Ungern, identified the Jews with the children of an evil materialism. We have seen that Western illuminates of a certain type were prone to anti-Semitism and that in at least two of the Slavonic prophets we have looked at, allied trains of thought were present. The particular sort of illuminated politics of which Roman Ungern-Sternberg was so extreme an exponent was, to a large extent, brought to the West by an influx of Russian refugees. The 19th-century Occult Revival can be shown to be inextricably connected with its origins.

Ossendowski is an interesting example of the connection. His doubtless mythical account of Ungern takes pains to make the point that the baron, after all, had "many Jewish agents"—in other words, that the accusations against him are not true. Yet Ossendowski undoubtedly believed in the myth that there was a conspiracy against right order; and it is quite probable that he agreed with the baron's definition of who was responsible. The mystical engineer also identified the magician Papus and other gurus of the court, as "Buddhist and masonic agents" and he seems, therefore, to have believed in a legend current in the West that the Freemasons were conspiring to overthrow society. To this he coupled Vladimir Soloviev's fear of "Buddhism" advancing from the East.[120]

But what is this of conspiracies, occultists, and anti-Semitism? It is a new sort of history, an irrationalist history, which found its hour in tsarist Russia and Nazi Germany. "Horoscopes, horoscopes, horoscopes," muttered Vasily Rozanov, dying at Sargeva Posad. "Oh, how terrible are their predictions. Is it indeed the whisper of the stars? Run historians, shut your ears."[121]

1. See my discussion of this in *The Occult Underground*, pp. 245 ff.
2. Siegfried Lipiner, *Uber die Elemente einer Erneuerung religiöser Ideen in der Gegenwart* (Vienna, 1878; a lecture given that year by Lipiner to the German Students Reading Club). On Lipiner, see Harmut von Hartungen, *Der Dichter Siegfried Lipiner* (thesis presented to Munich University, 1932).
3. Sergius Bulgakov, *The Orthodox Church* (tr. E. S. Crann, London, 1935), pp. 215, 100-101.
4. Quoted in preface to John Ilyich Serviev, *My Life in Christ* (tr. E. E. Goulaeff, London, 1897), p. viii. See also W. Jardine Grisbrooke, ed., *Spiritual Counsels of Father John of Kronstadt* (London, 1966).
5. George Gapon, *The Story of My Life* (London, 1905), pp. 115-16.
6. Nicolas Zernov, *The Russian Religious Revival of the 20th Century* (London, 1963). I have drawn heavily on this invaluable work.
7. Zernov, p. 100 for Tsaritsin. See also *The Mad Monk of Russia, Iliodor, Life, Memoirs and Confessions of Serge Michaulovitch Trufanoff* (New York, 1918), pp. 12-13, 50; J. S. Curtiss, *Church and State in Russia 1900-17* (N.Y., 1940), p. 379.
8. Nicholas Berdyaev, *Dream and Reality* (tr. Katharine Lampert, London, 1950), pp. 188-89.
9. Details and estimates from F. C. Conybeare, *Russian Dissenters* (Cambridge, Mass., and London, 1921). Compare the *Skoptsy* leader "Kondrati Salivanov" with Naundorff and the other pretenders to the title of Louis XVII of France.
10. See *The Occult Underground*, pp. 160 ff., 245 ff.
11. Harold Williams, *Russia of the Russians* (London, 1914), pp. 129, 132.
12. D. Stremoukhoff, *Vladimir Soloviev et son oeuvre méssianique* (Paris, 1935), pp. 19-26; Vladimir Soloviev, *Crise de la philosophie occidentale* (tr. M. Hermann, Paris, n.d.), p. 343; Stremoukhoff, *Soloviev,* pp. 37-38, 41-45.
13. E.-M. de Vogüé, *Sous l'horizon* (Paris, 1904), pp. 17-18.
14. Stremoukhoff, *Soloviev,* pp. 46 ff.
15. Oleg A. Maslenikov, *The Frenzied Poets* (Berkeley and Los Angeles, 1952), pp. 59-60.

16. See Vladimir Soloviev, *Lectures on Godmanhood* (tr. P. P. Zouboff, 1948; orig. 1877-84).
17. See Soloviev, *Russia and the Universal Church* (tr. Herbert Rees, London, 1948) and Stremoukhoff, *Soloviev,* pp. 122 ff.
18. Vladimir Soloviev, *War, Progress and the End of History* (tr. Alex Baksly, London, 1915), p. 227. There is some significance in the date of this translation—fifteen years after its author's death, the piece is resurrected in London of the First World War.
19. Maslenikov, *Frenzied Poets,* pp. 70-71 and p. 201.
20. Nicholas Arseniev, *Holy Moscow* (London, 1940), pp. 116-17.
21. Berdyaev, *Dream and Reality,* pp. 141-42.
22. On this cultural development, see Maslenikov, *Frenzied Poets,* D. S. Mirsky, *Contemporary Russian Literature, 1881-1925* (London, 1926), M. J. Olgin, *A Guide to Russian Literature* (London, 1921), and Camilla Grey, *The Russian Experiment in Art* (London, 1966); Ivanov quoted by James West, *Russian Symbolism* (London, 1970), p. 51 from his "Two Elements in Contemporary Symbolism" (1908).
23. Bernard Pares, *My Russian Memoirs* (London, 1931), p. 132; on Ivanov see Maslenikov, *Frenzied Poets,* pp. 198 ff.; Olgin, *Guide,* p. 174.
24. Berdyaev, *Dream and Reality,* p. 145.
25. Jean Chuzevill, *Dmitri Merezhkovsky* (Paris, 1922), pp. 16-17; see Merezhkovsky, *Peter and Alexis* (London, 1905).
26. Merezhkovsky, *Tolstoy as Man and Artist: With an Essay on Dostoievsky* (London, 1902), p. 161; Zernov, *Revival,* pp. 90-95.
27. V. V. Rozanov, *Fallen Leaves,* Bundle One (tr. S. S. Koteliansky, London, 1929), pp. 16-20, 150; E. Gollerbach, "V. V. Rozanov," in Rozanov, *Solitaria* (tr. Koteliansky, London, 1927), p. 40.
28. See, e.g., his *La Face sombre du Christ* (Paris, 1964) and *Solitaria,* p. 75.
29. Rozanov, *Solitaria,* pp. 103-4, 187.
30. Maslenikov, *Frenzied Poets,* pp. 25-26.
31. Merezhkovsky, "Religion et Révolution" in Merezhkovsky, Hippius, Filosofov, *Le Tsar et la Révolution* (Paris, 1907), pp. 222-24; Berdyaev, *Dream and Reality,* p. 208.
32. On Florensky, see N. O. Lossky, *History of Russian Philosophy* (London, 1952), pp. 176 ff. and V. V. Zenkovsky, *A History of Russian Philosophy* (tr. G. L. Kline, London, 1953), vol. II, pp. 875 ff.
33. Inayat Khan, *Confessions,* pp. 154-55.
34. Josephine Ransom, *History of the Theosophical Society* (London, 1938), pp. 16-18.
35. The petition is printed, and the debate can be followed in full in *The Complete Works of H. P. Blavatsky,* vol. I (ed. A. Trevor Barker, London, 1933), pp. 112-15.
36. Ransom, *Theosophical Society,* p. 18.
37. Bibliographical information in Geoffrey Baborka, *H.P.B., Tibet and Tulku* (Adyar, 1966), pp. 153-54. It appears not to have occurred to the

philosopher that the Abbé Huc was precisely the source from which H.P.B. acquired her information; quoted in Stremoukhoff, *Soloviev*, p. 217 note 7.

38. Vsevolod Soloviev, *A Modern Priestess of Isis* (tr. Walter Leaf, London, 1895). This is abridged from the original articles of 1892; Charles J. Ryan, *H. P. Blavatsky and the Theosophical Movement* (Point Loma, 1937), pp. 225-27.

39. Vsevolod Soloviev, *Priestess*, pp. 23, 219; see especially Leaf's abstract of Vera Jelikovsky's *H. P. Blavatsky and a Modern Priest of Truth*, pp. 287 ff.

40. *The Letters of H. P. Blavatsky to A. P. Sinnett*, pp. 227-28, dated 10 January 1887.

41. Ransom, *Theosophical Society*, p. 18; quoted in A. P. Sinnett, *Incidents in the Life of Madame Blavatsky* (London, 1913), pp. 107-8.

42. "Alba," "Theosophy in Russia" in *Theosophy in Scotland*, vol. I, pp. 40-41.

43. Paul Dukes, *The Unending Quest*, (London, 1951), pp. 49 ff. Of Russian musicians the most mystically inclined was Scriabin, who expected a Union of the male Creator-Spirit with the Woman-World. He, of course, was the "messiah of the union." See Martin Cooper, "Scriabin's Mystical Beliefs," in *Music and Letters* (1935), pp. 110 ff.; Sophie Bonneau, *L'univers poétique d'Alexandre Blok* (Paris, 1946), pp. 149-50, 154 ff.; Maslenikov, *Frenzied Poets*, pp. 112-14; quoted by Alec Brown in his preface to his translation of Remizov, *The Fifth Pestilence* (London, 1927), p. ix; Berdyaev, *Dream*, p. 17; Donald A. Lawrie, *Rebellious Prophet* (London, 1960), p. 128; Lawrie, *Prophet*, p. 88; Berdyaev, *Dream*, pp. 162, 188.

44. Savitch, *Marie von Sivers*, pp. 25-41; Wachsmuth, *Steiner*, p. 79; cf. Steiner, *Story of My Life*, p. 333.

45. Vyacheslav Ivanov, *Freedom and the Tragic Life* (tr. Norman Cameron, London, 1952), pp. 120 ff.; Berdyaev, *Dream*, pp. 190-94.

46. Berdyaev, *Dream*, p. 193; Savitch, *Marie von Sivers*, pp. 114-15. Returning from this course of lectures Berdyaev told an acquaintance that Steiner exuded "demonic power." Lawrie, *Prophet*, p. 127; Maslenikov, *Frenzied Poets*, pp. 84-94; Wachsmuth, *Steiner*, p. 232; Kobylinsky in *Psychische Studien* (1917), quoted Kully, *Wahrheit*, p. 303; Schwarz-Bostunitsch, *Doktor Steiner*, p. 26.

47. Maurice Paléologue, *An Ambassador's Memoirs* (London, 3 vols. 1923-25), vol. II p. 105.

48. Rene Füllöp-Miller, *Rasputin: The Holy Devil* (tr. F. S. Flint and D. F. Tait, London and N.Y., 1968). Despite the strictures passed on this book by Colin Wilson, it remains very useful. It is easy to detect the "dramatizations," and it is worth noting that the author edited a book with Friedrich Eckstein.

49. See *The Occult Underground*, chapters V and VII for a précis of Parisian occultism.

50. Philippe Encausee, *Le Maître Philippe de Lyon* (Paris, 1958), pp. 223-25.

51. *The Memoirs of Count Witte* (tr. and ed. Abraham Yarmolsinsky, London, 1921), p. 192; Papus, quoted Philippe Encausse, *Papus; sa vie, son oeuvre* (Paris, 1932), p. 43; Encausse, *Le Maître Philippe*, pp. 229-30.

52. Alexandre Spiridovitch, *Les dernières Années de la cour de Tsarskoe Selo* (Paris, 1928), vol. I, pp. 100-101; Witte, *Memoirs*, pp. 203-4; Encausse, *Le Maître Philippe*, p. 203, 231-33.

53. Henri Rollin, *L'Apocalypse de notre temps* (5th ed., Paris, 1939), pp. 375-76; Encausse, *Le Maitre Philippe*, pp. 224-25, 247.

54. Iliodor, *Mad Monk*, pp. 170-74, 175; cf. Füllöp-Miller, *Rasputin*, pp. 96-99.

55. Rozanov, *The Apocalypse of Our Times*, p. 184.

56. Iliodor, *Mad Monk*, pp. 94-95, 187 ff.; Füllöp-Miller, *Rasputin*, pp. 171 ff.; see, *e.g.*, M. V. Rodzianko, *The Reign of Rasputin* (tr. C. Zvegnitz, London, 1927), p. 8. Cf. Conybeare, *Dissenters*, pp. 343 ff. for the *Khlysty*.

57. Füllöp-Miller, *Rasputin*, pp. 100-103. Cf. note 84, this chapter. For the "yellow powder," see Iliodor, *Mad Monk*, p. 181. It should not be forgotten that this book was written at the instigation of the revolutionary Vladimir Burtsev, who played an important part in exposing the *Protocols of the Elders of Zion*—for which see next chapter. The best example of the conspiracy theory in action is in the report, *La Chute du régime tsariste: Interrogatoires par la commission extraordinaire du gouvernement provisoire de 1917* (tr. J. and L. Polansky, Paris, 1927).

58. On this, see Pierre Gilliard, *Thirteen Years at the Russian Court* (tr. F. A. Holt, London, 1921), pp. 81-83.

59. On this development, see Thais S. Lindstrom, *Tolstoi en France* (Paris, 1952); F.W. Bennings, *The Russian Novel in France, 1884-1914* (London, 1950); Helen Muchnic, *Dostoievsky's English Reputation: 1881-1936* (Smith College Studies in Modern Languages, vol. XX, part II 1938-39; Landmann, *Monte Verita*, pp. 26-27, 36-37, and passim.

60. George Woodcock and Ivan Avakumovic, *The Doukhobors* (London, 1968), pp. 111-12; Conrad Noel, *Byways of Belief* (London, 1912), pp. 115-16.

61. Hippius, quoted in Hans Erich Volkmann, *Die Russische Emigration in Deutschland, Marburger Ostforschungen*, Band 26 (Würzburg 1966), p. 125; see Alexander Eliasberg, *Russische Literaturgeschichte* (2nd ed., Munich, 1925), pp. 185 ff.; Charles Ledré, *Les Emigrés russes en France* (Paris, 1930), pp. 247-48; quoted in Michael d'Herbigny, S. J. and Alexandre Deubner, *Evêques Russes en éxil; 1918-1930, Orientalia Christiana*, vol. XXI, no. 67, January-March 1931, p. 22; Zernov, *Revival*, pp. 251-52.

62. D'Herbigny and Deubner, *Evêques russes*, pp. 263-69.

63. Zenkovsky, *History of Russian Philosophy* vol. II, p. 874; Zernov, *Revival*, p. 175.

64. Bulgakov, *Orthodox Church*, p. 219.

65. Vasily Rozanov, *L'Apocalypse de notre temps*, printed by Nathalie Reznikoff in her translation of *Le Face sombre du Christ* (Paris, 1964), p. 281.

66. Berdyaev, *The End of Our Time* (tr. Donald Atwater, London, 1933), pp. 11, 91, 109, and cf. Berdyaev, *The Bourgeois Mind* (tr. Countess Beningsen, London, 1934).
67. Simon Frank, *Die Russische Weltanschauung* (Darmstadt, 1962; orig. 1926), p. 13; Lev Shestov, *Athens and Jerusalem* (tr. Bernard Martin, Athens, Ohio, 1966), p. 375.
68. Merezhkovsky, preface to *The Birth of the Gods* (tr. Nathalie Duddington, London, 1925), pp. vi-vii; Merezhkovsky, *Jesus the Unknown* (tr. H. C. Matheson, London, 1933), pp. 36-37. The sequel, *Jesus Manifest* (London, 1935), is less eccentric.
69. I hope to give a reasonably complete Gurdjieff bibliography in my forthcoming study of the movement. The best books to start with are P. D. Ouspensky, *In Search of the Miraculous* (London, 1950), which gives an accurate account of Gurdjieff's teaching until he arrived in the West, and Fritz Peters, *Boyhood with Gurdjieff* (London, 1965).
70. See my *Occult Underground*, p. 245 ff.
71. Herman Keyserling, "Autobiographical Sketch," in *The World in the Making* (tr. Maurice Samuel, London, 1927), pp. 22-23.
72. Keyserling, "Utopians and Prophets" in *The Art of Life* (tr. K. S. Shelvankar, London, 1937), p. 104; Rudolf Kassner, *Die Mystik, die Künstler und das Leben*, in *Sämtliche Werke*, Band I (Pfullingen, 1969); for Kassner's Neo-Platonism, see his *Die Mystik*. Cf. Keyserling, *Creative Understanding* (New York and London, 1929), pp. 321-22, and "Autobiographical Sketch," p. 31; on Kassner generally, see Hans Paeschke, *Rudolf Kassner* (Pfullingen, 1963) and Kassner's own *Buch der Erinnerung* (Leipzig, 1938). See also his *Grundlagen der Physiognomik* (Leipzig, 1922).
73. Keyserling, *Reise durch die Zeit*, Band I, (Vaduz, 1948), pp. 101-03, 106.
74. Keyserling, *The Travel Diary of a Philosopher* (2 vols., London, tr. J. H. Reece, 1925), vol. II, pp. 364, 370; vol. I, pp. 117, 157-58.
75. Keyserling, "Autobiographical Sketch," pp. 67, 78; Mercedes Gallagher Parks, *Introduction to Keyserling* (London, 1934), p. 27; Landau, *God*, pp. 20-25.
76. Parks, *Keyserling*, pp. 29-30; Keyserling, *The Recovery of Truth* (New York and London, 1929), p. 352; Keyserling, "Reason and Religion" in *Problems of Personal Life* (tr. M. G. Parks, London, 1934), p. 212.
77. Landau, *God*, p. 167; cf. Pierre Frederix, "Un Petit Village d'Autriche," in *Graf Hermann Keyserling, ein Gedächtnisbuch* (Innsbruck, 1948).
78. Methodi Konstantinov, *La Nouvelle Culture et l'ère du verseau* (Paris, 1963), p. 92; Marianne Kohler, *A l'école de sagesse* (Paris, 1961), p. 186 note 1; Konstantinov, *La Nouvelle Culture* pp. 262, 168.
79. Konstantinov, *La Nouvelle Culture*, p. 92 and Petr Deunov, *La Vie pour le tout* (Sofia, 1939), pp.79 ff.; Konstantinov, *La Nouvelle Culture*, pp.

240-41; on Ivanov, see Kohler, *A l'école de sagesse*, pp. 183 ff. The first French-language publication of the Deunov group was in 1936.

80. Biographical sketch from W. Kwiatkowski, *Informations sur W. Lutoslawski* (n.p., c. 1917); MS note by the author in the British Museum copy of Lutoslawski, *El Personalismo* (Madrid, 1887); Lutoslawski, *Über die Grundvoraussetzungen und Consequenzen der individualistischen Weltanschauung* (Helsingfors, 1898), p. 28; Lutoslawski, "On the Difference between Knowledge and Belief as to the Immortality of the Soul," in *Journal of Speculative Philosophy* (December, 1893), pp. 437-39.

81. Lutoslawski, "In Search of True Beings" in *The Monist* (April 1896), pp. 351 ff.; *The Origin and Growth of Plato's Logic* (London, 1897), *Über die Grundvoraussetzungen*, and *Seelenmacht* (Leipzig, 1899), the last partly translated as *The World of Souls* (London, 1924); Lutoslawski, "Psychologie des Conversions" in *Comptes rendus du VI Congrès internationale de Psychologie* (Geneva, 1909), pp. 709-12.

82. Marion Moore Coleman, *Adam Mickiewicz in English* (Cambridge Springs, Pennsylvania, 1954), has an entry on Lutoslawski.

83. "The Polish Nation" in *The Quarterly Review* (October 1904), pp. 417-18.

84. See letters quoted Kwiatkowski, *Informations sur W. Lutoslawski*, pp. 12-14 and cf. William James, *Letters*, vol. II, and G. W. Allen, *William James* (London, 1967), p. 401.

85. Lutoslawski, "Polish Letters to a Hindu Devotee" in *East and West* (Bombay, November-December 1907), pp. 1087, 1089-90, 1238.

86. Lutoslawski, *Volonté et liberté* (Tlemcen, Algeria, 1912); and see his two articles in Hiram Butler's *Bible Review*, February 1910 and October 1911.

87. See Lutoslawski, *The World of Souls* (London, 1924), *Pre-existence and Reincarnation* (London, 1928), and *The Knowledge of Reality* (London, 1930).

88. Arnold Toynbee, *Acquaintances* (London, 1947), pp. 252-61.

89. For Mijatović, see his *Memoirs of a Balkan Diplomatist* (London, 1917); on Mitrinović, see Mairet, *Orage*, pp. vii ff; and Purdom, *Life Over Again*, pp. 266 ff.

90. Edwin Muir, *Autobiography* (London, 1954), pp. 174 ff; Willa Muir, *Belonging* (London, 1968), p. 41.

91. "M. M. Cosmoi on World Affairs" in *The New Age* (vol. XXVII, no. 11, 13 June 1921), p. 123; Purdom, *Life Over Again*, pp. 271-76; Mitrinović's Adler Society held a meeting every night of the week with a party on Saturdays.

92. *New Britain* began as a quarterly in October 1932, and on 7 June 1933, became a weekly under Purdom's editorship. The group also published a quarterly, *The New Atlantis* (for Western Renaissance and World Socialism) in October 1933 and January 1934, which became *The New Albion* (for British Renaissance and Western Alliance) in April 1934, and

reverted to being *New Britain* (for British Revolution and the Social State) in the autumn of that year. A silver-covered *New Europe* (through the Social State and Federation of Progress to the Dignity, Freedom and Happiness of Persons) appeared in September 1934. See also *The Meaning of New Britain* (Tracts of the New Order; no. 1 London, 1936). For S. G. Hobson's contribution, see his *Functional Socialism* and for E. A. Wilson, his MS autobiography in the British Museum.

93. See report in *The New Albion*.
94. Purdom, *Life Over Again*, pp. 155-56; *The New Atlantis* (October 1933), p. 15; Willa Muir, *Belonging*, p. 168; Purdom, *Life Over Again*, p. 280.
95. René Dupuis and Alexandre Marc, *Jeune Europe* (Paris, 1933), p. 165.
96. On *L'Ordre nouveau*, see J.-L. Loubet del Bayle, *Les Non-Conformistes des années 30* (Paris, 1969), pp. 79 ff.
97. Supplement to *The New Atlantis* (January, 1934).
98. Lutoslawski, "Polish Letters," pp. 1220, 1235; Lutoslawski, *Bolshevism and Poland* (Paris, 1919), pp. 4-5.
99. Merezhkovsky, Hippius, Filosofov, *Le Tsar et la révolution*, p. 132; "V. Ropshin" (Boris Savinkov), *The Pale Horse* (tr. Z. Vengerova, Dublin and London, 1917), p. 79, Mirsky, *Russian Literature*, p. 160, and cf. Savinkov, *Memoirs of a Terrorist* (New York, 1937).
100. M. K. Driewanowski, *Joseph Pilsudski* (Palo Alto, Calif., 1969), pp. 208-9. For Winston Churchill's estimate of Savinkov, see his *Great Contemporaries* (2nd ed., London, 1938), pp. 125-33. Cf. R. H. Bruce Lockhart, *Memoirs of a British Agent* (London, 1932), p. 182 and Geoffrey Bailey, *The Conspirators* (London, 1951); Stremoukhoff, *Soloviev*, p. 175 note 50 and Venceslas Lednicki, *Quelques aspects du nationalisme et du Christianisme chez Tolstoi* (Cracow, 1935), pp. 91-92, and p. 92 note 2.
101. See in sequence, Zenaida Hippius, *Mon Journal sous la terreur* (Paris, 1921), Merezhkovsky, *Joseph Pilsudski* (London, 1921), "Polish Messianism and Russia" in *Le Peuple crucifié* (Paris, 1921), pp. 191 ff. and *Le Regne de l'Antichrist* (Paris, 1921); Savinkov, *The Black Horse* (tr. Paul Dukes, London, 1924).
102. Henri Donjon, "Notre Ami l'assassin" in *Les Oeuvres libres* (October 1930), p. 320; sketch based on Vladimir Pozner, *White Despot* (tr. W. B. Wells, London, 1938), pp. 40-46; cf. George Stewart, *The White Armies of Russia* (New York, 1970; reprint of 1933 ed.), pp. 401 ff. and Dmitri Alioshin, *Asian Odyssey* (London, 1941), pp. 186-87. Keyserling, *Reise durch die Zeit*, vol. II, (Darmstadt, 1958), pp. 54-55 and Sven Hedin, *Ossendowski und die Wahrheit* (Leipzig, 1925), pp. 32-33 have useful information. For further comments on sources, see text above. I have not been able to use the substantial collection of materials in the Hoover Institute.
103. See Ossendowski, *From President to Prison* (London, 1925), and note by his collaborator, Lewis Stanton Palen, in *Man and Mystery in Asia* (London, 1924).

104. See Ossendowski, *From President to Prison,* pp. 197-200 and in particular his *Shadow of the Gloomy East,* (tr. F. F. Czarmoniski, London, 1925), which was written *without* Palen's collaboration.
105. Hedin, *Ossendowski,* pp. 29 ff. Cf. Ossendowski, *Men, Beasts and Gods* (London, 1924), pp. 299 ff. and Saint-Yves d'Alveydre, *Mission de l'Inde* (Paris, 1910).
106. Ossendowski, *The Shadow of the Gloomy East,* pp. 202-3.
107. For Keyserling on Ungern-Sternberg, see his *Reise durch die Zeit,* vol. II, pp. 53 ff., his letter to Vladimir Pozner printed Pozner, *White Despot,* p. 68, and conversation with Sven Hedin recorded Hedin, *Ossendowski,* pp. 19-20.
108. Ossendowski, *Men, Beasts and Gods,* p. 246.
109. Pozner, *White Despot,* pp. 122 ff., gives extracts from White newspapers covering this development, and M. A. Novemeysky, *My Siberian Life* (London, 1930), p. 303, records Ungern's cruelty at Dauria.
110. C. R. Bawden, *The Modern History of Mongolia* (London, 1968), pp. 216 ff.; E. H. Carr, *The Bolshevik Revolution,* vol. III (London, 1963), pp. 500 ff.; A. Lobanov-Rostovsky, "Russia and Mongolia," in *The Slavonic Review* (March 1927), pp. 518 ff.; J. Korostovetz, *Von Cingis Khan zur Sowjetrepublik* (Berlin and Leipzig, 1920), pp. 302-3; Alioshin, *Asian Odyssey,* pp. 219 ff.
111. Printed Ken Shen Weigh, *Russo-Chinese Diplomacy* (Shanghai, 1928).
112. Printed Ken Shen Weigh, *Russo-Chinese Diplomacy,* p. 200.
113. Alioshin, *Asian Odyssey,* pp. 256-57.
114. Ungern's Order No. 15, quoted J. Levine, *La Mongolie* (Paris, 1937), p. 136.
115. Ken Shen Weigh, *Russo-Chinese Diplomacy,* p. 200.
116. Keyserling, *Creative Understanding,* p. 276, and Carr, *Bolshevik Revolution,* vol. III, p. 514.
117. Pozner, *White Despot,* pp. 31-33 and cf. pp. 55-65.
118. Alioshin, *Asian Odyssey,* p. 264.
119. Bawden, *Mongolia,* p. 232; Alioshin, *Asian Odyssey,* pp. 230 ff.; Novomeysky, *Siberian Life,* p. 340.
120. Ossendowski, *The Shadow of the Gloomy East,* p. 96.
121. Rozanov, *Solitaria,* p. 158.

Chapter 4
The Conspiracy against the World

The Protocols of the Elders of Zion—The Occult, anti-Semitism and Conspiracy Theories—The Theosophical Society and the Plots of Jews and Jesuits—The "Secret of the Jews" and its Occult Sources—The Protocols and the Rival Gurus—The Illuminated Nature of Russian anti-Semitism—The Supernatural and the Myth of the Ipatyev House—Illuminated anti-Semitism comes West

THERE is a secret plot to take over the world. It is masterminded by an international syndicate of Jews, who make it their business to foment party strife, to upset the established social order, and promote international conflict. These men are called the Elders of Zion, and they delight in the destruction of conventional morality and the comforts of religion. Their particular agents are the Freemasons, but other secret societies exist to carry out their mission of subversion. So ruthless are the elders that they stop short of none of the repertoire of tricks normally reserved for mad scientists—the clandestine inoculation of diseases, for example—and are even now burrowing beneath the earth, their sinister purposes camouflaged as the construction of underground railways, to create a network of tunnels from which they can blow up the capitals of Europe. The goal of these elaborate preparations is the establishment of a Jewish despotism, whose total control over all aspects of human life will surpass the most gloomy precedents known to history.

Such is the burden of the document known as *The Protocols of the Learned Elders of Zion.* It has been known to be a forgery since the year after its first publication in the West in 1920. Some apology may seem necessary for returning to the *Protocols* after the study by Professor Norman Cohn.[1] But the occult has played a larger part in the genesis and propagation of this forgery than has been admitted, and the recognition of this fact can make plainer the devil-ridden universe in which such imaginings originate. Particularly it sheds light on the Nazi episode.

The first book to discuss in detail the section of the Underground in which the *Protocols* circulated was published in Paris in 1939 and was suppressed by the Germans after their conquest of France. Henri Rollin's *L'Apocalypse de notre temps* borrows its title from Rozanov's last desperate utterances. It demonstrates how the *Protocols* were written in France around the time of the Dreyfus case, were carried into Russia and published there to give substance to the semiofficial campaign against *Zhidmasonstvo*—the Freemasonic-Jewish conspiracy—and, after the Revolution of 1917, re-entered the West in the baggage of refugees to provide fuel for the flame of Nazi anti-Semitism. Professor Cohn and Professor Walter Laqueur[2] have added the weight of their researches to confirm Rollin's basic narrative. From its beginning in turn-of-the century French anti-Semitism, to its first application at the fall of the Russian autocracy and its apotheosis in the gas chambers, the myth of the Jewish conspiracy has been accompanied by the most extravagant elements of the occult underworld.

Anti-Semitism arose in 19th-century France as a political force at the same time as the Occult Revival reached its peak. In part, the two developments responded to the same stimuli. The 19th-century crisis of consciousness, experienced on one level, might result in an adoption of one or another of the current occult palliatives; on another level the danger to personal security could be perceived not as a cosmic threat but as a tangible, political menace, soon identified as Freemasons and Jews. The antagonism which vented itself so wretchedly against these groups was not so much a fear that these agencies would destroy society as a perception that the society which its defenders believed themselves to be protecting had already crumbled and that scapegoats had to be found. For such people the essence of Freemasonry or Judaism lay in their internationalism. The secure basis of the Nation-State, which had become the established form of government for much of Europe, was undermined by the existence of these bodies. One was explicitly devoted to international brotherhood; and the other had traditionally occupied an anomalous position in the body politic since the days of feudal legislation. Nor was this all. The Church had traditionally seen in the Masons the embodiment of secularist tendencies and threats to the Christian social order; and the identification of Jewry with the demon of negotiable capital was common to those who felt the security of landed property or traditional crafts vanishing in the imbroglio of industrialized society.

The reaction against insecurity might lead both to the underground of the occult and to the thesis that there existed a conspiracy to overturn established order. The two positions were compatible in terms of their strange logic, although they were by no means necessarily complementary. Edouard Drumont, the father of French anti-Semitism and author of its cardinal text, *La France juive* (1888), carried around with him a mandrake root and made a practice of reading the palms of the staff of his newspaper, the *Libre Parole*. In 1890 he denounced General Boulanger on the grounds of palmistry; and as early as 1881 he predicted disaster from an analysis of Gambetta's right hand.[3] One of Drumont's closest friends (and the financial editor of the *Libre Parole*) was Gaston Méry, an eccentric anti-Semite who in 1892 published a novel, *Jean Révolte*, preaching a holy war of the Celtic races of France against the Latins and the Jews who were ruining the nation.[4] In March 1897, Drumont sent Méry—otherwise incessantly involved in dueling—to write a story about the latest of the popular prophets who had taken public fancy. This was Mlle. Henriette Couedon, "the seeress of the Rue de Paradis," whose inspired utterances were very much in the line of French Catholic prophecy of a semipolitical nature. France was to be chastized for arrogance and impiety, and Paris to be especially punished. The Hotel de Ville and the Opéra were to burn down, the bourse was to be closed, and something unspecified and holy was to happen at the church of Sacré Coeur.[5] Méry became converted to the cult of Mlle. Couedon. In 1897 he founded an occult review, the *Echo du Merveilleux,* with another member of the staff of the *Libre Parole.* Drumont contributed articles to the *Echo* and gave it free advertising in his own paper.[6]

Not very far removed from this nest of illuminated anti-Semitism were the figures of Léo Taxil and his protégée Sophia Walden. This lady had been invented by Taxil and his colleagues as a source of information on the Satanic practices of the Freemasons. The reputation of the lodges as houses of devil worship was eagerly spread by numbers of clerics and was recognized by the Pope himself.[7] When Taxil eventually revealed his fraud in 1897, certain of his more fanatical supporters refused to abandon belief in the existence of the Satanic church and accused Sophia Walden's progenitor of having murdered her.[8] Before Taxil put an end to his deception, Méry had turned Drumont and the *Libre Parole* against the prophetess of Satanic masonry, lamenting that public interest was directed to Sophia Walden as opposed to his more deserving seeress. This provoked retaliation from Jules Doinel, a collaborator of Taxil, who retorted that Henriette Couedon was inspired, not by the angel Gabriel, but by "a mediocre, dull, second-rate Lucifer."[9] Even the originators of conspiracy theories found it difficult to agree.

For the general anti-Semitic public a synthesis was nonetheless contrived. This emphasis varied with the individual agitator, but the outline remained the same. The Jews had infiltrated the Masonic lodges and were manipulating the Freemasons from behind the scenes. Depending on the relative sophistication of the anti-Semite, the conspiracy might then be extended to include the Devil himself. As the frenzy grew, Jews began to adopt a circumspect attitude to Masonry.[10] This did nothing to allay the fears of their enemies. The agitation mounted from Drumont's publication of *La France juive* in 1884, through the scandals arising from the financial double dealing around the Panama Company in 1892—Drumont founded the *Libre Parole* the same year—to the high point of the Dreyfus case toward the end of the decade. The attempts of the Dreyfus family to clear the name of Captain Alfred Dreyfus in the face of the military establishment could be made to appear very like the machinations of the mysterious Jewish syndicate, which mythology supposed to be at the back of social disturbance. With the famous letter of Emile Zola headed *J'accuse* in January 1898, the shifty nature of the maneuvering of the military was laid bare, and the public could take up positions for or against.

It was at the height of the debate over Dreyfus—which was also related to the superstitious myth of the Judeo-Masonic conspiracy—that the *Protocols* were composed. From internal evidence, Professor Cohn has dated the forgery at about 1897 or 1898 and has even discovered that the forger probably did his work in the Bibliothèque Nationale. The *Protocols* are supposed to be the minutes of a meeting of the secret Jewish world government; and it has been known since 1921 that the unpleasant regime that they predict was constructed by adapting the *Dialogue aux enfers entre Montesquieu et Machiavel,* a satire on the authoritarian rule of Napoleon III, published in 1864 by the Paris lawyer Maurice Joly. One of the copies of the satire in the Bibliothèque Nationale "bears markings," writes Professor Cohn, "which correspond strikingly with the borrowings in the *Protocols.*"[11]

There is no possibility of doubting the date of the forgery or that the *Protocols* were composed somewhere in France. Their first publication was in St. Petersburg, in Krushevan's anti-Semitic paper *Znamya* during August-September 1903. In 1906-07 the *Protocols* appeared in popular format edited by G. Butmi and in 1905 they had been added to the third edition of *The Great in the Small,* a mystical work by Sergei Nilus, which was published at Tsarskoe Selo itself. It is probable that the forgery entered Russia with Yuliana Glinka (1884-1918), the daughter of a Russian diplomat who spent her time in Paris and St. Petersburg and was a Theosophist devoted to Madame Blavatsky.[12] It is possible to identify Yuliana Glinka in one of the best-known books of the Occult Revival, and when it becomes clear what sort of person she was the historian of the occult at once grows pensive. The reasons that give one pause must be reviewed.

The flight from reason, as I have suggested, might land the fugitive with one foot in the country of the occult and another in the land of conspiracy theories. But there is more to the coincidence of occultism and anti-Semitism than a common basis in the fear of change. This can best be initially expressed as "a similar quality of hate." In the ceaseless quarreling that besets occult groups, black and white are the only colors and the occultist's opponents are most viciously attacked. Such a general statement can be further refined. The hatred in the occultist and in the anti-Semite—we have already seen that they can coincide—are similar in degree, which is almost limitless; in object, which is undirectional; and in subjective effect, which is obsession—that is, such a hatred becomes the dominant feature of the hater's life, the cornerstone of his cosmology. Obviously, this generalization cannot be too vigorously applied. It becomes suggestive, however, when occultists and illuminates are discovered all along the path of anti-Semitism.

Dr. James Parkes distinguishes three basic forms of anti-Semitism: among peasants and proletarians a version that seems inherited from the superstitions of the Middle Ages; among the middle classes and the urban artisans, a recognition of the Jews as competitors; and among the land-owning aristocracy and ecclesiastics, a vision of Jews as the archmaterialists, the skeptical destroyers of culture and tradition.[13] Professor Cohn follows others in arguing "that whereas the Russians and Poles and Yugoslavs were decimated in the name of racist theories which were less than a century old, the drive to exterminate the Jews sprang from demonological superstitions inherited from the Middle Ages."[14] This would seem to argue the predominance of only one of Dr. Parkes's categories, while it is obvious that all three versions of anti-Semitism have been at work in the progress of the *Protocols* and the execution of the philosophy which lay behind the forgery.

But Professor Cohn is certainly more right than wrong in that the really dangerous aspects of modern anti-Semitism are without doubt superstitious and magical, although probably only a small proportion of anti-Semitic feeling is directly derived from the legacy of the Middle Ages. In the 19th and 20th centuries the chief repository of superstition has been the Occult Underground, and it is chiefly from this source that there stems the most vital element in modern anti-Semitism.

This argument implies yet another category of anti-Semitism

which interpenetrates the other useful distinctions and represents the dynamic that makes political programs out of passive attitudes. This is the category of fanatical belief and the instigation of murder. For although cynical politicians have certainly used anti-Semitic feeling in a completely amoral manner, pogroms and extermination camps are the products of faith. Just as more innocuous brands of antimaterialist politics have been identified as "illuminated" by their frequent association with the occult, there is an illuminated form of anti-Semitism, which is the most dangerous and can in the present century be identified by similar indicators.

The knowledge that the person who, in all probability, brought the manuscript of the Protocols from France to Russia was a Theosophist encourages a deeper examination of Theosophy. And there is yet another reason to examine more closely the connection between occultism and anti-Semitism. This becomes intelligible if we think of the not uncommon phenomenon of an anti-Semitic Jew, whom social pressures have driven into an unenviable position. In a similar fashion, renegade occultists are the most ferocious assailants of the occult. Because of the leading role played in many occult systems by the elaborate Jewish metaphysical system known as the Cabala, it would be perfectly logical (according to the strange laws operating in these regions) for a former admirer of Jewish mystical theology to turn upon the object of his veneration and see in the occult society which he has left, or been expelled from, part of a diabolical conspiracy of which he has been the victim.

An example of precisely this sequence of events can be found in the career of Miss C. M. Stoddart. For several years this lady was one of the three "ruling chiefs" of the English magical temple known as the Stella Matutina. Then suddenly, she reversed her values and wrote a series of anti-Semitic articles eventually published in 1930 as a book called *Light Bearers of Darkness*. All esoteric groups, she thought, were "consciously or unconsciously linked up with the Central Group which is acting behind the Third International of Moscow." This, of course, was the Jewish Freemasonic conspiracy.

> To bring about the unity of humanity, bound by the magnetic chain into the "Universal Republic" of the Grand Orient Judeao-Masonry, perverted sex consciousness by every means possible is necessary, such as illuminism, eurythmy,

nudity cults and dances etc., and perhaps in some groups psycho-analysis.[15]

The Hon. Ralph Shirley, the editor of the London *Occult Review*, deplored the anti-Semitic tendencies of the book, but he himself endorsed "the suspicion that the ranks of occultism are secretly working for disintegration and revolution. Positive proof in the shape of a group of occultists working with this object in view recently came under the notice of the present writer."[16]

Miss Stoddart was not the only English conspiracy-theorist to come from the ranks of occultism. Major-General Fuller, who had been a disciple of Aleister Crowley, developed an extraordinary magical anti-Semitism in the pages of Sir Oswald Moseley's *Fascist Quarterly*. The Jew, he wrote, hoped "to gain world domination under an avenging Messiah as foretold by Talmud and Qabalah." As a former member of a magical order—Crowley's Astrum Argentinum—Fuller knew all about the real significance of the Cabala. But now he alleged that "the Jews attack by Magic and Gold" and raked up one of the most celebrated occult scandals involving a magical order so as to justify his condemnation of a tradition to which he had once belonged.

In France, around the time of the forging of the *Protocols*, a similar apostasy occurred. Jules Doinel—the same who attacked Méry and Henriette Couedon from under the umbrella of Léo Taxil—was the founder of a Gnostic Church, of which one of the members was Papus. At the end of 1895 Doinel was reconverted to Catholicism. He then wrote a book under the pseudonym of Jean Kotska called *Lucifer démasqué*, which attacked occultism in general and in particular his own Gnostic Church and the Martinist Order of Papus.[17] In his reply Papus complained of the unsystematic way in which the campaigners against occultism "mixed up in the same salad the atheist Freemasons of the Grand Orient, the Spiritualists, the mystical groups and the Martinists, whose ancestors had themselves guillotined in '93 to defend Christianity against the secularising obscurantism which had already begun."[18] Of Doinel's *Lucifer démasqué* he wrote that it obviously had not been the unaided work of the former Gnostic. The book displayed traces of Taxil and his collaborators. Doinel, Papus wrote, "lacked the necessary scientific education to explain without trouble the marvels which the invisible world squandered on him." There had been only two possibilities open: conversion or madness. "Let us be thankful that the Patriarch of the Gnosis has chosen the first way."[19]

The propensity of occultists to do about-turns appears to have been recognized by those who wished to foster conspiracy theories. At any rate, when the German Foreign Office wanted to place the blame for the First World War, it turned to the best-known purveyor of mysticism in the German language: Gustav Meyrink.

In July 1917, Pastor Carl Vogl visited Meyrink to find his worktable covered with books on Freemasonry. The novelist told him an unusual story. He had been summoned to the Foreign Office in Berlin, where he had met an embassy official and two secret agents, including the former confessor of the queen of Bavaria. He was asked to write a novel that would blame the Freemasons for the outbreak of the war. It was to be translated into English and Swedish; 500,000 copies were to be printed; and it was to be sent all over the world. Meyrink was presented with a pile of books for his research, but he protested that possibly Gustav Frenssen or Ludwig Ganghofer would do the job better. This suggestion of the two fervently Germanic novelists must have seemed faintly ironical, for Meyrink had even published a parody of Frenssen's exaggerated celebration of peasant wisdom.[20] He was informed that if the tale was told by him it would be much more believable; and he took on the task. However, for one reason or another—according to Vogl, pressure from important Freemasons was responsible—a diplomat arrived in Starnberg to persuade Meyrink to drop the project. Pastor Vogl had held the instructions for the book in his hands: Meyrink had been directed to lay the blame for the war especially on French and Italian Masonry.[21]

If this official project foundered, the postwar period saw several attempts to follow the blueprint given Meyrink. One of the earliest was the occultist Karl Heise's *Die Entente-Freimaurerei und der Weltkrieg,* which made the villain "Anglo-Jewish Masonry" and on the first page noted the predeliction of Freemasons for the occult.[22]

It is expecting too much to find any great consistency in the no-man's land between occultism and anti-Semitism. There was even published in 1895 a book by a Catholic abbé accusing Edouard Drumont of being "not a Jew, but an Israelite" and insinuating that he was a member of a Rosicrucian organization that prostituted its female members. Every time Drumont wrote the word "Christ," cried the abbé, this must be taken as signifying "the unknown tribunal of Kadosch."[23] Drumont actually found these allegations worth replying to in his memoirs, which is a good indication of the territory in which he lived. With the necessary proviso that it is certainly not possible to fit every extravagance of a deranged mind into a neat pattern, it is always admitting defeat to condemn such extravagances as "mad." For whatever "madness" may be, it always has its own logic. The connection between occultism and anti-Semitism obeys certain rules.

Yuliana Glinka was not only a Theosophist: she was a secret agent. At least, for a period she had tried to be. In 1881-82 she had taken on the task of reporting on Russian terrorists exiled in Paris through her friend General Orzheyevsky, who was highly placed in the secret police. She was not very good at this and her cover was blown by the left-wing press.[24] If it was she who brought the *Protocols* into Russia —and there seems every reason to believe so—this was the second anti-Semitic document she had transported. The first, entitled *The Secret of the Jews,* is dated February 1895 and passed through the hand of General Orzheyevsky. It is a tract of muddled occultism, and while it is definitely a fabrication directed to the same ends as the *Protocols,* the impression it gives is remarkably different. Its paternity may become clearer as we examine Glinka and her Theosophical connections.

In June 1884, Glinka was living in Paris. Madame Blavatsky had just arrived from India, and Glinka received a letter full of scandalous gossip about H.P.B. The author of this letter was, like Glinka, a maid of honor at the Russian court and is referred to by Madame Blavatsky merely as "la Smirnoff." La Smirnoff wrote to Glinka that the foundress of the Theosophical Society had been banished from the Caucasus for theft and that her sister, Madame Jelikovsky, had destroyed her husband with unfaithfulness before leaving St. Petersburg for a life of sin in Odessa. The irate H.P.B. telegraphed the governor-general of the Caucasus to clear her good name and dispatched her informant Glinka together with Madame Jelikovsky to confront la Smirnoff in the Place Vendôme. The gossip was suitably discountenanced and the two ladies retired with great glee to inform Madame Blavatsky.[25] Yuliana Glinka was thus sufficiently concerned with Theosophy, or sufficiently a friend of Madame Blavatsky, to report to her gossip contained in a private letter. During the course of the year she met H.P.B. at least once again.

Glinka is not mentioned by name in Vsevolod Soloviev's account of his disillusionment with the Theosophical Society. But thanks to two passages in the letters of Madame Blavatsky, she is easily identified as the maid of honor, "Miss A."[26] Soloviev introduces her as a great friend of the secretary of the Paris Theosophical Society, Emilie de Morsier. Yuliana Glinka was

> continually surrounded by "phenomena" and miracles of all sorts; her marvelous stories of what happened to her at every step were enough to make one's head swim. She did not live in Russia and had lodgings in Paris; but she was continually vanishing, no one knew where, and was absorbed in some very complicated and intricate affairs of her own.

It is easy to guess something of the nature of Glinka's secret business, and possible to suspect Vsevolod Soloviev's account of his relationship with her. He writes that he left Paris on 24 August 1884 on his way to Elberfeld, where Madame Blavatsky was staying, and ran across Yuliana Glinka in Brussels. They decided to go together to visit H.P.B. "This point settled, we passed the rest of the day together, and in the course of the evening Miss A told me so much that was startling, marvelous and mysterious that I went off to my room with my head positively in a whirl, and though it was very late I could not get to sleep." The next morning they had arranged to start for Elberfeld, but Soloviev found Glinka standing in the middle of all her luggage, claiming to have lost her keys. A locksmith was called, opened a portmanteau, and discovered inside the bunch which would have opened the lot. By this time prostrated with nerves, Soloviev rested before embarking on his journey and had visions of unknown landscapes. When he and Glinka eventually caught the train for Elberfeld, he saw these landscapes pass by the carriage window.

Such inexplicable happenings had prepared the couple for H. P. Blavatsky and her masters. On their arrival at Elberfeld they were kept in front of brilliantly lit portraits of the Masters Morya and Kut Humi. In his hotel that night Soloviev awoke to see sitting beside him an exact representation of the Master Morya, who told the Russian "in an unknown but intelligible language" various matters of interest to himself. Soloviev discovered that he possessed "a great and growing magnetic force." At breakfast the next morning, Glinka told him that she too had seen the Master Morya, who had informed her that "we have great need of a little beetle like you." When the pair called on Madame Blavatsky, that sage lady claimed that she knew they had seen a Master. Glinka was amazed, but Soloviev was still skeptical, and his suspicions that he had been suggested into the experience were not allayed by Colonel Olcott's discovery of a Master's letter in his pocket. Madame Blavatsky persuaded him to stay and help her revise the manuscript of her latest series of articles for Katkov. Soloviev agreed, and while he was occupied at this task, Glinka, H.P.B., and Colonel Olcott sat in Madame Blavatsky's bedroom next door. A letter from the Master Morya fell at Glinka's feet. "This phenomenon secured her for the Theosophical Society."[27] The same day there arrived Frederic Myers of the London Society for Psychical Research, who induced Soloviev to communicate the "phenomenon" to the society.[28] It is this incident which positively identified Yuliana Glinka as "Miss A"; for Madame Blavatsky is on record as protesting to A. P. Sinnett that Soloviev later claimed "that the phenomenon of Mlle Glinka receiving Master's letter at Eberfeld when I was sick in bed, was produced with the help of *my aunt who detained* him in the drawing room while Olcott was throwing the letter on Glinka's head."[29]

We have, therefore, a clear indication of the sort of Theosophist Glinka was: credulous, easily impressed, and at all times "surrounded by phenomena." Soloviev, however, gradually began to dig in his heels. He refused to be sucked further into the swamp of uncritical faith, and in the course of his messy self-extrication from the Theosophical Society he precipitated a scandal of ferocious proportions. During this he outdid the wildest fantasies of la Smirnoff. He accused Glinka of being madly in love with the young Indian Theosophist Mohini Chatterji, affirmed that a member of the Paris Theosophical Society had tried to rape him, and threatened Madame Blavatsky with the continuing existence of her long-forgotten husband Nikifor Blavatsky, now "a charming centenarian." H.P.B. retaliated that Soloviev was a well-known gossip, and that he had seduced his present mistress when she was only thirteen.[30]

Besides these diverting innuendoes and the general dispute as to whether or not Madame Blavatsky was a fraud, lay another cause of war. This was the question of H.P.B. and the Russian secret service. The suspicion that she was "a Russian spy" had dogged her ever since her first arrival in India—it was also to attach itself to Gurdjieff and Ouspensky. But, according to Soloviev, in the autumn of 1885 H.P.B. asked him to propose her as a secret agent. When he returned to St. Petersburg, he was to transmit her request to the authorities and to tell them that she believed it perfectly feasible to use her position in India to raise a large rebellion against the English. (She had proposed a similar scheme, she said, "when Timashev was Minister.") Soloviev wrote that he promised to pass the request through their mutual friend, the editor Katkov.[31]

Madame Blavatsky, as always, had her riposte prepared. Soloviev, she wrote, had been the one to make the proposal of espionage. He was now "either crazy or acts so" because having compromised himself, he was afraid that Madame Blavatsky would discredit him in St. Petersburg.[32] When they had known each other in Paris Soloviev had tried "every day for five weeks" to persuade her to resume her Russian nationality—she was an American citizen —and to submit a "project" for subversion in India which he would pass on to St. Petersburg.[33] As her sense of persecution mounted, she maintained that Soloviev was quite capable of denouncing her to the secret police for treason. "All Russia knows it."[34] Out of this turmoil it is difficult to draw any definite conclusion; but it might be asked, why, if Soloviev was telling the truth, H. P. Blavatsky picked him, a journalist and historical novelist, in whom to confide her grandiose project? It is quite possible that Soloviev—who held the rank of groom of the chamber, the male equivalent to Glinka's maid of honor—was indeed involved in some of the shady activities of his traveling companion, and there are substantial grounds for thinking that the two had a much closer relationship than Soloviev indicates.[35] It is important, after discovering that Yuliana Glinka lived chiefly on the astral plane, to notice that the language of espionage and the secret police entered naturally into the abuse of Soloviev and Madame Blavatsky. Even assuming that *both* were lying, each could use the epithet "spy" and imagine that they might be believed. Whether or not H.P.B. or Soloviev ever joined Glinka on the roster of unofficial informants of the Russian government, the possibility was thought to exist, and—as we know in the case of Glinka—could easily coexist with Theosophy in the same person.

Theosophy, its doctrine, its foundress, and its adherents, can all be shown to have been involved in racism, conspiracy theories, and at least one anti-Semitic tract. This tract is of considerable importance, as it is one of the earliest anticipations of *The Secret of the Jews* and the *Protocols*. In order to understand how the Theosophical Society could have reprinted it in 1888 we must return to Madame Blavatsky and her doctrine.

Madame Blavatsky was by birth a Russian of the official classes, and it would be surprising if something of the anti-Semitic mythology of the Russian aristocracy had not rubbed off on her. She cannot be accused of any active anti-Semitism, but her attitude was that of her origins. In 1877 she was in New York, and on 25 September she published a letter in *The World* protesting against an article in the *New York Sun* which described the continuing persecution of the Russian Jews. The condition of the Jews, she wrote—and in this she was justified—had improved since the accession of Alexander II. But then the anti-Semitic myth takes over. In Kiev, she thought there were "more Jews than Gentiles": "pretty much all the trade is in their hands." The chief rabbi of Moscow had just been forced to publish an appeal to the Jews to be patriotic Russian citizens. And

> in 1870, during the *émeute* in Odessa, which was caused by some Jewish children throwing dirt into the church on Easter night, and which lasted more than a week, the Russian soldiers shot and bayonetted twelve Christians and not a single Jew: while—and I speak as an eye-witness—over two hundred rioters were publicly whipped by order of the Governor-General, Kotzbue, of whom none were Israelites. That there is a hatred between them and the more fanatical Christians is true, but the Russian Government can no more be blamed for this than the British and American

Governments because Orangemen and Catholics mutually hate, beat, and occasionally kill each other.

The fact that the Jews were not killed by the soldiery because they were themselves not rioting is passed over, and the blame laid at the door of the "fanatical Christians" whom H.P.B. detested. It is, thus, not a persecuting anti-Semitism, merely a passive acceptance of some elements of the myth. Her attitude to the Cabala was similar. She allowed it value but thought it should be stripped of its Jewish guardians. It may also be significant that she included in the references for *Isis Unveiled* (published in the same year as the letter about the Odessa riots) a book on human sacrifice among the Jews—a common topic of Russian anti-Semitism.[36]

If H.P.B. was to be believed, there was certainly a conspiracy plotting to take over the world; but it was a much older conspiracy than that of the Jewish Freemasons. The objects of her detestation, as befitted a rabid anti-Christian, were the Jesuits. In this she followed a widespread tradition of 18th-century pamphleteering against Jesuit plans for world domination, the basis of which was a tract entitled *Monte Secreta,* published in 1612 at Cracow by a renegade member of the order. She never tired of inveighing against "that crafty, learned, conscienceless, terrible soul of Jesuitism. . . . the hidden enemy that would-be reformers must encounter and overcome." She provided an interesting counterpart to the claims of the anti-Semites that the Jews were secretly manipulating Freemasonry by applying the same argument to the Jesuit attempt to control the Church. "They have succeeded. The Church is henceforth an inert tool, and the Pope a poor weak instrument in the hands of this Order." This diabolical Order made use of a secret cipher, and Madame Blavatsky quoted the *Royal Masonic Encyclopaedia* of Kenneth Mackenzie to the effect that "they may appear as Protestants or Catholics, democrats or aristocrats, infidels or brigands, according to the special mission with which they are entrusted. Their spies are everywhere." The clerical campaign against the Freemasons was organized especially to cover up the evil machinations of Jesuitry.[37] Madame Blavatsky transmitted her prejudice to her adherents. The devoted Theosophist Countess Wachtmeister thought that the Church was "fighting for life" against H. P. Blavatsky's *Secret Doc-*

trine,[38] and Annie Besant accused Rudolf Steiner of being a "pupil of the Jesuits."[39]

In the published correspondence of Madame Blavatsky there is an extraordinary document. It is undated and unsigned, although there can be little doubt that the style is that of H.P.B.—quite apart from its inclusion in an edition of her correspondence. It is headed "Private and confidential" and is rooted in her anti-Jesuit bias. It is unique in that it actually shows the application of this particular conspiracy theory to a specific political situation. After a preamble about the plotting of the Jesuit Order, the document warns that such conspiracies "have a much wider scope, and embrace a minuteness of detail and care of which the world in general has no idea." The only European statesman to keep himself informed of their activities is Bismarck, who contrives "to know accurately all their secret plottings through *his own private adept of the Schwarzwald.*" The purpose of the Jesuit plan is to plunge man back into his passive ignorance and to institute a "Universal Despotism." The Jesuits have been expelled from France and have transferred their headquarters to England, against which country they now direct the brunt of their evil efforts The Fenian agitation in Ireland is Jesuit-organized. The extremist and self-contradictory tone of the following extracts from the document is exactly in keeping with contemporary agitation directed against the Jews.

> The Jesuits have of late years candidly avowed that they hoped to succeed by enlisting ignorant democracies on their side. Accordingly, in 1885 W.E.G. plays the game of pandering to democrats by giving the suffrage to 2,000,000 of farm labourers. . . .
>
> If W.E.G. *be not a Jesuit,* we think he ought to be. His renewed advent to power was speedily followed by an insurrectionary meeting in Trafalgar Square. . . .
>
> The Jesuits have already been shown avowing their intention to excite revolutions to get what they think their rights. Now here are public speakers in England inciting to revolution. Ought you not then to come to the conclusion that these are Jesuit emissaries?
>
> Students of Occultism should know that while the Jesuits have by their devices contrived to make the world in general,

and Englishmen in particular think there is no such thing as Magic and laugh at *Black* Magic, these astute and wily schemers themselves hold magnetic circles and form magnetic chains by the concentration of their *collective WILL,* and when they have any special object to effect or any particular and important person to influence.[40]

"W.E.G." of course is Gladstone. The political tone of the document is exactly that of the author of the *Protocols* in its admixture of antimodernism and counterrevolution. The Jesuits replace the Jews as the Satanic conspirators because of H.P.B.'s dislike of Christianity, but the logic of the plot is the same. Because the audience addressed are occultists, there is the farrago of Jesuit "magnetic circles"; but such supernatural elements are not lacking in standard anti-Semitic propaganda. Obviously, the circular—for it reads as such—was concocted between 1885 and H.P.B.'s death in 1891. If its placing in the edition of her correspondence is anything to go by, it was written soon after the row with Soloviev, in late 1885 or early 1886. This approximate dating is quite enough to establish the occasion of Madame Blavatsky's manifesto. On 8 April 1886 Gladstone introduced his Irish Home Rule Bill into the House of Commons, and on 7 June the measure was rejected at the second reading; Gladstone resigned after the July elections had failed to confirm his mandate. The "Private and confidential" circular is undoubtedly directed against Gladstone's Home Rule policy—and it may be asked what H.P.B. thought she was doing in issuing such a document. It can be seen merely as a manifestation of her particular version of the conspiracy theory. Or if one is inclined to accept the story of H. P. Blavatsky's possible link with the Russian secret service, the circular resembles other attempts of the Russian police to discredit reform movements abroad as well as at home. It may have had certain results in occult circles—the Rev. William Aytoun, an alchemical clergyman involved with the Golden Dawn, subscribed to the theory that Gladstone was a Jesuit, and it is difficult to imagine another source for this idea. But the Jesuits were no longer the most satisfactory candidates for the role of disturbers of society, and other scapegoats were soon found.

In 1888 the Theosophical Publishing Society in London issued another document concerned with a conspiracy. This time it was directed against the Jews. *The Hebrew Talisman* was originally published in 1838: I have not myself seen a copy of the Theosophical reprint,⁴¹ but the date of publication, publishing house, and editor were recorded in 1927 in the anti-Semitic paper *The Patriot*. *The Patriot* thought that the tone of *The Hebrew Talisman* recalled that of the *Protocols,* and it printed sections of the pamphlet as a supplement for independent circulation. It also gave an extract from the introduction of the editor, Richard Harte.

> Through all the centuries, as they (the Jews) believe, Jehovah has been disciplining them and preparing them for their final triumph. Already the despised outcasts of a thousand years ago are the masters of kings and republics alike. There are a score of Jews today each one of whom is a greater power in the world than an army of a hundred thousand men. Were they to combine they could purchase Palestine ten times over, and then keep a million Christian workmen joyfully slaving at starvation wages for twenty years in doing the work of making the country once more a garden, while they stood by to superintend.⁴²

Richard Harte himself was a minor Theosophist, who in the year that he republished *The Hebrew Talisman* was a member of the Theosophical household at 17, Lansdowne Road in London. H. P. Blavatsky was finishing there her massive *Secret Doctrine,* and he had a hand in expanding the commentary on the spurious *Stanzas of Dyzan,* the product of Madame Blavatsky's imagination that is the book's crucial text. At the end of 1888 he traveled out to India and became temporary editor of *The Theosophist,* the magazine that his society published from Adyar; but at the end of 1890 he resigned his post over a difference of opinion.⁴³ His Indian career was distinguished only by the expediture of much time and money in constructing a boat which was propelled by a mechanism designed to reproduce the action of a fish's tail. Harte was an authority on hypnotism and hoped for the day when telepathy would be sufficiently developed to allow rapid two-way communication.⁴⁴ He remained a staunch admirer of Madame Blavatsky and thought that she had often been under the control of some supernatural entity. The only other anti-Semitic statement he made in print was his assertion that "the conception of the incarnation of a God for the salvation of men is a purely Aryan idea, absolutely and completely 'Pagan,' and nothing would have horrified the Jews themselves as a nation more than the notion of Jehovah having a son by a woman."[45] Needless to say, Harte himself was on the side of the pagans against the Jews.

The Hebrew Talisman, which Harte reprinted in 1888, is a satire originally published in London two years after the death of the financier Nathan Meyer Rothschild in 1836. A caricature of Rothschild forms a frontispiece. The middle of the 19th century was a great era for French polemics directed against the Rothschilds' rising fortunes. But with a single exception, the *Talisman* seems to be the only English example of the genre.[46] It is much more, however; for the occasion was only partly Rothschild's recent death. The satire is directed generally against the financial power of the Jews, with special reference to their recent dealings on the London Stock Exchange, and against the first Jewish Emancipation Bill, which was introduced in 1830. It is in the form of a story told by the Wandering Jew, a figure who was to appear frequently in mid-19th-century novels, and who had even been reported in 1830 as actually visiting England.[47] The Wanderer tells how he took the signet of Solomon from the Temple at Jerusalem to save it from destruction by the troops of the Emperor Titus, who had taken the city. At the moment of grasping the seal he was snatched away by supernatural power. He was given a mission "to teach the trampled Jew to become very mighty in despoiling his oppressors, very cunning in availing himself of their heart's leprosy—avarice." The power of the Talisman can ensure boundless riches. These are to be accumulated for the purpose of "making glorious the towers of Zion" and encouraging a return to Palestine.

> The bigotry of a whole people, and the cupidity of their tyrants could easily degrade the Jew in social condition; debar him from this or that privilege, condemn him to this or that burthen, and brand him with an outward and visible token of his debasement;—but the Jew could always amass wealth, preserve wealth, ... and sway the fate of the haughtiest and bloodiest of his oppressors. Aye! the Talismanic power has ever been at work; in every land hath its influence at some time been felt, in every land have I at some time made one of my people a mighty man, in the despoiling of the princes and the people who believe in the prophet of Nazareth.[48]

By the power of the Talisman, Necker was enabled for a time to support the extravagance of the court of Louis XVI. But the Wandering Jew withdrew the Talisman and unleashed the French Revolution. In London he bestowed the Talismanic power on Solomon Salvador but again withdrew the magical seal and selected Abraham Goldsmid. "Who among the elder frequenters of the great temple of Mammon which is called the Exchange, does not remember the golden box with which the hand of Goldsmid was perpetually occupied in his busiest and most important moments? It was his *talisman."* Unfortunately, Goldsmid, too, neglected the sacred task of resurrecting Zion, and the guardian of the charm

> found him incorrigible in his neglect of the cause of our people and our God; and even while he was wassailing at his luxurious villa in the neighborhood of Morden, the words of power went forth from my lips, and his talisman had departed from him for ever. Large rewards were vainly offered for what all but himself supposed to be a mere toy, a mere thing of effeminate luxury; but those rewards were offered in vain. He appeared upon the Exchange without his palladium; bargained, lost, and saw absolute ruin looking at him with steadfast and unpitying eyes. *Ten days he bore this* AND THEN BLEW HIS BRAINS OUT! None can be false to our cause and prosper.[49]

Not content with attributing the sensational suicide of Abraham Goldsmid to his Talisman, the author moved on to Rothschild. Who was it, he asked, who secured the downfall of Napoleon? Blucher and Wellington? Pshaw! "Simply Nathan Meyer Rothschild, armed with the Talisman." Rothschild had provided Lord Liverpool with the money needed to bribe the French deputies to abandon Napoleon. But as he then betrayed his original bargain with the British prime minister for a restored Palestine and settled for a Jewish Emancipation Bill in England, the Wanderer withdrew his sanction, and Rothschild "never ventured upon the Exchange again."[50]

Who the author of this elaborate mystification was is not known. Such indications as are contained in the text only tell us that the writer was very well informed about Jewish affairs and was conceivably present at the capture of Frankfort by the Napoleonic armies.[51] The original authorship is unimportant, as it is clear why

Richard Harte reprinted the pamphlet toward the end of the century. Its wide-reaching anti-Semitism, anti-Zionism, and, above all, its emphasis on the financial power of the Jews, well fitted the pattern of Jewish conspiracy literature that was growing up. For a Theosophical audience, moreover, the Jewish power was seen to be actually supernatural. Besides using the legendary magical relic of Solomon's seal, *The Hebrew Talisman* contains much pseudo-Jewish magical lore. Such is the reference to the "Wondrous and invaluable root BAARA," which can only be drawn from the earth if sprinkled with human blood and, when aided by a spell engraved on the Talisman, "is potent exceedingly in tasking the hidden powers, and in discovering the most hidden things."[52] In the secret world of conspiracy theories it is permissible to wonder whether the plot detectors themselves go armed with the root BAARA as well as with a dark lantern.

From H. P. Blavatsky's publication of *The Secret Doctrine* in the year that Harte reprinted *The Hebrew Talisman,* there existed for any Theosophist a powerful sanction for one or another doctrine of race supremacy. This lay in H.P.B.'s formulation of a doctrine of cosmic evolution, which entailed belief in a series of successive races, each embodying a different spirit and stage of evolution. The day of the "Sixth Root Race" was approaching. But throughout the world still remained representatives of archaic races which had been left behind on the cosmic spiral and were to die out in obedience to natural law. Such teaching was obviously open to distortion. For example, in England the Theosophist Isabelle Pagan published in 1937 a work ominously entitled *Racial Cleavage.* The book is essentially harmless, much of it written on the principle that "foreigners are *very* foreign." But it will soon be seen how such premises might provide less aimless cannoneers with an addition to their arsenal.[53]

When Yuliana Glinka passed to her protector the manuscript known as *The Secret of the Jews,* she was not only fulfilling her function as a good secret agent and loyal anti-Semite. She was probably also proceeding in accordance with her private inclinations as an occultist and a member of the Theosophical Society. Her contribution was a sort of memorandum, which does not attempt to provide the spurious authenticity of the *Protocols* or the novelistic appeal of *The Hebrew Talisman.* It was dated 10 February 1895, and was handed to General Orzheyevsky so that he should pass it on to General Cherevin, the commander of the Imperial Guard, who had the ear of the tsar. Cherevin disappointed the conspirators. He avoided possible accusations of suppressing evidence of state by placing the report in his files and leaving a copy to the tsar in his will. When the document was later discovered, Stolypin (who was minister of the interior in 1900) was found to have written in the margin "this is a form of propaganda wholly inadmissable by the government."[54] With the manuscript was a letter from Orzheyevsky to one Pyotr Alexandrovitch:

> I consider it essential that you should peruse the enclosed material, and request that you acquaint yourself with it, and pay special attention to its contents.
> It encloses exclusive material which confirms an invisible link between the Jewish faith and Freemasonry.
> In this sphere, I am forced to keep under constant surveillance those of our people who hold the highest posts, and even those whom considering the responsibilities they hold, it would seem should have a clearer understanding of similar questions which are not only of State, but of world importance.
> Recently, one of our Ministers in conversation with me about the revolutionary movement expressed the opinion—"Bloody Masons . . . they're the root of all evil. They rejoice that the people are idle and drunk. They're trying to negate and destroy everything."
> To my question, "How do they manage this, and what is their ultimate goal?" the minister, after a moment's thought, replied, "What should one say—simply *le néant*" [nothingness].[55]

The Secret of the Jews is an odd and interesting production. It consists of four distinct elements jumbled together. There is a preamble on the origins and significance of Judaism, to which is attached a short section of "occult history" of a familiar pattern. A long rigmarole about the structure of Freemasonry and its relationship with Judaism forms the body of the memorandum. The final pages are devoted to an analysis from the point of view of a conspiracy-theorist of how the forces of subversion are operating against Russia. This contains direct recommendations which are of considerable interest. Before discussing the contents in greater detail, it is important to emphasize that *The Secret of the Jews* is not directed at a popular audience. It takes the form of a report from a person possessed of "secret information" who wants this information placed before higher authority.

The sources of the interpretation of Jewish history are quite easy to identify; for the result is a scrambling of two or three strains of contemporary occultism. The author begins with a survey of the evolution of monotheism and its cultivation within "one all-embracing, world-wide religious brotherhood" (which included the Indian and Chaldean Magi and the Egyptian hierophants). This doctrine was introduced to the Jews by Moses, who instituted a ceremony of initiation—circumcision—and a grade structure symbolizing three different levels of understanding: for the ordinary people, for their leaders, and for the priesthood. The essence of the doctrine was taken from the Emerald Tablets of Hermes Trismegistus; and Moses also adopted the Egyptian system of hieroglyphs. The result was that the inner meaning of the religious symbolism was known only to the Essenes, the esoteric community of Jewish adepts. Among this community Jesus spent his youth and learned their secret doctrine. His mastery of this lore partly accounts for the rapid spread of Christianity. The untimely death of the apostle John robbed the Christians of their true understanding of the fundamental hidden truths, for it prevented their transmission from high priest to high priest. Christianity as such continues only on the "second level" of understanding. However, when the Roman Emperor Titus sacked Jerusalem in AD 70, a small community of Essenes was living isolated in the desert. And it is from this group, the custodians of the secret religion of antiquity, that the present clandestine organization of Jewish Freemasonry is descended.[56]

Of the various general occult allusions scattered about the document, some could have been derived from anywhere: the Emerald Tablets of Hermes, for instance, and a reference to the mystery religions of Serapis and Eleusis. But the insistence on the role of Moses and the deliberate organization of the Jewish people into a community of the chosen could have been taken at this period from only one distinct line of occult speculation. This began with the writings of Fabre d'Olivet (1767-1824), passed through those of his adaptor, Saint-Yves d'Alveydre (1842-1909), and was again incorporated in the writings of Saint-Yves' disciple, Papus. The most likely source, however, is Saint-Yves's *Mission des Juifs* (1884), but given an anti-Semitic twist. Saint-Yves declares explicitly that the Jews "have been the salt and the ferment of Life amongst Christian peoples, and they remain absolutely unresponsible for the Evil in the general government." In contrast, the author of *The Secret of the Jews* takes over the idea of the special organization of Jewish society around an esoteric religion but attributes the flight from Egypt to the natural indignation of the Egyptians at Jewish religious agitation and the impending threat of a gigantic pogrom. This complete reversal of the original occultist's attitude of reverence for Jewry is also typical, for example, of Miss Stoddart's *Light Bearers of Darkness*.[57]

We return to the surviving Essene community. It was their lot to reorganize the Jewish people after the fall of Jerusalem and to lead the nation in its predestined penitential mission to expiate the sin of the crucifixion. The best way of easing the position of condemned Jewry was to hasten the spiritual evolution of the rest of humanity and so to shorten the duration of God's curse. This meant encouraging the spread of Christianity, but also—and here *The Secret of the Jews* takes wing for the thin atmosphere in the upper reaches of illogic—undermining the Christian faith in those countries already professing it. At the same time the Jews preserved their traditional exclusiveness. They concentrated their political energies on the elaboration of a worldwide secret society to direct operations.

The memorandum then traces the activity of this secret society throughout history. At the coronation of Charlemagne in the year 800 a deputation arrived from the "Old Man of the Mountain"—who is represented as a Jew—proposing a joint attack on Islam. The Crusades were arranged on the advice of an Israelite delegation which wished to see Jerusalem exalted as the capital of the world and the seat of the papacy; and they resulted in the establishment of the Knights Templar, whose mission was to resurrect the Temple of Solomon in the Jewish interest. At this point the Jewish secret society had begun its work of recruiting collaborators among the Christians. This it was to continue through various occult groups and, eventually, among the Freemasons. The achievements of the secret society to date—Humanism, the French Revolution, the

American War of Independence, the expulsion of the Turks from Europe, Capitalism, the unification of Italy, the 1848 International—are merely masks for the ultimate goals of Jewry.[58]

From its occult premises, *The Secret of the Jews* thus contorts itself through some attempts at "occult history" until it emerges with a condemnation of occult societies very much like that made by the repentant Gnostic Jules Doinel. The association with anti-Masonic propaganda is then easy. This kind of occult history is of a type familiar to readers of Margaret Murray, the witch Gerald Gardner, and the Sufi Idries Shah, in which any secret and intriguing association can be seen as carrying the thread of the true doctrine. In the case of anti-Semitic propaganda, the "true doctrine" is that of the supposed false plot. The "Old Man of the Mountain" is a figure from anti-Semitic mythology, who occurred as early as the notorious Simonini letter of 1806;[59] while the Templars are largely occult preserve. There is little point in giving details of the memorandum's theories about the supposed connection between Freemasons and Jews. Although they much impressed General Orzheyevsky they are indistinguishable from countless other anti-Masonic tracts. The author's survey of the contemporary activities of the Jewish-Masonic society in Russia is more interesting.

According to the author, by 1895 the conspiracy has come to concentrate on a few main methods of attack. These are the encouragement of the liberal bourgeois intelligentsia and of all secularist elements of society; the introduction of the capitalist system and the destruction of the landed nobility; and the incitement of discontent among the peasantry (which had been dissatisfied by a fault in the reform program of February 1861, which gave the peasant insufficient land while improving his possibilities of collective action). The villains of the piece are the liberal intelligentsia, the capitalists, and the socialists. *The Secret of the Jews* then makes two recommendations. All the subversive agencies must be vigilantly watched; and, as the best way of enlightening the well-disposed elements of society, a popular summary and exposure should be printed of the Jewish plot against the whole Christian world and against Russia in particular.[60]

This is exactly what did happen in the case of the *Protocols*, although not with government backing. It is not possible to see the

Protocols as an "official response" to the proposal of *The Secret of the Jews,* because we do know that the memorandum was pigeonholed. But if we accept the story of how Yuliana Glinka brought the text of the *Protocols* to Russia after handing over *The Secret of the Jews* to General Orzheyevsky, we are entitled to ask whether the author of the memorandum had not become impatient with the lack of response to the original suggestion and had decided to take matters into his or her own hands. For the author of *The Secret of the Jews* it may not be necessary to look any further than Glinka herself. The document is a report, not a fabrication and would come easily from the lady perpetually "surrounded by phenomena." Of the three occultists from whom the author might have drawn the vision of early Jewish history Papus may well have had his finger in the pie. But it is worth noting that Glinka's friend Vesevolod Soloviev probably knew Saint-Yves d'Alveydre personally, and this in the year that he published *The Mission of the Jews.* Different parts of the report might have come from different hands, but the more "occult" opening section came not only from an occultist, but a *Russian* occultist—the use of the term "*god-seeking*" and mention of the expectation of Antichrist seem to show this.[61] A reference at the end of the report to the policy of the "new regime" indicates that the occasion of the memorandum was the advent of a new tsar. Nicholas II succeeded his father, the reactionary anti-Semite Alexander III, in November 1894, and was crowned in May 1895. The date of *The Secret of the Jews* places it in the period between accession and coronation, and the tone of the document shows that it was possibly designed to discredit modernizing policies—such as those of Count Witte—with the advisers of the new monarch. The memorandum is not directed specifically against Witte. There does not seem to be a specific attack on the gold standard, as has been suggested. This is unsurprising as Count Witte (who had become minister of finances in 1892) did not introduce this particular measure until 1897.

We come at last to the *Protocols* and the confusion surrounding them. It would be foolish as well as unnecessary to try to emulate Professor Cohn and Henri Rollin, whose conclusions may be quickly summarized. The *Protocols* attack liberalism and the industrial society; specifically, they attack the introduction of the gold standard and the modernizing policies of Count Witte, which are stigmatized as being exactly those of the secret Jewish world government.

These targets approximate, as we have seen, to the targets of *The Secret of the Jews*. In France the circle surrounding Juliette Adam and her *Nouvelle Revue* was implacably opposed to Witte and his policies; in Russia the diehard conservatives and reactionaries were concerned to alienate Witte and the tsar. Yuliana Glinka was Juliette Adam's close friend and the link between the two groups. She probably brought the *Protocols* to Russia when she returned sometime after the middle of the 1890s and was exiled to her estates in the government of Orel. This banishment took place because Glinka was suspected of complicity in a book published by Juliette Adam in Paris in 1886 under the pseudonym of "Count Paul Vasili." This had provided unwelcome revelations on the life of the imperial Russian family and the aristocracy. Professor Cohn has argued convincingly that Glinka passed a copy of the *Protocols* to the marshal of the nobility for her district, Alexei Sukhotin, who turned the foregery over to Filip Stepanov, the procurator of the Holy Synod. Stepanov (according to his own testimony) reproduced the *Protocols* in hectograph, then had them printed without any indication of place or date, sometime at the end of the 1890s.[62]

To complicate the issue, there appears on the scene the historian's nightmare, a professional double dealer. Pyotr Alexandrovich Ratchkovsky was from 1884 to 1902 the head of the foreign section of the Russian secret police. His headquarters were in Paris, and he delighted in counterrevolutionary activities of an uncanny deviousness. Ratchkovsky kept exiled Russian terrorists under strict surveillance, and when it came to a really dangerous situation he was preferred by the French President Loubet over his own security officers. His methods extended to instigating terrorist bomb attacks and promoting forgeries exposing himself. It is really not possible to make any statement for certain about Ratchkovsky's responsibility for any particular covert act; on a few points, however, his stance was consistent. These concerned his counterrevolutionary activities on behalf of the Okhrana and action above and beyond the call of duty in the way of instigating pogroms. He is supposed to have unwaveringly loyal to the beleaguered Count Witte, but it is a matter of some doubt how far this loyalty extended. When Count Witte, disturbed by anti-Semitic agitation, gave the order to destroy all the printing presses concerned in such enterprises, he was unable to silence the secret organization of Ratchkovsky which maintained itself in a priviledged position outside the normal channels.⁶³ But while Ratchkovsky is *a priori* a likely contender for the dubious honor of having forged the *Protocols,* it must be agreed that (at least during his period in Paris) the secret policeman was not likely deliberately to assault his own government—and it was against Witte that the *Protocols* were directed.⁶⁴ It remains possible that the Okhrana and their sinister chieftain were somehow involved.

There is a plethora of testimony pointing toward them, although most of it is unspecific and apparently based on the fact that Ratchkovsky was recognized as a likely person to have had a hand in an anti-Semitic forgery. Very little trust can be placed in claims by tsarist police officers to have forged the *Protocols* themselves. But Ratchkovsky is known to have participated in an intrigue in which it is thought that the *Protocols* were used. This odd conspiracy was part of the ceaseless game of chess that we have seen played around the Russian court, in which the pawns were magicians and mystics and the principals those concerned to influence the throne. Ratchkovsky was called in to assist the party gathered around the Grand Duchess Elisabeth Feodorovna whose business it was to replace the little captain of the Lyon fire brigade, Monsieur Philippe. Early in 1902, when the chief of the Okhrana visited St. Petersburg he brought a detailed report on Philippe. It denounced him as an agent of the *Alliance Israelite Universelle*—a Jewish philanthropic society whose name sounded sinister enough to anti-Semites to be used as the title of their imaginary band of conspirators. A report of some kind did in fact reach the tsar, who informed Philippe that he believed none of it. But in the end he was forced to give in and cease inviting the healer to Tsarskoe Selo.⁶⁵ If Philippe was exiled, Ratchkovsky was for a time disgraced: he was recalled from France and deprived of all offices. This did not prevent his vindictive nature from making the last years of Philippe a misery. He was haunted by secret agents, his correspondence was opened, his standing was ruined with the French authorities; Philippe's death in 1905 can be directly attributed to the machinations of Ratchkovsky.

Where do the *Protocols* come in? The mystagogue which the group who enlisted Ratchkovsky's aid had selected as their ambassador to the tsar was Sergei Alexandrovich Nilus. It was Nilus who published the *Protocols* in 1905 in the third edition of a book describing his conversion to Orthodoxy, *The Great in the Small*. The Grand Duchess Elisabeth Feodorovna, a highly religious woman who had founded an unofficial religious community, was impressed by the original publication. She made the acquaintance of Nilus with the idea of introducing to the court a mystic in the Orthodox tradition, instead of the dubious occultists who dominated it. Nilus was a landowner who had been converted from atheism after losing his fortune, and he had taken to the life of the wandering Russian pilgrim rather in the manner of Dobrolyubov. The grand duchess had him introduced to a maid of honor at Tsarskoe Selo by the name of Helena Ozerova; it was intended he should marry her so as to qualify according to the Orthodox rule to be ordained priest. The plan was for Nilus to be made imperial confessor; but this was foiled by Philippe's supporters. They replied to the grand duchess's stratagem by exposing several reasons why Nilus was an unsuitable candidate for the priesthood. Nilus had to leave the court, but Helena Ozerova—whom he was later to marry—performed a service for him that was to prove an essential link in the diffusion of the *Protocols*. When the new edition of Nilus's book was submitted to the censor, it ran into trouble because of the anti-Semitic complications. Through Ozerova's intervention the edition was passed, and even then the censor stipulated that all personal names must be removed from the appended *Protocols* themselves.[66]

One of these names—that of a rival secret agent, Akim Effront—has been taken by Professor Cohn as confirming the story of Ratchkovsky's responsibility for giving the *Protocols* to Nilus. Nilus himself said in 1917 that the *Protocols* came to him from Alexei Sukhotin; it has also been claimed that his source was Filip Stepanov.[67] Sukhotin or Stepanov, it makes no difference—this is the channel of communication which sees the forgery entering Russia with Yuliana Glinka. If the inclusion of Effront's name among the agents of the Jewish world conspiracy is taken as evidence of Ratchkovsky's meddling hand, it is also possible to see both him and Nilus using the *Protocols* as a device to link Philippe with the

Jewish-Freemasonic world conspiracy. It is not possible (and Professor Cohn has pointed this out) to see Ratchkovsky as instigating the forgery in order to implicate Philippe. Philippe was a faith healer and a Martinist; it will be remembered that his disciple Papus is supposed to have enrolled the tsar as a member of his Martinist order. Philippe's opponents would certainly have lost no opportunity of attacking Martinism as a manifestation of the Jewish plot. But Martinism remains uncondemned by the *Protocols'* sweeping condemnation of every possible *bête noire*. At the most, therefore, all Ratchkovsky did was use an already-existing forgery to suit his general purposes or urge on Nilus the publication of an anti-Semitic forgery in 1905, when he himself was busy inciting pogroms in defiance of Count Witte—and when he had long ago defeated Philippe, who in fact died in August 1905, one month before the book of Nilus, containing the *Protocols* but still in manuscript, was passed by the Moscow censor.

It is fairly clear that Ratchkovsky as a prime mover in the affair—as in so much of his devious career—is a gigantic red herring. Although there is every reason to think that he may have had something to do with the *Protocols* at some stage in their diffusion, he did not forge them to discredit Philippe; he did not bring them to Russia; and if he had a hand in their publication, it was probably only that inspired by his general anti-Semitism. So I return again to Glinka, whose transmission of the *Protocols* to Sukhotin, Stepanov, and thus to Nilus remains the only credible channel of communication. Now, if the *Protocols* contain no attacks on Martinism, Glinka's previous production, *The Secret of the Jews,* most certainly does.

> The First Crusade brought into existence the first order of knights—*the Knights Templar*—founded with the mystic mission of resurrecting the *Temple of Solomon.*
>
> This cult which seemed to be so alien to the Christian Brotherhood, symbolises the first victory of the Jews in their attempts to attract Christians to work unwittingly for the benefit of secret Jewish religious aims.
>
> Since that time, the Jewish secret society has been trying, under various names—*Gnostics, Illuminati, Rosicrucians, Martinists* etc.—to have invisible influence on the subsequent

course of Jewish history. The basic principles have remained the same: to undermine fundamentals, sow discord, and incite intellects; in a word, endlessly serving as the fermenting agent in the crumbly, amorphous mass of the Christian people.[68]

Some recapitulation is necessary to understand the precise significance of the attack on occultism in *The Secret of the Jews*. The document is dated 1895, the year of the defection of the Paris Gnostic Jules Doinel and his exposure of occult groups as part of the Satanic conspiracy. Papus, besides being a Martinist, was a member of Doinel's Gnostic Church and was deeply affected by the incident. He was also a disciple of Saint-Yves d'Alveydre, from whom as we have seen, the author of *The Secret of the Jews* drew a considerable amount of material. There is further confirmation of this in the extract cited above.

The author uses the metaphor of the Jews being the *ferment* in the body of Christian people, which is exactly that used in a good sense, by Saint-Yves d'Alveydre, when absolving Jewry from blame for political troubles. Papus is thought by his disciples to have introduced Saint-Yves d'Alveydre to Grand Duke Peter, and he certainly made the ideas of his "intellectual master" well known in Russian mystical circles. It is exceedingly likely that the author of *The Secret of the Jews* was an occultist infected by the current suspicion of the occult—possibly a renegade like Doinel or even a time-server like Meyrink.

We have suspected the author of the document to be Glinka herself. We know her to have been an occultist, and if she acted only as colporteuse of *The Secret of the Jews* or the *Protocols* she was certainly an anti-Semite, an attitude which her Theosophy may have encouraged. Could Glinka have turned on the teachings of Saint-Yves and Papus, or (like her friend Vsevolod Soloviev) left the Theosophical Society because it was anti-Christian? It is quite possible. For in these realms of rapidly changing allegiance from one master to the next, all is uncertain. It is impossible to see in the attack on Martinism in *The Secret of the Jews* an assault on Papus and Philippe, except incidentally; for it was only in 1896 that Papus sent his message to the tsar and five years later that he and Philippe set foot in Russia for the first time. But—even if Glinka was not the author—the root of the trouble lies without doubt in French occultism and its links with Russia.

Of the three branches of the Theosophical Society in Paris in 1884, one was a Spiritualist group, one a "scientific" society of occultists; and the third (the "Theosophical Society of the East and West") a branch of Theosophy proper. The president was the Duchesse de Pomar, the secretary Mme. Emilie de Morsier, and the membership included such celebrated occultists as Edouard Schuré, Albert Jounet (Barlet), and Charles Richet. Three Russian names appear on the list of members: Princess Olga Wolkonsky, Countess Marie Balowska, and a Madame Jakouleff. In a membership list written shortly before July 1887 Glinka's name can be found. In the same year the name of Papus also appears as a member of another Theosophical organization.[69] By this time, Vsevolod Soloviev had succeeded in breaking up the original society" of the East and West" and had seduced Emilie de Morsier and some of the original members from their allegiance: in 1892 he could still refer to Mme. de Morsier as "one of my true friends." Glinka had apparently survived this test of loyalty to Madame Blavatsky; unfortunately her name then disappears from the records. But in 1888 there was conflict in the Paris Theosophical Society between one party led by Papus and another led by Felix-Krishna Gaboriau, who controlled the magazine. The result was that Colonel Olcott dissolved the existing branch and refounded the Paris group in a way that was favorable to Papus and his friends. Papus meanwhile founded the *Groupe Indépendent des Études Esoteriques.* His independent line of conduct annoyed Madame Blavatsky, and in 1890 he was finally expelled from the society.[70] In this cut-and-thrust there was plenty of scope for the brewing of enmity, and, if Glinka remained a stalwart supporter of Madame Blavatsky, there is plenty of reason to represent her as a possible opponent of Papus. If this was so, however, her enmity probably did not show itself until 1895; for it seems that Glinka's close friend Juliette Adam may have been in relations with Papus during the period 1891-92.

All authorities on the *Protocols* have united in the opinion that the forgery emanated from the circle of Juliette Adam and the *Nouvelle Revue.* This is one of the initial reasons for supposing the story that Glinka took the document to Russia to be correct. From this has come the suspicion that the forger was a publicist and politician known as Elie de Cyon (Tsion), a known opponent of Witte and in many other ways a likely guess. Once more it is Professor Cohn who has shown that de Cyon, a humane man and an opponent of pogroms, could not possibly have produced the *Protocols* as they stand; instead he suggests that, when Ratchkovsky burgled de Cyon's villa in Switzerland in 1897, he discovered a satire directed against Witte and gave it an anti-Semitic bias.[71] But, apart from the inherent unlikeliness of the procedure, the satire would after all still be directed against Witte, in whose interests Ratchkovsky was burgling the villa. This introduces yet a further step between the group of the *Nouvelle Revue* and the appearance of the *Protocols* in Russia via Glinka and Stepanov. Ratchkovsky would have had to have given his adulterated forgery to Glinka, a friend of Juliette Adam and the burgled Tsion, who could not have failed to have recognized his own work had it come his way, however altered. Tsion appears as red a herring as Ratchkovsky, and distracts attention from Juliette Adam herself.

At the end of October 1855, Vsevolod Soloviev called on Juliette Adam about a story of his called "The Magnet" appearing in the *Nouvelle Revue*. At this time he had not completely broken with Madame Blavatsky, and he wrote to her from Paris on 8 October:

> I have made friends with Madame Adam, and talked a great deal to her about you; I have greatly interested her, and she has told me that her Revue is open not only to theosophy but to a defence of you personally if necessary. I praised up Madame de Morsier to her, and at the same time there was another gentleman here who spoke in the same tone, and Madame Adam wished to make acquaintance with Madame Morsier, who will remain in Paris as the official means of communication between me and the *Nouvelle Revue*. Yesterday the meeting of the two ladies took place; our Emilie was quite in raptures.

Later, in a more skeptical frame of mind, Soloviev wrote that he had found Madame Adam talking of how she was a pagan and worshipped the pagan gods; he had been hard put not to laugh. This pagan cult of Juliette Adam in fact culminated in a book of 1888 called *Un rêve sur le divine* which constructed her own occult synthesis. The book attracted the attention of occult circles—indeed Madame Adam was said by the anti-Masons to entertain such gentry as Papus and the Gnostic Fabre des Essarts in her salon. In 1892, Papus lectured on the merits of her book, and it was rumored by her opponents that Juliette Adam was a member of that magician's *Groupe Indépendant des Études Esoteriques*. But the pagan Madame Adam became increasingly Christian. Around 1903-04 articles began to appear hailing the reclamation of this fervent French patriot by the Catholic Church. Indeed, Juliette Adam's religion was linked with her patriotism, for she saw French Catholicism as part of her racial heritage and directly opposed to the *Kultur* of Bismarck.[72]

The name of Juliette Adam was associated with Papus and his group *after* the magician's quarrel with Madame Blavatsky, and *before* the general crisis in the French occult world which resulted from the defection of Jules Doinel in 1895. In the minds of those addicted to conspiracy theories, occultists only became fully associated with the Jewish-Masonic plot after this incident. If the author of *The Secret of the Jews* were indeed Glinka, there is nothing in the facts to contradict the idea that in 1895 she had decided either that occultism was in reality part of the diabolic conspiracy, or that it should appear to be so. The conversion of her friend Juliette Adam from a heterodoxy hospitable to Theosophy to an eccentric Catholicism might well be part of the same process of revulsion with the occult. Glinka, of course, was by no means the only Parisian Russian with occult learnings. There seem to have been few who were free of them.

Emilie de Morsier (whom Vsevolod Soloviev introduced to Juliette Adam in 1885 and who was to remain his contact with the *Nouvelle Revue*) initiated a lasting communication between "progressive" ladies in Paris and those of St. Petersburg, when in 1892 she and a Russian friend collaborated on raising funds for the relief of the famine which devastated Russia that year. Madame de Morsier died in 1895, but the contacts established survived her.[73] One result of her efforts was a magazine, *La Revue des femmes russes* (1896-97), edited from Paris by Olga Besobrasova, who was prominent in mystical and progressive circles. The *Revue* at first bore a sphynx at its masthead and contained contributions by Raymond Nyst and Count Leonce de Larmadie, both associated with the magician Péladan. From the Russian end, Countess Ina de Kapnist reported a special interest in new university courses for women in "psycho-physics" and a general interest in Spiritualism. In March 1897 the *Revue* reported the first annual general meeting of the "Société d'Aide Mutuel des Femmes de St. Petersburg," which was as near as the aristocratic Russian ladies—as opposed to the intelligentsia—were allowed to come to "Progressive" activities. It was patronized by, among others, the Grand Duchess Militza and John of Kronstadt, who gave the group his blessing; and the same meeting recorded the election of a new member, the maid of honor "C. S. Oserow" (who might well have been a relation, if not a misprinting, of Helena Ozerova).[74] The mystical atmosphere of the whole undertaking must have suited its editress splendidly. She was able to serialize her own synthetical *The New Religion,* which laid particular stress on Pythagoras and the Cabala: its authoress knew all the texts of contemporary occultism, such as Saint-Yves d'Alveydre, Fabre d'Olivet, the alchemist Louis Lucas, and of course, Papus.[75] Olga Besobrasova is discovered in 1898 contributing to the Paris Theosophical magazine, and in 1901 her volume of mystical poems carried a preface by Paul Adam, a member of the *Ordre Kabbalistique de la Rose-Croix*—and also an anti-Semitic novelist.[76]

In the circles from which the *Protocols* originated in France; in those in which they were received in Russia; and in the communication between the two milieux there was a substantial dose of the mystical. Almost any of the illuminated Russians might have written or provided the material for *The Secret of the Jews*. But could they or Glinka or any of the other mystics in contact with Juliette Adam have produced the more dangerous—because relatively more down-to-earth—*Protocols?* For there is almost nothing in the *Protocols* to suggest the mystical: they are adapted from a political satire, and where they describe horrors which do not originate in Joly's vision of the rule of Napoleon III they are directed solely toward substantiating the legend of a tangible Jewish plot to establish a global despotism.

Almost the only "occult" thing about them is the appendix, which the early Russian editions carried. This dilated on the Symbolic Serpent, which was supposed to demonstrate the march of Jewish conquest. The serpent was drawn on a map, with its tail in Palestine, its body encircling Europe and its head in Russia, through which it would pass to join the tail and complete its victory. This conception is said by one of the oddest Russian anti-Semites to have originated in the writings of the defrocked clergyman Hippolytus Liutostansky;[77] but the motif is also present in French anti-Masonry. Both sources probably took the symbol from a misapplication of contemporary occultism, in whose idiom Olga Besobrasova could ask, in the *Revue des Femmes Russes* of 1896: "Does not the esoteric theosophy of the temples of Isis and Horus, symbolized by the serpent squeezing the universe in its coils incorporate in an obscure cult, the highest religion. . . ?"[78] In several occult systems the serpent symbolizes wisdom and eternity: it appears in Cabalistic diagrams and on the seal of the Theosophical Society.

The Symbolic Serpent apart, the *Protocols* are the least occult document of militant anti-Semitism that it is possible to imagine. It is probably for this reason that they have been so effective. But in Glinka the forgery has a common factor with the memorandum entitled *The Secret of the Jews,* which gives the appearance of being produced by a renegade occultist, in a year of occult apostasy. That document, it will be recalled, ends with a recommendation that there should be printed and circulated a popular exposure of the Jewish conspiracy in Russia. Glinka later returns with a document which is eventually put to just that use. This is scarcely coincidence.

Because illuminates of the type who cultivate and believe in anti-Semitism are apt to write in the manner of *The Secret of the Jews,* it does not follow that they cannot write otherwise, or that they cannot persuade others to do their writing for them. Who actually discovered Maurice Joly's satire on Napoleon III and decided that it would make good anti-Semitic material will probably never be known. But one case is known in which an illuminate concocted an attack directed both at Count Witte and at a conspiracy aimed at undoing the Russian regime: and he had the sense, although he was an experienced man of letters, to secure the collaboration of a professional jouranlist skilled in polemic. This illuminate was none other than the magician Papus.

In late October 1901—the month after Monsieur Philippe was introduced to the tsar and tsaritsa, when both he and Papus had returned from their respective Russian visits—a series of articles under the pseudonym "Niet" began to appear in the *Echo de Paris,* for which Papus was primarily responsible. He attacked Witte; he attacked Ratchkovsky, whose operations in Paris were circumstantially surveyed; he attacked the machination of a sinister financial syndicate that was trying to disrupt the Franco-Russian alliance. It is quite clear that this syndicate, which is identified with that responsible for the scandal of Panama, is Jewish. In terms of policy, this broadside conformed with the policy of Juliette Adam and her associates. It was this series of articles that aroused Ratchkovsky's abiding ill-humor against the hapless Philippe, who was naturally associated with Papus: not only was the spy's political master attacked, but his *amour propre* was at stake. In the articles of Niet, the primary target was the "hidden conspiracy," about which the public was hideously uninformed and unperceptive.

> It does not see that in all conflicts whether arising within or between nations, there are at the side of the apparent actors hidden movers who by their self-interested calculations make these conflicts inevitable. For example, is it necessary to remember the role of the Jesuits in the wars of Louis XIV and the revocation of the Edict of Nantes? Again, it is known that the French Revolution was planned in 1740 by the Duc d'Antin and his friends, begun by the publication of the Encyclopaedia, organised in 1773 by the foundation of the Grand Orient, to hatch out for all to see in 1789.
>
> Lastly, no one is any longer unaware that the *Risorgimento* of Italy was contrived long before by the Carbonari associations, in the same way as the *Mafia* is trying to establish—and perhaps will establish sooner or later—a Republic on the other side of the Alps.
>
> Everything which happens in the confused evolution of nations is thus prepared in secret with the goal of securing the supremacy of a few men; and it is these few men, sometimes famous, sometimes unknown, who must be sought behind all public events.
>
> Now, today, supremacy is ensured by the possession of gold.
>
> It is the financial syndicates who hold at this moment the secret threads of European politics. . . .

> A few years ago there was thus founded in Europe a financial syndicate, today all-powerful, whose supreme aim is to monopolise all the markets of the world, and which in order to facilitate its activities has to acquire political influence. Let us remember in passing that the notorious Cornelius Hertz was one of the principal agents of this international association, whose centre is at London and whose most important ramifications are at Vienna and in Germany.

Nothing could better illustrate the reasoning behind conspiracy theories than this introductory passage. From the mention of Hertz (heavily involved in the Panama scandal) and the covert reference to the Rothschilds, it is obvious that the Anglo-German financial syndicate the authors go on to describe is supposed to be fundamentally Jewish. They take elements from current anti-Masonic agitation by combining their conspiracy with the myth of the all-powerful British Secret Service—which was sometimes said to stand behind the Masonic lodges. The object of this unholy alliance is to weaken the ties that bind Russia to France (because this is the greatest obstacle to British imperialism). In France the agents of this syndicate concentrate on anti-Russian propaganda. In Russia they have infiltrated the Minstry of Finances—Witte—and the General Staff: in particular they have forced the adoption of a system of loans, of deflation and of financial trickery so that the Russian army can be stopped at any moment at the will of the sinister "trust." Tsar Nicholas II knows nothing of this—why his minister of finances and his General Staff circumvent all his most generous projects. "May we be able," Niet concluded his introduction, "to preserve the Russian Emperor—so loyal and so generous—from the evils which this syndicate of financiers visited on us in our recent troubles: this syndicate which at the present controls the destinies of Europe—and of the world."[79]

The elaboration of this theme proved particularly distressing to Witte and Ratchkovsky. From St. Petersburg Witte dispatched a huge bribe to prevent the *Echo de Paris* from publishing a second series of articles.[80] Ratchkovsky then began his campaign against Philippe. If the result was the death of the Lyonais mystic, his friend and pupil Papus was made of sterner stuff. Under pressure the imperial couple had renounced their beloved Philippe, but continued to see Papus. The legend told by the disciples of Papus is that when the Revolution of 1905 broke out in Russia, one of the highly placed friends of the magus ordered him to the Russian court. The day after his arrival, Papus evoked the spirit of the reactionary Tsar Alexander III before the tsar and the tsaritsa. Nicholas was advised by the spirit not to make any concessions to the liberals and was told that revolution would nonetheless break out again: "It doesn't matter! Courage, my son! Don't give up the struggle!"[81] Take or leave this story—most commentators have left it, and the authority is that of the credulous French ambassador Paléologue—it is probably an accurate reflection of Papus's political advice. This echoed the counsels of Monsieur Philippe, whose warnings against granting a constitution are recalled in the letters of the tsaritsa.

Papus—what was he really up to? Occultist, *guru en titre* in the shoes of Monsieur Philippe, and believer in conspiracy theories, his role is, on the face of it, equivocal. From his papers it is known that he furnished documentation to the tsarist authorities on the subject of Masonic activities (for example, to the tsar's ambassador in Rome). He had once himself written Masonic textbooks. But the whole tenor of his Martinist propaganda was that Freemasonry was atheistic in contrast to the esoteric Christianity of Louis-Claude de Saint-Martin. The confusion is no greater than is customary in occult regions. His friends among the Paris occultists thought that in his Martinist activities, Papus was *deliberately* meddling in European politics; and, according to Victor-Emile Michelet, most of the Balkan princelings were Martinists.

This is not so farfetched as it sounds when we remember the part played by the Montenegrins in introducing mysticism to the Russian court. It is a typically occult boast to claim influence over heads of state—but then we know that Papus did in fact exercise such influence in Russia. Then there is the question of the row of decorations Papus claimed: three of these are verifiable in works of reference, comprising an ancient Portuguese order and two recently instituted decorations from Venezuela and Turkey. On the whole, these seem products of *folie de grandeur.* But there remains the certainty that the magus saw himself as a power behind thrones. His Martinist policies fitted easily the preconceptions of Russian "idealist" reactionaries. He castigated "our epoch of scepticism, adoration of material forms, so vitally in need of a frankly Christian reaction, independent of all the priesthoods."[82] In his association with the Montenegrins and the mystics of Philippe's party in both Russia and France, Papus (like his master, Philippe) certainly accepted their view of Russian politics. The articles of Niet, for which the magus was largely responsible, express precisely the standpoint of the Russian right wing.

In July 1920 a Warsaw newspaper accused Papus himself of fabricating the *Protocols* with the aim of discrediting Monsieur Philippe. This cannot be true, because of the magician's unwavering loyalty to Philippe, and because a manuscript of the *Protocols* shown by Sergei Nilus to Count du Chayla appeared to the latter definitely to have been written by a Russian.[83] But, as regards the magician's essential attitude, there is little to prevent the speculation. In 1896, around the time of the forging of the *Protocols,* Papus was in cordial relations with the illuminated anti-Semite Gaston Méry. The *Sociétè des Sciences Psychiques* had appointed a committee to investigate Méry's protogée, the seeress Henriette Couedon—whose prophecies, incidentally, included the information that someone was trying to poison the tsarevich and that the Jews were soon to make a concerted move. On the committee, Papus found himself upholding the claims of Mlle. Couedon against the anti-Mason and collaborator of Léo Taxil, Charles Hacks (alias "Dr. Bataille").[84] It was 1896, the year of the tsar's visit to France, when Papus sent his message on behalf of the French Spiritualists, and it is possible that even then his conspiracy theory had been formed.

As for his collaborator, the other half of Niet, this was Jean Carrère, a journalist. A note discovered among the papers of Papus apportioned responsibility as that of "Papus for the material, and Jean Carrère for the drafting," while Carrère's wife sold the articles to the *Echo de Paris*. Jean Carrère (1865-1932) began life as an anarchist Bohemian associated with the Symbolist poets. In 1891 Jean Renard wrote of him that "he believes in the Ideal, in the infinite, in Job, in a pile of unremarkable things." Around the middle of the 1890s, Carrère underwent a conversion. He became a fanatical *Félibre*—an adherent of the movement for Provençal culture headed by Mistral—and in 1898 published an answer to Zola's *J'accuse,* blaming degenerate art for leading France astray. He became increasingly attached to Drumont and the *Libre Parole,* and, when he was sent to South Africa in 1901 as a war correspondent, he was well prepared to receive the anti-Semitic views put about by the supporters of Sir William Butler which inspired Henry Hamilton Beamish. His collaboration with Papus followed hard on his return from South Africa, and throughout the articles of Niet there are found obvious references to the hidden action of a financial syndicate in inciting the Boer War. There is even a section on "The Tsar and the Transvaal." Carrère subsequently served as a war correspondent in Italy and became associated with d'Annunzio, but was latterly prevented from much energetic activity by ill health. When Papus was in search of his collaborator, it was thus to a known anti-Semite that he turned. There is no doubt that their views coincided.[85]

The lines are converging. We are within a hair's breadth of a solution to all these complexities when we recall that one of the starting points for this chapter was that "the quality of hate" of anti-Semites and occultists is often the same. Although Papus was an anti-Semite, associated with the group around the Montenegrins, it was logical for Ratchkovsky and Philippe's opponents to try to use Nilus and his edition of the *Protocols* to exclude Papus and Monsieur Philippe from the counsels of the empire—to associate *them* with the conspiracy imagined by Niet. But (as we have noted), in the Nilus edition of the *Protocols* there is no mention of Martinism, which Papus was assiduous in representing as opposed to Freemasonry. In the more popular editions of the *Protocols,* published under the editorship of G. Butmi, Martinism generally—and Papus and Philippe by name—are represented as attached to the universal Jewish conspiracy. Martinism, Butmi declared, was responsible for all revolutions. He attacked the reputation of Martinism as the sworn enemy of Freemasonry and the representative of "pure Christianity." It was "the most Jewish" of all occult orders, and its representatives were those responsible for advising the governing classes to adopt self-destructive policies. The political stance of Butmi is as clear as it could possibly be. His main assault is on an organization called the "Great Universal League," which he claims has just been founded in St. Petersburg, headed by "sorcerers and dangerous agitators" like Philippe and Papus, who had come to

Russia *"to make adepts among the members of the highest society who were seeking in Martinism for a support against Judaism."*⁸⁶

From his own distorted point of view, Butmi suspected rightly. This seems exactly what must have happened. The Montenegrin group won favor with their own reactionary gurus, and the Grand Duchess Elizabeth Feodorovna attempted to counter with Nilus. At the same time Butmi and his associates tried to displace Philippe and Papus by attaching their names to the *Protocols.* When it is remembered that Ratchkovsky was returned to favor in 1905 and given a police post in Russia, which he used to print anti-Semitic propaganda (and to assist Butmi and others in the founding of the ultra-right-wing "Union of the Russian People"), the division of the parties becomes clearer. On the one hand the Montenegrins and their friends: occultists, aristocratic, and using Philippe, Papus, and Martinism as a transcendental sanction for their anti-Semitism. On the other hand, Butmi and his colleagues of the "Union of the Russian People," using brutal methods, repugnant to most of the aristocracy, printing the *Protocols* as a popular incitement to pogroms (and wishing incidentally to displace the reigning gurus). Attached to this party is Ratchkovsky, who, in Paris, has begun a lasting personal feud with Papus and Philippe. A third group intervenes in the shape of the Grand Duchess Elisabeth Feodorovna and her circle, representing the Orthodox element, which wishes to displace the Martinists and substitute Nilus. Again the *Protocols* are used, but without specific mention of the Martinists and this time incorporated in a well-produced mystical work aimed directly at the tsar. It is obvious that this more subtle approach, if not exactly that of the "Union of the Russian People," could not but meet with its approval. Whether Ratchkovsky or Stepanov/Sukhotin transmitted the *Protocols* to Nilus, all parties possibly involved in the transaction were united in their objects.

What is interesting is that Papus and the Martinists had fired the first shots in this war. These were the articles of Niet in the *Echo de Paris* attacking Witte and Ratchkovsky. To most reactionaries in Russia, attacks on Witte would have been perfectly acceptable. To Ratchkovsky, on the other hand, they constituted a personal affront. But even without Ratchkovsky, the Russian right wing might have become disquieted at the provenance of the Martinists. The author of *The Secret of the Jews* had included them as early as 1895—before there had been any contact between Papus, Philippe, and the Russians—in the list of occult agencies through which the Jewish conspiracy worked. If the *Protocols* are seen as the result of the appeal in *The Secret of the Jews* for a popular exposure of the Jewish plot, we can explain Glinka's carrying the *Protocols* to Russia as part of this express plan. Who provided her with the forgery is quite impossible to guess. If she wrote *The Secret of the Jews*, she would undoubtedly have been on the lookout for material to use for this specific purpose. It would be chasing will-o'-the-wisps, however, to pursue the inquiry any further.

Glinka's exact role in the episode must remain a matter of speculation. It is safe to assume that, by the time she transmitted *The Secret of the Jews* to General Orzheyevsky, she concurred with its opinions, even if she did not actually write it. When she brought the *Protocols* to Russia, she would therefore be perfectly prepared to see a forgery, which was perhaps designed as a popular exposure of the Jewish plot, used in a campaign against the Martinists and Montenegrins. Not only did Nilus probably derive his copy of the *Protocols* from Stepanov's private publication, but it is likely that the version printed in 1903 by Krushevan in *Znamya* came from Glinka as well.[87] This version was used by Butmi for his two popular pamphlets on the Jewish conspiracy. It thus came about that the recommendation of the shelved memorandum, *The Secret of the Jews*, was adopted unofficially ten years after that production had briefly seen the light of day.

This is the only explanation that fits the facts. It may contain too many ifs and buts to be regarded as proven; but it is the most likely. It surely shows the importance of examining the occult Underground: an importance magnified by the presence in that Underground of the indispensable quality of *belief*. The actual forger of the *Protocols* may have been a cynical *pogromtschik*, but his object was to induce *belief* in others. The fact that anti-Semites are often frighteningly sincere men is frequently passed over—probably because of fear of what this discovery means for a general vision of man. We have seen how the *Protocols* were transmitted through illuminated circles, and how the battle of the magicians was that in which they were at first deployed. The case is reinforced by the continued role played in both anti-Semitism and the propagation of the *Protocols* by representatives of the illuminated point of view.

The "Union of the Russian People," with its notorious bands of bully-boys, the Black Hundreds, was the leading Russian anti-Semitic organization. The union was founded in 1905 by a St. Petersburg doctor, A. Dubrovin, as the successor to a number of similar right-wing groups. Its membership was drawn from the sort of elements who were to give the German Nazis their support: a few aristocrats, some churchmen, many declining petit bourgeois, and the violent flotsam that drifts on the top of urban life. The union was chiefly concerned with whipping up mass discontent against foreigners, the intelligentsia, and Jews. Generally speaking, the union and the Black Hundreds were looked down on by the monarchists, for whom Count Witte's opinion can stand:

> The bulk of the party is dark-minded and ignorant, the leaders are unhanged villains, among whom there are some titled noblemen and a number of secret sympathisers recruited from the courtiers. Their welfare is made secure by the reign of lawlessness, and their motto is: Not we for the people, but the people for the good of our bellies.[88]

Deeply involved in this unbeautiful assembly were Krushevan, the instigator of the terrible pogrom at Kishinev in 1903 and the first publisher of the *Protocols;* and Butmi, the editor of the popularized editions. The most effective leader of the Union of the Russian People was Vladimir Mitrofanovich Purishkevich (1870-1920), a landowner and former government official, who attempted to use his redoubtable energies in stemming the liberal tide. In the Duma, he and his equally notorious colleague, Nicholas Yevgenievich Markov (known as Markov II), caused ceaseless disturbance in an effort to discredit parliamentary government entirely. From about 1908, when the Revolution of 1905 had been forgotten and the activities of the union became less necessary to the powers that were, the Black Hundreds began to decline. Purishkevich founded his own organization, the "Union of the Archangel Michael." Dubrovin and Markov II were at daggers drawn, each leading rival groups and denouncing each other to the police for "sympathizing with the Jews."[89]

From the "Union of the Russian People" emanated the force behind organized anti-Semitism. The leaders of the Black Hundreds may have been cynics of the worst possible type, but they naturally made use of any anti-Semitic material lying to hand. One of the most potent elements was the illuminated body of opinion which could be led to attack the Jews either through inherited Christian tradition or through the association of anti-Semitism with the irrationalist reaction of the time. The Orthodox church, as a pillar of the established regime, contributed several high-ranking clerics to the leadership of the Black Hundreds (for example the Bishops Antoni of Volhynia and Hermogen of Saratov, or the Metropolitan Vladimir of Moscow). After the publication of Sergei Nilus's version of the *Protocols,* Vladimir ordered that a sermon quoting the forgery should be read in all of Moscow's churches. When Dubrovin and his supporters held a congress in Kiev in October 1906, proceedings were opened by a Te Deum sung by the Metropolitan of the city, and Vladimir of Moscow sent a telegram wishing the union success. There were many other instances of clerical support for the Union of the Russian People. In March 1905 the Holy Synod ordered its bishops to "permit and bless" the participation of clergy in the union's activities. After the pogrom of Kishinev, the holy John of Kronstadt accused the Jews of bringing persecution on themselves.[90] The Russian church certainly harbored social reformers among its members, but its alliance with the anti-Semites was strong.

The obvious reason is that the Orthodox church was, as always, concerned to prop up the Orthodox regime. But there is probably a further explanation. This can be illustrated by the example of the monk Iliodor, who from his Pochaeivskaya Monastery published a number of anti-Semitic newspapers, including the local organ of the Black Hundreds. Iliodor's *The Vision of a Monk* portrayed an apocalyptic battle between the "holy Black Hundred" and a revolutionary army of the urban proletariat, students, and Jews. Yet on his own admission, the monk had never seen a Jew until he went to the United States. He describes his hate in blood-curdling terms:

> The Jews I hated with every fibre of my soul. In the Jew I saw only the descendents of the priests of Judaea, who pursuing their trivial personal interests, had condemned to death the greatest Jew that ever lived. Of the Jewish scholar, the

> Jewish artist, the Jewish author and the Jewish inventor, I knew nothing. All I had been taught about the Jews was this: the Jew drinks human blood, the Jew regards it as a pious deed to kill a Christian, the anti-Christ will spring from Jewish stock, the Jew is accursed by God, the Jew is the source of all the evil in the world. Much hatred of Jews was thus based wholly on religious fanaticism.[91]

Iliodor went to elaborate lengths to instill in his hearers a superstitious fear of Judaism. He led anti-Semitic "missions" all over the country. He hired river steamers on the Volga, which he packed with his devotees. On one occasion he prepared an immense model of a dragon from whose mouth jumped children he had clad as demons. He preached that from the dragon of revolution came the devils of devastation, starvation, and death; and at the end of his sermon he incited the crowd to burn the symbolic monster.[92] Better than any accumulation of examples perhaps, this shows the atmosphere in which the anti-Semitic clerics worked, and the nature of their convictions. These convictions were used by men like Dubrovin, who was in direct contact with Iliodor.

The most notorious incident in the annals of Russian anti-Semitism is the Beillis case of 1911-13. A Jew, Mendel Beillis, was made the scapegoat for the murder of a small child in Kiev. At a higher pitch of hysteria, the case was the Russian equivalent to the Dreyfus trial. From the early activity of the Kiev branches of the "Union of the Russian People" and Purishkevich's "Union of the Archangel Michael" to the propaganda of of Dubrovin and Markov II during the trial itself, the anti-Semites appealed to "Orthodox Christians." The prosecution called in a notorious Roman Catholic priest as an "expert witness" in cases of Jewish ritual murder. Always the appeal was to the apocalyptic, to the religious aspect of anti-Semitism. Such manipulation of the illuminated factor could not but strike a chord of response in the minds of the Illuminated intelligentsia. Although few of the more famous names would have anything to do with the *pogromtshchiki,* certain intellectuals did respond.[93] Vasily Rozanov was one of the most eminent among them. His strange sexual mysticism had given the Jews pride of place as the race who had harnessed the power of the universe. But by a typically "occult" inversion of attitude, Rozanov hated Jews and wrote articles calling for pogroms after the Beillis trial.

Around the throne, where illuminates clustered thick, anti-Semitism was a natural corollary. The mystics who came from the "black Ignatiev" salon and from the other mystical groups knew the political message they must preach.[94] Count Witte wrote:

> The Emperor is surrounded by avowed Jew-haters, such as Trepov, Plehve, Ignatiev and the leaders of the Black Hundreds. As for his personal attitude to the Jews I recall that whenever I drew his attention to the fact that anti-Jewish riots could not be tolerated he either was silent or remarked: "But it is they, the Jews (His Majesty always used the opprobrious *Zhidy* instead of *Yevrei*) that are to blame." The anti-Jewish current flowed not from below upward, but in the opposite direction.[95]

It was fostered, however, by the gurus whom various interested parties propelled toward the throne. According to Iliodor, almost all the mystics who held sway in the period when the "holy fools" dominated the court preached against the revolutionaries and Jews. He records a rumor—untrue but significant—that when the crowd led by Father Gapon was fired upon in 1905 it had been the mumbling Mitya the Blissful who had given the order. Rasputin was certainly one of the chief instigators of anti-Semitism in court circles, and denunciations of Satanic Jewish revolutionaries pepper his correspondence.[96] It has been plausibly suggested that Rasputin was deliberately planted at court by Ignatiev and Black Hundred sympathizers.[97] The tsaritsa was in communication with Dr. Dubrovin as late as December 1916 and wrote to the tsar that Dubrovin found it a shame that his inflamatory *Russkiye Znamya* could not be sent to the troops at the front, adding "I agree." Significantly, a letter of the previous day had mentioned the name of the revered master from Lyon in connection with Alexandra's attempts to stiffen her husband's backbone: "Remember even Mr. Philippe said one dare not give constitution."[98] Whether primitive Russian holy men or comparatively sophisticated Western mystics, the gurus at the Russian court almost all brought with them political views of a reactionary type; and probably that is why their sponsors chose them. Such views carried all the more conviction by seeming transcendentally justified.

Among these anti-Semitic illuminates was Sergei Nilus, who had been expected by certain interested parties to become the tsar's confessor. Nilus was thoroughly representative of the type of holy fool. After he had to leave court, he settled down with his new wife, Ozerova, and a former mistress at the monastery of Optina Pustyn. Here he associated with the friends of Mitya the Blissful and edited the diary of a visionary. The Revolution passed him by in a hermitage in South Russia, and he led a wandering life until his death in 1930.[99]

Nilus connected his manuscript of the *Protocols* with the expectation of the coming of Antichrist which, as we have seen, was quite common in the Russian religious revival of the time. The subtitle of his book *The Great in the Small* (in which the *Protocols* were inserted) was *Antichrist Considered as an Imminent Political Possibility,* and the King of the Jews whom the *Protocols* describe was obviously Antichrist in person. This had been more or less the opinion of the writer of *The Secret of the Jews,* who saw in the common expectation of Antichrist a euphemism for the arrival of the despot of World Jewry. Nilus buttressed his own convictions with the apocalyptic visions of St. Seraphim of Saratov, Merezhkovsky, and Vladimir Soloviev. He concocted a symbolic system that enabled him to detect the mark of Antichrist in almost any geometrical design—including commercial trademarks. This latter method of "research" was also very popular among German anti-Semites; but the sense of apocalypse and the reality of the advent of Antichrist are purely Russian. Indeed, in the appendix to the 1905 edition of *The Great in the Small,* Nilus included an appeal for the summoning of the Eighth Ecumenical Council, which might have been derived directly from Vladimir Soloviev himself.[100]

Totally in keeping with this incense-filled atmosphere is the fact that when it was decided that affairs were completely out of hand and that Rasputin—the latest and most powerful of gurus—had to go, his murderers themselves subscribed to the conspiracy theory. Principally, these were Vladimir Purishkevich and Prince Felix Yussupov. For Purishkevich, Rasputin was the evil counsellor, and thus naturally in the pay the of Jews; the tsaritsa was a German and, of course, under the influence of a German-Jewish conspiracy.[101] Yussupov believed in a mysterious syndicate called "the greens," who operated from Sweden, and he thought them to be Jews. He was himself illuminated to a surprising degree. As a child he had made predictions, seen ghostly trains where no lines ran, and intensively studied occultism and Theosophy. He took up a system of exercises designed to enable him to master himself and then dominate others; while at Oxford he developed a distressing form of second sight which allowed him to predict deaths. In particular he was devoted to the Grand Duchess Elisabeth Feodorovna, whom he regarded as a saint. After the murder of Rasputin, the grand duchess consoled him that the deed was justified as ridding the world of a fiend incarnate. Yussupov recorded, on her authority, that at the time when he and Purishkevich had finally succeeded in their task "priests had suddenly gone mad, blaspheming and shrieking; nuns ran about the corridors howling like souls possessed and lifting their skirts with obscene gestures." It is worth recording the fact that the prince appears to have believed in the *Protocols,* and that his story of their origin leads once more to an occult source. According to Yussupov, one of the neighbors of his family in the Crimea, a Countess Kleinmichel, had found the Hebrew manuscript in her library and sent it to Moscow to be translated. Countess Kleinmichel was famous for her Spiritualist séances, read Swedenborg assiduously, and, when forced to leave Russia by the Revolution, stayed with the Theosophical family of Wachtmeister in Sweden.[102]

It is an unbroken chain, this association—occultism, anti-Semitism, and back to occultism again. There seems little enough substance to Yussupov's narrative, but again the *Protocols* are attached to an illuminated source. The story that really launched the *Protocols* contains similar ingredients of occultism and conspiracy theory.

On 17 July 1918 the imperial family—now no longer imperial, and the tsar called Colonel Romanov—were murdered in the Ipatyev house in Ekaterinburg by a body of men supposedly under a Jewish commissar. By chance, the tsaritsa had recently been sent a copy of Nilus's book containing the *Protocols,* and it was one of the articles listed by the magistrate deputed to take an inventory. Almost as sinister, in the eyes of conspiracy-theorists, was the discovery of a subsequently notorious symbol in the Ipatyev house. Pierre Gilliard (the French tutor to the imperial family) writes in his memoirs of how he

> noticed on the wall in the embrasure of one of the windows of Their Majesties' room the Empress's favourite charm, the

swastika, which she had put up everywhere to ward off ill-luck. She had drawn it in pencil, and added, underneath, the date 17/30 April, the day of their incarceration in the house. The same symbol, but without the date, was drawn on the wallpaper on a level with the bed.

The swastika was already known through the theories of German racists as symbolizing the supremacy of the Aryans over the Jews.[103] The combination of swastika and *Protocols* was to prove more than enough for distracted anti-Semites to see the iron fists of Jewry —much as Charles Maurras was to scream, when sentenced for collaboration, "It's the revenge of Dreyfus."

The swastika must be disposed of as quickly as possible. Generally speaking, a symbol of good luck, widely diffused throughout prehistory, the swastika was resurrected by turn-of-the-century occultists interested in the Orient. It appears on the seal of the Theosophical Society. In Germany, Ernst Krause, in a book called *Twiskoland* published in 1891, called attention to the swastika as a particularly Aryan symbol; in fact, the Jews have certainly also used it. There followed, hard on the heels of Krause, the Austro-German racists Guido von List and Lanz von Liebenfels who had definite connections with the occult revival and used the swastika as a leading symbol in their illuminated anti-Semitism. Their theories may have penetrated Russia and influenced the Russian anti-Semites. I can find no evidence for the assertion that Guido von List's ideas had reached Russia. But Lanz von Liebenfels claimed that in 1904 he had sent copies of his *Theozoologie* to "several of the most distinguished Russian gentlemen in the closest proximity to the tsar (Baron Frederiks, Prince Urussov, and several Baltic barons at the Imperial court)." Frederiks was the minister responsible for court protocol and favored a pro-German policy; Urussov was an opponent of anti-Semitism but around 1904 was making general inquiries from any writers on the Jewish problem; and the Baltic barons ring true. Lanz claimed to have spoken personally with those to whom he sent his book; but the result was that his *Theozoologie* was banned and he himself threatened with imprisonment.

Nonetheless, there are indications that something of the racist view of the swastika came to Russia and stayed. A biography of Purishkevich published in Leningrad in 1925, when the racist associations of the swastika were not familiar outside Germany, carries the symbol on the cover. The swastika also appears on the stamps of the Mongolian Republic of von Ungern-Sternberg. In the melée around the Ipatyev house and a plot which was hatched to rescue the tsar, there are further indications that the swastika may have come to represent for the Russian right wing something of what it eventually signified in Germany.[104]

The real launching of the symbol may have been the legend of the Ipatyev house itself. The tsaritsa's use of the swastika carried no anti-Semitic overtones. She was not an anti-Semite, and the object was her good-luck charm. But the confused attempts made by the friends of the imperial family to extricate them from their confinement took place under the sign of the tsaritsa's talisman. The swastika became the symbol of the rescue organization. How real this organization was is difficult to say, particularly as the verdict is bound up with the later conspiracy theories of paranoid White officers. The two main actors in the tragedy were Boris Nikolaievitch Soloviev, representing the friends of the tsaritsa gathered around Anna Vyrubova; and Sergei Vladimirovitch Markov, a distant cousin and the agent of Markov II.

Boris Soloviev was the son of a minor official of the Holy Synod. It is tempting to try to link him with the family of Vladimir Soloviev, but the name was common. According to his adversary Paul Bulygin, (the former commander of the dowager empress's bodyguard), Boris shared the inclinations of his famous namesakes. After studying at Berlin, he became secretary to a German tourist and traveled with him to India. Here he left his employer and went to the Theosophical headquarters at Adyar where he remained for about a year. The Great War found him once more in Russia, where he volunteered for the army and fell in with Anna Vyrubova and her friends who shared his occult interests. His father was a friend and neighbor of Rasputin, and Boris Soloviev was the candidate whom the *staretz* favored for his daughter's hand. The marriage between Matriona Rasputin and the young Theosophist actually took place in September 1917. At the request of Anna Vyrubova and other monarchists, Boris Soloviev left for Siberia to act as the official representative of the royalist organizations. Here, according to his opponents, Soloviev made contact with one Father Alexis and represented to the imperial family that there were 300 loyal officers ready to free them. This organization—said by Bulygin to have been completely nonexistent—was dubbed by the tsaritsa, the "Brotherhood of St. John of Tobolsk" and was to identify itself by her personal good-luck charm—the swastika.[105]

Another emissary arrived from Finland, where Markov II had set up his headquarters. This was the young lieutenant S. V. Markov, who at that time was instructing his agents to help the Bolsheviks to overthrow the provisional government as the first step to restoring order. According to Bulygin, S. V. Markov was used as camouflage by Soloviev—who was in fact a Bolshevik agent—to convince members of other monarchist organizations that the plot to free the imperial family was proceeding satisfactorily. Perhaps Soloviev, Markov, and the imperial family were the only people ever to use the identification sign of the swastika. But the references to Markov II by the younger Markov show that he regarded his anti-Semitic relative as the "Head of the organization which had made it its mission to protect and free the imprisoned Imperial family" and that the sign of the swastika was that of "our organization."[106] If there was a conspiracy, it failed, and the imperial family was taken to Ekaterinburg and murdered.

The result was that the White Russians had to find a scapegoat. The energetic S. V. Markov had contrived to make contact with German relatives of the tsaritsa and the elements of the German General Staff surrounding Ludendorff and Hoffmann who were contemplating a royalist restoration in Russia. He was consequently seen as part of the German-Jewish conspiracy. As for Soloviev, whose role was indeed suspicious, his marriage to Rasputin's daughter made him more suspect still. The magistrate Nicholas Sokolov (who devoted the remainder of his life to collecting evidence about the murder of the imperial family) had Soloviev and his wife arrested in Vladivostok as they were preparing to emigrate. From Soloviev's captured diary Sokolov constructed a remarkable theory, which passed into White Russian mythology. Soloviev had married Matriona Rasputin to ingratiate himself with monarchist circles, and he kept his wife under his control by means of hypnosis. If the diary extracts quoted by Sokolov are correct, there seem to be some grounds for this otherwise unbelievable suspicion.[107] For the

Whites, the identification of Soloviev and Matriona Rasputin with the German-Jewish conspiracy was further assured when it was discovered that, after they were eventually able to leave Russia, the couple had stayed with a Jewish friend of Rasputin. In 1921 Bulygin denounced Boris Soloviev to Markov II and other emigré leaders in Berlin.[108] Five years later Rasputin's son-in-law died in Paris as the result of an attack by White Russians in the street.

Suspicion of Boris Soloviev may well have been justified. Documents found on him in Vladivostok indicate that he was a complete opportunist. Some of the vehemence against him undoubtedly came from the supporters of Markov II, whose own activities had been less effective than might have been expected. But the German-Jewish conspiracy that was concocted by White Russian illuminates to explain the deaths of the imperial family acquired a particularly diabolical cast from its constant association with the supernatural. The marriage of Soloviev to Rasputin's daughter, his hypnotic control over her, and the devotion which Rasputin's former devotees still showed to their dead master—for Rasputin's spirit was said still to haunt the séance room of Anna Vyrubova and her set—all these details filled in the outline drawn by the tale of the *Protocols,* the swastika, and the Jewish commissar. Such an atmosphere could only have been generated in Russia at that time of apocalypse or in Germany a few years later. But this species of mythologizing has still not been completely buried. Wilder and wilder grow the stories, such as a recent tale that Rasputin and his associates were directed through a "Green center of Moravian flagellants" by a colonel of German intelligence. It seems that it was a "Moravian flagellant" who had given the tsaritsa her swastika in the first place.[109] Whatever Boris Soloviev was trying to do, he was a denizen of that shadowy land between Theosophy and espionage which was occupied by Yuliana Glinka. The story demonstrates that not only do illuminates profess an extraordinary quality of hate but that their suspicion of "occult powers" in others may mobilize this hate against them. Yussupov's vision of Rasputin as the incarnation of Satanic powers and the semisupernatural nature of the deceptions attributed to Boris Soloviev remain an essential part of the myth.

In the legend of the Ipatyev house there were, thus, several important elements. The presence of the *Protocols* and the "Jewish" executioners form the first and most important. The use by the tsaritsa of the swastika and its possibly wider significance as a symbol of resistance to "Jewish Bolshevism" among right-wing Russians form the second. The third element is that of a fundamental irrationalism—the conspiracy was that much easier to believe if coupled with the use of magic by a traitor within the ranks of the heavenly host. This irrationalism was perpetuated in the West. The Russian-American anti-Semite Leslie Fry (Paquita Shishmarev) interpreted the scrawls on the wall of the Ipatyev house as evidence "that the murder of the tsar was committed by men under the command of occult forces; and by an organization which, in its struggle against existing power resorted to the ancient cabbalism in which it was well versed."[110]

In the diffusion of the *Protocols* throughout the White Russian armies the means employed were those of organized propaganda. Purishkevich distributed an edition to the armies of General Denikin on the Don. The forgery was assiduously cultivated in the Crimea. In Siberia, Admiral Koltchak printed the *Protocols* and was himself obsessed by the Judeo-Masonic conspiracy.[111] Illuminates—who actually *believed* in the conspiracy—were essential to the propagation of the myth. In exile, Merezhkovsky had visions of a struggle between the Pentacle and the Cross, but he thought Lenin and Trotsky to be "blind instruments of mysterious forces" rather than part of an active conspiracy. In Mongolia, the anti-Semitism of the mystical Ungern-Sternberg was notorious. Grigori Bostunitch lectured to the armies of General Denikin, and he purveyed a very "occult" brand of anti-Semitism. He had written a pamphlet on Rasputin, commented on the *Protocols*, and analyzed the conspiracy of the Freemasons. His theories included the suggestion that Fabre d'Olivet had been ritually murdered; it is significant that he should attach importance to Fabre d'Olivet, an obscure figure to all but French occultists and a very few illuminated anti-Semites like the author of *The Secret of the Jews*. Vladimir Soloviev, who himself had in fact been attracted to the Jews, is made by Bostunitch to denounce the conspiracy. It is scarcely surprising to find that he ended up in the *SS*, where he was known as Schwartz-Bostunitch.[112]

It is intriguing to discover that at the same time as propagating conspiracy theories Bostunitch had continued his own activities in occultism. His first esoteric teacher, he tells us, was in the Caucasus in 1917-18; when he emigrated he spent time in Bulgarian Theosophical circles. The only esoteric teacher who is known to have been in the Caucasus at that time was Gurdjieff, and it is more or less certain that any Bulgarian contacts would have been associated with "the Master" Petr Deunov. On his arrival in Germany, Bostunitch fell in with the Anthroposophists, met Rudolf Steiner personally, and came deeply under his influence. In a Viennese magazine of 1925 he wrote an obituary on Steiner, praising him as "one who fought Evil"; and three years later (in a second edition of his book on Freemasonry) he apologized for having in the Russian edition called Steiner a "black magician." In 1929 he changed his allegiance and issued a pamphlet against Anthroposophy of an especially vicious sort. This sudden reversal of values and the consequent association of the abandoned idol with the power of darkness—Steiner immediately became part of a Jewish-Masonic conspiracy of sex-magicians—are exactly in keeping with the process we have already observed as common among occultists.[113]

Schwartz-Bostunitch is an extreme case, but this illuminated *SS*-man does show the extent of what was possible. There were many others—marginally less eccentric but equally fanatical—who arrived, like Bostunitch, in the West, and set about propagating the Russian view of the occult conspiracy. In Germany their effect was much the same as that of alcohol on certain drugs: they potentiated an already powerful mixture.

1. Norman Cohn, *Warrant for Genocide* (paperback ed., London, 1970). The text of the *Protocols* can be found in Leslie Fry, *Waters Flowing Eastward* (4th ed., London, 1953).
2. Walter Laqueur, *Russia and Germany* (London, 1969), pp. 50-125.
3. Robert F. Byrnes, *Antisemitism in Modern France,* vol. I (New Brunswick, 1950), p. 144.
4. Gaston Méry, *Jean Révolte* (Paris, 1892). "Combien de gens se sentiront Celtes quand je leur aurai dénoncé Méridional, une nombre d'indifférents se sont réveilles socialistes quand Drumont leur a dénoncé le Juif" (p. 68).
5. See Gaston Méry, *La Voyante de la rue de paradis* (Paris, 1896-97), p. 33.
6. Byrnes, *Antisemitism,* p. 145.
7. See *The Occult Underground,* pp. 144 ff.

8. Eugen Weber (ed.), *Satan Franc-maçon* (Paris, 1964), pp. 216 ff.
9. Quoted Byrnes, *Antisemitism,* p. 316.
10. See Alec Mellor, *Our Separated Brethren, the Freemasons* (London, 1964), pp. 263-65.
11. Cohn, *Warrant,* p. 113.
12. Cohn, *Warrant,* pp. 109-10. Cf., for example, Schwartz-Bostunitsch, *Jüdischer Imperialismus* (3rd ed., Leipzig, n.d.).
13. James Parkes, *The Emergence of the Jewish Problem 1878-1939* (London, 1946), pp. 195-96.
14. Cohn, *Warrant,* pp. 11-12.
15. "Inquire Within," *Light-Bearers of Darkness* (London, 1930), pp. 23, 201. Nesta Webster, *Secret Societies,* pp. 3-24, identified the Great Conspiracy with Gnosticism. The sexual innuendoes used against the Jews are also used by propagandists against occultism; see chapter I for the accusations against Steiner.
16. Shirley in *The Occult Review* (June 1930), p. 362.
17. On the apostasy, see Pierre Geyraud, *Les Petites Eglises de Paris* (Paris, 1937), p. 78 and Fabre des Essarts, *Les Hiérophantes* (Paris, 1905), p. 17. Doinel lost none of his eccentricity by becoming ecclesiastically orthodox. He was to be seen wandering around Carcasonne in a hat trimmed with episcopal purple, with Gnostic insignia on his chest and wearing a large amethyst on his finger. He died in 1903.
18. Papus, *Le Diable et l'occultisme* (Paris, 1895), p. 10. Cf. Georges Bois, *Le Péril occultiste* (Paris, 1899).
19. Papus, *Le Diable,* pp. 24-25.
20. *Gustav Meyrink contra Gustav Frenssen* (Munich, 1908).
21. Eugen Lennhoff and Oskar Posner, *Internationales Freimaurerlexicon* (Zurich, Leipzig, Vienna, 1932), pp. 103-5, quoting Carl Vogl, *Aufzeichnungen und Bekenntnisse* (Vienna and Berlin), which I have been unable to obtain. My attention was drawn to this passage by Mr. Ellic Howe.
22. Karl Heise, *Die Entente-Freimaurerei und der Weltkrieg* (2nd ed., Basel, 1920; orig. 1919). For Heise, see Chapter VI.
23. Charles Renaut, *L'Israélite Edouard Drumont et les sociétés sécretes actuellement* (Paris, 1895).
24. Cohn, *Warrant,* p. 110.
25. See letter of H. P. Blavatsky to M. Bilière printed Blech, *Société Théosophique en France,* pp. 138-40.
26. Compare Soloviev's account of the Eberfeld miracles with Madame Blavatsky's assertion that the lady in question was "Mlle de Glinka." *Letters of Madame Blavatsky,* p. 268, and cf. corroboration of Countess Wachtmeister, *Letters of Mme. B.,* p. 273. Throughout Vsevolod Soloviev's *Modern Priestess of Isis* read "Miss X" = Madame Fadeyev; "Mme Y" = Vera Jelikovsky; "Miss A" = Glinka.
27. Vsevolod Soloviev, *Priestess,* pp. 34, 74-76, 80-85, 90.
28. See SPR *Proceedings* (vol. III, 1885), pp. 393-95.
29. H.P.B. to A. P. Sinnett, *Letters,* p. 208.

30. *Letters*, pp. 184, 192-93, 208.
31. Vsevolod Soloviev, *Priestess*, pp. 114-15, pp. 169-71. It is interesting that not only paranoid colonial officials believed that H.P.B. was implicated in the Russian secret service—Rudolf Steiner believed that the Theosophical Society had been taken over by Russian-oriented politics.
32. *Letters of H. P. Blavatsky*, p. 208.
33. Vsevolod Soloviev, *Priestess*, pp. 311-12.
34. *Letters of H. P. Blavatsky*, p. 192.
35. This is because, although it is certain that Glinka was Soloviev's companion on the visits to Eberfeld, the visitors are twice described as "the Solovievs"—see Blech, *Société Théosophique en France*, p. 115, and William Kingsland, *The Real H. P. Blavatsky* (London, 1928), p. 219. Kingsland places "the Solovievs" in quotation marks because of "an ancient scandal." It would follow that Glinka was the person whom H.P.B. accused Soloviev of seducing at the age of thirteen. Cf. *Letters*, p. 208. Soloviev claimed not to have seen Glinka for some years before the Eberfeld affair; and their relationship must remain conjectural.
36. H. P. Blavatsky to *The World* (24 September 1877), printed in *The Complete Works*, vol. I, pp. 156-57; H. P. Blavatsky, *Isis Unveiled* (Point Loma, ed. 1919), vol. II, pp. 69-70, note 1107. The book referred to is Friedrich Wilhelm Ghillany, *Die Menschenopfer der alter Hebräer* (Nuremberg, 1844). Ghillany (1842-46) appears to have believed that the Jews still practiced ritual murder, and he advocated a reform of Judaism—to put it mildly. The anti-Jesuit bias was shared by several of H.P.B.'s mystical compatriots, for example, Olga Besobrasova—for whom see this chapter—and at the Karlovtsy Council the pope was described as "the Black Pope, head of the Jesuit Order."
37. Rollin, *L'Apocalypse*, pp. 30-32; Blavatsky, *Isis Unveiled*, vol. II, section II, p. 352; Iliodor, *Mad Monk*, p. 355, pp. 369-72, 397.
38. Wachtmeister to A. P. Sinnett, *The Letters of H. P. Blavatsky*, p. 265.
39. This, of course, may have stemmed from the idea that Steiner, as an Austrian Catholic, was educated by the Jesuits; but the sense in which it was meant is quite clear.
40. Document headed "Private and Confidential" in *Letters of H. P. Blavatsky*, pp. 230-31; all extracts, *Letters*, pp. 232-33.
41. Mr. Francis King, who discovered the existence of the pamphlet in the first place, has seen one, nor is there any reason to doubt the editors of *The Patriot*, who were rather put out by finding an "exposure of World Jewry" by an organization that their ideologist, Mrs. Webster, told them was linked with the Jewish conspiracy.
42. "The Hebrew Talisman," supplement to *The Patriot* (8 September 1927), p. 1.
43. William Kingsland, *The Real H. P. Blavatsky* (London, 1928), pp. 230-33; Ransom, *Theosophical Society*, p. 252 and p. 254; see supplement to *The Theosophist* (October, 1890), pp. ii-iii, and cf. Ryan, *Theosophical*

Society, pp. 252-53, where Harte is said to have quarreled with Madame Blavatsky over the question of whether the Theosophical Society should appeal to a wider audience.

44. See Richard Harte, *The New Psychology* (3rd. ed., London, 1903), especially p. 127; and *Hypnotism and the Doctors* (2 vols. London, 1902-03).

45. Harte, *Lay Religion* (London, 1894), p. 45. For his opinion of H.P.B., see pp. 16-17.

46. The other is a sermon by a very dissenting clergyman—see John Styles, *The Mammon of Unrighteousness* (London, 1836). *The Hebrew Talisman* of 1838 is a pamphlet of 47 pages, undated, anonymous, and printed by W. Whaley, 12 Holywell Street, The Strand.

47. Joseph Gaer, *The Legend of the Wandering Jew* (N.Y., 1961), pp. 59, 122 ff.

48. *The Hebrew Talisman,* pp. 18-20.

49. *The Hebrew Talisman,* pp. 26-27.

50. *The Hebrew Talisman,* pp. 43-45.

51. See *The Hebrew Talisman,* pp. 27-30, for a very circumstantial account of the seige. The suicide of Abraham Goldsmid is historical. There was a legend of a Jewish mystic who lived with the Goldsmid family to whom he gave a box which was not to be opened until a certain date. Of course the box was opened prematurely—and the suicide was supposed to have been only one of the disasters that befell the family. See Moses Margouliouth, *The History of the Jews* (3 vols. vol. II, London, 1851), pp. 144-45. This story passed into the mythology of anti-Semitism—see Nesta Webster, *Secret Societies and Subversive Movements* (7th ed., London, 1955), pp. 185 ff.

52. *The Hebrew Talisman,* p. 11.

53. See Blavatsky, *The Secret Doctrine* (London, 1888), vol. II, pp. 779-80. Cf. Isabelle Pagan, *Racial Cleavage* (London, 1937). For an application of Theosophical race theories of a more sinister sort, see remarks on Lanz von Liebenfels in Chapter VI.

54. John Gwyer, *Portraits of Mean Men* (London, 1938), pp. 69-70; cf. Cohn, *Warrant,* pp. 114-15.

55. Text of *Tavnya Yevrestia* in Yuri Dyelevsky, *Protokoly Sionskikh Mudretsov* (Berlin, 1923), pp. 138 ff. I am greatly indebted to Liz Cowgill for a translation of the document (p. 137).

56. Dyelevsky, *Protokoly,* pp. 139-44.

57. See in particular Fabre d'Olivet, *The Hebraic Tongue Restored* (tr. N. L. Redfield, London and New York, 1921; orig. 1815); Saint-Yves d'Alveydre, *Mission des Juifs* (Paris, 1884). Cf. the comments of Léon Cellier, *Fabre d'Olivet* (Paris, 1953); Saint-Yves d'Alveydre, *Mission des Juifs,* p. 912. For another occult expression of loyalty to the Jews, directed against Drumont, see Lady Caithness, *Théosophie Sémitique* (Paris, 1889); Dyelevsky, *Protokoly,* p. 139.

58. Dyelevsky, *Protokoly*, pp. 145-49.
59. Cohn, *Warrant*, pp. 31 ff.
60. Dyelevsky, *Protokoly*, pp. 154-58.
61. Vsevolod Soloviev, *Priestess*, p. 29; Dyelevsky, *Protokoly*, pp. 141, 144.
62. See Cohn, *Warrant*, pp. 108 ff.
63. Rollin, *L'Apocalypse*, pp. 462-64.
64. This is the verdict of Professor Cohn.
65. Cohn, *Warrant*, p. 92; Rodzianko, *Rasputin*, p. 2; Encausse, *Le Maître Philippe*, p. 242.
66. Rollin, *L'Apocalypse*, p. 34, pp. 382-84.
67. Cohn, *Warrant*, p. 117.
68. Dyelevsky, *Protokoly*, pp. 148-49
69. Blech, *Société Théosophique*, pp. 35, 144-48.
70. Vsevolod Soloviev, *Priestess*, pp. 30-32; Ransom, *Theosophical Society*, pp. 250-51. Papus was noted for joining any occult society that came his way and inventing those that did not.
71. Cohn, *Warrant*, pp. 116-17.
72. Vsevolod Soloviev, *Priestess*, pp. 288-89. 326; Juliette Adam, *Un Rêve sur le divine* (orig. 1888), 2nd ed. bound with *Paienne* (Paris, 1903), p. 261; "Dr. Battaille," *Le Diable au 19e. siècle* (2 vols. Paris, 1896), vol. II, p. 950. Cf. Winifred Stephens, *Madame Adam* (London, 1917), p. 211.
73. Isabelle Bogelot, "Emilie de Morsier et la fondation de l'Adelphie" in *La revue des femmes russes* (Paris), tome 1, nos. 5-6, pp. 193 ff.
74. Ina de Kapnist, "Echos de Russie" in *La revue*, tome 2, nos. 1 and 2, pp. 86-93, 163 f.
75. Olga Besobrazova, "La Religion Nouvelle" in *La revue*, tome 1, nos. 9-12.
76. See Olga Besobrazova, *Poèmes mystiques* (Paris, 1901), and in *Le Lotus bleu*, vol. IX, no. 8. On Paul Adam's anti-Semitism, see in particular *Le Mystère des foules* (Paris, 1895), in which the lust of a Jew for another man's wife causes war between France and Germany. It was very popular in occult circles.
77. Schwartz-Bostunitch, *Jüdischer Imperialismus*, p. 220.
78. Besobrazova, in *Le Revue des femmes Russes*, tome 1, no. 11. p. 462.
79. "Niet," *La Russie d'Aujourd'hui* (Paris, 1902), pp. 6-7, 12, 46. This is a compilation of the newspaper articles. Cf. Alec Mellor, *Separated Brethren*, pp. 265-66. Sometimes even the Salvation Army was involved in the conspiracy theories.
80. Rollin, *L'Apocalypse*, pp. 355-56.
81. Encausse, *Papus*, pp. 31-33.
82. Rollin, *L'Apocalypse*, p. 363; V.-E. Michelet, *Les Compagnons de la hiérophanie* (Paris, n.d.), p. 41; Encausse, *Papus*, p. 51. I have identified the Imperial Order of Mejdie (Turkey, founded 1852), the *Ordre royal et*

militaire du Christ (ancient Portuguese) and the honor of *Chevalier de L'Ordre de Bolivar* (Venezuela, founded 1857); Papus, quoted in Encausse, *Papus,* p. 51.

83. Rollin, *L'Apocalypse,* pp. 363 ff.; du Chayla quoted in Cohn, *Warrant,* p. 100.

84. Gaston Méry, *La Voyante de la rue de paradis* (Paris, 1896-97), first collection, pp. 121 ff., 169 ff., second collection (no. 7 onward) p. 162.

85. Encausse, *Le Maître Philippe,* p. 240; Jean Renard, *Journal 1887-1910* (Paris, 1960), p. 77; Jean Carrère, *Affaire Dreyfus—réponse à Emile Zola* (Paris, 1898). His thesis was summarized in *Degeneration in the Great French Masters* (tr. Joseph McCabe, London, 1922) praising the "healthy" art of Mistral and the Parnassians. "All these geniuses are clear, radiant and beautiful....," p. 236. Juliette Adam was sympathetic to the *Félibrige*—in 1896 she published Mistral's *Poème du Rhone* and for many years kept a property in Provence. It is worth noting that a lady who was possibly Glinka claimed to have received the *Protocols* from a journalist who had stolen them from the Jewish headquarters in *Nice*—why Nice? It may also be significant that Fabre d'Olivet was seen by the *Félibres* as a precursor, and that from 1883, when a book by J. Donnadieu was published, the occultist was placed—a little doubtingly, it is true—in their heroes' gallery. See Cellier, *Fabre d'Olivet;* Rollin, *L'Apocalypse,* p. 363; for Butler and Beamish, see chapter III.

86. Butmi, quoted in Rollin, *L'Apocalypse,* p. 363. My italics.

87. See the story of the journalist Menshikov told by Professor Cohn, *Warrant,* p. 111.

88. Walter Laqueur, *Russia and Germany* (1969), pp. 79-80; Witte, *Memoirs,* p. 129.

89. Laqueur, *Russia and Germany,* pp. 86-87.

90. Laqueur, *Russia and Gemany,* pp. 84-85; Cohn, *Warrant,* pp. 73-74; Curtiss, *Church and State,* pp. 260-61; Curtiss, *Church and State,* pp. 260-61, 268-69, 271-72; Gapon, *Story of my Life,* pp. 115-16.

91. Gapon, *Story of my Life,* p. 204; Iliodor, *Mad Monk,* pp. 41-42.

92. Iliodor, *Mad Monk,* pp. 42-43.

93. On the case itself see Alex B. Tager, *The Decay of Czarism* (Philadelphia 1935), and Maurice Samuel, *Blood Accusation* (London, 1967); Laqueur, *Russia and Germany,* p. 84.

94. Füllöp-Miller, *Rasputin,* pp. 88-90; Curtiss, *Church and State,* p. 370.

95. Witte, *Memoirs,* p. 190.

96. Iliodor, *Mad Monk,* p. 176; e.g., on his indictment by the Duma: "Darling Papa and Mama, the cursed devil is overpowering. And the duma serves him. It contains many revolutionists and Jews." Iliodor, *Mad Monk,* p. 193.

97. Hans von Eckhardt (born Riga, 1890), *Russisches Christentum* (Munich, 1947), p. 285.

98. *Letters of the Tsaritsa to the Tsar, 1914-16* (London, 1932), pp. 456-57.

99. See Cohn, *Warrant*, pp. 96-107.
100. Dyelevsky, *Protokoly*, p. 144; Cohn, *Warrant*, pp. 100-102, 319; Leslie Fry, *Waters*, p. 180.
101. See Vladimir Purishkevich, *Comment j'ai tué Raspoutine* (tr. Lydie Krestovsky, Paris, 1924) and compare another version translated by Mikhail Purishkevich in *Les Oeuvres libres* (August 1953). The two versions differ substantially.
102. Felix Yussupoff, *Lost Splendour* (tr. A. Green and N. Katkoff, London, 1954), pp. 106, 254; see Countess Kleinmichel, *Memories of a Shipwrecked World* (tr. V. Legard, London, 1923) and Serge Obolensky, *One Man in his Time* (London, 1960), pp. 26-27, 138.
103. Gilliard, *Russian Court*, p. 274; photograph p. 276; Norman Cohn follows Henri Rollin.
104. Rollin, *L'Apocalypse*, p. 70; Cohn following Rollin; Wilfried Daim, *Der Mann, der Hitler die Ideen gab* (Munich, 1958), p. 99; see A. A. Mossolov, *At the Court of the Last Tsar* (ed. A. A. Pilenco and E. W. Dickes, London, 1935), pp. 109-10; see Prince S. D. Urussov, *Memoirs of a Russian Governor* (London and New York, 1908). The liberal Urussov had been appointed governor of Bessarabia just after the pogrom of Kishinev with instructions from Plehve for "less speech-making and less philo-Semitism"; Daim, *Der Mann*, pp. 99-101; Laqueur, *Russia and Germany*, p. 336 note 4; G. Franz-Willing, *Die Hitler-Bewegung*, vol. I (Munich, 1962), p. 84.
105. Paul Bulygin, *The Murder of the Romanovs* (London, 1936); cf. Marie Rasputin, *The Real Rasputin* (tr. Arthur Chambers, London, 1929).
106. Sergei Vladimirovitch Markov, *How We Tried to Save the Tsaritsa*, (London and New York, 1929), pp. 82 ff., 202.
107. Nicholas Sokolov, *Enquête judiciaire sur l'assassination de la famille impériale russe* (Paris, 1926), pp. 132-34.
108. Bulygin, *Murder*, p. 211.
109. See Paléologue, *Memoirs*, vol. III, p. 173, for the story of the crazy Prince Kurakin and cf. Anna Viroubova, *Journal secret* (tr. M. Vaneix, Paris, 1928), p. 304 for her devotion to her "master" after his death; the remarkable "Moravian" theory is that of Victor Alexandrov, *The End of the Romanovs* (tr. Sutcliffe, London, 1966). However, even the normally careful Henri Rollin fell into the trap of accepting a conspiracy theory.
110. Fry, *Waters*, p. 186.
111. Cohn, *Warrant*, pp. 128 ff.
112. Merezhkovsky, "La Croix et le Pentagramme" (tr. de Gramont, Paris, 1921), in *Le Peuple Crucifié* (pp. 212-18); Schwartz-Bostunitsch, *Jüdischer Imperialismus*, pp. 69-70; see Laqueur, *Russia and Germany*, pp. 122 ff., and the forthcoming work of Ellic Howe, *The Lunatic Fringe in Germany, 1890-1925*.
113. Schwartz-Bostunitch, *Doktor Steiner*, p. 3; Karl Heyer, *Wie man gegen Rudolf Steiner kämpft* (2nd ed., Stuttgart, 1932), pp. 90-94.

Chapter 5
The Magi of the North

The Underground in Power—"völkisch" Occultism—The Mystic Dietrich Eckart—The Spirituality of Gottfried Feder—Alfred Rosenberg and Russian anti-Semitism—Rudolf von Sebottendorff and the Thule Bund—Adolf Hitler and "völkisch" Occultism—The Ludendorffs and the Conspiracy Theory—The Fate of the Mystics after the Machtergreifung—*Rosenberg's Aryan Atlantis—Himmler's Occult Fantasies—The* Deutsches Ahnenerbe—*Hitler and Hörbiger—Other Realities and the Divine Sanction*

NAZI Germany presents the unique spectacle of the partial transformation of the Underground of rejected knowledge into an Establishment. In the process, the Underground was considerably altered, and the nature of this change is not the least significant fact about the Nazi period. Despite all compromises with the demands of power, the seekers of "other realities" did partly succeed in establishing a different vision of the world from that of the pragmatic, materialist Establishment, which the First World War had shown to be so damaged. This success is probably why the Nazi party continues to attract attention despite all the unpleasant aspects of studying it at all. Other realities cultivated by established governments are rare indeed.

The Nazi universe was, of course, largely a matter of chance; it was formed from various irrationalist elements, which were to hand and lent themselves to political application. Very much of the propaganda, at least, was similar to the approach of English illuminated politicians: the new universe was to be anti-Establishment in the sense of being anti-individualist, antimaterialist, and antirationalist. Occultism, mysticism, and the religious impulse characterize the illuminated attitude. What is more, because some portion of the German Underground's vision of a new heaven and a new earth found its way into the necessary synthesis with power, some very peculiar elements of previously rejected knowledge crawled out into the light of day.

Because the attainment of German nationhood had come comparatively late, the glories of this status had been the subject of panegyrics by those concerned with any reality but that of the present. When, after the First World War, it could be represented that the nation was corporately in peril, a nationalism of the most visionary kind arose. At the same time German illuminates felt the pull of the tide which ran through the whole European Underground, toward rejection of the Establishment culture which had failed. This again pressed reformers in the direction of the ideal, because the Establishment which had governed in Germany by *Realpolitik* could be seen as the quintessence of the old order of the rule of force and the pursuit of profit. This gave the Underground its chance.

As we have seen, the growth of apocalyptic cults and the popularity of the occult were fostered by the misery of material conditions in the confused period immediately after the Great War. Because of the peculiar factors that encouraged an illuminated nationalism in Germany, a great deal of the transcendental impulse behind the occult revival was given a specifically nationalist twist.

Within the ranks of the *völkisch* movement are to be found several influential prophets of a nationalist occultism. The word *völkisch* carries overtones of "nation," "race," and "tribe," as well as the more antiquarian associations which cling to the English ideas of "folklore" or "folk dancing"; "folk," however, is an adequate translation. The movements which can be called *völkisch* have already found their historian,[1] but it has not been sufficiently emphasized that the sort of attitudes these men adopted were in many respects derived from theories of the Occult Revival. The forms their rebellion took were associated with the new "spirituality" of Progressive thought.

For example, Julius Langbehn's enormously influential book *Rembrandt als Erzieher* (1890) made a hero of the Swedish mystic Swedenborg and coupled him with the 13th-century Meister Eckhart; the contemporary cult of Germanic mystics like the obscure Jacob Lorber is part and parcel of this veneration. When applied to nationalist principles the mystical doctrine of the dissolution of the self in the Godhead has interesting results. The individual subject of the state must dissolve his personal identity in that of the people, the *Volk*.[2] This is precisely the doctrine we have already observed in the Guild Socialist Ramiro de Maeztu without emphasizing its mystical origins. Langbehn himself was attracted to the Theosophy of Madame Blavatsky but ended his life in a Catholic religious order. The prominent *völkisch* publisher Eugen Diederichs cultivated Oriental mysticism and theories of a return to the soil. When he established his publishing house in Jena he originally intended to call it "theosophical," and he believed in mystical fluids uniting the individual with the community. His friend and associate Martin Buber developed ideas similar to those of Diederichs on the basis of Jewish Hasidic mysticism. Once more the keynote was that the self must be absorbed into the Divine.[3] With such currents of thought other idealisms, like that of the *Wandervögel*, mingled: Diederichs and his Sera circle sent a greeting to the Hohe Meissner meeting composed in hexameters.[4]

Like the more generally Progressive Underground, whose concern was an unspecified new life rather than the resurrection of *Volk*, the *völkisch* idealists constructed their own Utopias. Buber and his disciples took Monte Verita one summer for a conference. The romantic Theosophist "Fidus" (Karl Höppner)—whose *völkisch* paintings of the young heroes and heroines of the new era were exceedingly popular[5]—was one of the visitors to the Ascona colony.[6] There were also purely *völkisch* Utopias, some following the theories of Adolf Damaschke and the money reformer Sylvio Gesell (in fact, Gesell bears a distinct kinship to British rebels against the financial system like Arthur Kitson and C. H. Douglas). Then there was the settlement of Eden, founded in 1893, which was based on a system of profit sharing and an internal barter economy. Eden increasingly emphasized the exclusively Aryan nature of its elite and celebrated what its directors imagined were ancient German festivals. The doyen of German anti-Semitism, Theodore Fritsch—who was also, quite typically, absorbed in designing garden cities—attempted to apply the ideas of Eden to founding a settlement for his own *Hammerbund*. His friend Willibald Hentschel—yet another pupil of Häckel—projected a Utopia called *Mittgart* under the presiding spirit of the Aryan god Artam who gave his probably concocted name to the influential *Artamanen Bund*.[7]

In many ways the *völkisch* idealists obeyed the same impulses as the illuminates who were not concerned with the state of the "nation" or the "race." The two elements can be easily confused. Thus Rudolf Steiner observed how Langbehn's book *Rembrandt als Erzieher* passed in the Theosophical circles he frequented as a work of deep "spiritual" import: a verdict with which Steiner did not at all agree.[8] In a similar way Rom Landau could see Keyserling as a guru of general "spiritual" significance; while to at least one historian he has appeared an important *völkisch* thinker and preparer of the way for Nazism.[9]

The distinguishing characteristic of *völkisch* spirituality was, of course, its racial emphasis. We have already seen how the teachings of H. P. Blavatsky's *Secret Doctrine* embodied the idea of the occult destinies of each particular race; and it is worth noticing that the Theosophical Society was at one time called the "Theosophical Society of the Arya Samaj." The Arya Samaj was a body of Hindu revivalists with whom Colonel Olcott and Madame Blavatsky had allied themselves. Although the connection did not last very long it persisted in terminology—for example, in 1883 a New York branch of the Theosophical Society was formed by William Quan Judge called the "Aryan Theosophists of New York" and had as its first object the promotion of *Aryan* and other Eastern religions.[10] The word "Arya," in fact, is Sanskrit for "noble," and the term had been applied by anthropologists to the most ancient Indo-European race. But it is common knowledge how the vision of the Aryan race was ultimately applied, and it is within a Theosophical setting that the theories of the Viennese racialists Guido von List and Lanz von Liebenfels can best be understood.

Guido von List (1848-1919) was the son of a businessman and a keen Alpinist. His mystical ideas took long to germinate.[11] In 1889 he published his novel *Carnuntum,* which extolled the sacredness of Vienna on the grounds that it had been the home of Gluck, Hayden, Mozart, Beethoven, and the discoverer of the "Odic force," Baron Reichenbach. It was also the place where, according to an ancient prophecy, the coming church of the Aryans would arise to spread throughout the world. In 1891 von List published a work of "archaeological occultism," which placed a romantic interpretation on Germanic landscapes and prehistoric relics like runic inscriptions and burial mounds.[12] In the same year he was inspired to compose a pantheistic and Germanic catechism. Von List's god, *Allvater,* was honored by leading a virtuous life, working, and serving the *Volk.* The last of his Ten Commandments read, "To your *Volk* and Fatherland be true unto death."[13] Von List gradually developed a system of interpreting runes, symbols, peasant carvings, and coats of arms to discover the esoteric religion of the "Ario-Germans." In 1905 the Guido von List Society was founded, which included among its members the Theosophist Franz Hartmann, whom von List's biographer—himself a prominent Theosophist—describes as "very honored among us." In 1910 Hartmann placed von List's ideas in a class with *Isis Unveiled* and remarked on their correspondence to Indian tradition.[14]

Guido von List and his society were in the mainstream of the occult revival. Friedrich Wannieck (who financed the group) wrote to von List in December 1914 that he had lost his son in the war and was seeking consolation from a Spiritualist medium. This medium was a Fraülein von Rantzau, with whom Franz Hartmann had been closely associated. Both Wannieck's son and Hartmann himself spoke through the medium commending von List's work. At the same time the society counted on its books the names of General Blasius von Schemua, the chief of staff of the Austro-Hungarian army, and Dr. Josef Neumayer, a former mayor of Vienna.[15]

List's ideas filtered into *völkisch* and occult thought in Germany as well as Austria. Philipp Stauff, the president of the Guido von List Society, adapted his master's theories to the interpretation of carved beams on old houses. He was a member of the group around the Munich newspaper that later became the official Nazi organ under the name of the *Völkischer Beobachter.*

Another line of communication between Vienna and Munich was a charlatan whom the Guido von List Society always referred to as "the exalted Tarnhari." Tarnhari presented himself to the Viennese in 1911 as the head of the still-surviving family of the Volsungs—whose family traditions appeared to tally strangely with the discoveries of von List. It seems that von List and his adherents expected great things from this hereditary descendent of ancient Teutonic prowess.[16] Despite all Germanic trappings, von List's ideas were thoroughly those of the Occult Revival. His symbolic interpretations—in which the swastika and the "sun-wheel" played a great part—led him to the discovery of the sacred primeval language of the secret Aryan priestly caste, the "Armanen."[17] This secret caste professed an esoteric religion which the popular worship of Wotan concealed. It incorporated belief in *karma* and reincarnation and found its supreme expression in the Cabala, which von List's disciples maintained was not at all Jewish, having originated in Gothic Spain. The teachings of the Freemason Kerning were modern versions of the ancient secret religion.[18]

Near to von List in spirit and sharing supporters with him—Schemua belonged to his organization and he himself belonged to von List's—was Adolf Lanz, alias Jörg Lanz von Liebenfels (1874-1954). Lanz von Liebenfels was a renegade Cistercian monk. He was expelled from his monastery in 1899, and almost immediately he developed a romantic attachment to the Germanic past and a prejudice against the Jesuits. He founded the Order of the New Templars on the model of the Roman Catholic hierarchy and set about collecting castles as centers for his order of "Aryan heroes." In 1907 the New Templars acquired their first fortress, Burg Werfenstein on the Danube. By the 1920s they had accumulated three more, to say nothing of a house in Salzburg and a "cell" in Hungary. Lanz gathered great support in *völkisch* circles through the issue of his racist magazine *Ostara.* The specifications for members of the New Templars laid down in the magazine went far beyond the simple formula of "blonde hair and blue eyes," and included slender hands and feet and an elongated cranium. Lanz proposed the founding of colonies of the pure-blooded far from the corrupting influence of the towns, and he compiled a handbook for prospective colonists. He exercised considerable influence over Strindberg, claimed a protracted correspondence with Lord Kitchener, and (as we have seen) tried to convert several Russian nobles to his doctrine of "Ariosophy."[19]

Ariosophy was a teaching of eclectic occultism, whose cardinal text was Lanz von Liebenfels's *Theozoologie* of 1904. Almost any reasonably "Germanic" occult text was appropriated. For example, numbers 7-10 of the Ariosophical Library were devoted to Lanz's elaboration of the monumentally boring Jacob Lorber under the title of "the greatest modern Ariosophical medium." To his racism and *völkisch* principles Lanz added an interesting method of scriptural interpretation which entailed reading "Angel" as "Aryan Hero" every time the word was used.

"The Aryan hero," wrote Lanz, "is on this planet the most complete incarnation of God and of the Spirit." The enemy of the Aryan hero was the Tschandala, the underman, whose political organization was democracy and who favored free competition and materialism. The coming age of Aquarius would see the purification of the Aryan hero from the sin of mixing his blood with that of such ape-men. According to a friend of Lanz, the prior of the Order of the New Templars was in touch with H. P. Blavatsky and Annie Besant.[20] His racism is peculiarly important because it shows the transition between the general possibilities implicit in Madame Blavatsky's *Secret Doctrine* and their practical application.

The Secret Doctrine was published in German translation the year before Lanz's *Theozoologie,* and the Ariosophist found much material in its pages to justify his position. Through his method of scriptural interpretation, Lanz discovered a series of subhuman races that existed in the time of the Assyrians. There had been for example the Pagutu, a race of river-men. He was convinced that the authoress of *The Secret Doctrine,* with its basis of "root-races" and "subraces," had known all about them: the Pagutu—was it not obvious?—had been one of her Lemurian root-races. "When H. P.

Blavatsky wrote her inspired Anthropogenesis" (the first part of *The Secret Doctrine*), Lanz mused, "she was almost a generation ahead of her time and of anthropology. Today for the first time work on the latest material has brought to light results which show a completely amazing identity with those of the spiritual Theosophist."[21] Lanz taught that men had not evolved from apes—apes were degenerated men. H.P.B. herself had recognized the "unfruitfulness" in the mixing of races.[22]

In 1918 Lanz was in some manner involved in the Hungarian revolution and seems to have narrowly avoided being shot. During the late 1920s he was the center of a group of *völkisch* occultists that included Ernst Issberner-Haldane (a palmist and astrologer), Rudolf John Gorsleben (the translator of a version of the Edda known in Munich *völkisch* circles merely as "the Gorsleben Edda"), and the ubiquitous and highly illuminated anti-Semite Grigori Schwartz-Bostunitch. They acknowledged Lanz as "our Leader and Teacher" and published a *völkisch* paper to spread the gospel.[23] In 1938 Lanz was forbidden to publish by the Nazis; and it is possible that this ban was connected with the personal influence of Lanz on Hitler, a story to which we shall soon return.

In Munich similar theories held sway. In Schwabing there was another side to the posturings of the occultists and prophets, a side that one witness called "Secret Germany," where the Bohemian atmosphere nourished projects certainly of a Utopian nature, but also of practical application under conditions of crisis.[24] Ludwig Derleth's project of a new order dwelling in the *Rosenburg* has already been compared to the Order of the New Templars. The emphasis placed by the Munich Cosmics on the disruption of bourgeois standards and their use of the symbolic interpretations of Bachofen are similar to the methods of Guido von List and Lanz von Liebenfels. Ludwig Klages became a great influence on the youth movement; but possibly the most influential member of the Cosmics was Alfred Schuler, whose personal doctrine of the sacredness of the blood had been symbolized by the sign of the swastika ten years before Lanz von Liebenfels raised his swastika banner on Burg Werfenstein. The 1890s revival of Bachofen took on new life in the 1920s, with lectures given by Schuler, the propaganda put about by Klages, and a crowd of young disciples. Of these an example is

Bertha Eckstein-Diener, who wrote under the names of "Helen Diner" and "Sir Galahad," translated the American mystic Prentice Mulford, and, apart from interpreting Bachofen into a feminist history of culture, produced occult novels and a denunciation of Slav Messianism. This she naturally saw as transmuted into Russian Communism, the epitome of mob rule and an expression of the Chosen People of Jewry. Her profoundest veneration went out to "the most obvious aristocrat of his time," the French Catholic magician, Joséphin Péladan.[25] This was merely one of the possible syntheses of elements to hand. The presence of the occult in Munich should not be thought to have ended with the First World War.

Hitler himself must be ignored until the stage is fully set, because one of the most telling arguments for classing the early Nazi movement as "illuminated" is the constellation of ideas that presided over its birth. There is no longer much dispute over who or what in terms of ideas most helped Hitler to develop the *Deutsche Arbeiterpartei* of Anton Drexler into a force able to attempt a coup in 1923. There was his own orientation up till that time and the general confusion both of present conditions and plans for an improved future. In Munich the men who influenced or helped him beyond any question were the engineer-economist Gottfried Feder, the Bohemian playwright and mystic Dietrich Eckart, and two fugitives from the Russian Revolution, Alfred Rosenberg and Max-Erwin von Scheubner-Richter. Indispensable pieces in the game that was played up till the failure of the Beer-Hall Putsch were the representative of the old order betrayed, General Ludendorff, and the amalgam of occult-*völkisch* opinion around the *Thule Bund* of Rudolf von Sebottendorf.

Dietrich Eckart (1868-1923) was born the son of a lawyer in Neumarkt in the Oberpfalz. He went to the University of Erlangen to study medicine, and his chosen field is connected with his addiction to morphine, contracted while still at university. His friend Alfred Rosenberg wrote of him: "Without the sweet poison he could not live, and applied the whole cunning of a possessor of this craving to get himself dose after dose. Eventually he was taking daily measures from which a normal man, not possessed of such bear-like strength, would have died." Eckart had to give up his medical studies and took the cure in a sanatorium. He determined on a writing career; lived as Bohemian an existence as he could contrive in the town of his birth; and first published in 1893. Two years later his father died, and Eckart quickly ran through his inheritance. He moved from artistic circles in Leipzig and Regensburg to Berlin, where he settled in 1899. Eckart became the Bayreuth correspondent for several newspapers and wrote novels and political verse. Eventually he broke through with a play, *Familienvater* in 1905-06, and he made a reputation as a *völkisch* playwright with a translation of *Peer Gynt,* a historical drama *Henry the Hohenstaufen,* and his widely acclaimed *Lorenzaccio.* After another spell in a sanatorium, Eckart married and moved to Munich where he became a fixed star in the Schwabing firmament.[26]

Eckart was an archetypal Bohemian and an emotional cripple. To his early morphine addiction and his later overindulgence in alcohol—which probably killed him—he added a contempt for women. As Rosenberg said: for Eckart, Woman was nature and no more.[27] Eckart's anti-Semitism had burgeoned in Berlin. The lack of success that attended his first attempts to have his plays produced was attributed to the same Jewish conspiracy as lay behind the early hostility of theater critics.[28] From December 1918, Eckart issued at his own expense and very largely wrote *Auf gut Deutsch,* an anti-Semitic news sheet, which he was forced to distribute personally. This activity brought him into contact with Gottfried Feder, Alfred Rosenberg, the *Thule Bund,* and Hitler.

It is important to see this man not as a "precursor of Nazism" or "an influence on Hitler," but as a creature in his own right, for only in this way will the nature of Eckart's influence become apparent. Nazi studies of the playwright and "veteran fighter" unite in presenting him as a mystic and seer rather than as an orthodox exponent of *völkisch* ethics, and there is every indication that they are correct.

> Dietrich Eckart was never a politician in the usual sense. As a politician he remained—as he did as poet—a seer of essentials, and from this standpoint he passed judgment on men and events. With the politics of everyday and their advancement, with practical *Realpolitik* and its hypocrisy and readiness to compromise, he had nothing to do.[29]

Eckart was a seeker of other realities. He especially admired Schopenhauer for his adoption of the Hindu doctrine of *maya*—that the world is illusion. According to Rosenberg, the *Cherubinischer Wandersmann* of the mystic Angelus Silesius was Eckart's Bible.

The basis of Eckart's doctrine was Christian mysticism. Man must free himself from the world and deny the supremacy of matter, which is illusion. Only death will break the spell under which humanity labors. This negation of the world has its opposite in the teaching of world affirmation, whose greatest representative Eckart saw as the Jew. Christ, for Eckart, was an incarnate revelation; but his teaching had been overlaid by St. Paul and others with the Jewish gospel of the Old Testament from which proceeded all evil. Belief in the true God, on the other hand, was essential to all Germans.

In Dietrich Eckart mysticism and racism were inseparable; and his most definite personal views later caused his friends and panegyricists much embarrassment. Rosenberg complained that even in purely political articles, Eckart would keep dragging in Christ. In 1941 a study of Eckart was published, which stigmatized the Nazi hero's beliefs as "dangerously Indian." Eckart's curiosity extended further than Angelus Silesius, and he considered himself well able to denounce the "Theosophical Society ... which never knew—and still does not know—what Theosophy really means."[30] A curious feud took place between the *völkisch* playwright and the Anthroposophists, which is worth examining in a little detail because it reveals the milieu in which Eckart moved.

In Schwabing all elements of the idealistic Underground could come together. Rudolf Steiner and his followers were as free to make converts as the *völkisch* prophets, and an example may help to show how closely the various "idealists" and illuminates brushed against each other.

Until after the First World War the Schwabing home of the novelist Helen Böhlau (1859-1940)[31] was a center of *völkisch* prophets, and nationalist sentiment. Apart from a series of novels describing life in medieval Germany, Helen Böhlau published in 1896 what she considered her best novel, suggestively entitled *Das Recht der Mutter*—the reference is to Bachofen's *Mutterrecht*. The author found the inspiration for this book in her husband, Omar al Raschid Bey, yet another German-Russian of mystical temperament. He had become a naturalized Turk in order to marry her. Apart from presumably keeping another wife elsewhere, Omar's peculiarities extended to going around in Turkish dress. "He is a philosopher," wrote one of the couple's friends, "and although he objects to calling his philosophy and comparative religious sciences theosophy (a certain odium always attaches itself to this word), it is nevertheless extremely like it." This opinion was that of Princess Helen von Racowitza, a devotee of H. P. Blavatsky, whom she had known in New York at the time of the founding of the Theosophical Society and again in London at the close of H.P.B.'s life. When Princess von Racowitza was not using her title she became plain Frau von Schewitsch, and as such is mentioned by Rudolf Steiner as the hostess to gatherings at which he was able to find a sympathetic hearing when he was building up his Anthroposophical movement.[32] By easy stages the inquirer moves from Helen Böhlau and her salon of illuminated nationalism, through the mysticism of her Slav-influenced husband, to Theosophy, and finally to Steiner.

Eckart himself was approached by Steiner's agents on a political rather than a transcendental footing. The publisher of *Auf gut Deutsch* had founded a political organization directed against Jews and Communists, which he called the *Deutsche Bürgervereinigung*. By May 1919 this organization was advertised across the front page of the *Münchener Beobachter*. This was the month in which army and Freikorps units entered Munich and overthrew the workers councils of the Left, which had governed the city since the assassination of Kurt Eisner at the beginning of the year. Bloody revenge was taken by the occupying forces because of a dozen hostages murdered by the Communists. For Eckart the importance was that the murdered hostages had belonged to the Thule Society, with which he was connected by ties of sympathy if not yet by actual membership. The tide of politics had turned to the Right, and Eckart and his *Bürgervereinigung* were among those who might be assumed to profit from this. In July 1919, Eckart wrote in *Auf gut Deutsch:*

> Recently I have been asked incessantly what I think of *Dr. Rudolf Steiner*. My answer confined itself to the facts that many years ago in Berlin when he was enthused by Nietzsche I once heard him speak from a miraculously suspended dais; that recently an "Appeal" concocted by him came my way signed by a number of "eminent" names which was nonetheless completely without content, indeed thoroughly con-

fused; and lastly, that I saw him as a Jew whom I wouldn't trust across the street. In the meantime I came somewhat more closely in contact with him through the visit of one of his disciples, an artist, who had several times vainly sought me out in the offices of the *Deutsche Bürgervereinigung,* finally to reconcile himself however, to my flat—apparently for him not nearly sufficiently neutral territory. In ten minutes we had both said all we would ever say to each other, I really don't need to enlarge. Whether he was sent by Steiner himself in the hopes of being able to use my supposed influence for his Munich plans, I don't know, but I believe so; at least the persistence with which I was sought out in the *Bürgervereinigung* argues strongly for it.[33]

The chances are that Eckart was right. During the troubled year of 1919—in which form of government succeeded form of government, giving place to no government at all—Rudolf Steiner had decided that spiritual science should enter politics. His panacea was called the "Threefold Commonwealth," and the theory had first been outlined by Steiner to Count Otto Lerchenfeld in 1917. Together with another Anthroposophist, Count Ludwig Polzer-Hoditz, Steiner and Lerchenfeld had elaborated the scheme for Polzer-Hoditz to communicate to the German emperor. Through Polzer-Hoditz's brother the plan reached the emperor that November, but nothing further came of the project till 1919.

Steiner's original strategy might be compared to that of Papus, who also tried to influence thrones. This is a somewhat ironic comparison, considering that the design for the Threefold Commonwealth was taken lock, stock, and barrel from Papus's "intellectual master," Saint-Yves d'Alveydre. Saint-Yves had called the system "Synarchy"—by which he said he meant "Totalism," the association of everyone with everyone else, as opposed to Nihilism, the association of no one with nobody. The basis of the theory is an analogy of human society and the human body. In both there are said to be three systems—the "eating," "living," and "thinking" (in the words of Papus); the "transformers of material," the "rhythmic system," and the "head-system" (in the terminology of Steiner). In terms of the State this meant the division of government into three equivalent functions: economic life; legislature and judiciary; and the directing force (interpreted by Papus as authority and instruction, and by Rudolf Steiner as the spiritual life of the nation).[34] In France the occult publisher Chamuel had issued a series of "synarchical" works. But Steiner had no need to go beyond Saint-Yves or Papus for his material.

In 1919 the fully elaborated plan was ready to be applied to a Germany boiling with revolution. Steiner's opponents were unanimous that the Anthroposophist thought that his time had come. In April 1919 *The Threefold Commonwealth* was published in book form, and 80,000 copies were sold in the first year. Steiner's attempts to interest statesmen ensnared Prince Max of Baden, the last imperial chancellor, but this time Steiner addressed his chief efforts to the workers. He lectured to trade unions and established organizations to campaign for the Threefold Social Order in both Germany and Switzerland. The Stuttgart-based Union for the Threefold Social Order published a weekly paper. It was, therefore, as an organized political force that the Anthroposophists took the field.

The "Appeal" that Eckart had read almost certainly had to do with the Threefold Commonwealth, and Steiner stated in 1922 that the book embodying the theory had been written specifically for "the time Spring 1919 and the place South Germany." On 7 May two of Steiner's followers—probably Dr. Carl Unger and the industrialist Emil Molt—approached the Württemberg state president, the Social Democrat Blos, and tried to persuade him that Steiner would make a good addition to the state government. Blos strongly disapproved of Steiner and rejected his advances.[35] It is more likely than not that Eckart was deliberately approached by the Anthroposophists in a similar fashion.

With Eckart the Anthroposophists had no success. Indeed they had stirred up a hornet's nest. The hostility and indifference that met the later efforts of Steiner to engage a mass audience can in part be attributed to the work of Eckart and other *völkisch* agitators. By the time the Anthroposophist lectured to those involved in the Saar Plebiscite in 1921, his standing had been irreparably damaged. In two attacks in *Auf gut Deutsch* in July and December 1919, Eckart set the style for all subsequent polemics against the Anthroposophists. Steiner was a Jew from Galicia, he insisted; his society was built on love of money and megalomania. Eckart reprinted large sections of a pamphlet by the Russian-German Max Seiling accusing

Steiner of "sexual magic," and he revived accusations that had been the cause of the first attacks on Steiner during the Great War. These consisted of a fatuous theory that when Steiner had met General Helmuth von Moltke just before the 1914 Battle of the Marne, he had somehow mesmerized his sympathizer into military ineptitude. This was soon to be given a contemporary turn and Steiner represented as the agent of the Jewish-Masonic-Communist conspiracy. "Whether it's Preuss or Hirsch or Steiner," wrote Eckart, "the spirit's the same even when it goes disguised in a Theosophical beard."

In the course of his attacks Eckart revealed himself to be very well informed on internal Theosophical politics and occultism generally: for example, denying Steiner's book *Theosophy* any more value than "Brandler's *Okkultische Lehrbriefen.*" "Brandler" was Karl Brandler-Pracht (b. 1864) a central figure in the German astrological revival and a practitioner of what Ellic Howe has described as a "primitive" brand of occultism. Brandler-Pracht had been in Munich during 1908-09, when he had quarreled with the Steinerites in the Theosophical Society (who, of course, considered themselves immeasurably his superiors).[36] Eckart's cut was, therefore, both subtle and revealing. To refer in familiar terms to "Brandler" shows that the leader of the Deutsche Bürgervereinigung was quite at home in the rapidly growing Occult Underground.

Why did the Anthroposophists approach Dietrich Eckart? He was known to be a mystic, fond of "philosophizing" as his friends described him. He was a Schwabing character, and in a good political position. It might reasonably have been expected that Eckart's call for a more "spiritual" politics would have found favor. After all the Threefold Commonwealth was well-received in other illuminated circles. A review in the English *Guildsman* gave Steiner a guarded welcome, and the theory was later to form the basis of the economic policy of Dmitri Mitrinović's "New Britain."[37] Steiner's vaguely medievalist praise of the guilds might be expected to endear itself to a supporter of the economic theories of Gottfried Feder. Furthermore, the analogy with the human body and the whole concept of the political organism working together must have seemed tailor-made for the prophet of a less materialist and more organic, more *völkisch* society.

We can learn much from the violence of Eckart's rejection of the Anthroposophists. To react so strongly—he was not the only *völkisch* thinker to do so—he must have taken them seriously. Indeed he was right, for Germany seemed prepared to consider any alternative to her previous unfortunate system. But, in a way, the *völkisch* reaction was an admission that both camps were operating on the same level. And a proportion of the *völkisch* rage came from the realization that here was another vision of the universe which claimed to be "spiritual." Did not the prophets of the *Volk* have a monopoly of spiritual politics, were not they alone truly *geistreich*?

It was not necessarily illogical for Steiner's disciple to approach Eckart. The accusation of being "Indian" rather than German which was leveled at Steiner was later to be applied to Eckart himself. Steiner was not really alien to *völkisch* thought. He was a friend of the painter Fidus, and he had already made an effort to ingratiate himself with supporters of an organic nationalism by propounding a doctrine of "folk-souls" in the early days of the First World War. The British folk-soul was, naturally enough, the expression of pure materialism—the German, alone of all such corporate entities, communed directly with the spirit.[38] This was further trespassing on the sacred preserves of *völkisch* orthodoxy. Eckart chose to regard Steiner as internationalist and Communist—hence a Jew of the conspiracy to be hated with the hate of an illuminate for rejected associates.

Eckart's anti-Semitism sprang from his peculiar Christianity. His biographers have insisted upon the place of Christ in Eckart's theology, and it is odd to find this true. Christ was made the man of action. Christ did not temporize when his country was occupied, shouted Eckart; Christ did not try to form alliances with impure elements in his society. He threw the Jewish (!) money changers out of the temple and went on to oppose his own government. The Crucifixion was by no means the culmination of Judah's hate for everything "poured down from Heaven." This malevolence expressed itself in the 20th century in the Masonic conspiracy and the *Alliance Israélite Universelle*. In his search for comrades in the fight against the Jew, Eckart soon discovered the Britons and their incomparable founder, Henry Hamilton Beamish. In June 1920 the *Völkischer Beobachter* carried an article on the Britons' news sheet

Jewry über alles, for which Eckart was probably responsible. In a November number of *Auf gut Deutsch* its editor disclosed that through a friend—who signed himself Kurt Kerlen—he was keeping in touch with various anti-Semitic organizations in Britain. They had revealed to him that the latest dastardly move of the Jews was the financing of the Irish movement—for was not de Valera a Portuguese Jew? On 23 January 1923, the *Völkischer Beobachter* reported a meeting of the Nazi party in the Zirkus Krone attended by several thousand. There were two guests: Hitler's chauffeur Emil Maurice (who had emerged from prison after attempting some unspecified move against the Mannheim Stock Exchange) and Henry Hamilton Beamish (refugee from the English courts and the prosecutions of Sir Alfred Mond). Beamish was introduced to the meeting as "an English mineworker" and moved the *Beobachter*'s reporter to enthuse on the possibilities of international cooperation between anti-Semites.[39] The presence of the obscure Beamish testifies to the enthusiasm with which Eckart cultivated his anti-Semitism and yet more surely identifies him—as if further identification were needed—as a member of the international Underground. Goffried Feder (1883-1941) was Eckart's first contact with another who was to stand high in the councils of the early Nazi party. Feder was born in Wurzburg of an academic family and in 1904 qualified in Munich as an engineer. He specialized in working with reinforced concrete, and in 1908 he founded his own firm, which carried out contracts in Bulgaria, Italy, and Russia as well as in Germany. "As a young engineer and contractor with too little capital for ambitious projects I soon learned to know the iron grip of impersonal moneymaking." His experiences abroad taught him how quickly small states ran into debt, and the First World War increased his concern over the financial situation. Personal experience led to generalizations; and after approaching bankers with his own solution for the mounting national debt, Feder sent a memorandum on his financial proposals to the Marxist government of Bavaria on 20 November 1918. This "Manifesto for the Abolition of the Interest-Slavery of Money" was directed at familiar targets: encroaching materialism and the "Golden International." It is worth noting that at the same time in England another engineer, C. H. Douglas, was expanding similar theories into the doctrine of Social Credit.

The villain of the piece Feder called "Mammonism."

> By Mammonism is to be understood, first, international money-power, the supra-national financial arbiter which lords it over every right of self-determination of peoples, International Capital, the so-called Golden International. Next, a spiritual orientation which has come to dominate the most far-flung groups of people, the insatiable acquisitive urge based on a purely temporal view of life which has led to an appalling degeneration of all moral standards and must lead further still.[40]

The Manifesto ended on a grandiose note: *"Give me your hands, workers of all countries, unite!"* In August 1919 the document was printed in the *Völkischer Beobachter;* and in September, Eckart and Feder founded the German Union for the Abolition of Interest Slavery. They had already taken their first joint action, for on 5 April, just before the proclamation of the Bavarian Council Republic, Eckart had composed a leaflet entitled "To all Workers!" on the basis of Feder's manifesto, and the two had distributed this throughout Munich from automobiles. The leaflet was directed "to everyone who works, doesn't matter at what or where, as long as they just work" and—seemingly as an afterthought—"to all reasonable men." It combined Feder's dislike of usury and anonymous capital with Eckart's anti-Semitism, and it represents their first strategic synthesis of the anti-Semitic myth with an appeal for more "spiritual" standards. The root of all evil is "capital lent at interest," and the "Golden International" which caused the war is manipulated by Jews.[41] Eckart seems to have been responsible for the passages which refer specifically to Jewish bankers; for Feder's anti-Semitism was a rather more ethereal affair.

In 1933, when he had very nearly slipped out of sight, Feder made two pronouncements on the Jewish question. He wrote that though the Nazi was by definition an anti-Semite, it was not the Nazi way to plunge headlong into Jew-hating without making inquiries from the experts. Jewry, however, was the representative of the materialistic spirit, the direct opponent of those who wished to abolish interest slavery. But at a meeting of his German Union for the Abolition of Interest Slavery (27 May 1920), Feder had said, in reply to a questioner, that his projected reform "was not a question of race.

Obviously however the Jewish question is connected with the solution of the problem, for representatives [of Jewry] stand in the first line of attack—which is their own fault."[42] In other words, Feder initially conceived his mission as that of combating materialism, not Jews, and his later statements are evidence of how fatally easy it was to progress from the appeal to the spiritual instincts of man to a positive identification of the agents of evil. It was not to be expected that Feder could escape the contorted logic that his anti-Semitic friends supplied. But the way in which his theories and those of Eckart fitted like two pieces of a jigsaw puzzle points to the dangers of an illuminated position. Feder's "spirituality" identifies him also as a seeker for "other realities." In 1930 he made a speech in the Reichstag which warned his audience to have no truck with the "political atheism" of the Left and in this respect to conform to the wishes of the Vatican. They must not forget the center of gravity of the whole enterprise, he cautioned—this was *"the religious basis of our movement,* which can be recognized through the highest innate qualities of man, through sacrifice, devotion, through sacred anger."[43] If we dismiss this merely as the rhetoric of propaganda—which, of course, it also was—we run the risk of imagining that Feder disbelieved his own theories. Nothing could be further from the truth.

Alfred Rosenberg was born into a merchant family of Riga in 1893. With Rosenberg and his fellow refugees from the collapse of tsarist Russia, we are back on the trail of Russian mysticism, its illuminated anti-Semitism, and its supreme expression in the *Protocols.* It is no coincidence that the Baltic areas from which Rosenberg came provided not only the mystics whom we have already noticed, but also many of the more influential *völkisch* prophets and supporters of the idea of German expansion (like Paul Rohrbach, Julius Langbehn, and Paul de Lagarde). To the political reasons which led these "German colonists" to advocate the greatest possible unification of the *Volk,*[44] was added the mystical bent that Russian culture generally and their homeland in particular, seemed to nourish. Contact between Russian mystical circles and *völkisch* opinion had been established long before the Revolution of 1917, which sent Slavonic idealists scurrying to the West. An important example is that of Arthur Moeller van den Bruck, whose book *The*

Third Reich (1923) coined the phrase that forms its title to describe a new "spiritually reformed" Germany based on metaphysical premises. Moeller van den Bruck met his second wife, the Lithuanian Lucy Kaenick, in Paris in 1902 and began a romanticized attachment to things Russian. Through his wife's sister, he met Merezhkovsky, and together they produced the first complete German translation of Dostoievsky. At that time Merezhkovsky was proclaiming a new age for his new Christianity in accordance with the medieval prophecies of Joachim of Flora (who had dreamed of a *tertius status*), and it is almost certain that his influence played a part in Moeller's attempt to usher in an empire of the spirit.[45]

Rosenberg was educated in Reval, and in 1910 he went to the Technische Hochschule in Riga to study architecture. Here he joined the student corps "Rubonia," which may have been one source of his anti-Semitic opinions; the previous year he had discovered Houston Stewart Chamberlain. In 1915 he married and moved to Moscow when the Riga Hochschule was transferred to the Russian capital to remove it from the area of German occupation. In Moscow he lived with a family of Cadet sympathies and seems to have absorbed their political opinions, regarding the Cadets as leading the fight against the tsarist system. He also acquired something of the White Russian theory that Rasputin and the "Dark Forces" were part of the conspiracy of subversion.

> In his great speech of Winter 1916, the [Cadet] leader Miliukov attacked openly for the first time the "Dark Forces" by which he meant Rasputin and the supporters of a separate peace with Germany. The Conservative Markov [II] answered him unbendingly but cleverly and prophesied the most frightful consequences for Russia. The banned speech of Miliukov was secretly printed and distributed throughout Russia, but it had to have Markov's speech attached to it. I was able to glance through both speeches in F-'s house.

Sometime in 1917—as Rosenberg was later to claim—"an unknown hand" placed on his desk a copy of Sergei Nilus's book *The Great in the Small,* with its translation of the *Protocols of the Elders of Zion.* This seems to have been a revelation. Apart from scraps of art criticism, Rosenberg wrote nothing until 1923 that was not connected with the *Protocols* and the Jewish conspiracy. During 1917

Rosenberg's sources of money dried up and he had to think of leaving Moscow. He returned to Reval with his wife and eventually left for Germany with the retreating forces of occupation. His last act in his Baltic homeland was to give a lecture on "the Jewish question" some hours before he left. From Berlin he made his way to Munich, where there seemed more hope of getting work.[46]

It is now established beyond any doubt that Russian emigrés were at the bottom of much of the anti-Semitism that blossomed suddenly after the Russian Revolution. The convenience of the conspiracy theory in explaining the collapse of the old order in Russia was also appreciated by Western sympathizers like the journalists Robert Wilton and Victor Marsden. It is rare to find an anti-Semitic source after 1917 which does not stand in debt to the White Russian analysis of the Revolution. The *Protocols* arrived in Germany under the wing of P. N. Shabelsky-Bork and Colonel F. V. Vinberg—both of whom were greatly influenced by the legend of the Ipatyev house and devoted to the tsaritsa. From Vinberg the *Protocols* were passed to the *völkisch* anti-Semite Ludwig Müller von Hausen, who published six editions of his German translation in 1920. Many other Russian right wingers arrived in Germany with anti-Semitic beliefs firmly entrenched.

Among "straightforward" emigrant anti-Semites like General Netchvolodov and Markov II,[47] there were naturally the more "illuminated" members of the right wing. One of these was the Catholic General A. Cherep-Spiridovich, who had been convinced of a worldwide Jewish conspiracy as early as 1914. Then he had seen the *Germans* as the chief agents of the Semitic plot, and he blamed Bismarck for his own financial ruin—caused by the collapse of his shipping business on the Volga. Spirodovich appeared to think of himself as an agent of heaven: in 1903 he had tried to influence the papal conclave, and after the Armistice had been signed ("thanks to my advice") he spent three years in the British Museum carrying out research into the machinations of "the Anti-Church or the executors of Satan's will—the Jews."[48] Cherep-Spiridovich later operated from the United States. In Germany a man of a similar stamp—according to the general "a brilliant Slav author"—was Gregori Schwartz-Bostunitch, who had decided that he was a Balt, a scion of the race which had produced Rosenberg and Keyserling. About 1925

Bostunitch began to work for Rosenberg, but he later switched allegiance to Heinrich Himmler.[49]

Alfred Rosenberg was one of many Russian and Baltic emigrants, and by no means the most conspicuous, when he arrived in Munich in December 1918. Through a Frau von Schrenck, another Baltic refugee, he was introduced to Dietrich Eckart, who was looking for writers on the Jewish question. Rosenberg began to write for *Auf gut Deutsch;* his material was drawn from the traditions and publications of the Russian emigrants. Rosenberg formed a fast friendship with Eckart, whose mystical preoccupations he, to some extent, shared: before leaving Russia he had been preoccupied with Schopenhauer and Indian philosophy. His correspondence with two fellow-members of his old student corps in Riga led to the arrival in the circle of Eckart and the Munich right wing of Max-Erwin von Scheubner-Richter (1884-1923), a German Balt with aristocratic connections and considerable pull with the Russian emigration. Von Scheubner-Richter's first effort at securing cooperation between German and Russian right wingers was in 1920, when he was sent by several Bavarian firms to negotiate with Baron Wrangel's army in the Crimea.[50] Eckart recorded Scheubner-Richter's return with hopes of an eventual White victory. What—asked the publisher of *Auf gut Deutsch*—was the attitude of Wrangel's forces to the Jews? All officers and most men were dead against them, was the reply. "And the Allies?" "Almost only Jewish officers in the Crimea, English as well as French."[51] This invaluable contact man—the description is Professor Walter Laqueur's—the drummer up of funds, joined the Nazi party in the spring of 1920, when Rosenberg introduced him to Hitler. Meanwhile, Eckart, Rosenberg, and Feder came together in the Thule.

The Thule Society was a cover organization disguised as a "Germanic Studies group" run by the art student Walter Nauhaus for a branch of the Germanen Order. The Germanen Order was founded in 1912 as an "Aryan" anti-Semitic group composed of members of the already-existing *Hammerbund* of Theodore Fritsch. At the end of 1917 Rudolph von Sebettendorff was appointed head of the order's Bavarian branch and began to build up its moribund Munich lodge on the basis of the Thule Society. Sebottendorff (1875-1945)—alias Adam Glauer, although he claimed to have been adopted by a Baron von Sebottendorff under Turkish law—was a drifter and adventurer whose chief preoccupations were astrology and occultism. According to Ellic Howe, the leading authority on Sebottendorff, the Freiherr was probably familiar with Sufi and other texts of Islamic esotericism. This partly accounts for a deep occult coloring to the activities of the Thule; although a certain amount of mysticism was present in its parent Germanen Order. For example, Hermann Pohl, a leader of the Germanen, circularized his members calling for a religious revival. The Munich branch of the Germanen Order was inaugurated by Sebottendorff on 17 August 1918 in the fashionable Munich hotel, the Vier Jahreszeiten. Its activities went forward with much emphasis on ancient Germanic subjects and a talk from Sebottendorff on the occult uses of the pendulum.[52]

In June 1918 Sebottendorff acquired for his Germanen Order the publishing house of Franz Eher. The firm owned the *Münchener Beobachter,* a small weekly newspaper, which the *Thule Bund* promptly transformed into an anti-Semitic broadsheet. In the contributions which decorate its early pages along with swastikas, S-runes, and all the paraphernalia of *völkisch* symbolism is found the headline: "Down with the *Tschandalen!*" To the theories of Lanz von Liebenfels, which gave birth to this term, was added the influence of Guido von List: Philip Stauff contributed a touching obituary describing how his master had died in his arms.[53]

In July Sebottendorff left his intrigues in Bavaria to devote himself to occultism proper. He became the editor of the *Astrologisches Rundschau* and published several books on astrology and occultism. Chief among these was his so-called *History of Astrology* (1923), which is nothing of the kind and only uses astrology as a peg on which to hang Sebottendorff's version of occult prehistory—mostly adapted from Guido von List and Lanz von Liebenfels. Sebottendorff seems to have believed that the stars prophesied great things for the Germans and asked rhetorically: "Whether the Germans especially must give to the world a new species? It almost seems like it." At the same time as proclaiming the German mission for the new astrological eon, Sebottendorff decided that the pure Aryan religion was in his day represented by—of all people—Bô Yin Râ. In 1923 Sebottendorff returned to Turkey. The following year was published his *Praxis of old Turkish*

Freemasonry, in which the Freiherr attributed the moral strength of the Moslem peoples to their practice of Islamic alchemy.[54] It is possible, if there is any truth in the rumor that Meyrink practiced "Sebottendorff-exercises," that they were derived from this source.

With the esoteric Freiherr presiding over the Germanen Order, one can be reasonably certain of two things: that his colleagues would share his tastes to some degree, and that these pursuits would separate the Thule Society from the realities of politics. Sebottendorff's misleading account of the Thule is interesting in that it makes clear that he shared the concern of Eckart and other *völkisch* friends with the political efforts of Rudolf Steiner. The Anthroposophist appeared as a significant part of the Munich political scene. I have myself talked to a former member of the Thule who met Steiner several times in Schwabing. It is clear that other members of Sebottendorff's *völkisch* circle were as concerned as the Freiherr at the possibilities of Steiner's tentative. Thus a front-page article in the *Münchener Beobachter*—now called the *Völkischer Beobachter*—in late August 1919, characterized Steiner's movement as "Jewish" and drew attention to a papal directive forbidding Catholics to have anything to do with Theosophy or Anthroposophy.[55] Eckart was at home in these circles, as were both Feder and Rosenberg. From this connection at least one historic result was the purchase in December 1920 from Sebottendorff's colleagues of the *Völkischer Beobachter* by Eckart on behalf of the newly founded National Socialist German Workers' Party.

A second result of the agitation of the Thule was the arrival in Munich *völkisch* circles of Adolf Hitler. A member of the Thule Society called Karl Harrer was deputed by his colleagues to form an alliance with the workers, to try to spread the *völkisch* message. Harrer (1890-1926), a sports writer, was impressed with the locksmith Anton Drexler, who had recently started a Munich branch of a worker's party founded in Bremen in 1916. Together with Drexler, Harrer founded a "workers' circle," which grew into a "workers' party." In January 1919, in the rooms of the Thule Society in the Vier Jahreszeiten, the group became the "National Socialist German Workers Union," and the title was altered to "party" a year later. From the Thule Society Drexler took as members Dietrich Eckart, Gottfried Feder, and Friedrich Krohn (a dentist of *völkisch*

The Magi of the North 299

leanings). On 12 September 1919, Gottfried Feder gave a lecture on economic problems in the Sterneckerbräu at which was present Corporal Adolf Hitler, who forgot his role as "information officer" so much as to make a fifteen-minute speech and afterward to join Drexler's party.[56]

Hitler's career up to this time is in outline very well known, although in detail the information is woefully uncertain and the authorities agree only on certain points. Hitler's birth in Braunau am Inn in 1889, his schooldays in Linz, the period of mendicant Bohemianism in Vienna from 1907 to 1913, and his short stay in Munich before the outbreak of the war have provided little certain indication of the real mentors—or even of the surroundings—of the future dictator. The example of Dr. Leopold Pötsch (an anti-Semitic schoolmaster of Linz), the inspiration of the notorious Carl Lüger (the anti-Semitic mayor of Vienna), and the impression made by the massed processions of the Austrian Social Democrats have all been cited as influences. No doubt all are correct. But there is some further evidence, which has usually been dismissed *a priori* as fantastic but which deserves a more extended airing in the general context of the early Nazi party and of what little we know about the nature of the young Hitler. The resentful, under-educated aspiring architect and hack artist who tended to live withdrawn from the world, the denizen of that sub-Bohemia of skid row, was quite likely to be attracted by the underground of rejected knowledge. It is known that Hitler carried with him into power one rejected theory which very definitely belonged to the underground of Central Europe—this apart from the various racial theses, which were also widely diffused—and I shall maintain on the basis of new evidence, that this theory was known in Hitler's early circle in Munich.

Enough has been said already about the connection of occultism and mysticism with the type of politics I have called "illuminated" to show that there is a case for considering seriously all evidence pointing in this direction. And enough has been said about Eckart, Feder, Rosenberg, and the Thule Society to show that they come under the "illuminated" classification. In this context the well-known fact that Hitler turned to vegetarianism is extremely suggestive.

The engineer Joseph Greiner is not a witness on whose authority one would care to rely heavily. In 1947 he published a book called *Das Ende der Hitler-Mythos,* which was banned by the Allied forces of occupation and has since been proved untrustworthy on many important points of detail—so much so that it has sometimes been doubted whether Greiner knew Hitler at all. Nevertheless both other sources of personal information on the young Hitler—*armer Teufel* Reinhold Hanisch and Hitler's Linz school-friend August Kubizek—have also been caught out in inaccuracy and distortion. Greiner claimed to have known Hitler in Vienna, when the future dictator was living in a men's hostel in the Meldemanstrasse—but Franz Jetzinger (who rejects Greiner's story as being concerned merely to detract) claims Greiner was in Berlin at the time. Nevertheless, it seems that the Nazi archives were informed of a publication of Greiner's in 1938, and Konrad Heiden, writing in 1944, mentions Greiner as one of Hitler's companions in misfortune. The leading authority on the subject of Hitler's early life is Werner Maser, who thinks that Greiner is virtually worthless as a source, yet occasionally uses his account when it is supported by documents. And Sir Alan Bullock in his biography of Hitler must have relied on Greiner for his impression of Hitler's studies in a Vienna public library. For nowhere else is there found the information that Hitler was interested in the occult.[57] With the greatest reservations, let us look at Greiner's story.

Hitler, he says, was interested in Yoga and Indian fakirs. He compared these to Christian mystics and was particularly impressed by their powers of strengthening the will. In an effort to strengthen his own he tried holding his hand in the flame of a gas jet. "At that time in Vienna there were several open lectures held on occultism which Hitler attended." The results, says Greiner, included a belief that mediums could move objects from a distance, and several experiments in water divining, which were made by Hitler in the Wienerwald. Astrology, graphology, and number mysticism occupied his attention, together with physiognomy and the study of hypnosis. In places, Greiner's recollections altogether exceed the bounds of probability: for example, Hitler is said to have drawn up his own horoscope in the Meldemanstrasse, and Greiner then goes on to give an astrological interpretation of Hitler's birth, which is obviously supposed to be Hitler's own.[58] But inherently, there is nothing improbable among a society of rejects in a concern with occultism, and if Greiner did know Hitler at any time during his Vienna period, this acquaintanceship is itself suggestive. For whether or not Hitler was able to make astrological delineations, Greiner himself was evidently well read in occult literature and fully able to draw up a horoscope himself. Although nothing can be relied on, the possibility remains that Greiner's account is a reflection of a general interest in the occult among the down-and-outs among whom Hitler lived.

A somewhat more reliable connection is made by Wilfried Daim between the young Hitler and the *völkisch* racist Lanz von Liebenfels. In May 1951, Dr. Daim and two companions visited Lanz von Liebenfels in Vienna; this was three years before the prophet's death. Lanz told his visitors that one day in 1909 Hitler called on him in his office and said that he regularly bought Lanz's *Ostara* in his local tobacconist in the Felberstrasse. Lanz sent Hitler away with copies of his magazine and two kroner for his fare home. Dr. Daim discovered that Hitler had indeed been living in the Felberstrasse until August 1909, and that there was a tobacconist two doors down from his lodging. The former prior of the Order of the New Templars was still considerably annoyed that he had been forbidden to publish by the *Führer,* and he claimed that many Nazi racists had plagiarized his ideas without acknowledgment. Daim connected this story with Hitler's statement that he had bought his first anti-Semitic tracts in Vienna and has discovered what seem to him to be correspondences between issues of *Ostara* and *Mein Kampf.* This would tie in with Lanz's statement that he had a great influence on a journalist who was imprisoned with Hitler in the Landsberg jail after the failure of the 1923 putsch and who "edited" *Mein Kampf.* A friend of Lanz supplied the name: Dietrich Eckart.[59]

Again, there is nothing inherently improbable in the connection of Hitler or Eckart with Lanz—Eckart had been a supporter of the occult charlatan Tarnhari. But it would be dangerous to accept more than the simple narrative of Hitler's arrival at Lanz von Liebenfels's office. Even this must be treated cautiously, although there was no reason for Lanz to lie; for in 1951 any connection with Hitler could have been, at the very least, inconvenient. It is possible to discount Greiner's evidence as sensationalism, and to accuse Rudolf von

Sebottendorff of trying to jump on the Nazi bandwagon (by claiming that his Thule Society had inspired the NSDAP), but it is not possible to write off Lanz. He was evidently so far removed from reality that it was still more important to him to establish his racist priorities than to lead an undisturbed existence. After his discovery, Wilfried Daim wrote to Joseph Greiner to see if he could throw any light on Hitler's contact with Lanz. Greiner not only confirmed that Hitler read *Ostara* but added to his published memoirs some information that he said his publishers had asked him to exclude. This story made Hitler the discussion partner of one Grill, another inmate of the Viennese men's hostel. Grill (said Greiner,) was a lapsed Catholic priest, the son of a Polish-Russian rabbi, who preached a religion of brotherly love. All life, he believed, was animated by cosmic rays; and man achieved a sort of immortality in his children. He and Hitler would have long metaphysical discussions, with Grill trying to cure Hitler of his hatred of the Jews. In his account of their interview, Daim altered some details to test Greiner, and sent a memorandum for the engineer to sign: Greiner corrected the details Daim had changed.[60]

We are left with the impression that there might be more to the stories of Greiner than has been admitted, and certainly there is a strong possibility that Hitler read *Ostara* and once met Lanz von Liebenfels. The keenness of historians to play down and even to suppress such stories is a natural reaction to most investigators of the "occult," who are always eager to claim that Hitler's "occultism" was his guiding force. Circumstances alter, however, if the object is merely to establish that rejected knowledge interested Hitler and thus to draw some conclusions about his type of personality in a specific historical situation.

Hitler returned to Munich after the war, and here again he has been associated with an adept of the irrational. Alfred Schuler gave a series of lectures in Munich in 1922-23 in the house of Hugo and Elsa Bruckmann. The Bruckmanns had taken up Hitler, and it is generally accepted that the Nazi leader's frequent visits to their house entailed hearing Schuler in full mystical flight.[61] According to Joseph Greiner, Hitler had cultivated in Vienna a combined veneration for Rome and the swastika, which sounds very like the resurrected Bachofenism of the Cosmics and other *völkisch* occultists.[62] This may well be fantasy; and there is a great difference between stating that Hitler probably heard Schuler lecture and maintaining (as has been done) that this was the source of his inspiration of his adoption of the swastika. Attempts to trace responsibility for the adoption of the swastika by the Nazi party are bound to be fruitless, for the sign was so widely diffused among *völkisch* organizations that nothing can be said except that Alfred Schuler, Lanz von Liebenfels, and Guido von List were three of the earliest propagandists of its renewed symbolic significance.

The influence of the Thule Society should not be entirely overlooked. According to the very well informed Dr. Georg Franz-Willing, in Hitler's early days in Anton Drexler's National Socialist German Worker's party the future leader came into conflict with the Thule member Karl Harrer. Harrer wanted the party to be organized on a secret lodge structure like Sebottendorff's Germanen Order—which was run on lines familiar to Freemasons and was sedulously ceremonial. Hitler, says Franz-Willing, was by no means opposed to the concept of an order, but he held out for realism, although Drexler was sufficiently struck with the idea of an order to support the party's decision of January 1921 to exclude women from the movement. Between 1919 and 1921 Hitler also read copiously in the *völkisch* library established by the Thule member Friedrich Krohn, which ran to 2,500 titles.[63] Then Karl Harrer left the NSDAP, and by the end of 1921 Hitler dominated no "secret lodge" but a political party with a mass following.

His chief support came from the returned soldiery, the men bred in the ethics of violence, Captain Ernst Röhm and the Freikorps. He referred in scoffing terms to the *völkisch* movement.

> It is typical of such persons [Hitler wrote] that they rant about ancient Teutonic heroes of the dim and distant ages, stone axes, battle-spears and shields, whereas in reality they themselves are the woefullest poltroons imaginable. For those very same people who brandish Teutonic tin swords that have been fashioned carefully according to ancient models and wear padded bearskins, with the horns of oxen mounted over their bearded faces, proclaiming that all contemporary conflicts must be decided by the weapons of the mind alone. And thus they skedaddle when the first communist cudgel appears.

Repeatedly, Hitler wrote in *Mein Kampf*, he had had to warn his followers about such impractical "wandering scholars." In the party program, he deliberately excluded the word *völkisch*, because it was so imprecise: "It is just as general as the word 'religious,' for instance."[64] He was out for a mass following and a severely practical approach. But because of the peculiar conditions prevailing in Germany after the First World War, it would have been surprising if the illuminated approach had not played a large part in the early days of the Nazi party. Although it might not take the guise of Teutonic swordsmen intent on discovering the quickest route to Valhalla, there were less lumbering possibilities.

We have already seen that Hitler himself may have been no stranger to irrationalist opinion; and that Dietrich Eckart, Gottfried Feder, and Alfred Rosenberg—all following different versions of the quest for "other realities"—met in the Thule Society, dominated by Rudolf von Sebottendorff, an irrationalist of the most extreme sort. In the new quest for practicality, the *völkisch* image was dropped. But particular illuminates survived in surprising numbers: Eckart, the only man of education whom Hitler would allow to advise him; Feder, the maker of the "unalterable" party program and the economic theorist whose lectures opened Adolf Hitler's eyes; Rosenberg, the editor of the *Völkischer Beobachter* and later the "party Philosopher," dragging in his train von Scheubner-Richter and the Russian emigration from which came money, ideological fuel for the crusade against communism, and, above all, the terrifying *Protocols* in which Hitler implicitly believed. These are mystics, irrationalists, protagonists of spiritual revolution, the kind of men of whom the *Völkische* in bearskins were only caricatures. In the period up to the Beer-hall Putsch other supporters of Hitler can be detected in similar attitudes. We shall then discuss how much of the illuminated approach or the relics of devotion to rejected knowledge was borne by the Nazis into power.

Erich Ludendorff, the "War Lord of the World War," met Hitler in Berlin in 1920 when Hitler and Dietrich Eckart flew to the capital in the hope of assisting at the triumph of the right-wing Kapp Putsch. That August, Ludendorff moved to Munich and became the totem of the *völkisch* parties. It has been argued that his *Kriegführung und Politik* (1923), with its vision of the state in arms, was a leading influence on Hitler and perhaps the only positive vision the Nazi leader possessed.[65] In October 1923, the field marshal met the woman who was to become his second wife. This was only a few days before the unsuccessful putsch of 9 November 1923, in which the aging soldier was to take part, and the political atmosphere in Munich was charged with tension. Mathilde von Kemnitz was a devotee of the occult conspiracy theory. Of their meeting Ludendorff wrote:

> The part played by the Jews in the decline of our *Volk*, no less that of Rome, stood clearly before me, and I was discovering the role of the Freemasons. The other secret brotherhoods, the nature and influence of Christianity and other insane positions of an occult sort remained at that time hidden from me.

Frau Mathilde von Kemnitz visited Ludendorff in the company of Gottfried Feder. Apart from the specific political arrangements that were the main subject of their conversation, the three talked of the horrible news brought to Frau von Kemnitz by a German-Russian pastor from the Volga. He claimed to have discovered documents written in Hebrew, proving that the Russian revolution was the work of world Jewry.[66]

Who was this woman who was to enlighten Ludendorff as to the role of the occult orders in the collapse of Germany? Most important, she was a friend of Gottfried Feder. It was in Feder's company that Ludendorff first met her, and it was Feder who introduced her book *Triumph des Unsterblichkeitswillens* (1921) to the field marshal. "Putzi" Hanfstaengel records an incident in Gottfried Feder's house when Hitler tried to stop Frau von Kemnitz from philosophizing about the spiritual reawakening of the German people. Perhaps, he said, some philosopher would one day make a system of what his party did. "This, unfortunately, was just the opening his partner needed. Rising to her full height—she was wearing a sort of chiffon tent and every outline of her massive person was clearly visible—she announced: 'But Herr Hitler, that philosopher already stands before you.' This was too much, even for Hitler, who tore his eyes away from her silhouette and stood up to go."[67] It was Feder, too, who discussed Mathilde von Kemnitz's feminist activities in the *Völkischer Beobachter*. In June 1920, Frau von Kemnitz issued invitations to a women's congress in Munich, and in December she published five these for a World League of Nationalist Women. Evidently Feder thought his friend's position left much to be desired; at the end of 1920 she was still an "integrationist" on the Jewish question and dared to protest at the use of force. Feder concluded that despite these aberrations they were both fighting for the same cause and recommended his readers to study her manifestoes.[68] Certainly Frau von Kemnitz later adopted a more militant stance.

Her type should be by now familiar: the manufacturer of conspiracy theories and opponent of occultism who uses all the most extravagant weapons in the occultists' own armory.

Mathilde von Kemnitz was the daughter of a theologian and Orientalist, Professor Bernhard Spiess. After her first husband (a Dr. von Kemnitz) had been killed in an avalanche, she herself went into medical practice. She studied under the Munich psychiatrist Emil Kräpelin and distinguished herself by penetrating the séances held by the psychical researcher Baron von Schrenck-Notzing to expose their unscientific procedure. Her pamphlet on *Moderne Mediumforschungen* was published in 1914 and marked the beginning of a career devoted to opposing magical orders and psychical research. In the summer of 1914 she attended a psychical research congress in Berlin as a "scientific opponent" and during the 1930s devoted much labor to denouncing astrology as a practice decisively connected with pollution of the bloodline. At the same time, she attacked the conspiracy of the Jesuits, declared Christianity to be a non-Aryan importation from the Orient, and preached her own religion of "German God-Knowledge."

Her idea that Christianity originated in the Far East came from the late 19th-century romancer Louis Jacolliot. Jacolliot's works furnished H. P. Blavatsky with no less than fifty-nine plagiarized passages, and he shared H.P.B.'s prejudice against the Jesuits. He never published his sources, and he was soon written off as a forger. Mathilde von Kemnitz made the unlikely claim that her father, Professor Spiess, had verified Jacolliot's sources and thus proved Christianity unworthy of those of German blood.[69]

After the first meeting of Ludendorff and this illuminated lady, their acquaintanceship prospered. In Ludendorff's company Frau von Kemnitz visited Hitler in the Landsberg prison. At the joint request of the field marshal and Goffried Feder, she spoke on the religious problem at the Nazi Party Congress at Weimar in 1924. The tone of her speech was that the communal life of the *Volk* was an expression of the "holy idea of the Cosmos." In 1926 she and Ludendorff were married. "This was a profound turning-point in my life," wrote Ludendorff, "indeed in the life of our people, perhaps of all peoples. Some day historians will establish this."[70] For the warlord it meant chiefly that he became converted to his new wife's obsession with the magical conspiracy against the moral tone of the *Volk*. Jointly they conducted research and mounted attacks on the demons of Theosophy, Rudolf Steiner, Mazdaznan, and the O.T.O. An obsession developed with the secret signs of Freemasons and with the Jewish tradition of Cabalistic number mysticism called Gematria. Thus Mathilde Ludendorff discovered a Freemasonic "magic square" which had been printed next to a newspaper report of the tsar's murder. Her husband maintained that the double cube was favored by the designers of Freemasonic memorials, and he pointed to just such a memorial where the Nazi march to the Feldherrnhalle had been fired on by troops. Similarly, Mathilde Ludendorff added up the date of the tsar's murder at Ekaterinburg on "Cabalistic" principles and discovered that it totaled 15—for some reason a secret Jewish number. It was also the number, declared the field marshal, which could be obtained by assigning numerical values to the letters of the word *Weltkrieg* and once more performing a simple sum.

Rudolf Hess was another participant in the march to the Feldherrnhalle whose tendency to mysticism was widely known. Hess had been born in Alexandria in 1896 and served in the same regiment as Hitler during the First World War. On his return to Munich he became heavily involved with the Freikorps and the confused fighting of the year 1919; naturally, he was also a member of the Thule. Eckart inscribed a copy of his *Lorenzaccio* to Hess, praising those who "soar boldly above the age." At least in respect of his weakness for certain sorts of occultism, particularly fringe medicine, Hess remained solidly anchored in his generation. In 1938 he addressed the International Conference on Homeopathy in Berlin, and when he arrived in Scotland in 1941 his pockets were stuffed with peculiar remedies for illusory illness. One of his doctors reported the Nazi leader's explanation of these.

> He confided in us that for years he had carefully followed out Rudolf Steiner's injunctions about not eating vegetables grown under artificial conditions, and that he had had a special greengrocer who delivered farm produce reared on natural manure. This opening into the world of the occult provided an opportunity for observing that he had for years been interested in Steiner's anthroposophy and related magical topics, notably astrology and the prophecies based upon it, as well in herbalist lore which to some extent is founded upon the mystical doctrine of "correspondences."[71]

We have already noted that Eckart, von Sebottendorff, and others of their circle were concerned about the influence of Anthroposophy, and it is significant to find that by his own admission a former member of the Thule was sympathetic to Steiner's doctrines. A similar fascination with unorthodox theories led Hess to become the disciple of the geopolitician Professor Karl Haushofer. The leading authority on Hess has shown that his voice in party councils was heard less and less as his mysticism increased.[72] This rings true both in terms of personal psychology and as a particular instance of what was more generally occurring. After the Nazis attained power, it was inevitable that the more illuminated attitudes which had accompanied them during their rise would be dropped (or at the very least greatly transformed) owing to the exigencies of government.

The occult has been defined as "rejected knowledge" and its adepts termed "irrationalist." This is historically justified in that it can be shown that the occult consists of an amalgam of theories which have failed to find acceptance with the establishments of their day; and the Establishment of the late 19th and early 20th century was still precariously rationalist. If a rationalist or materialist viewpoint equips a man for anything, it is the struggle for survival: thus we are presented with the spectacle of casualties from the battle for existence taking refuge in a "spiritual" interpretation of life. But irrationalist theories may become the property of more than a small minority owing to a situation of anxiety; and, although some of these ideas can be adapted to the necessities of survival, to incorporate others in such a synthesis is quite impossible. The Nazis were to show that the conspiracy theory of history and the idea of racial supremacy were quite capable of being joined to—and indeed out of all proportion reinforcing—the ethics of material survival. On the other hand, the vaguer idea of a "spiritual revolution" or a "religious basis," while it may provide an extra dynamism for a political movement, has little to do with the everyday business of governments. Whereas something of the transcendental impulse adhered to the Nazi party in power, the more basic manifestations of the flight from reason—Spiritualism, for example—would merely have proved embarrassing. The men who counted when the Nazi party had become an Establishment were those who were skilled in manipulating power. But because the Nazis in their early days possessed some of the characteristics of an illuminated movement, they attracted elements of the Underground of rejected knowledge—and when the Nazi party became an Establishment, some parts of the Underground by accident became Established with it.

What happened to the old illuminates? Most were dropped, suppressed, or had died by 1933. Dietrich Eckart died in 1923 and kept only a niche in the National Socialist hall of fame. Von Scheubner-Richter fell in the November putsch in the same year; and with him died the close collaboration beteeen the Russian emigration and the Bavarian right wing, which might have provided fresh material for German irrationalism.[73] Rosenberg did survive, and he preserved something of the legacy. The Ludendorffs were tolerated, but they never exercised any influence after the failure of Hitler's putsch; and Hitler prided himself on having kept Mathilde von Kemnitz out of the Reichstag.[74]

Gottfried Feder dissolved into the background. He formulated the "unalterable" party program in 1924 and fought a running battle with a persistent libel—at least *he* claimed it was a libel—until 1932. This concerned the fact that Feder, carrying out his designated function of "finance minister" in the putsch of 8-9 November, had issued an order freezing all financial transactions and nationalizing the banks. By a strange coincidence, a letter of Feder's reached his own bank on 8 November, withdrawing the bulk of his personal deposits. Not until September 1932 was he able to silence criticism in the press.⁷⁵ His economic theories were never seriously applied, and, although comparable approaches seemed to attract the party hierarchy for brief periods, Feder's influence was negligible. For example the "Universalist" economics of Othmar Spann, inspired by a Catholic view of the "body of Christ" and a semimystical vitalism, attracted Rosenberg, Robert Ley, and others, but were ultimately condemned; and it is difficult to see the similarity of Feder's theories as accounting for this attraction. Feder himself filled a minor governmental post, held a chair at the Technische Hochschule in Berlin, and spent the years before his death in 1941—how predictable his absorption is—in designing "New Towns."⁷⁶

The Thule Society fell completely under Hitler's ban on *völkisch* activities. Occasionally it would be remembered as an early comrade-in-arms by some *alter Kämpfer,* like Eckart's friend, the painter Albert Reich. It had never really been anything more than a meeting place, although Sebottendorff had been involved in his quota of political intrigue and had helped in the recruiting for the Freikorps Epp. Even the extreme irrationalists became disillusioned with his overloaded esotericism. One example is that of Fritz von Trützschler, a member both of the Thule and of Eckart's *Deutsche Bürgervereinigung.* He had appeared in Munich at Easter 1919, distributing leaflets calling for a spiritual revolution and advocating "mysticism as politics." Von Trützschler was scathing at Sebottendorff's lack of success in gathering funds and accused him of "crocodile tears" over his famous murdered hostages. He decided that there was more hope of a resurrected Germany in a society which he himself founded to purify the German language than in the turgid ceremonial of the Thule. Sebottendorff returned to Munich for a while in 1933 and was arrested for a short period early the next year before returning to Turkey. In 1936 Julius Rüttinger, the founder of the Germanen Order, was informed that he could not hold Nazi office because he had been a member of the order; which verdict "simply corresponds to the basic attitude of the NSDAP towards Freemasonry."⁷⁷ Impotent and inconvenient, the Thule was forgotten.

A similar fate overtook stray occultist thinkers, whom the party had inevitably absorbed. A good example is Arthur Dinter, whose immensely popular novel *Sin against the Blood* (first published in

1918) provided the classic statement on the evils of marriage between Aryans and Jews. Its sequel, *Sin against the Spirit* (1921), contained the admission that Dinter had been occupied with Spiritualism from 1914, when a fallen comrade contacted him at a séance. The spirit revelations that pepper the novel had been made to Dinter himself or to a Munich circle of the 1890s, and Dinter gave the address of a Spiritualist organization in Hamburg to which his readers might apply. By 1922 he was asserting that Spiritualism was "the metaphysics of the racial theory" and its necessary corollary. Dinter had a strong connection with Julius Steicher, and from 1924 to 1927 he was Nazi *Gauleiter* of Thuringia. In 1927 his enemies had him removed. Dinter founded the Deutsche Volkskirche, whose symbol combined cross and swastika. Although condemned by the party, Dinter's sect survived until 1937; and it is clear that, despite his fervent anti-Semitism, its leader found his true métier in the world of religion rather than that of politics.[78]

After the Nazi accession to power, the burgeoning sects of the German Reich were gradually prohibited. They could be seen as part of the international conspiracy controlled by Jews, and this made a convenient excuse for disposing of sources of divided allegiance. But the comprehensiveness of the authoritarian action gives food for thought. By 1936, not only comparatively large sects like the Anabaptists, Seventh Day Adventists, and the Weissenberger had fallen under the axe, but also Mazdaznan, "Sheep and Shepherd," the *Bund der Kämpfer für Glaube und Wahrheit* and even the *Gottesbund Tanatra*. The occultists proper were rounded up in 1941 in response to a decree dated 4 July and signed by Heydrich. This was directed against Anthroposophists, Theosophists, Ariosophists, Christian Scientists, faith healers, astrologers, occultists, Spiritualists, "followers of the occult theory of rays," and "fortunetellers, fake or otherwise (no matter which type)." It ordered the *Gauleiters* to intern such parasites in concentration camps. Ellic Howe has shown that the Nazi authorities evidently decided to make Hess's known interest in astrology and mysticism the public explanation of his flight to Scotland. Arrests and interrogations followed.[79] After this point there was little future for adepts of rejected knowledge in the Third Reich.

Unless, of course, they were adepts of the sort of previously rejected knowledge on which the Reich itself was built. There is little point in adding to the many accounts of the "Final Solution," the culmination of a *believing* anti-Semitism. The racial theory is also too well known to need any further discussion. But in support of the argument that the Third Reich, to some extent, represents the Underground become Establishment it is suggestive to glance at less well-known beliefs held by three illuminates who survived: Hitler himself, Rosenberg, and Heinrich Himmler.

Hitler's utterances record many of the attitudes which characterize not only illuminated politicians but also occultists pure and simple. On the night of 25-26 January 1942, he mused: "I imagine to myself that one day science will discover in the waves set in motion by the *Rheingold,* secret mutual relations connected with the order of the world." A moment of passing fancy, certainly; but also the magical doctrine of correspondences and the musical analogy used by the Rosicrucians and Gurdjieff. In *Mein Kampf,* the *Führer* gave vent to the complaint which is heard time and time again among occultists: "The so-called intellectuals still look down with infinite superciliousness on anyone who has not been through the prescribed schools and allowed them to pump the necessary knowledge into him." His obsession with secret societies extended to the idea that it might be possible to make an alliance with the Ku Klux Klan. This is attested by Hanfstaengl and by Kurt Ludecke, who was actually sent on an embassy to Hiram Evans, the Imperial Wizard of the Invisible Empire. In the context of Rudolf Hess and his captivation by fringe medicine, it is very significant indeed that Hitler did not become a vegetarian until *after* he started his political career. At his political meetings, Hitler recalled, he used to drink stein upon stein of beer; after he gave up meat he only needed a sip of water. In 1942 he was well equipped with a barrage of arguments and statistics on behalf of vegetarianism.[80]

It is difficult to know how far to believe the accounts of Hermann Rauschning, the former *Gauleiter* of Danzig. No historian has cast serious doubts on his book *Hitler Speaks;* yet it almost goes against the grain to accept it. If Rauschning's record is true, Hitler believed in the popular occult doctrine of the emergence of a new type of man on the evolutionary spiral. Man was separating into two types: the man of the new age and the undeveloped creature. "I might call the two varieties the god-man and the mass animal. . . . Man is becoming God—that is the simple fact. Man is God in the making. According to Rauschning, "there were only a few people, mostly women, among whom he used to talk in this style."[81]

It has been argued by Louis Pauwels and Jacques Bergier in their book *The Dawn of Magic* that Hitler was primarily motivated by such eccentric mystical and cosmological ideas, and to these authors belongs the credit of pointing out the possible application of Rauschning's words. The trouble with *The Dawn of Magic* is that it is itself written from an occult viewpoint. It is exaggerated, underresearched, and erratic on many points, such as the nature and influence of the Thule Society or Himmler's *Ahnenerbe*. Its authors are occasionally right and often have the advantage of an expert knowledge of occult patterns of thought. But they are wrong in suggesting that Hitler's private beliefs controlled his military actions or his short-term plans. What does seem possible is to divine from such beliefs the sort of man Hitler was and the sociological territory from which he sprang. If we accept Rauschning, then there is absolutely no doubt that Hitler believed in a theory of occult evolution of a Theosophical type, out of which would emerge a "god-man"—a term used particularly by *Russian* occultists. Science, says Rauschning's Hitler, must become once more a *Geheimwissenschaft*. This is usually translated as "secret science." But it is nothing more or less than the term used by German esotericists for their "occult sciences." There is further confirmation that the *Führer* did believe in this sort of doctrine embedded in the story—which the authors of *The Dawn of Magic* succeed in burying beneath a mountain of fantasy—of Hitler's undoubted adherence to the Cosmic Ice Theory of Hanns Hörbiger. Fantasy is not necessary; but to make such beliefs comprehensible, we should first consider the mysticism of Rosenberg and Himmler.

Alfred Rosenberg ought not to have survived the transition from Underground to Establishment. He did so because of a double failure in the ranks of the Nazi party. There was no "Russian expert" and there was no Ideologist. The death of von Scheubner-Richter in 1923 had deprived Hitler of his chief link with the Russian emigration; and Rosenberg was the only candidate who seemed fitted to pronounce on Germany's all-important relationship with the East. At the same time, he represented the victims of the "Jewish" revolution. Dietrich Eckart—the obvious candidate for the role of philosopher—also died in 1923, and for a time Hitler seems to have hoped for something from the German Christians led by Reich Bishop Müller. That movement threatened to become unruly, and in January 1934 Rosenberg was created the *Führer's* overseer of the *"geistigen und weltanschaulichen Schulung und Erziehung der Partei,"* a truly untranslatable title embodying notions of philosophical, spiritual, and intellectual tutorship, which cannot be rendered word for word in English.

Rosenberg's *Myth of the 20th Century* had sold over a million copies by 1944. It has been the fashion to discount its representative qualities and to point out that Hitler privately described Rosenberg as quite unintelligible. Yet Hitler elsewhere defended Rosenberg as "the most acute thinker in questions of *Weltanschauung.*" Rosenberg's organization could declare without contradiction that the *Myth* was the most important Nazi text after *Mein Kampf.* Hitler's self-distancing from Rosenberg's production may well have been a tactical maneuver. According to Rosenberg, he gave Hitler the *Myth* on its completion in 1929. Five months later he received it back from his leader with the comment that is was most ingenious, but that he wondered how many of the party comrades would be able to understand it. Understand it or not, they naturally bought the book. It is not generally realized that *The Myth of the 20th Century* is merely the most "official" expression of a body of irrationalist opinion quite widely diffused through Germany between the wars. Rosenberg had written one section of what became his book before leaving Moscow in 1917; in 1919 he finished a section on German idealist philosophy; but he seems to have written the bulk of the *Myth* in the 1920s.[82]

The Myth of the 20th Century is written in homage to Houston Stewart Chamberlain. "Racial history," declared Rosenberg, "is both natural history and spiritual mysticism." By *Myth,* he intended the meaning of Georges Sorel, of a complex of ideas that symbolized the guiding spirit of the age. This, of course, was the death of Materialism and Individualism and the submersion of the grasping individual in the all-embracing *Volk.* The ideas that accrued to

Rosenberg's history of the Aryans—it is really "occult history" —were curious in the extreme. First, there was Atlantis. It was very probable, he thought, that Atlantis had really existed and had been the original home of the Aryan race.

> And these waves of Atlantean people travelled by water on their swan and dragon ships into the Mediterranean, to Africa; by land over Central Asia to Kutschka, indeed, perhaps even to China, across North America to the south of the Continent.

It was crucial to Rosenberg's Atlantis that it lay in the extreme north. For he then went on to explain the symbols of Middle Eastern religion—like that perennial *völkisch* favorite, the "Sun-Wheel"—as based on racial memories of the Arctic sun. Races other than the Aryan had resulted from a mixing of Atlantean blood with already existing primitive strains.[83]

This sort of Atlantis speculation had greatly affected German theorists of history and anthropology. The anthropologist Leo Frobenius published in 1926—naturally enough, with the *völkisch* and Theosophical publisher Eugen Diederichs—his *Die Atlantische Götterlehre,* which argued that various symbols widely diffused round the Bight of Benin had all come from a common Atlantean source. One of these symbols was the swastika. Although Oswald Spengler never published anything on the subject, in his private musings on prehistory he used the idea of Atlantis as a working hypothesis. The most successful popularizers of the Atlantis legend were the occultists. H. P. Blavatsky and the British Theosophist Walter Scott-Eliot had started the fashion, and in Madame Blavatsky's account of occult evolution, her third and fourth races had been made to live on the now-submerged continents of Atlantis and Lemuria. In Germany, Rudolf Steiner added by his clairvoyant investigations to Atlantis literature. Among the Russian emigration Dmitri Merezhkovsky used the idea of Atlantis as a crucial point in his "new Christianity." *The Myth of the 20th Century* was published in 1930; in October 1931, an exhibition of "trance paintings" of Atlantis could been seen in Berlin. After the publication of the *Myth,* occultists continued to parade their speculations, usually based on Merezhkovsky and Steiner.[84]

Naturally the *Völkische* had adapted the vision of the occultists to whom they were so much akin. The most important of such theorists was Professor Hermann Wirth, whom Rosenberg used as a source, and who was eccentric almost to the point of insanity. Wirth was more closely attached to Himmler and will be discussed in connection with the *SS* leader. Some of his arguments were used by Albert Herrmann, professor of geography at Berlin University, who became convinced that a tract of desert in Tunisia had once been covered by the sea and was the former site of the capital city of Atlantis. Herrmann was quite open about his aim; this was to abolish "the dogma that our most ancient ancestors were primitive barbarians." Even Herrmann was embarrassed by over-credulous supporters of the thesis, like Karl Georg Zschaetzsch, whose *Aryans* had been published as early as 1920 and might have served as a blueprint for Rosenberg's speculations. Here Atlantis was madly identified both with Asia and the home of the Norse gods, Asgard, and it was stated flatly that the blond-haired, blue-eyed race were Atlanteans.[85] In this sort of occult racism, Rosenberg's "history of the Aryans" has its roots.

Another sure indication that Rosenberg is using occult techniques of history is his method of opposing Roman Catholicism. Beside all the "martyrs of free research" and the "heroes of Nordic philosophy" who have opposed the suffocating power of Christianity must be set "the Albigensians, Waldenses, Cathars, Arnoldists, Stedingers, Huguenots and reformed Lutherans," who represent the struggle of the Aryans for freedom of belief. Such a catalogue of heretics is a common device of occultists, concerned either to demonstrate the continuity of their particular version of the "Secret Tradition" or to display the sins of past Establishments. In his memoirs Rosenberg recalls how, once, on a trip to Brittany, he had wanted to go south to investigate the homeland of the Cathars, who had always interested him. He makes it clear that he sees his favorite heretics as representatives of the "true doctrine." This partisanship of the historical Underground is all of a piece with Rosenberg's insistence that the new total "German knowledge" must incorporate "every occurrence (like somnambulism, clairvoyance, etc.)" which present methods did not explain.[86] Once more this is the perpetual cry of the 19th- and 20th-century occultist: a call for synthesis and an accommodation with unreason.

For Rosenberg the supreme hero of the race is the German mystic. "For the first time and in full consciousness in the German mystic . . . appeared the new, the reborn Teutonic man." Meister Eckhart is the supreme example of this type, and Rosenberg finds something of his calibre in Dietrich Eckart's hero Angelus Silesius. The influence on Rosenberg of his old friend Eckart is undoubtedly seen in the contrast made between the enlightened soul of Germanic mysticism and the Jew, the creature of the world. Rosenberg defines freedom as "organic freedom"; freedom in accordance with the old neo-Platonist idea of the world-body transformed to suit the demands of racist ideology into the body of the *Volk*. He declares that Paracelsus would have approved of this new vision of occult community, this "freshly-awakened Myth of our life."

Paracelsus was the hero of a book that was published in 1926 and that bears comparison with Rosenberg's *Myth*. It does not seem possible to argue a direct influence, and the differences between the two books are as evident as the similarities. But the two stand directly in the same tradition of semioccult philosophy. The earlier book is *The Rise of the West* by John Macready, which was written in direct answer to Spengler's *Decline of the West* and published in German at Leipzig. Nothing can be discovered about the author, except that he was an Englishman who had earlier lived a long time in Germany and found it impossible to have his book published in England. Macready seems almost as "Germanized" as Rosenberg's master, Houston Stewart Chamberlain. His book opposes to the material decline of the West the prospects of a spiritual and religious rebirth. Beside racists like Chamberlain and de Gobineau, Macready sets vitalists like Bergson, Driesch, and the German Romantics. In the Spiritualist movement which the World War has called into life in England, he sees the first stirring of a new attitude. But his real hero is Madame Blavatsky, the main opponent of his chief enemy, Charles Darwin. Atlantis, Paracelsus, and the legend of Steiner's influence on von Moltke jostle each other in his pages. Macready preached what he called a "transcendental Monism." Naturally his book does not carry the specifically Nazi superstructure of Rosenberg's; but within their limits, and with all the divergences, the two reached the same conclusions. Materialism must at all costs be abandoned. "As certainly as the perplexity of Reason in the World War begot the falling away from God, so certainly true Socialism can conquer only through the feeling of unity in mankind—in the feeling of oneness with the God of 'immaterial' eternal life."[87] For Macready the cementing factor was God, for Rosenberg the transcendental *Volk;* many of their preconceptions were the same.

Linked with the occult philosophizing of Rosenberg were the preoccupations of Heinrich Himmler. Himmler's position as an irrationalist in control of the Nazi regime's bluntest instrument is really quite extraordinary. Only recently has the full extent of his irrationalism become apparent. A reading list from Himmler's early years shows that he was—predictably—occupied with literature of the conspiracy theory, like Friedrich Wichtl's *Weltfreimaurerei, Weltrevolution, Weltrepublik* (1919) or Dietrich Eckart's *Bolshevism from Moses to Lenin* (1924) and Artur Dinter's *Sin against the Blood*. It also shows that as Himmler veered away from his early devotion to Christianity, the transcendental impulse found another expression, and he became preoccupied with occultism. Soon after its appearance, he read Carl Du Prel's *Spiritualism* (1922) and commented: "a scientific little book with a philosophical basis that allows me really to believe in Spiritualism." About the time of the Hitler putsch (during which he carried the standard of Ernst Röhm's *Reichskriegflagge*), he was reading a compendium of miracles dealing with astrology, hypnosis, Spiritualism, and telepathy. In February 1926 he read Karl Heise's *Okkulte Logentum,* which had been published five years earlier. He concluded that he had greatly profited by its argument that there were good and evil principles, which manifested themselves in human organizations. Heise was a Zürich bookshop assistant who specialized in revealing the Freemasonic conspiracy and exposing the "sexual magic" of orders like the O.T.O.[88]

On top of this dose of "basic mysticism" Himmler gulped down draughts of *völkisch* medicine. The Utopian Willibald Hentschel had provided the inspiration—and elements of the youth movement the enthusiasm—for the *Artamanen Bund*. The *Artamanen* were founded in 1923 with the object of establishing Guilds of Nordic peasants. These were to form settlements on the Eastern borders of the *Reich* to hold back the incursion of the Slav undermen. The members of the *Bund* began by working on the land with the aim of raising enough money to form their own settlements. In 1924 the first colonists departed for Saxony, and the reaction of the *Artamanen* to the strangulation of Nordic man by urban civilization attracted many *Völkische* and future Nazis. Among these were Himmler, who became the leader of the *Bund* in Bavaria; the future minister of agriculture, Richard Walter Darré; and Rudolf Hess, who was to become the *kommandant* at Auschwitz. Even before the foundation of the *Artamanen,* Himmler had been impressed by the *völkisch* ideal of settling in the East and had tried to add a knowledge of Russian to his agricultural education.[89]

Thus Himmler was yet another who combined an interest in the occult revival with an illuminated nationalism. His personal beliefs were at least as odd as those of Hess. The masseur Felix Kersten records how Himmler was interested in nature cures and medieval herbalists; he knew the works of Albertus Magnus and was proud that Paracelsus was a German. The *Reichsführer SS* was also a believer in *karma* and reincarnation, and he declared that he would really like to be minister for religious affairs. Himmler fancied himself the reincarnation of his namesake Henry the Fowler—or possibly, on occasion, Henry the Lion. He supported a cult of Teutonic heroes with shrines at Quedlinburg, the burial place of Henry the Fowler; the Externsteine, a rock in the Teutoburgerwald, which was the favorite hunting ground for German archaeological mystics; and a memorial to the Stedingers near Gruppenbühren dedicated in 1934 by himself and that other lover of heretical doctrine, Alfred Rosenberg. The reason for this cultivation of racial traditions seems to have been Himmler's particular version of reincarnation, which entailed belief that man would be reborn in his family. One Karl August Eckhart represented this as the ancient doctrine of the Germanic peoples in his book *Temporal Immortality* published in 1937. Himmler ordered 20,000 copies for the *SS* but was forced to cancel the order on political grounds. In a speech at Dachau in November 1936, Himmler told his assembled *Gruppenführer* that "we have all seen each other somewhere before, and in the same way we will see each other again in the next world."[90]

This seems to argue that Himmler had a vision of his *SS* as a sort of time-defying order of heroes with a special mission: a concept not unknown among occult bodies. It would be strange if the private beliefs of the *Reichsführer* had not affected the organization that he led. Notoriously, he did regard the SS as an order, which would spread the Nordic ideal throughout the world and act as an improving agency for the bloodline. Their opponent, Bolshevism, organized as it was by Jewry, was no mere eruption of the last fifty years. The struggle in which the SS were engaged had been going on for as long as there had been life on the planet. Himmler's vision of the progress of this diabolical conspiracy—it really seems to have appeared *diabolical,* in the supernatural sense—began with a massacre of Persians by Jews in Biblical times, progressed through the witch persecutions—directed against "the mothers and maidens of our people"—and moved toward Bolshevism by way of the Freemasonic French Revolution.[91]

His order was equipped with the ceremonies Himmler deemed necessary. The first ritual question asked of an SS candidate was what he thought of a man who did not believe in God; and the condemnation was absolute. The use of runes, of symbolism and ceremonial, was deliberate. The SS-man progressed through various grades with appropriate ceremonies: the program laid down for him was not only a comprehensive educational plan based on Social Darwinian principles, but a ritual with definite party feast days and observances. The structure of the SS has been compared to that of the Jesuits—Hitler called Himmler "my Ignatius"—and it well may be that Himmler derived some inspiration from this source. Felix Kersten was told by a member of Himmler's staff that SS uniforms and ranks could only be understood as in direct emulation of the opposing power of Freemasonry. If this represents Himmler's own opinion it may have coincided with that of Hitler. Rauschning's report is explicit: Hitler claimed to have taken ideas from the Catholic church and the Freemasons that included "the hierarchical organisation and the initiation through symbolic rites, that is to say without bothering the brains but by working on the imagination through magic and the symbols of the cult."[92]

Himmler's sanctuaries for his order were called *Ordensburgen.* The secrecy surrounding these institutions has given rise to all manner of fantasies. Belief in the importance of ceremonial and in secrecy as an aid to its effectiveness probably accounts for most of the isolation. What little is known shows the ceremonial to have been of a most uninspired kind. For example, at Wewelsburg, which by the end of the war had cost Himmler some thirteen million marks, there was a crypt containing a well in which a wooden plaque bearing the arms of dead *SS-Obergruppenführers* was to be burned. The ashes would then be placed in an urn, which stood on one of the pedestals lining the wall.[93]

Rosenberg provided guest lecturers for the *Ordensburgen:* the names of these lecturers show them to have been a predictable bunch. Darré lectured on politics, together with Philipp Bouhler, the editor of Hitler's speeches. Ribbentropp dealt with foreign policy. Under the heading of "Art and Culture" came Hubert Schrade, an authority on Christian iconography who wrote a megalomaniac survey of German national memorials; and Richard von Kienle, a rather less demented student of ancient German history, one of whose publications carried a foreword by Himmler. Experts on the racial question included Wilhelm Grau, the director of research into the Jewish problem at the Reichsinstitut for the History of New Germany; his associate Karl Georg Kuhn, who was certain that Jewish emigration into the United States was the latest phase in the conspiracy; and Professor Julius Andree from Munster in Westphalia, the leading expert on the Externsteine.[94] "Philosophy and Weltanschauung" was supervised by the well-known Nazi philosopher Alfred Baümler, with the cooperation of, among others, Hans Alfred Grunsky of Munich and Ernst Krieck of Heidelberg. There is nothing apparently "occult" here, although a fair quantity of *völkisch* mysticism naturally had a place in the curriculum. On the other hand, Himmler used his organization to foster projects of an occult nature, to make propaganda for pseudo-sciences and rejected knowledge, which he cultivated as a private interest. So, while it is wrong to look at the *SS* as more than slightly influenced by their *Reichsführer's* mysticism, it is possible to gain a deeper insight into the nature of the Nazi leadership by examining the process by which such causes were brought to their attention.

The chief refuge of eccentrics and rejected theories was the organization known for short as the *Deutsches Ahnenerbe* which Himmler made part of the *SS*. This institute was the culmination of a series of attempts made by Professor Hermann Wirth to give his pseudo-academic ideas some sort of official framework. Wirth was a German-Flemish specialist in the more abstruse aspects of prehistory. He maintained that a pure monotheistic religion embodying the notion of the Eternal Return and originating in Atlantis could be followed by a trail of symbols. He described his method as "a combination of science and religion" and Alfred Baümler maintained that "to whomever perceives this (symbolic) trail there appears a new dimension of reality." Wirth derived evidence for his ideas from the Edda, and also from a notorious late-19th-century forgery called the "Ura-Linda Chronicle," whose supporters overcame the fact that it was written on modern paper by arguing that it had been copied from a genuine 10th-century source. Even Alfred Rosenberg had his doubts about the Ura-Linda Chronicle. But these did not prevent him from using Wirth's theory of a Northern Atlantis in his *Myth of the 20th Century*. Wirth's eccentricities were personal as well as scholarly, and visitors to his house at Doberan passed a sign reading "Please walk softly and don't smoke: a deep breather lives here." The professor believed that his wife was a clairvoyant, and when Friedrich Hielscher called at Doberan for a vegetarian meal, he was greeted by the total silence of his hostess, who sat impassively with her brow bound with a golden fillet, while Professor Wirth interpreted her thoughts by telepathy.[95]

It was through the racist Johann von Leers that Wirth met Himmler, and in early 1935 the *Deutsches Ahnenerbe* was founded as a private institute of learning with Himmler as curator. Gradually Wirth himself was elbowed out of positions of authority, and control of the *Ahnenerbe* passed to one of his former disciples, Wolfram Sievers, who was responsible to Professor Walter Wüst, deacon of the Philosophical Faculty at Munich. By 1939 the *Ahnenerbe* was a fully "coordinated" branch of the *SS* and part of Himmler's personal staff.[96] Its chief functions were financing and publishing "Germanic" researches along the lines initiated by Hermann Wirth —symbols, runes, and mythological archaeology remained its chief preoccupations. For example, a bibliography was compiled of an eccentric anthropologist called Grünwedel on whose works Rosenberg relied. During the war the *Ahnenerbe*'s function as the instrument of Himmler's pseudoacademic interests drew the organization out from its harmless if pointless activities, and the always-present racist overtones—*Ahnenerbe* means "ancestral heritage"—became coupled to the most infamous experiments in crank medicine. For example, at Dachau, Dr. Sigmund Rascher used inmates of the concentration camp for his research program designed to discover the best method of reviving pilots who had been shot down in freezing water—and he did this under the aegis of the *Ahnenerbe.* Because of his responsibility for these and other activities, Wolfram Sievers was condemned to death by the Nuremberg tribunal. His friend and former colleague Friedrich Hielscher has claimed that Sievers and others of the *Ahnenerbe* formed a resistance group led by himself which on several occasions planned to assassinate Himmler.[97] The important fact is that the *Ahnenerbe* contained within it the entire spectrum of rejected opinion from the religiously inclined Hielscher on the one hand to the cold-blooded Rascher on the other.

An impression of its activities can be gained from the diaries of Sievers. For example, on 6 January 1944, he was in Munich and had an especially busy day. At 9:30 he spoke to his "South-East Office" in Salzburg, at 10:00 attended to administrative matters and half an hour later met Dr. Eduard May in the Hotel Vierjahreszeiten. With May, another medical student who was carrying out unorthodox "research" into malaria at Dachau, he drove from Munich to the concentration camp and held a series of meetings, which discussed the apportioning of funds for Christmas expenses, the hiring of a flat in Vienna for a "malaria institute," and the newly completed *Volksmikroskop* (which may have had something to do with Himmler's belief that a view of the mystical correspondence between microcosm and macrocosm would be encouraged by putting microscopes or telescopes into the hands of as many people as possible). By 3:15 Sievers was back in Munich, again spoke to Salzburg, and at 4:00 visited Professor Wüst at the university to talk about the *Ahnenerbe* publishing firm and their Sven Hedin Institute for Asian Exploration.[98] This was only six months before the Allied invasion of Normandy. In the summer of 1944 Sievers's activities were still following a similar pattern.

It would be easy to show the unorthodox nature of the studies more openly pursued under the aegis of the *Ahnenerbe;* but once again it is the occult which provides the best indicator of the emergence of rejected knowledge. Most of the occult records of the *Ahnenerbe* have vanished; they were filed with the "Secret" documents and were no doubt destroyed with them. One story of which the record survives is that of the Freiherr Strömer von Reichenbach (perhaps a relation of the Reichenbach of the Odic force). In March 1938 Strömer was billed to give a lecture in the Central Library for Occult Science in Berlin-Charlottenburg. An *SS-Scharführer* reported this forthcoming lecture to his *Sturmbannführer,* and thus information on Strömer filtered through to Himmler himself, who passed it to Professor Wüst for evaluation. An unidentified *Obersturmbannführer* wrote to Himmler (14 July 1937) giving the *Reichsführer* Wüst's glowing opinion of Strömer's work—needless to say, Himmler had previously made his own attitude quite clear to Wüst. Wüst linked the name of Strömer von Reichenbach with those of Nietzsche and Spengler. Strömer's work appeared to him "as a new expression of the really Nordic theory of the eternal return" and the professor added some comparisons with the idea of Samsara and the "Iranian" concept of successive ages of history.[99]

Who was this genius whose intellect rivaled Nietzsche and Spengler? Strömer von Reichenbach lived near Nuremberg and was the originator of a theory of history he called "historionomy." He had worked at this theory since the 1890s and had compiled a series of charts containing over 22,000 of the "essential dates" of world history. Historionomy was racial history, and as such became popular in *völkisch* circles. Strömer maintained, for example, that colonists living far from their homelands—or, of course, Jews in Germany—were subject to the influence of periodical laws which he had calculated from his date charts, and which applied exclusively to *races.* In 1913 Strömer had hoped to see his charts published in conjunction with his friend Max Kemmerich—another manufacturer of historical laws who claimed telepathic abilities up to a few hundred kilometers. But the project had fallen through, and he had been reduced to publishing sections of his great work in a small mystical publishing house run by a son of Heinrich Lhotzsky, in the Ariosophical library, and in his own Historionomical Company in Constance.[100]

Apart from the obvious appeal of a theory of racial determinism and the occult overtones of Strömer's calculations, Himmler and the *Ahnenerbe* must have been chiefly attracted by the Freiherr's success as a prophet. In 1919 he predicted the overthrow of the existing regime for 1929-33 and the emergence of a "German Cromwell" between 1935 and 1939. In 1924, with Hitler in the Landsberg prison, his sympathies had become quite plain, and he hailed the advent of the Great Man as imminent. After the Nazi accession to power, Strömer claimed to have prophesied not only the advent of Hitler, but many less earth-shaking events, such as the murder of the German ambassador in Lisbon.[101] It was suggested that the *Ahnenerbe* publish his work, and Strömer sent Himmler a touching letter expressing the joy of a "seventy-year-old scholar" at achieving such exalted recognition. Nothing came of the project; and perhaps the reason can be found in ominous rumbling made by Himmler's aides that "the great work" must not be allowed to fall into the wrong hands. Embarrassingly enough for the inventor of historionomy, he had predicted a monarchist restoration for 1940-44.

Although the *Ahnenerbe* was not the only Nazi organization to inquire into the occult, it was easily the most credulous. Rudolf Hess had applied for a vast grant to establish a Central Institute of Occultism; but this never materialized.[102] Rosenberg's department, in its function as ideological watchdog, inquired into out-of-the-way theories and occasionally became briefly interested. One such instance was when a certain Johannes Lang applied in December 1938 for permission to lecture on the Hollow World Theory of Koresh (Cyrus Reed Teed) which had a certain vogue in Germany between the wars. Lang was discovered to be an official in the Berlin Patent Office and to have committed the unpardonable sin of publishing a horoscope of Hitler. After consideration the *Reichsleitung* Rosenberg replied that the Hollow World theory was "a completely unscientific explanation of outer space."[103] In contrast, the *Reichsführer-SS* and his *Ahnenerbe* were actively engaged in pushing a cosmological theory no less eccentric than that of Koresh. The reaction of even Rosenberg's department to the overtures of the Hollow Earthers shows in comparison just how divorced from reality some of the *Ahnenerbe* were. It should be said that not only Himmler, but Adolf Hitler himself was deeply interested in the World Ice Theory of Hanns Hörbiger, and that perhaps the *Ahnenerbe* had therefore little choice.

Hanns Hörbiger (1860-1931) was born in Lower Austria. His family moved to Hungary when he was a child. Hörbiger began life as a blacksmith's apprentice, then came to Vienna to study engineering. He invented a patent valve, which enabled him to set up his own firm, and by the outbreak of the First World War he had become rich enough to devote his time to his hobby of astronomy. Hörbiger had his first intimation of the Cosmic Ice Theory in 1882, when he wondered whether a comet which appeared that year could be made of ice. Some ten years later a vision in the early hours of the morning gave him the clue to the secrets of the cosmos. By 1906 Hörbiger's theory was complete, and he had succeeded in convincing Philipp Fauth, a private astronomer who specialized in observation of the moon. Hörbiger and Fauth published their *Glazialkosmogonie* in 1912, and disciples set about making their unorthodox views known to the world of learning. Even a study favorable to Hörbiger makes it clear that Cosmic Ice became an obsession with its originator. He once had to take a rest cure on the advice of a doctor who tried to tell him that it really did not matter whether or not the moon was made of ice; and he bombarded the astronomers of Europe with letters and telegrams, followed by doubtless equally welcome visits.[104]

The basis of Hörbiger's theory is that the universe is filled with "cosmic building stuff." This occurs in the form of hot metallic stars and light gases—chiefly hydrogen and oxygen existing as H_2O, ("in its cosmic form"), ice. When a block of Cosmic Ice plunges into a hot star, a vast explosion ensues, which generates a stellar system. Such systems are governed by further Hörbigerian laws, chiefly that of spiral motion toward the central sun. This results in the ceaseless capture of small fragments resulting from the original explosion by larger bodies in the system. In this way the Earth has captured several of the dozen small planets originally existing between it and Mars. These earlier moons spiraled down on to the Earth with cataclysmic results. Our present moon was captured some 13,000 years ago, and the tragedy of its descent will inevitably repeat the great horror that occurred when the earlier moon crashed, of which memories are preserved in myths and legends.[105] Hörbiger's sources—apart from Heraclitus—are uncertain. But resemblances have been observed between his idea of successive moons and the theories of Madame Blavatsky.[106] These probably stem from a common source in Charles Fourier, who also believed in previous moons that had fallen on the earth. Hörbiger's Cosmic Ice was decisively rejected by the learned establishment and itself spiraled toward the Occult Underground. It is to be found, for example, in the writings of Egon Friedell, who thought that it was "in subterranean agreement" with Relativity and belonged to "the category of didactic poetry."[107] To his "scientific" ideas, Hörbiger coupled a metaphysics that included a Platonic World-Soul, the influence of Nietzsche, and a belief in a separate world in which the laws of Cosmic Ice did not apply. These considerations were at once attractive to the European Underground.

Völkisch thinkers of the sort who followed Hermann Wirth and speculated about Atlantis gleefully pounced on the idea of a previous moon crashing on the earth. This conveniently explained why their beloved continent, the *Urheimat der Arier,* had sunk beneath the waves. The chief among these romancers was the surveyor Edmund Kiss, a *völkisch* playwright who was known as "the poet of Atlantis" and contrived a synthesis of Wirth and Hörbiger.[108] For mythological evidence of the fall of an earlier moon the *Völkische* pounced on their "Nordic Bible," the Edda, well-known from the translation by Rudolf John Gorsleben, an anti-Semitic friend of Dietrich Eckart. Gorsleben himself entered on a Wirthian explanation of prehistory, and others reinterpreted this in Hörbiger's favor. The first "popular" (as opposed to pseudo-scientific) presentation of Cosmic Ice was that of the engineer Heinz Voigt in 1920, and the doctrine earned a classification in the German index of books published for the following five years. Uncritical acceptance of Cosmic Ice was rivaled only by the adulation accorded Hörbiger himself. His life, wrote one of his devotees, showed itself "an astonishing compendium of tragedy, heroism, patience and unexampled industry."[109]

Himmler and the *Ahnenerbe* naturally determined to make this theory their own. Hermann von Hase, the publisher of the *Ahnenerbe's* magazine *Germanien,* was a disciple of Hörbiger and a friend of Kiss. In late summer 1936 Kiss was planning a journey to Abyssinia to undertake investigations into Cosmic Ice. Himmler came to hear of this and allowed him to carry out his research through the *Ahnenerbe*. At the same time, Hörbiger's collaborator,

Philipp Fauth, was taken up by agents of the *Reichsführer* and a certain Dr. Hans Robert Scultetus placed in charge of the *Ahnenerbe* department concerned with weather forecasting, which made its predictions on the basis of Cosmic Ice. Himmler lost no opportunity of making propaganda for his favorite pseudo-science. He tried to suppress attacks on Hörbiger, ordered Hörbigerian experiments to be made on the German expedition to Nanga Parbat, and sent literature to high-ranking party officials.[110] But because of the impossibly quarrelsome nature of occultists and adepts of rejected knowledge in general, no sooner had the interest of the *Reichsführer* in Hörbiger become known than the theorists of Cosmic Ice began a ferocious dispute among themselves.

At Bad Pyrmont on 19 July 1936, the leading representatives of the new cosmology signed a document known as "the Pyrmont Protocol." Those included Alfred Hörbiger, Philipp Fauth, Heinz Voigt, Edmund Kiss, and Dr. Scultetus.

Some extracts from the "Protocol" follow.

> 1. The undersigned are convinced that the Cosmic Ice Theory of Hanns Hörbiger is in its basic form the intellectual gift of a genius, and extremely valuable for all mankind both from the practical point of view and from that of *Weltanschauung;* and for us Germans of quite especial importance as a really Aryan treasure of the intellect....
>
> 4. The undersigned think it right and proper to put into practice the incontrovertibly proved deductions from the Cosmic Ice Theory and suggest for this purpose primarily weather-forecasting. They think it wrong, however, to waste time and money on areas which are not really related to Cosmic Ice and are mostly of a fantastic nature....
>
> 6. The undersigned heartily welcome the fact that *Reichsführer-SS* Heinrich Himmler is taking the Cosmic Ice Theory under his protection.
>
> 7. The undersigned consider it their duty to see to it that the applications of the Cosmic Ice Theory, now that it is under the *Reichsführer's* protection, appear only in a fashion corresponding to the position of the *Reichsführer SS*. The cause must always rank above personal considerations. All reports must command the strictest standard of scientific procedure and confine themselves to relevant material.

8. In order to coordinate and apportion correctly the tasks selected, the assembled researchers into Cosmic Ice must put themselves under an intellectual director of Cosmic Ice who is alone responsible to the *Reichsführer SS*. The undersigned suggest for this position Hanns Robert Hörbiger, the eldest son of the founder of the Cosmic Ice Theory, and are prepared to recognize his leadership. Hanns Robert Hörbiger is not only the bearer of the name of Hörbiger, but was taught by the Master himself ... as his deputy Dr. Scultetus is suggested....

10. The undersigned declare that the following gentlemen
Captain von Etzdorf (rtd)
Georg Hinzpeter
Hanns Fischer
are not collaborating, *on their own initiative and according to their own opinions,* on the proposed work....[111]

Von Etzdorf, thought the signatories, should be suppressed completely, as he would damage the *Reichsführer's* project of having Cosmic Ice accepted by the scientific Establishment. Georg Hinzpeter and Hanns Fischer might be useful if put to work under the stern supervision of Dr. Scultetus.

Hanns Fischer had other ideas. He was an obvious target for the "scientific" specialists in Cosmic Ice, as he had been one of the founders of Hermann Wirth's first pseudo-academic institution, and he was certain that Hörbiger's theory represented the proof of astrology.[112] A month after the signing of the "Pyrmont Protocol," news of the document reached him and he flung back an irate letter to Himmler. He accused the Pyrmont group of acting behind his back and exposed the maneuver as a cunning move by the publisher of *Germanien* to secure the monopoly of books on Cosmic Ice—no doubt a lucrative market if sponsored by the *Reichsführer-SS,* Fischer was not prepared to work under Hanns Robert Hörbiger. As the *Reichsführer* knew, Hörbiger was a Catholic. But more sinister still, he had published an essay for the Grand Lodge of the Druid Order, a sort of "druid freemasonry" to which he belonged.[113] Not unnaturally, little more was heard of "Brother Hörbiger," who however, was still publishing after the war—which is more than can be said for Hanns Fischer or indeed almost any of the theorists of Cosmic Ice.[114]

Within the *Ahnenerbe,* Scultetus pursued his eccentric meteorology and kept Himmler informed on the progress of his pet theory. In August 1936 he sent Himmler the weather forecast by Cosmic Ice principles to impress Göring and General von Milch. Just over a year later he wrote excitedly that Cosmic Ice had now been given "official recognition" by the allocation of a class in the German equivalent of the Dewey Decimal library index.[115] Progress was made in Nazifying the theory, a process that had begun when in New Year 1936 the *Illustrierte Beobachter* gave space in three successive issues to the works of *Meister* Hörbiger. It continued the next year with the publication by Rudolf von Elmayer-Vestenbrugg of a pamphlet on Cosmic Ice as part of the series *Kämpfschriften der Obersten S.A. Fuhrüng.* Elmayer-Vestenbrugg used at least one other pseudonym, was a propagandist of colonial expansion, and the Nazi biographer of Ritter von Schönerer. In his S.A. handbook, the Cosmic Ice Theory finds its most Nazified expression: it is coordinated with Rosenberg's revised version of Atlantis, which incorporates some probably apocryphal stories about Hörbiger's careful experimentation, and concludes that here at last is a German scientific world-picture.[116] "The Theory of Relativity is to it [Cosmic Ice] as the Talmud to the Edda."

It is now well known that Hitler himself believed in Hörbiger and Cosmic Ice. In several conversations in 1942 he made his position quite clear. Hörbiger was comparable to Copernicus, and Hitler would set up in the ideal city that he proposed to build at Linz an observatory dedicated to Hörbiger as one of the three great cosmologists. The *Führer* was also convinced that a great disaster had long ago struck the world when civilization was already advanced, and he considered Hörbiger to have explained the Flood.[117] How did Hitler come in contact with this theory? There are indications in the following letter of February 1937 from *Hauptsturmbannführer* Bruno Galke of Himmler's personal staff.

> Dear Frau Gahr,
> Enclosed I send you three books by Kiss
> *The Sea of Glass*
> *The Last Queen of Atlantis*
> *Spring in Atlantis*
> which the firm has ordered for you as a friendly gesture.

Please place the books in your library—they all deal with the Cosmic Ice Theory, and will certainly greatly interest you as indeed you have often discussed the Theory with the *Führer*. They are three of the best books that have ever been written about Cosmic Ice.[118]

The *Führer* might be Himmler—but he is referred to elsewhere in the same letter as the *"Reichsführer-SS"* and it was always Hitler alone who was "the *Führer*". Nor—in view of Himmler's sending Cosmic Ice literature to prominent Nazis like Göring and Darré, which he did, in fact the month after the letter to Frau Gahr—does it make sense for a *Leiter* of his personal staff to send anyone books in order to influence Himmler. If Hitler was in the habit of talking to Frau Gahr about Cosmic Ice, who was she?

Karoline Gahr at the period the letter was written kept a small workshop in Munich which occasionally turned out badges for the *SS*.[119] She was the widow of the goldsmith Otto Gahr, one of Hitler's early cronies in the Nazi party, who had designed the standards of the S. A. to Hitler's specification and had died in 1932. Both in *Mein Kampf* and in his 1942 conversations, Hitler talked fondly of Otto Gahr. It is not at all improbable for Hitler to have discussed a theory in which we know he believed with the widow of his old party comrade who was herself still helping the cause. Kurt Ludecke tells in his memoirs of a visit to Otto Gahr while the goldsmith was making the S.A. standards. The context in which he sets his visit is that of Hitler's custom in the early days of spending time talking to his humblest and most devoted followers. "They were men from the most modest homes, like his own, men who knew nothing of the great world beyond their own towns, but were sincere, enthusiastic, loyal, looking upon Hitler not only as a genius but as an inspired prophet. To understand these men was largely to understand Hitler and his power."[120]

If Adolf Hitler and Karoline Gahr had discussed the Theory of Cosmic Ice, where did they get it? There is no real way of telling, but one probable source is Edgar Dacqué. Professor George Mosse has shown that a book "by a savant of Munich," which Hermann Rauschning mentions as attracting Hitler, was almost certainly Dacqué's *Urwelt, Sage und Menschheit*. In this book Dacqué uses the theory of Cosmic Ice to explain the flood. Moreover, Hitler admitted in January 1942 that he had once himself owned "a work on the origins of the human race. I used to think a lot about such matters."[121] Edgar Dacqué (1878-1945) was a paleontologist who in 1915 became professor and custodian of the Bavarian State Paleontology Collection. By the publication of *Urwelt, Sage und Menschheit* in 1924 he began an attempt which was to occupy him for the rest of his life, "to forge together as best I can religion, science, and life." The influence of Schelling and Schopenhauer completed with that of Jakob Böhme and Meister Eckhart. An even stronger influence may well have been the Theosophical Society, for Dacqué was one of those who signed an application for a charter from that organization to revive its dormant Munich section around the turn of the century.

Dacqué's musings on the significance of revolution were undoubtedly influenced by Theosophical ideas. He prophesied the death of "the century of mechanistic tyranny" and the advent of the "magical viewpoint" (the source of "creative culture"). By 1938 Dacqué's picture of "magical paganism" had been somewhat overlaid with a Christian gloss, but the mysticism that remains has analogies with that of Klages and Schuler.[122]

If Dacqué was the source of first instance for Hitler's knowledge of Hörbiger, the Nazi leader could not have come across the theory until the year of his imprisonment in the Landsberg jail. We do not know *when* he discussed Cosmic Ice with Frau Gahr, but there is a tortuous connection, which may show that Hörbiger became known quite early in *völkisch* circles. An "old friend" of Hanns Hörbiger was Ottokar Prohaszka, Prince-Bishop of Szekesfehervar in Hungary, who is said to have been heavily influenced by Hörbiger.[123] Prohaszka (1858-1927) played a leading part in the counterrevolution after the Hungarian uprising of Bela Kun. He was a convinced anti-Semite who saw Jews and Freemasons at the bottom of all the disturbances of 1918-19. Prohaszka's principles eventually became the ideology of the right-wing Arrow Cross Party's "Group of National Reconstruction," and for a brief period the bishop was president of the Hungarian majority Party of Christian Union. When Kurt Ludecke was sent by Hitler to attend a congress of Hungarian Nationalists in Budapest at Christmas 1924, his address was scheduled between Prohaszka and the extreme racist Julius

Gömbös (who had been in touch with Hitler since the end of the previous year). Prohaszka appeared as the hero of an article in the *Völkischer Beobachter* as early as September 1920; and his essay "The Jewish Question in Hungary," first published in 1920, was printed in German in 1921 in the Hamburg journal *Hammerschläge*.[124] Because Hörbiger is found almost invariably with a racist implication attached, because his supporters without exception praise him as a "really German" spirit, because he called one of his sons by the archaic name of Attila, there is a distinct chance that the Hörbiger-Prohaszka connection and the popularity of Cosmic Ice among the *Völkische* coincide with the conjunction of Hungarian and Bavarian anti-Semitism in the early 1920s. But further than this it is impossible to go.

What, then, is the relationship between Nazism, the occult, and the concept of "illuminated politics"? The Occult Revival had expressed itself in peculiar forms in Germany and the *völkisch* movement drew much inspiration from the resurrection of mystical ideas. The trio of Eckart, Feder, and Rosenberg, which was so influential at the birth of the Nazi party, displays the illuminated characteristics that in a more extreme form were shown by the less significant Thule Society. Because the Nazi party was founded during a period of anxiety in an area which was exceptionally open both to inherited *völkisch* irrationalism and an influx of Slav-inspired conspiracy theories, it naturally bore upward with it idealistic, irrationalist, and occult ideas from the Underground in which the party had its origin. Because of the demands of operating effective government, the irrationalists were almost by definition excluded from power. But in the private beliefs of Hitler, Himmler, and Rosenberg there remained much of the irrationalism of their earlier days, which they were generally able to separate from their exercise of power. The possibility should by no means be ruled out that Hitler, Himmler, and Rosenberg did want to put into practice some of their more occult beliefs; that Hitler did see his New Order as the next step in evolution, that Rosenberg did believe that his *Myth* could persuade people to study Meister Eckhart and submerge themselves in the *Volk*. As for Himmler, his vision of reality was quite obviously far removed from that of the rationalist universe—often, as his indiscriminate patronage of rejected knowledge makes clear, almost *deliberately*. These were men of the twilight who brought twilight subjects with them into the sun; and in this lies their significance.

Karl Kautsky's famous analysis of the rise of Christianity might be applied to certain sections of the early Nazi movement: "the *organization* . . . attained victory by *surrendering* its original aims and defending their opposite."[125] The lesson for illuminated politicians may be the old one of "power corrupts." The illuminates who were swept into Nazism and who ended in the *SS* or preaching a "new reality" to the universities probably really believed that they were effecting an "idealistic" revolution. In many ways the Nazi reality does represent illuminated politics in power, and thus transformed. Add a prolonged period of isolation, culminating in a total war—what other sort of war could an illuminated government contemplate?—and the self-created pressure of real and illusory enemies forced the *Reich* into a policy of external aggression and internal massacre. The Nazi reality became the only interpretation of experience from which the ordinary German could derive social support. There is material for psychological (rather than historical) studies in the fact that the Nazi organizations most responsible for carrying out the "Final Solution" were often—like certain sections of the *SS* and the *Einsatzstab Rosenberg*—under the direction of or associated with iiluminated elements. The extermination of the Jews marks the point at which some Germans proved in the most indisputable way that they had made a transition from an ill-defined but existing Established reality to a world whose values—and no doubt whose subjective appearances—were totally other.

The psychology of power and conquest is not the field of this book; but even here the driving force may to some extent have been derived from an imagined transcendental sanction. On the night of 12-13 January 1942, Hitler said to Bormann: "Mark my words, Bormann, I'm going to become very religious." Bormann replied: "You've always been very religious."[126] Hitler at once proceeded to indulge in fantasies about becoming the great khan of the Tartars. But it is not these that are significant so much as Bormann's reply.

In Dietrich Eckart's last fragmentary publication, *Bolshevism from Moses to Lenin,* Hitler's friend gave his particular version of the anti-Semitic gospel in the form of a dialogue between Hitler and himself. The views attributed to Hitler (while of course not certainly his) are probably an approximation of an Eckart-Hitler consensus. They include the theory—put in the mouth of Hitler, and claimed as original—that the Jews left Egypt because of an impending pogrom. We have already seen this idea expressed in that unpublished document of illuminated anti-Semitism, *The Secret of the Jews*.

"We want Germanity, true Christianity, order and planned breeding," says Eckart. There is never an enemy (the Hitler character is made to say) so implacable that we cannot obey Christ's instructions to love him—but Christ never intended us to love mere animals. And then the characters in the dialogue mutually decide that "we are both Catholics."[127] There is also probably some significance—beyond the obvious one for Catholic Bavaria—in the number of articles in the early *Völkischer Beobachter* on the theme "Can a Catholic be an anti-Semite?"

The idea that the transcendental impulse can carry politicians and their followers into "other realities" must not be taken too far. It is certain that if Hitler was borne into the realms of occult belief by his irrationalist ideas, he also determined to use the appeal of the transcendental sanction as a weapon in a very concrete struggle for power. We have seen how both Hitler and Himmler admitted their reliance on the power of ritual. At lunch on 14 October 1941, these two illuminates discussed the question of religion. "The notion of divinity gives most men the opportunity to make concrete the feeling they have of supernatural realities," Hitler said. "Why should we destroy this wonderful power they have of incarnating the feeling for the divine that is within them?" But he also expressed his horror at the possibility that the Nazi movement would acquire a religious character and institute a form of worship.[128] This is not the opinion of the convinced irrationalist of popular superstition. Both belief and manipulation were present in variable quantities.

To some extent the illuminated attitude and an affection for rejected knowledge are found in other Fascist movements. This is clear enough in Belgian, Hungarian, and Romanian Fascism, to say nothing of the more well-known brands in France, Italy, or Spain. The Marxist explanation that "reactionary" forces naturally allied with each other against the inevitable rise of the proletariat has influenced our writing of history much more than is explicitly admitted. There is obviously some truth in it; but on occasion the really important factor may well have been the need for a transcendental sanction felt by illuminated politicians. In Italy the interesting and mysterious figure of Giulio Alessandre Evola wrote on the Hermetic tradition, preached an "imperialism of the blood," and had some influence on the ideology of Italian Fascism.[129] In Norway, Vidkun Quisling emerged from the lunatic fringe of politics with his *Nasjonal Sammlung*'s ideology of blood and soil. Quisling's philosophy seems to have been based on a "Universalism" not unlike Häckel's monism or the universalism of Othmar Spann. In 1929 he published a pamphlet on the significance of the existence of life on other worlds—a preoccupation in at least one German *völkisch* sect—and after his conviction for treason, he repeated the statement that the universe was controlled by "a divine power connected with the inhabited planets." Quisling seems to have been convinced that he was engaged in a struggle between the powers of light and darkness—and some of his statements to this effect read very like those of Ungern-Sternberg! According to a former editor of the British *Church Times,* Quisling was one of Frank Buchman's converts to Moral Rearmament—which secured some of its greatest successes in the Scandinavian areas.[130] Whether or not this was the case, the similarity of approach between the two opponents of "moral Bolshevism"—the phrase was actually used by Buchman—is significant from the point of view of the effect of the transcendental impulse. It is probably this common search for a divine sanction that led to Buchman's relatively insignificant contact with the Nazis and the rumor recorded by Fritz Thyssen that Himmler was a member of the Oxford Groups.[131]

And as always, the man on the street or the *Strasse* was interested in other things. Even in the *SS* there were complaints that the "educational" sessions were poorly attended.[132] But something of the transcendental attitude did surface briefly in Germany, and with it some illuminates. Those who became converts to the Nazi ethic, however, were usually of a very definite type: irrationalists in the most derogatory sense of the word, undiscriminating and ill-educated in the processes of rational thought. Yet such people were not the only products of the flight from reason. Men and women of the greatest sophistication also reacted against the materialist-rationalist interpretation of life. From their deliberations have come some valuable—and even dominating—elements of modern culture.

1. George L. Mosse, *The Crisis of German Ideology* (London, 1966). Cf. his earlier essay "The Mystical Origins of National Socialism" in *Journal of the History of Ideas* (January-March 1961), pp. 81 ff. to see how he has modified an earlier thesis, which remains significant.
2. Mosse, *Crisis*, pp. 40 ff.
3. Mosse, *Crisis*, pp. 52-63.
4. Laqueur, *Young Germany*, pp. 32-37.
5. On Fidus, see Mosse, *Crisis*, pp. 84-86.
6. Landmann, *Monte Verita*.
7. Mosse, *Crisis*, pp. 108 ff, for German Utopians.
8. Steiner, *Story of My Life*, p. 134.
9. See R. d'O. Butler, *The Roots of National Socialism* (London, 1941).
10. Ransom, *Theosophical Soceity*, p. 188.
11. See Johann Baltzli, *Guido von List* (Leipzig, 1917).
12. Guido von List, *Deutsch-Mythologische Landschaftsbilder* (Berlin, 1891).
13. Von List, *Der Unbesiegbare* (Leipzig, 1898).
14. Baltzli, *Von List*, pp. 45-46.
15. Wannieck to von List, 12 December 1914, quoted in Baltzli, *Von List*, pp. 184-85.
16. Baltzli, *Von List*, pp. 47, 185.
17. See von List, *Die Religion der Ario-Germanen in ihrer Esoterik und Exoterik*, reissued in *Deutsche Wiedergeburt*, Band III, (Berlin, 1921); and *Der Übergang vom Wuotanismus zum Christentum*, Band V (n.d.).
18. Baltzli, *Von List*, pp. 50, 55.
19. On Lanz see Wilfried Daim, *Der Mann;* Daim, *Der Mann*, p. 271.
20. Lanz von Liebenfels, Meister Amalrich, and Meister Archibald, *Die ariosophiische Kabbalistik von Name und Ortlichkeit* (Ariosophische Bibiliothek, Heft 15), p. 1; Daim, *Der Mann*, pp. 180, 120-21.
21. Jörg Lanz von Liebenfels, *Die Theosophie und die assyrischen Menschentiere* (Bibeldokumente, Heft II), p. 5.
22. Von Liebenfels, *Die Theosophie*, p. 26. See passage quoted in *The Occult Underground*, p. 92.
23. Daim, *Der Mann*, pp. 159-60. For Issberner-Haldane see Howe, *Urania's Children*, pp. 111-12. For Gorsleben see this chapter below.
24. Fuchs, *Sturm und Drang*, p. 82.
25. Gerd-Klaus Kaltenbrunner, "Zwischen Rilke und Hitler—Alfred Schuler," in *Zeitschrift fur Religions- und Geistes-geschichte*, Band XIX (1967), p. 336. See Carl Albrecht Bernouilli, *Johann Jakob Bachofen und das Natursymbol* (Basel, 1924), which is dedicated to Klages; Joseph Campbell, introduction to Helen Diner, *Mothers and Amazons* (New York and London, 1965). E. K. Winter, "Bachofen-Renaissance" in *Zeitschrift für die gesamte Staatswissenschaft*, Band 85 (1928), pp. 316 ff.; see Helen Diner, *Mothers and Amazons*, "Sir Galahad," *Die Kagelschnitte Gottes* (Munich, 1921), and Bertha Eckstein-Diener, *Idiotenführer durch die Russische Literatur* (Munich, 1925); Eckstein-Diener, *Idiotenführer*, p. 116.

26. Alfred Rosenberg, *Dietrich Eckart, ein Vermächtnis* (4th ed., Munich, 1937), pp. 13-14; Albert Reich, *Dietrich Eckart* (Munich, 1933), pp. 22-62.
27. Rosenberg, *Eckart*, p. 16; Wilhelm Grün, *Dietrich Eckart als Publizist* (Munich, 1941), p. 44.
28. Reich, *Eckart*, p. 52; Rosenberg, *Eckart*, p. 21.
29. Adolf Dresler, *Dietrich Eckart* (Munich, 1938), p. 36.
30. Rosenberg, *Eckart*, pp. 22-23, 32; Grün, *Eckart*, pp. 42-48, 69; Dresler, *Eckart*, pp. 15 ff.; Eckart, "Der Adler des Jupiters" in *Auf gut Deutsch*, 12 December 1919, p. 668.
31. Fuchs, *Sturm und Drang*, p. 100.
32. See Helen Böhlau, *Das Recht der Mutter* (Berlin, 1896), and Friedrich Ulrich Zillman, *Helen Böhlau* (Leipzig, n.d. but c. 1919); Helen von Racowitza, *An Autobiography* (tr. Cecil Marr, London, 1910), p. 415; Steiner, *The Anthroposophic Movement*, p. 143.
33. *Völkischer Beobachter*, 17 May 1919; Eckart joined the Thule some time in 1919; Eckart, "Ein eigentümlicher Theosoph," in *Auf gut Deutsch* (11 July 1919), p. 222.
34. Wachsmuth, *Steiner*, pp. 315-18; Saint-Yves d' Alveydre, *Mission des ouvriers* (3rd ed., Paris, 1884); Rudolf Steiner, *The Threefold State* (London, 1920), and Papus, *Anarchie, indolence et synarchie* (Paris, 1884).
35. E.g., Kully, *Die Wahrheit*, p. 206; Wachsmuth, *Steiner*, pp. 356 ff. Steiner, 29 August 1922, quoted Savitch, *Marie von Sivers* p. 133; Kully, *Die Wahrheit*, pp. 206-9.
36. For this hostility, see Rittelmeyer, *Steiner*, p. 117, and Wachsmuth, *Steiner*, pp. 397-98 for Steiner's lecturing to those involved in the Saar Plebiscite. Cf. Kully, *Die Wahrheit*, p. 209; see, e.g., Wachsmuth, *Steiner*, pp. 242-43; Eckart, "Der Adler des Jupiters," p. 327; Eckart, "Ein eigentümlicher Theosoph," p. 671; Howe, *Urania's Children*, pp. 81 ff.
37. *The Guildsman*, June 1920. "There are some good ideas in his book and we shall make haste to steal them."
38. See H. W. Schomerus, *Die Anthroposophie Steiners und Indien* (Leipzig, Erlangen, n.d.); Christian Gahr, *Die Anthroposophie Steiners* (Erlangen, 1929), pp. 38-39; Steiner, *The Soul of the People* (London, 1936). Originally lectures delivered in Berlin in November 1914. These were sent to Prince Max of Baden together with the theory of the Threefold Commonwealth. See Wachsmuth, *Steiner*, p. 357.
39. Richard Euringer, *Dietrich Eckart* (2nd ed., Hamburg, 1938), p. 15; Eckart, "Mittendurch," in *Völkischer Beobachter* (3 February 1923), p. 5; Eckart, *Das ist der Jude* (Munich, 1920); "Ein Völkischer Beobachter in England" (9 June 1920). See Grün, *Eckart*, bibliography for 1920; Eckart, "Jewry über Alles," in *Auf gut Deutsch* (26 November 1920); Hansjörg Maurer, "Versammlung im Zirkus Krone," *Völkischer Beobachter* (24 January 1923), pp. 2-3; Franz-Willing, *Hitlerbewegung*, p. 131; also short

note in school text, *Nationalsozialistische Weltanschauung* (ed. Martin Iskraut, Leipzig, 1934), pp. vii-viii.

40. Gottfried Feder, *Kampf gegen die Hochfinanz* (2nd ed., Munich, 1933), p. 12; Feder, "Das Manifest zur Brechung der Zinsknechtschaft des Geldes" in *Kampf*, p. 51; see *Münchener Beobachter*, 9 August 1919, p. 2 and Feder, *Kampf*, p. 111.

41. Feder, *Kampf*, p. 97; Reich, *Eckart*, pp. 69-71; Eckart and Feder, "An alle Werktätigen," in Feder, *Kampf*, pp. 96 ff.; see also Feder, *Die Juden* (Munich, 1933), and in *Das neue Deutschland und die Judenfrage* (Leipzig, 1933).

42. "Aus der Bewegung," *Völkischer Beobachter* (29 May 1920), p. 4; Feder on 4 December 1930, in *Kampf*, p. 282.

43. On the Balts see Laqueur, *Russia and Germany*, pp. 30 ff.

44. H. J. Schmierescott, *Arthur Moeller van den Bruck und der revolutionäre Nationalismus in der Weimarer Republik* (Göttingen, 1967), pp. 127-28.

45. Reinhold Bollmus, *Das Amt Rosenberg und seine Gegner* (Stuttgart, 1970), pp. 21, 256 note 32.

46. Rosenberg (ed. Serge Lang and Ernst von Schrenck), *Porträt eines Menschheitsverbrechers* (St. Gallen, 1947), p. 33; Günter Schubert, *Anfänge nationalsozialistischer Aussenpolitik* (Cologne, 1963), pp. 11-12, 167-69. Cf. F. Th. Hart, *Alfred Rosenberg* (Munich, 1933), pp. 36-37; for this development see Cohn, *Warrant*, pp. 138 ff., Laqueur, *Russia and Germany*, pp. 50-125.

47. See A. Netchvolodov, *L'Empéreur Nicolas II et les juifs* (Paris, 1924), and Nikolaus Markov, *Der Kampf der dunklen Mächte* (Erfurt, 1935).

48. See A. Tcherep-Spiridovitch, *Vers la débacle* (Paris, 1914) and *The Secret World Government* (New York, 1926).

49. Laqueur, *Russia and Germany*, pp. 122-25. See Bostunitch, "Der letzte Theologe," p. 67, where he quotes Heinrich Lhotsky on the Balts: "Vergiss nie, dass du Arier bist und Sonnenwege wandeln musst." Both Lhotsky and Johannes Müller may have absorbed anti-Semitic influences while with the Mission to the Jews in Russia.

50. Laqueur, *Russia and Germany*, pp. 58 ff. for Scheubner-Richter and cf. also Paul Leverkühn, *Posten auf ewiger Wache* (Essen, 1938), pp. 184 ff. For Rosenberg in Munich, see Laqueur, *Russia and Germany*, pp. 68 ff. and Bollmus, *Amt Rosenberg*, pp. 18 ff.

51. Eckart, "Jewry über alles," p. 42.

52. Howe, *Urania's Children*, p. 86. Mr. Howe's forthcoming *Lunatic Fringe* will enlighten us as to the elusive *Freiherr* and his associates. Meanwhile, see Reginald H. Phelps, "Before Hitler Came: Thule Society and Germanen Orden" in *Journal of Modern History* (March-December 1963), pp. 245 ff.; Phelps, *Journal*, pp. 250-51.

53. See "E.H.," "In eigener Sache" in *Münchener Beobachter* (1919, no. 4), p. 3, and Philip Stauff in *Münchener Beobachter*, 24 May 1919.

54. Rudolf von Sebottendorff, *Geschichte der Astrologie* Band I (Leipzig, 1923), p. 37; Sebottendorff, *Die Praxis der alter Türkischen Freimaurerei* (Leipzig, 1924).

55. Sebottendorff, *Bevor Hitler kam* (Munich, 1933), pp. 222-23, 260. N.B. the strictures of Howe, *Urania's Children*, p. 86 on this book; *Völkischer Beobachter* (23 August 1919), p. 1.

56. Franz-Willing, *Hitler Bewegung*, pp. 64-66. Cf. Sebottendorff, *Bevor Hitler kam*, p. 73.

57. For verdicts on Greiner's unreliability, see Franz Jetzinger, *Hitler's Youth* (London, 1958), p. 11, 136 note 1, 143; Werner Maser, *Die Frühgeschichte der NSDAP* (Frankfurt-am-Main, 1965), pp. 8, 67 note 92; also Maser's *Hitler's Mein Kampf* (tr. R. H. Barry, London, 1970), pp. 61, 209. But cf. Maser passim, and Konrad Heiden, *Der Führer* (tr. Ralph Manheim, London, 1944), p. 55. Cf. Alan Bullock, *Hitler, a Study in Tyranny* (rev. ed., London, 1962), p. 35.

58. Joseph Greiner, *Das Ende der Hitler-Mythos* (Zurich, Leipzig, Vienna, 1947), pp. 86-94.

59. Daim, *Der Mann*, pp. 15-23.

60. Mosse, *Crisis*, p. 77, pp. 31 ff., 246-47.

61. Kaltenbrunner, "Zwischen Rilke und Hitler," p. 163; Boehringer, *Stefan Georg*, p. 109; Mosse, *Crisis*, p. 76, Salin, *Stefan Georg*, p. 194.

62. Greiner, *Hitler-Mythos*, pp. 84-86.

63. Franz-Willing, *Hitler Bewegung*, pp. 67-73, p. 78, p. 82; Maser, *Frühgeschichte*, p. 149.

64. Hitler, *Mein Kampf*, tr. James Murphy (London, 1939), pp. 302, 318.

65. Ernst Nolte, *Three Faces of Fascism* (New York, 1965), pp. 412-15.

66. Erich Ludendorff in *Mathilde Ludendorff: Ihr Werk und Wirken* (Munich, 1937), pp. 40-41.

67. Ernst Hanfstaengl, *Hitler: The Missing Years* (London, 1957), pp. 84-85.

68. Feder, "Das Weibes Kulturtat" in *Völkischer Beobachter* (9 December 1920), p. 3. Cf. Ludendorff, *Mathilde Ludendorff*, p. 110 ff.

69. For these sources see Johannes Hertel, *Von neuen Trug zur Rettung des Alten* (Berlin, 1932), and Louis Jacolliot, *The Bible in India* (London, 1870). For the biography of Mathilde von Kemnitz, see Erich Ludendorff, *Mathilde Ludendorff*, pp. 178 ff. and Hertel, *Von neuen Trug*. For Mathilde von Kemnitz and occultism, see her *Moderne Mediumforschung* (Munich, 1914), and her *Der Trug des Astrologie* (Munich, 1932).

70. Erich Ludendorff, *Mathilde Ludendorff*, pp. 43 ff.

71. See Erich and Mathilde Ludendorff, *Die Judenmacht: ihr Wesen und Ende* (Munich, 1930); Ilse Hess, *Prisoner of Peace* (London, 1954), p. 54; J. R. Rees (ed.), *The Case of Rudolf Hess* (London, 1947), p. 35.

72. James Douglas-Hamilton, *Motive for a Mission* (London, 1971), p. 125.

73. For Scheubner-Richter's role in coordinating the activities of Russians and Germans see Laqueur, *Russia and Germany*, pp. 62-68, 105 ff. Cf. also Volkmann, *Emigration*.
74. *Adolf Hitler's Table Talk, 1941-1944* (London, 1953), p. 252.
75. Feder, *Kampf*, pp. 150-54.
76. Franz Neumann, *Behemoth* (London, 1942), pp. 187 ff. on Spann, see D. Vikor, *Economic Romanticism in the 20th Century* (London, 1932). Spann's complete works are published from Graz; see in particular the *Fundament der Volkswirtschaftslehre* (Gesamtausgabe, Band 3, 1967) and *Der wahre Staat* (4th ed., Vienna, 1938). Cf. *Erkenne dich selbst* (Gesamtausgabe Band 14) for the mystical premises on which Spann based his theories. Within the ambit of this sort of economic speculation the English Guildsmen found a hearing. A series of "Schriften der Englischen Gildenbewegung" was published at Tübingen and at least two university theses were devoted to Guildsmen after the Nazis came to power. See Feder, *Die neue Stadt* (Berlin, 1939).
77. Albert Reich and O. R. Achenbach, *Vom 9 November, 1918 zum 9 November, 1923* (Munich, 1933), p. 20; Fritz von Trützschler, *Armes Volkstum* (Berlin, 1920); Howe, *Urania's Children*, p. 87 note 1; quoted in Phelps, *"Before Hitler came,"* p. 261.
78. Artur Dinter, *Die Sünde wider den Geist* (Leipzig, 1921), pp. 235-44; Dinter, *Die Sünde wider die Liebe* (Leipzig, 1922), p. 329; Peter Hüttenberger, *Die Gauleiter* (Stuttgart, 1969), pp. 13-14 and pp. 42-46. Cf. Dinter, *Die Deutsche Volkskirche* (Leipzig, 1934).
79. See documents printed in J. S. Conway, *The Nazi Persecution of the Churches* (London, 1968), pp. 370-74, listing sects banned up till December, 1938, pp. 370-74; 378-82; Howe, *Urania's Children*, pp. 192 ff.
80. Hitler, *Table Talk*, p. 251; Hitler, *Mein Kampf*, p. 191; Hanfstaengl, *Hitler*, p. 41; Kurt Ludecke, *I Knew Hitler* (London, 1938), pp. 195-96; Hitler, *Table Talk*, pp. 231, 442-43, 572.
81. Hermann Rauschning, *Hitler Speaks*, pp. 240-42.
82. Bollmus, *Amt Rosenberg*, pp. 54 ff., 113 ff., 25-26, 39, 255 note 27.
83. Rosenberg, *Der Mythus des 20 Jahrhunderts* (Munich, 1934), pp. 25-27.
84. See Spengler, *Frühzeit der Weltgeschichte*, ed. M. Schröter and A. M. Koktanek (Munich, 1966), pp. 210 ff.; A Bessinertiny, *Das Atlantisrätsel* (Leipzig, 1932), p. 147; Bessinertiny with Ernst Uehli, *Atlantis und das Rätsel der Eiszeitkunst* (Stuttgart, 1930).
85. Albert Herrmann, *Unsere Ahnen und Atlantis* (Berlin, 1934); Karl Georg Zschaetzsch, *Die Arier* (Berlin, 1920).
86. Rosenberg, *Mythus*, p. 88; Lang and Schrenck, *Menschheitsverbrechers*, pp. 111-12; Rosenberg, *Mythus*, pp. 220 ff., 251, 259.
87. John Macready, *Der Aufgang des Abendlandes* (Leipzig, 1926), p. 632. See the analysis of Ernest Seillière in *Morales et religions nouvelles en Allemagne* (Paris, 1927), pp. 126 ff.
88. Josef Ackermann, *Heinrich Himmler als Ideologue* (Göttingen,

Zürich, and Frankfurt, 1970), pp. 34 ff. This is invaluable in showing the possible extent of Nazi mysticism. Cf. Werner Angriss and B. F. Smith, "Diaries of Heinrich Himmler's Early Years" in *Journal of Modern History* (September 1959); C. A. Bernouilli, *Bachofen,* p. 456.

89.   Josef Ackermann, *Himmler,* pp. 196-99; Mosse, *Crisis,* pp. 116-20; Heinz Höhne, *The Order of the Death's Head* (tr. Richard Barry, London), pp. 48-49.

90.   Felix Kersten, *The Kersten Memoirs* (London, 1956), pp. 38-39, 151-52; Josef Ackermann, *Himmler,* pp. 63 note 132, 64, 68-69 and note 166. See Karl August Eckhardt, *Irdische Unsterblichkeit,* (Weimar, 1937). Eckhardt was associated with Ernst Krieck and Walter Wüst—see this chapter; speech printed in Josef Ackermann, *Himmler,* p. 245.

91.   Speech quoted Ackermann, *Himmler,* p. 101. See Heinrich Himmler, *Die Schutzstaffel als antibolschewitstische Kampforganisation* (Munich, 1936).

92.   Himmler, *Die Schutzstaffel,* p. 27. "Ich halte ihn für überheblich, grossenwahnsinnig und dumm; er ist nicht für uns geeignet"; Himmler, *Die Schutzstaffel,* pp. 101-07; Kersten, *Memoirs,* p. 29; Rauschning, *Hitler Speaks,* p. 237.

93.   Höhne, *Death's Head,* p. 152.

94.   Document from *Amt Schulung* in Bundesarchiv Koblenz, file no. NS 15/51 neu; see Hubert Schrade, *Das Deutsche Nationaldenkmal* (Munich, 1934) and *Bauten des Dritten Reiches* (Leipzig, 1939); Richard von Kienle, *Germanische Gemeinschaftsleben* (Stuttgart 1939), which was published by the *Ahnenerbe.* See Wilhelm Grau, *Die Judenfragen in das deutschen Geschichte* (Leipzig, 1937); K. G. Kuhn also wrote on the "Jewish question." Julius Andree, *Die Externsteine* (Münster, 1936) is a typical example of Externsteine literature.

95.   Alfred Baümler (ed.), *Was bedeutst Hermann Wirth fur die Wissenschaft?* (Leipzig, 1932), pp. 92-93; see Hermann Wirth, *Der Aufgang der Menschheit* (Jena, 1928), and Albert Hermann, *Ahnen und Atlantis,* pp. 23 ff.; Friedrich Hielscher, *Fünfzig Jahre unter Deutschen* (Hamburg, 1954), p. 288.

96.   Michael H. Kater, *Das Ahnenerbe, die Forschungs- und Lehrgemeinschaft in der SS,* thesis presented to Heidelberg University, 1966. A vital piece of research for those seeking to understand Nazi irrationalism.

97.   Hielscher, *Fünfzig Jahre,* passim, esp. p. v.

98.   "Forschungs- und Lehrgemeinschaft 'Das Ahnenerbe' Tagebuch 1944 geführt von Reichsgeschäftsführer SS Standartenführer Sievers." Bundesarchiv Koblenz file NS/21/Vol II.

99.   Correspondence in Koblenz file NS21/409/G/81/2, in particular letters of unidentified *Scharführer,* 18 July 1937 and 29 August 1937; and *Obersturmbannführer* to *Reichsführer SS,* 14 August 1937.

100. Strömer von Reichenbach, *Was ist Weltgeschichte?* (Ludwigshafen,

1919), and Max Kemmerich, *Das Kausalgesetz der Weltgeschichte* (2 vols., Munich, 1913-14).

101. Strömer von Reichenbach, *Was wird?* (Ludwigshafen, 1919), and also *Erfüllte Voraussagen der Historionomie* (n.d., n.p.).

102. Howe, *Urania's Children*, p. 192 note 2, quoting Helmut Heiber, *Walter Frank und sein Reichinstitut für Geschichte des neuen Deutschlands* (1966).

103. See letter of *Reichsleitung Rosenberg* to Wendorff of *Amt Wissenschaft* in Bundersarchiv file NS 15/219 neu. For Koresh, see Martin Gardner, *Fads and Fallacies in the Name of Science* (New York, 1957), pp. 22-27.

104. Georg Hinzpeter, *Der Sieg der Welteislehre* (Breslau, 1936), pp. 180-88.

105. Chiefly from H. S. Bellamy, *Moons Myths and Man* (2nd ed., London, 1949). I do not recommend any of the German works, for reasons which should be clear; but those interested might try Philipp Fauth, *Der Mond in Hörbigers Welteislehre* (2nd ed., Leipzig, 1938).

106. See William A. Jones, *Blavatsky and Hörbiger* (London, 1950).

107. Friedell, *Kulturgeschichte Ägyptens*, pp. 46-49; *Cultural History of the Modern Age*, vol. III, pp. 463-65.

108. Edmund Kiss, *Die kosmische Ursachen der Völkerwanderung* (Leipzig, 1934). Cf. A. G. Högbom "Die Atlantislitteratur unserer Zeit" in *Bulletin of the Geographical Institute of the University of Upsala* (1941), pp. 46 ff.

109. Rudolf John Gorsleben "Hochzeit der Menschheit" in *Illustrietre Beobachter* (1937), Folge 3. Wilhelm Asendorpf, *Die Edda als Welteislehre* (Krefeld, 1933). On Gorsleben, see Dietrich Eckart, *Das is der Jude*, p. 54 note 2; Hans Wolfgang Behm, *Hörbigers Welteislehre* (Leipzig, 1938), p. 219.

110. Kater, *Ahnenerbe*, pp. 63-64, 351-53. Josef Ackermann, *Himmler*, pp. 46-67.

111. The "Pyrmont Protocol" in Bundesarchiv Koblenz file NS 21/Vol 716.

112. See Hans Fischer, *Rhythmus des kosmischen Lebens: Das Buch vom Pulsschlag der Welt* (Leipzig, 1925).

113. Hans Fischer to *Reichsführer-SS*, 21 August 1936 in Koblenz NS 21/Vol 716. The connection of the younger Hörbiger with the Druid Order leads to the speculation that Lewis Spence—thought to have belonged to a Druid Order and who wrote copiously on the related Atlantis problem—may have belonged to this organization.

114. One of the two Viennese Hörbiger societies was liquidated by the Nazis; another survived under the chairmanship of Manfred Rieffenstein. The only member of the committee of the Berlin Society to survive was Hinzpeter, still alive in 1949. See *The Research Centre Group*, fly sheet issued by Egerton Sykes (London, 1949).

115. Scultetus to *Reichsführer-SS* 18 August 1936 (via Bruno Galke) 13 September 1937. In Koblenz files NS 21/Vol. 714 and 716.
116. Rudolf von Elmayer-Vestenbrugg, *Rätsel des Weltgeschehens* (Munich, 1937). This is almost identical to his *Die Welteislehre* (Leipzig, 1938). The author also used the name "Elimar Vinibert von Rudolf." Quite possibly both are fictitious.
117. Hitler, *Table Talk,* pp. 248-50, 324, 445.
118. Galke to Frau Gahr 3 February 1937 in Koblenz file NS 21/Vol. 715/G. Cf. letter printed by Helmut Heiber, *Reichsführer!* (Stuttgart, 1968), p. 47.
119. Franz-Willing, *Hitlerbewegung,* p. 86 note 47.
120. Ludecke, *I Knew Hitler* (London, 1938), p. 93.
121. Mosse, *Crisis,* pp. 306, 356 note 32; Edgar Dacqué, *Urwelt Sagen und Menschheit* (Munich and Berlin, 1928), pp. 158 ff. for *Welteislehre,* and Hitler, *Table Talk,* p. 248.
122. See *The Vahan;* Dacqué, *Urwelt, Sagen und Menschheit, Natur und Seele* (Munich and Berlin, 1926), esp. pp. 21-22 and *Das verlorene Paradies* (Munich and Berlin, 1938).
123. Hinzpeter, *Welteislehre,* p. 189.
124. On Prohaszka, see William Juhasz, "The Development of Catholicism in Hungary in Modern Times" in *Church and Society 1789-1950* (ed. Joseph N. Moody, New York, 1953) and C. A. Macartney, *October Fifteenth* (2nd ed., Edinburgh, 1961), pp. 28-32, 498. See, also Prohaszka, *The Jewish Question in Hungary* (The Hague, 1920) and Friedrich Heer, *God's First Love* (tr. Geoffrey Shelton, London, 1970), p. 339. Ludecke, *Hitler,* p. 243 and *Völkischer Beobachter,* 23 September 1920, "Ein antisemitischer Bischoff," p. 4.
125. Karl Kautsky, *Foundations of Christianity* (London, 1925), p. 461.
126. Hitler, *Table Talk,* pp. 203-4.
127. Eckart, *Bolschevismus von Moses bis Lenin* (Munich, 1922), esp. pp. 22-23 and pp. 30 ff.
128. Hitler, *Table Talk,* p. 61.
129. Nolte, *Three Faces,* pp. 321, 630 note 17. Cf. chapter VIII.
130. See Hans-Dietrich Loock, *Quisling, Rosenberg und Terboven* (Stuttgart, 1970); Ralph Heims, *Quisling* (London, 1965); *E.g.,* Quisling's article "A Nordic World Federation," in *British Union Quarterly,* vol. I, no. 1 (January-April 1937); Sidney Dark, *Not Such a Bad Life* (London, 1941), p. 230.
131. Fritz Thyssen, *I Paid Hitler* (London, 1940), p. 189-90.
132. Höhne, *Death's Head,* pp. 154-55.

Chapter 6
The Hermetic Academy

The Discovery of the Unconscious—Freud and the Occultists—The Status of Hypnotism—The Eccentricities of Wilhelm Fliess—Psychoanalysis and Psychical Research—Freud as Secularizer of the Occult—The Occult Experiences of Jung—Basilides the Gnostic—The Analysis of Kristine Mann—The Eranos Conferences—J. W. Hauer and the Nordic Faith Movement—Spiritual Progress and Education—The Occult and the New Educational Fellowship

EINSTEIN'S General Theory of Relativity was not formulated until the First World War; and not until Relativity was accepted was the post-Newtonian universe of law finally overturned. This universe of law had found its culminating expression in the late-19th-century scientific Establishment which, as seen by its opponents, insisted on the primacy of a crude materialism and allowed no other arbiter of truth than the rigors of observed experiment. To a large extent, of course, this scientific Establishment and its criteria existed—it existed more surely than the "Establishment of materialism and individualism," which the idealistic politicians intended to overturn. But the scientific Establishment was elevated into a great bogeyman by those who saw their human dignity or religious preconceptions placed under the writ of "Victorian materialism." The Occult Revival of the late 19th century was one symptom of a reaction against the harsh supremacy of the universe of law. By the period between the two wars, the successors of the 19th-century occultists had eagerly adopted Relativity, and popular works like Sir James Jeans's *Mysterious Universe* convinced numberless adherents of the many occult groups that "the scientists were coming round." It was important to convert the scientists, because the irrationalists of the early Occult Revival had never been able to forget that they were opposing the great pundits of their day, and the next generation frequently combined both rationalist and irrationalist superstitions.

If the tyranny of the scientific Establishment was understandably exaggerated, its restrictions had been effective not only in prescribing a skeptical attitude and an experimental method but in *limiting the territory investigated*. The standards of controlled experiment and conclusion could only be applied to certain subjects—the physical world in its broadest sense. What then was the status of man himself? The alternatives seemed clear: either to accept the implications of the idea that he was simply the highest animal, or to take refuge in orthodox religion, which for some two centuries had been suitably isolated from the inconvenient probing of Established science. Against this artificial dualism the occultists again reacted. Amid a welter of romanticism and hysteria could always be heard a number of voices calling plaintively for a philosophy that would unite religion and science and provide an explanation both convincing and comforting of man's place in the universe. Because of the fundamental content of such systems, Eastern religions or Western occultism of a neo-Platonic, Gnostic, or Hermetic character could be seen as fulfilling this need. As part of the same process there occurred a fundamental turning point in man's vision of man. The restricted area of investigation prescribed by the scientific method was expanded immeasurably. The direction of man's vision broadened from an exclusive concentration on things outside himself to include a concern with his perceptible nature and his interaction with his fellows.

From this swiveling of the attention have come modern psychology and sociology, as well as countless variations on areas of inquiry that were already accepted. Man himself was under the microscope—but not with the beady eye of T. H. Huxley fixed sternly to the other end of the instrument. The new sort of investigator was convinced that there was more to humanity than met that beady eye, that there were motives and actions that could not be expressed merely in terms of surface pressures, that beneath the obvious demands of survival and procreation lurked undefined chains of cause and effect, which resulted in man's being far from the master in his own house. The term *unconscious* became of the highest importance. An inquirer might once more assume that man—that is, the investigator himself—*was not capable of perceiving his entire nature.* And he might do this, he thought, without abandoning the strict criteria of "scientific proof" which had stood him in such good stead in his forays through the physical universe. At the same time, and as part of the same process of altered vision, the irrationalist reaction produced two results that became inextricably bound up with man's inquiry into the submerged part of himself. In the shape of the occult and Oriental systems, which had come to be so much in vogue, there was available a mountain of literature dealing with precisely the problems which the investigator into the unconscious found confronting him and to which the Christian answers had long been forgotten or discredited. On a less profound level, public interest in Spiritualism and the supernatural had resulted in attempts to apply the criteria of 19th-century science to the appearance of "ghosts" or communications from the "Summerland." The plain result is that psychoanalysis, psychical research, and the more religious aspects of the Occult Revival can by no means be disentangled.

Indeed, it is doubtful whether they should be. The area of investigation—the Unconscious, the unperceived part of a man—might appear in essence the same, although the premises of inquirers might greatly differ. If a psychoanalyst of the type familiar in the West is faced with a patient whose relatives believe him to be "possessed by a devil," the fact that he may diagnose a "split personality" does not alter the symptoms displayed. And if such a diagnosis is made it owes a great deal to the Cinderella of psychical research. It has been argued that the whole development just outlined—a certain redirection of scientific attention—has involved giving new names to old ghosts. That is, that what might in the 12th century have been called an evil spirit might after Freud be simply known by another term. Occultists—and some psychoanalysts —have naturally hailed this concentration on the immaterial as presaging a new age. Whereas Rom Landau decided that the "spiritual problems" of man between the wars required a resort to fashionable gurus like Keyserling, Ouspensky, or Krishnamurti, varieties of psychoanalysis could fulfil something of the same need. This is clear from a summary of the mood of the interwar period made by Carl Gustav Jung.

> We cannot suppose that this aspect of the unconscious or of the hinterland of man's mind is something totally new. Probably it has always been there, in every culture. Each culture gave birth to its destructive opposite, but no culture or civilization before our own was ever forced to take these psychic undercurrents in deadly earnest. Psychic life always found expression in a metaphysical system of some sort. But the conscious, modern man, despite his strenuous and dogged efforts to do so, can no longer refrain from acknowledging the might of psychic forces. This distinguishes our time from all others. We can no longer deny that the dark stirrings of the unconscious are effective powers—that psychic forces exist which cannot, for the present at least, be fitted in with our rational world-order. We have even enlarged our study of these forces to a science—one more proof of the earnest attention we bring to them. Previous centuries could throw them aside unnoticed; for us they are a shirt of Nessus which we cannot strip off.
>
> The revolution in our conscious outlook, brought about by the catastrophic results of the World War, shows itself in our inner life by the shattering of our faith in ourselves and our own work ... the old dream of the millennium, in which peace and harmony should rule, has grown pale.[1]

We have seen that some people still entertained that dream. But Jung's verdict and the importance ascribed to psychoanalysis are indisputable. Once more the crisis of the First World War is invoked to show the primacy of unreason; and Jung claims that a science has been invented to deal with the unrecognized forces, which in their darker aspects have caused the tragedy. This insistence that his own analytical psychology or the psychoanalysis of Freud form part of a new "science" must be kept in mind as we examine some neglected aspects of their emergence. For the pioneers of the Unconscious were as concerned as their occultist contemporaries with the supremacy of materialist science; and Freud in particular took the greatest care not to become publicly associated with the more "occult" or "mystical" aspects of that redirection of human attention in which he was a central figure.

In discussing the historical origins of psychoanalysis, two traps must be avoided. The first is to attempt the sort of "psychoanalytical biography," which analysts alone are qualified to attempt or judge; and the second is to become overwhelmed by the multiplicity of Freud's philosophical ancestors. It has been observed that "the general conception of unconscious mental processes was *conceivable* (in post-Cartesian Europe) around 1700, *topical* around 1800, and *fashionable* around 1870-1880,"[2] and that Freud's insistence on the sexual basis of neuroses was the main factor in arousing opposition to psychoanalysis. It is notorious that Freud's intense eagerness for originality led him not to carry out thorough reading on his crucial *Interpretation of Dreams* (1900) until *after* his conclusions were formed. Therefore it becomes all the more important to relate the origins of psychoanalysis to the "general intellectual climate" in which speculation about the Unconscious took place.

In 1868 Eduard von Hartmann published his *Philosophy of the Unconscious,* which raised the problem of unconscious mental processes. Rudolf Steiner's reaction to his first reading of von Hartmann has already been noted. *Nothing,* he felt, should remain unconscious. Steiner's deduction was that he should find some way of making conscious the unconscious processes—which is what his "spiritual perception" amounts to. It is well worth while to examine the occult affiliations of psychoanalysis, a cure for neurosis which Freud thought to consist of bringing the conscious mind to a recognition of the suppressed causes of illness. Occultists, Spiritualists, and hawkers of proprietary brands of Theosophy were interested in precisely the same problems, although their final conclusions might and did take a very different form. Thus, the Spiritualist Carl du Prel's *Philosophy of Mysticism,* first published in 1885 (and Freud included it in the bibliography of *The Interpretation of Dreams*), defines its author's central problem as "the question whether our Ego is wholly embraced in self-consciousness."[3] It had better be made clear at the start that this relationship between the Occult Revival and psychoanalysis is no mere intellectual construction based on similarities of approach or of conclusion. It begins with the fact that Sigmund Freud was "an old friend" of Friedrich Eckstein.

This information is contained in a footnote in Ernest Jones's biography of Freud, and the source given is Dr. Siegfried Bernfeld. Dr. Bernfeld is dead, but it is possible to be certain that his Eckstein was indeed our old friend the devoted Wagnerian and follower of Madame Blavatsky. The footnote gives Eckstein's nickname of "Fritz," and a paper by Dr. Bernfeld is almost explicit in referring to the varieties of rebellion practiced among Freud's friends at the University of Vienna. There were those, he writes, who "led queer existences in coffee houses and vegetarian restaurants." Eckstein was able to remember that when Freud left school in 1873 and heard the lecture that convinced him to become a doctor he wrote a newspaper review of the occasion that had so impressed him. This review remains untraced, but it indicates that Eckstein, although a few years older than Freud, was indeed "an old friend." Certainly both men knew Victor Adler, although Freud's contact with the latter nearly ended in a duel. The occasion of this was a heated attack mounted by Freud in a student debating society against Adler's idealism. The future psychoanalyst had recently been converted from his early attachment to the romantic doctrine of *Naturphilosophie* and had become a rabid materialist. Freud himself does not seem to have been a candidate for membership of the clique in Megalomania Café, although his friendship with Eckstein was long-lasting.

How else explain the appearance of Eckstein in the *Almanack of Psychoanalysis* published in the 1930s by the Freud group in Vienna? In 1930 Eckstein contributed an article entitled "The Unconscious, Heredity and Memory in the Light of Mathematical Science." He argued from progress in genetics that psychoanalysis might one day be capable of a mathematical formulation. His starting point was Leibniz, and he claimed that as early as 1918 he had written a popular article embodying "a mathematical formulation and analysis of the Unconscious," which had, not surprisingly, been ignored both by biologists and psychoanalysts.[5] Six years later Eckstein surfaced again in the same yearbook, writing on "Older Theories of the Unconscious." This once more began with Leibniz but dwelled on the Neo-Platonists in a manner that might be expected of an associate of Jung rather than of Freud. Plotinus was seen as the founding father of all theories of the Unconscious. According to Plotinus, all "higher" knowledge is based on an intuitive-regressive emergence into consciousness of the unconscious, of contents that occur "somewhere in the soul" and that we are only able to recognize when they have permeated the entire being. And precisely in this lies its shattering, purifying effect and its significance for the spiritual renewal of mankind. "Up, let us fly to the beloved land of the Father!"[6]

In his memoirs (published the same year as the article), Eckstein mentions Freud only in connection with their mutual friend Christian von Ehrenfels (1859-1932). Von Ehrenfels, like Friedrich Eckstein, was a mathematician and a Wagnerian; Eckstein wrote his obituary in the *Neue Freie Presse*. But like Freud he was a sexual eugenist, and he christened the founder of psychoanalysis and himself "Sexual Protestants." In 1908 Freud published a paper in which he used von Ehrenfels's book on *Sexual Ethics* as his starting point. Both agreed in their views on the custom of monogamous marriage.[7] For the greater part of his career von Ehrenfels was professor of philosophy at Prague, producing his best known book on ethics in 1897. In the present context his important work is the *Cosmogony* (1916), in which he outlined nothing less than a new religious system. At least von Ehrenfels seemed to think it was new. It was in fact a redefinition of the idea of God in Neo-Platonic terms and an expression of von Ehrenfels's hope "for a new and even far lovelier variant of Christianity." Compare Eckstein's description of the emergence of unconscious contents according to Plotinus with von Ehrenfels's account of the evolution of Deity: "With the arising of human intellect (and probably of similar processes on other heavenly bodies) consciousness of self awoke in God, and there dawned a phase of immanence in his work."[8] The philosopher also believed in "over-souls," which represented personalities composed of many human souls.

It would be difficult to argue that Freud derived his ideas to any notable extent from his friendship with Eckstein or Ehrenfels. What the connection does show is that Freud's destruction of his papers may have covered up evidence of contact with others working on the periphery of his own field, although with different premises. Friedrich Eckstein's lack of reference to psychoanalysis in his memoirs seems to show that the contribution he made the same year to the *Almanack of Psychoanalysis* was not greatly influenced by Freud's discoveries except in point of terminology. It emphasizes the fact that the school of divine philosophy to which he belonged, when furnished with the concept of the unconscious mind—which (as Lancelot Law Whyte has written) had already been considered in twenty-six aspects by Eduard von Hartmann when Freud was twelve[9]—could lead to conclusions that anticipated some basic theories of psychoanalysis. Such philosophy, of course, had nothing to do with Freud's discovery of his complexes and only a tenuous connection with therapy. But there are a few other interesting coincidences. First, it has been argued that Freud was indebted to Empedocles for his concepts of the life and death instincts; and it is known that Friedrich Eckstein and his "Pythagorean" friends were devotees of Empedocles.[10] Then there is the question of Eckstein's attempt to work out a mathematical basis for the Unconscious. This will assume new significance in the context of Freud's debt to Wilhelm Fliess. Finally, the odd fact should be noted that the house in which Freud was staying in 1895, when he had the idea that underlay his theory of the interpretation of dreams, was Schloss Bellevue at Grinzing, the scene of the Viennese Theosophists' summer colony seven years before.

Freud's first steps away from Vienna and toward psychoanalysis were made when he went to Paris in August 1885 to study under Jean-Martin Charcot at the Salpêtrière. A measure of Freud's success in establishing his creation as an independent science is that it is so frequently forgotten that psychoanalysis emerged from the study of hypnosis. The investigation of the altered states of consciousness induced by the hypnotic trance led to other psychologies which have not fitted the materialist temperament so well as that of Freud.

Charcot (1825-93) represented the 19th-century scientific Establishment's coming to terms with hypnosis. The phenomena that are now defined as "hypnotic" emerged from the faith-healing activities of Mesmer at the turn of the 18th and 19th centuries, and the movement of which Charcot was the final product had been begun by James Braid in England in the 1840s. The object was to remove the "hypnotic" phenomena from the occult complexities in which the Paracelsian Mesmer had entangled them. Charcot exercised himself to produce an explanation of the symptoms he studied in terms of neurophysiology—in other words, with a completely materialist theory, in which a subject easily hypnotized was seen as physically ill and successive stages of hypnotism rigorously classified.

Charcot had arrived at the Salpêtrière in 1862; and it was not until 1884 that his theories were challenged by Hippolyte Bernheim (1840-1919), the president of the Nancy Medical Society. Bernheim attacked Charcot's system of classification. Together with Dr. Ambrose Liébault he proposed a theory that Liébault had proved amply in his medical practice—that the hypnotic state was produced psychologically, by *suggestion,* and that Charcot's belief that hypnosis was connected with illness was a largely accidental result of the concentration on hysterics at the Salpêtrière. A few months before his death Charcot wrote an article on faith healing in which he appeared to concede defeat. He admitted the principle that "hysterics" were easily suggestible.[11]

The reaction of Charcot against the irrational aspects of hypnosis was counterbalanced by the continued borrowing by occultists of the phenomena of hypnotism. The Spiritualist epidemic that had originated in America in 1848 very quickly appropriated the idea of the Mesmeric trance. To the revelations transmitted by "spirits from the next world" was added the whole parcel of dubious medical practice attached to the popular Mesmeric movement. By the last half of the 19th century this could include phrenology (there was also a half-breed specialty known as "phrenomagnetism"), hydrotherapy, and any number of questionable pursuits of a magical or fortune-telling nature. Most of these occupations flourished in America, where itinerant Mesmerists had little trouble in fascinating backwoods communities with slick talk and the title of "professor." An example is the "Electrical Psychology" of John Bovee Dods, who used the human aura in some peculiar fashion to make contact with his patient and believed that all the phrenological organs were duplicated on the spiritual plane. In Europe such systems were less well known, although Richard Harte, the Theosophist who published *The Hebrew Talisman,* can be found as late as 1902 to be of the opinion that "Adam must have been in a magnetic slumber when the Lord performed the very serious operation of the extraction of a rib."[12]

Despite the efforts of Charcot and the Salpêtrière school, it proved impossible to deny the assertions from Bernheim and Liébault at Nancy that hypnotic phenomena were to be explained on psychological grounds. For a respectable doctor who wanted to use the beneficial effects of hypnosis in his practice, this presented grave problems. The capitulation of the Salpêtrière meant the end of the program to incorporate hypnotism into the materialist world picture. Shortly after Charcot's death hypnotism declined altogether as a subject of medical interest in France, and this may be partly attributed to the fact that it was temporarily unsafe to venture further into debatable territory. However, occultists continued to be interested in hypnotism, and they were not all of the calibre of Dr. Dods or Richard Harte. On 7 June 1884, just over a year before Freud came to study with Charcot, Colonel Olcott of the Theosophical Society had called at the Salpêtrière and seen Charcot himself. This meeting took place because one of Charcot's assistants, Dr. Raymond Combret, was a member of the Paris Theosophical Society of the East and the West, presided over by the Duchesse de Pomar.[13]

Thus, in venturing into the field of hypnotism—even in the stronghold of Charcot's materialist interpretation—Freud was knowingly putting himself at risk, and he should not have been surprised at the opposition he received. In October 1886, Freud presented a paper, "On Male Hysteria," to the Vienna Medical Society, and criticism was vociferous. Among the critics was Theodore Meynert, who had a perpetual feud with a certain Dr. Leidesdorf, known as a hypnotizing doctor. Freud worked with Leidesdorf—and Meynert began to refer to Freud as if he were "merely" a hypnotist, "working in this place as a trained practitioner in hypnosis."[14] To make matters worse, in 1889 Freud visited Bernheim at Nancy. He was converted from his allegiance to

Charcot and translated Bernheim's book on *Suggestion*. The same year Freud defended hypnosis against the slanders of its opponents.

> They have not tested the new therapeutic method and employed it impartially and carefully as one would, for instance a newly recommended drug; they have rejected hypnosis *a priori* and now no acquaintance with that procedure's invaluable therapeutic effects hinders them from giving the most biting and unjustified expression to their dislike of it, whatever that may be based on. They immensely exaggerate the dangers of hypnosis, they call it by one bad name after another.[15]

By changing his allegiance from the Salpêtrière to Nancy, Freud had placed himself against the materialist interpretation of hypnosis. He had evidently branded himself in the eyes of his more prejudiced brethren as a man who dealt in quackery and intangibles. His defense of hypnotism is *as hypnotism,* and it is interesting to compare the Theosophist Richard Harte. Some years later Harte published a book called *Hypnotism and the Doctors,* and it was dedicated to demonstrating that "the history of the treatment which hypnotism has received at the hands of the doctors is a long story of ignorance, prejudice, cruelty, stupidity, and conceit on their part."[16] Two men may undoubtedly support the same cause for very different motives, but the sort of cause they support may indicate much. Hypnosis was rejected by a large proportion of the medical establishment—it has never really achieved acceptance. It therefore attracted adepts of pure irrationalism like Richard Harte as well as those like Freud concerned with its therapeutic implications. Not only might Freud be tarred with the same brush as Dr. Dods and his Electrical Psychology, but in the indefiniteness of his own ideas at the time and of ideas about hypnosis generally there may well have been something in the accusations of his opponents. In making fun of Dods, there is the danger of giving such pioneer theorists much less than their historic due. Dr. Dods was invited to deliver nine lectures to the United States Senate; and in the speculations of some other products of the popular Mesmeric movement (like Laroy Sunderland and William Fahnstock), there is much good sense. In the "spiritual science" of P. P. Quimby (the progenitor of Mary Baker Eddy's

Christian Science) may be found an anticipation of Freud's idea of the traumatic experience and also of the cathartic method of cure.[17]

Freud came to use the hypnotic state to avoid the "censor," which prevents the analyst from discovering those repressed experiences which in his system are said to cause neuroses. But eventually he abandoned hypnotism because of the embarrassing discovery that one of the side effects of the hypnotic transference might be to provoke amorous advances from his patients. He substituted placing his hand on the patient's forehead—which might, in fact, induce a light hypnosis—and developed his method of dream interpretation as another means of penetrating the hidden areas of the unconscious. It has been argued that Freud gave up hypnosis because it was not a field in which he could satisfy his "desire for originality."[18] Whatever the truth of the matter, the idea of reaching hidden areas of the mind was implicit in many of the theories of hypnosis before Freud took over the concept and developed his own special means of analysis. The founder of psychoanalysis can also be seen to have searched for congenial theories in the borderland between medicine and occultism during his relationship with Wilhelm Fliess.

Freud met Fliess in 1887, while he was still very much occupied with hypnosis. Wilhelm Fliess (1858-1928) was a nose-and-throat specialist with a large practice in Berlin. He was sent by Joseph Breuer—Freud's teacher and first collaborator—to hear Freud's lectures on neurology. An intimate friendship developed, which lasted until the turn of the century—and the correspondence between Freud and Fliess has provided rich material for the history of psychoanalysis. This includes the draft of a "Project for a Scientific Physiology," which was the earliest attempt by Freud to formulate his ideas and the basis on which he was to build.[19] The Freud-Fliess letters also show that Freud was so completely under the spell of Fliess that he temporarily accepted some of his friend's more eccentric theories and tried to combine them with his own developing system.

Fliess discovered that he was able to cure certain illnesses by administering cocaine to the nasal mucous membrane. He then made a tenuous and unjustified connection between this part of the nose and the genital area, and jumped wildly to the conclusion that all life was governed by periods of 28 and 23 days, which were connected with the menstrual cycle. At the same time he developed the notion that all human beings were bisexual. To take first the magic numbers 28 and 23 and Freud's acceptance of them: in 1896 Fliess sent Freud a draft of his first paper on the theory of periodic cycles. At first Freud voiced some slight criticism. But he was responsible for sending Fliess's paper to the Viennese publishers who issued it the next year. By December 1896, Freud was attempting to use the 28-day period to explain the development of the neuroses he was studying (the wording of this passage has been suppressed by the editor of the correspondence). Gradually the relationship between the two men cooled and Freud saw less importance in the theory of his friend—although in May 1900, he was still able to praise "the beauty of the conception, the originality of the ideas, the simple coherence of the whole."[20]

Wilhelm Fliess used his periodic laws in the most far-reaching way, and his methods of reducing almost any period of time to multiples of his two crucial numbers are, to say the least, suspect. For example, Fliess argued that creativity went in cycles. Thus, Gustav Fechner had discovered a certain formula when he was $18,083 = 23 \cdot 28^2 + 28 + 23$ days old. As the theory developed it became clear that the chief conclusion was a comprehensive determinism, which particularly affected individuals of the same family.

> Following the periodic cycles through generations of the same blood teaches us to interpret the substance of life as a coherent whole whose pulsations flow through all individuals who carry within themselves the inheritance of a generation. The birthday of a great-grandson is already settled with the day of his ancestress's death.

By 1918 Fliess was maintaining that the year—the precise calendar year, for example, 1926—could be used as a significant period over which to compare births and deaths in different families. Three years before his death he waxed poetical over *The Miracle of the Year.*

> Yes, miracle! Or is it not a miracle, if over many years we always see the first flowers on a rose-bush at the same date, or at the most with a discrepancy of one or two days, if we notice the remarkable regularity with which the swallows

arrive on the first or second of May and leave on the first of August?[21]

It is no coincidence that after the publication of his first large work, *The Course of Life,* in 1906, Fliess changed publishers and issued his works under the imprint of the Theosophical and *völkisch* publisher Eugen Diederichs of Jena. The insistence of Fliess on the mystical link of the blood was obviously attractive to *völkisch* thinkers. It is interesting that Gustav Wyneken, a prominent figure in the youth movements, possessed a copy of the book which first placed emphasis on this aspect of Dr. Fliess's theory—*Of Life and Death,* published by Diederichs in 1909.[22] The ideas of Fliess also became the property of occultists, who were attracted both by the obvious connections of the Fliess periods with astrology and the current occult fascination with prophecy engendered by disturbed times. The historical studies of Strömer von Reichenbach are almost identical in method to the laborious calculations of births and deaths published by Fliess. Egon Friedell compared this "similar system of fatalism" to that of the Babylonian numerologists. The theories of Fliess began to appear tangled up in occult bibliographies with Berdyaev, Franz Hartmann, Eliphas Lévi, Papus, Max Kemmerich, Hermann Wirth, Rudolf Steiner, Lanz von Liebenfels and Hans Hörbiger. By the second edition of *The Course of Life* in 1923, its author had tacitly recognized the camp in which he stood:

> Indian antiquity could have drawn up the theory which will be put forward in this work. The necessary assumptions were completely present. Its deduction needs no laboratory and no microscope. It is based on simple observation of nature and its instrument is the human intellect.

Such observation led to the conclusion that human life was completely regulated by the day and the year, the rotation and the orbit of the earth. As early as 1906 Fliess had recognized the inevitability of his being branded a mystic. By 1923 he was complaining bitterly that his theories had been neglected by the scientific Establishment. Perhaps, he wrote, his ideas would soon find a hearing among those who were ready.

> Or else I must say with Kepler: It doesn't worry me whether my work is read now or only later. It's nothing to me to wait

a century for my readers, when God himself waited six thousand years for his discoverer. I will conquer. I have stolen the hidden treasure of the Egyptians. I resign myself to my holy wrath.[23]

There is, of course, nothing inherently unrespectable about a fascination with periodicity or cycles in purely scientific terms. In fact, at the same time as Wilhelm Fliess was elaborating his theories, the Swedish Nobel Prize winner Svante Arrhenius was investigating the effect of the moon on the menstrual cycle, having earlier established lunar influence over thunderstorms.[24] But the extension of the Fliess theory into an all-embracing determinism represents a capitulation to the fashion for cyclic theories so prevalent among the occultists and those in search of reassurance, among whom Fliess's theory fell.[25] A certain similarity of viewpoint was probably there from the start. Fliess's idea that all nature was linked together has been traced to the late Romantic school of *Naturphilosophie* (by which Freud also was greatly influenced). This implied an "organic" vision, a reliance on the idea of a world-body.[26] Goethe was the great traditional exponent of this attitude, and his sources were those of occult tradition. The lecture that persuaded the young Freud to become a doctor was, in fact, nothing less than a reading of Goethe's essay on Nature. That perpetual Goethean, Rudolf Steiner, was tutor to a Viennese family where Joseph Breuer (Freud's teacher and collaborator) was a regular visitor.[27] In 1886, Steiner delivered his first lecture in the Vienna Goethe Union—where (as I have already noted) he met Friedrich Eckstein. There is neither evidence nor need to argue a direct connection. It is merely important to realize that the atmosphere in which Freud, Fliess, Eckstein, and Steiner lived was influenced by similar considerations and that there is a certain connection and even coherence in their outlook.

Another point of contact between the approach of Fliess and that of occult pursuits is his use of numbers. They are manipulated in a way which many of his opponents have denounced as "number mysticism."[28] We have already recorded that Friedrich Eckstein (another friend of Freud from the early days) published in 1918 what he claimed was a mathematical formulation of the unconscious; and we also know that Freud tried to adapt the numerology of Fliess to the progressive development of neurosis. This in itself is significant.

But it becomes even more so when we remember the episode of Eckstein, his mathematician friend Oscar Simony, and their unsatisfactory séances with Henry Slade, the protégé of Baron Hellenbach. Hellenbach himself was a friend of Simony, and in Spiritualist matters was a follower of Carl du Prel. In 1882 Hellenbach had published in Vienna a treatise called *The Magic of Numbers,* in which he argued a periodicity in all human activities and demonstrated to his own satisfaction how the tetragram controlled both his own life and the career of Napoleon. Hellenbach also maintained that there was a periodic law governing human growth. He based his claims on the numerological theories of a Viennese surgeon and occultist, Franz Liharzik, who had published an elaborate exposition of his ideas in 1865. Liharzik's numerology was derived from Athanasius Kircher and Ramon Lull, to say nothing of Pythagoras.[29] Ideas of the significance of *number* itself and of periodicity in human life were very much part of the Occult Revival at the time when Freud was developing psychoanalysis, and they were expounded in Freud's hometown.

In this context the numerology of Fliess begins to take on a new appearance, as do the accusations of his critics. Wilhelm Fliess was a man whose theories were substantially akin to those of the Occult Revival, and in such circles he found his only public. Freud's association with him has always been a matter for amazement in psychoanalytic circles. But only a detailed acquaintance with the background of such theories reveals to what extent Freud's friend was an adept of the Underground of knowledge.

Like other rejected theories, the "Fliess periods" acquired followers and became a cult. One of his supporters wrote in 1918: "The importance of Fliess periodicity research stands nowadays beyond all contradiction. The circle of his disciples and collaborators grows undiminished." Significantly, criticism leveled at Fliess was also used to damage Freud. For example, in 1910 the two—by then estranged—friends were labeled "New Pythagoreans" by a writer in a scientific publication who made short work of Fliess's calculations and strongly criticized his use of the year as a "Great Mystery." This critic thought that just as Freud's psychology made everything depend on sex, so did Fliess's biology. That is, the starting point of the Fliess concept of cyclic determinism was the menstrual cycle, and his theory incorporated the secondary idea of bisexuality. Just as it is significant that the opposition to Freud was based on his stressing the sexual origins of neurosis, it is also important that the interest of both Fliess and Freud coincided in the field of sexual investigation. This may partly account for Freud's otherwise odd statement in a letter to Fliess (New Year's Day, 1896) that they were "both doing the same work," and it emphasizes the fact that the collaboration of the two men was seen by the—admittedly blinkered—Establishment as similar and subversive.[30]

In the interchange of ideas that occurred between Sigmund Freud and Wilhelm Fliess, Fliess's secondary theory of "bisexuality" was also discussed. After some initial doubts, Freud was completely won over. He announced to Fliess in August 1901, that he was about to write a book called *Bisexuality in Man*. Fliess had already become rather disturbed about Freud's jealousy, and it seems fairly certain that the psychoanalyst's known trait of forgetting inconvenient discoveries by other people was responsible for the fracas which followed. A pupil of Freud, Dr. Herrmann Swoboda, learned from his teacher of the "bisexual theory," and he informed a friend named Otto Weininger. On the basis of this plundered idea, Weininger wrote his book *Sex and Character,* which Freud read in manuscript in 1901. The book was published in 1903; and in October of that year Otto Weininger shot himself. When Fliess discovered that his theories had been plagiarized and that the channel of communication had been Freud, a quarrel developed, which led to the breaking off of their friendship altogether in 1904. A polemical battle broke out between the supporters of Fliess and Swoboda during which Freud's name was not unexpectedly dragged in the mud. This did not prevent Swoboda from continuing to publish books based on the Fliess theory—he even carried on a correspondence with Fliess—and eventually this former pupil of Freud issued an immense work on the significance of the periodic recurrence of the number 7 which might have been elaborated straight from Baron Hellenbach.[31]

Otto Weininger (c. 1880-1903) is a tragic figure. He was a Jew who became a Christian on the day he obtained his doctorate in 1902. His religious conversion seems to have been genuine. But it carried a sad corollary, for Weininger was deeply convinced by German *völkisch* ideology, venerated Wagner, and despised his own race. His suicide in 1903 came as the climax to a period of intolerable mental pressure at the end of which he told his friend, Swoboda, that he saw three possibilities open to him: the scaffold, suicide, or the achievement of a mystical quest. His book *Sex and Character* had an enormous circulation particularly among illuminated groups: it combined his tortured anti-Semitism and distaste for women with the prophecy that there would emerge from this "Jewish century" a great founder of a new religion. Weininger went on to elaborate a symbolic theory of the universe, which acknowledged his debt to Plato, adopted the analogy of microcosm and macrocosm, and declared that character could be discovered from astrology. It is clear both from his posthumous works and from *Sex and Character* that Weininger was acquainted with occult and Theosophical groups. There are even indications that he saw himself as the great prophet whose advent he predicted.[32]

Lessons can be learned both from the fact that it was Weininger who adopted the Fliess theory and from its popularity under its new guise. The *Naturphilosophie* that influenced Fliess and the early Freud derived from the Romantic—which is to say very much an occult—world-picture. One of the traditional elements in this world-picture is the idea of polarity.[33] An almost contemporary discussion of the problem is the book of the French magician, Joséphin Péladan, *Traité des Antinomies* (1901). Whereas Fliess had confined the concept to the idea that each human being incorporated masculine and feminine elements, at least one of his disciples extended the idea of polarity throughout all creation.[34] Weininger attempted to express his version of the bipolar theory through some almost meaningless mathematical formulae. The real crux of the matter is not his algebraical window dressing but the significance that he himself attributed to the idea of bisexuality. As soon as he introduced the concept, he compared it to traditional thought: to the hermaphrodite and the suggestion of one of the Gnostics about a "man-woman." In his book Weininger saw "the germs of a world-scheme . . . allied most closely with the conceptions of Plato, Kant, and Christianity."[35] So, once more, the theories of Fliess gravitate to the occultists and mystical philosophers. Yet again someone connected with Freud's progress toward psychoanalysis is seen to have belonged to their number. More correctly, two figures: Weininger, who showed Freud his manuscript; and, to a lesser extent, Swoboda, Freud's pupil.

The following conversation, recorded by Jung, took place in Vienna in 1910.

> I can still recall vividly how Freud said to me, "My dear Jung, promise me never to abandon the sexual theory. That is the most essential thing of all. You see, we must make a dogma of it, an unshakeable bulwark." He said that to me with great emotion, in the tone of a father saying, "And promise me this one thing, my dear son, that you will go to church every Sunday." In some astonishment I asked him, "A bulwark—against what?" To which he replied, "Against the black tide of mud"—and here he hesitated for a moment, then added—"of occultism." . . . I knew that I would never be able to accept such an attitude. What Freud seemed to mean by "occultism" was virtually everything that philosophy and religion, including the rising contemporary science of parapsychology, had learned about the psyche. To me the sexual theory was just as occult, that is to say, just as unproven an hypothesis, as many other speculative views.[36]

The date has some importance in the development of Freud's attitude to the occult. Leaving aside for the moment Jung's analysis of Freud's motives, what might Freud be chiefly concerned about in his use of the term *occult?* We have defined the occult as "rejected knowledge," and to a strict materialist both the Gnostic and Oriental doctrines of the recent revival and more accepted transcendental teachings might be seen as included in the term. But in this context there is no doubt that the chief fear of Sigmund Freud was directed against the area of inquiry known as "psychical research" and was defined in the terms of the London Society for Psychical Research established in 1882 "to investigate that large body of debatable phenomena designated by such terms as mesmeric, psychical, and spiritualistic." This is what Jung later termed "the rising contemporary science of parapsychology." The fact that we have already in a single paragraph three terms for one subject shows the difficulty confronting anyone at all who takes an interest in the field. In Germany, the term *Okkultismus* was used up until the Second World War to describe both members of esoteric groups and parapsychologists (*wissenschaftliche Okkultisten*). The English word *occultism* could have something of the same ambiguity. The phrase *psychical research,* although its meaning is now certain, merely shows the necessary interpenetration of supposedly normal, abnormal, and paranormal aspects of the mind—for what after all, *is* this psyche, which is being investigated? The confusion becomes acute when, for example, *The Brighton Herald* could print a report in 1913 of a talk by Mgr. Robert Hugh Benson on "Psychology" at the Brighton Pavilion—and the reader discovers that the versatile prelate's view of "psychology" was as a term covering the phenomena of the séance room.[37] The word *parapsychology,* which Jung used in his memoirs, is unambiguous. It is derived from the French *metapsychisme,* a coining in which the psychical researcher Charles Richet had been anticipated by that most eclectic of all gurus, Wincenty Lutoslawski.[38]

Freud initially tried to circumscribe the area of his inquiries, and he was naturally cautious about the wagonload of mystics and those in search of faith dragged along the path marked "occultism." At the same time he was dismally conscious that he might at any point along his road have to deal with the supposedly "supernatural"; and on several occasions he did face up to this task. It was difficult to ignore subject matter that presented itself as part of his elected specialty. Frederic Myers, one of the founders of the Society for Psychical Research, had preceded Freud by some years in recognizing the importance of the unconscious mind. His theory of the "subliminal self" was first outlined in the *Proceedings* of the SPR in a paper of 1888. Myers discussed the "Daemon" which was said to have inspired Socrates. He referred to the "messages which are conveyed to the conscious mind from unconscious strata of the personality."[39] This was followed by a long series of papers during the period 1891-92 in which Myers argued that

> that group of facts which the scientific world has now learnt to accept (as the hypnotic trance, automatic writing, alternations of personality and the like), and that group of facts, for which in these *Proceedings* we are still endeavouring to win general scientific acceptance (as telepathy and clairvoyance), ought to be considered in close alliance and correlation.

Referring to the fact that hypnotized subjects showed themselves dislocated from their normal personalities, he wrote: "I conceive it possible that . . . I may assume these various personalities under one single consciousness."[40] The term "subliminal," meaning "beneath the threshold," Myers later defined as "all that takes place . . . outside the ordinary margin of consciousness."[41]

From the point of view of the early Freud, the approach of Myers left much to be desired, particularly as the Englishman insisted on nailing to the masthead of his "subliminal self" a Neo-Platonic metapsychology. But it is important to notice that the two men were attempting in a similar fashion to map the unconscious regions of the mind—and that, therefore, the phenomena which have been more exclusively associated with each were in fact objects of necessary mutual concern. Thus, after Breuer and Freud published the "Preliminary Communication" to the *Studies in Hysteria* in January 1893, Myers gave a full account of the paper at a meeting of the London SPR that April. Thus, Freud accepted membership of the SPR in 1911 and five years later of the American society.[42] The very nature of Freud's concerns and the matrix of psychoanalysis itself meant that the possibly supernatural could by no means be excluded.

There was all the more reason for exercising care to admit for consideration only the *phenomena* that might be classed as occult or "supernatural," and to exclude the *philosophy*.

Myers is an extreme example of the early psychical researcher involved in finding a way to reestablish his lost religious faith. But many of his active colleagues in the SPR shared his approach. It is an attitude that has tended to dominate psychical research and to which the most publicized parapsychologist of the 20th century, Dr. J. B. Rhine, is no exception. Rhine's interest in psychical research grew out of his need "to find a satisfactory philosophy of life, one that could be regarded as scientifically sound and yet could answer some of the urgent questions regarding the nature of man and his place in the natural world." Rhine, at first, had aspirations to the ministry. When he became disillusioned with his Christian faith, he and his wife decided to become professional foresters as "the woods seemed to offer a free and natural life." The turning point came when they heard Conan Doyle lecture on "Spiritualism." Although they remained unconvinced, even the possibility of attaining Doyle's faith was exhilarating. After a period of experiment with mediums, the Rhines came into contact with the vitalist William McDougall, who had arrived in the United States in 1920 and initiated psychical research at Harvard. From this contact sprang the famous card-guessing tests for Extra Sensory Perception carried out by the Rhines at Duke University and over the results of which there is such disagreement. It is remarkable how Rhine's conclusions from his inconclusive experiments in telepathy are almost identical to the equally doubtful theories of Frederic Myers.[43]

This excursion is necessary to show that parapsychology as such has so consistently presented traps to the "scientific" investigator that Freud's mistrust of the supposedly "supernatural" aspects, which his chosen subject made it difficult to avoid, was a perfectly natural condition. If Freud had been forced to defend himself so heatedly over the relatively acceptable question of hypnosis, his circumspection over the ambiguous connotations of "the occult" is understandable. In the German-speaking countries academics and medical men were no more immune to the attractions of occultism than their Anglo-Saxon colleagues. Zöllner had started the fashion with his experiments with Henry Slade. At one of his sittings he had persuaded Gustav Fechner to be present—and as it is known that Freud freely admitted his debt to Fechner, he would undoubtedly have been aware of the Zöllner experiments. Freud would have also known that the psychologist William Wundt had assisted at one of Zöllner's séances, had twice pronounced unfavorably on the phenomena, and that his powerful opinion was shared by his pupils—for example, Hugo Münsterberg (1863-1916), who lectured at Harvard and categorically denied the existence of psychic phenomena. Most influential of all in determining Freud's attitude to the occult was probably the succession of occult scandals with which Europe was as familiar as England and America. For example, in 1900 there occurred the first exposure of the celebrated "flower medium," Anna Rothe, who had obtained a large following even among contributors to *Psychische Studien*.[44] The arguments that caused the greatest reverberation in the later days of psychoanalysis were those which centered around the work of the Munich psychical researcher Schrenck-Notzing.

Albert, Freiherr von Schrenck-Notzing (1862-1929) qualified as a doctor with a thesis on hypnotism. According to one of his friends, he married "the richest heiress of Württemberg" and afterward (in the words of another) "ran a large house but a small practice."[45] He published several works on psychopathology but, after the founding of the Munich Psychological Society in 1892, became associated with Carl du Prel and determined to study Spiritualist phenomena by scientific means. As early as 1887 he had published a survey of telepathic experiments and issued two other books concerned with the phenomena of mediums. His main work of 1914, the *Phenomena of Materialisation,* contains records of sittings with several mediums said to produce "materialized" apparitions, notably one known by the pseudonym "Eva C." Six weeks after this publication Mathilde von Kemnitz published her *Moderne Mediumforschung,* containing records of a séance that she had attended the previous summer with another of Schrenck's mediums. This displayed the amazing credulity of the Freiherr and the complete lack of control exercised during the sitting. Mathilde von Kemnitz had been deputed to search the medium, who immediately claimed she did not understand what was required of her; and those present at the séance were chiefly friends of Schrenck-Notzing. To her pamphlet was attached a letter from Dr. Walter Gulat-Wellenberg, who revealed that "Eva C" (the heroine of Schrenck's book on the phenomena of materialization) was well-known under other names, that she was accompanied everywhere by an obvious confederate, that her vaunted materializations were retouched photographs from the Paris newspaper *Le Miroir,* and that Charles Richet had exposed her activities in Algeria some years before. Schrenck-Notzing issued a weak rejoinder. It took the line that a recently qualified physician could hardly be supposed capable of overturning the giants of modern science like Crookes, Lodge, and—by implication—himself.[46]

From this moment on, Schrenck-Notzing was ranked with the occultists of the most credulous sort. His self-defense became ever more improbable. By 1920 he was still upholding the belief that "Eva C" had produced materialized spirits, and he argued that the two-dimensional appearance of Eva's cut-out photographs was explained by "a general law that a *continuation of the materialization of organic parts, beyond the field of vision of the observers, is non-*

existent." Attacks on Schrenck's later experiments with the Schneider brothers grew more and more vocal, and in the year before his death the Freiherr was suing two of his opponents in the courts. In 1927 Count Carl von Klinckowstroem diagnosed, on the basis of Schrenck's example, what he called "the Occultists' Complex." This "manifests itself in the occultists' becoming used to the miracle of mediumship and getting entangled in its dogmas and absurd hypothesis so that they become completely unreliable for level-headed interpretation and report of the evidence." Around the time of Schrenck's death, there appeared a number of pamphlets protesting at the penetration of rationalist science by the criteria of "faith" and at the damage done to genuine parapsychology by credulous researchers. Schrenck-Notzing's friend and colleague, Albert Moll, a leading authority on hypnosis, deliberately restrained his criticism but characterized the Freiherr as "an example of being led astray through ambition and sensationalism." Klinckowstroem bemoaned the fate of parapsychology. Another doctor warned that the supremacy of the white race was founded on rationalism, and that surrender to the mystical was a portent of doom.[47]

None of this concern on the part of the scientific Establishment would have remained unknown to Freud, particularly as Schrenck-Notzing had contributed some useful studies on sexual pathology and because psychologists, medical men, and authorities on hypnosis were continually involved. As psychoanalysis gradually gained acceptance, the dangers of dealing with "occultism" of any description would have presented themselves ever more forcibly. It is, therefore, significant that Freud altered his attitude as the years advanced *in favor* of considering the supernatural: and even he could not escape the influence of the outburst of irrationalism which followed the First World War. Apart from Jung, at least two of Freud's close psychoanalytical associates were interested in the forbidden areas: Sandor Ferenczi and Wilhelm Stekel.

Six days after he had finished *The Interpretation of Dreams* in 1899, Freud noted a case of a prophetic dream being apparently fulfilled. He explained it as an instance of a dream being manufactured after the event to which it really referred. In March 1908, he described three cases that might seem to have indicated thought transference at a meeting of the Vienna Psychoanalytical Society, but he still excluded the possibility of telepathy. Then he met Jung, was profoundly shaken by some apparently paranormal events, which Jung himself provoked, and (perhaps in response to warnings from other friends) administered to his most brilliant disciple his warning against the "black tide of occultism" in 1910. Yet in the very same year the founder of psychoanalysis began some half-hearted inquiries himself, in the company of Sandor Ferenczi. They visited a Frau Seidler in Berlin, who claimed to be able to read letters blindfolded. She correctly guessed that a letter she was given came from Vienna; but Freud later realized that the place of origin was written on the envelope. Both he and Ferenczi were obviously ignorant of the correct procedure for protecting themselves against fraud. Freud told Ferenczi that Frau Seidler must possess a "physiological gift" for perceiving others' thoughts. "I am afraid you have begun to discover something big, but there will be great difficulties in the way of making use of it," he wrote to Ferenczi. The attitude of caution was maintained the next year when he warned his friend against "undue eagerness" in his "occult studies."[48]

This warning was probably necessary. The first paper ever written by Ferenczi dealt with the occult (1899), and Ernest Jones records that much correspondence between Freud and Ferenczi—who until 1932 was as close to Freud as anyone—was on occult topics.[49] After his visit with Freud to Frau Seidler, Ferenczi made further tests with her and also with a Hungarian Theosophical medium called Frau Jelinek. These unsatisfactory experiments were replaced by a collaboration between Ferenczi and a homosexual patient who, the analyst claimed, could approximately guess his thoughts. Prophesying a revolution in analytical technique, Ferenczi wrote to Freud that he himself was a mind reader, and about 1912 tried to convince Ernest Jones that they were in mental contact. His next enthusiasm was the talking horse of Elberfeld called "Clever Hans." But he was deterred from investigating the animal's supposed telepathic abilities by discovering the vast body of literature on psychical research. In November 1913, he introduced a "Professor" Alexander Roth into the Vienna Psychoanalytical Society but failed to persuade Freud to give this clairvoyant a testimonial. After the war Ferenczi's occult studies continued. In 1925 he took part in apparently convincing experiments in thought transference with Freud and his daughter Anna. Freud continued to allow the more cautious members of the psychoanalytical movement to influence him against letting Ferenczi publish his results. The resulting conflict was a major cause of the breach between the two men. The Hungarian ended by believing he was being successfully psychoanalyzed via telepathic messages sent from America by a former patient.[50]

Despite Freud's initial caution, there is no doubt that Ferenczi's influence was a leading factor in changing his attitude to the "occult." It would be to credit Freud with powers more than human to suppose that he could have resisted altogether the irrationalist influences which pressed so hard around him. Postwar Vienna was as full of anxiety as anywhere else in the defeated countries; indeed even confirmed mystics could be scathing at the expense of popular occultism. Franz Blei wrote in his autobiography in 1931: "In Vienna the 'occult phenomena' deserved well of a spectacular number of officers, which made the 147-year-old Dr. Eckstein call the whole complex 'sub-lieutenant's metaphysics.' As everyone in Vienna knows, Dr. Eckstein also knew the Count de St Germain. There are some who say that he himself *was* the Count."[51] Despite such warnings before his eyes Freud moved decidedly from a position of restraining Ferenczi to a position where he himself had to be restrained.

In the summer of 1921 Freud was invited to act as coeditor to no less than three different periodicals devoted to psychical research. To one of the invitations—from Hereward Carrington of New York—he replied that "If I had my life to live over again I should devote my life to psychical research rather than psycho-analysis." That September he delivered a paper on "Psycho-analysis and Telepathy" to a small circle of his closest associates in the Harz Mountains; and he evidently thought the paper important enough to be read again—although he let himself be persuaded not to carry out this plan.[52] It is in fact a deliberate statement of his position on the burgeoning occult revival.

Freud told his audience of the invitations he had received from psychical researchers, recorded various instances in which prophecies had *not* come true, and discussed the "strong resistance" he felt to talking about occultism at all.

> It no longer seems possible to keep away from the study of what are known as "occult" phenomena.... The impetus

towards such an investigation seems irresistibly strong.... It is a part expression of the loss of value by which everything has been affected since the world catastrophe of the Great War, a part of the tentative approach to the great revolution towards which we are heading and of whose extent we can form no estimate; but no doubt it is also an attempt at compensation.

Freud saw very clearly the similarities between the occult approach and that of psychoanalysis.

> It does not follow as a matter of course that an intensified interest in occultism must involve a danger to psycho-analysis. We should, on the contrary, be prepared to find reciprocal sympathy between them. They have both experienced the same contemptuous and arrogant treatment by official science. To this day, psycho-analysis is regarded as savoring of mysticism, and its unconscious is looked on as one of those things between heaven and earth which philosophy refuses to dream of. The numerous suggestions made to us by occultists that we should cooperate with them show that they would like to treat us as half belonging to them and that they count on our support against the pressure of exact authority. Nor, on the other hand, has psycho-analysis any interest in going out of its way to defend that authority, for it itself stands in opposition to everything that is conventionally restricted, well-established and generally accepted. Not for the first time would it be offering its help to the obscure but indestructible surmises of the common people against the obscurantism of educated opinion. Alliance and cooperation between analysts and occultists might thus appear both plausible and promising.[53]

But on closer inspection Freud saw pronounced difficulties in the way of an alliance. The occultist was a believer who was searching for reasons to support his faith, while the analyst was essentially a child of exact science. "Analysts are at bottom incorrigible mechanists and materialists, even though they seek to avoid robbing the mind and spirit of their still unrecognized characteristics." The analyst could not go about deliberately looking for occult phenomena, because this itself would impair his impartiality. However, "if occult phenomena force themselves upon him" he would not evade them. The analyst must discipline himself to attend to his proper subject. "Precisely because it relates to the mysterious unconscious" psychoanalysis itself could not hope to escape the catastrophic consequences of a collapse in intellectual values resulting from a triumph of irrationalism over rational science. Freud gave three reasons for concealing his remarks from a wider audience: a dislike of swimming with the tide, the fear of "distracting attention from psychoanalysis," and the fact—telling in itself—that he was being perfectly frank.[54]

The title of Freud's statement on occultism, "Psycho-analysis and Telepathy," was to some extent a bow in the direction of his former colleague, Wilhelm Stekel. Stekel's *The Telepathic Dream,* first published in 1920, either then or in a later edition appeared in a series called "The Occult World," which included discussions of the astral plane, the Odic force, Yoga, and the Cabala, besides works by Schrenck-Notzing and Arthur Grobe-Wuchitsky (this last an adept of occult numerology). Stekel had broken with Freud in 1912. But the coincidence of their mutual interest in telepathic dreams around 1920-21 indicates that there were strong pressures forcing analysts toward the paranormal. Stekel became interested in telepathic dreams after he himself had undergone a hallucination. He had been lying in bed very ill when a voice suddenly spoke to him: "In two weeks you will die! Use the time well!"[55] The prediction was not fulfilled, but the incident aroused Stekel's interest in psychical research. It turned him from a position of pure materialism to a wholehearted acceptance of telepathy. In his discussion of the cases he had collected, Stekel made great use of Myers, Gurney, and Podmore's *Phantasms of the Living,* and he contrived to explain the existence of telepathy in dreams through the agency of the "N-Rays," which had recently been "discovered" by Professor Blondlot at Nancy.* He thought that every human being gave off rays, which transmitted emotions like love or hate, and he imagined that by this occult commonplace he could also explain hypnotism. He attacked his former master openly:

> The telepathic dream contradicts Freud's theory. It is

---

*Blondlot announced his discovery in all good faith, but it was soon proved that if his rays existed, they could be seen only by his own eyes.

never a wish-fulfillment. So orthodox psychoanalysis does not want to recognize the telepathic dream.

Because of this, Freud and his immediate circle doubt the existence of the telepathic dream. I cannot understand this doubt and am forced to trace it back to a prejudice against all occult questions. . . . Anyone who today does not believe in the telepathic dream makes himself a laughing-stock.[56]

Freud struck back in 1922. He argued that even if Stekel's thesis had been adequately proved, it would not affect his theory that a dream was a wish fulfillment. Even supposedly telepathic dreams must be subject to analysis like any other. Analysis and occultism could not be mixed, and there were "powerful and mysterious instincts" fighting on the side of occultism. Yet his own attitude gave evidence of hesitation. Freud denied belief in "telepathy in the occult sense," but he referred to "the incontestible fact that sleep creates favorable conditions for telepathy."[57] Three years after this reply to the renegade Stekel, Freud, Anna Freud, and Ferenczi carried out their own experiments in thought transference and, at the same time, Freud sent out a circular in which he declared how impressed he was with certain telepathic experiments published in the SPR *Proceedings*. On 15 March 1925, he wrote that "the matter is becoming urgent for us." This naturally alarmed these analysts who preserved the attitude of the earlier Freud and were concerned for the status of the new science. Ernest Jones dispatched a counter-manifesto warning against the dangers in this change of approach. In correspondence with Jones, Freud admitted his complete "conversion" but advised him to say that this matter was Freud's own private affair.[58] The conversion of the founder of psychoanalysis was by no means sudden—for as early as his 1921 pronouncement on matters occult, Freud had encouraged his listeners to collect instances of dreams that, when analyzed, seemed to show a possible telepathic content.[59]

Freud's final stance on the paranormal, as far as it is known, is contained in an essay of 1933. He maintained a belief in telepathy, while qualifying some of his earlier statements; and he came to see psychoanalysis as paving the way for an explanation of the phenomenon on purely physical grounds. He thought that telepathy might be the vestigial remnant of an earlier method of communication, which had been replaced by speech.[60] As regards his ideas on how his "conversion" affected his own system, he had, in the full flush of his enthusiasm in 1925, written a note on "The Occult Significance of Dreams" for inclusion in his *Interpretation of Dreams,* describing his own methods of experiment. Freud hinted at a complex means of attributing telepathy after first having analyzed the associations of the person to whom the thought was supposed to have been transmitted.[61] The possibilities of falsely attributing telepathic effects scarcely bear thinking about.

In 1926, the year after Freud issued his circular on the importance of telepathy, his journal *Imago* printed no less than four articles concerned with possibly occult phenomena. Obviously, the directions of the Master's interest greatly affected the disciples, although all were careful to achieve a correct position with regard to analytical dogma, and an editorial note stated that psychoanalysis pronounced neither for nor against the reality of such phenomena.[62] The most common Freudian attitude to the occult was to analyze it "according to the canons of the Master." But the nature of these canons and the man himself have so far been left out of this discussion. Without entering on a superfluous explanation of Freudian tenets, some attention must be paid to the means by which Freud sought to penetrate the depths of the Unconscious.

The essential elements of Freudianism include the assertion that there is an unconscious, that neuroses are sexually determined, that dreams are wish-fulfillments and can be symbolically interpreted, and that a cure for neurosis may be brought about by removing the mental block protecting a traumatic experience. We have seen that the possibly "occult" in the form of the revival of occult philosophy, the opting for rejected knowledge of a kindred nature, and a fascination with parapsychology had been present while Freud was developing psychoanalysis, and that a significant number of his associates shared such preoccupations. What of the system that emerged?

The unconscious has to be reached when the censor is asleep. Troublesome experiences and facts that the analyst could interpret were first obtained through light hypnosis, later merely by establishing a position in which the transference could be affected, and also by the interpretation of dreams. Freud's system does not use hypnosis to effect a cure, merely to obtain information. This is the characteristic that distinguishes psychoanalysis from all other systems of "mental healing" that derive from the use of hypnosis. Yet, in the premise that the healing must be done in the unconscious, Freudianism was not unique.

For example, in 1893, the year in which Freud and Breuer published their "Preliminary Communication" on hysteria, Thomson Jay Hudson issued his *Law of Psychic Phenomena* in London and Chicago. Hudson (1834-1903) had been a barrister and a journalist; at the time his book was published, he was chief examiner in the United States Patent Office. *The Law of Psychic Phenomena* sold over 100,000 copies. Its author stated his object as being "to assist in bringing Psychology within the domain of the exact sciences" and was concerned above all with paranormal phenomena, dreams, and hypnotism. Much of the book, however, was devoted to elaborating Hudson's theory that man "has two minds": an "objective mind," which is the directing force, and a "subjective mind," which is "constantly amenable to control by suggestion" and "incapable of inductive reasoning." Hudson considered telepathy a proven fact, and he proposed a system of mental healing by telepathy—"the communion of subjective minds"—during sleep, when the directing mind was in abeyance. It is easy to see that Hudson's "subjective mind" is, in some aspects, equivalent to the Freudian unconscious, and also that the proposed method of healing corresponds to Freud's idea of evading the censor, even anticipating the idea that the barriers preventing access to the unconscious are lowered during sleep. But Hudson wrapped his theories up in the paraphernalia of the Occult Revival, and he incurred the hostility of scientists by the determination to make this—otherwise remarkable—theory serve as a bulwark for religion. Freud's contribution is, on the face of it, entirely secular, and his methods sometimes worked. But if, in relation to Freud, Hudson's idea of healing by telepathy seems fatuous, it should be remembered that, in 1912, Ferenczi was contemplating the same principle.

Freud's followers place great stress on his work on the interpretation of dreams. Dreams have been traditionally the preserve of priests and soothsayers, and to such associations is added the fact that, from the point of view of the patient, there is no reason to suppose a connection between the reported memories of a night's surrealism and the problems with which the patient consults an analyst. There are two questions to be distinguished here: the first about the *method* of dream interpretation, the second about the status of the analyst himself. As to the method, the inventor admitted "My presumption that dreams can be interpreted at once puts me in opposition to the ruling theory of dreams and in fact to every theory of dreams with [a] single exception...."[63]

"One day, I discovered to my great astonishment that the view of dreams which came nearest to the truth was not the medical, but the popular one, half involved though it was in superstition."[64] As in his estimate of the relationship of psychoanalysis and the occult, Freud had no illusions as to where he stood—against the conventional materialists and in danger of being branded a "witch doctor." His interpretation of dream symbols was as traditional as his insistence that dreams could be interpreted at all. Two French critics once observed:

> Dreams of snakes, trees, flowers, gardens, teeth, eyelids, the navel, columns, caves, boxes, torches, and lamps had in the Renaissance the same meaning as the symbolism of Freud. Like him, the ancient authors had decided that the same dream was open to two different and opposing interpretations and possessed this idea of contradiction which is no discovery of modern psychology. Perhaps they came at it by examining the subjective content of a dream which is so different for the same depiction.[65]

To some extent, the analyst, as the interpreter of dreams, embodies the powers of the soothsayers who went before him. Again, Freud recognized this in his reflections on dreams and the occult. "Since dreams themselves have always been mysterious things, they have been brought into intimate connection with the other unknown mysteries."[66] The comparison between psychoanalysts and witch doctors has been made both by analysts themselves and by respected anthropologist (among others, Lévi-Strauss).[67] Curiously enough, it is usually made the excuse for attacking Freud rather than for taking the witch doctor more seriously. In terms of function and in terms of cure, it is easy to discover parallels between the operation of analyst, priest, and magician. Freud himself wanted to establish psychoanalysis independently of both science and religion. In November

1928, he wrote to the Zurich pastor, Oskar Pfister, about his brainchild. "I should like to hand it over to a profession which does not yet exist, a profession of *lay* curers of souls who need not be doctors and should not be priests."[68] Despite his concern to gain the acceptance of the scientific Establishment, Freud did not wish analysis to become part of that Establishment, and his own antireligious position did not apparently preclude him from an implicit acknowledgment of affinities between analyst and priest.

The idea of the psychoanalytic cure was based on the notion of removing repressions, a theory in which Freud found he had been anticipated by Schopenhauer. Freud writes that the psychoanalyst attempts *"to restore an earlier state of things."* To define this Freud adapts a Platonic myth. This refers to the search of all living beings for their natural complement. For Freud this became the sexual search, and the desired integrity was to be attained through the satisfaction of the libido.[69] This traditional theory—without the sexual interpretation—would have been very familiar to the contemporary mystics influenced by the Occult Revival, the Platonic tradition, and various ideas of polarity. It is easy to show that the idea was in fact applied to medicine by figures of the Occult Revival. In 1893—the year of Hudson's *Law of Psychic Phenomena* and of Breuer and Freud's "Preliminary Communication"—the Theosophist Franz Hartmann (a friend of Eckstein, who had settled in Austria) published in London a work on *Occult Science and Medicine,* largely based on Paracelsian precepts. His definition of disease shows plainly the idea of restoring the lost equilibrium. *"Disease is the disharmony which follows the disobedience to the law; the restoration consists in restoring the harmony by a return to obedience to the law of order which governs the whole."*[70] That Freud was acquainted with what he called "obscure and ancient medical ideas" we know from a letter to Fliess,[71] and it is more than likely that he knew of Paracelsian medicine.

A pattern begins to emerge of psychoanalysis embodying ideas that the Occult Revival would have quite understood—but with a considerable difference from the occult originals. In psychoanalytic theory and practice, ideas are encountered which are *secularized* versions of ideas that found their traditional expression in the language of contemporary occultism. This is not to say that such was Freud's intention. But enough has been said about his attitude to the occult to show that contact existed, and indeed that it could not be avoided. The theories were available, and either subconsciously or semiconsciously influenced Freud's interpretation of the Unconscious, a system which he had to take great care not to have condemned out of hand. (An analogy could be made with the process of chemistry developing from alchemy, but not an analogy which saw only virtue in the exact science, neglecting alchemical symbolism.) It is well known that Freud considered religions as examples of "delusional transformation of reality,"[72] and the hypothesis can therefore be advanced: that Freud's psychoanalysis incorporates elements of traditional thought, which reached him by way of the Occult Revival, but with the religious top-dressing shorn off and applied to the practical problem of curing neurosis—although Freud could not altogether exclude the traditional associations of the "cure of souls."

In writing the history of occult and mystical groups in Western Europe it is always wise to see what the state of Jewish mysticism is at any given time. Jewish mystical tradition has provided a rich source of inspiration for non-Jewish mystics, and it has remained well insulated from the more obvious currents of nonrationalist thought. It has recently been argued at length that Freud's system represents the secularizing of certain trains of thought embodied in the Cabala: that Freud's reversed vision was to some extent influenced by the interior traditions of his Cabalistic inheritance.[73] This cannot be regarded as proven, but there may well be some truth in the theory. If so, the conclusion would be that "what was happening" in Jewish mysticism was to some extent its secularization—in other words, Freud himself. It has been suggested that a mediator may well have been Eduard von Hartmann, whose *Philosophy of the Unconscious* owes a considerable debt to mystical ideas and who was himself an expert on Hasidism.[74] Another authority is concerned to demonstrate the affinities of Freud, the Cabala, and Leibniz—the philosopher to whom Friedrich Eckstein attributed the idea of the importance of the unconscious during illness.[75] The indications are consistent, but final proof is lacking. If we are to accept the hypothesis of Freud's coherence with an occult revival on the one hand and his parallel native tradition on the other, it will largely depend on how we choose to regard both the man and his theories of sexuality.

It is obvious that, in the broadest sense, sexual upheaval was part of that crisis of consciousness which was the chief cause of the Occult Revival. Changing patterns of life and society also affected family life and sexual mores. Certainty in sexual relationships was as irreparably damaged as certainty in divine ordering; the uncertainties were twins and followed roughly the same development in time. A rough indication of changing sexual attitudes can be found in the progress of pornography. By 1660, writes one authority,

> almost all the themes of later pornography are present; within a completely amoral attitude, in which all perversions are welcome if they gratify the senses . . . these take place within a tightly knit family circle, with the shocking suggestion that all the conventional relationships of society are merely a façade for personal gratification.[76]

By the last half of the 19th century "matters came to a head." A pornography industry had grown up, in which the view taken of sexuality was the "mirror image" of that held by the Establishment.[77] This flourishing pornographic underworld has little connection with the Underground of Progressive opinion. But the alteration in sexual values reflected in one way by the pornographers was naturally echoed in another by those concerned to overthrow the Established order. Many of the Utopian colonies were based on free love, and it became an article of belief among the artists and camp followers of Bohemia. It was noticed by sexologists that "in times of upheaval," like the French and Russian Revolutions, the abolition of sexual restraint was an inevitable consequence.[78]

Thus, at the time when Freud's studies of hysteria began to convince him that there was a sexual basis for the neuroses, the topic of sexual freedom was a common one in Progressive circles, the possibilities of a new sexual ordering were quite apparent—and therefore the agonies over "the sexual question" increased. The topic was ready to hand as a stick with which to beat the Establishment. While in Russia Vasily Rozanov delighted to shock his hearers with his religion of cosmic semen, in Vienna Freud created opposition by insisting on his own theories of sex. Jung's analysis of why Freud demanded that he make a "dogma" of the sexual theory suggests that for Freud the idea of the "libido" was a "hidden god," what Jung called a *"numinosum"*—a holy or sacred power—but that Freud could nonetheless "regard the new numinous principle as scientifically irreproachable and free from all religious taint."[79] What little is known about the apparent link between certain aspects of sex and religion seems not to rule out this possibility. Ivan Bloch has documented the correspondence throughout history of "secret arts, voluptuousness and unnatural vice"— and there may well be a common denominator in the religious and the sexual dynamics. Francis King has shown that sexual theories of magic played a part in the 19th-century Occult Revival,[80] and interests in sexuality and the supernatural do frequently go hand in hand.

There exists at least one example of compatibility between Freudianism and the sexual side of the Occult Revival. In a review in *Imago* in 1913, the Freud group's expert on occult matters, Herbert Silberer, discussed Hargrave Jennings's *The Rosicrucians,* which had been published in German translation the year before. Jennings was obsessed with phallic symbolism. Steeples, pyramids, standing stones—all represented the phallus, the "reason for religion." As might be expected, this interested Silberer, who recommended the book as a good read, although not as a work of scholarship or an account of the Rosicrucians—indeed it is neither. But the theme was interesting "for psycho-analytic research," and, although the book bore no relation to psychoanalysis at all, Silberer admitted that "a superficial observer "might think *The Rosicrucians* was a psycho-analytic treatment of the theme.[81] It would be naive to connect Jennings's lunacies directly with Freud. But the fact that an analyst himself could make the comparison shows that the "Phallic theory"—which antedated Freud's sexual theory by ten years and was part of the lunatic fringe of occultism—could be thought to have dangerous similarities.

Freud himself had once constructed a phallic religion of which he wrote to his friend Dr. Wilhelm Fliess:

> I am toying with the idea that in the perversions, of which hysteria is the negative, we may have the remains of a primitive sexual cult, which in the Semitic East may once have been a religion (Moloch, Astarte).

I am beginning to dream of an extremely primitive devil religion the rites of which continue to be performed secretly, and now I understand the stern therapy of the witches' judges. The links are abundant.[82]

Just as Hargrave Jennings went chasing round the countryside pursuing phallic symbols in the architecture and maintaining that the phallic theory was "the necessary mystic groundwork of all religion," so Freud promenaded the mythical landscape and halted to examine the witches. He decided that the stories of the witches were similar to those told by his patients, as was the symbolism. Thus, the witches' broomstick is "the great Lord Penis." The "stern therapy," presumably burning alive, of the witches' judges seems somewhat excessive for a mere neurosis. It is difficult to understand exactly what connection the "devil religion" bore in his mind to the sexual imagery of the witches—it is certainly not called for by his interpretation of the witch confessions. Freud's dream of his "extremely primitive devil religion" is little better than Hargrave Jennings's vision of the Rosicrucians. His speculations on the witches preoccupied him to the extent that he ordered a copy of the *Malleus Malleficarum,* and he troubled his mind with problems which have perplexed other "discoverers" of a witch religion like Margaret Murray—"If I only knew why the devil's semen in witches' confessions is always described as 'cold.' "[83] In the event, Freud's interest in the Devil culminated in a perfect example of "Orthodox Freudianism" published in 1923, in which he analyzed a 17th-century Satanic pact as a case of "demonological neurosis."[84] This brilliant intellectual construction is a far cry from his earlier speculations. But the seemingly needless presence of the prototypically "occult" idea of a secret religion in Freud's early formulations is suggestive evidence of the sort of theories from which his ideas evolved. The 1923 paper represents the witch speculation in a secularized form.

Because of information deliberately destroyed or withheld, it is impossible to be certain of this argument; but within its context a number of Freud's personality traits assume significance. His cult of Rome, whatever the reasons in his own case, was shared by contemporaries like Alfred Schuler and Lanz von Liebenfels; his collection of Egyptian idols may signify more than antiquarianism; according to Ernest Jones his interest in mystical numbers predated his friendship with Fliess, and one leading source of occult numerology is the Cabalistic tradition of *Gematria*. In 1907 Freud was invited to contribute to a symposium on "ten good books." He included among the "most important" a work of Agrippa's pupil, Johann Wier, on witchcraft, and another on the list was Merezhkovsky's *Forerunner*. To his disciple Max Eitingon, he wrote in November 1922 that he was "perplexed to distraction by the Bacon-Shakespeare controversy and by occultism."[85] This association of the Baconian red herring with Freud's current fascination for telepathy is once more *exactly* the sort of combination of interests that is found in the Underground of rejected knowledge. The man who started the whole Bacon–Shakespeare quarrel, Ignatius Donnelly, was also the first popularizer of the Atlantis legend in the 19th century. Although Freud's own allegiance was given to the Earl of Oxford and to a somewhat saner argument,[86] the fact that he could be "perplexed to distraction" by the problem is extraordinarily revealing. The view of Freud as a secularizer of rejected but emergent traditions also finds some sanction in his organization of "the Committee" of his closest adherents who functioned as the watchdogs of orthodoxy. They formed a "secret society" of seven and wore gold rings in which they mounted Greek intaglios given them personally by Freud.[87]

The Committee was formed to protect psychoanalysis from the speculations of individuals who dared to transgress the party line. Its immediate cause was the heretical behavior of C. G. Jung. If Freud did secularize occult ideas, Jung's defection represents merely a reversion to the originals: he can be seen as the culminating point in the whole of the occult revival.

Carl Gustav Jung was the son of a Swiss country pastor, and the differences between himself and Freud cannot better be expressed than in their origins. The security of Jung's early religious upbringing collapsed; and he began to seek a substitute while studying medicine at the University of Basel. Like Freud he entered medicine as a compromise, as he had nourished both scientific and philosophical interests. At the end of 1895—his second term in the university—he came across a book on Spiritualism in the library of a friend's father. Determined to discover the truth of such matters, Jung embarked on a comprehensive course of occult reading. "Names like Zöllner and Crookes impressed themselves on me, and I read virtually the whole of the literature available to me at the time." Besides German idealists and mystics he devoured seven volumes of Swedenborg. Some three years later, his thoughts were turned once more to the paranormal when two apparently meaningless explosions took place in his home. One split a solid wooden tabletop and another shattered the blade of a carving knife. A few weeks later Jung heard of some relations who had formed a circle for table turning around a fifteen-year-old girl medium. For two years Jung attended the weekly séances, and the material he gathered became his doctoral thesis.[88]

Meanwhile, he discovered psychiatry by way of Krafft-Ebbing, and by 1905 he had progressed from the post of assistant at the Burghölzli Mental Hospital in Zürich to senior physician at the Psychiatric Clinic. His superior at the Burghölzli was Eugen Bleuler, who was interested in hypnosis, and for a time Jung was in charge of the hypnotism clinic. Like Freud, Jung abandoned hypnotism, in his case because of the uncertain factors involved and his distaste for "magical" methods of cure. Soon after he had been appointed to head the Psychiatric Clinic, he became a determined supporter of Freud's (at that time) unpopular views, and from 1907 to 1913 both he and Bleuler formed part of the entourage of the eminence in Vienna.[89] The breach between Freud and Jung has often been discussed. The chief cause was the conflict between Freud's insistence on the sexual theory and Jung's philosophical leanings in other directions. As early as 1908 Karl Abraham is supposed to have warned Freud about "the tendency to occultism, astrology and mysticism in "Zürich,"[90] and in retrospect one of the most interesting aspects of the relationship between Jung and Freud is why it occurred at all.

Jung, in fact, started his investigations into the human mind where Freud was to finish. The experiments with the girl medium "Miss S. W." not only provided Jung with his first insights into the formation of subsidiary personalities but encouraged his reading in the *philosophical* aspects of occultism. Jung was not interested in what he considered "the obvious autonomy" of the spirit rapping that surrounded the medium, but rather in the content of her communications. These were broadly divided up into two categories: (1) what Jung called the "Romances," which involved tales of reincarnation in which the medium had once been the Seeress of Prevorst and also mistress of Goethe; and (2) the elaboration of a complex cosmology of a Gnostic type. The Romances are very like the "clairvoyant investigations" of the Theosophical Bishop Leadbeater and the similar productions of Hélène Smith—which Jung discovered only later.[91] The mystical system devised by Miss S. W. involved a Prime Force manifesting through matter and producing both good and evil agencies. Jung derived this structure from hearsay, Kant, and a fascination with the Seeress of Prevorst. "Naturally I worked through the occult literature so far as it pertained to this subject, and discovered a wealth of parallels with our gnostic system, dating from different centuries, but most of them scattered about in all kinds of works, most of them quite inaccessible to the patient."[92] By the time that Jung caught the medium cheating and broke off the séances, he had acquired not only an insight into the phenomena of different personalities in trance but a thorough grounding in the philosophical bases of contemporary occultism.

Throughout his life, Jung himself was to be subject to paranormal experiences; and these naturally played a great part in orienting his system. From the visions which punctuated his childhood, through the episode of the exploding table, to the dreams and mystical experiences of Jung's later life, the supernatural was never far away.[93] The most spectacular incident occurred in the presence of Freud himself. On a visit to Vienna in 1909, Jung asked Freud for his opinion on parapsychology, and the older man gave vent to a thorough condemnation of the whole approach "in terms of so shallow a positivism that I had difficulty in checking the sharp retort on the tip of my tongue." Jung began to feel as if his diaphragm "were made of iron and were becoming red-hot." And at that moment a loud explosion went off in the bookcase beside the two men. Jung told Freud that this was "an example of a so-called catalytic exteriorisation phenomenon." In answer to Freud's angry denial, he predicted a second explosion, which duly occurred. "Freud only stared aghast at me."[94] Later Freud wrote to Jung explaining the incident away; but by the summer of 1911 he had so far been influenced by Ferenczi's occult enthusiasms as to tell Jung that when it came to "the perilous step of publication" he would like them to act jointly.[95] At exactly the same time Jung told Freud that he could not accept the exclusively sexual theory. He published a paper on "Symbols of the Libido," which led to a complete break with the founder of psychoanalysis in 1913. Whatever the personal motives in this conflict,[96] there is no neglecting the ostensible cause. The facts were that the intellectual traditions to which Jung and Freud belonged were completely alien to each other—it is neither denigratory nor generalizing to call Freud a "classical" and Jung a "romantic" figure[97]—and to assert that what Jung took from Freud was in essence a *method* of interpreting the unconscious while the interpretations themselves came from his occult sources.

The break with Freud precipitated Jung into a period of what he himself called *Sturm und Drang,* during which he practiced as a psychiatrist without producing much in the way of theory. In 1917 came the *Psychology of the Unconscious,* which he described as "an intuitive leap in the dark" containing "no end of inadequate formulations and unfinished thoughts"[98]; and the crucial work of this period is not strictly psychological at all. Jung has described how he let himself down into his own unconscious and carried out an extraordinary journey of exploration among the contents. Finally, in 1916 there came a period when the Jung household seemed to be oppressed by "ghostly entities." Jung's son had an anxiety dream, and his daughters were haunted. Then occurred another of the paranormal experiences with which Jung's life was filled.

> Around five o'clock in the afternoon on Sunday the front-door bell began ringing frantically. It was a bright summer day; the two maids were in the kitchen, from which the open square outside the front door could be seen. Everyone immediately looked to see who was there, but there was no one in sight. I was sitting near the door bell, and not only heard it but saw it moving. We all simply stared at one another. The atmosphere was thick, believe me! Then I knew that something had to happen. The whole house was filled as if there were a crowd present, crammed full of spirits. They were packed deep right up to the door and the air was so thick it was scarcely possible to breathe. As for myself, I was all a-quiver with the questions: "For God's sake, what in the world is this?" Then they cried out in chorus, "We have come back from Jerusalem where we found not what we sought."[99]

"The dead came back from Jerusalem, where they found not what they sought. They prayed me let them in and besought my word, and thus I began my teaching." Jung's strange book *VII Sermones ad Mortuos* begins with the words of the spirits to him, and appears to indicate that he had accepted the role of occult teacher rather than analyst of a more conventional pattern. In three evenings Jung wrote the book in an apparently semiautomatic fashion. Its subtitle describes equally its contents and the rest of Jung's work: "The Seven Sermons to the dead, written by Basilides in Alexandria, the City where the East touches the West." Basilides was a Gnostic writer; Alexandria, the city of Neo-Platonism and alchemy; and the synthesis of Oriental and Western traditions was to occupy much of Jung's time. Most of the elements of Jung's thought are contained in the *Seven Sermons,* couched in the language of a religious revelation. The book is based on neo-Gnostic premises and is almost impossible to summarize. Jung begins with the Pleroma, in which "there is nothing and everything" and about which "it is quite fruitless to think." *We* are distinguished from this "ground of being"—the phrase is of course not Jung's—and this distinctiveness is man's essential attribute. He must at all costs *distinguish* himself, following the "principle of individuation," or run the risk of falling back into the Pleroma and losing all individual being. Man is the mediator between the world of gods and "the inner world." He must free himself from the bondage of "Abraxas," the name—originally the supreme principle of Basilides and other Gnostics—used to designate the "illusory reality" of "force, duration, change." Even a slight acquaintance with Gnostic or Oriental thought is enough to see that such systems contributed much to Jung's own, although Jung introduced significant changes, notably the idea of *individuation* as the necessary way of "spiritual progress." Both in the context of Jung's break with Freud and in the wider sense of the contemporary emergence of occult thought, the words of Jung-Basilides betray an awareness of his positions: "For redemption's sake I teach you the rejected truth, for the sake of which I was rejected."[100]

The rings that Freud's Committee wore contained classical Greek intaglios given them by Freud. Jung wore an Egyptian "Gnostic" ring, whose symbols he had changed so as to Christianize them.[101] He certainly knew contemporary cults that were explicitly Gnostic, and he considered the Occult Revival to be comparable to "the flowering of Gnostic thought in the first and second centuries after Christ." "There is even a Gnostic church in France today, and I know of two schools which openly confess themselves Gnostic." Jung's statement that he studied the Gnostics "between 1918 and 1926" is misleading in that we have already seen that he had made quite an extensive search through Gnostic literature while observing his spirit medium. By the time he wrote the *Seven Sermons* he had obviously already been strongly influenced by Gnostic theology. Reference to German Gnostic schools recalls that General Ludendorff was shocked to find that (*c*. 1930) "Abraxas" armlets were sold by a Frau von Platen in Berlin. Jung's mention of *l'Eglise Gnostique de France* is interesting in that Jules Doinel's Universal Gnostic Church became involved with the O.T.O., several of whose members became Gnostic prelates. The Gnostic Catholic Church which resulted has its present headquarters not far from Zürich where Jung himself lived.[102]

It is clear that Jung's affinities with the more religious elements of the Occult Revival were considerable and without doubt extended to direct contact. When, after the First World War, disciples came to Zürich for training or analysis, the attraction of Jung's psychology for the illuminated type of mind at once became apparent. For example, to take only the interest shown in Britain: William McDougall had become interested even before the war; Maurice Nicoll left Jung for Gurdjieff; and when Jung held seminars on dream symbolism in 1923 and 1925, they were reported by the Theosophist and writer on magic W. B. Crow.[103] Jung's psychology represents to many a restatement of the ideas at the core of occult tradition in terms accessible to those ill at ease with religious language. The point can be most strongly made by examining the way in which Jung was inspired to compare the stages in the "alchemical process" with those he observed during the course of his patients' "individuation."

Jung's account in his memoirs conflicts with his earlier statements. At the end of his life he was convinced that the impulse to investigate alchemy had come from one of his own dreams in which he was "trapped in the 17th century." Insight into the meaning of the alchemical process came after he read the *Secret of the Golden*

Flower, supposedly a text of Chinese alchemy sent him by his friend Richard Wilhelm. But in the earlier essay, *A Study in the Process of Individuation,* Jung interpreted a series of paintings executed by one process, and he told another story. The third of a series of 24 paintings, wrote Jung, "brings in a motif that points unmistakably to alchemy and actually gave me the definite incentive to make a thorough study of the world of the old adepts.[104] The picture in question consists of a sphere, and in the corner a snake. The sphere is surrounded by a "vibrating" silver band with the figure twelve on it. It is important to follow Jung's exact words in conversation to his patient:

> As if asking a question, I made the remark: "Then it is the vibrations of the band that keep the sphere floating?" "Naturally," she said, "they are the wings of Mercury, the messenger of the gods. The silver is quicksilver!" She went on at once: "Mercury, that is Hermes, that is the Nous, the mind or reason, and that is the animus, who is here outside instead of inside. He is like a veil that hides the true personality."[105]

The question of the "animus" being inside or outside refers only to the technical details of that particular analysis. The real significance is that not Jung but his patient suggested the symbolism of Mercury and quicksilver. Jung, with his prior occult knowledge, at once associated Hermes with alchemy, the Hermetic science, and set about elaborating the comparison that suggested itself. Jung gives sufficient details in his account of this analysis for us to identify the patient, and as she has been dead for over twenty years there seems little harm in exploring her affiliations. "Miss X" was academic, educated in psychology, and in 1928 came to Europe to study under Jung. She was fifty-five at the time of the analysis, the "daughter of an exceptional father," and some sixteen years after the analysis had been carried through she became fatally ill of cancer.[106] Thus, if we can find an unmarried American lady who fits the description and the dates of 1873-1944/5, we are on the way to discovering one source of Jung's interest in alchemy. The odds are that she formed part of the group of American analysts who came over to Zürich between the two World Wars for training analyses.[107] One of these fits the details so well that there is no possibility of doubt. This is Kristine

Mann (1873-1945), the daughter of "a remarkable father," Charles Holbrook Mann (1839-1918), in his day the chief intellectual of the Swedenborgian New Church in America.

Kristine Mann herself published little except various articles during the war years on the subject of public health and hygiene. She took a B.A. in 1895 and taught English at Vassar, where another pioneer of Jungian analysis in America, Eleanor Bertine, was one of her pupils. Together they studied medicine and received their M.D.'s in 1913 at Cornell University. In 1919 Eleanor Bertine organized analysts to speak at the International Conference of Medical Women, at which Kristine Mann was present. In due course they both found their way to Jung, and subsequently practiced as analysts in New York.[108] It is less Kristine Mann herself who is important, than her upbringing at the hands of the "remarkable father" who so impressed himself on Jung's consciousness during his daughter's analysis. The chain of associations that the identification of Kristine Mann as Jung's patient sets off is quite complicated. But it is, I believe, worth following it to the end.

Charles Holbrook Mann entered the ministry of the Swedenborgian Church of the New Jerusalem in 1865, and in 1877 he took up the editorship of the *New Church Messenger,* which he held for twenty-five years. In 1914 he left his ministry and announced the formation of a new sect, which was to abandon ritual and take for its slogan "religion in the workshop." Mann greatly influenced the elder Henry James and was the recognized leader of Swedenborgian thought on social and economic questions of the day. His significance with regard to analysis is that the New Church was particularly interested in sex education and mental healing, and the theories of Mann in many ways form an anticipation of psychotherapeutic procedure. In fact, the Swedenborgians liked to think that Swedenborg himself "out-Freuds Freud." Mann wrote a book called *What God Hath Cleansed* defending "the correct use" of the sexual organs as "the highest, the purest and the most holy of all the external parts of the body." The New Church also adopted many of the trappings of the popular Mesmeric movement, including hydrotherapy, homeopathy, and the healing methods of P. P. Quimby. The Swedenborgian pastor Warren Evans set up a Mind Cure Sanitorium, and (with Quimby's disciple Julius Dresser) founded the

Boston Metaphysical Club, which developed into the New Thought movement. The next New Church attempt at establishing a Swedenborgian system of healing was by Mann himself.[109] In his book *Psychiasis* (1900) Mann attempted to formulate a doctrine of the "healing of the body through the soul" as "the expression of the regenerating man's spiritual state." Even as early as 1887, he was proclaiming with remarkable lucidity the imperfect state of the so-called mind cure. "What the limitations of this system are, in what precise field it is properly to be applied, where it can come into orderly use and where it becomes an abuse, where it is the Lord and where it is the power of magic that produces the effect are questions as yet to be decided."[110]

There was every likelihood that the daughter of this forerunner of psychiatry would become an analyst herself. But what is the connection of alchemy with the Swedenborgian near miss at establishing a systematic mind cure? In 1858 in New York, Ethan Allen Hitchcock had published his *Swedenborg: a Hermetic Philosopher,* the year after his *Remarks upon Alchemy and the Alchemists.* Hitchcock served as a major general in the Civil War; but according to his biographer, in the middle of councils of war and social occasions he would be concerned with "abstruse speculations concerning the mysteries of nature." In 1854 Hitchcock picked up an alchemical text in a New York bookshop, discovered the symbolic interpretation of alchemy, and accumulated an alchemical library of nearly 300 books. In 1866 he had visions of the Philosopher's Stone as "a kind of revelation. . . . Personally, I have much to fear from it before I can look forward to its benefits." *Swedenborg: a Hermetic Philosopher* is sympathetic to the New Church and deploys an extensive argument to show that Swedenborg derived a large part of his philosophy from alchemy, "although he misinterpreted a point in connection with it."[111] Almost certainly, therefore, the theory that aligned Swedenborg with the alchemists would be known in New Church circles, to say nothing of the probability that the New Church was perfectly aware of the resemblances in any case.

It is stretching coincidence too far to argue that when Jung recorded the suggestion of Hermetic symbolism in Kristine Mann's painting by Miss Mann herself, the New Church background is irrelevant. It is quite possible that Jung's account of the genesis of his alchemical ideas results from the sort of "forgetting" in which Freud also indulged. For Jung also admits, "Oddly enough, I had entirely forgotten what Herbert Silberer had written about alchemy."[112] We have met Silberer before, reviewing Hargrave Jennings's phallic musings. He specialized in applying the Freudian interpretation to folktales, occultism, and religion. In 1914 (the year after his review of *The Rosicrucians*) Silberer published *Problems of Mysticism and Its Symbolism,* in which he discloses that he had discovered for himself the religious significance of alchemy—from the works of Ethan Allen Hitchcock. Hitchcock had suggested to Silberer comparisons with the Vedanta and several other points in an analysis which also depended on Eliphas Lévi, Papus, Rama Prasad, a translation of *The Red Book of Appin* by Bertha Eckstein-Diener, and the *Geheime Figuren.* In his study of an alchemical parable, Silberer discovered three possible interpretations. These were the psychoanalytical (Freudian-sexual); the chemical; and what he called the "anagogic," which was simply a recognition of the Hermetic intention in the first place.[113] Silberer himself then moved some distance away from Freud. It is distinctly odd that Jung—who, as he freely admits, had valued Silberer highly—had "forgotten" his predecessor's anticipatory work.

We are returning by a circular route to the treatment of Kristine Mann by Jung, during the course of which Miss Mann painted the alchemical picture. The nature of the treatment in this particular case is clarified by a knowledge of the New Church connections. Ethan Allen Hitchcock claimed that he had met Swedenborg many times "in the spiritual world." But it is doubtful whether this refers to a real vision as opposed to "conversations" with his works. "I was chiefly induced to make the acquaintance of Swedenborg by certain encomiums upon him by his friend *Mr. Wilkinson* whom I met in the spiritual world also, some 12/13 years ago, and who in fact introduced Swedenborg to me. The philosopher had a veil over his face." "Mr. Wilkinson" must have been James John Garth Wilkinson (b. 1812), a convinced Swedenborgian, a friend of Emerson, a homeopath who produced the first printed edition of Blake. He was one of the New Church members most interested in mental healing.

In the same year as Hitchcock gave the world his interpretation of Swedenborg, Wilkinson wrote in a paper edited by his friend Thomas Lake Harris:

> Let involuntary drawing be introduced then as a normal employment into asylums, and let the class of patients upon whom the spirit-cure is to be tried be those who are only functionally deranged, and especially those who are suffering from disappointed affections, and in general mental and affectional causes.... Let each drawing be kept, dated, and numbered, as marking a progress of state.[114]

Garth Wilkinson was suggesting that a form of "spirit drawing" or "automatic writing" be used as therapy, although "if you choose to say it is your own spirit I have no objections." Well over half a century later, Jung is discovered using precisely this method as an index to his patients' progress on the path of individuation. Remembering that he himself had read "seven volumes of Swedenborg," it is permissible to wonder whether this Swedenborgian excursion had not taken him into the land of the New Church thinkers on his own initiative. In his memoirs Jung contrasts his own philosophical background with that of Freud, whose "intellectual history often seemed to begin with Du-Bois-Reymond and Darwin," while he, Jung, possessed "some knowledge of the history of psychology" and was "especially familiar with the writers of the eighteenth and early nineteenth century." Possibly on his American trip in 1909, Jung's interests may have led him to pick up something of New England Transcendentalism in the bookshops. Or just possibly Kristine Mann suggested some details of her own treatment.

All these possibilities must be seen as unlikely if we accept Jung's claim that he had begun the process of painting in stages as an aid to his own inner development soon after he had written the *Seven Sermons,* and a Swedenborgian source is by no means ruled out. The coincidence of the New Church tradition emerging in Jung's professional life is continued not only in methods and men, but also in terms. Thus Garth Wilkinson uses the same Platonic terminology as Jung when describing Swedenborg's doctrine of the relations between Body and Soul: "There is an image-and-likeness psychology in man himself, for the soul is the archetype of the body as God is the archetype of the soul."[115] The fact that the Jungian archetype bears little relation to the word as used in Garth Wilkinson's conventional argument points the moral that Jung's system was an adaptation of tradition rather than a direct rendering of it into modern dress. It also suggests a solution to the problem of Jung's relationship with the Occult Revival and previous systems of mind cure.

The solution probably lies somewhere between the explanation of direct influence and that of independent discovery. The system of Freud had its roots in the scientific study of hypnotism and in the tradition that sought to take the *phenomena* of hypnosis away from the popular Mesmerists and more occult practitioners of mind cure. It was totally in keeping with this line of thought that when Freud found himself inevitably in confrontation with the "paranormal," his interest took the direct form of psychical research. On the other hand, Jung began with psychical research. He accepted from the start the "paranormal." He confronted it in his own life, and paid attention to the *content* of earlier theorists of immaterial reality as well as those of the contemporary Occult Revival. Because of this difference in emphasis, Jung—either through knowledge of writers like the American Swedenborgians, or through the wide reading we know he carried out in their sources—developed a different concept of the meaning of unconscious mental processes. Freud followed Charcot, then Bernheim, but he always retained some of the Charcot in his attempts to map the unconscious. Jung can be seen as the heir to the still unsecularized attempts to established a mind cure, and thus he had natural ties with those whose less successful efforts in the same direction were based on similar premises.

There is no need to attack Jung's originality by insisting improbably that he took the idea of a succession of paintings from Garth Wilkinson. His own explanation that he spontaneously developed the method as a guide to his own unconscious is perfectly plausible. But it is certain that the tradition to which Jung belonged was obvious to fellow-adepts, who came to Jung as the preferred modern interpreter of traditional metaphysics. From such contact with like-minded spirits, Jung must have derived stimulus, inspiration, and ideas. The case of Kristine Mann with her New Church background is a perfect instance of this process. For her alchemical painting to suggest to Jung the connection between his "individuation process" and the alchemists, three elements were necessary.

First, that Miss Mann should have had the background to incorporate Hermetic symbolism in her painting to start with (although this can no doubt be disputed); next, that she should herself have suggested the interpretation to Jung; and, not least, that Jung should have been sufficiently well read in occult literature to recognize the parallel presented to him.

By the time that Jung came to make his fuller pronouncements on alchemy in the 1940s and 1950s, there could be no doubt where he stood. *Psychology and Alchemy* is reinforced by wide reading on the alchemical side of the Occult Revival: Mrs. Atwood, A. E. Waite, Arthur Avalon, Manley Palmer Hall, G. R. S. Mead, and Lewis Spence crowd each other in his bibliography. In his idea that medieval alchemy was "rather like an undercurrent to the Christianity that ruled on the surface," he is certainly indebted to A. E. Waite. And in the notion that "the central ideas of Christianity are rooted in Gnostic philosophy," he is repeating the argument of Anna Kingsford and Edward Maitland, who had been so influential with their "esoteric Christianity" in the days of the high Occult Revival. In 1936 Jung compared Edward Maitland's idea of God as a male-female duality to his own concept and to a vision in the Hermetic literature from which Maitland and Kingsford also derived much inspiration.[116] The contrast with Freud, who read Anna Kingsford's account of her dreams as a case history, is pointed.[117] But it should be noted that Jung was to some extent himself a secularizer. He knew full well that the religious symbolism of alchemy had been most thoroughly known to the writers of the Occult Revival, and he was careful to claim originality only in perceiving "the psychological meaning of alchemy." He used it as a model for the completed "individuation process" which, he maintained, did not display itself in any single case.[118] All that is necessary is to read instead of *individuation process* the phrase, so beloved of occultists, *spiritual progress;* to make certain other small changes of terms, and the reader is back with Mrs. Atwood and her *Suggestive Enquiry* of 1850.[119]

Because Jung shared some of his sources with the occultists and his psychology held attractions for them, the circles in which Jungian theory became popular in the German-speaking countries are predictable. Jung's first propagandist was the Munich psychotherapist Gustav Heyer, who had connections with the George circle and with Freiherr von Schrenck-Notzing.[120] The extraordinarily close link between the supporters of Jung and German mysticism of the 1890s is exemplified in the Eranos Conferences.

In a specially constructed auditorium at her "Casa Gabriella" on Lake Maggiore, Olga Froebe-Kapteyn (1881-1962) initiated annual meetings at which scholars, mythologists, and psychologists of Jungian sympathies have expounded their views of the spiritual problems faced by modern man. The presiding spirit is that of Jung, and an extraordinary harmony of outlook has seemed to prevail at the meetings. Olga Froebe commented in 1954:

> Like all spiritual manifestations of an age, Eranos too is the response to an inward summons and necessity.... From its start, Eranos has been integrated by virtue of the force that C. G. Jung once termed "the sympathy of all things."... Only this "sympathy" can explain the manner anyway in which our speakers have been brought to us. It has each time been something like a providential coming together of scholars who were intuitively moving in the same direction and open to the same ideas.[121]

This apparently miraculous harmony of voices can be explained simply by the fact that many of the scholars present have their intellectual roots, like Jung, in the Occult Revival. The Eranos Conferences take place in Ascona, and Olga Froebe-Kapteyn, "this mysterious nun-like muse," was the friend and protectress of Ludwig Derleth.

When Ludwig Derleth contemplated establishing his *Rosenburg* in the dark days of the First World War, one of the places he naturally considered was Ascona, the center of the Progressive Underground and the home of Monte Verita. Olga Froebe-Kapteyn had visited Derleth in Munich, and in 1922 the Schwabing Napoleon stayed at Ascona with his friend. Together they traveled to Rome that year, and it is quite clear that it was the stimulus of Derleth that inspired Olga Froebe's interest in symbols and the ancient world. In 1937 she was still writing to Derleth of her reverence for him. The ever-present tendency of the Eranos scholars to see themselves as an élite is perfectly prefigured in Derleth's vision of his order as the "golden society" elevated above all associations of the century.[122]

The troubled life of Monte Verita entered a new phase in 1926. Eduard Freiherr van der Heydt—who had visited Frau Olga Froebe in her Casa Gabriella and been impressed with Monte Verita three years before—bought the colony and turned it into a meeting place for artists. Van der Heydt was attracted by Krishnamurti, and his prospectus for Monte Verita recalled the old days. To Ascona came visitors like Gropius, Moholy-Nagy, and Jung himself. There was considerable contact between this new incarnation of Monte Verita and the Casa Gabrielle. And in 1930 Ascona saw Olga Froebe-Kapteyn send out invitations for a "Summer school for Spiritual Research," which seems to have been her first conception of the role of the Eranos Conferences. This school was to offer free courses which would be "of very actual help to students," and it defined its purpose as "a summer school for the study of Theosophy, Mysticism, the esoteric Sciences and Philosophies and all forms of spiritual research."[123]

In the years before Jung and his followers established themselves as the guiding lights of the Eranos Conferences, the meetings were directed by a much more "occult" hand. In late 1930, Olga Froebe-Kapteyn invited Alice Bailey and her husband to come from the United States and spend the summer lecturing at Ascona. Alice Bailey was the head of a schismatic Theosophical organization based in New York and known as "the Arcane School." She is best known for the series of lengthy tomes, which a Tibetan master is supposed to have dictated to her. From 1931 to 1933 she and her husband were the guests of Olga Froebe-Kapteyn. They succeeded in building up a large audience among the Bohemian population of Ascona, despite Alice Bailey's disgust with "the peculiarly decadent and objectionable people who lived on the shore of the lake." The prophetess warned her daughters against the many "groups from Germany and France whose ideas were anything but nice or clean." She retired to New York after the 1933 session when Jung and his friends arrived. In Alice Bailey's words: "The place was overrun by German professors and the whole tone and quality of the place altered. Some of them were most undesirable, and the teaching given shifted from a relatively high spiritual plane to that of academic philosophy and a spurious esotericism."[124]

At Eranos the occult did take on a more academic form, and the meetings became a series of lectures on topics of a "spiritual" nature. Over the mythological speculations of Eranos has hovered the spirit of Bachofen, most particularly in the symposium held in 1938 on "The Great Mother," to which Jung, Louis Massignon, and Heinrich Zimmer contributed, as well as another consistent Eranos lecturer, Gustav Heyer, whose inspiration was taken directly from the philosophy of Ludwig Klages. Specialists in Eastern religion combined with authorities on Western occultism such as Professor Rudolf Bernouilli, who was (like Jung) a Fellow of the Zurich Technische Hochschule and who gave papers on alchemy and the number mysticism of the Tarot. After the death of Jung a dominating figure in the Eranos Conferences has been Mircea Eliade (born 1907) who has renounced his earlier vocation of writing novels "in order to inculcate a new comprehension of *homo religiosus.*" Eliade had spent six months in an *ashram* at Rishikesh, and his Romanian novels of the 1930s were the center of a "transcendental movement."[125] His book on Yoga argues a connection with alchemy, and he is best known for his scholarly work on the Myth of the Eternal Return. In fact the theories of Jung have passed into the hands of the modern representatives of the 19th-century Occult Revival. Jung's psychology inspires the inheritors of those traditions which once inspired him. The Eranos Conferences are a compendium of all the elements of the Occult Revival, and an extension of all the elements of Jung's work.

Eranos may well owe much to Count Keyserling's Darmstadt conferences. Some of the lecturers at the School of Wisdom later found their way to Ascona. In the early 1920s there was close contact between the developing theories of Jung and the eclectic entourage of the Baltic philosopher. Jung met Richard Wilhelm in the early 1920s at Darmstadt, and in 1923 Wilhelm came to Zurich to give a talk on the ancient Chinese book of divination, the *I Ching.* From this meeting sprang Jung's commentaries on Wilhelm's translation of the *I Ching* and *The Secret of the Golden Flower.* Another contact between Jung and Darmstadt was Oskar Schmitz, who was responsible for introducing Jungian psychology to Keyserling and who possibly provided the stimulus for Jung's later investigation of astrology—much in the same way as Kristine Mann *plus* Richard Wilhelm may have triggered the association with alchemy in Jung's already well-stocked mind.[126] It is not necessary to delve into every one of Jung's restatements of traditional or Oriental thought. His prefaces to Evans-Wentz, his introduction to Suzuki's study of Zen, his mythological interpretations, all fit the pattern already observed. However, one neglected influence on Jung must still be discussed, because it throws much light on the vexed question of his relationship with the Nazi regime. The connection can only be understood with the knowledge that Jung's psychology had come to represent a focal point for the scholarly mystics of the period between the wars.

Through the activities of Gustav Heyer, Jung met Jacob Wilhelm Hauer and was more influenced by him than it has been thought politic to admit.[127] In 1932 Hauer held a week-long seminar on Yoga in the Zurich Psychology Club, and in 1934 he spoke at the Eranos Conference on "Symbols and Experience of the Self." Jung's own standpoint on Yoga is ambivalent. He thought it "one of the greatest things the human mind has ever created," but it was not for the West.[128] His interest in Yogic psychology can be partly traced to Hauer; but the German's greater influence on Jung is shown in Jung's conception of the Self. Hauer's 1934 Eranos lecture concerned itself largely with the number symbolism, laying particular stress on the four-symbol, the quaternity or "tetrakys." In 1937 Jung referred to Hauer as one of the two sources of his own discussion of this problem. The psychologist then went on to talk of the "whole" of man: both conscious and unconscious aspects. He had chosen, he said, the term "self" to designate this "total man in accordance with Eastern philosophy, which for centuries has occupied itself with the problems that arise when even the gods cease to incarnate."[129] Again, Jung's source for this conception of "Eastern philosophy" is Hauer.

At the 1934 conference, Jung had first expanded on the topics of "The Archetypes and the Collective Unconscious." Hauer at once adopted both conceptions to argue that there existed a collective *racial* unconscious which manifested itself in racial symbolism.[130] The year before this lecture, Hauer had founded the Nordic Faith Movement.

Jacob Wilhelm Hauer was born in Württemberg, attended a missionary college at Basel, and went to India, where he is said never to have converted a single Indian. He returned to Europe with great enthusiasm for Yogic philosophy and took a First in Greats at Oxford. In 1921 he left the Lutheran pastorate for a chair at Tübingen. On his arrival at the university, he founded a *völkisch* Bible-study group which, five years later, became part of the Youth movement proper. In 1928 Hauer took up the editorship of a magazine called the *Kommende Gemeinde,* which had as its symbols the Gothic arch and the Sun-Wheel. At the last meeting of the society which published *Kommende Gemeinde,* two of the speakers were Ernst Krieck and Martin Buber[131]—on the one hand, a future Nazi philosopher and lecturer at *Ordensbürgen* and, on the other, a friend of Eugen Diederichs and the reviver of Hasidic mysticism. In 1933 Hauer took it upon himself to unite all the non-Christian *völkisch* religious groups. He received widespread support for his proclaimed belief in the divine mission of Germany: in 1935 Hauer and Count Reventlow were the principal speakers at a rally of 10,000 sympathizers in the Berlin *Sportpalast*. But even the vehement anti-Christian standpoint of the Nordic Faith Movement did not in the end save it from condemnation by the Nazis or its leader from an enforced resignation.[132]

Hauer was one of the earliest opponents of Anthroposophy, denouncing it as a "crime against the spirit." In his polemics he demonstrates not only his knowledge of Indian religion and a mastery of the doctrines he is attacking, but also a thorough grounding in Hermetic texts. He had even read Hargrave Jennings. Hauer collected his Nordic Faith Movement together under a pledge of having no Jewish or colored blood or Freemasonic affiliations. In the *Sportpalast* he was heard praising the virtues of Blood and Soil, and acclaiming the heroic *SS*-man. In 1935 he could see Adolf Hitler as "the genius of our people."[133] What had he to do with Jung?

Jung's uncritical supporters will answer: nothing, except a chance coincidence of views. This is not the case; for, as we have seen, the two used each other's ideas and derived inspiration from each other's psychologies. The manner in which Hauer adapted the idea of the "collective unconscious" to express his own opinion on the community of the race is exactly that in which Dietrich Eckart or Alfred Rosenberg took up the analagous concept of the unity of all souls in God. Indeed in 1934—the year after the publication of Rosenberg's *Myth of the 20th Century* and the year in which Hauer spoke at

Ascona to the assembled Jungians—Hauer published a study of the Bhagavad Gita which defines God as the All, declares that the recognition of this leads to the *grosse Heimkehr,* and in other respects conforms to Rosenberg's interpretation of the same text. For Hauer, the "God-possessed German soul" was a mode of being that transcended political categories and resulted in the mystical unity of the *Volk.*[134]

Jung and Hauer were illuminates of similar traditions. This is the key to Jung's conduct while the Nazis were in power. And only against the background of Jung's relationship with Hauer can the psychologist's essay *"Wotan"* be understood. This piece, published in 1936, declared that the archetype of Wotan, the ancient Germanic god, creator of strife and worker of magic, was moving in the communal unconscious. Jung saw his Wotan impulse moving in the *völkisch* irrationalists, and in a note (added after the war) he revealed a knowledge of Klages, Schuler, and Stefan George. Germany was "possessed," he announced, using the very metaphor with which Hauer had defined his position. Jung disapproved of the "German Christians" and advised them to join Hauer's Nordic Faith Movement, which was composed of "honest, well-meaning people" who admitted to being "God-possessed." Hauer himself was "possessed," and Jung regarded his German creed as "the tragic and really heroic effort of a conscientious scholar" whose actions were directed by the disrupting force of Wotan. "There are people in the German Faith Movement who are intelligent enough not only to *believe* but to *know* that the God of the *Germans* is Wotan and not the Christian God."[135] Jung's essay is on the one hand, an explanation of world events in terms of his complicated psychology, and, on the other, a lament and apology for a kindred spirit in the grip of unconscious forces he could not control.

There is no need to accuse Jung of pro-Nazism on account of this essay, but the potentiality was there. Jung's theories drew strength from and in their turn inspired the illuminates of Central Europe. In Hauer can be seen a close associate and a member of the same illuminated circle who applied theories like Jung's to a racial doctrine. Jung's psychology could seem to lend itself to anti-Semitism and its founder made continual references to a difference between the psychology of races—again a point of agreement with Hauer. This has not unnaturally led to accusations that Jung collaborated with the Nazis in assuming the presidency of the International Medical Society for Psychotherapy, the organization that supervised "coordinated" psychiatric activities under the Nazi regime. There is little doubt that Jung assumed the position because he was asked to and in order to keep psychiatric activities from being suppressed.[136] But the significance of the episode does not end with a decision as to whether or not Jung was anti-Semitic or pro-Nazi. The real importance of the accusations lies in the fact that Jung's accusers—once the hysteria is penetrated—had discerned a fundamental similarity between Jungian views and views associated with the Nazi regime. This once again shows the dangerous possibilities implicit in an illuminated viewpoint.

When he assumed the editorship of the *Zentralblatt für Psychotherapie* in 1933, Jung wrote: "The differences which actually do exist between Germanic and Jewish psychology and which have long been known to every intelligent person, are no longer to be glossed over, and this can only be beneficial to science."[137] In so doing he did not unambiguously compromise himself—as he was forced ever afterward to remind his attackers, he had for years been arguing the differences between the psychology of different races. Yet, it was an odd statement to make with no malice aforethought in that time and place. Jung, as a German-Swiss, naturally attracted favorable comment from Nazi psychologists in contrast with Freud.[138] Although his was not a "Nazi psychology," it did incorporate the racial theory. The comparison that suggests itself is with the English illuminated politicians. Some did become anti-Semitic; some did not. Jacob Hauer became anti-Semitic; Jung probably did not. But the illuminated positions which they held in that time and place carried similar dangers, and if his critics have falsely accused Jung of holding "Nazi views," this is at least partly because the Zürich psychologist talked in the language of contemporary illuminism—in whose alarming accents certain criminally eccentric politicians in Germany had also been thoroughly schooled.

Because of Jung's intellectual standpoint, his vision of the analyst's role was more explicitly magical then Freud's. As early as 1913 he admitted that "indeed we must rate those doctors wise—worldly-wise in every sense—who know how to surround themselves with the aura of a medicine-man. They have not only the biggest practices, but also get the best results." The fundamental position may well be sound medical sense and has little to do with illuminism. But when Jung-Basilides took up his teaching it was very much in the manner of the medicine men he recommended. An Eastern commentator has described Jung:

> In spite of being a deeply religious man, surcharged all over, and suffused with the richness of experience, he donned the robe of a psychologist and a doctor. He would not have done this had he been in the East.

This goes some way to explaining the "cultism" which even supporters of Jung have observed with displeasure. It is a condition not at all altered by explaining that "a gifted analyst is bound to be surrounded by people with strong transferences."[139] The statement is quite true, but it merely raises in a new form the question: what is an analyst?

In the case of Jung himself—speaking entirely of his function—there was a perpetual conflict between his role as an interpreter of essentially religious traditions and his early training as a scientist. He introduced Evans-Wentz's translation of the Tibetan *Book of the Great Liberation* with the remark that "yoga in Mayfair or Fifth Avenue, or in any other place which is on the telephone, is a spiritual fake." He complained that his critics "ignore the fact that as a doctor and scientist, I proceed from facts which everyone is at liberty to verify. Instead they cite me as if I were a philosopher, or a Gnostic with pretensions to supernatural knowledge." But such illumination is precisely what Jung did claim. "Religious experience is absolute," he wrote.

> It cannot be disputed. You can only say that you have never had such an experience, whereupon your opponent will reply, "Sorry, I have." And there your discussion will come to an end.

The student of the occult was always present, as when Jung decided that there were no Western equivalents to the Tibetan *Book of the Dead* "except for certain secret writings which are inaccessible to the wider public and to the ordinary scientist." By self-definition, therefore, Jung was *not* an ordinary scientist, although it is only possible to guess with which esoteric groups he was in contact.[140]

With Jung, elements present even in Freudian psychoanalysis are made explicit. It is no function of this book to discuss how far either the Freudian or the Jungian maps of the unconscious—or the projections of any psychic cartographer—correspond to close observation of the psychic processes. There is certainly no intention of detracting from the benefits derived from all good doctors and healers of souls. However, it is essential to realize that while the outer forms of irrationalism had penetrated political Establishments, the interior content of Underground systems of thought had begun to penetrate academies. The widest breach in the rationalist front was inevitably in the terrain of psychology and psychiatry, because of the nature of the subjects studied and the historical circumstances in which that study took place. Theories deriving from psychoanalysis, or developing parallel with it, have absorbed some of the same influences. Of these the most significant has been the New Education.

The builders of the brave new worlds of the Progressive Underground were most naturally concerned with the education of the children who would one day inhabit their Paradise. Doctrines of "spiritual revolution" found their natural outcome in attempts at reeducation; of "spiritual evolution," a good analogy in the educational progress of the child.

The pioneer of the altered attitude to education was Maria Montessori (1869-1952) whose vision of a race of Superchildren bordered on the apocalyptic. "The outcome . . . is the New Child, a superior being, giving promise of a New Humanity, with powers of mind and spirit hitherto unsuspected." Many of the developments already discussed were part of the movement toward the New Child. In Germany, Langbehn's *Rembrandt als Erzieher* was followed by Carl Götze's *Child as Artist* and Götze's educational work based on the principle that the child was a natural creative artist who must have his powers liberated through education. The youth movements, and the groups with which Rolf Gardiner and the Springhead Ring were in contact, also formed parts of the movement for "liberated" education—that is, designed to evoke the powers of the child rather than imposing adult standards upon him. In America the "Junior Republics" in which children governed themselves were set up. The idea was also tried in England with a "little Commonwealth" in Dorset. The Order of Woodcraft Chivalry and the Kibbo Kift were very much part of the educational movement and embodied a commitment to reestablishing "natural man."[141]

The theories of the psychologists provided added impetus. Freud's conclusion that neuroses were produced by repressions fitted excellently with the ideas of those who wanted to recreate natural man; while Jung was a central figure in the minds of educational reformers after the First World War, as his psychology was particularly favorable to ideas of "spiritual evolution." Jung accepted the Biogenetic Law and may have been more influenced by his contact with G. Stanley Hall than he cared to admit. He lectured at conferences of the New Educators in 1923 and 1924, and his views on educational development very closely coincide, for example, with those of Ernest Westlake of the Order of Woodcraft Chivalry.

Occultists and religious reformers also concerned themselves with the children of the future—for they, after all, were the custodians of the idea of "spiritual progress." Johannes Müller and Heinrich Lhotzky both put forward educational theories. The leading exponent of occult ideas of education has been Rudolf Steiner; and in 1962 there were almost seventy schools run on Anthroposophical principles in various parts of the world. Steiner himself also lectured to the New Educators, and (according to the *Manchester Guardian*) a conference attended by Steiner at Oxford in 1922 found in him "its central point." Steiner's principles were based on his occult theories, and it is easy to see how these could coincide with less esoteric ideas of evolution. "We must know on what part of the human being we have especially to work at a certain age, and how we can work upon it in the proper way," he wrote. "We can awaken what is in the child, but we cannot implant a content into him."[142] Such a coincidence of ideas makes it comprehensible that the organization that carried the flag of the New Education throughout Europe sprang from the Theosophical Society.

In 1914 a committee of Theosophists under Bishop George Arundale of the Liberal Catholic Church—a former tutor of Krishnamurti—decided to start a Theosophical School. The site chosen was—where else?—Letchworth Garden City. To the Theosophical tenets of *karma* and reincarnation were added the more generally "progressive" ideas of Arts and Crafts, Montessori theory, and Dalcroze Eurythmics. A general vegetarian diet was the rule and the pupils governed themselves through a "moot." The Theosophist Beatrice Ensor, an inspector of schools, was inspired by the Letchworth experiment and founded the Theosophical Fraternity of Education in 1915. She established a magazine to propagate enlightened ideas; and in 1921 she held a meeting of her fraternity in Letchworth, when it was decided that next year they should organize a general conference of educators at Calais which the Theosophists would run, although themselves keeping in the background. In 1921 the Calais conference was held, the name of the Theosophical paper changed to *The New Era,* and the New Educational Fellowship established. Its first object was "to prepare the child to seek and to realize in his own life the supremacy of the spirit."[143]

The New Era secured contributions from both occultists and educators. Beatrice Ensor shared the editorship with the celebrated A. S. Neill, and the entire spectrum of the Progressive Underground contributed to its pages. There was Isabelle Pagan of *Racial Cleavage* and Cloudesley Brereton, who wrote for G. R. S. Mead's Theosophical magazine *Quest.* There were articles by the Jungian therapist Esther Harding and the ubiquitous Patrick Geddes. The president of the Arts and Crafts Association joined the leader of a new French youth movement and Wilhelm Stekel—a friend of Neill—in a remarkable synthesis of "advanced opinion." Beatrice Ensor and the Theosophists were never quite submerged by the more practical educators. In April 1923, Mrs. Ensor contributed an editorial that noted approvingly the efforts of A. Conan Doyle and E. L. Gardner to capture the fairies.

> We have recently come across other children who see fairies, and we are trying to obtain more photos. It is a very beautiful idea that Nature's laws are operated through the cooperation of beings who, while not belonging to our human order of evolution, are nevertheless working side by side with humanity in the building up of our world . . . it would seem as though we were now beginning to reawaken at a higher level the sense organs which enabled the folk of yore to see clairvoyantly "the little people."[144]

Mrs. Ensor followed her beautiful thoughts by some tips for teachers on the education of the psychic child. Despite caustic comments from A. S. Neill on such vagaries, the New Educational Fellowship continued to interest people attracted to the occult and the transcendental. Adolphe Ferrière (1879-1960), who had been eminent in European New Education since just after the turn of the century, was a leading light in the Continental NEF. Ferrière was an advocate of an antirationalist approach to life, who considered that "realist politics are a mistake. They are an encroachment of reason on the healthy intuition." His educational interests led him to a concern with psychological types long before Jung published his book of that title in 1920. Ferrière agreed with Jung but thought the psychologist's theories incomplete. He devised a more extensive theory for himself, which he proposed to use in the service of the New Education. In its completed form this was based on what Ferrière considered "the essential element in religion." This was "the longing for union with creator." In such a union each person would find "the complete fulfilment of his own being."[145] This illuminated educator was responsible for introducing an expert on astrology to the adepts of the New Education.

The astrologer was Karl Ernst Krafft (1900-45), whose strange career has been exhaustively charted by Ellic Howe.[146] Ferrière had been interested in astrology since the days of the First World War, and by 1924 he had discovered a pamphlet written by Krafft, with whom he began a correspondence. Krafft's vast statistical researches into the relationship between the planets and humanity might, thought Ferrière, help his enquiries into the methods of determining character. This interest is exactly in line with the interest of illuminated intellectuals like those attending the Darmstadt School of Wisdom or the Eranos Conferences at Ascona. One of Krafft's specialties was called "Cosmobiology." When two issues of a *Yearbook for Cosmobiological Research* appeared in 1928 and 1929, Krafft's fellow-contributors included Richard Wilhelm, Edgar Dacqué, and Sigrid Strauss-Kloebe, who lectured on astrology at Eranos. At the Conference of the New Educational Fellowship at Elsinore in August 1929, Krafft was introduced as a "psychologist of Zürich," and in the same program as talks by Montessori, Piaget, and Decroly, he gave two lectures on "The Relation between

Astronomical, Meteorological and Biological Phenomena" and "The Possibility of Connecting Characterology with Cosmobiology." Krafft was followed by Ferrière, who suggested an explanation of "cosmobionomic phenomena" in terms of radiation and predicted the possibility of a neutral theory of types based on "the fundamental radio-active characteristics of the human being."

Krafft wrote to Ferrière that "many members" of the NEF were concerned with astrology and welcomed its renaissance. As an outcome of the conference, Ferrière tried to set up an international committee for research into typology with Krafft as its president. Some members of standing were secured, but a protracted campaign to attract the interest of Jung was unsuccessful. A single result of the committee was a joint publication by Krafft and Ferrière under the auspices of Ferrière's Swiss educational organization, which contains in embryo almost all Ferrière's formulations on the idea of types.[147]

The efforts of illuminated educationalists combined with successful attempts by psychologists to secularize certain occult concepts. Together they have produced remarkable effects. These results cannot be appreciated without the knowledge that those responsible have almost invariably been influenced by the Occult Revival. The illuminated attitude produces interesting variations on the theme common to all periods of history, that "the times are out of joint." While illuminated politicians attemped to alter the social structure of reality, illuminated psychologists and educators tried to restructure souls and minds. The identity of their aims was well expressed by Adolphe Ferrière in a letter to Romain Rolland.

> The old religions, under the cover of their symbols, were right: man has lost this contact with the cosmic order—mathematical or intuitive—which the animals have managed to preserve well away from mankind—and little children, too! Jean-Jacques Rousseau—he knew it well.[148]

1. C. G. Jung, "The Spiritual Problem of Modern Man," in *Modern Man in Search of a Soul* (London, 1933), pp. 234-35.
2. Lancelot Law Whyte, *The Unconscious before Freud* (London, 1962), pp. 168-69.
3. Carl du Prel, *The Philosophy of Mysticism* (tr. C. C. Massey, London, 1889), vol. I, p. xxiii.

4. Ernest Jones, *Sigmund Freud, Life and Work* (3 vols., London, 1953-57), vol. I, p. 31 note 1; Siegfried Bernfeld, "Sigmund Freud, M.D.," in *International Journal of Psychoanalysis* (July 1951), p. 208.

5. Friedrich Eckstein, "Das Unbewusste, die Vererbung und das Gedächtnis im Lichte der mathematische Naturwissenschaft," in *Almanach der Psychoanalyse* (Vienna, 1930), pp. 44-60.

6. Eckstein, "Altere Theorien des Unbewussten," in *Almanach der Psychoanalyse* (1936), pp. 241-44.

7. Eckstein, *Alte Unnennbare Tage*, p. 119; *Neue Freie Presse* (15 September 1933); Jones, *Freud*, vol. II, pp. 51, 328.

8. Christian von Ehrenfels, *Cosmogony* (tr. Mildred Focht, New York, 1948), p. 210.

9. Whyte, *Unconscious*, p. 164.

10. Garfield Tourney, "Empedocles and Freud, Heraclitus and Jung," in *Bulletin of the History of Medicine* (1956), pp. 109 ff. Eckstein, *Alte Unnennbare Tage*, p. 105.

11. For the Nancy-Salpêtrière controversy and the general position of hypnosis at the time, see particularly Konrad Wolff, "Magie und Rationalismus in der Hypnose" in *Antaios*, vol. II (1961), pp. 348 ff. Robert G. Hillman, "A Scientific Study of Mystery" in *Bulletin of the History of Medicine* (March-April 1965), pp. 163 ff. Jerome M. Schneck, "J-M. Charcot and the Theory of Experimental Hypnosis," in *Journal of the History of Medicine* (July 1961), pp. 297 ff.

12. Richard Harte, *Hypnotism and the Doctors*, vol. II, pp. 224 ff., vol. I, p. 121.

13. Hillman, "Study of Mystery," pp. 180-82; Blech, *Société Théosophique*, p. 37.

14. Walter A. Stewart, *Psycho-analysis: The First Ten Years* (London, 1969), pp. 13-14; Standard Edition of Freud, vol. I, p. 95, note 2.

15. Sigmund Freud, review (1889) of August Forel's *Der Hypnotismus*, in Standard Edition, vol. I, pp. 91 ff.

16. Harte, *Hypnotism and the Doctors*, vol. I, p. vii.

17. On these systems see Harte, *Hypnotism*. For Quimby see my *Occult Underground*, pp. 121-23.

18. Schneck, "A Re-evaluation of Freud's 'Abandonment of Hypnosis,' " in *Journal of the History of the Behavioural Sciences* (April 1965), pp. 191 ff. Cf. Freud, "An Autobiographical Study" in *The Problem of Lay Analysis* (tr. James Strachey, London, 1928), pp. 189 ff.

19. Cf. opinion of Walter Stewart, *Psycho-analysis*, p. 3.

20. Freud, *The Origins of Psycho-analysis: Letters to Wilhelm Fliess* (ed. Ernst Kris, London, 1954), pp. 179 and note 1, 318.

21. Wilhelm Fliess, *Der Ablauf des Lebens* (Leipzig and Vienna, 1906), p. 251; Fliess, *Vom Leben und vom Tod* (2nd ed., Jena, 1914), p. 105; Fliess, *Das Jahr in Lebendigen* (Jena, 1918); Fliess, "Das Wunder des Jahres," in *Zur Periodenlehre* (Jena, 1925), p. 50.

22. Copy with Wyneken's signature in the Warburg Institute Library, London.
23. Fliess, *Ablauf des Lebens*, p. 529; Friedell, *Kulturgeschichte Ägyptens*, p. 267; see Eugen Georg, *Verschollene Kulturen* (Leipzig, 1930), published by Voigtlander, the *Welteislehre* specialists; Fliess, *Ablauf des Lebens* (Leipzig, 1923), p. viii.
24. Michael Gauquelin, *The Cosmic Clocks* (London, 1969), pp. 97 ff.
25. E.g., Eugen Georg, *Verschollene Kulturen;* Hans Künkel, *Das grosse Jahr* (Jena, 1922). Hanns Fischer, *Rhythmus,* uses Arrhenius but not Fliess. Also G. W. Surya (i.e., D. Giorgiewitz-Weitzer) *Das Übersinnliche in der Weltkreis* (Freiburg in Breisgau, 1921).
26. See Iago Galdston, "Freud and Romantic Medicine" in *Bulletin of the History of Medicine* (December 1956), pp. 489 ff. and Bernfeld, "Freud's Earliest Theories and the School of Helmholtz," in *Psychoanalytical Quarterly* (1944), pp. 431 ff.
27. Steiner, *The Story of My Life,* p. 138.
28. See Freud, *The Origins,* p. 9.
29. Lazar, Baron Hellenbach, *Die Magie der Zahlens* (Vienna, 1882) and Franz Liharzic, *Das Quadrat* (Vienna, 1865).
30. Richard Pfenning, *Grundzüge der Fliessschen Periodenrechnung* (Leipzig and Vienna, 1918), p. 1; Hans Henning, "Neupythagoräer" in *Annalen der Naturphilosophie* (1910), pp. 219 ff.; Freud, *The Origins,* p. 41.
31. A full account of the scandal is Vincent Brome, *Freud's Early Circle* (London, 1967), pp. 5-13. Cf. Richard Pfenning, *Wilhelm Fliess und seine Nachentdecker* (Berlin, 1906), and Hermann Swoboda, *Das Siebenjahr,* Band I (Vienna and Leipzig, 1917).
32. On Weininger, see David Abrahamsen, *The Mind and Death of a Genius* (New York, 1946) and Swoboda, *Otto Weiningers Tod* (Vienna and Leipzig, 1923), Otto Weininger, *Über die Letzten Dinge* (Vienna and Leipzig, 1904), pp. 113 ff.; *Taschenbuch und Briefe an einem Freund* (ed. A. Gerber; Leipzig and Vienna, 1919), pp. 27-28, where he claims to be the founder of "the only true pathology of self-cure through God." *Sex and Character* (London, 1906), pp. 276-78, 330 for his occult experiences.
33. See Galdston, "Romantic Medicine," pp. 500-501. Note his comment (p. 503) that the Romantics would have found Freud's metapsychology "familiar," although "naive."
34. Hans Schlieper, *Der Rhythmus des Lebendigen* (Jena, 1909).
35. Weininger, *Sex and Character,* pp. xi, 10.
36. C. G. Jung, *Memories, Dreams, Reflections* (ed. Aniela Jaffé, London, 1967), pp. 173-74.
37. *The Brighton Herald,* 24 May 1913.
38. Lutoslawski first used the term in a book on Plato published in Polish in Cracow in 1902. See his *Knowledge of Reality* (London, 1930), p. 198 note.
39. F. W. H. Myers, "The Daemon of Socrates," in *Proceedings* of the SPR, vol. V (1888-89), pp. 522 ff.

40. Myers, "The Subliminal Consciousness," in *Proceedings* of the SPR, vol. VII (1891-92), pp. 299-301 ff. The other papers under this title are in *Proceedings,* vol. VIII, pp. 333 ff., and vol. IV, pp. 3 ff. There is a concluding paper on "The Subliminal Self" in vol. XI, pp. 334 ff.
41. Myers, *Human Personality and Its Survival of Bodily Death* (London, 1903), vol. I, p. 15.
42. Breuer and Freud, "Studies on Hysteria" in the Standard Edition, vol. II (London, 1955), pp. xiv-v; Jones, *Freud,* vol. III, p. 425.
43. J. B. Rhine, *New Frontiers of the Mind* (London, 1938), pp. 44-66; Rhine, *The Reach of the Mind* (London, 1948), p. 169.
44. Anton Müller, "Medizin und Okkultismus um die Jahrhundertwende," in *Zürcher Medizingeschichtliche Abhandlungen* (Neue Reihe Nr. 48), pp. 16-17. For the association of Fechner with occult tradition, see *The Occult Underground,* p. 229; also H. F. Ellenberger, "Fechner and Freud," in *Bulletin of the Menninger Clinic* (July 1956), pp. 201 ff.; Anton Müller, "Medizin und Okkultismus," p. 27; see Erich Bohn, *Der Fall Rothe* (Breslau, 1901), and Bohn with Hans H. Busse, *Geisterschriften und Drohbriefe* (Munich, 1902). Busse was the cofounder with Klages of the Graphological Society—see chapter II—and used his talents to expose "Spirit messages."
45. Albert Moll, *Psychologie und Charakterologie der Okkultisten* (Stuttgart, 1929), pp. 18 ff. Franz Blei, *Erzählung eines Lebens* (Leipzig, 1931), p. 403. For further personal reminiscences of Schrenck, see Gerda Walther, *Zum anderen Ufer* (Remagen, 1960).
46. Mathilde von Kemnitz, *Moderne Mediumforschung* (Munich, 1914). Gulat-Wellenberg's letter on pp. 71 ff. Protocol of sitting of 13 July 1913, pp. 50 ff.; Albert v. Schrenck-Notzing, *Der Kampf um die Materialisationsphänomene* (Munich, 1914).
47. Schrenck-Notzing, *Phenomena of Materialisation* (tr. E. E. Fournier d'Albe, London, 1920), p. 283; various articles, notably those printed in Schrenck-Notzing, *Gesammelte Aufsätze zur Parapsychologie* (ed. Gabrielle von Schrenck-Notzing, Leipzig, 1929), pp. 133, 140 ff. and report of the settlement of one of Schrenk's law suits, "Vergleich in der Privatklagsache Schrenk-Notzing gegen Kiesewetter," *Zeitchrift für parapsychologie* (May 1928); Karl von Klinckowstroem, "Zur Psychologie des Okkultisten," in *Waldenburger Schriften,* vol. VIII, (1927), pp. 68 ff.; Moll, *Okkultisten,* p. 18; Klinckowstroem, "Die Krise im Okkultismus" in *Die Medizinische Welt,* no. 50 (1928); Heinrich Schole, *Okkultismus und Wissenschaft* (Göttingen, 1929).
48. Freud, "A Premonitory Dream Fulfilled," *Standard Edition,* vol. VI, pp. 623-25; Jones, *Freud,* vol. III, pp. 410-12; vol. II, p. 188.
49. Jones, *Freud,* vol. II, p. 411. For the Freud-Ferenczi relationship, see Brome, *Freud,* pp. 195 ff.
50. Jones, *Freud,* vol. II, pp. 412-22, 436.
51. Blei, *Erzählung,* pp. 404-5.

52. Jones, *Freud,* vol. III, pp. 419-20.
53. Freud, "Pyschoanalysis and Telepathy," in the Standard Edition, vol. 18 (London, 1955), pp. 177, 178-81. The manuscript dates from August 1921, and was first published 1941.
54. Freud, "Psychoanalysis," pp. 178-81.
55. Wilhelm Stekel, *Der Telepathische Traum.* The edition I saw was no. 2 of the series "Die Okkulte Welt," but it was undated and may not have been the original publication. For his crucial experience, see p. 43.
56. Stekel, *Der telepathische Traum,* p. 17.
57. Freud, "Dreams and Telepathy," in the Standard Edition, vol. 18, pp. 197 ff. See especially pp. 219-20.
58. Jones, *Freud,* vol. III, pp. 420-24.
59. Freud, "Psychoanalysis and Telepathy," p. 190.
60. Freud, "Dreams and Occultism," in the Standard Edition, vol. XXII (London, 1964), pp. 31 ff.
61. Freud, "The Occult Significance of Dreams," in the Standard Editon, vol. XIX, pp. 135 ff.
62. *Imago,* vol. XII (1926), p. 434.
63. Freud, *The Interpretation of Dreams,* the Standard Edition, vol. V, p. 96.
64. Freud, "On Dreams" in *The Interpretation of Dreams,* the Standard Edition, vol. V, p. 635.
65. M. Laignel-Lavastine and Jean Vinchon, "Les Symboles traditionels et le Freudisme," in *1-er Congrès de l'Histoire de l'art de guérir, Liber Memorialis* (ed. Tricot Royer and Van Schevensteen, Antwerp, 1921), pp. 165-66.
66. Freud, "The Occult Significance of Dreams," p. 135.
67. E.g., Claude Lévi-Strauss, "Witch-doctors and Psychoanalysis" in *UNESCO Courier,* pp. 8, 10.
68. Freud to Pfister 25 November 1928 in *Psychoanalysis and Faith* (ed. H. Meng and Ernest Freud, London, 1963), p. 176.
69. The argument of Walter Riese in "The Pre-Freudian Origins of Psycho-analysis," reprinted from *Science and Psychoanalysis* (1958).
70. Franz Hartmann, *Occult Science and Medicine* (London, 1893), p. 10. The italics are Hartmann's.
71. Freud, *The Origins,* p. 145.
72. Freud, *Civilisation and Its Discontents* (tr. Jean Riviere, London, 1930), p. 36.
73. David Bakan, *Sigmund Freud and the Jewish Mystical Tradition* (Princeton, Toronto, London, 1958).
74. Donald Capps, "Hartmann's Relationship to Freud: a Reappraisal," in *Journal of the History of the Behavioural Sciences* (April 1970), pp. 162 ff.
75. Robert Couzin, "Leibnitz, Freud and Kabbala" in the same journal (October 1970), pp. 335 ff.

76. D. F. Foxon, "Libertine Literature in England," in *The Book-Collector* (1963), p. 304.
77. Steven Marcus, *The Other Victorians* (London, 1966), p. 283.
78. Clifford Howard, *Sex and Religion* (London, 1925), p. 28.
79. Jung, *Memories,* p. 175.
80. Ivan Bloch, *The Sexual Life of Our Time* (tr. Eden Paul, London, 1908), pp. 113 ff.; King, *Sexuality, Magic and Perversion.*
81. Herbert Silberer in *Imago,* vol. II (1913), pp. 593-94. See Hargrave Jennings, *The Rosicrucians: Their Rites and Mysteries* (London, 1893), and cf. his *Phallicism* (London, 1894).
82. Freud, *The Origins,* p. 189.
83. Freud, *The Origins,* p. 188; Margaret Murray, *The Witch-cult in Western Europe* (London, 1962), pp. 178 ff.
84. Freud, "A Seventeeth-Century Demonological Neurosis," in the Standard Edition, vol. XIX, pp. 72 ff.
85. Jones, *Freud,* vol. III, pp. 410, 419, 453.
86. Freud's interest—Jones, *Freud,* vol. III, p. 476—was ensnared by "Looney." This was J. Thomas Looney, author of *Shakespeare Identified* (London, 1920).
87. See Brome, *Freud,* pp. 154 ff.
88. Jung, *Memories,* pp. 119-20, 126-28.
89. On this period, see Jung, *Memories,* pp. 135 ff. and E. A. Bennett, *C. G. Jung* (London, 1961), pp. 22 ff.
90. Jones, *Freud,* vol. II, p. 156.
91. Jung, *On the Psychology and Pathology of So-called Occult Phenomena* (1902) in *Complete Works,* vol. I, pp. 36-39; *Memories,* p. 186. "Miss Miller" seems to be "Hélène Smith" of Flournoy's *From India to the Planet Mars* (tr. D. B. Vermilye, London and New York, 1900).
92. Jung, "On the Psychology and Pathology," p. 88, and *Memories,* pp. 127-28.
93. Jung's own account in *Memories* should be supplemented by the criticisms of Sir Cyril Burt in the *Journal of the SPR* (December 1963), p. 163 ff.
94. Jung, *Memories,* pp. 178-79.
95. See letters from Freud to Jung printed in *Memories,* pp. 395-97.
96. Brome, *Freud,* pp. 118 ff. has analyzed these.
97. Freud's affection for Rome, his classical references, his insistence on clarity, and a (sometimes deceptively) precise presentation are almost directly opposed to Jung's knowledge of occult philosophy—at the root of the "Romantic" world-view—his Gnostic sources, denial of reason, and often diffuse style.
98. Jung in a letter quoted in H. R. Philip, *Jung and the Problem of Evil* (London, 1958), p. 322.
99. Jung, *Memories,* pp. 215-16.
100. Jung, *VII Sermones ad Mortuos* (tr. H. G. Baynes, 1925), p. xix.

101. Miguel Serano, *C. G. Jung and Herman Hesse* (tr. F. MacShane, London, 1966), p. 101.
102. Jung, "The Spiritual Problem of Modern Man," p. 238; Jung, *Memories,* p. 226; Erich Ludendorff, foreword to Mathilde Ludendorff, *Induziertes Irresinn* (n.d., n.p.), p. 68; according to Francis King, Papus (who was a bishop in the Universal Gnostic Church) had Masonic honors conferred on him by Theodore Reuss. In return, Papus consecrated Reuss as a Gnostic potentate, and thus the line of succession passed into the O.T.O. See King, "Wandering Bishops," in *Man, Myth and Magic.*
103. McDougall in *A History of Psychology in Autobiography* (ed. C. Murchison, Worcester, Massachusetts, 1930-36), p. 211; G. Stewart Prince, "Jung's Psychology in Britain" in Michael Fordham (ed.), *Contact with Jung* (London, 1963), p. 49 and W. B. Crow, *The Science of Dreams* (Adyar, 1935).
104. Jung, *Memories,* pp. 228 ff.; Jung, "A Study in the Process of Individuation" (developed from *Eranos-Jahrbuch* paper of 1930), in *The Archetypes and the Collective Unconscious, Collected Works,* IX (London, 1959), p. 305.
105. Jung, "Individuation," p. 306.
106. Jung, "Individuation," pp. 290, 344.
107. On the beginnings of Jungian analysis in the United States, see Alma A. Paulsen, "Origins of Analytical Psychology in the New York Area," in Fordham, *Contact,* pp. 186 ff.
108. Paulsen, "Origins of Analytical Psychology," and Paulsen, Obituary notice on Eleanor Bertine in *Journal of Analytical Psychology* (July 1968).
109. Marguerite Beck Block, *The New Church in the New World* (New York, 1932), pp. 160-68, 303-4, 340-41, 350-52.
110. Charles H. Mann, *Three Sermons on the Healing of the Body through the Soul* (New York, 1887), and *Psychiasis* (Boston, 1900). Anyone who imagines the current *Honest to God* interpretation of Christianity (Dr. John Robinson *et al.*) to be new would do well to read Mann's *The Christ of God* (New York, 1897).
111. See I. B. Cohen, "Ethan Allen Hitchcock of Vermont," in *Proceedings of the American Antiquarian Society* (April-October 1951), pp. 34 ff.; E. A. Hitchcock, *Swedenborg: a Hermetic Philosopher* (Boston, 1857).
112. Jung, *Memories,* p. 230.
113. Herbert Silberer, *Problems of Mysticism and Its Symbolism* (tr. S. E. Jelliffe, New York, 1917). This book, together with Rudolf Kassner's *Die Mystik, die Künstler und das Leben* greatly influenced Hugo von Hofmannsthal. Apart from the commonly known fact that he committed suicide, I have been able to discover little about Silberer, who may well be a significant figure.
114. Hitchcock, *Swedenborg,* p.119; C. J. Wilkinson, *James John Garth Wilkinson* (London, 1911); quotation in Block, *New Church,* p. 351.

115. Jung, *Memories,* pp. 184, 222-25; James John Garth Wilkinson, *The Soul is Form and Doth the Body Make* (London, 1890), pp. 16-17.
116. Jung, *Psychology and Alchemy* in *Collected Works,* vol. XII (London, 1953), pp. 23, 35; Jung, "Concerning the Archetypes with Special Reference to the Anima Concept" (1936), in *The Archetypes,* pp. 64-65 and note 24. Jung says that Maitland probably did not know the *Poimandres;* Maitland certainly did. See passage quoted in my *Occult Underground,* p. 278.
117. See bibliography to *The Interpretation of Dreams.*
118. Jung, *Psychology and Alchemy,* p. 23 and *Mysterium Conjunctionis* in *Collected Works,* (London, 1963), pp. 555-56.
119. See *The Occult Underground,* p. 275.
120. Käthe Bügler, "Die Entwicklung der analytischen Psychologie in Deutschland" in Fordham, *Contact,* pp. 23 ff. For Heyer, see references in Gerda Walther, *Zum anderen Ufer.*
121. Quoted from Joseph Campbell, foreword to *Man and Transformation* (London, 1964), pp. 5-6.
122. Jost, *Derleth,* pp. 99-101, 136. Lothar Helbig, "Ludwig und Anna Maria Derleth," in *Derleth Gedenkbuch,* p. 70; Derleth, *Das Buch vom Orden,* p. 101.
123. Robert Landmann, *Monte Verita,* pp. 206 ff.
124. Manifesto printed in Landmann, p. 226.
125. See *Eranos-Jahrbuch* (1938) and cf. G. R. Heyer, *The Organism of the Mind* (tr. E. and C. Paul, London, 1933); Bernouilli, "Die Zahlenmystik des Tarotsystems," in *Eranos-Jahrbuch* (1934); Eliade's diary, quoted by George Uscatescu, "Time and Destiny in the Novels of Mircea Eliade," in J. M. Kitagawa and C. H. Long (eds.), *Myths and Symbols: Studies in Honor of Mircea Eliade* (Chicago, 1969), p. 398; on Eliade, see E. M. Cioran in Kitagawa and Long, *Myths and Symbols,* pp. 407 ff. and Basil Munteanu, *Geschichte der neueren Rumänische Literatur* (Vienna, 1943), pp. 165 ff.
126. Jung, *Memories,* p. 405; Howe, *Urania's Children,* pp. 94-95 and notes p. 95, suggests that Schmitz was probably responsible for Jung's real "conversion" to astrology in the early 1920s. For an approach to astrology approved of by Keyserling, see Olga von Ungern-Sternberg, "Die Korrespondenz von Makro und Mikrokosmos," in *Der Leuchter,* vol. VI (1925).
127. Bügler, "Die Entwicklung der analytischen Psychologie in Deutschland," brackets Hauer with Richard Wilhelm and Heinrich Zimmer as three of the great influences on Jung.
128. Jung, "Yoga and the West," in *Psychology and Religion, Complete Works,* vol. II (London, 1950), pp. 529 ff.
129. Jung, "Psychology and Religion," in *Complete Works,* vol. XI, p. 52 and note 20, p. 82 and note 31. Cf. Hauer, "Symbole und Erfahrung des Selbsts," in *Eranos-Jahrbuch* (1934).

130. Hauer, *Eranos-Jahrbuch,* p. 60 and his *Deutsche Gottschau* (Stuttgart, 1937), pp. 44 ff.
131. Hans Buchheim, *Glaubenskrise im dritten Reich* (Stuttgart, 1953), pp. 157-61. Cf. T. S. K. Scott-Craig and R. E. Davis, *Germany's New Religion* (London, 1937), pp. 22-23.
132. Conway, *Persecution,* pp. 106 ff.; Buchheim, *Glaubenskrise,* pp. 162 ff.
133. See J. W. Hauer, *Werden und Wesen der Anthroposophie* (Stuttgart, 1922); Conway, *Persecution,* pp. 106-8.
134. Hauer, *Eine indo-arische Metaphysik des Kampfes und der Tat* (Stuttgart, 1934).
135. Jung, "Wotan" in *Civilisation in Transition, Complete Works,* vol. X (London, 1964), p. 191.
136. Brome, *Freud,* pp. 142-53, discusses the controversy. The opposing points of view are put by Ernest Glover, *Freud or Jung* (London, 1950), pp. 142 ff. and Ernest Harms, "Carl Gustav Jung—Defender of Freud and the Jews," in *Psychiatric Quarterly* (April 1946).
137. Printed in *Civilisation in Transition,* p. 533.
138. E.g., Kurt Ganger, quoted in George Mosse, *Nazi Culture* (London, 1966), pp. 199, 223-24. But cf. the *Ordensbürgen* lecturer, Hans Alfred Grunsky, *Seele und Staat* (Berlin, 1935), pp. 97 ff.
139. Jung, *Freud and Psycho-analysis, Complete Works,* vol. IV (1961), p. 255; A. U. Vasuvada, "Analytical Psychology of C. G. Jung and Indian Wisdom," p. 141; Jane Wheelwright, "A Personal Experience," in Fordham, *Contact,* p. 227.
140. Jung, "A Psychological Commentary on the *Tibetan Book of the Great Liberation,*" in *Psychology and Religion,* p. 500; Jung, foreword to Victor White, *God and the Unconscious,* p. 307. Jung, "Psychology and Religion," pp. 104-5; Jung, "Commentary on the *Tibetan Book of the Dead,*" p. 524.
141. Montessori, quoted in William Boyd and Wyatt Rawson, *The Story of the New Education* (London, 1965), pp. 23, 27-29. For one school conducted on OWC and K.K. lines, see Dorothy Revel, *Cheiron's Cave* (London, 1928), and Ernest Westlake, *The Forest School.*
142. E. A. Hinckelman and M. Ademan, "Apparent Theoretical Parallels between G. Stanley Hall and Carl Jung," in *Journal of the History of the Behavioural Sciences* (July 1968), pp. 254-57; see Jung, "Child Development and Education" and "Analytical Psychology and Education," in *The Development of the Personality, Collected Works,* vol. 17 (London, 1954); Lhotzky, *The Soul of Your Child* (London, 1902). For Müller's theories, see Willy Scheel, *Innerliche Schulreform* (Munich, 1920); Hemleben, *Steiner,* p. 125; Steiner, *The Education of the Child in the Light of Anthroposophy* (London, 1965; orig. 1909), p. 25; Steiner, *Study of Man* (London, 1947; orig. 1919), p. 34.
143. An account of the school is in Armstrong Smith, *Some Ideals in Co-*

Education (London, 1919); Boyd and Rawson, *New Education,* pp. 70 ff., 78.

144. *The New Era* (4-14 April 1923), p. 156.

145. Adolphe Ferrière, *La Loi de progrès* (Paris, 1915), p. 660; see Ferrière, *Psychological Types and the Stages of Man's Development* (London, 1958), and his *Activity School* (London, 1939).

146. See Howe, *Urania's Children,* part 2, passim.

147. H. A. Strauss (ed.), *Jahrbuch für kosmobiologische Forschung* (Augsburg, 1928), p. 29; reports in William Boyd and Muriel MacKenzie, *Towards a New Education* (London and New York, 1930), pp. 387-90 and cf. *New Era* (October 1929), p. 215; Krafft to Ferrière from Elsinore, 28 October 1929; Howe, *Urania's Children,* pp. 145-46. Of Ferrière's numerous publications, his *Symboles graphiques de la Typocosmie* is worth noting. It was published in 1940 at La Sallaz sur Lausanne by the Editions de la Forge. This argues a possible connection with followers of Lutoslawski, who moved his Forge to Lausanne in 1912.

148. *Romain Rolland* (Neuchatel, 1969), published by University of Geneva.

Chapter 7
The Great Liberation

Liberation and Society—Modern Art and the Occult Revival —America imports Bohemia—Drugs and the Occult— Timothy Leary and Ken Kesey—Underground Occultism— Haight-Ashbury and the Hippies—New Forms of Illuminated Politics—Reich, Marcuse, and Metaphysical Liberation—R. D. Laing and the Dialectics of Liberation

THE idea of "freedom" often has most tangible associations— let me out of here, give me enough to eat, create the opportunities for me to use my abilities to benefit myself or others. Always beside these easily understood demands has run another. It is an apocalyptic definition of freedom, which has its roots in various pre-Christian religious conceptions. And in this century it owes direct allegiance to the irrationalist reaction and the occult revival of the 1890s. It is notorious that no two men will ever agree on what "freedom" is: for the anarchist of the turn of the century it signified the dissolution of all legal and social bonds, but for the believer in Hitler's Germany, it meant a liberation from the vagaries of fate augmented by the anarchic and profiteering systems of Western liberalism. Each definition represents "freedom"; and each embodies definitions of what "unfreedom" is. It is the purpose of this chapter to imply that in many such definitions of free and unfree, the tangible meaning of the word "freedom" has its inevitable corollary in a conception of personal "liberation" from *the condition of being human*—a rejection of the helplessness, mutual isolation, and mortality of man.

This liberation is liberation of a mystical or occult nature. In its Western form it is to be found in the Gnostic systems. The cardinal tenet is that man contains God, a spark of the divine somehow entrapped in matter—and that he can only effect his salvation by realizing and rejoining the Godhead from which he sprang. This is also the position at the root of the most serious occult systems. It may be that there is an innate Gnosticism in humanity, which throws up the idea of man's divine origins from time to time in different forms to provide a consoling myth for an intolerable predicament. The idea is even found in orthodox Christianity—all myths of the Fall from grace embody some idea of a possible return to Heaven. In this century, with the presentation of traditional religious positions in secular form, there has emerged a secular Gnosticism beside the other great secular religions—the mystical union of Fascism, the apocalypse of Marxist dialectic, the Earthly City of social democracy. The secular Gnosticism is almost never recognized for what it is, and it can exist alongside other convictions almost unperceived. Thus, the Fascist or the Communist or the anarchist may cherish unknown to himself a vision of personal liberation, which in imagination fuses with the communal definition of "freedom" to which he nominally subscribes. It was the characteristic of the Sixties, however, to produce a form of secular Gnosticism, which took on a relatively independent existence and which defined "liberation" in terms that without doubt derived directly from the occult revival or its influence.

This "pure" form of secular Gnosticism is found among the "Counterculture," the "Youth movement," and parts of the "New Left."

So far we have discussed the coincidence of occultism and politics in terms of "illuminated politics," implying a politics that has a religious complexion and obeys a transcendental scale of values. The counterculture was packed full to bursting with the occult and mystical elements which indicate the illuminated attitude, and certain of its most cherished and supposedly "relevant" theories—the term of the self-proclaimed pragmatic wing of the movement in opposition to the out-and-out mystics—derived directly from the secularized Gnosticism of the occult revival. These concepts had been floating around for at least a century. But not until the 1960s did the Gnosticism become sufficiently secularized to provide the motor force for a widespread theory of everyday living. The Underground of the Sixties was often concerned with illuminated politics of a particular—Gnostic—form, whereas the illuminated politicians of the first half of this century more often put their idealism at the service of a political cause that made more concessions toward the aspirations of society at large.

Present-day illuminates are the obvious heirs of earlier illuminated politicians. We have already examined *almost every tenet* cultivated among the contemporary Underground. Insistence on a "natural" way of living, anti-industrialism, vegetarianism, protection of the environment, "organic" community, and spiritual evolution—all combine with occult enthusiasms and the political cause of the movement. The specific political objectives of any given time account for most of the differences between the later Underground and that of the 1890s—and in what follows some obvious differences are taken for granted. My concern is to point the similarities and to argue that the Gnostic-occult idea of "liberation" is one common denominator of Underground groups. The Progressive Underground of the 1890s—equally concerned with spiritual evolution and spiritual revolution—was also the habitat of occultists and practitioners of strange religions like those from which the Underground of the 1960s derived its fundamental illuminism and much of its ideology. Because the Underground of the 1960s was a development from earlier Bohemias, those earlier Bohemias are important as a source of inspiration for contemporary idealists. Both the myth of Bohemia and the real configurations of that landscape have played a part in the growth of the modern Underground, and the occult has formed part both of the legend and the reality. The societies on which the Underground of the last decade were based had their own ideas of "liberation," and the occult preoccupations of Eckstein's Vienna, Symbolist Paris, or the Munich of the Cosmic Circle have had an inevitable effect on their spiritual descendants. "Modern" culture as a whole is so indebted to artists and writers who found their inspiration in the turn-of-the-century Occult Revival that the avant-garde of today necessarily makes use of "esoteric" ideas without realizing their nature. In order to understand how the social criticism of the modern Underground is of a predominantly Gnostic nature, it would be useful to outline—very briefly—how the occult has affected some influential theories of modern art.

The eccentric American critic T. H. Robsjohn-Gibbings published in 1948 a book called *Mona Lisa's Mustache.* This was the first work to call attention to the occult connections of modern art. Robsjohn-Gibbings was largely concerned with a polemic against the recently opened New York Museum of Modern Art, and his idiosyncratic fulminations contributed to bury his book. He also labored under the ideological effects of the recent war and made an equation which must have seemed preposterous to some: "modern art" = occultism = Fascism. The equation is preposterous as it stands, but the truth it conceals is great. Robsjohn-Gibbings had fallen into the trap of overstating his case; and, at the same time, he made the same mistake that is made by those who call, for example, Jung's psychology,—or, for that matter, the Social Credit Party—"Fascist." What both Jung and Social Credit have in common with some sorts of Fascism is the illuminated attitude. And exactly the same is true of modern art. Considerable occult influence has sometimes been behind modern theories of art, but these are not identical with Fascism.

Robsjohn-Gibbings placed considerable stress on the Futurist doctrines of Marinetti and their associations with the Italian Fascists. But he had only to examine the attitude of distaste shown by the typically "illuminated" group around Orage in their encounter with Futurism to see that those with a penchant for the occult need not be tarred with the brush of "modern art."

To be fair, if we alter his equation to read "occultism = much original modern art = occasionally illuminated politics," we can see how the error arose. There is considerable excuse for the mistake when the career of someone like Guilio Evola—whom Robsjohn-Gibbings did not cite as an example—is considered. Evola turns up everywhere. He preached an "imperialism of the blood," influenced Italian Fascism, and had his works translated into German under the Nazis. He wrote on alchemy and the Hermetic tradition. He is quoted by Jung in this connection. He played a part in the revival of Bachofen. Anada Coomaraswamy sent a pamphlet by him to Eric Gill. Of course he appears in the history of modern art, although there is disagreement as to his status: Hans Richter thinks him a "second-generation Futurist," while Tristan Tzara incorporated him in the legions of Dada—whatever they were.[1]

Illuminated art derives from occultism, and much modern art is indirectly illuminated or directly occult. There is no place here for aesthetics, and my intention is only to show the connection of much influential modern art with the occult. This alliance began in Paris of the 1890s when—as I have shown in my book on the subject[2]—the occult revival coincided exactly with the Symbolist movement, and the Symbolists drew a great part of their inspiration from the occultists. Occult theories resulted in the conception of the artist as a saint and a magician, while his art became less and less representative of ordinary reality and hinted at things beyond. From this departure of the Symbolists from the universe of agreed discourse for private or superior worlds has sprung the tampering with "everyday" reality which has become so central a feature of modern art. Naturally, similar developments were going on elsewhere, just as the reaction against the tyranny of Reason occurred in other places. But Paris remained the hub from which the magic influences radiated, the center of artistic and occult experiment.

After the initial breakthrough, the development of modern art followed the epidemic of unreason, and it was often linked directly to the proliferating cults. Germany and Russia saw important developments, in which a central figure was Vasili Kandinsky. Kandinsky arrived in Germany in 1896 from a humdrum life as a lawyer, and, after a series of false starts, he settled in 1908 near Munich. In 1910 he painted the famous watercolor that, despite all counterclaims, has still the best title to be called "the first abstract picture." Sixten Ringbom has recently explored in detail some of

Robsjohn-Gibbings's speculations. He has shown beyond all doubt that Kandinsky was influenced in his complicated theories of the significance of color by the ideas that Rudolf Steiner derived from Goethe, and in his moves toward abstraction by the Theosophical book *Thought Forms,* in which emotions are given pictorial substance.[3] Kandinsky attended lectures by Steiner in Murnau and Berlin. The library he left behind him includes the works of Steiner as well as several on Spiritualism—Aksakov, Du Prel, Kiesewetter, Zöllner—and miscellaneous trapping of the idealistic revolution in the form of books by Baron Hellenbach, Hübbe-Schleiden's periodical *Sphynx,* and a tract entitled *What everyone should know about vegetarianism.*[4]

In 1911 Kandinsky and Franz Marc organized the first *Blaue Reiter* exhibition in Berlin, the year before Kandinsky published his Theosophically inclined book, *On the Spiritual in Art.* Marc himself was greatly influenced by Kandinsky's occult color theories. He saw art as religion and abstract art as "second sight." He himself hoped for "liberation from the sense-illusions of our ephemeral life."[5]

The coincidence of art and occultism was, of course, not universal. But it was a definite part of the idealistic Underground, which drew its sustenance from the same revolt against reason as had inspired the Symbolists. In Germany, as in France, critics proclaimed the "death of naturalism." As early as 1891 Hermann Bahr had announced his belief that naturalism would go down before "a neurotic romanticism: I would rather say, through a mysticism of the nerves." In the Bohemian circles that had taken to their hearts Wagner's views on art and religion the more specific ideas of Rudolf Steiner found their natural home. Kandinsky and Marc had been anticipated in their mysticism by the Expressionist group *Die Brücke* founded in Dresden in 1904. Its leading spirit, Edvard Munch, was in close touch with Strindberg in the mid-1890s when the playwright was in contact with Lanz von Liebenfels. It is possible to endorse Robsjohn-Gibbings: "From the Rhine to the Baltic, the religious symbolists, religious socialists, idealistic art-lovers, occultists and Buddhists found their way." We have already seen this true in terms of general irrationalism, and it remains true in terms of irrationalism in art. By the end of the First World War, even an apologist for the religious mission of art who was fascinated by Steiner and Soloviev could deplore the way in which spiritual aspirations had been "distorted" into "pure spookiness and occultism."[6]

Such tendencies came together in the early days of the Bauhaus, which Walter Gropius established in Weimar in 1919. Although Gropius and the style with which he is associated later became severely attached to functionalist principles, at the time that he founded the Bauhaus he was considerably influenced by ideas of the religious mission of art, which at that time were common currency. "Art is sacred," he wrote in 1919, "it is rare, without purpose; it wanders the loveliest ways far in advance, is born and understood in the highest ecstasy." The early programs of the Bauhaus included "joint planning of extensive utopian building projects—cultural and spiritual centres—with far-reaching objectives."[7] In the concept of a new sort of cooperation and artistic training for which the early Bauhaus stood, there are many parallels with the English Arts and Crafts movement, including a romanticized attachment to handicrafts and the nobility of labor. Within this atmosphere it was natural that the specifically occult would play a part.

The designer and supervisor of the Bauhaus "Preliminary Course" was Johannes Itten (1888-1967), who taught at the Bauhaus till 1923. In the 1930s he was listed as the leading Mazdaznan lecturer in Germany.[8] His vision of the world in crisis led to a strange introductory course, in which breathing exercises and meditation were prominent features. He was obsessed with the vision of doom purveyed by Spengler's *Decline of the West:*

> I was conscious that technical-scientific civilisation had come to a critical point. The slogan, "unity of art and technology" did not seem to me to be able to solve the problem.
>
> I studied Eastern philosophy, occupied myself with Persian Mazdaism and primitive Christianity. Thus I came to the opinion that an internally-directed thought and spiritual strength must provide the counterweight to our outwardly-directed scientific research and technologising.
>
> George Muche came to a similar conclusion through his war experience and we worked amicably together. We were looking for the basis of a new way of life for ourselves and our work. At that time I was laughed at because I did breathing

and concentration exercises. Today it has become perfectly accepted for many people to occupy themselves with Eastern philosophy.[9]

Itten began his courses only when all were thoroughly prepared by breathing exercises. To his camp of idealists belonged, to some extent, also Klee, Kandinsky, Muche, and Oscar Schlemmer (who delivered compulsory courses in "Anthropology"—which consisted of astrology, phrenology, physiognomy, and graphology). Itten designed a "uniform," or monastic habit, for the Bauhaus; it was rather like the outfit worn by Eric Gill. The Bauhaus even possessed a special dance called "Itten-Muche-Mazdaznan." Alfred Arndt recalls: "Serious and dignified, the 'mazdaznaners'—their chief was Master Itten—ate much garlic and gargled often." When Arndt took over a studio from a "mazdaznaner," he found a straw pallet and a blue circle on the wall five feet in diameter. The circle served as an aid in concentration exercises, which were a part of the creed of the "mazdaznaners." Not only the practitioners of Mazdaznan were influenced by the sense of the sacred: at Christmas 1919 Gropius himself served dinner to his pupils, and Arndt commented: "Just like the washing of feet."[10]

Although the greater part of such mysticism left the Bauhaus with Itten, the organization continued to be associated with adepts of the irrational. During the 1920s, the influential Dutch group *De Stijl* (of which the leading figures were Theo van Doesburg and Piet Mondrian) formed an alliance with the Bauhaus. The influence that originally bound the founders of *De Stijl* together was a mystical mathematician, Dr. M. H. J. Schoenmaekers, who believed himself able to partition the world into its component elements. His theories gave the *Stijl* artists the incentive toward their use of mathematical form and primary colors. Holland had always possessed a strong body of Theosophists, and the Dutch section was the first section of the Theosophical Society to receive an independent charter from the parent group. Mondrian himself joined the Theosophical Society in 1909, and he kept a portrait of Madame Blavatsky in his studio. Holland was also the European headquarters of Krishnamurti's Order of the Star in the East; and among the books that Mondrian kept until his death was Krishnamurti's *At the Feet of the Master,* together with some lectures of Steiner.[11]

The presence of Kandinsky in the later Bauhaus is a reminder that the traditions of Slav irrationalism have contributed to the irrational currents in modern art. It would be surprising if the circles around Diaghilev's *World of Art* had not been influenced to some extent by mysticism. In this group is found, for example, the Lithuanian M. K. Ciurlionis, who was much impressed by contemporary esotericism, and who around 1907 was beginning to try to "paint music."[12] When the confusion of the Bolshevik Revolution had been sorted out, the same fate awaited the idealist artists as awaited the writers of the "spiritual" traditions. When Kandinsky's plans for art education in Russia were again and again turned down by official cultural organizations, he left for the Bauhaus; and other protagonists of a spiritual art either emigrated or relapsed into silence. The channels through which their influences ran were those of Western irrationalism. For example, the "Suprematist" Kasimir Malevich published a book in the Bauhaus series as late as 1927, after having retired increasingly into teaching activities. There was little else to do other than maintain silence or publish abroad, for one who in 1920 had been proclaiming that man's perfection lay in God, that "God was not cast down."[13]

The occult revival was, thus, linked with the quest for a "spiritual" art; and, to a certain extent, such ideas of art followed the flag of esotericism. However, as the 1930s approached, political necessity and utilitarianism became the watchwords of the day. There remained one tradition—apart from the works of those individual artists who owed allegiance to the earlier idealism—that continued to question the premises on which ideas of political expediency or material satisfaction were based. It is probably incorrect to refer to a "tradition," because this compendium of unreason began with the intentionally indefinable—Dada. Dada, writes Hans Richter, was "the creation of a state of affairs which made new products possible." In this deliberate break with the accepted methods of doing, being, and creating, sense and non-sense were irremediably mixed. Dada was no less a revolt against reason for being wrapped in a language that reason itself denied. When Hugo Ball, Tristan Tzara, and Richard Hulsenbeck began to give their anarchic displays in 1916 at the Cabaret Voltaire in Zurich, the *confusion* was directed against an *order* which the performers despised. Whereas Itten and others of his opinion might look with horror at the mechanized civilization that engulfed them and take refuge in the spiritual highlands, the Dadaists proceeded from a similar horror to attempt to destroy the constricting system of meaning which upheld the detested and Established order of things. But, precisely because of their revolt against accepted reality, the Dadaists—and more often their Surrealist successors—could not avoid the perennial solutions to the perennial problem: "What is real?" Thus Hugo Ball declared, "What we call Dada is foolery, foolery extracted from the emptiness in which all higher problems are wrapped."[14]

The aims of the Dadaists were to shock the bourgeoisie and to induce a sense of self-outlawry through their rejection of conventional standards. This did not absolve them from the natural human wish to find meaning in the world, even if it was not the meaning of accepted society. Just as the Symbolists of the 1890s had shocked the bourgeosie with nonsense poems and foregathered with occultists—those more purposeful irrationalists of Bohemia—the Dadaists were unable to escape the same pattern. In late 1916, in sympathy with a waiters' strike in their usual café, the Dadaists of Zürich moved to the Café Odéon, where they met Erich Unger, a student of the Cabala. Unger introduced them to Dr. Oscar Goldberg, who was a numerologist attempting to complete an esoteric interpretation of the Pentateuch. Hans Richter put Goldberg in contact with a wealthy friend who subsidized his researches. This was not an "important" or "influential" contact of the Dadaists, but it illustrates that those seeking anti-Establishment interpretations of existence inevitably meet—both literally, and along the line of their inquiries. Hugo Ball (1886-1927) the "originator" of Dada, if anyone is to have the title, was well read in the literature of mysticism and Eastern philosophy, and he particularly admired Boehme. After the first appearance of Dada in Zürich, Ball and Emmy Hennings settled down with the rest of the German emigration in Ticino—the canton of Ascona—and studied the literature of the Russian idealists. From Merezhkovsky, Rozanov, and Soloviev, Ball moved on to the church from which they sprang. In 1923 he published a study of *Byzantine Christianity,* which contained lives of St. John Climacus, Dionysius the Areopagyte, and Simon Stylites.[15]

Not only did Dada have a necessary external connection with nonrational ways of thought, but it possessed an interior identity. This is clearly discernible in Hans Richter's discussion of the Dada obsession with chance and the magical power of art. Richter sees the "true" Dadaists as attempting to achieve a balance between conscious and unconscious forces. In 1918 Tristan Tzara introduced him to the Norwegian painter Viking Eggeling, who was experimenting with similar conceptions and who based his work on a philosophy embodying the old occult idea of polarity. They decided that they must "resolve the polarities" and create the bridge between consciousness and unconsciousness. Richter's description of this "new" truth reveals completely why occultism and Dada have a fundamental affinity.

> At the time we were convinced that we had set foot in completely unknown territory, with musical counterpoint as its only possible analogy.
>
> In fact, however, this idea of the "unity of opposites" has been known under the name of "contingence," for a very long time. But what we had found still constituted a "discovery." Our scientific and technological age had forgotten that this contingence constituted an essential principle of life and of experience and that reason with all its consequences was inseparable from *un*reason with all its consequences. The myth that everything in the world can be rationally explained had been gaining ground since the time of Descartes. An inversion was necessary to restore the balance.
>
> The realization that reason and anti-reason, sense and nonsense, design and chance, consciousness and unconsciousness, belong together as necessary parts of a whole—this was the central message of Dada.[16]

Out of the Dada revolt and the Symbolist inheritance, André Breton and his associates constructed Surrealism. Like Dada, Surrealism was not "art," but a philosophy concerned with liberating man from a false consciousness. Breton's studies had begun with the occultists: Ramon Lull, Nicholas Flamel, Fabre d'Olivet, Fulcanelli, and Eliphas Lévi. These became entangled with the work of more modern explorers of the irrational. Around 1919 Breton's occult interests merged with Freudianism and a particular fascination with the phenomena of trance writing—possibly based on a reading of Pierre Janet's *Psychological Automatism* (which relied partly on Frederic Myers). In 1919 Breton and Philippe Soupault produced in *Les Champs Magnétiques* the first example of automatic surrealist writing. In so doing they were producing something which, while perhaps new in the realms of literature —although briefer attempts had been made by the Dadaists in Zürich—was not so in the world of art. Several painters—among them Picasso—have claimed to paint in a semitrance. Particularly in Germany there was, even before the First War, substantial interest in the artistic productions of mediums. For example, Hans Freimark's *Mediumistische Kunst* (1914) came to the typically Surrealist conclusion that the genius and the medium shared the same sources of inspiration. By the end of 1922 "an epidemic of trances" had broken out among the future Surrealists.[17]

The occult connections of Surrealism are frequently denied by latter-day "Surrealists" who have not bothered to study the substance of their inheritance. At the end of the Second World War, Breton returned to his early occult preoccupations. Another leading ornament of Surrealist iconography, Antonin Artaud (1896-1948), lapsed increasingly into a private world of magical symbols that continually changed significance; for Artaud it was always difficult to decide whether or not he believed in his numerology and his magical universe.[18]

The union of occultism, psychoanalysis, and personal experiment with trance was symptomatic of Surrealism rather than constituting its essence; and indeed so was art itself of any description. I shall return at the end of this chapter to the manner in which Surrealism has transmitted its conception of "liberation." For the moment the important factor is that the movement embodied occult elements and was in every sense the direct heir of Dada and (to a lesser degree) of the earlier attempts to arrive at a "spiritual" standpoint through art.

Occult tradition was as much part of Bohemia—both the inherited myths and the present reality—as it had been in the 1890s, and its philosophies still formed the core of attempts to free the mind from the vision induced by circumstances. By the 1930s the occult had been joined by psychoanalysis and theories deriving from it—fresh proof of the kinship of such apparently different systems and more ammunition for those who wished to destroy the fabric of bourgeois reality. These were further reinforced by a reverence for the experience of madness and a cult of the primitive. Among the ever-increasing number of Americans who began during the 1920s and 1930s to frequent European artists' quarters, elements both of the myth and the reality of Bohemia were naturally absorbed. After the Second World War (and the G.I. Bill), a culture, its dreams and artifacts were engorged entire. Dada and Surrealism as "movements" or "influences" or "trends" crossed the Atlantic and were absorbed into the consciousness of American artists, and the Bauhaus emigrated en bloc. Theories of occult liberation arrived with the artists in the New World.

American esotericism does not appear to have had much connection with illuminated politics until the past decade, and the most obvious reason is that the funds, organization, and drive needed to initiate any orthodox "political" movement in the United States have proved prohibitive for illuminated politicians. But the same rules of like-calling-to-like apply to the American situation; and one very good reason for the lack of occult groups in Progressive circles was the lack of such Bohemian political circles altogether. There was no lack of occultists. America had given birth to many of the movements that played a part in the 19th-century occult revival—Spiritualism, Christian Science, innumerable cults of Christian derivation had arrived in Europe from America. The Theosophical Society in America broke off from the Annie Besant-dominated European and Asian group and established itself in California. Initiates from various magical orders had returned across the Atlantic ever since S. L. Macgregor Mathers of the Golden Dawn had started to initiate Americans for fees in Paris. During the 1930s and 1940s followers of Aleister Crowley began to build up support of Crowley's brand of magic. When Progressive circles did begin to develop in the 1920s and 1930s, the esotericists found their natural place. Thus the doctrines of Gurdjieff and Ouspensky penetrated the avant-garde. Margaret Anderson and Jane Heap of the *Little Review* left for France and the master himself, while others gathered around Orage in New York. The potential for illuminated politics was there. For example, there was Alfred William Lawson (born 1869), who was a typical exponent of rejected knowledge—in this case of an individualistic "physics," which Lawson claimed governed the universe according to laws of suction and pressure—and he sprang into the public eye in the 1930s with an economic doctrine known as "Direct Credit," which resembled the theories of Major Douglas.[19] Lawson did manage to whip up a remarkable amount of support—16,000 people attended a parade he held in 1933 in Detroit. This points the moral that another essential factor for the fusion of pure irrationalism with political or social thinking is a sufficient anxiety level. Lawson found his hour—as Hargrave did in England—with the Depression.

For America to display the patterns of behavior that we have observed in Europe, three factors were necessary. There must be a high level of anxiety to induce the crisis of consciousness which in Europe had been kept at an extreme of tension since the end of the last century. There must be a broadening of Bohemian culture to provide the natural launching pad for the exploration of other realities. And for irrationalist views of politics or society to obtain a wide hearing some way must be found to overcome the obstacles to political organization in the United States. With the momentary fusion of all anti-establishment forces in the late 1960s, all these conditions were fulfilled. Anxiety had been mounting since the immediate postwar era.* Bohemia had become the myth it had been so long in Europe and was at last based on a sufficient material reality. And the solution to the political problem was found by a new sort of political grouping—*around the myth itself.* Through the publicity of the mass media and particularly of television, the infinite desirability of Bohemia was projected as it had never been in Europe. And the rebellion against the Established, materialist, rationalist order of things in America took the form of an extension of the Bohemian life-style and an application of the Bohemian critique of society to the political situation as a whole. This critique has always been powerful and has been adopted by *Realpolitik* revolutionaries for their own ends since the middle of the last century. In essence it is the creed of spiritual revolution, a *unio mystica* of humanity and a liberation from the flesh.

So—into the American consciousness came the artistic occult, as a natural corollary of the importation of Bohemia. In the magazine *View,* which began publication in New York in September 1940 and

---

*For a discussion of the symptoms of this crisis see the next chapter.

prominently featured the views of the Surrealists surrounding Peggy Guggenheim, the irrational was a key element. In the first number the front page carried a photograph of Pavel Tchelitchev, an artist perpetually involved with the occult. Tchelitchev had brought his esoteric tastes—he actually imitated the style of 17th-century alchemical texts—out of his native Russia.[20] *View* printed a telegram from Julien Lévy to Tchelitchev describing the evil omens his Tarot pack had shown for the future of a friend.[21] In the autumn of the next year an interview with André Breton appeared; he mused on the supernatural powers attributed to Hitler and the prevalence of Nostradamus prophecies in his own prewar circle. Surrealism continued, he said, as "*alienation of sensation* in full accord with the precept of Rimbaud to become a 'seer.' " The same issue published a letter from Pierre Mabille in Guadeloupe calling for "a new orientation of the being and a 'hermetic' knowledge of metaphysics." Side by side with this stood a heart-rending appeal from Artaud in the lunatic asylum—he could not get heroin and his communications were cut by the police, who "bar the roads in the occult, no less than in the real."[22] As the war progressed, the magical elements noticeably increased in the pages of *View*. Kurt Seligman began to serialize the material that he was to publish in 1948 in his *The Mirror of Magic*, and the editorial of *View* proclaimed explicitly: "Seers, we are for the magic view of life."[23] In the autumn of 1946, Seligman published a symposium on "Magic and the Arts," which included every sort of definition of the magical approach, ranging from the concision of Marcel Duchamp ("Anti-reality!") through the labored profundities of Parker Tyler, to the enigmatic opinion of Edgar Varese (who cited Hoëne-Wronski and thought magic to be "corporealisation of the intelligence that is in sound").[24]

One writer who ended up on the West Coast contributed as much as any of the East Coast refugees from Hitler's Europe toward introducing a sense of the magical into American Bohemia. This was Henry Miller. Miller became interested in the occult in the mid-1930s, and his later interest extended to announcing that he would hang framed photographs of Gurdjieff and Hermann Hesse beside each other on the wall. Around 1935 Miller was reading Steiner, Eliphas Lévi, Madame Blavatsky, and the Tibetan series of Evans-Wentz. He met Keyserling, Dane Rudhyar, and the extraordinary astrologer Conrad Moricand (who became a good friend). In a number of *View* in early 1942, Miller told how after an evening with Moricand he had fallen through a glass door and gone to the hospital. The next day Moricand had appeared with Miller's horoscope, announcing that the indications had been for death, not injury. After the war, Miller had Moricand as a guest in his home in California, a disastrous episode, which he has fully described.[25]

Neither the occultism of the *View* group nor that of Henry Miller can be seen as having a direct effect on the hospitality of American artists to the miraculous. Yet artists of the postwar generation necessarily absorbed the occult preoccupations of their predecessors as part of their education. The accumulated traditions of European Bohemia meant not only that the occult was a subject which fascinated some of the more influential artists but that the philosophies which informed their work were based on esoteric ideas. We have seen how occult ideas of liberation and spiritual revolution permeated the artistic movements to which the postwar generation looked. Both in the myth of the *vie de Bohème* and the reality, the topics had a recognized place. But the place they had was a place in an imported European fashion. And when America began to originate its own distinctive forms of Bohemianism instead of being content to play host to the foreign avant-garde, the fashion was transformed. Despite this transformation, the Bohemia of the "beatniks" could not escape the influence of earlier Bohemias.

Two factors about the Beat Underground are important from the point of view of this inquiry. First, unlike that of American Bohemians of the 1920s and 1930s, the political stance of the more intellectual Beat could be expressed simply by a rejection of "square society" and an identification with the socially rejected—an attitude made famous by Norman Mailer in his essay, "The White Negro." Any political commitment by the Bohemians of the 1930s was liable to have been to the Communist party.[26] Secondly, although a mutual dissatisfaction with Established society had sometimes sent the denizens of the traditional Bohemias of Europe into the company of semi-criminal elements, European Bohemia was permissive and accepting but intellectually fastidious. Partly because of the attitude exemplified by Mailer's "White Negro," but mostly because of the central position occupied by marijuana in the beatnik culture (and the consequent interest of semicriminal drug dealers), the Beat Bohemia may have incorporated—although there is no means of being statistically certain—a larger proportion of unmotivated hangers-on than Bohemias of the traditional pattern. This resulted in a fairly large Beat "proletariat," who might conform to the expected patterns of behavior, make all the right noises, but fail to understand the language. Thus, in the summer of 1960, one estimate of the Beats in Greenwich Village made only one sixth "habituated to reading (none seem addicted)" and guessed that at least as many in this particular Bohemia were writing as in earlier artists' colonies.[27] It would be unwise to make too much of this, for lack of solid evidence. But it is quite certain that with the development of the Beatnik culture into that of the Hippies, the huge publicity given to this colorful Bohemia drew in many more existential window shoppers than did the traditional European Bohemias or Greenwich Village of the 1930s. The process seems to have begun with the Beats. From the point of view of the developing Bohemian critique of society, it had one important result: the use of language, inherited from earlier Bohemias, that dealt with highly sophisticated and esoteric concepts of "liberation," but with the meaning of the language forgotten, conventionalized, or misapplied, by a considerable number of camp followers or hangers-on.

At the same time as the American Beat culture developed an inchoate Bohemian critique of society—untied to Party lines—a particular Beatnik form of illuminism emerged in the adoption of Zen.[28] The romanticized use of Zen in the novels of Jack Kerouac created what was for America a new figure: the wandering scholar with religious leanings, more vagabond than academic. He had long been known in the literature of Europe, where he appeared in novels like Hesse's *Narziss und Goldmund,* and had found particular favor with the *Wandervögel.* Kerouac converted the character into a "Dharma Bum," who rode freight trains across the continent seeking enlightenment. The moving spirit of American Zen seems to have been the West Coast poet Gary Snyder, who passed his interest on to Kerouac and Allen Ginsberg in San Francisco in the 1950s. Kerouac describes Snyder as embodying both the inherited traditions of 1930s protest and the new vision of Zen. He was

> a kid from eastern Oregon brought up in a log cabin deep in the woods with his father and mother and sister, from the beginning a woods boy, an axman, farmer, interested in animals and Indian lore so that when he finally got to college by hook or crook he was already well equipped for his early studies in anthropology and later in Indian myth and in the actual texts of Indian mythology. Finally he learned Chinese and Japanese and became an Oriental scholar and discovered the greatest Dharma Bums of them all, the Zen Lunatics of China and Japan. At the same time, being a Northwest boy with idealistic tendencies, he got interested in oldfashioned I.W.W. anarchism and learned to play the guitar and sing old-worker songs to go with his Indian songs and general folksong interests.[29]

In this portrait, Kerouac identifies a type who was to become more and more familiar to Americans: the rebel who combined a detestation of social ills with a religious search. Sometime after this description, Snyder himself left for Japan to study Zen with the leading practitioners of the discipline. But it is more the Zen-and-rosewater marketed by Kerouac that influenced Bohemia than serious religious study. The other chief figure in arousing interest in Zen in the United States was Alan Watts, who has deplored the shallowness of the Zen commitment of many camp followers in an essay "Beat Zen, Square Zen and Zen," which has become as celebrated as Mailer's "White Negro." Watts is a product of the European occult revival, and it is worth noticing that even in the creation of the "typically American" version of Bohemia by the Beatniks, neither the occult revival nor the inherited traditions of Bohemia could be excluded. Even Kerouac, the "creator" of the Beat legend, felt keenly his French-Canadian roots, and his novels—particularly the later ones—are studded with references to the archetypal Bohemians of Paris. In Watts—who appears, incongruously besuited, at a Beat party in *The Dharma Bums*—the emerging counterculture of California discovered a popularizer of Zen who had emerged indirectly from the Theosophical Society.

In 1903 an International Buddhist Society had been founded, following the period spent in the East by Allan Bennett, alias the "Bikkhu Ananda Metteya," who had passed into Buddhism from the magical activities of the Golden Dawn. An English Buddhist

Society was formed in 1907, but by 1924 the chief association for the dissemination of Buddhist doctrine in England was the Buddhist Lodge of the Theosophical Society, founded by the eminent lawyer and judge Christmas Humphreys. In 1936 Alan Watts took over the editorship of the Buddhist Lodge's magazine, *Buddhism in England,* at the age of sixteen, and the same year, he published his *Spirit of Zen.* The father of this prodigy, L. W. Watts, was the treasurer and vice-president of the Buddhist Lodge;[30] and Alan Watts also sat at the feet of Dmitrije Mitrinović. In 1938 the younger Watts left for the United States and became a doctor of theology and an Anglican counselor at Northwestern University. Then he moved to San Francisco from where his influence spread first throughout the Beatnik, then throughout the hippie world. As has been rightly pointed out,[31] it is more the influence of Watts than the more learned message of the leading Zen authority for the West, D. T. Suzuki—whose second wife was American—that has been responsible for spreading Zen ideas. Watts by no means confined himself to Zen and was himself the modern representative of those "mediators between East and West" who first became prominent in Europe and America in the middle of the last century.[32]

If this were in any sense a thorough survey of Bohemian characteristics or even of the development of Bohemian ideas, much more attention would have to be paid to the political causes adopted by Bohemia at any given time, statistical evidence produced for the composition of the disaffiliated community, very many writers and artists more than mentioned. Here it is only necessary to note that by the time of the hippie explosion, American Bohemia had developed into an independent culture superficially unlike its European predecessors, yet inevitably owing allegiance to their achievements. Occult and religious elements occupied the place they have held in every Bohemia; and the specific political causes of previous generations of intellectuals were replaced by the general opposition of way-of-life to way-of-life that had also been traditional in Bohemian Europe.

By the end of the 1950s the Beats were moving out of their headquarters in North Beach, San Francisco, into New York's Greenwich Village and out again into the Lower East Side. In San Francisco itself they made for the area around Haight-Ashbury, traditional low-rent area favored by San Francisco State students and conveniently located next to the "pan-handle" of Golden Gate Park. With a further increase in the burden of anxiety, increased publicity for an "alternative" way of life, and the emergence of a vast semi-educated group of school leavers and dropouts whose opportunities for romanticism had been nourished as never before—a generation was produced that was devoted to the *image* through television, cinema, and large and uncritical reading while shielded from the strong winds of reality. The stage was set for the deposition of the kings of Bohemia and the proclamation of the republic of Woodstock Nation.

With a suitable change of key, the Progressive Underground of the 1890s might have been quite at home in Beatnik California: exchanging the vegetarian restaurants and cafés of Paris, Munich, and Vienna for the Chinese cooking of San Francisco and the cellars of North Beach; listening to records of Charlie Parker rather than concert performances of Wagner. But, if the inhabitants of Monte Verita could have fitted with ease into the pads of Venice West, they would have been even more familiar with the society of Haight-Ashbury, where a resurrected form of Christian Socialism combined with every form of mysticism under the sun. Familiar, that is, except for one aspect, certainly the most distinctive: the economy based on the new drug LSD.

Norman Cohn has suggested that certain medieval movements that combined revolutionary millennarianism with mystical anarchism are, in a secularized form, "with us still."[33] In the last five years of the 1960s, a form of illuminated politics developed among the young, which gives more insight into the state of mind of a mystical revolutionary than has been possible at any earlier date, because its viewpoints were expressed in direct and unambiguous language. Detailed examination of Hippies, Yippies, and variations on the theme of rebellious youth proves Professor Cohn extraordinarily accurate in his assessment. Reading the underground newspapers of 1966 and 1967, in which the story of the movement is buried, nothing is so striking as the overwhelming impression of joy and hopefulness, the real sense of "liberation" achieved or about to be achieved. Whatever the political activists have subsequently written, the main factor in inducing this unparalleled euphoria was without doubt LSD. Although the gurus of the "consciousness-expanding" drug were not by any means the sole instigators of the hippie revolt—as simplified accounts once made them seem—they were certainly very influential.

Drugs have been used in most cultures to dislocate man's sense of ordinary reality, or at least to give relief from the humdrum world. Frequently the strange effects of such substances have been associated with the divine. Visions, dreams, and prophecies can be ascribed to the effects of drug-induced consciousness. The occult revival knew all about drugs, and marijuana was a recognized weapon in the "sorcerer's armory" of Stanislas de Guaita or Baudelaire.[34] The chief aspect of drug action examined during the occult revival was the effect of ether or nitrous oxide, which was widely thought to induce mystical experiences and earned the name of the "anesthetic revelation." John Addington Symonds experimented with chloroform, and the prophet of esoteric Christianity, Anna Kingsford, experienced her visions under the influence of the same drug. In 1880 Professor William Ramsay (a Fellow of the Royal Society who was subsequently knighted) carried out experiments in which he anesthetized himself at least fifty times. They induced in him a condition of rather disappointing mystical insight—that is, Ramsay did not find his Berkeleyan revelation to his liking. In June 1893 he read a paper on his experiences to the Society for Psychical Research and was followed by Edward Maitland, who recounted the visions of Anna Kingsford. Those stimulated to try the effects of either for themselves were sufficiently numerous to hold a symposium on the topic in 1904.[35]

The most prominent supporters of the "anesthetic revelation," however, were to be found in America. These were William James of Harvard and the inventor of the term "anesthetic revelation," Benjamin Paul Blood. Blood was born in the 1820s and spent most of his life in New York State, where he died at the age of 86. In 1860 he had a revelation under anesthetics, which he describes as "an *initiation* historically realized as such, into the oldest and most intimate and ultimate truth. Whoever attains and remembers it, or remembers of it, is graduated beyond instruction in spiritual things." After repeating the experience at intervals, Blood produced a pamphlet on *The Anaesthetic Revelation* in 1874, which attracted many correspondents with corroborative evidence (including the poet Tennyson). Blood was emphatic that his insight had nothing to do with philosophy. The basis was simply that one's self existed, nothing more. He wrote in 1910: "Sinai and Calvary were but sacred stepping-stones to this secular revelation." On the appearance of Blood's pamphlet, William James reviewed it very favorably, and began a correspondence with the author. By 1896 James was writing to Blood that he had distributed copies of one of his pamphlets after a seminar in "speculative psychology." The last article James was to publish during his lifetime dealt with Blood, and the psychologist admitted that *The Anaesthetic Revelation* "fascinated me so 'weirdly' that I am conscious of its having been one of the stepping-stones of my thinking ever since."[36] Apart from their influence on James's thought, the visions of Blood stimulated the Harvard professor to try for himself the effects of nitrous oxide. His own mystical insight was embodied in his influential *Varieties of Religious Experience* (1902), and James's conclusion has served ever since as a text for those in search of "other realities."

> It is that our normal waking consciousness, rational consciousness as we call it, is but one special type of consciousness, whilst all about it, parted from it by the filmiest of screens, there lie potential forms of consciousness entirely different.[37]

Aleister Crowley, as the chief inheritor of the traditions of Symbolist Magery, was rather more indiscriminately concerned with drugs. Opium, cocaine, heroin, ether—he indulged and overindulged. Crowley's interest in drugs went further than simple dissipation, and his magical experiments were paralleled by those he undertook with drugs, notably what was then called *Anhalonium Lewinii*. This name for peyote, or mescaline, commemorates Ludwig Lewin, the first investigator of the Mexican cactus from which the drug is derived. After Lewin published his first study of this strange agent of visions in 1886, others (most notably Havelock Ellis) experimented with its effects, and Crowley followed suit. When in the U.S.A. during the First World War, Crowley visited the Parke-Davis factory in Detroit. He noted in his *Confessions*: "They were kind enough to interest themselves in my researches in *Anhalonium Lewinii* and made me some special preparations on the lines indicated by my experience which proved greatly superior to previous preparations."[38] There is firsthand evidence that Crowley introduced Aldous Huxley to mescaline in pre-1933 Berlin.[39] This is interesting and significant; for it indicates that Huxley's wide reading in mystical matters was supplemented by practical experience before he arrived in the United States in 1937—that yet another link with the occult revival can be made. (The more accepted story—that Huxley started experimenting with mescaline in 1953 under the supervision of Dr. Humphrey Osmond—may of course be true, without affecting the present argument.) It is certain that Huxley's book *The Doors of Perception*, which resulted from his later experience, had more effect than almost any other element in stimulating interest in what Osmond later called "pyschedelics."[40]

In the spring of 1943, Dr. Albert Hofmann, working in his laboratories at the Sandoz Corporation in Basel, accidentally absorbed a small quantity of lysergic acid diethylamide, a substance that he had synthesized while researching into the chemical constituents of the fungus ergot. Hofmann experienced hallucinatory effects and experimented on himself with a larger dose of LSD. Through Hofmann and Sandoz yet further hallucinogens were located. An American couple penetrated a Mexican Indian ceremony in which a hallucinogenic mushroom was used. On a second expedition the pair took an expert on fungi, who identified and afterward grew a culture of the mushrooms in his Paris laboratory. Some of these mushrooms he sent to Hofmann, who again experimented on himself and eventually synthesized the active constituent of psylocibin. He also discovered the hallucinatory properties of the morning glory seed. It was LSD, however, as manufactured primarily by Sandoz, which was responsible for the epidemic of mysticism which broke out on the American West Coast. According to John Wilcock's column, *Other Scenes,* most of the LSD reaching California in the spring of 1966 was made at the Sandoz plant in Switzerland, sold to buyers in Czechoslovakia, and delivered to the United States through Mexico. At this time there was no law against the use of LSD, and the drug naturally gravitated into the hands of the religiously inclined and the innumerable cults that have made California their headquarters since the end of the last century.

It was also natural that the apparently mystical experiences produced by the drug should themselves generate religious aspirations in official researchers. Thus, in December 1966, in the issue which announced the celebratory dedication of Haight-Ashbury by Diggers and hippies, the *Berkeley Barb* carried an article by Thaddeus and Rita Ashby, who had been responsible for research carried out by Sandoz in Mexico into problems of LSD and creativity, Their article, entitled "Did Jesus Turn On?", argued that Christ *did* turn on, that much Biblical poetry was produced by psychedelics, and announced that "Paradise must always be recreated." "The young people we meet in the LSD 'underground' seem to be groping towards such a renewal of religion." The Ashbys' own version of religious renewal ideally involved living in a house with a "tree-room" open to light and air, and a "womb-room" packed with psychedelic equipment for visionary experiences.[41]

From one relatively early survey of LSD use, a good idea can be gained of how the drug originally became diffused. LSD was at first thought to produce a "model psychosis": that is, to duplicate the effects of schizophrenia. Accordingly, it was to psychiatrists and medical men that the drug was of greatest interest. In the particular survey in question, three groups of LSD users were examined: an "informal professional" sample, over one-third of whom were initiated by a single psychiatrist member of the group; a group around a "religious-medical center" of a sort similar to Leary's; and a black market sample, all of whom had been introduced to the drug by a single person, himself in touch with people who fitted into one of the other two categories examined. Although research workers had the opportunity to try LSD as early as 1950, in this particular survey the first LSD use occurred in 1956. The next year the drug began to be used in clinical study on patients, and the group which obtained its LSD on the black market first used it in 1959. The religious-medical center had LSD available in 1960. A single survey of course proves nothing about the general pattern, but there is little to show that this sample cannot be taken as typical for the beginnings of the cult of LSD. One interesting aspect is that despite the relatively early opportunity to take LSD, the first use even among the "professional" group did not take place until 1956. It is possible that this may have been linked with the publication in 1956 of Huxley's sequel to *The Doors of Perception* entitled *Heaven and Hell*. This is reinforced by the survey's conclusion that even a sample of private patients introduced to LSD by their psychiatrists developed the characteristics of an "in-group" after having read Huxley, Alan Watts, or other theorists of mystical experience.[42]

Timothy Leary was the moving force behind the popular LSD movement. Leary (born 1920) has dated the beginnings of his religious quest to January 1959. He was living in Spain, having resigned from his university job and in a state of disillusionment. He contracted a venereal disease, and during the ensuing illness, decided that he had undergone a process of mystical rebirth. In August 1960 he ate several hallucinogenic mushrooms in Cuernavaca in Mexico and returned to his offices in the Center for Personality Research at Harvard—the university of William James—with a new conception of what his work should be. Leary knew all about the anaesthetic revelation of William James, "who had mystic experiences using nitrous oxide and saw God and scandalized people by running drug parties in Boston's scruffy Back Bay."[43] At this point, Leary had not yet read Huxley's accounts of his visions under mescaline, although two of his graduate students had been running tests with the chemical. One of these introduced him to *The Doors of Perception* and *Heaven and Hell*. During October and November 1960, Leary planned a series of experiments in conjunction with Huxley himself, who, by a strange coincidence, was staying in Boston. It is quite obvious that two factors conditioned the subsequent experiments: Leary's already-formed idea of "the possibilities of mind-free consciousness" and the influence of Huxley during the planning stage.

> We were not to be limited by the pathological point of view. We were not to interpret ecstasy as mania, or calm serenity as catatonia; we were not to diagnose Buddha as a detached schizoid; nor Christ as an exhibitionist masochist nor the mystic experience as a symptom; nor the visionary state as a model psychosis. Aldous Huxley chuckling away with compassionate humor at human folly.
> And with such erudition! Moving back and forth in history, quoting the mystics, Wordsworth, Plotinus, The Areopagite, William James. Ranging from the esoteric past, back into the biochemical present.[44]

In other words, Leary absorbed Huxley's own view of the significance of drug-induced experiences and took good note of his sources, those of Romanticism, Neo-Platonism, and the occult revival. His program expanded to include treatment of prisoners with a view to rehabilitation. But alongside the research arose a determination to *turn people on.*

The beginnings of the Bohemian use of hallucinogens probably date from Leary's initiation of Allen Ginsberg in December 1960. This produced in Ginsberg a determination to proselytize. Shortly afterward, Leary gave his magic mushrooms to another hero of the Beatnik era, the poet Charles Olson. Marijuana had been the drug of the Beatnik culture, and even then it had acquired religious connotations from its association with the Buddhism of Kerouac, Snyder, and Ginsberg. But the real eminence of the Beatnik drug world was William Burroughs, the son of the calculating-machine dynasty whose powerful book *Junky* had described his adventures with drugs much more potent than marijuana. Burroughs had taken up residence in Tangier, which became a place of pilgrimage for Beats like Kerouac on their way to Europe. It was logical that Leary and his new convert Ginsberg would approach the Grand Panjandrum of Junk, who was already experimenting with flickering and flashing lights to achieve "druglike" effects, which were to become familiar. In the summer of 1961, Leary, his colleague Richard Alpert, Ginsberg, and Gregory Corso held a mushroom session in Tangier. This was followed by an unsuccessful trip made by Burroughs to America and his rejection of the Harvard group's psychedelics. But contact with the leaders of the Beat Bohemia had been made, and it symbolized the directions that the drug religion was to follow. Ginsberg left for India and the ashrams of the Ganges.

In November 1961 Leary was given LSD by an academic dropout called Michael Holingshead, who had taken the drug while working with a New York doctor. Soon afterward, the Harvard experimenters tried another chemical that produced visions, DMT. Both of these drugs resulted in experiences which were far more vivid and ecstatic than those caused by the magic mushroom. At Easter 1962, Leary and a Harvard Ph.D. student called Walter Pahnke gave a group of experimenters psylocibin in the chapel of Boston University and precipitated mystical experiences. Gerald Heard and Alan

Watts arrived at Harvard, told Leary of the Traditions of European occultism, of Madame Blavatsky, of Gurdjieff and Ouspensky. They all warned Leary that the classic technique of the occultist was the only one to ensure survival. Those who know, don't speak. Leary, on the other hand, felt the mantle of the guru clasped around his shoulders. "I found myself getting poetic and dogmatic. I know it is a real reality! I know it is the Divine message." He took to frequenting a Hindu ashram in Boston. Then he was asked to give LSD to Hindu devotees, and during the course of the session, Leary became convinced that "we are all Hindus in our essence." A process of mutual conversion began between him and the inmates of the ashram. Leary's growing respect for Hindu mythology was accompanied by the growing respect of the Vedantists for Leary. When their guru was away they would visit him for advice, and gradually he accumulated a following of those searching for a spiritual leader.

> The slow, invisible process of becoming a guru, a holy man, had begun. It would be four years before I could openly admit to it. Accept my divinity, my divine election. . . . How ironic and ludicrous that an American Irishman should be forced into sainthood!

In the summer of 1962 he left once more for Mexico, and next year he was sacked from Harvard, whose authorities found it dangerous to have a valuable mystic on the staff. In succession he established the "Castalia Foundation"—named after the Order imagined by his hero Hermann Hesse, the "International Foundation for Internal Freedom," and the "League for Spiritual Discovery," with its headquarters at Millbrook, New York, where Leary and his followers were living at the time of the great drug explosion. There was time after the disruption of his Castalia Foundation for a trip to India, where he went to study under Sri Krishna Prem. "Relax," he told his colleague Richard Alpert, "sit back, have a ball. . . It's done now: watch it happen."[45]

What was "done" was the broadcasting of LSD to the four winds. Leary claims that Albert Hofmann, the synthesizer of the chemical, had at once realized the spiritual implications of his discovery. Concealing himself under the guise of a scientific researcher he had "initiated a high-level, ethical, gentleman's conspiracy of philosophically-minded scientists to disseminate LSD for the benefit of the human race." Leary himself and Alan Watts—whose *Joyous Cosmology* (1962) proved to be the LSD equivalent to Huxley's propaganda for mescaline—joined with other semiacademics to provide the publicity. The chemical itself was the chief problem. Whether or not Hofmann himself was ever involved, some scientists fairly certainly did cooperate. The most influential evangelist of LSD was one Al Hubbard, who had made a fortune from uranium and planned to set up a network of medically approved LSD clinics around the country. He was responsible for converting Humphrey Osmond to the religious interpretation of the LSD experience. Hubbard's pilot project at Menlo Park, California, which (according to Leary) "turned on several hundred of the most influential people in the San Francisco Bay Area" was closed; and Leary himself failed to persuade Sandoz to put an "ecstasy pill" on the market. By 1962 he had, nevertheless, contrived to set up "a loose but effective" distribution system for free LSD. Then he met a distinguished scientist, whom he calls "Dr. Spaulding" and describes as "one of the ten leading chemists in the country," who claimed to be part of a well-established conspiracy that had been stockpiling LSD. "Spaulding" then sent Leary enough of the chemical to last four years.[46]

Partly through the efforts of Hubbard, partly through the natural receptivity of California, partly through the Beatnik preparation, LSD took its greatest toll in San Francisco. With the question of LSD-supply so paramount, the activities of private "chemists" came to be of increasing importance, and San Francisco possessed the most important private manufacturer of LSD in America. This legendary figure, known as Owsley and rumored to possess the full name of "Augustus Owsley Stanley III," produced a fair proportion of the LSD used in the Haight-Ashbury culture. Leary has recorded a monologue by Owsley in which the Underground supplier expressed his belief that the Van Allen Belt was "the higher intelligence protecting earth from lethal solar radiation" and that LSD had been activated by this supreme intelligence as the counterforce to nuclear fission.[47] Owsley was also responsible for some of the public success of the Acid Tests conducted in San Francisco in 1965 and 1966 by Ken Kesey, the most remarkable of all LSD gurus.

Kesey (born 1936) attracted public notice in 1962 with his first novel, *One Flew over the Cuckoo's Nest*. Before that, he had been a schoolboy hero and a college athlete. He arrived at Stanford University, California, on a creative writing fellowship in 1958.[48] At Stanford, Kesey met a young psychologist with whom he volunteered to take part in experiments with the newly discovered psychedelics—then called psychomimetics because of the theory that they mimicked schizophrenic states. Kesey was among the first to be turned on, and soon the Bohemian community in Stanford was ordering peyote from Mexico and trying out the strange chemicals Kesey smuggled out of the hospital. Bohemia became Cockaigne. Richard Alpert arrived after he had begun to work with Leary; and equally important, Neal Cassady joined the circle. Cassady was the original Beat, the hero, "Dean Moriarty," of Kerouac's *On the Road*: the model for the Bohemia that was ending and a main protagonist of that which was to begin. In 1963 Kesey moved to La Honda near Palo Alto, California, and early the next year the legendary adventure began.

From the bare description of what Kesey and his Merry Pranksters did, it is difficult to make the point that what developed was—far more than in the case of Leary with his explicit reliance on the traditions of the Orient and European occultism—a 1960s, Americanized version of the perennial occultist dream of a forcing house for souls. In the spring of 1964, Kesey and his friends crammed themselves, a jungle of electronic equipment and film cameras, and a quantity of LSD, marijuana and whatever else they could lay their hands on, into a pre-war schoolbus painted with Day-Glo and bearing a sign on the front reading *"Furthur."* They set off across the continent for New York. During the trip, if we are to believe Tom Wolfe—and if we disbelieve him there is much in the whole hippie episode which makes no sense at all—the Merry Pranksters subtly changed in their conception of themselves. They became a band of truth seekers bent on extending their own consciousness with the help of drugs and a perpetual surrealism, and bent on turning others on. Back in California after their strange expedition, Kesey formed a curious alliance with the Hell's Angels—and, even more significantly, a radical faction of Unitarians tried to form one with him. Owsley turned up, with his vast resources of LSD and a passion for electronics that was as great as the Pranksters' own.[49] Ginsberg had already become part of the group with a newly acquired Hinduism, which included chanting the *Hare Krishna* mantram. All the elements that go into the popular conception of the "hippie" had coalesced around Kesey.

In December, 1965, Kesey began his series of "acid tests." They used his particular notion of "expanding consciousness"—LSD, provided by Owsley, music by an Owsley-sponsored rock group called the Grateful Dead, and Kesey's electronic gadgetry and stroboscopes—in an attempt to put the message of consciousness expansion over to the greatest number of people. The greatest result of these experiments was to start a new fashion in a decoration for discothèques and dances, and it becomes increasingly difficult to analyze who did and who did not believe in the grand metaphysics of the enterprise. The climax of the attempt at proselytizing, turning on, (and partly just having a ball) came at the end of January 1966. Kesey, the Grateful Dead, and Rock's number-one impresario, named Bill Graham, staged a three-day "Trips Festival"—LSD was still not illegal—which attracted large numbers of people and sparked off the high period of "hippie" culture in Haight-Ashbury.[50]

The widespread use of LSD was inextricably associated with occult and mystical groups through a two-way process. Because the leading gurus of LSD identified the drug-induced experience with the mystical experience of saints and ecstatics, those who used the drug did so in an atmosphere that was likely to put them in contact with theories of the occult or the unorthodoxly religious. And because the traditional irrationalist Underground has naturally been concerned with mystical experience, some of its members jumped at what appeared to be the chance to induce the vision of truth that years of unassisted meditation had not brought them. The result was that the components of the late 19th-century occult revival—which provided the most accessible range of mystical goods on offer—pervaded certain sections of the hippie Underground. It was by no means universal, but it formed a substantial element present from the beginning. Thus Timothy Leary wrote a tongue-in-cheek article on the responsibility of Englishmen for the psychedelic revolution, which embodies a high proportion of truth: but this is because most of the Englishmen he mentions who are not contemporary gurus were leading figures of the occult revival. It is quite possible to agree with Leary's judgment when he writes that "the English in India got turned on" or thanks "William Blake and A. R. Orage for Alan Watts."[51] If "turning on" is made equivalent to a state of mystical consciousness and occult interpreters are invoked to the adept's aid, Leary's position is perfectly clear.

The occult factor became prominent throughout the underground press and particularly in papers in any way concerned with events in the Haight-Ashbury. Messiahs of every description combined with earnest seekers of liberation and syncretisms more bizarre than any yet devised. As John Wilcock noted in April 1966, California "is a renowned haven for faddists, individualists and nuts of every kind. . . . There's always some screwball out here who's got some new cult or ism working and a band of happily unrealistic acolytes around him who are now convinced that they've discovered the True Path to everlasting health, wealth and satisfactory orgasm."[52] The traditional hospitality of Bohemia to occultism was extended as the vision of Haight-Ashbury spread over America from the West Coast and eventually to Europe.

The spectrum of hippie irrationalism stretched from revamped fundamentalist Christianity to detailed knowledge of the works of Jung. *The Los Angeles Free Press* printed in March 1965, at the very beginning of the restive stirrings in Bohemia, a letter from Sam Shapira, "The Living World Messiah," who declared the existing American order to be "corrupt, criminal, diabolical from late John F. Kennedy and present Lyndon Johnson down." The Living World Messiah denied any identity with Jesus but claimed "to be heaven's called and anointed world Messiah or Christ by direct descending speech from the canopy of heaven witnessed" and demanded that in his honor all other religions cease to function. Sporadic items of metaphysical interest on the West Coast included the Church of the Awakening founded by Doctors John and Luisa Aiken in 1963, which was based in New Mexico and used psychedelics; and "Charlie Brown," otherwise known as Charles Artman, and "Little Eagle," who claimed to be a member of the Native American Church and kept its (legal) sacrament of peyote in a locket around his neck. Charlie Brown Artman was a figure of note in the first issue of the *Berkeley Barb* of August 1965—when the *Barb* was almost exclusively concerned with the student revolution in progress on the university campus. He was the son of an Iowa miner, and he believed in the advent of the new age and the dawning of a state of "Christ-awareness." His arrests range from that of February 1966 for living in a tepee on Berkeley Heights displaying a sign reading "Impeach Lyndon Johnson" to that of two years later for a traffic offense in Salt Lake City. During the latter proceedings Charlie Brown demanded solitary confinement in order to meditate, and his supporters expected "another out-of-sight, turned-on trial." Heroes from the worlds of pop, protest, and the church testified to the occult significance of the New Age. In September 1967 Bishop James Pike agreed that mystical experience and psychedelic initiation were identical. In November of the same year the folksinger Buffy Sainte-Marie—who has a degree in the history of religions—proclaimed in Jungian terms: "I'm dedicated to Satan and Jehovah—my God is Abraxas, the god of evil and of good."[53]

With the burgeoning of the underground press in 1967, occult and mystical attitudes found further outlets of expression. For example, in August 1967 the paper *Indian Head* of Santa Ana, California, published articles on Bhakti Yoga, Alan Watts, and Velikovsky's cosmology. The next issue was chiefly concerned with the economic-political analyses of Dr. Marcuse and Professor J. K. Galbraith, but by three numbers further on, the accent had shifted again to occultism and psychedelia, with discussions of Atlantis and the problems of taking LSD on a surfboard. The same year saw the beginning of the gloriously zany *Buddhist Oracle*—full title: the *Buddhist Third Class Junkmail Oracle*—of Cleveland, Ohio, which carried advertising for all manner of esoteric literature, such as Crowley's *Book of the Law*. The sanest magazines of reform could be invaded by weird and dubious cults. Thus, the usually practical *Modern Utopian* could consider the antics of the "Church of the Virgin Mother," which involved widespread transvestitism and claimed to explore the possibilities of parthenogenesis. In the late summer of 1967, the London *International Times* published an eccentric letter in which the writer claimed that Arnold Bennett—he meant Allan Bennett—had "invented methedrine."[54] The classical aims of the occultists' quest were bent into the oddest forms and overlaid with a heavy aroma of whatever drug might suit the fancy. The Montreal paper *Logos* printed an article describing its author's journey to the East which culminated in three weeks in a South Indian ashram where he was physically mauled by his guru. The next issue included a "Letter from Katmandu," which concentrated exclusively on the "heavy drug scene." "Hash, grass are sold in government shops. Meth and other things can be had at the pharmacy and the 'Doc' is always willing to shoot you up with morphine or heroin. In addition there is opium, bhang, acid, mescaline, psylocybine, STP and some other way out things. There are many worlds just here." Although drugs may have been the principal route by which the occult entered Bohemia, once the mystical had become an accepted part of the scene, it was not necessarily connected with drugs or improbable extravagance. Thus, the clear-headed occult column begun in 1969 by Elfrida Rivers in the New York *East Village Other* was adept at knocking dangerous lunacies on the head. How necessary this approach was is shown by the columnist's weary resignation in the face of letters asking for the name and address of "an experienced witch": some version of this petition arrived almost every week.[55]

Whether in traditional or modernized form, with or without drugs, the occult has remained a consistent part of the modern Underground. Both the Leary and the Kesey experiments produced yet further esoteric organizations. At Leary's base at Millbrook, the headquarters of the "League for Spiritual Discovery" was set cheek by jowl with the Sri Ram Ashram and the Neo-American Church of Art Kleps, whose surrealistic figure had lurched into Millbrook in 1963.

Kleps (born 1928) had been an educational psychologist and, according to the various reports of his activities to appear in the underground press, seems to have spent most of his time at Millbrook in an inebriated state. Leary described him as "a clumsy manipulator, a blatant flatterer, a bully to the willingly weak, the world's most incompetent con-man. He is in short a sodden disgrace to the movement." The object of the Neo-American Church was to have LSD accepted as a sacrament. Its members would thus be given comparable legal status with the Native American Church, whose Indian peyote religion was sanctioned by law. Kleps named his "priests" Boo-Hoos and issued a paper called *Divine Toad Sweat*—the sweat of a toad was supposed to contain some psychedelic chemical. On one level he declared that "the discovery of LSD may be taken as the intervention of God in human history"; and, on another, he offered to seal for $1,000 a certificate stating that "the chief Boo-Hoo never heard of you and regards you with indifference." The antics of Kleps introduced a welcome note of hilarity into psychedelic evangelizing. Once when he was in jail he contrived to make a Boo-Hoo of the son of a judge then occupied in trying to chase the Learyites out of the country. To Kleps also belongs the reputed distinction of having the Kleenex on which he had just blown his nose scooped up by narcotics agents for analysis.[56]

After the Trips Festival of January 1966, Ken Kesey had himself smuggled over the Mexican border, while his group continued the explosive Acid Tests which he had devised. One of the acquisitions to the Pranksters in this period was Hugh Romney, a former actor and inhabitant of the Beatnik world who had dropped out of the New York scene and met Kesey during the first Acid Tests. From this point, Romney says, he "went to work for the pudding"—the pudding being the Intergalactic World Brain (or any other new term for God that happens to appeal). Romney ended up in the hills with a commune called the Hog Farm. He developed an elaborated version of Kesey's techniques. His "original Tarot on wheels" first set out at the end of 1968. Romney described it as "a group mind-bank" designed to produce children with universal capacities. What appeared to be a combination of group therapy, communal living, spiritual forcing house, and experiment in cooperative education had an eclectic selection of sources among which the occult revival is prominent. In 1967 Romney marveled at the books which "keep appearing, like the *I Ching* and the Bible, the *Wind in the Willows*, the *Book of the Hopi*, the *Secret of the Golden Flower, Stranger in a Strange Land* and *Siddartha* and the rest of Hesse and the last of Jung and all of Evans-Wentz and *Mount Analogue*, the *Urantia Song*, consummate *All and Everything* and still they keep coming."[57] Even more than Kesey's Pranksters, the Hog Farm represented an updated version of the occult quest, and their debts to Jung and Gurdjieff are especially obvious. In method the Hog Farm may have been following Gurdjieff; in theory, Jung.

Other groups coalesced round figures who had little to do with the LSD-inspired cults but still became pivotal points of the

Underground. An example is the group that published the Boston *Avatar* from June 1967. The *Avatar* ran a regular astrology column and another called "The Aquarian Age." It attracted contributions like that from one reader who decided that "An area designated for para-psychological and occult study coupled with programs designed to bring together factions now split over psychedelics, socio-economic trend interpretation, theological re-assessment of spiritual experience in a natural setting such as Colorado or Montana would be a groovy thing, I think." The center of this enterprise was Mel Lyman, the author of the *Autobiography of a World Savior* and producer of apocalyptic utterances on current problems. Lyman's pronouncements were completely unlike anything published on the West Coast; this World Savior had pronounced himself all in favor of "hard work" against occult trends. Nevertheless, his ideas of mission were intriguing: "sometimes I'm the AVATAR, sometimes I'm asleep," he announced; and in March 1968 the Avatar circle declared, "Today we simply incorporate ourselves as Mel Lyman." In answer to a correspondent who challenged him to explain his mission he replied: "I know God's plan, and I will reveal it to mankind, step by step, as God reveals it to me. That makes me a world savior." It is unsurprising that when the savior left AVATAR there was wailing among his devoted readership. A tragic letter from "Kathy" began, "Mel! I love you! I need you so bad! In 3 days I'll be 17 (yes, only a mere child). Maybe I don't matter to you, but I've always felt that you loved us all, no matter what. I may not have made it this far if not for you." Lyman's reply is explicit enough: "You have to lose me to find me in YOU."[58]

The center in which all such apocalyptic aspirations fused and from which they radiated, combined with politics and rearranged as a potent myth, was Haight-Ashbury. From the turn of the year 1965-66, when Kesey's Acid Tests became the Trips Festival, this San Francisco Bohemia gradually developed the characteristics that marked the image of "hippie" in the eyes of the public and of countless imitators. The term *hippie* was coined by Herb Caen, the columnist on the *San Francisco Chronicle* from "hippy-dippy," otherwise "bebopping jerk." It is strange that Caen, who also named the Beatniks—from "beatitude"—should have pounced on the hippie style of dancing as the distinguishing characteristic and ignored the related search for enlightenment.⁵⁹ Apart from the use of drugs and exotic clothing, the characteristics of hippie culture with which people are most familiar—through the musical *Hair* if in no other way—seem to involve much chanting of *Hare Krishna* and mutterings about being in the Aquarian age. It is worth recording how these catchphrases passed into Bohemia.

When Alan Ginsberg was given psylocibin by Timothy Leary in 1960, it marked a turning point in his life. One of the results was that he stopped writing for publication. In 1966, as he confessed: "I took a lot of LSD and psylocibin previous to leaving for India and, well, I was in a slightly disordered state of mind. I thought it was absolutely necessary for me to drop dead in order to obtain complete enlightenment—for my ego to vanish entirely and for my person to vanish entirely and everything about me to vanish entirely in order to be perfect." He left with his companion Peter Orlovsky and Gary Snyder on his own journey to the East and wandered around India meeting gurus and smoking marijuana. He visited the Dalai Lama and the Swami Shivananda of Rishikesh. It was Shivananda who recommended the chanting of the *Hare Krishna* mantra as an exercise, and Ginsberg was later impressed by hearing the same phrase on the lips of a woman saint on the banks of the Ganges.⁶⁰

The real importer of the chant into the United States was Swami Bhaktivedanta (born 1897), who arrived in America in 1965 on a missionary expedition and started to give lectures on "Krishna Consciousness" in the Lower East Side of New York. He met Howard Wheeler, a teacher of English at Indiana State University, who introduced Ginsberg to the circle. Bhaktivedanta gradually acquired popularity among the New York Bohemians, and Ginsberg suggested that the fifteen "initiated disciples" of the Swami begin chanting in Tompkins Square, which the New York hippies had selected as their open-air meeting place. Wheeler distributed leaflets:

STAY HIGH FOR EVER
No More Coming Down
Practice KRISHNA CONSCIOUSNESS
Expand your consciousness by chanting
the
TRANSCENDENTAL SOUND VIBRATION

During the Peace Parade of 5 November 1966, Ginsberg and

Wheeler led the chanting of the mantra, and distributed leaflets to thousands. Krishna Consciousness had arrived; and in January 1967 its missionaries came to Haight-Ashbury, which had been expectantly waiting for them.[61] Wheeler wrote:

> During the spring and early summer of '67, Haight culture was at its peak. We were flying high with mantra, and thousands opened up to us. We splashed in the Haight pond with a mammoth mantra-rock dance at the Avalon. Swamiji and Ginsberg danced on the stage with upraised hands. Multicolored lights swirled across huge wall slides of Krishna and Rama. The Grateful Dead, Moby Grape and Big Brother blared away. Even Tim Leary garlanded one of us and salaamed, "A beautiful night, a beautiful night." Five thousand hippies, teenie-boppers and Hell's Angels stood reverently when Swamiji entered and listened attentively while he talked.
>
> Every Sunday we chanted in Golden Gate Park and hundreds joined, holding hands and dancing in a ring. At any time of day I could walk down Haight Street playing cymbals and chanting and pick up at least a dozen enthusiasts. People were also attracted by our free prasadam [food] program and we would feed dozens daily. The Rhada Krishna Temple quickly became a dynamic influence in Haight-Ashbury life.[62]

From this success, the Krishna Consciousness movement expanded until it had centers in eight cities on the North American continent and four in Europe; and this rapid diffusion of the doctrine was an indication of how swiftly other related ideas might spread. To American Bohemia, such as it was, Hinduism *seemed* new; and in the precise form of "Krishna Consciousness" indeed was new. But it was the recurrence of a phenomenon that had been in progress ever since the end of the 19th century.[63]

The idea of the age of Aquarius is simply a statement of astrological fact. That is, a subscriber to astrology believes not only in the links between the heavenly bodies and life on earth but also in an elaborate superstructure of periods, including that of a "master period" of the Great Year, which is generally thought to last for about 36,000 ordinary years. The earth is at present at the end of the Great Year governed by the astrological sign Pisces, and due to begin the next Great Year, dominated by the characteristics of Aquarius. The precise dating of the change-over varies considerably with the individual astrologer and the system of calculation he employs. But the fact that the earth is due to enter a new astrological eon is not at all the invention of the hippies and could well have been calculated in the 16th century—or in ancient Chaldea well before the birth of Christ. To say that the change is due in "about the year two thousand" means little; for variations of a few hundred years count for nothing in the calculation of a Great Year. In the more esoteric sections of the 19th-century Progressive Underground, the calculations were naturally biased toward an earlier advent of the new age; in pre-Nazi Germany the age of Aquarius was sometimes timed to coincide with the arrival of the Thousand Year Reich. In all cases the Aquarian characteristics were thought to be diametrically opposed to those of the preceding age—for confusion, harmony; for the pursuit of material profit, the brotherhood of man.

The occultism of Haight-Ashbury might well merely have produced a consensus of opinion among the astrologically inclined indicating the arrival of the Aquarian Age. In fact, one particular astrologer who lived in the Haight seems to have been chiefly responsible for popularizing the idea. His name was Gavin Arthur, otherwise Chester Alan Arthur III. He was the great-grandson of a United States president and a direct link with the European astrological revival. Arthur (born 1902) had passed through a varied career, which included gold mining in Alaska, the world of American high society, and Paris in the 1920s before he came to live in Haight-Ashbury. He had been given Edouard Schuré's *Great Initiates* at the age of 19 and had dabbled in astrology for thirty years before a Jungian psychiatrist in San Francisco persuaded him to cast her patients' horoscopes as an aid to analysis. Gavin Arthur was at this time a counselor at San Quentin prison, and he began to use astrology in his prison work. His astrological book, *The Circle of Sex,* was less his claim to fame than the fact that he had predicted the death of President John F. Kennedy before the elections sent him to Washington and Dallas.[64]

Arthur saw himself as a Jungian astrologer and foretold the arrival of the Aquarian age for the year 2260. The earth had, nevertheless, entered a "new age of culture" in 1940. To this quite orthodox astrological tenet, Arthur added the equally orthodox belief in spiritual evolution, a doctrine that he supported by a conflation of R. D. Bucke's *Cosmic Consciousness*—a well-known text of the 19th-century occult revival, which owed much to the New England Transcendentalists and Walt Whitman—and the theories of Korzybsky's General Semantics. These theories he adapted to term minerals as one-dimensional, plants as two-dimensional, animals as three-dimensional and humans as four-dimensional modes of being. By implication, a new five-dimensional form of life for the new age was evolving. Arthur vaunted his intellectual ancestry: he had "sat at the feet of Edward Carpenter, who sat at the feet of Whitman."[65]

It was to the theories of Gavin Arthur that the enthusiast in the *San Francisco Oracle* was indebted when he watched the "Be-in" of 14 January 1967. "Not since the vast empire-armies of old Persia has there been such an exotic massing for a common purpose" he wrote. "Not since the last day of the Christ has the purpose been so gentle and so strong. Not in the 26,000 years have the aborigines of a new mankind gathered in recognition of their heritage and their gig."[66] The mood of apocalypse—as well as the success of the idea of Haight-Ashbury—also derived from the Diggers, but the occult and religious factors that came together at one place and time were at least as responsible; and apocalyptic feelings generated by other causes reactivated interest in the occult. Before considering the Diggers and the social-political aspects of the Hippie Myth, some further results of the combination of LSD-cults, occultism, and Oriental religion should be noticed.

Gavin Arthur was by no means the only guru to pronounce for the idea of spiritual evolution. It was a cardinal tenet of those who followed Timothy Leary. How far anyone followed Leary completely is an open question, but his ideas could not help but be influential. Some six months after Kesey began his Acid Tests, LSD was declared illegal in the State of California—on 6 June 1966—and soon afterward, Leary and Alpert delivered a "manifesto for an inner revolution" to an enthusiastic crowd. In October a writer in the *Berkeley Barb* wrote that "Timothy Leary comes to us as apostle and martyr of the new religion. Let us respect him, but let us take Spartacus, not Christ, as our model." The split between the political activists and the mystical drop-outs was obviously present from the start; but the important thing about Haight-Ashbury was the temporary fusion of ideas. A moving spirit behind the Haight's vision of itself was Ron Thelin, the owner of the Psychedelic Shop on Haight Street, a center of the new culture. Thelin was behind the most distinctively "hippie" paper to emerge from the Underground, the *San Francisco Oracle,* and he was far from an opponent of Leary.[67] In the pages of the *Oracle* the rationale of a new "mutant consciousness," which might be produced by LSD, was elaborated together with the idea that Haight-Ashbury was the center of the new developments. Was LSD producing a new subspecies? To some it seemed like it:

> *Mutants! Know now that you exist!*
> *They have hid you in cities*
> *And clothed you in fools' clothes*
> *Know now that you are free!*[68]

Richard Alpert called the Haight-Ashbury a "very high energy center," and "the purest reflection of what is happening in consciousness, at the leading edge in the society." The *Oracle's* column, "Gossiping Guru," thought it apparent that "a real and viable synthesis of Eastern and Western modes of consciousness is taking place and the result is sure to be the most powerful cognitive tool ever to fall into the hands of men of good will." Astrology not only predicted the new age, but possibly an avatar. In early 1967 the Oracle carried a request for further information about "Him who was born on February 5th, 1962, when 7 planets were in Aquarius." According to some sections of opinion there had been a great convocation of adepts on the inner planes to prepare for this Messiah![69] The triumph of the new consciousness was seen in the "gathering of the tribes" (14 January 1967) for the Human Be-In in Golden Gate Park. By this point, the hippie culture had become defined and could do nothing but expand or decline. In fact it did both.

From the point of view of the individual's role in society, this new Bohemia produced a new version of the dream of the 19th-century occult revival: "liberation," "spiritual evolution," "expanded consciousness." It did this partly by using something of its Bohemian inheritance, partly by absorbing the occult tradition, mostly by adapting such ideas into a new form. It was nonetheless the Progressive Underground—spattered with Day-Glo paint, stoned out of its mind, dancing with a frenzy that some have compared to the outbreaks of dancing mania in the Middle Ages—but recognizably the same creature. Its critique of society was derived from sources similar to those of earlier undergrounds of opposition to materialist Establishments. Because of this, the junction between the representatives of the new consciousness and the radicals who demanded a less materialist, less individualist society was made on the basis which our story has identified again and again: a common idealism, a common pursuit of cities not of this world, a common unity of the implicitly "spiritual" against the legions of Mammon. The union of all such elements took place in San Francisco, and Haight-Ashbury possessed a particular kind of illuminated politics in the shape of the Diggers.

The Diggers were responsible for the "love" part of Haight-Ashbury, just as the occult and drugs were responsible for ideas of an emergent new consciousness. The hippie culture based on drugs and a new Bohemianism flourished during 1966. But it was only recognized in December of that year when the Diggers staged a ceremony to mark the "Death of the old Haight and the Birth of the New Haight." A step further was the Be-In of 14 January, and the idea that the whole ethos would flower in the "Summer of Love." The mass media moved in, and the myth of the hippie was born. The anticipated influx of teenagers and summer hippies exceeded all expectations. Tourists began to frequent Haight-Ashbury, where gentleness quickly evaporated under the pressure of too many people and a shortage of marijuana, which gave criminal groups and pushers of horror-drugs like methedrine the chance to infiltrate. In October 1967, Thelin closed his Psychedelic Shop, and the Diggers held another ceremony designed to mark the death of "Hippie, son of Mass Media" and the birth of the "Free Man." This was also the month of the antiwar demonstration against the Pentagon.

The Haight was never to be resurrected, but what there was of value had by this time been grafted on to a zany version of *Realpolitik* and developed into a new idealistic critique of society. By the time most of the world had heard of hippies the species was transmogrified, but the myth was spread abroad. It should be emphasized that the *vision* of Haight-Ashbury has been much more influential than the *reality,* which by the summer of 1967 had degenerated into a state which, by all reports, was more like the rotting of the old society than the incubation of the new.[70]

A policeman shot a young Negro at Hunter's Point in San Francisco on 27 September 1966 and sparked off a three-day race riot, which resulted in curfews and a dislocation of normal living. The situation inspired some members of the San Francisco Mime Troup, a radical organization that specialized in trying to involve people going about their normal business in political action. The night after the shooting the first of the Digger manifestoes appeared. This emanated from a group within the Mime Troup; and it gradually became known that the Diggers would provide free food for those stranded by the curfew.[71] The tradition begun that night continued into 1967, until the influx of people and an acquired habit of looking to the Diggers for help temporarily submerged these exceedingly practical Utopians. In Haight-Ashbury a free store was opened under Digger direction, and it was the Diggers who organized the ceremony in December to inaugurate the new Haight and provided quantities of food for those attending the Be-In.

Who or what were the Diggers? They issued a series of flysheets of a surrealistic nature—such as an orange sheet headed COOL CRANBERRY HORSE—HAIRED MOUTH CLUTTERED WITH APPLE CORES. They signed their correspondence with the name of George Metetsky, the "mad bomber" who had terrorized New York in 1957 and announced: "Regarding enquiries concerned with the identity and whereabouts of the Diggers: We are happy to state that the DIGGERS are not that."[72] They took great pains to deny any member the status of "leader." Diggers proclaimed themselves against cars, the economics of excess, and the exploitation of the Haight-Ashbury culture by the "hip merchants" who were cashing in on the psychedelic fashion. Yet they were by no means opposed to the drug-induced idea of the "revolution in consciousness." They were indeed enthusiasts: "total drug-oriented mad ones, who are mad to live/mad to talk, mad to be saved... people who have ridden the crest of Kerouac's bum's romance and slammed to earth wailing love!" Part of the hippie community, but determined on action rather than sitting around stoned and looking "spiritual," the Diggers "in a sense became a new morality, the opposite of industrial capitalism." While the hippie entrepreneurs saw the Diggers as a community service, the Diggers themselves were out to make their new morality the basis of the community. The idealistic plan could not work, and by May 1967 the Diggers issued a leaflet denouncing the "weak-kneed series of cabals which expect someone to take care of their living . . . some revolution!"[73]

The basic facts about the Diggers are that they combined practice with an approach that did not contradict the "new consciousness" theory; and that they derived their inspiration from the original Diggers led by Gerard Winstanley, who had settled on St. Georges Hill at Cobham in Surrey in 1649. The parallel is extraordinarily true both in terms of ideals and historical period. The Diggers, Ranters, and Levellers of the English Protectorate combined in varying degrees theories of social equality, simplicity of living, and religious illumination. In a transformed situation all these ideals could be discovered among the Haight-Ashbury Diggers. The original 17th-century Diggers embodied in the form of a social gospel various illuminist tendencies that had been present in the heretical millennarianism of the Middle Ages and that burst forth when the crises of Renaissance and Reformation shattered the solidarity of the medieval edifice. The traditions of direct illumination on which the millennarians of Cromwell's day drew had some affinities with heretical doctrines labeled "occult," which emerged at the same period as Winstanley's Diggers. It is an interesting coincidence, if no more, that in response to a similar crisis, both the occult and political illuminism once more emerged from their underground habitations and explicitly acknowledged their ancestry.[74] The parallel with the 17th century is still drawn by certain underground groups.

Under pressure in the summer of 1967, some of the Diggers began to advocate revolution, claiming to follow Winstanley's later practice.[75] It is still not certain how "activist" the Diggers were. One of their leading members, Emmett Grogan, gives a confused impression of their ideology, based on Artaud, LSD, Winstanley, and sheer bloodymindedness. The Diggers' liberation was liberation from the Underground itself, but they naturally made use of its ready-made rhetoric.[76]

Nostradamus and the Cabala, Christianity and LSD, free food and the simple life—all were natural bedfellows in this particular situation. The addition of Christian principles should surprise no one. The traditions of American Protestantism—which have more recently produced the fundamentalist reaction of the "Jesus Freaks"—are sufficient parentage. In Haight-Ashbury Christianity might clothe the apocalypse as well as Vedanta. "If Jesus were alive today he would live in the Hashbury—the new Jerusalem." In April 1966, the *Berkeley Barb* carried a reproduction of a poster which made explicit the comparison which so many reporters—unable to abandon the adjective "Christ-like"—had been romantically implying. "REWARD for information leading to the apprehension of Jesus Christ," it read. "Wanted for sedition, criminal anarchy, vagrancy and conspiring to overthrow the Established Government. Dresses poorly. *Said* to be a carpenter by trade. Ill-nourished, has visionary ideas. Associates with common working people, the unemployed and bums."[77] The use of metaphor or analogy, is halfway to proclaiming identity. In such a situation the adoption of Digger principles was a perfectly logical step.

In many ways the Diggers were themselves a continuation of the turn-of-the-century Progressive Underground. In attempting to convert Haight-Ashbury to their ethical position, they were trying to extend the idea of the earlier Utopian communities over a larger urban area. The free food the Diggers supplied came partly from two farms operated by sympathetic communes outside San Francisco. Exactly as the illuminates of Munich took to the countryside during the First World War, those who had aquired a taste for communal living in Haight-Ashbury began during 1967 to head for the Utopian hills. The main exodus took place in the late summer, although the commune had been recognized much earlier as an alternative to the existence of urban Bohemia. The insistence on the simple life, the adoption of the rejected cause of the Indians, and a respect for ancient ceremony induced by the ingestion of peyote, resulted in the glorification of the Tribe as the ideal unit for living. The Be-In was advertised as a "gathering of the tribes," and the *Oracle's* reporter

The Great Liberation 461

added to his account of the festival an appeal for "growing space for the healthy, organic harmonious evolution of the Tribe." "Let's make Haight love together and then move to the country where love is hanging out waiting." Communes themselves might incorporate almost any variety of the various possible Underground syntheses: naturally the illuminated element has also become involved with communes, too.[78] But, whereas the transcendental impulse is constricted and passive within a commune, in the political movement that developed from the Haight of Diggers and hippies, the passive rejection of the Establishment practiced by communards was turned into an active revolt.

At the same time as the hippie culture was developing in Haight-Ashbury, the nearby University of California at Berkeley was undergoing a series of convulsions. These began in the autumn of 1964 and were partly the product of disillusionment and frustration felt by civil right workers after the failure of the CORE project in the South. The details of the student and so-called "Free Speech" Movement do not concern us here. Student revolt is nothing new, and recent European history shows many correspondences with what happened in America in 1965-68.[79] What is important is the junction that took place between some of the more orthodox student radicals, associated with the nationwide protest against the war in Vietnam, and the spiritual dropouts and Utopians of Haight-Ashbury.

Students have always been honorary citizens of Bohemia, and in a time of disaffection they naturally began to investigate Haight-Ashbury. Conversely, influences more associated with Bohemia started to affect student conceptions of political protest. In a debate in November 1965 over tactics for the large protest march in Oakland against the Vietnam War, Alan Ginsberg's pacifist proposals were barely defeated. These included the use of "masses of flowers," Christian crosses, and Jewish stars; the chanting of mantras and carrying "Zen" signs. The chairman of the Vietnam Day Committee to whom this proposal was put was Jerry Rubin, who had been living at Berkeley and was heavily involved in the agitation connected with the Free Speech Movement. Rubin became the leading figure in the junction between the radicals of Berkeley and the hippies of Haight-Ashbury. When he and his fellow-activists were invited to a conference at a hippie Buddhist temple, they arrived at the idea of the "Be-In" to create "a union of love and activism." At a press conference just before the Be-In, Rubin told reporters that the radicals "share common identity with the community of Haight-Ashbury," and his own account of the festival is clear in what it seemed to him to signify. Those taking part "believed that our energy would *turn on the world*." All the protest movements "led to deeper discoveries—that revolution did not mean the end of war or the end of racism. Revolution meant the creation of new men and women."

At the Be-In people recognized "that they were not alone," and this process seems to have resulted in a deep and lasting impression made by the hippie ethic—which means both the advocates of the new consciousness and the Diggers—on the student radicals. One observer compared the Be-In to the orthodox protest demonstrations he had attended and made the significant comment that although "the composition of the crowds was nearly the same, control of events had moved from politicos to the straight hippies."[80] Rubin's adoption of the idea of creating new men and women represents the transplanting of hippie ideas into the radical mind. We are back in the country of spiritual revolutions, and these are much-traveled roads.

Rubin moved from the West Coast to New York to become project director of the National Mobilization demonstration at the Pentagon in October 1967. At that demonstration—for which the *East Village Other* called for the presence of "Mystics, saints, Artists, Holymen, Astrologers, witches, sorcerers, warlocks, Druids, hippies, priests, shamen, ministers, rabbis, troubadours, prophets, minstrels, bards, roadmen"[81]—a pop group and assorted "shamen" ostensibly tried to levitate the Pentagon through a semimagical ceremony. This astute piece of image building stemmed from the group around Abbie Hoffman, a former civil rights worker at that time trying to practice the Digger eithic in New York. It fascinated reporters, entranced commentators like Norman Mailer, and marked the beginning of a brief period of surrealist political activity whose techniques were incarnated in the "Yippie!"—Youth International Party—movement, dreamed up by Hoffman, Rubin, and Paul Krassner the following New Year. Yippie!, which was designed as "a cross-fertilization of the hippie and New Left philosophies," had the long-term aim of developing "a model for an alternative society" and the short-term object of massing as many elements of the underground as possible at the Democratic Convention in Chicago that August. Hoffman and Rubin both declared that they aimed to create a *myth* of the Yippie—an all-purpose, hippie-surrealist revolutionary who would attract recruits at the same time as provoking the opposition. In Rubin's words:

> A new man was born smoking pot while besieging the Pentagon, but there was no myth to describe him. There were no images to describe all the 14-year-old freaks in Kansas, dropping acid, growing their hair long and deserting their homes and their schools. There were no images to describe all the artists leaving the prison of middle-class America to live and create art on the streets.
> The Marxist acidhead, the psychedelic Bolshevik. He didn't feel at home in SDS, and he wasn't a flower-power hippie or a campus intellectual. A stoned politico. A hybrid mixture of New Left and hippie coming out something different.[82]

The Yippie was a myth, like the hippie who went before him; but this time deliberately created. Both Rubin and Hoffman invoked Marshall McLuhan to support their choice of techniques: the "medium is the message" and thus the creator of myths. There is little difference between this McLuhanite idea of image building and the "myth" of Georges Sorel, which provided so many of the European Fascist leaders with a source of inspiration. The myth, the political image, the living symbol with all its indefinite and unconscious connotations is a powerful tool in the hands of politicians. But the myth must correspond to some degree of actuality: it must answer to needs which are in fact felt, and it must allow some possibility of success to those who try to live up to its legends. It is, therefore, significant in itself, in the support it attracts, and in what its manipulators set out to achieve.

The choice of technique—the myth itself—is suggestive because it had been previously used by politicians who appreciated the power of irrational forces to move men. The "hippie" and "New Left" elements of which the myth was composed both contributed to form the Yippie and his objectives. In case it is thought that most of the irrationalism came from the hippie element, it is worth quoting a report about Lawrence Lipton's film of the massive Oakland Vietnam Day march in Berkeley in February 1966.

> One member of the audience asked Lenny [Lipton] why he used religious music in the first scene, when the demonstrators were beginning their march. He didn't like the equation of irrational religion with the Vietnam Day Committee. We were rooting for Lenny's answer and he came through very well. He explained that there was an element of emotional fervor to the demonstration and emotionality is not necessarily derogative.
> We cheered because deep in our hearts we knew we had some irrational motivation, some emotional craving. And down went the self-righteous activist, and the audience cheers. The demonstrators do come off as supremely heroic despite Lipton's claims to the activist that "he would have put halos round the heads of all the marchers if it would have been possible."[83]

A similar collective irrationalism is displayed in the hippie-derived cult of mass gathering for rock dances and festivals. Even in Haight-Ashbury, this point was made. For those who were not concerned with the expansion of consciousness, rock dances provided a possible way of simply losing the self. In October 1966 the pop columnist Ed Denson compared the success of vast rock concerts with the Nuremberg rallies—a comparison that is often made by opponents of the Underground and that holds only insofar as there is a common denominator of irrationalism. "Man seems to like to gather together in large groups and lose individual identity in the higher union of the whole." Denson also recognized the nature of this flight from the self. "The emergence of the Frisco rock scene has marked a partial return towards the religious or the blues type of experience."

We have seen sufficient examples of hippie irrationalism to expect the fundamental anxiety that almost always induces a widespread rejection of the rational. In its most basic form this could find expression in the fear—which became widespread among West Coast hippies at the beginning of 1969—that California was destined to sink like Atlantis beneath the sea, as prophesized by the faith healer Edgar Cayce. In its more elaborate forms, such anxiety encouraged the pervasive mysticism in sections of the Underground. Far from Haight-Ashbury or any comprehension of what the consciousness-expanders meant, Underground mysticism developed into the worst possible nonsense. *OZ* summed up the situation in 1969: "Today's mystics seem muddled, yet reason shakes them hardly at all (and they don't believe in verbal communication). It is faith itself they want to believe in, the very *act* of believing they affirm."[84]

The creation of the Yippie was a strategy partly directed at the irrational impulses expressed both in New Left and hippies. The honeymoon period of happy surrealism, of throwing away money at the New York Stock Exchange, of "street theater," lasted only till the battle for which the Yippies had been preparing in Chicago in August 1968. With the violence and the ensuing bitterness, the Underground once more polarized. On the one hand, there were the passive dropouts; on the other, there were the elements with tangible grievances and tangible goals, like the Black Panthers, together with militant revolutionaries like the Weathermen concerned with ideology and bombs. During 1969 Abbie Hoffman announced that killing a policeman was a sacramental act. Timothy Leary was interviewed as an expert on sacraments, and he voiced his doubts while admitting that it might be "some people's *karma*."[85] It was only for a short time that the attempted fusion of politics and transcendentalism succeeded; but the brief period of Yippie tactics left an enduring legacy. This legacy was the myth. Although the aims and methods of the Yippie organizers soon changed, their theories were to some extent borne out. Part of the Yippie myth was the idea of *liberation,* which pervaded every aspect of the Underground and provided a useful blanket concept under which any rebel could cloak specific discontents. Beside all practical and tangible grievances, however, sat the occult idea of liberation—of total freedom from all human restrictions, or equally from the restrictions of being human.

This idea passed into the underground from the Hippies, Diggers, and Yippies. All the LSD-cults, the Oriental religions, the occult doctrines, if properly understood, contain the element of *liberation* from the prison of the personality, individual loneliness, and ultimately matter. Such philosophies had long been in the air as a result of the 19th-century occult revival. They had coalesced via Leary, Kesey, and innumerable other gurus in Haight-Ashbury, were projected accidentally by the media-created myth of the hippie and the deliberately-projected myth of the Yippie—and their implications stuck. The original object of self-transcendence was often left implict or distorted. Jerry Rubin wrote that "there is no such thing as an antiwar movement," there were "movements for liberation, for freedom." Abbie Hoffman possessed "the knowledge that the institutions and values of imperialism, racism, capitalism and the protestant ethic do not allow young people to experience authentic liberation."[86] Such demands for the imponderable of total freedom had previously been met by specifically mystical or religious adaptions of the transcendental impulse. The contribution of the Yippies—and, to a lesser extent, of the hippies—had been the identifying of the "repressive" agency with a particular social system. In the original form of the theory it was not capitalism, "Amerika," or the Protestant Ethic that was seen as the factor hampering man's self-liberation, but the human condition defined as matter, illusion, or a Gnostic Demiurge. With the spread from Haight-Ashbury of both hippies and of the hippie myth, such ideas became an integral part of the "alternative society," and, with the impulsion given by Yippie! and other activist groups, the ethic of liberation was applied to reinforce a neo-Marxist criticism of society.

The progress of Hoffman and Rubin reveals how the political activists learned from the "spiritual" dropouts. Further impetus was given to the idea of liberation by some of the gurus of psychedelic Bohemia who themselves extended or adapted their spiritual disciplines to the exigencies of a social critique. One of these was Gary Snyder. He argued that Buddhist thought had been too much concerned with dispelling ignorance by psychological methods. If the sociological conditions are attended to as well, the result is "a Buddhist Anarchism." Ginsberg agrees. "Whereas one lone nut saying 'I am the Lamb' can be clapped in jail one cat coming up among 5 thousand people dressed in caps and bells saying 'I am the Lamb' and *act on it* because they're not afraid to be the Lamb because they know that everybody knows it already." The most influential of all such exponents of a social liberation was Alan Watts, whose *Psychotherapy East and West* (1961) is a remarkable exposition of the theory that Eastern "ways of liberation" are all, in fact, methods of reorientating human perception of a world whose constituents are governed by social institutions. Thus the Hindu doctrine of *maya*—that man is trapped in a web of illusion—"lies not in the physical world but in the concepts or thought forms by which it is described." Psychotherapy can perform the same function as Eastern methods of liberation. For Watts, "the aim of a way of liberation is not the destruction of *maya* but seeing it for what it is, or seeing through it." For those who have taken over and misunderstood the concept, the reverse often appears to be true: yet it seems that in the original Yippie! idea of spiritual revolution there was much of the Watts approach. Thus Hoffman: "So what the hell are we doing, you ask? We are dynamiting brain cells. We are putting people through changes."[87]

The distinctively Yippie approach—the zany disregard for society's values and the deliberate attempts to shock unthinking participants in accepted reality—had been preceded in Europe by the Dadaists and Surrealists. With the development of an extensive American Bohemia, it was inevitable that imported versions of spiritual protest against material abuse would combine with a spontaneous rediscovery and reinterpretation of just such positions. We have seen how the occult was perpetually present both in Bohemian Europe between the two world wars and in the Europeanized Bohemias of America that preceded the hippie upsurge. In the Yippie critique of society, the occult was mobilized and became not merely an index of a generally illuminated approach, but the very source of the particular attitude itself. In Europe the occult sources of the idea of "liberation" are much easier to see, stemming, as they do, chiefly from Surrealism. It has therefore seemed more important to concentrate on the American movement of "liberation," whose origins are not so clear.

It was natural that Yippie!—and the more passive hippie culture—should independently develop Surrealist and Dada techniques of protest. It was natural, too, that as the American myth spread to the Progressive Underground of Europe the older established rationale of idealistic revolution would affect America and itself undergo a process of transformation into an active political creed. Abbie Hoffman makes his affinities clear when he shouts in triumph at the success of the Pentagon demonstration: "Artaud is alive at the walls of the Pentagon, bursting the seams of conventional protest, injecting new blood into the peace movement."[88] Artaud, apart from his theories of theater, which attracted Hoffman, is a natural hero of the irrationalist Underground; his magical preoccupations had even led him to take part in a peyote ceremony in South America. However, he was also—*de facto* if not in name—very much part of the Surrealist opposition to things-as-they-are. A brief analysis of the relationship of Surrealism and the modern Underground will indicate the direction of developments in Europe.

The Surrealists had issued a declaration on 27 January 1925 denying that they had anything to do with literature, although they were "quite capable, when necessary of making use of it like anyone else." If Surrealism was not a literary or artistic movement, what was it? To this question there were two main answers:

> 2. *Surrealism* is not a new means of expression, or an easier one, nor even a metaphysic of poetry. It is a means of liberation of the mind *and of all that resembles it.*
> 3. We are determined to make a Revolution.[89]

For André Breton there followed a long period of coquetting with the Communist Party, because the Marxist gospel seemed to him to provide a means of attaining social liberation. At the end of 1933, Breton, Crevel, and Eluard were expelled from the French Communist Party, and the odd alliance was at an end. Its progenitors remained convinced that Surrealism was a revolutionary force. The idea of liberation and the occult associations of Surrealism have a familiar consistency, and it is unsurprising to find that the successors of Surrealism have played a prominent part in European movements for "liberation."

In 1957 the first Situationist International was founded in Paris. Its members affirmed that surrealism had been for them "the beginning of revolutionary experience." To the question why one could not be a Surrealist today, they answered simply "in order not to be bored." They intended to take steps toward a movement more liberating than Surrealism itself, a standard to which Breton had declared he would rally if it could ever be unfurled. Both in East and

West, culture appeared to the Situationists as "a series of faked up repetitions." Their position—which demanded "complete freedom of information and creation"—would under any form of government remain the same. The Situationists have attempted to maintain a strict party line, although a series of alignments and expulsions have encouraged variations on their ideas. Situationist echoes reverberated through the Underground. Thus in 1962 the Munich artists group *Spur* was expelled from the Situationist International. One of its members, Dieter Kunzelmann, was later to help found the Berlin Kommune I, a German commune that ranked high in the list of Underground beatitudes.

The Amsterdam Provos, who in 1965 began a campaign of political Dada, Surrealism, and anarchy, owed much to the activities of Constant (born 1920), an avant-garde painter and writer who had been involved with the Situationist-oriented *Cobra* group and for a time was himself a Situationist.[90] Constant proclaimed an era of play and adventure, an idea taken up by the Provos in their campaign against the Establishment. Yet another Situationist connection was with the British poet Alexander Trocchi's "sigma" group, which organized the poetry festival "Wholly Communion" in 1965 at the Albert Hall in London.

As for the Situationists themselves, they published a review which anticipated the techniques adopted by much of the Underground press: strip cartoons and naked beauties accompanied excursions into severe theory. In early 1966 they were approached by a group of students who had friends recently elected to the students union of Strasbourg University and were in search of an ideology. The Situationists drew up a brochure in an attempt to reconcile the warring factions in the would-be subversive group. The students then used student union funds to publish the brochure *On the Poverty of Student Life* and decorated the university walls with a subversive comic strip. The use of union funds was made the cause of a scandal by the authorities, and the theories of the Situationists became the model for university rebels. When the discontents at Nanterre erupted at the beginning of 1968, the hard core of revolutionaries turned to Situationist theory. Both in the Nanterre rebellion and the "student revolt" proper of May 1968 in Paris, Situationist slogans—"Power to the Imagination," "Take your Desires for Reality"—which had previously been printed only in the Situationist bulletin found their way on to walls. The style of revolution in May 1968 owed a great deal to the Situationists; and, although in the internecine squabbling of various revolutionary groups the Situationists often tend to be despised, they have probably had more influence than is admitted on subsequent eruptions of the Underground. They themselves estimated that in May 1968 there were only about ten Situationists and their *"enragé"* supporters in Paris, yet they boasted of the creation of an illusory "vague and mysterious Situationist menace."[91]

Situationist theory provided the main Underground link with Surrealism. Situationists see society as a "spectacle." "Everything that used to be directly lived has moved away into a representation."[92] They accept much of Marx—especially the ideology of alienation—but little of Marxism. There must be a liberation from the power of the spectacle, a redefinition of reality, a recovery of "the totality of everyday life." The Situationist analysis is at once amazingly detailed and inaccessible. One thing is clear: in a very complex form it reaffirms the necessity for "liberation" from an illusory state of consciousness. The "society of the spectacle" is seen as both cause and effect of the system of production, but it might quite simply be expressed as *maya,* the illusion which must be overcome. Throughout all transformations from Surrealism to Situationism, the idea of overcoming appearances has held constant; and traditional occultism and mysticism agree very well with this position. The new revolutionaries do not forget their masters. André Breton's last pronouncement on Surrealism cited the esotericist René Guénon—who began his career as a disciple of Papus—and the Situationist Raoul Vaneigem's *Traite de Savoir Vivre* (1967) actually includes a chapter with the same title as one of Guénon's books.[93]

No one who has spent time reading the varied, contradictory, and self-abusive publications of "the Underground" would care to maintain that the creature was anything but a Questing Beast with an infinity of heads, each one browful of theories. But if there was any unity at all among its members, this was provided by the concept of liberation. This concept has been associated with occult and "spiritual" movements, and it was capable of such universal application only because it originally applied to universals. Old-fashioned revolutionaries were caught up in the Underground; many thousands of concerned people marched against the Vietnam War without knowing anything of Kesey; there have been shoals of pseudohippies, with no knowledge of the theories of love and liberation, and malcontents or disaffiliates of every description who were merely fed up with something they called "the System." Yet beside every specific and perceived grievance lay the other, irrational desire for "liberation," and among the Underground itself there were a few who realized what the term meant.

Until it took to guns, the Underground of Europe and America was, in every respect, the inheritor of the traditions of spiritual revolution which European progressives and Bohemians had earlier transmitted. The style of life—rebellious, provoking, communal; the transcendental aspirations and ideas of spiritual evolution; the coincidence of rejected knowledge and rejected politics in the areas where all opposition fuses—all conformed to the familiar pattern. The problem faced by the late Sixties was exactly that of earlier idealist revolutionaries—the necessary synthesis with power. When the Dutch Kabouters (Gnomes), who succeeded the Provos, won five seats on the Amsterdam city council, they at once offered to give one back on the grounds that they now had too much influence. It was less likely that the Underground would be co-opted by the system it was trying to circumvent than that—as happened to the idealists of the period between the world wars—it would become the victim of an alternative system. The idea of liberation has become internalized, and it may vanish altogether. But there have been powerful forces supporting the Great Liberation, and the disappearance of the idea is unlikely. For—owing allegiance in the last resort to the same esoteric sources—the idea of liberation has become a commonplace in those circles that derive their inspiration from the illuminated psychologists and educationalists who were discussed in the last chapter.

It is difficult to believe that the experiments in "liberating" the powers of the child begun by the new educationalists have been completely without influence on the children thus educated. This is not to indulge in the strange brand of pseudoanalysis cultivated by those who derive the youth revolution from Dr. Spock's instructions on weaning. It is to restate the truism that what is avant-garde for one generation is taught to the next in the schools. By the third generation, it has become an accepted part of the unperceived assumptions on which everyday life is based. A common theory among post-1945 British Conservative opinion was to blame the success of Socialism on "the schoolmasters." This was an interesting and half-true appreciation of the principle of inheritance and transformation of ideas. The methods of liberationist education have passed into educational practice; and the idea is generally accepted that the abilities of the child must be "liberated," rather than certain facilities instilled. This implies the assumption that there is something to liberate—a suggestive metaphysical idea, which has undoubted associations with the occult connections of the New Education.

The chief theorists of such liberation are indebted to the psychoanalysts and analytical psychologists. Those who descend from Freud have rejected their master's conviction that repression was necessary for the advancement of civilization. Their grounds are that civilization as constituted is unsatisfactory. This has led to a number of attempted syntheses of Marx and Freud, and the most notable are those of Wilhelm Reich and Herbert Marcuse. In the context of this book, only a few important points should be noted.

There is an "official" Wilhelm Reich. This Reich attempted to characterize Fascism as the outcome of sexual repression, developed the concept of "character armor" inhibiting the natural relationship of persons, and advocated the cultivation of the orgasm. This Reich was the friend of A. S. Neill, the welcome ally of progressive education, and the hero of the Dionysian underground, which sometimes seemed to have adopted the orgasm as a political principle. The admirers of the official Reich prefer to draw a veil over the last years of Reich's life. When the Nazi seizure of power made it impossible to carry out his work of sex-reform in Germany, Reich fled to Scandinavia, where he made experiments that he claimed resulted in the discovery of "bions," or "energy vesicles." In 1939 he arrived in the United States and continued his research into the nature of the life force: naturally, he found it. This was "orgone energy," and it resembled nothing so much as Reichenbach's Odic force or Mesmer's animal magnetism. Orgone energy charges organic substances, living tissues, especially blood corpuscles, and it kills bacilli and protozoa. It acts differently from the known forms of electromagnetic energy. It accounts for a number of astronomical phenomena: the Northern Lights, lightning, the atmospheric disturbances of shortwave transmission at times of increased sun spot activity. It accounts for the light phenomena of many flowers and of wood undergoing bionous disintegration, of the sexual organs of many insects, and for the blue coloration of many frogs in a state of sexual excitation.[94]

The discovery of orgone energy led Reich to believe he had discovered a cure for cancer in his "orgone accumulators." Later he believed that he could control cloud movements and hence the weather. At the very end of his life he was convinced he was in communication with beings from outer space. Supporters of the official Reich have denied that this later period has any relationship to the master's earlier work; opponents have been content to denounce Reich as "mad." In contradiction to both these points of view, the facts show that Reich's later ideas—with the exception of the beings from outer space (and they will be discussed in the next chapter)—were a natural development of his earlier theories. The experiments that discovered the "energy vesicles" resulted from Reich's attempts to put his psychology on a biological basis. It was no doubt an extravagant and unjustified leap to the discovery of the life force, but it was a logical progression—or at least consistently illogical. Reich's view of the liberating role of the orgasm in society led him to search for the life-giving energy responsible. Like so many protagonists of liberation, he ended by discovering God.

On visits to his laboratories in Rugely, Maine, Reich became friendly with a seventy-year-old guide called Herman O. Templeton, who was one of the first to use Reich's "orgone accumulator." Reich was astounded to find that this backwoodsman had intuitively divined the appearance of his "bions." Templeton was "religious in the good sense of the word."

> When I asked him one day whether he believed in God, he said: "Of course he is everywhere, in me and all around us. Just look there," and he pointed across the lake to the blue

against the distant mountains.* "I call it *Life,* but people would laugh at me, so I don't like to talk about it."

In other words this woodsman also knew of the existence of the biological energy in the atmosphere.[95]

Reich's identification of the orgone energy with God is again only a logical extension of his search for a life-force. The repeated persecution he had undergone undoubtedly helped to turn his mind to the preoccupations of his later years. But the concern of the sexual liberator with the divine was the result of no sudden jump. Reich's *Murder of Christ* (1953) is perhaps "paranoid," and it virtually identifies the author with Christ; but it is also consistent with the pattern of Reich's mystical development. The bibliography includes Christian theology and works on Hindu and Buddhist thought, as well as a document issued by the "Rosicrucian" organization AMORC. Reich's description of the plight of the unliberated man uses the same metaphor as several neo-Gnostics. "*It is possible to get out of a trap. However, in order to break out of prison, one must first confess to being in a prison. The trap is man's emotional structure,* his character structure."[96]

A similar "Gnostic" idea of liberation is found in Herbert Marcuse. Marcuse (born 1898) obtained his Ph.D. in Berlin in 1922, and his theories betray the inheritance of his formative years. Again, there is something of a conflict between an "official" (if subversive) Marcuse and the unofficial philosopher. The official Marcuse is another mediator between Marx and Freud, a product of the *Institut für Sozialforschung,* the pupil of profoundly Germanic Hegelians.

He is obviously a revolutionary, although not particularly original: many of his ideas can be found in the writings of his former colleagues, Theodor Adorno and Max Horkheimer.[97] Marcuse's concepts have strong connections with the Situationist idea of liberation and have probably influenced the French analysis. This is the well-known Marcuse of *Eros and Civilization* (1955) and *One-Dimensional Man* (1964). There is another Marcuse, who is seen in his later publications.

This is the Marcuse who has described himself as "an absolutely incurable and sentimental romantic."[98] His concept of "liberation"

---

*Reich's "orgone energy" is supposed to be blue in color.

involves the dissociation of the individual from the communal illusions of society, and Marcuse has compared the process to the LSD "trip":

> The "trip" involves the dissolution of the ego shaped by the established society—an artificial and short-lived dissolution. But the artificial and private liberation anticipates, in a distorted manner, an exigency of the social liberation: the revolution must be at the same time a revolution in perception which will accompany the material and intellectual reconstruction of society, creating the new aesthetic environment.[99]

So there is to be a "revolution in perception"—a "spiritual revolution"—which is analogous on a social scale to the private and momentary liberation from self achieved by LSD. The proposition could hardly be more plainly put. The liberated universe cannot be described in terms of the ordinary universe. But the nearest Marcuse can come to its definition is "society as a work of art"; and art alone, he thinks, gives some idea of the transformative vision. It is telling that Marcuse sees as "the signal" for this alteration in perception "the great artistic rebellion in the period of the First World War," and he chooses to quote Franz Marc of the *Blaue Reiter* as his text for the creation of the new aesthetic society.[100] Thus, the quest of the early Bohemians for a "spiritual" art and society returns to the revolutions of the new Bohemia in the form of a pronunciamento by one of their most revered prophets. It would be untrue to portray Marcuse as a mystic, but he has certainly transposed into rational-seeming language ideas that have previously found a semimystical expression. His view of the status of a philosopher is as a "liberator," whose duty is to bring home to those he teaches the Platonic allegory of the Cave—essentially that man is imprisoned and has no idea of his true potentialities—and to assist in "abolishing the entire structure of established existence."[101]

What is this liberated viewpoint if not "another state of consciousness"? Reich might define it as attainable by the perfect orgasm. Marcuse, while allowing the erotic element its place, advocates life as a work of art. Another of Freud's adaptors, Norman O. Brown, performs astonishing contortions to produce a "mysticism of the body," in which he conflates Ferenczi and Jacob

Böhme. Because the thing itself is self-contradictory, it is only describing it to say paradoxically that Brown's theories represent a "secular Gnosticism." Almost every critic of Brown has noticed his mysticism—it is hard not to do so—and Marcuse himself has delivered a stinging rebuke, which reminds the reader of Freud's own admonitions to his followers.[102]

Another line of "liberationist" theories stems from C. G. Jung. Jungian analysts are prone to lamentation about the lack of acceptance of their school of thought as compared to the relative popularity of Freud. However, Jung has exercised a strong, though often unperceived, influence among the Underground. For example, in the phrase which was at one time so popular, "total experience"—used among other applications to describe the "psychedelic" effect of rock dances with amplified music and stroboscopic lights—there is a direct use of a Jungian term.[103] Jungian ideas passed through several mediators—notably the British psychologist Eric Graham Howe, whose influence has been exercised on both Henry Miller and Alan Watts; and R. D. Laing (born 1927), the center of the modern group of "liberating" psychiatrists.[104] Although Laing and his chief collaborator, David Cooper, have derived inspiration from other sources, the basis of their early approach was the Jungian view that "neurosis tends towards something positive,"[105] and, in particular, that schizophrenia itself is a therapeutic process begun by the situation in which the apparently "afflicted" human finds himself. To this is added the idea that people are labeled as "mad" and attempts made to "cure" them for the purposes of maintaining a false consciousness in the sense of the Situationists or Marcuse. Society is, in fact, an unconscious conspiracy to suppress the nature of man.

In social terms this devolves into a conflict between Us—the dissociated being, struggling to recover his true nature—and Them—the possibly well-wishing but ultimately destructive Establishment. Laing writes: "It is just possible that a further transformation is possible if men can come to experience themselves as 'One of Us.' " Or, in language that does not pay attention to some distinctions which no doubt would be drawn by Laing, the supposedly individual personality must be transcended and a contact made with something which could be seen as universal humanity or God.

Some of the phenomena labeled "schizophrenic" are examples of "*a natural way of healing our own appalling state of alienation called normality.*" This position leads Laing to endorse much of Reich, the extent of whose neglect "cannot be explained rationally."[106]

Laing, Cooper, and their associates called a congress on the "Dialectics of Liberation," which was held in London in July 1967. Besides the organizers, speakers included Stokeley Carmichael, Dr. Marcuse, Allen Ginsberg and other formulators of the idea of "liberation," including Paul Goodman and Simon Vinkenoog. Laing and Cooper had become convinced that their position coincided with contemporary political struggles for "liberation"—the "Us" were definitely defined as Cuba and North Vietnam and the "Them" as the American Imperialists.[107] This facile identification of a particular political system with the repressive forces alienating man from himself enabled the Laingians to align themselves with the international Underground. And it does not take an opponent of Laing's psychology, or a supporter of the Vietnam War, to see the absurdity of this assumption. Nevertheless, for a fortnight that July—it was the summer of Haight-Ashbury's decline—London witnessed a union of "liberated" elements that represented something of an "Intellectual Be-In." The congress was roundly criticized by those supporters of complete irrationalism who had abandoned thought altogether. Despite such criticism, the Dialectics of Liberation was a landmark in the history of the Underground.

The same ideas that led Laing and Cooper to ally themselves with theorists of political liberation resulted in the rapprochement with LSD cults and the theorists of spiritual liberation. In the early days of LSD it was thought that its "psychomimetic" properties would make it useful to psychiatrists. In fact, the Laing group did at one time use LSD in therapy. Laing first met Leary as early as 1964; and David Cooper was writing about the American drug movement in early 1966 before Britain had really become aware of what was going on across the Atlantic. Another factor that encouraged the adoption of Laingian views by an enthusiastic body of lay supporters was the very redefinition of "madness" upon which the approach rested. The Surrealists had long before attached value to the experiences of madness, and there were obvious points of similarity between the

Underground cult of Artaud and Cooper's opinion that the tortured genius "had more to say relevant to madness than all the text-books of psychiatry."[108]

Religious and occult analogies are very important to the Laingian approach. Cooper compares the situation of acute bewilderment which precedes schizophrenia to the state of "no-mind" induced by the Zen *koan*. There are ways of being able to "liberate ourselves into a more real, less stereotyped future," but these incur the risk of being thought mad; and in a present in which Christ would "end up largactilised and electro-convulsed on a 28-day detention order (Mental Health Act, 1959)," the implications do not need to be stressed. Laing is even more explicit. He states that the "normal" condition of perceiving oneself as a coherent permanent "I" is "a preliminary illusion, a veil, a film of *maya*." If the ego—the "instrument for living in *this* world"—is broken up, the person may be catapulted into states of other reality. States of reality that do not relate to the external world are classified as "mad"; and this includes the perception of the Divine. "The fountain has not played itself out, the flame still shines, the river still flows, the spring bubbles forth, the light has not faded. But between *us* and It there is a veil which is more like fifty feet of solid concrete. *Deus absconditus*. Or we have absconded."[109]

Other realities—they all talk of them or imply them. Leary and Laing are explicit in their use of the term; others prefer "expansion of consciousness" or "liberation." It is liberation from that which is, which presumes that there exists or can be created that which is other. The concept of liberation can *almost always* be associated with an esoteric source, either directly or through a mediating or secularizing agency. Specific forces of repression, of course, generate countermovements, which find fine slogans in the theology of total liberation; and there have undoubtedly been numbers of those who could be identified with "the Underground" who would disavow any of the theories discussed in this chapter. All that can be said is that much of the Underground was heading—though it may not have realized it—toward a "spiritual" and esoteric revolution. Urged by assumptions implicit in the idea of liberation and the explicit supernatural logic of some of its prophets, the counterculture also came to seek the Heavenly City.

But in seeking the liberation of the individual through the destruction of social *maya,* the advocates of the new apocalypse appear to have made one signal error. In the original form, the idea of liberation is Gnostic in nature. That is to say, it is world-rejecting. At the center is the divine spark trapped in heavy matter. The situation could be described as a point enclosed within a circle. In the original idea, the circle is broken and the spark escapes *through a different way of looking at the circle.* This is what is meant by "revolution in consciousness." The trapped human executes some spiritual acrobatics and sees that he is not trapped after all—all the time the circle was broken, and indeed he may have created it himself. But this change in the relationship of the point (Man) and the circle (Matter) is achieved through operations taking place within the individual—within the point. The circle is illusion, nothing more. The theorists of social liberation are trying to produce the necessary changes in the point by manipulating the surrounding circle, the existence of which has traditionally been seen as the product of wrong being, of a wrongly perceived relationship of man and universe.

The construction of a new social reality would seem to be, from the point of view of all systems of liberation, merely another artifact of illusion. On the other hand, the exponents of material reform proclaim that to concentrate on "spiritual" goals is to distract attention from goals that are realizable in the present. Both the spiritual aspirants and the social reformers seem to have admirable motives which it is not for this book to judge. But the application of the spiritual theory to material ends must finish in disaster. If it is the social system which prevents man from "experiencing liberation," the construction of a new social system—even the system which defines itself in opposition to that which has previously existed—is merely to reforge the fetters which have been struck off. "Even a cowherd may by realization attain Liberation," says the *Tibetan Book of the Great Liberation.* And even the wisest and the best intentioned may bury themselves yet further in the mire.

1. Hans Richter, *Dada* (London, 1970), pp. 199, 201.
2. See *The Occult Underground,* pp. 153 ff., 281-85, 362-63.
3. Sixten Ringbom, *The Sounding Cosmos* in *Acts Academia Aboiensis* (Humaniora), vol. 38, no. 2 (Abo, 1970), and "Art in the Epoch of the Great

Spiritual" in *Journal of the Warburg and Courtauld* Institutes (1966), pp. 386 ff.
  4. Ringbom, "Art in . . . the Great Spiritual," p. 394 and list printed on p. 418.
  5. Ringbom, "Art in . . .," pp. 409-10, and cf. Klaus Lankheit (ed.), *Franz Marc* (London, 1960).
  6. Hermann Bahr, "Die Uberwindung des Naturalismus," in *Zur Uberwindung des Naturalismus,* (Stuttgart, 1968), p. 87; for Steiner's pronouncements on art, see *Art in the Light of the Mystery Wisdom* (London, 1970), and *Architectural Forms* (London, 1936); see Otto Benesch, *Edvard Munch* (London, 1967), pp. 17 ff. At the time of their friendship in Berlin, Strindberg was writing a story called *Tschandala*—the term is that of Lanz von Liebenfels (see chapter V); T. H. Robsjohn-Gibbings, *Mona Lisa's Mustache* (New York, 1948), p. 76; G. F. Hartlaub, *Kunst und Religion* (Leipzig, 1919), p. 45.
  7. Gropius quoted in Wolfgang Pehnt, "Gropius, the Romantic" in *The Art Bulletin,* September 1971, p. 301.
  8. Scheurlen, *Sekten.*
  9. Johannes Itten, *Mein Vorkurs am Bauhaus* (Regensburg, 1963), pp. 11-12, 17.
  10. Ringbom, "Art in . . . the Great Spiritual," p. 413; Alfred Arndt, "Life at the Bauhaus," in *50 Years Bauhaus* (London, 1968), p. 312.
  11. Hans L. C. Jaffe, *De Stijl* (London, 1970), pp. 17-18, 55; Ringbom, "Art in the . . . Great Spiritual," p. 414.
  12. On Ciurlionis, see Nicolai Worobiow, *M. K. Ciurlionis* (Leipzig, 1938), and Camilla Gray, *Russian Experiment,* p. 118.
  13. Kasimir Malevich, "God is not cast down," in *Essays on Art* (London, 1970), pp. 188 ff. Gray, *Russian Experiment,* pp. 234-35 and 248 ff. for ideological squabbles among artists.
  14. Richter, *Dada,* pp. 32, 67-68, 218.
  15. Hugo Ball, *Die Flucht aus der Zeit* (Lucerne, 1956), pp. 18-19, *Byzantinisches Christentum* (Munich and Leipzig, 1923); Emmy Hennings-Ball, *Hugo Balls Weg zu Gott,* (Munich, 1931), especially p. 77.
  16. Richter, *Dada,* p. 64.
  17. See Ana Balakian, *André Breton, Magus of Surrealism* (New York, 1971), pp. 28-35, and Maurice Nadeau, *The History of Surrealism* (London, 1968), p. 83; Hans Freimark, *Mediumistische Kunst* (Leipzig, 1914).
  18. On Artaud, see Bettina L. Knapp, *Antonin Artaud, Man of Vision* (New York, 1969), which gives an excellent picture of an alternative reality slipping out of control.
  19. On Lawson, see Martin Gardner, *Fads and Fallacies,* p. 69 ff.
  20. See Parker Tyler, *The Divine Comedy of Pavel Tchelitchew* (London, 1970).
  21. *View* (New York), vol. I, no. 1 (September 1940). It was to some extent against artists of the *View* brand that Robsjohn-Gibbings directed his attack.

22. *View*, vol. I, nos. 7-8 (October-November 1941).
23. *View*, vol. III, no. 1, p. 5. For other such articles, see Pierre Mabille, "The Destruction of the World," vol. I, nos. 9-10; Hilary Arn, "Nostradamus against the Gods"; Lionel Abe, "The Politics of Spirit," vol. I, nos. 11-12, etc. Kurt Seligman, *The Mirror of Magic* (New York, 1948), reveals a complete knowledge of the basic 19th-century French occultists: Wronski, Fabre d'Olivet, Alina d'Eldir, Albert Poisson, Wirth, Papus, Saint-Yves d'Alveydre.
24. Seligman, "Magic and the Arts," in *View* (Fall, 1946), pp. 13-16.
25. George Wickes (ed.), *Lawrence Durrell-Henry Miller, a private correspondence* (London, 1963), p. 347; Sidney Omar, *Henry Miller: His World of Urania* (London and California, 1968), p. 63; Alfred Perles, *My Friend, Henry Miller* (London, 1955), p. 132. Henry Miller, *Big Sur and the Oranges of Hieronymus Bosch* (London, 1958), pp. 245 ff., 260; Henry Miller, "A Night with Jupiter," in *View* (February-March 1942), p. 5.
26. For a comparison between the Beats and their predecessors, see Lawrence Lipton, *The Holy Barbarians* (London, 1960), pp. 263 ff.
27. Ned Polsky, "The Village Beat Scene," in *Hustlers, Beats and others* (London, paperback ed. 1971), pp. 173-74, 176 ff.
28. Polsky, *Hustlers, Beats and others*, p. 174; Lipton, *Barbarians*, pp. 244 ff.
29. Jack Kerouac, *The Dharma Bums* (orig. 1958, paperback ed. London, 1969), p. 11.
30. Christmas Humphreys, *Sixty Years of Buddhism in England* (London, 1968), pp. 20-40. Other heroes of Kerouac—for example, Dwight Godard, compiler of *A Buddhist Bible,* published in the United States in 1928—are also the heroes of the European Buddhists.
31. Theodore Roszack, *The Making of a Counter-Culture* (London, 1970), p. 132.
32. An additional factor in spreading consciousness of Zen in America was undoubtedly the occupation of Japan. After 1945 there was a great increase in East Asian studies, and it is interesting that Zen properly entered England after the Second World War, when Christmas Humphreys—who had been sent as a counsel to the War Crimes Trials in Tokyo—visited Suzuki. It is symptomatic of the close links between the Occult Revival and the coming of Zen to the West that at the time of his trip Humphreys was preparing a new edition of the *Mahatma Letters to H. P. Blavatsky,* and that his journey included a visit to the headquarters of the Theosophical Society at Adyar near Madras. See Humphreys, *Via Tokyo* (London, 1948).
33. Norman Cohn, *The Pursuit of the Millennium* (London paperback ed. 1970), p. 286.
34. See *The Occult Underground.*
35. For Symonds, see William James, *The Varieties of Religious Experience* (paperback ed., London, 1968), pp. 376-77. For Anna Kingsford and others, see *The Occult Underground;* B. P. Blood, *Pluriverse* (London, n.d.), pp. 217-25. Cf. *Journal* of SPR June 1893, pp. 94-96.

36. Blood, *Pluriverse,* p. vii; for Tennyson's letter to Blood, see pp. 215-17, and Hallam, Lord Tennyson, *Tennyson, a Memoir,* vol. II, pp. 158-59; Blood, *Pluriverse,* p. xxiv; *Letters of William James* (London, 1926), vol. II, p. 39; William James, "A Pluralistic Mystic" reprinted in *Memoirs and Studies* (London, 1911), p. 373.

37. James, *Varieties of Religious Experience,* pp. 373-74.

38. See, e.g., Symonds, *Beast,* pp. 160 ff.; *The Confessions of Aleister Crowley* (ed. Symonds and Kenneth Grant, London, 1969), p. 768. The editors note (p. 934, note 4) that Crowley had been taking the drug "for some years."

39. The source is a former disciple of Crowley.

40. As his correspondence shows, Huxley kept in touch with almost every prominent member of the mystical underground. At first there were Gerald Heard and Christopher Isherwood, later Alan Watts and Timothy Leary. Huxley himself was prone to accepting every chance-blown scrap of rejected knowledge: for example, the Bates system of sight-training and Dianetics. See *The Letters of Aldous Huxley* (ed. Grover Smith, London, 1969) and Laura Huxley, *This Timeless Moment* (London, 1969).

41. Sidney Cohen, *Drugs of Hallucination* (paperback ed., London, 1970), pp. 26-27, 32-35; John Wilcock, "Other Scenes," in *Berkeley Barb* (22 April, 1966), p. 7; Thadeus and Rita Ashby, "Did Jesus Turn On?," *Berkeley Barb* (23 December 1966); Thadeus and Rita Ashby, "Ecstatic Living" in *The Alchemist* (Manhattan, Kansas) vol. I, no. 3 (December 1968), reprinted from San Francisco *Oracle.*

42. Richard Blum, Eva Blum, and Mary Lou Funkhauser, "The Natural History of LSD Use" in *Utopiates* (ed. Blum, London, 1965), pp. 23-38, 55-56.

43. See Timothy Leary, *High Priest* (New York, 1968), pp. 2-60 (p. 60 quoted).

44. Leary, *High Priest,* p. 66.

45. For Ginsberg, see Leary, *High Priest,* pp. 110 ff.; for Olson, p. 143 ff.; for Burroughs, pp. 214 ff.; for the "Good Friday Experiment," pp. 304 ff.; for Watts and Heard, p. 288; quote on p. 300; see Leary and Ralph Metzner, "Poet of the Interior Journey," in Leary, *The Politics of Ecstasy* (London, 1970), pp. 146 ff.; Norman Hartweg, interview with Richard Alpert in *Berkeley Barb* (3 September 1965), p. 9.

46. Leary, *High Priest,* pp. 110-12; "God's Secret Agent AOS 3" in *Politics,* pp. 225 ff..

47. Leary, "God's Secret Agent."

48. The main source for information on Kesey is Tom Wolfe, *The Electric Kool-Aid Acid Test* (paperback ed., New York, 1969). This book needs no recommendation to its already large public, and only those who have had anything to do with Kesey-type experiments can judge whether the atmosphere it creates is authentic. However, from the point of view of a student of strange religions, Wolfe has conveyed better than any other writer the

sense of living within another order of experience induced by a novel scale of values. Ouspensky's *In Search of the Miraculous* has something of the same atmosphere, but is primarily concerned with exposition. There are one or two novels of the 19th-century Occult Revival which induce the claustrophobia and even the aspiration. But Wolfe's head-over-heels prose shows something which it is surely important for a 20th-century historian to understand—how people still believe in miracles.

49. For Owsley and Kesey, see Wolfe, *Acid Test*, pp. 188-89.
50. Wolfe, *Acid Test*, pp. 222 ff., and Ralph J. Gleason, *The Jefferson Airplane and the San Francisco Sound* (New York, 1969).
51. Leary, "The Magical Mystery Trip" in *Politics of Ecstasy*, pp. 88, 96.
52. Wilcock, in *Barb*, 22 April 1966, p. 7.
53. "The Messiah Speaks," *Los Angeles Free Press*, vol. 2, no. 11; *Berkeley Barb*, vol. 3, no. 11, p. 6; on Charlie Brown Artman, see *Barb*, 1/1 (August 13, 1965) and 2/20 (20 May 1966); and *Electric News* (Salt Lake City) 1/3, p. 51; *Helix* (Seattle, Wash.), 2/2/ (29 September 1967); *Distant Drummer* (Philadelphia) vol. 1, no. 1 (November 1967), p. 2.
54. See *Indian Head* (Santa Ana, Calif.) vol. I, nos. 4, 5, 8; *Modern Utopian*, vol. I, no. 3, pp. 29 ff.; *International Times*, no. 18 (13 August-13 September), p. 2.
55. David Ryan in *Logos*, vol. II, no. 2 (July 1969); reprinted from *International Times;* also "Letter from Katmandu" (August 1969), p. 2; Elfrida Rivers, "Emanations," *East Village Other*, vol. IV, no. 39 (27 August 1969), p. 13.
56. Leary, Review of the Neo-American Church Catechism and Handbook in *East Village Other*, vol. II, no. 19, (19 August - 1 September 1967), p. 9; Walter Bowart in *Berkeley Barb* (17 June 1967), p. 9 (reprinted from EVO), "The Way to God" in *Modern Utopian* vol. I, no. 1, and EVO vol. III, no. 4 (1-15 January 1968), p. 5.
57. Wolfe, *Acid-Test*, pp. 241 ff., and Richard Strauss, "A strroool trooomnmn down Memory Lane with Hugh Romney" in *Oracle of Southern California* (January 1968), pp. 6 ff.; Al Katzman, "Hog Farm in Open Celebration' in *Logos* (April 1969), p. 7A and 14A; Hugh Romney in *EVO* (week ending 17 August 1967), p. 10.
58. *Avatar*, vol. I, no. 3 (7 July 1967); see *Avatar*, nos. 18-24 (February - May 1968).
59. On Caen and his terms, see *EVO*, vol. II, no. 22 (1-15 October 1967), p. 3.
60. Ginsberg in *Los Angeles Free Press*, vol. III, no. 3 (21 January 1966); "Reflections on the Mantra," in *The Alchemist* (November 1968), p. 19 (reprinted from *Fifth Estate*).
61. Howard Wheeler, "The Hare Krishna Explosion," in *The Alchemist* (March 1968); Mukunduh Das Adhikary in *San Francisco Oracle*, p. 8.
62. Wheeler, "Hare Krishna," p. 10.
63. See Wendell Thomas, *Hinduism Invades America* (New York, 1930).

64. *L.A. Free Press,* vol. IV, no. 33 (8-24 August 1967), p. 16 and *San Francisco Oracle* (January 1967), p. 4.
65. *Oracle* and Arthur, "Evolution and Cosmic Consciousness," reprinted from *Oracle* in *The Alchemist,* vol. I, no. 2 (November 1968). On Alfred Korzybsky, see Gardner, *Fads and Fallacies,* pp. 281 ff. Gardner's arguments here should be watched as carefully as Korzybsky's own.
66. *S.F. Oracle* (January 1967), p. 7.
67. *Berkeley Barb,* vol. III, no. 14, and vol. II, no. 25, vol. III, no. 11 (16 September 1966), and Leary, *Politics,* p. 301.
68. Ted Berk, "Manifesto for Mutants" in *S.F. Oracle* (January 1967).
69. *S.F. Oracle* (5-15 November 1966) for Alpert, p. 3 and pp. 10-11; and "Gossiping Guru," "The Stoned Age," p. 6. See January numbers for the idea of Avatar.
70. For a description of what happened during the "summer of love" see Nicholas von Hoffman, *We Are the People Our Parents Warned Us Against* (paperback ed., New York, 1969), and Helen Perry, *The Human Be-In* (London, 1970). Hoffman, while not unsympathetic, concentrates on Haight-Ashbury as a culture based on a drug-economy. It is an excellent antidote to the naïve enthusiasm of Helen Perry, who does show what was expected of the hippie ethic and makes the interesting point that Haight-Ashbury to some extent acted as a sort of "automatic psychotherapy" for people out of control. Perry also compares the hippies to the New England Transcendentalists. The much-praised account by Joan Didion, "Slouching towards Bethlehem" in the book of the same title (London, 1969), is quite useful, but lacks perspective. The best sources are, of course, the Underground Press—*Barb, Oracle, East Village Other, Fifth Estate*—and they should be compared with more jaundiced accounts like Didion's or Hoffman's. There is an anthology of the early underground press, heavily edited by Jesse Kornbluth, *Notes from the New Underground* (New York, 1968) in which see pp. 284-300 for the decline of Haight-Ashbury.
71. On Digger origins, see *Barb* (21 October 1966), p. 3; Perry, *Human Be-In,* pp. 52 ff.
72. See *Barb* article, note 115. I have not been able to find a copy of the *Digger Papers* in which these manifestos were printed, but see notes immediately following.
73. "Diggers Do," in Kornbluth, *New Underground,* pp. 209-10; Alex Foreman and F. P. Salstrom, "Revolution, Diggers' Style," in *Distant Drummer* (3-10 October 1969), p. 4. For two manifestoes from the *Digger Papers,* see Peter Stansill and David Z. Mairowitz, BAMN (London, 1971).
74. See Cohn, *The Pursuit of the Millenium,* pp. 287 ff.; for the earlier crisis of Renaissance and Reformation, see my earlier *The Occult Underground.*
75. Foreman and Salstrom, "Diggers' Style."
76. Emmett Grogan, *Ringolevio* (London, 1972), pp. 232 ff.
77. *Modern Utopian,* vol. II, no. 4; *Barb,* 2-14 April 1966.

78. William James Collins and David Lee Carson, "A Speed-Freak Mythology," in *Avatar* (15 October - 4 November 1969), p. 9; Thelin, "The Community of the Tribe," in *Oracle* (January 1967), p. 15; William Hedgepeth, *The Alternative* (New York and London, 1970).

79. For the Berkeley troubles, see Hal Draper, *Berkeley, the New Student Revolution*, (New York, 1965). 1848 saw the first "student government" in Vienna and at the same time an outbreak of mysticism and millennarianism (e.g., the movement of Ganneau in Paris, for which see *The Occult Underground*, pp. 304 ff.) See also pp. 245 ff. and pp. 308-9 for corresponding roles of Poland and Vietnam in idealistic revolutionary movements.

80. Ginsberg, in *Barb* (19 November 1965), p. 4; *Oracle* (5-15 November 1968); *Barb* (13 June 1967), p. 3; Jerry Rubin, *Do It!* (London, 1970), p. 56; Ed Denson in *Barb*, vol. IV, no. 3, p. 4.

81. *EVO* (1-15 October 1967).

82. For Hoffman's contact with Diggers, see Abbie Hoffman, *Revolution for the Hell of It* (paperback ed., New York, 1970), pp. 37 ff.; Rubin, *Do It!*,, p. 106, quote on p. 82.

83. *Barb* (4 February 1966), pp. 1, 7.

84. Ed Denson, "The Holy Barbarians," in *Barb* (21 October 1967), p. 6; see Elfrida Rivers in *EVO* (30 April 1969) who replied to a correspondent that those who believed were "looking as damn silly as the original Millerites," and also underground press for early April that year; "Transcendentalism Is In," in *Oz*, 17 (London, 1969), p. 20.

85. Leary in *EVO*, vol. IV, no. 27, p. 18.

86. Rubin, *Do It!*, pp. 246-47; Hoffman, *Revolution*, pp. 5-6.

87. Snyder, "Buddhist Anarchism," in *Buddhist Oracle* (November - December 1967); Ginsberg, "Consciousness and Culture," in Joseph Berke (ed.) *Counter-Culture* (London, 1969), p. 178; Alan Watts, *Psychotherapy East and West* (London, 1971), pp. 9, 51. It is odd that this influential—and in any case remarkable—book should have taken ten years to reach England. Hoffman, *Revolution*, p. 31. Another parallel between yippie-style revolutionaries and occultists is the insistence that in order to understand their speciality one must take part in it.

88. Hoffman, *Revolution*, p. 46. His debt to Artaud is quite explicit. See p. 105 ff. for application of Theatre of Cruelty principles to the Chicago demonstration; Hoffman, *Woodstock Nation* (New York, 1969), p. 153.

89. Translated by Richard Howard in Maurice Nadeau, *Surrealism*, p. 240.

90. *Internationale Situationiste* (July 1958), pp. 5-6. Facsimile of entire review reprinted Amsterdam, 1970; Stansill and Mairowitz, BAMN, p. 131. On *Kommune I*, see Rainer Langhans and Fritz Teufel in Berke, *Counter-Culture*, pp. 104 ff.; Simon Vinkenoog, "A Rap on the Highroad to Happiness," in Berke, *Counter-Culture*, p. 153.

91. *Internationale Situationiste* (December 1958), pp. 4 ff., 31-32; no. 11

(October 1967), pp. 23 ff., "Nos buts et nos methodes dans le scandale de Strasbourg"; and "Strasbourg 1966" in Berke, *Counter-Culture,* pp. 197 ff.; *Internationale Situationiste,* September 1969, p. 26. Cf. Patrick Seale and Maureen McConville, *French Revolution 1968* (London, 1968), and Stansill and Mairowitz, BAMN, pp. 131 ff., 109.

92. The theory, which I will not attempt to summarize, and which is—for at least one persistent reader—very difficult to understand, has been translated into English in the form of Guy Debord, *Society of the Spectacle* (Detroit, 1970), and Raoul Vaneigem, *The Totality for Kids* (London, n.d.).

93. Breton, "Du Surrealisme en ses oeuvres vives" (1953), in *Manifestes du surrealisme* (Paris, 1962), p. 187, note 1. Guénon took over *L'Initiation* from the disciples of Papus; Vaneigem, *Traité de savoir vivre* (Paris, 1967). See chapter, "Le regne du quantitif," pp. 88 ff. and René Guenon, *The Reign of Quantity.* The Situationists have a fondness for the theories of Fourier, who has always had a strong following in the illuminated underground. See *The Occult Underground,* pp. 343-44. Breton himself, towards the end of his life, became very concerned with Fourier. See Jean Gaulmier's edition of Breton's *Ode à Charles Fourier* (Paris, 1961). Vaneigem opposes the "universal harmony" of Fourier to the "perverted harmony" of present conditions (in *The Totality,* section 25). Marcuse applauds the new Fourierism in "The End of Utopia" in *Five Lectures,* (London, 1970), and the idea of "creative play" which was broached by John Hargrave is common to Situationists, Provos, and to stray mavericks like Richard Neville of *Oz*—see his *Playpower* (London, 1971).

94. Wilhelm Reich, "About the History and Activities of our Institute," in *Journal of Sex Economy and Orgone Research* (March 1942).

95. Reich, "Experimental Orgone Therapy of Cancer," in *International Journal of Sex-Economy,* vol. II, no. 1, p. 88.

96. Reich, *The Murder of Christ* (Rugeley, Maine, 1953).

97. See Max Horkheimer, *Eclipse of Reason* (New York, 1947).

98. Marcuse in "The End of Utopia," p. 82.

99. Marcuse, *An Essay on Liberation* (London, 1969), p. 37.

100. Marcuse, *Liberation,* p. 41.

101. William Leiss and others, "Marcuse as Teacher," in *The Critical Spirit* (ed. K. H. Wolff and Barrington Moore, Jr., Boston, 1967).

102. Norman O. Brown, *Life Against Death* (London, 1970). See especially last chapter. Almost every commentator on Brown notices his mysticism. Marcuse himself has criticized this trait in "Love Mystified," in *Negations* (London, 1968).

103. Ed Denson, "The Holy Rockers," p. 6. The expression "total experience" may come from a mistranslation. Might "experience of totality" come nearer Jung's intention?

104. E. Graham Howe, *The Open Way* (London, 1939), and *Cure or Heal* (London, 1965), which has an interesting preface by Laing.

105. On this, see Jolande Jacobi, *The Psychology of C. G. Jung* (6th ed., London, 1967), p. 101.
106. R. D. Laing, *The Politics of Experience* (paperback ed., London, 1970), pp. 83, 137; Laing, review of Reich, *The Function of the Orgasm* in *New Society* (28 March 1968), p. 465.
107. David Cooper, introduction to his edition of *The Dialectics of Liberation* (London, 1969) and in the same book, Laing, "The Obvious," pp. 13 ff.
108. Leary, *Politics,* pp. 94-96. Cooper, "The Drug Movement," in *New Statesman* (4 March 1966); Cooper, *Psychiatry and Anti-Psychiatry* (London, 1967), p. 33.
109. Cooper, *Psychiatry and Anti-Psychiatry,* pp. 17, 23; Cooper, "Poetic Justice," in *TLS* (28 July 1967), p. 687; Laing, *Politics,* pp. 117-18.

Chapter 8
A Grammar of Unreason

Rationalists and Irrationalists—The Private Worlds of Occultists and Illuminated Politicians—Writers and Readers of Fantastic Literature—The Nature of Imaginary Worlds—Their Connection with the Occult—Flying Saucers—The Search for Otherness and the Creative Imagination—Conclusion

WHAT is the reasoning which governs irrationalism, and what are the laws that hold in a country where no laws run?

The "irrationalists" discussed in this book range from the supporters of the most puerile and simplistic ideas to adherents of elaborate and potent philosophies. All will resent being lumped collectively with the others; and the first step toward more fully defining the nature of "unreason" is to justify this arrangement. On their varying levels, then, the reactions we have called "irrational" probably represent *the responses of specific types of men in certain historical situations.* Perhaps the irrationalist response is a possibility for all men. Yet it is probably more likely for some than for others. It is also obvious that personal crises may trigger off irrationalist reactions. But we have largely been concerned with collective irrationalism, and irrationalism on a collective scale implies a collective, historical cause. This has been broadly defined as anxiety caused both by the fear of change and the perception of change that has, in fact, taken place. The general type of historical situation favorable to the spread of unreason is clear.

Such a situation may occur in restricted areas over a short period of time; but it seems that collectively the West has experienced three large outbreaks of unreason. The first may be described as the "crisis of Zero AD" and denotes the period both before and after the birth of Christ when a wave of magical speculation overwhelmed the achievements of Greek rationalism. The second may be called "the Renaissance/Reformation crisis" and refers to the upsurge of the irrational when the medieval synthesis collapsed. The third crisis is that of the 19th and 20th centuries, which has been the subject of discussion and can be thought of either as a "crisis" in its own right or as a development of the crisis of Renaissance and Reformation.[1] It is quite probable that, since the Reformation, the "crisis of consciousness" that I have defined historically may have become a problem to be faced by every thinking human being. But the three general crises represent times when the pressures on the individual have become strong enough to precipitate a flight from reason on a massive scale.

It is much easier to define the historical situation than to define the "specific type of man" who is most liable under pressure to become an irrationalist.

The word *reason,* or *rationalism,* has been used throughout as a purely descriptive term and implies by itself no value judgment. Thus an "irrationalist" means someone who does not subscribe to a "rational" system of thought. The very fact that one of the primary concerns of this book has been to show that irrational systems obey internal logics should be enough to disabuse any inquirer who is inclined to see in the term "irrationalism" an equivalent to the words "lunatic" or "absurd." The word "irrationalism" and not "a-rationalism" has been used because a cardinal characteristic of the systems we have been discussing is active opposition to the rational, and in no sense are they neutral. What is this Reason they oppose?

To attempt to give the term too wide-ranging a significance would be foolish. It is very easy to argue that no such thing as "the age of Reason" ever existed, although to a considerable extent the label retains its use. Reason was the creed of the age which supplanted the late Renaissance, saw the beginnings of scientific thought, *Realpolitik* and the ethic of profit. If one must attach class labels to ideas—and they are only useful in the most obvious sort of history—one might say that theocracy had in several variants been the strategy of feudal and aristocratic regimes, sweet reason the song of the emergent bourgeoisie, and irrationalism an accompaniment of the "revolt of the masses." There are a thousand holes in this interpretation, but also a residuum of truth. Reason was the "ideology" of Western Europe from the later 17th to the later 19th centuries. Of course during this period of time there were countless "irrationalists"—there may even have been many more numerically than the protagonists of reason. Yet it was this system that became extended, codified, and eventually made a dogma: the dogma of late Victorian materialism, which we have seen as to some extent an illusory construction, but which again bears some relationship to the facts. Against what was perhaps a caricature of Reason, the irrationalists revolted.

Rationalism is a method of thought supremely adapted to the tangible, material problems of existence. Where all irrational systems cede primacy to rational codes is in the business of daily life and the mechanisms of survival. I doubt whether any of the irrational systems can equip a man to survive the world more fully than the commonly accepted usage of the mind. This would be hotly denied by occultists, mystics, and some orthodoxly religious, who might go on to claim that the so-called "rational" systems are imperfect and incomplete, as they take account of man only as a biological organism or finite animal. There seems to be truth in the argument that "man cannot live by bread alone," that he *needs* some security beyond the assurance of coping with the problems of physical survival. But these basic problems must first be solved by any creature on earth regardless of his celestial origins or aptitude for metaphysics. It is not much good being proficient in Cabalistic exercises or Pyramidology if one's body is wasting away from plague, hunger, or cold. The irrationalist obviously does not entirely reject the logic of survival—there is a case for regarding some instances of collective irrationalism as automatic self-preservation—but he does frequently abandon the implications of that process of thought best adapted to ensure his physical well-being in favor of other ways of relating to what appear significant data.

The type of person who has become an irrationalist during the past hundred years has rejected the dominant mode of thought of over a century ago, and with it some potentialities for material success. It is exactly in the area of material problems in which the greatest possible measure of understanding is possible between men. It might be said that there is a "universe of agreed discourse" within which human beings communicate, and outside this the myriad private universes of each human being. At its most basic—and most common—level, the agreed discourse is merely that which the human animal has evolved for the production of food, shelter, and the propagation of his species, together with the means of maintaining a limited cooperation without which none of these activities could develop. To this might be added the shared experience of operating a human organism. The various private universes belonging to individuals comprise the patterns of thought and modes of being of single creatures, and these universes can be communicated to other individuals only to the degree in which their own private worlds correspond to the first. By rejecting the most certain possibilities of shared experience the irrationalist departs from the universe of agreed discourse and lodges himself within a private world.

On the one hand, then, there is the communally accepted world obeying the ethics of survival, in which the rationalist approach is very effective. On the other, there are the private universes of each human being, for the ordering of which is necessary only a system of thought corresponding to the values on which its user places a premium. It often happens that a number of private universes are found to coincide sufficiently to enable an extended definition of reality—supplementary to the limited universe of material needs—to be adopted by a group of individuals. Thus, there arises a mutually accepted alternative reality or private universe, whose participants derive support from mutual affirmation of its standards. Occasionally such subsidiary realities attract so large a following that their enthusiasts begin to hold their interpretation of life as the only possible vision and seek to impose their version of "agreed discourse" on top of the basic language of human communication. The argument can be applied to the most orthodox communities of opinion, although if the "private universe" is that subscribed to by, say, the Union of Small Shopkeepers, the distinction is scarcely useful, as it merely states the obvious. But the idea of the development of private universes, secessionist realities, does show what irrationalists of different kinds have in common. The illuminated politician persuades his supporters to participate in a vision of reality that is not simply that of the lowest common denominator. The occultist or mystic opts out of the bothersome business of material reality and constructs his own. He may do this according to a system already in existence—in which case he will share the "private universe" of others of his persuasion—or he may be content to remain in his own personal version of reality. The rationalist may talk of "madness" or "eccentricity." When faced with a shared interpretation of life with which he cannot come to terms he refers to "shared delusions" or "mass psychosis."

This theory of "private realities" is not put forward as either original or universally applicable. It is merely an aid to description; and in its terms the illuminated politicians and the occultists can be seen to have something in common other than a specific concern with esoteric doctrine or rejected knowledge.

Dr. Wolfgang Treher has gone much further in his study, *Hitler, Steiner, Schreber.* He has made a detailed and convincing comparison of the private worlds of Rudolf Steiner and Adolf Hitler. Treher considers both Hitler and Steiner to have been schizophrenic, and in comparable ways. He has suggested dates for the beginning of the illness suffered by each and compared the private universes occupied by Hitler and Steiner with a personal account of a schizophrenic world written by the lawyer and politician Daniel Paul Schreber.[2] We also possess valuable information from the psychiatric examination of an illuminated politician who was also an occultist: Rudolf Hess. The first description of Hess after his flight to Britain mentioned "a paranoid attitude towards his present surroundings only partly accounted for by reality." His examiner noted "the general impression of having his mind fixed on some far-away inner topics which was apt to produce a sense of withdrawnness and lack of contact with reality, except in certain narrow segments of experience in which his inner world and his outer interests fused."[3]

Both in a comparison of Hitler with Steiner and in a study of Hess, psychiatrists have thus come to the conclusion—not very startling, after all—that all three were divorced from ordinary reality: perhaps "schizophrenic." It is, therefore, significant that Aleister Crowley himself saw similarities between his own gospel of Thelema and Hitler's projected new order.

There are two versions of a story, which was believed by Crowley and some of his followers, about Hitler's reliance on Crowleyan principles. One is impossible, and the other extremely unlikely. They both center on Marthe Künzel of Leipzig (head of the German branches of the O.T.O and Crowley's Astrum Argentinum), who was told by Crowley in 1925 that the country which first adopted Crowley's *Book of the Law* as its official text would become the leading nation of the world. The two versions of the story state either that Marthe Künzel was a friend of Rudolf Hess, whom she interested in *The Book of the Law* when he and Hitler were imprisoned in Landsberg; or that "about 1926 or 1927" she became convinced that Hitler was "her magical child" and somehow managed to present him with a copy of Crowley's publication.[4] The idea that Hess was a friend of Marthe Künzel is not in itself far-fetched, and it would have been perfectly possible for her to visit Hess in the Landsberg jail. However, the term of imprisonment served by the Nazi leaders ended in December 1924; and although an earlier date for her obsession is not ruled out, the legend does seem to associate the supposed attempt to pass *The Book of the Law* to Hitler with Crowley's pronouncement to his disciple in 1925. There is no real trace that Hitler had ever heard of Crowley's Law of Thelema. The whole story is rendered even more improbable by a letter from Marthe Künzel to Crowley, in which she tells him of her political awakening: this was caused by observing how closely Hitler's thoughts followed Crowley's principles, and there is not a word about her responsibility for this coincidence.[5]

Some time between 1942 and 1944, Crowley annotated his copy of Rauschning's *Hitler Speaks,* noting correspondences between the ideas of Hitler as recorded by Rauschning and his own *Book of the Law.* Like all supposedly "prophetic" writings, *The Book of the Law* requires much interpretation, although Crowley himself was, at any rate, fairly clear as to what it meant. A cardinal point is his famous

"Law of Thelema," "Do what thou wilt shall be the whole of the Law."[6] In much of Hitler's amorality the magician found resemblances to his own creed. From the fact that Crowley could—evidently in all seriousness—point to numerous connections between his own enigmatic proclamations and the ranting of Hitler, two main points can be deduced. First, the eldritch reality occupied by Hitler held attractions for Crowley, the occupant of an equally strange universe. Secondly, although it is in the highest degree unlikely that Marthe Künzel came anywhere near influencing Hitler, there were, in fact, certain similarities between the two visions of reality.

Crowley marked for attention all the passages where Hitler is reported by Rauschning to have referred to a new world-order or the collapse of the old system of values. These are general apocalyptic expectations with which both might indeed well have agreed. But Crowley, of course, saw correspondences everywhere. When Rauschning recorded Hitler's confession of manipulating mass fanaticism, Crowley commented: "This policy was surely implied by Aiwas in the Book, with its slogans, its feasts and its freedoms. All we need is shouter No. 1." The "correspondences" he noted are naturally often quite impossible—on one occasion, when Rauschning wrote of the Röhm purge that "Hitler bided his time, then struck like lightning," Crowley juxtaposed verse nine of Book Three of the *Book of the Law:* "Work! withdraw! Upon them!" (Actually, the original reads,"*Lurk,* withdraw....") On page after page Crowley took Hitler's side against Rauschning, acclaiming the magnetism of the Leader's presence and the rumors that Hitler had a room decorated with "obscene nudes." To Hitler's declaration that it was time to "protect the strong against the weak," Aleister Crowley added an enthusiastic "Yes!"[7] Although, by the end of his reading, Crowley had decided that Hitler had probably become a "Black Brother," he persisted in fostering the legend that the similarities of which he was convinced had been inspired by Marthe Künzel and his own sacred text.

We have seen enough examples of the attraction that occultism proper has for a certain sort of politician not to be surprised that Crowley thought that he and Hitler had much in common. The two men inhabited different realities; but these were equally opposed to that of the Rationalist Establishment and shared a small number of assumptions. Of course, Crowley's megalomania led him to exaggerate the similarities out of all proportion; and the differences are at least as significant. Whatever the opinion of the world about Crowley, he did have considerable personal gifts and some creative ability. This could hardly be said of Hitler. If we class them both as "irrationalists," we must also remember that many geniuses who could never be described as anything but "men of good will" have also inhabited private universes divorced from the consensus of humanity. But almost all the irrationalists have been concerned with initiating *change* of some kind. A further examination of the areas from which they derive their inspiration shows interesting pointers to the motives of those who desert the reality of Reason for the more exotic pastures of their private worlds. The solution seems to lie in a question of the *imagination*. And if it seems odd to jump abruptly to a consideration of fantasy and science fiction, it should be remembered that this type of literature is, above all others, concerned with the imagination and the creation of other realities. It can also be shown to have substantial connections with the occult, and with illuminated politics.

There is a consistent link between people interested in the occult and readers of science fiction. Both the occult and fantastic literature can be said to provide an escape from the universe of reason and limited possibilities into realities which are bounded only by the imagination.

Historically, the coincidence of the literature of other worlds and the occult is as marked as it is in individuals. The 18th-century Romantics combined an interest in occultism with the cultivation of the Gothic novel, whose supernatural horrors were related to the Freemasonic "Rosicrucianism" of William Godwin and influenced Francis Barrett's compilation of magical lore, *The Magus* (1801). The occult revival of the turn of the 19th and 20th centuries is inseparable from the rapid increase in literature dealing with ghosts, the fantastic, and the supernatural; and it is easy to link the growth of this fashion—extraordinarily influential in England and America—with the mounting crisis of consciousness. Thus, one authority (writing in 1917) noticed the "marked" influence of

Spiritualism and psychical research on literature and observed that this was connected with the growth of a literature of miracles dealing with the First World War. In the reaction against Reason during the first half of the 20th century, the literature of Europe sought to return to archetypes in the novels of Hermann Hesse and Franz Kafka, while English writers leaned heavily on a taste for the miraculous. This latter development was brilliantly analyzed by Antal Szerb in a largely forgotten book, *The Search for Wonder* (1938), in which he related even such relatively "established" authors as Virginia Woolf, D. H. Lawrence, Eric Linklater, and the Powys brothers to the more explicitly fantastic writers, such as James Branch Cabell. He saw the development as the culmination of the process that had begun with the Symbolist revolt against naturalism and as part of the search of European man for an indefinable freedom or *liberation*—"Whoever first names this freedom, whoever expresses what we all wish for and desire, will be the Messiah of the century."[8] It is, therefore, possible to relate the wave of fantastic literature to the historical situation that produced the occult revival.

The subject matter of fantastic literature relies on the staples of ghosts, magic, diabolism, and the supernatural: such preoccupations might be said to define the category. The reason for this is simply that such literature has very largely been written by occultists, or at least by those attracted to the occult. Thus in the middle of the last century Eliphas Lévi's friend Alphonse Esquiros concocted a fantastic novel called *The Magician* (1838), while in England Bulwer Lytton expressed a form of "Rosicrucianism," particularly in his novel *Zanoni* (1842). The French magus Joséphin Péladan wrote a long series of esoteric novels. Arthur Machen belonged very briefly to the Golden Dawn, was a friend of the mystic A. E. Waite, and himself underwent mystical experiences.[9] Even where occult connections are least expected, they can be found in writers of fantasy at all periods. One of the reasons is undoubtedly the usefulness of the parable or fable form as a teaching story. Two examples among the heroes of the modern cult of the fantastic will be enough to show the ways in which esoteric symbolism is incorporated in fantasy: E. R. Eddison and Hope Mirrlees.

Eddison (1882-1945) was a distinguished British civil servant who wrote an early fantasy, *The Worm Ourobouros* (1921) before retiring in 1937 to devote himself to literature. He produced an unfinished trilogy set in the imaginary land of Zimiamvia and composed of *Mistress of Mistresses* (1935), *A Fish Dinner in Memison* (1941), and *The Mezentian Gate* (1958). In Eddison there is no occult*ism* as such, but much occult *philosophy*. Thus, *The Worm Ourobouros* celebrates the theory of "eternal recurrence" elaborated by Nietzsche and given further fictional expression by P. D. Ouspensky's novel *The Strange Life of Ivan Osokin* (1947). The Zimiamvian trilogy is a festival of metaphysics, not only in the philosophy of the learned Dr. Vandermast, but in the very construction of the work. All or most of the chief characters in the land of Zimiamvia are incarnations or aspects of Zeus and Aphrodite, evil or capricious as well as benevolent. Within this framework the hero Lessingham—himself an aspect of Zeus—experiences "Days and Nights of Zimiamvia"—a concept taken from the Hindu "Days and Nights of Brahma" and signifying the illusory experiences of the god Brahma entrapped in *maya*. Eddison's philosophy is a form of Neo-Platonism. Its author is convinced that the world is illusion and a game. In fact, in *A Fish Dinner in Memison* the world in which we ordinarily live is shown as created by the Zimiamvian deities over the supper table for motives rather like those of Peter Pan when he thought that "to die would be an awfully big adventure."[10]

Hope Mirrlees is a minor author in the fantastic canon, and her only "pure" fantasy, *Lud-in-the-Mist* (1926), was reissued in 1970. *Lud-in-the-Mist* deals with a crisis in the life of the sleepy, prosperous town of the title. Its inhabitants are concerned to deny the existence of Fairyland, which borders their country and has obscure connections with a previous regime of a magical nature. The crisis results from the eating of "fairy-fruit" by children of the town, and in the ensuing story the humdrum materialist inhabitants of Lud-in-the-Mist are brought to recognize the existence of the irrational. There are frequent suggestions of an esoteric symbolism, which is made explicit at the close of the book in a chapter called "The Initiate." Hope Mirrlees published two other novels and was associated with the Bloomsbury group. She was a close friend of Jane Harrison (1850-1928), a vitalist student of mythology influenced by the revival of Bachofen and whose book *Themis* had a wide circulation in illuminated circles like those of the Kibbo Kift.[11] Late in life Jane Harrison became associated with Prince Mirsky and the Russian emigration, as did Hope Mirrlees; acknowledgments made by the latter in a biography published in 1962 may indicate a conversion to Christianity.[12] This provides yet another example of the constant relationship of illuminate with illuminate.

While the novels of Crowley or Péladan might reasonably be expected to contain occult symbolism and while it is comparatively easy to detect esoteric symbols if the language is known, it is perhaps not so obvious that many occult texts are very similar to outright fantasies. The sort of pseudohistory that Madame Blavatsky took over from Fabre d'Olivet and incorporated in *The Secret Doctrine* has had both occult and fantastic descendents. On the one hand, Rudolf Steiner turned his clairvoyant perception on the lost continent of Atlantis and—in a spiritual science fiction quite devoid of literary style—somehow found it relevant to his occult history to describe Atlantean airships. On the other Robert E. Howard (1906-36), an early writer for the science fiction pulp magazines, produced an endless series of stories set in the period between the sinking of Atlantis and the beginnings of recorded history. He called it "the Hyborean age," in an obvious reference to another of H. P. Blavatsky's lost continents, which had originally been called the "Hyperborean" land. The epidemic of Atlantis fiction in Germany was paralleled in the English-speaking world, although in England Atlantis had naturally no political importance. Sprague de Camp, an authoritative historian of science fiction, has observed that the Mars created by Edgar Rice Burroughs is very like the Atlantis described by H.P.B. and Walter Scott-Elliot, although he thinks it unlikely that Burroughs had read any Theosophical works.[13]

Whereas in fantastic literature the reader knows that he is dealing with fiction, in occult texts the disciple is given to understand that he is confronted by reality. The borderline between fiction and fact often becomes exceedingly blurred for the occultist; and it is no coincidence that just as occultism has inspired fantasy, works of fantasy have themselves inspired esoteric cults. It is possible that Madame Blavatsky—who certainly became overwhelmed by reading Fenimore Cooper—also derived some of her inspiration from the novels of Bulwer Lytton. In 1894 Frederick Spencer Oliver published a novel called *A Dweller on Two Planets,* which gave rise to a crop of legends that peopled Mount Shasta in California with a horde of Lemurian magicians. From this source came some of the inspiration for G. W. Ballard's I AM cult, which flourished during the 1930s and still has devotees. Most recently of all has appeared a book called *The Necronomicon* based on the forged *Fourth Book of Occult Philosophy* of pseudo-Agrippa. It has apparently found some favor with occultists.[14] But, as every afficionado of science fiction and fantasy is aware, the *Necronomicon* was invented by the sepulchral imagination of the horror-story writer H. P. Lovecraft (1890-1937), and it has its existence entirely in his pages. The occult world must await with anticipation the appearance of Lovecraft's other imaginary masterpiece, the prehuman *Pnakotic Fragments*.

The beginnings of the modern American science fiction movement once more confirm the impression that "dabblers in other realities" represent *specific types in a specific historical situation.* We observe a situation of anxiety, occult connections, and a blurring of distinction between different orders of reality. The crisis that really introduced science fiction to the American public has a specific time and date: 8:00 - 9:00 PM. on the 30th of October, 1938. During this hour Orson Welles made his famous broadcast of H. G. Wells's *War of the Worlds*. This caused panic in the Eastern states in America. Among those who actually believed that the earth had been invaded, there was damage to property and limbs; in Harlem there was praying in the streets, and many guardian angels were seen. Some people refused to believe in Martians but reported sighting Zeppelins. Patrick Moore records two other examples of "science fictional" rumor started by broadcasts—both post-Second World War—in the U.S.A. One dealt with the end of the world, another with the moon falling on the earth[15] (and it sounds as if it were Hörbiger-inspired*). At the time of the Welles broadcast, four specialist science fiction magazines were established, and a fifth was starting. Within the next eight months, seven more were launched. The war caused an inevitable retrenchment, but the unstable conditions of the postwar period sent the number of magazines up once more to over twenty.[16]

The amazing effect of the Welles broadcast has been linked to fear of an approaching war, and it seems reasonable to connect the

---

*Jane Gaskell has issued a trilogy of Atlantis novels based on Hörbigerian premises.

rise in the popularity of science fiction with similar cause. It was after 1945, in the tension of the Cold War and the period of the McCarthyite campaign, that science fiction established itself as a permanent feature of the literary landscape. Science fiction writers themselves often attribute this rise in popularity to consciousness of the atomic bomb. The results of opinion polls on the public attitude to the bomb suggest that they may have been right. For example, an article published in 1953 concluded that the Bomb had "strikingly *little* place in the conscious life of the American people" but admitted that there was much "illogical and unstable thinking" among those questioned. In one survey half the people who claimed not to be worried about the Bomb indicated that covertly they did in fact consider it a grave threat.[17] Such a reservoir of repressed fears was bound to result in unusual manifestations, and it is not unreasonable to assume that the science fiction boom was one of these. As to the readership, surveys have shown a definite bias toward scientists and technologists (opinions here vary).[18] Although, in the nature of things, there is no statistical evidence, it seems clear that science fiction has formed the natural stamping ground for those pseudo-scientists who would earlier have been respected members of the occult underworld, and that certain perennial occult beliefs have taken shape—sometimes posing as literature, sometimes not even supposed to be fictional—in the world of science fiction. In other words, American anxiety during the 1950s resulted in the grouping of irrationalists around a literary movement devoted explicitly to other worlds. This is not to say that "science fiction is the occult transformed." It is to say that science fiction—particularly in the 1950s—contained substantial occultist elements.

First, consider the question of the content of modern science fiction and esoteric doctrines. The original term, "scientifiction" was coined by the inventor Hugo Gernsback for the scientific fantasies which he published in his technical journals from 1911 onward. The difference between science fiction and fantasy was once much debated, although the distinction is clear. If the hero travels from London to Bogota by magical means it is fantasy, but if he uses a matter-transmitter it is science fiction. We have already seen how fantastic literature often contains esoteric references, and mechanized fantasy can be no less subtle. Thus, Daniel Galouye's *Dark*

Universe (1962), takes place in a world after the Big Bang, where survivors who have taken refuge below the ground act out the different parts of Plato's myth of the Cave. Of the countless superman stories, most, like A. E. van Vogt's *Slan* (1953), appear to be pure entertainment with no ulterior motive. Yet van Vogt himself has been very much part of the underworld of rejected knowledge, and from certain authors any story of "men like gods" must be suspect. Arthur C. Clarke's *Childhood's End* (1953), dramatizes the Teilhardian idea of humanity reaching "Point Omega" and evolving out of the human condition and into "the Overmind." Robert Heinlein's Gnostic book *Stranger in a Strange Land* (1961), has as its hero that familiar creature the barbarian appalled by "civilization"—yet as the visiting Martian deploys his energies on raddled earth the message is not just "change the world," but "thou art God." There are also an increasing number of symbolist, semioccult, neo-Jungian concoctions, whose meanings are based on the construction of mood and are essentially indescribable. What, for example, can be said of the extraordinary *Fourth Mansions* (1969) of R. A. Lafferty, except that it combines a title and texts from Saint Teresa of Ávila with magic, telepathy, occultism, the hidden hand in history, and a secret plan of the Almighty?

These authors and their stories are—with the exception of A. E. van Vogt—separated by a considerable distance from the bedrock of early science fiction. The earlier builders of other realities were less metaphysical. Yet even van Vogt—whose stories are "basic pulp magazine" science fiction, falling over themselves to provide a shock for every installment—has attempted to incorporate unorthodox theories in his work. Van Vogt has written a series of novels about *The World of Null-A*—the book of that title was first published in 1948—in order to dramatize the ideas of Count Alfred Korzybsky's General Semantics. Null-A is the world of 2560, when the Institute of General Semantics has reorganized human thought processes on its "non-Aristotelian" principles. According to van Vogt, the book did much to publicize Korzybsky's school of thought.[19] As for General Semantics itself, it can, in one aspect, be seen as yet another quest for breaking through a wrong perception of the world and attaining perfect health and sanity. Korzybsky believed that correct practice of his system of psycho-philosophy would result in the improved bodily and mental health of the student. Van Vogt seems still to be interested in General Semantics, although for a time he switched his allegiance to Scientology.

Another science fiction figure who was at one time involved in Scientology is John W. Campbell, who became editor of *Astounding Stories* in 1937. At first, Campbell's interest in the unorthodox concentrated on the pseudosciences. In the period after the war these became particularly prevalent as—according to one medical writer—"on to the market had poured a vast quantity of surplus electrical equipment, easy to get and cheap for fashioning into awesome contrivances." Campbell's personal attempt at fashioning one of these miraculous contraptions was to contruct a "Hieronymus machine"—the celebrated "black box" of "psionics"—which he demonstrated to the New York Science Fiction Convention in 1956. The machine is supposed to be based on a combination of electronics and extrasensory perception and is used for diagnostic and healing purposes.

Between 1960 and 1962 Campbell carried on a campaign on behalf of an invention for converting rotary motion into unidirectional motion, which was called "the Dean device." Of the inventor (Norman L. Dean, a successful businessman) Campbell wrote—in a manner that smacks of the terminology of General Semantics—that "being an amateur, he does not have any appreciable emotional investment in the validity of Newton's Laws; he had no block against challenging them." The National Aeronautics and Space Administration refused to test the device. But Campbell claimed that "some engineering companies" had taken up Dean on his recommendation and found that his invention worked. Eventually, a laboratory under official contract was persuaded to undertake the test. The Dean device refused to perform. Campbell was forced to make a grudging climb-down, claiming that the main point of his campaign was that, whether or not Dean was preposterous, he should have been given the chance to show what he could do. In fact, Campbell had originally had wistful ideas that Dean's invention might have been used as an all-American space drive. "It would have been nice if in response to Sputnik I, the United States had been able to release full photographic evidence of Mars Base I."[20]

J. W. Campbell and A. E. van Vogt both became involved in the cult founded by their fellow science fiction writer L. Ron Hubbard. Hubbard (born 1911) wrote Westerns and sea stories before he published his first piece of science fiction in 1938—interestingly enough, the year in which he claims that he began his search for truth. This search culminated in an article, "Dianetics, the Evolution of a Science," in the May 1950 number of *Astounding Science Fiction*. The magazine was edited by Campbell, who had been treated for sinus trouble by Hubbard according to the new system of mental healing he claimed to have discovered. The same year there appeared Hubbard's book *Dianetics*, which had an instant popular success. Dianetics expanded quickly among science fiction enthusiasts. Even the medical man who wrote the preface of Hubbard's book—and whose sister Campbell later married—had written science fiction. A. E. van Vogt became the head of Hubbard's Californian organization and in 1955 still believed in the value of the system. Campbell himself resigned after less than a year's allegiance. After a period of schism, Hubbard's dianetics evolved into a new system called Scientology, of which dianetics is now regarded as a preliminary formulation. Of this first stage of Scientology, Professor S. I. Hayakawa wrote: "It appears to me inevitable that anyone writing several million words of fantasy and science fiction should ultimately begin to internalize the assumptions underlying that verbiage. This appears to be what happened to Hubbard."[21] It is not recorded what A. E. van Vogt thought of this semantic analysis.

Scientology has proved no less popular than dianetics and has attracted support among fashionable rock groups and film stars. The cult possesses a headquarters at East Grinstead in Surrey. It has branches throughout the world and a fleet of three ships. On Hubbard's flagship (formerly the Glasgow-Belfast ferry) is based the "Sea Org," the "most valuable and dedicated group of beings on this planet." The basic assumptions of Scientology are that an "auditor" (therapist), using a machine called an "E-meter" which is something like a lie detector, can clear away various blocks that prevent the "pre-clear" (patient) from achieving full control of his abilities. The beginnings of this idea were incorporated in Hubbard's dianetics and are similar to the Freudian therapist's object of removing repressions through discovering traumatic experiences. Hubbard went further. In his "processing" he went back and back, first discovering that the most damaging experiences occurred in the womb before a child was born, and soon concluding that his patients had experienced previous incarnations. From recovering records of Scientologists' past lives, it was but a short step to declaring that the constant particle of this series of incarnations—the so-called Theta being—was trapped in a universe to which its nature was intrinsically superior. Hubbard's aim is to liberate these Thetans. There are lurid accounts of how Thetans have fought against the bodies in which they are entrapped with an assortment of weapons straight from the pages of a space opera. Hubbard apparently expects a battle to break out when ordinary humans discover the existence of a number of "liberated Thetans" and has warned his troops that they "need reinforcements" before they can "get spectacular."[22]

Hubbard's science-fictional Gnosticism has exactly suited the temper of the times. The scandals that have accumulated around Scientology[23] are less important than the pedigree of the cult. In an expanded version of his original article on dianetics, Hubbard has related his search through various paths of mysticism before evolving his own theories.

> In a lifetime of wandering around many strange things had been observed. The medicine man of the Goldi people of Manchuria, the shamans of North Borneo, Sioux medicine men, the cults of Los Angeles and modern psychology. Amongst the people questioned about existence were a magician whose ancestors served in the court of Kublai Khan and a Hindu who could hypnotize cats. Dabbles had been made in mysticism, data had been studied from mythology to spiritualism. Odds and ends like these, countless odds and ends.[24]

Presumably it was one of the "dabbles" which led to Hubbard's association with Jack Parsons. Parsons was a chemist who was one of the founders of the California Institute of Technology, and he had been a follower of Crowley since 1939. In 1946 Parsons and Hubbard attempted to conduct a magical operation on Crowleyan principles. The aim was to persuade a spirit to incarnate itself in a child, which Parsons was to father. Hubbard was to act during the operation as a clairvoyant reporter of proceedings. Parsons thought the experiment had been successful, but his friendship with Hubbard was shattered in the summer of the same year when Hubbard withdrew the bulk of the money from their joint account and bought a yacht. Parsons eventually secured the boat when Hubbard was forced to put into Miami by a storm, and (according to Francis King) this is the last recorded association of Hubbard with magic; and Hubbard claims that he entered an association with Parsons on the orders of the FBI.[25] If Hubbard's mystical adventures led him through such esoteric paths, it is unsurprising that the doctrine with which he emerged was, in essence, an amalgam of psychoanalysis and occult tradition packaged in a box complete with a novel machine like those so much in vogue among pseudoscientists and the fringes of the science fiction world.

Scientology was not the only example of old ideas in modern dress. A widely diffused belief, which had more than a little to do with occultism and science fiction and was certainly inspired by the same conditions of anxiety, concerned the sighting of flying saucers, which began in 1947 and continued through the mid-1950s. Because of their assumed nature, saucers were naturally allied to science fiction (although it is rare to find a story written about the sightings, as the writers of science fiction had moved on to greater marvels some considerable time before). Yet this vision in the skies attracted the most eminent irrationalists. Wilhelm Reich began to communicate with flying saucers through his "cloud-busting" machine and believed that he had taken part in "the first battle of the universe" in association with his celestial visitors. C. G. Jung made a brilliant comparison of the saucer epidemic with the visions of the Mons Angels and the apparitions of Fatima and argued that the cause of the rumors was "a situation of collective distress." At least one supporter of the saucers has since argued that the Fatima apparitions were saucer people. Whereas Jung's interest was critical and detached, Gerald Heard—who has also written on the religious significance of science fiction—became a saucerite who believed that the saucers were powered by some way of harnessing magnetic forces and were manipulated by tiny bee-like creatures from Mars. Heard specifically connected the arrival of the saucers with atomic explosions: "we put out a finger to beckon attention on any watching fellow-planet that we were out for trouble and able to give it!"[26]

Flying saucers were taken up immediately by adepts of various cults, particularly in California. The most celebrated is probably George Adamski, who claimed to have traveled in a spaceship. Adamski made a world tour in which he was granted an audience by Queen Juliana of the Netherlands. His books inveigh against the appropriation of his saucers by mystics; yet he himself runs very true to type. Adamski's anxiety about the human condition was evident as early as 1937 when he published a pamphlet called *Satan, Man of the Hour,* which declared that "the first perversion of the cosmic principle took place in Lemuria." In 1940 he established a colony near the Mount Palomar observatory, and one of the "witnesses"—one is reminded of Joseph Smith and the angels—to Adamski's meeting with the saucer people was a member of his cult.[27] A British equivalent that has transferred its activities to California is George King's Aetherius Society. King (born 1919) took up Yoga exercises in 1944, but it was not until ten years later that his mission began. The prophet was told by a voice: "Prepare yourself! You are to become the voice of Interplanetary Parliament." King's activities include the "charging" of mountains with power—these include the magician-haunted Mount Shasta in California. His chief task is to act as a channel of communication for extraterrestrial intelligence. He visits the planets in his astral body—an opportunity for several near-illiterate attempts at science fiction—and his followers seem to have adopted millennarian expections which would earlier have been couched in religious terms. Their hope is that they will be removed from earth by spaceship in the event of a nuclear catastrophe.[28]

Every conceivable occult theory has accumulated round the saucer cults. Thus a writer in the *Flying Saucer Review* in 1961 suggested: "Is it not plausible to suggest that Count St. Germain was a missionary from space, an avatar from Venus with remarkable powers...?" As recently as 1970 an article in the same magazine has declared that the Cabala can provide useful insights for saucer devotees.[29] Of course there are saucer theorists who disagree with all the claptrap talked by such occult sections of the saucer movement:

> In certain mystical and pseudo-mystical circles, both in the USA and Canada, to a lesser extent in Great Britain, there is being foolishly propagated an illusion that all the mysterious

and elusive entities of the flying saucers are benevolent superbeings, radiating an unearthly love and understanding....

There is a dangerous illusion! a Californian pipe or opium dream!

There are saucers, not manned by "little men" or captained by women, but by entities no one knows or has ever seen, whose irresponsible behavior takes the form of arson on quite a large and dangerous scale. They seem to have heat-ray projectors recalling those of H. G. Wells' "Men from Mars," all brain and no bowels.[30]

The universe in which flying saucers are real is not very far from the private worlds of some science-fiction enthusiasts. Hugo Gernsback (born 1884), the coiner of the word "scientifiction," seems to have been profoundly influenced by an experience that occurred at the age of nine, when he developed a fever after reading a translation of *Mars as the Abode of Life* by Percival Lowell. Staggered by the implications, Gernsback became delirious and is described as "raving about strange creatures, fantastic cities and masterly engineered canals of Mars for two full days and nights."[31] It is worth remembering that one of the most famous cases of turn-of-the-century psychical research involved a reincarnation of the subject on Mars. Whereas Gernsback's dissociation from ordinary reality was an involuntary process, the editor of *Amazing Stories*, Raymond Palmer, used the susceptibility of some of his readers to build up a large circulation among the "lunatic fringe" in the period of anxiety just after the war. In 1944 Palmer received a letter entitled "A warning to Future Man" from Richard Shaver, a Pennsylvania welder. Palmer rewrote the letter under the title "I remember Lemuria" and collaborated with Shaver in a series of stories based on his correspondent's imaginings. Shaver accepted his fantasies as reality, and for a time Palmer cooperated with this belief. The editor even claimed to go in fear of the sinister beings called "deros," who in Shaver's cosmology implanted evil thoughts in the mind of man. After the collapse of the hoax, Shaver took to writing straightforward science fiction.[32]

The hard-core followers of science fiction present several characteristics that remind the observer of a religious cult proper. They organize themselves in enthusiastic groups of "fans" and describe themselves as "addicts." C. S. Lewis suggested that the experience of reading Rider Haggard could provide a substitute for religion, and Gerald Heard has claimed that science fiction represents an extension of consciousness.[33] There are facets of fantasy and science fiction that go some way toward providing an explanation of the problems of an "illuminated viewpoint."

The Search for Otherness was the title which science fiction writer Henry Kuttner once gave to a collection of his stories. It is in the nature of "otherness" that the solution may lie. Fantastic fiction provides the most explicit rendering of "other realities." But because there are substantial grounds for believing that there is a correspondence between the science fiction world and that of the occultists whom we have used as an index of the "illuminated" attitude, it is possible to use the explicit creation of other realities to interpet private worlds whose "otherness" remains implicit.

The "search for otherness" necessarily applies also to social reformers. There is a particular genre of Utopian fantasy that is the natural vehicle of expression for plans for social reform. From Bacon's *New Atlantis* and More's *Utopia* itself, the pedigree of the imagined society is directly traceable down to modern science fiction. The Progressive Underground has frequently used fantasy as a means of communicating its ideas. For example, Edward Bellamy's *Looking Backward* (1888) and Richard Jefferies's *After London* (1885) were powerful influences on the Progressive Underground of the 1890s. Progressive causes, mysticism, and fantasy could be combined in the same person. For example, E. H. Visiak (E. H. Physick), the author of the fantastic novel *Medusa* (1929), once precipitated a mystical experience by dwelling obsessively on the evils of vivisection. Among modern inhabitants of the progressive Underground science fiction is immensely popular, as it embodies the aspirations both of the Utipian illuminates and of those concerned with an "expansion of consciousness." Ken Kesey was influenced both by Arthur Clarke's *Childhood's End* and by Robert Heinlein's *Stranger in a Strange Land.* It is from this latter book that the expression "grokking" comes. It probably transferred itself into the hippie world through Kesey and was at one time widely used in Underground circles to express a state of empathy or harmony with a person or a situation. Kesey's own use of the word "fantasy" to describe each latest far-fetched project is paralleled by Abbie Hoffman's proclamation about the exorcism of the Pentagon: "Fantasy is freedom!" The cult of J. R. R. Tolkien's *Lord of the Rings* is too well-known to need any emphasis. There has even been published an Iowa underground newspaper called *Middle Earth*, whose political comments plunged its readers into the fantasy world of its presiding spirit.

> The skirmish on Madison, on the edge of Mirkwood led to a temporary setback and numerous after-the-fact strategy sessions, but larger lessons were learned by the expedition to the Pentagon (magic figure of black sorcerers) which lies in Mordor, realm of the Dark Lord, whose name is unspeakable.[34]

The popularity of Tolkien—and to a lesser extent, of his friends Charles Williams and C. S. Lewis—emphasizes once more the religious or occult connections of fantasy. All three writers subscribe to a form of Christianity: Catholicism for Tolkien, for Williams an interesting personal mysticism which probably owed a lot to his early occult studies, and for Lewis a Neo-Platonic form of Christianity that was not above accepting some of Williams's unorthodox theories. The three formed a group they called "the Inklings," which met regularly and included a leading Anthroposophist, Owen Barfield.[35] It is no coincidence that a circle of fantasy writers, which has associations both with mysticism and the attitudes of the English illuminated politicians, has become popular as part of the search for otherness conducted by today's idealistic revolutionaries.

Whether such would-be revolutionaries find inspiration in the symbols of the generally spiritual journeys portrayed by Tolkien or Lewis, or in the more obvious moral lessons in *Stranger in a Strange Land*, it is essentially the *otherness* that they seek. This argues that fantasy is not merely an unhealthy escape, that the *otherness* is in some fashion fruitful. The capacity to appreciate otherness—and, more powerfully, to fashion for oneself an otherness—is the process of imagination. Without such imagination, the capacity to envisage a state of affairs other than that obtaining, *no change is possible.* There is a distinct relationship between the private worlds that are constructed simply to exclude the abhorred present and those that are rooted in the wish to change the present altogether. Both subscribe to the wish to abolish that which is, to replace the old by a new reality. The problem is to know how to evaluate alternatives.

It is difficult to conceive that the universe of agreed discourse could have imposed upon it a supplementary vision that demands the existence of flying saucers. But it must be insisted that this is not at all impossible, and that in Nazi Germany ideas just as strange attained wide currency. The reality of Nazism is as much the result of the ability to imagine something *other* as the best intentioned Utopias of the most charitable social reformers. A tortured imagination may produce visions of great power. A case in point is that of the fantasy writer M. P. Shiel, who never quite recovered from being crowned "King of Redonda" on his fifteenth birthday in 1880. Redonda was an atoll covered in guano. But despite the small size of his childhood kingdom, Shiel admits that "the notion that I am somehow the King, King of kings and the Kaiser of imperial Caesar, was so inveterately suggested to me that I became incapable of expelling it."[36] Shiel's megalomaniac novels are remarkably successful in impressing their obsessive worlds on the reader; yet they are also riddled with an unpleasant anti-Semitism and authoritarian propaganda. His late novel, *The Young Men are Coming* (1937), contains a prophecy of the victory of a British neo-Fascist movement based on the Divine Law as revealed by an extraterrestrial Egg.

There may be able but perverse adepts of the imagination. The Theosophist Hübbe-Schleiden—who was concerned with German expansionist propaganda—also translated Brigadier Chesney's pioneer piece of science fiction *The Battle of Dorking* (1871) under the gloating title *Englands Ende in der Schlacht bei Dorking*. Hitler himself was an avid reader of imaginative literature. Like Madame Blavatsky he was enthusiastic about Fenimore Cooper, but after reading *The Last of the Mohicans,* he took up the German writer of Indian stories, Karl May. He read all of Karl May and recommended others to try Jules Verne. Symptoms of a search for "other realities" are completely in accordance with what we know of Hitler.

On the one hand, the attempt to make a private world part of ordinary reality may produce the nightmare of the concentration camps; on the other perhaps a garden of earthly delights. It may be wondered if the difference between such heavens and hells is not the same as that between "good" and "bad" art: a disparity in the quality of the creative imagination. Hitler wanted to become an architect; and, although his watercolors show some talent, his patronage of Albert Speer gives the lie to Hitler's estimate of himself as an artistic genius. Possibly this fact has something to do with the sort of political universe he created. Although he was a man of extraordinary abilities, his particular imagination played Germany false.

If there is truth in the idea that illuminates—whether occultists or politicians—have a special relationship with the imagination in their pursuit of other realities, we might expect to find an extraordinary amount of creative work accomplished by such people. This is in fact the case, not only with reference to the illuminated artists and psychologists we have already discussed but even in the realms of mechanical invention. Hugo Gernsback was an inventor (he coined the word "television"), Hörbiger made his fortune with an invention, Arthur Kitson and Lanz von Liebenfels filed numerous patents, and Alfred William Lawson—who has only appeared in this book peripherally—built the world's first passenger airliner. Rudolf von Sebottendorff was concerned (like the 19th-century occultist J. M. Höene-Wronski) in the development of a tank; and John Hargrave patented in 1938 the navigating device that forms part of the Concorde airplane. What can be said of such creative and imaginative capacities without straying too far into the province of the philosopher?

The occult has been used throughout this book as the index to "a certain type of man"; and there seems to be some evidence that this type of man has sometimes privy access to the springs of inspiration. Esotericists make much play with the phrase "creative imagination," as originating in Paracelsus. The implications can best be described in the words of John Hargrave, an artist, an authority on Paracelsus, and—according to the classification of this book—an illuminated politician.

> It is obvious to anyone (or ought to be) that, but for the few freaks, cranks, originals, and odd-men-out, mankind in the mass would still be without fire, without the lever, the wheel,

the club, throwing-stick, bow, bolas, cat's cradle, net, plait, loom, dug-out, paddle, spade, and all the other discoveries, inventions and devices that have enabled man to enslave metals, plants, animals, and finally—himself. This final enslavement he calls "civilization" and today it is a worldwide, semi-mechanized serfdom dominated by the fear of atomic catastrophe on the one hand and the fear of manmade poverty on the other.

We stand on the threshold of an Age of Abundance and Leisure, and the failure to pass through the doorway into the New Solar Civilization, the coming Sun-Power Age, is a failure of man's imaginative faculty.

This bears directly upon our subject, for the entire structure of the Paracelsian teaching and practice is founded upon one reason-shattering statement: *that by his god-like faculty of imagination, and by means of Resolute Imagination, man can accomplish all things.*[37]

From this point of view, it is clear that the exercise of the creative imagination is different from the operation of its admittedly close relative, escapist fantasy. The creative mind makes forays out of the universe of accepted reality into private worlds of the imagination with the object of bringing back a portion of what is discovered there and using the treasure-trove to enlarge an established vision. The escapists—of whom the anxiety-driven occult extremists form the best examples—become trapped in their imagined worlds, even assuming that they once wished to return and fructify the commerce of their fellow-beings. According to Henry Corbin—who, although he has written a book called *Creative Imagination in the Sufism of Ibn Arabi*, seems also to rely on Paracelsus for his treatment of the doctrine—imagination "induces knowledge."[38] It would follow that a wrong imagination induces wrong knowledge. The observation of history appears to bear this out.

In 1924 the Surrealists proclaimed that the imagination had been enslaved; and in 1968 Situationist slogans echoed them. Has our creative imagination been as stultified as irrationalists of all kinds tell us? It may be necessary to the dynamics of our inspiration that the heavenly city is kept perpetually before us. They have been ringing in the age of Aquarius since the last century. It may never come, but it is essential to keep ringing; for without that distant angelus life would be a sad and dreary place. The hope for something better, something different; the prodding, nudging, shoving force that irritates man to change by inducing visions of a reality other than that of the present: this might—in the imagination of this writer at least—be the explanation of all art, all religion, all philosophy. In the same way that the occult provides an indicator to illuminated politics, it may provide an index to the mechanics of inspiration. But if a temporary departure from the universe of agreed discourse is necessary for change, for progress, for the fertilization of life with new possibilities, the departure should be temporary only. Let anyone try as he likes to attain a more objective consciousness, a mystical synthesis, a union with God. But let it be a personal striving for achievement—as in the artist's search for inspiration—rather than an attempt to define the truth for all men. If this book demonstrates anything, it shows that the mechanics of political inspiration can go horrifyingly wrong, and that it is possible to end up in the universe peopled with the demons of *The Protocols of the Elders of Zion* as easily as in the realm of freedom after the withering away of the state.

This is no place to pronounce on the personal quests of the occultists. The impression remains that most become trapped in their private worlds and produce sadly little evidence of the power of imagination. There are too many attempts to destroy reason rather than to extend it. The historical development with which this book has been concerned contains the most inspiring and the most dangerous of visions. The flight from reason, by departing from certain fixed categories and opening the floodgates of the imagination, may contain within itself the potential for expanding the limits of human existence. It is more than likely that it will, instead—as has happened in the past—shipwreck man on a desert island separated from all that is humanly satisifying by an ocean of illusion. Unreason exists to be made reasonable, and reason to be extended by the discovery of possibilities initially outside its comprehension.

There may exist theories of the creative act that would throw light on the process of social imagination. There is one implied in the Book of Ecclasiasticus, where we are admonished to praise those who have *found out* musical tunes. Let us go consciously but cautiously in search of new possibilities. For every musical tune discovered, there are a hundred potential cacophanies. After all, it was the blast of trumpets that brought down the walls of Jericho.

1. See *The Occult Underground* for development of idea of crisis.
2. Wolfgang Treher, *Hitler, Steiner, Schreber* (Emmendingen-in-Breisgau, 1966). This is almost the only detailed discussion of the psychology of an occultist. I would not accept it all, but there is much of great interest (e.g., the passage on pp. 21 ff. on the significance of belief in the Cosmic Ice Theory).
3. Rees, *Hess*, p. 32.
4. Information from a former disciple of Crowley, based on a letter of Crowley. Note by Crowley in the front flyleaf of his copy of Hermann Rauschning, *Hitler Speaks*—annotations reproduced in the copy in the Warburg Institute Library.
5. From letter of Marthe Künzel to Aleister Crowley, copied in the above.
6. Crowley, *Liber L vel Legis*, in *The Equinox*, vol. I, no. 10, pp. 11 ff. and commentary in no. 7, pp. 384 ff.
7. Crowley's copy of Rauschning, pp. 141, 166, 209.
8. See Edith Birkhead, *The Tale of Terror* (London, 1921); Dorothy Scarborough, *The Supernatural in Modern English Fiction* (New York and London, 1917), especially pp. 199 ff., 280-83. See pp. 251-52 for a perceptive comment on the birth of science fiction; despite its irritating style, this is a useful study; Anton (Antal) Szerb, *Die Suche nach dem Wunder* (Amsterdam and Leipzig, 1938), pp. 37 ff.
9. On Esquiros and Péladan, see *The Occult Underground;* for Machen's mystical experiences, see his *Autobiography* (London, 1952), pp. 269-74 and Aidan Reynolds and William Charlton, *Arthur Machen* (London, 1963), pp. 78-79.
10. Eddison deserves a better critical press. His present popularity will no doubt produce some commentary. See Eddison's letters prefacing *A Fish Dinner in Memison* (New York, paperback ed., 1968) and *The Mezentian Gate* (London, 1965), pp. 127 ff. and "The Prose of E. R. Eddison" in *English Studies* (1949).
11. See Jane Harrison, *Reminiscences of a Student's Life* (London, 1925), *Alpha and Omega* (London, 1915), *Themis* (reprinted London, 1963).
12. Hope Mirrlees has remained elusive, and the American publisher of *Lud-in-the-Mist* was unable to trace her.
13. L. Sprague de Camp, *Science Fiction Handbook* (New York, 1953), p. 66. Even the improbable Dr. Hanish wrote an "Atlantean" fantasy—see his illiterate *Aetalonia, the Land of Lords* (n.p., 1937).
14. See *The Occult Underground*, pp. 83-84 and notes; De Camp, *S.F.*

Handbook, p. 50. Ballard's publications are elusive in Europe; see Kohler for an account of the *I AM* doctrine in France.

15. Patrick Moore, *Science and Fiction* (London, 1957), pp. 168-70; de Camp, *S. F. Handbook,* pp. 15 ff. for the effect of the Welles broadcast on science fiction.

16. De Camp, *S. F. Handbook,* pp. 17-19.

17. Elizabeth Donvan and Stephen Willey, "Some Attitudinal Consequences of Atomic Energy," in *Annals of the American Academy of Political and Social Science* (November 1953), pp. 108 ff. A useful summary: Sylvia Eberhart, "How the American People feel about the Atomic Bomb," in *Bulletin of the Atomic Scientists* (June 1947), pp. 146 ff.

18. See de Camp, *S. F. Handbook,* p. 129; John W. Campbell, "The Place of Science in Fiction," in Reginald Bretnor (ed.), *Modern Science Fiction* (New York, 1953), pp. 212 ff. and Kingsley Amis, *New Maps of Hell* (paperback ed., London, 1963), pp. 50-51.

19. See the foreword to A. E. van Vogt, *The World of Null-A* (London, 1970).

20. James Harvey Young, "Device Quackery in America," in *Bulletin of the History of Medicine* (March-April 1965), p. 159; Martin Gardner, *Fads and Fallacies,* pp. 346-47; on the Dean device, see Campbell's articles in *Analog* (British edition), October 1960, January and April 1961, and February 1962.

21. On the origins of Scientology, see de Camp, *S. F. Handbook,* pp. 93 ff. and Gardner, *Fads and Fallacies,* pp. 263 ff.; S. I. Hayakawa, "From Science Fiction to Fiction Science," in *ETC* (1951), p. 280.

22. L. Ron Hubbard, *Scientology, a History of Man* (London, 1954). There is a booklet describing the gadget, *The Book Introducing the E-Meter* (East Grinstead, 1966).

23. The primary "inside source" for Scientological activities is Cyril Vosper, *The Mind Benders* (London, 1971), which was recently the subject of a prolonged action in the British High Court. See also *Hansard* (6 March 1967) for a Parliamentary debate on the cult, and Donovan Bess, "Total Freedom and Beyond" in *The Nation* (29 September 1969).

24. Hubbard, *Dianetics: the Evolution of a Science* (Edinburgh, 1968), pp. 16-17.

25. King, *Ritual Magic,* pp. 162-65.

26. The science fiction camp maintained its distance from the saucer cults. See the entertaining picture of saucer fanatics in Fritz Leiber, *The Wanderer* (London, 1964); I. O. Reich, *Wilhelm Reich* (London, 1969), pp. 119 ff., 151; C. G. Jung, *Flying Saucers* (London, 1959), and B. le Poer Trench, *The Flying Saucer Story* (London, 1968), pp. 75 ff.; Gerald Heard, *The Riddle of the Flying Saucers* (London, 1950), p. 143.

27. See Adamski and Leslie Adams, *Flying Saucers have Landed* (London, 1953) and *Flying Saucer Farewell* (New York and London, 1962), for "Satan, Man of the Hour," pp. 175 ff.

28. See George King, *You are Responsible* (London, and L. A., 1961) and *Life on the Planets* (London, 1959); Patrick Moore, *Science and Fiction,* p. 132.
29. See W. R. Drake, "Count St. Germain," in *Flying Saucer Review* (March-April 1961) and Ivor Mackay, *UFOs and the Occult* in vol. XVI, no. 5.
30. Harold T. Wilkins, *Flying Saucers on the Moon* (London, 1954), p. 69.
31. Sam Moskowitz, *Explorers of the Infinite* (New York, 1963), p. 229.
32. De Camp. *S. F. Handbook,* pp. 92-93.
33. C. S. Lewis "On Stories," in *Of Other Worlds* (London, 1966), p. 16. Gerald Heard, "Science Fiction, Morals and Religion," in Bretnor, *S. F.,* pp. 244 ff.
34. See I. H. Visiak, *Life's Morning Hour* (London, 1968), pp. 211-12; Tom Wolfe, *Acid Test,* pp. 123, 147; Abbie Hoffman, *Revolution for the Hell of It,* p. 47; quote in *Middle Earth* (Iowa City, 2 October 1967), p. 2.
35. On the Inklings, see Jocelyn Gibb (ed.) *Light on C. S. Lewis* (London, 1965). On Charles Williams, see Mary Hadfield, *An Introduction to Charles Williams* (London, 1959); Anne Ridler (ed.), Charles Williams, *The Image of the City* (London, 1958). Barfield's approach is best seen in his *Romanticism Comes of Age* (London, 1944). Whereas the religious or occult attitude of the others is not in doubt, Tolkien's is less obvious. But see F. Léand, "L'Epopée religieuse de J. R. R. Tolkien" in *Études Anglaises* (July-September 1967).
36. Hitler, *Table Talk,* pp. 316-17.
37. Hargrave, *The Life and Soul of Paracelsus* (London, 1951), pp. 14-15.
38. Henri Corbin, *Creative Imagination in the Sufism of Ibn Arabi* (London, 1970), especially pp. 3, 179-82.

Index

Aberhart, William, 123, 125
Ackerman, Robert, 60
Adam, Juliette, 239, 244-46, 249
Adamski, George, 507
Adler, Victor, 45, 47, 350
Adyar (Theosophical center), 29, 36, 65, 180, 183, 263
Ahnenerbe, 313, 321-25
Aiken, John and Luisa, 447
Aksakov, Count Alexander, 159-60
Alioshin, Dmitri, 202-3
Alpert, Richard, 443, 445, 455, 456
A Modern Utopia (Wells), 92
Anderson, Margaret, 180, 429
Anesthetic revelation, 437-38
Anthroposophy: definition and origin, 66-70; examples of application, 71, 103; headway in Russian Symbolist circles, 164-66; schools sponsored, 404; storms of controversy, 71-72; unsuccessful overtures to German spiritual politics, 285-90
Antichrist, coming of: a main focus of late 19th century Russian mysticism, 153-154, 157; as Bolshevism, 197, 202-3; ties to Russian anti-Semitism, 238, 257-58, 260
Anti-Semitism, English, 128-34, 219-20, 226-33
Anti-Semitism, French, 214-19
Anti-Semitism, Russian: Glinka, 217, 222-25, 233-38; influence of Alfred Rosenberg in Germany, 293-96; part of religious revival, 260; use of swastika as racist symbol, 262-64
Anti-vivisection, 25
Apocalypse, 18, 41, 154, 157, 202-3, 260
Apostolic Congregation, 29
Aquarius, Age of, 48, 281, 453-55, 513-14

Ariosophy, 281
Arndt, Arthur, 424
Artamanen Bund, 318-19
Artaud, Antonin, 428, 431, 459, 467-68, 478
Arthur, Gavin (Chester Alan Arthur III), 454-55
Artman, Charles (pseud. Charlie Brown), 447-48
Aryan hero, 281
Aryanism, 32-33, 52, 69, 191, 195, 231, 262, ch. 5
Ashby, Thaddeus and Rita, 440
Ashebee, C. R., 105-6
Astrology, 15, 296-98, 311, 406-7
Atlantis fiction, 315-16, 327, 499, 500
Automatic writing, 392, 427-28

Baba, Sri Meher, 24, 104
Bachofen, J. J., 48, 49-50, 51, 52, 282-83, 285, 498
Back-to-the-land movements, 54-61, 83-103
Baden-Powell, Robert S. S.: *Scouting for Boys*, 88; 84, 86-88, 89
Badmaev, Shamzaran, 171, 173-74
Baha'i, 85
Bahr, Hermann, 45, 47, 57, 62, 422
Bai, Radda. *See* Blavatsky, Madame H. P.
Bailey, Alice, 396
Baker, Richard St. Barbe, 101-2, 117
Ball, Hugo, 58, 425-26
Balmont, Konstantin, 156, 165
Barrett, Francis: *The Magus*, 496
Bauhaus, 423-26, 429
Bayreuth, 44, 45, 46, 59
Beamish, Henry Hamilton, 130, 253, 290-91
Beat Underground: Age of Aquarius, 454-55; American phenomenon, 432-33; focuses of liberation, spiritual evolution, expanded consciousness, 456-58; hippies, 457-62; influence of Watts, 435; Krishna Consciousness, 452-53; messianic phase, 447-51; mysticism based economically on drugs, 436, 442; shifts in headquarter locations, 435-36; Yippies, 462-68
Beillis, Mendel, 258
Bellamy, Edward: *Looking Backward*, 103, 508
Belloc, Hillaire, 108, 115-16, 132
Bely, Andrei, 153, 155, 156, 164, 165, 166
Bennett, Allan (Bikkhu Ananda Metteya), 434, 448
Berdyaev, Nicholas, 156, 158, 164, 165, 177-78, 196, 358
Bergier, Jacques and Pauwels, Louis (*The Dawn of Magic*), 313
Bergmann, Emil, 31
Bergson, Henri, 17-18
Bernfeld, Siegfried, 350
Bernheim, Hippolyte, 353, 354-55
Bertine, Eleanor, 389
Besant, Mrs. Annie, 25, 36, 38, 40, 43, 67, 116, 183, 228, 281
Besobrasova, Olga, 247, 248
Bey, Omar al Raschid, 285-86
Bhagavad Gita, 43, 400
Bhaktivedanta, Swami, 452
Biogenetic law, 83-84, 104, 118, 404
Bisexuality, 361-62
Black Hundreds, the, 256-59
Black Ignatiev salon, 167, 171, 259
Blätter für die Kunst (George), 48, 49
Blavatsky, Madame H. P.: Atlantis speculation, 315, 499; anti-Semitism, 226-27, 229-33; application of ideas in Germany, 30, 277, 281-82, 317; hatred of Jesuits, 227-29; *Isis Unveiled*, 52, 160, 187, 227, 279; pen name "Radda Bai," 160; plagiarism of Jacolliot's works, 306; relationship with Glinka, 222-25, 244; scholarly leaning, 24; *The Key to Theosophy*, 160; *The Secret Doctrine*, 62, 227, 230, 233, 278, 281-82, 499; ties to Central European mysticism, 43, 46, 60, 66; ties to

pseudohistory, 69, 499; ties to Russian mysticism, 159, 160-63, 171, 186. *See also* Theosophical Society, Theosophy
Blok, Alexander, 155, 163
Blood, Benjamin Paul, 437-38
Boadicea Clubs, 192
Böhlau, Helen, 285
Böhme, Jacob, 32, 152, 332
Bolshevism-as-Antichrist, 197, 201-2
Boltwood, Charles, 123-24
Bombastus Works, 31-32
Bormann, Martin, 334
Bostunitch, Grigori (pseud. Schwartz-Bostunitch), 166, 266-67, 295-96
Brandler-Pracht, Karl, 289
Branford, Victor, 104
Braun, Philipp, 56
Breton, André, 427-28, 431, 468, 470
Breuer, Joseph, 356, 359, 375
Britons, The, 130-31
Brown, Norman O., 475-76
Bruckmann, Hugo and Elsa, 302
Brückner, Anton, 46
Brunton, Paul, 38
Bryussov, Valery, 155, 159, 163-64
Buber, Martin, 58, 277, 399
Buchman, Frank, 25-26, 336
Buchner, Eberhard, 29
Bull, Father Paul, 113
Buddhist Lodge, 435
Bund der Kämpfer für Glaube und Wahrheit, 31-32, 311
Burroughs, Edgar Rice, 499
Burroughs, William, 442
Butmi, G., 217, 253-54, 255, 256

Cabala, 219, 227, 247, 280, 372, 378, 460, 507
Caen, Herb, 451
Café Griensteidl (Megalomania Café), 45, 47, 62
Campbell, John W., 503-4
Caractacus Clubs, 192
Carpenter, Edward, 82, 106, 455

Carrére, Jean, 252-53
Cassaday, Neal, 445
Catholic Apostolic Church, 29, 73-74
Cayce, Edgar, 464
Celtic Nationalism, 95
Central European irrationalism: in Ascona, 57-61; in Dornach, 72; in Munich, 47-55; in Prague, 36-41; in Vienna, 41-47, 75-76
Chamberlain, Houston Stewart, 182, 294, 314, 317
Change-through-anxiety, 15-16
Charcot, Jean-Martin, 352-56
Cherep-Spiridovitch, General A., 295
Chesterbelloc, 115
Chesterton, Cecil, 132
Chesterton, G. K., 108, 115-16, 132, 133
Christ-as-rural-redeemer, 103
Christian fantasy literature, 510
Christian sectarianism, 15, 29, 31-34
Christian socialism, 105, 112-17, 119-28
Church Socialist League, 113
Ciurlionis, M. K., 425
Clarke, Arthur C., 502
Cohn, Norman, 133, 214, 217, 218, 238, 241, 245, 436
Cole, G. D. H., 109, 111-12
Colonies, German, 54-61
Conrad, Michael Georg, 48
Coomaraswamy, Ananda, 116
Cooper, David, 476-78
Cooper, Fenimore, 499, 511
Cosmic Circle of Munich, 47-55, 282
Cosmic Ice Theory, 326-31
Cosmobiology, 406-7
Cottingley, Yorkshire dale of, 24
Crane, Walter, 105
Crisis of Consciousness, 8-19
Crowley, Aleister: activities with drugs, 438-39; analyst of *Hitler Speaks*, 494-96; developer of magical anti-Semitism, 220; *The Book of the Law*, 494-96; theoretician of the magical powers of sex, 61; type of Symbolist magus, 25, 127

522   Index

Cycles of time, 18, 20

Däbritz, Max, 31
Dacqué, Edgar, 331-32, 406
Dada, 421-27
Daim, Wilfried, 301-2,
Das, Bhagavan, 116
Darré, Walther, 102
Davenport, Charles, 87
Davidson, Thomas, 103
Dean, Norman L., 503
Decadence. See Symbolism
Demant, Father, 124
Denson, Ed, 464
Derleth, Ludwig: *Rosenburg*, 54-55; 48, 52-55, 395-96
Deunov, Petr, 186-87, 267
Deutsches Ahnenerbe. See Ahnenerbe
Die Brücke, 422
Diederichs, Eugen, 277, 315, 358, 399
Diggers, the, 457-61
Dinter, Arthur: relationship with Nazis, 311; *Sin against the Blood*, 310-11, 318; *Sin against the Spirit*, 311
Dissident Christians, 29
Distributist League, 115-16
Dobrolyubov, Alexander, 158-59
Dods, John Bovee, 353, 354, 355
Doesburg, Theo van, 424
Doinel, Jules, 216, 220-21, 237, 243, 268
Dornach, 61, 72, 166
Doukhobors, 149, 174-75
Dostoievsky, Fëdor, 152, 153, 157, 174
Douglas, Major C. H., 112, 117, 119-21, 123, 131, 133-34, 193, 291
Douglasites, 112
Dowie, John Alexander, 29, 73, 74
Doyle, Arthur Conan, 24, 365-66, 405
Dream telepathy, 372-76
Drexler, Anton, 283, 298-99, 303
Driesch, Hans, 17
Dreyfus case, 132, 217-19, 262
Drumont, Edouard, 215-16, 221-22
Dubrovin, A., 256

Eastern cults: as manifestations of occultism, 15, 24-25; Bhagavad Gita, 43, 400; Emerald Tablet of Hermes Trismegistus, 152, 235; English Buddhist Society, 434-35; Freud's phallic religion, 380-82; Jung's ambivalence toward, 402; Kerouac's Zen-and-rosewater, 433-34; Krishna Consciousness, 452-53; Suzuki, 435; The Great Mother, 397; Theosophist promotion of Krishnamurti and Buddhism in general, 25, 67, 73, 348, 435; Ungern-Sternberg's Central Asian political mysticism, 198-201; Watts's central prominence in U. S. Buddhism, 434-35
Eckart, Dietrich, 132, 283-93, 296, 298, 301, 304, 309, 333, 334-35
Eckstein, Friedrich, 41-47, 60, 62, 75-76, 146, 350-52
Eddison, E. R., 497-98
Effront, Akim, 241
Ehrenfels, Christian von, 351
Elan vital, 17
Eliade, Mircea, 397
Eliot, T. S., 117, 124
Ellis, Havelock, 438
Emerald Tablet of Hermes Trismegistus, 152, 235
Empedocles, 45, 352
Encausse, Dr. Gérard (pseud. Papus), 53, 167-69, 170-71, 199, 220, 243, 244, 246, 248-55, 350
English Array, 134
English Buddhist Society, 434-35
English Mistery, 134
Ensor, Beatrice, 405-6
Eranos Conferences, 395-97
Erdsegen, 60
Ernst Ludwig, Grand Duke of Hesse, 184
Eugenics, American and British, 87-88, 193
Eunicke, Anna (Anna Steiner), 64-65

Eunicke, Emmy, 64-65
Eva C, 38, 367
Evans-Wentz, W. E., 18, 24, 398, 403
Evola, Giulio, 336, 421

Fabian Society, 103, 106-7
Fahey, Mgr. Denis, 134
Fairy lore, 18-19, 405
Fascism, 126-28, 335-36, 420
Fauth, Philipp, 326, 328
Fechner, Gustave, 357, 366
Feder, Gottfried, 283, 284, 291-93, 296, 298, 299, 304, 305-7, 309-10, 333
Ferenczi, Sandor, 369-70, 373
Ferrière, Adolphe, 406-7
Fertility research, 103
Figgis, Father J. N., 113
Filosofov, Dmitri, 155, 156
Fischer, Hanns, 329
Fleischauer, Ulrich, 130
Fliess, Wilhelm, 352, 356-61
Flight from reason, 20th century: as category of thought, 7-10; as outgrowth of crisis of consciousness, 10-19; as a response in Central Europe, ch. 1; as a response in Eastern Europe, ch. 3; as a response in England, ch. 2; as a response in German-speaking Europe, ch. 5; as a response of certain European scholars and early psychic researchers, ch. 6; as the reincarnation of esoteric Gnosticism, as the response of modern European art, as a response in American society, and as the widespread attempt to escape from matter, ch. 7; as third great historic outbreak of irrationalism in the West, as the construction of private worlds of reality in illuminated politics and fantastic literature, and as a potentially subhuman force, ch. 8; in the form of conspiracy-theory responses, ch. 4
Florensky, Pavel Alexandrovic, 159
Flying saucers, 506-8

Folk movement, German. *See Völkisch* occultism
Fordham, Montague: *Mother Earth*, 101; 104, 105, 108, 113, 116, 127, 193
Fourier, Charles, 327
Frank, Jacob, 146
Franz-Willing, Georg, 303
Freemasonry: as alleged agent of Judaism in a world conspiracy, 213-17, 241-42; as alleged co-conspirator, with Jesuits, against Bismarck, 33; as continuator of occult teachings, 29; as secular religion, 12; attributed "accomplishments," 236-37; connection to Gothic novel, 496
Friedenstadt, 55-56
Frere, W. H., 113
Freud, Anna, 373
Freud, Sigmund: association with Eckstein, 350-52; association with Fliess and biology-based theory of life, 357-61; association with the occultist Ferenczi, 369-70; constructor of a phallic religion, 380-81; conversion to belief in telepathic dreams, 373-74; disagreement with Jung, 384-85; essential elements of theoretical system, 374; in favor of alliance between psychoanalysis and occultism, 371-72; secularizer of rejected occult traditions, 382; studies of hypnosis, 354-56; *The Interpretation of Dreams*, 349, 350; theory of religion as delusional, 378; unsuccessful proselytizer of Jung to his sexual dogma, 363; Viennese associates and ideological sources, 350-52
Friedenberg, Raphael, 58
Fritsch, Theodore, 278
Froebe-Kapteyn, Olga, 395-96
Fuller, Major General, 127, 193, 220

Gahr, Karoline, 330-31, 332
Gahr, Otto, 331

Galouye, Daniel, 501
Galton, Francis, 87
Gapon, Father, 148, 259
Gardiner, Rolf, 95-103, 118-19, 127, 128, 403
Geddes, Patrick, 104, 139, 405
George, Henry, 103, 113
George, Stefan, 48-51, 58
Germanen Order, 296-98
German folk movement. *See Völkisch* occultism
German Union for the Abolition of Interest Slavery, 292
Gernet, Madame Nina de, 163
Gernsback, Hugo, 501, 508, 512
Gill, Eric, 116, 424
Ginsberg, Allen, 433, 442, 445-46, 452, 466
Ginungagapp, 21
Gladstone, William Ewart, 228-29
Glinka, Yuliana, 217, 222-25, 233, 238-39, 241-46, 248, 255, 265, 269
Gnosticism: alleged as one front for a Jewish conspiracy, 242-43; definition of, 418; influence on Jung, 386-87, 413; Jung's ambivalence toward, 402; principles found in *Stranger in a Strange Land*, 502; recurring secular expressions in 20th century, chap. 7
Godwin, William, 496
Goethe, Johann Wolfgang von, 62-63
Goetsch, George, 96
Goldberg, Oscar, 426
Goldschmid, Abraham, 232
Gold standard, 121
Goodman, Irene, 102
Gore, Bishop Charles, 113
Gorsleben, Rudolf John, 282
Gottesbund Tanatra, 32-33, 35, 311
Götze, Carl, 403
Graalhohe, 56
Graham, Bill, 446
Gräser, Karl, 58, 59
Great Mother, the, 397
Great Universal League, 253-54

Green Shirt movement, 122-23, 127
Greiner, Joseph, 299-302
Grith Fyrd camps, 118-19, 193
Grogan, Emmett, 459-60
Gropius, Walter, 423, 424
Guaita, Stanislas de, 168, 176, 437
Guénon, René, 470
Guild of Handicraft, 105-6
Guild socialism, English, 105-7, 113-19. *See also* Progressive Underground
Gurdjieff, Georgei Ivanovich, 25, 108, 121, 179-81, 267, 429, 431, 450
Gurus, 24-25

Häckel, Ernst, 65, 83-84
Haight-Ashbury, 435-36, 440, 444, 446, 447, 451, 454, 456-58
Hain, Friedrich (*Vater* Hain), 31, 35
Hall, G. Stanley, 83, 404
Hanisch, Otto (Ottoman Zar-adusht Ha'nish), 32, 55
Ha'nish, Ottoman Zar-adusht. *See* Hanisch, Otto
Harbottle (Hargrave), 91
Hare Krishna, 452
Hargrave, John: art work for *Everyman*, 104; change in emphasis of Kibbo Kift, 119, 121-22, 134, 135; enthusiasm for Seton's woodcraft and scouting ideals, 86-87, 117; formation and development of the Green Shirt Movement for Social Credit, 122-25, 127-28; formation and organization of the Kindred of the Kibbo Kift, 89-94, 102; German admiration for Hargrave's ideas, 100; *Harbottle*, 91; interest in eugenics, 87-88; *Lonecraft*, 87; offshoots of the Kift, 94-99; *Summertime Ends*, 122-23; *The Confession of the Kibbo Kift*, 93, 122; *The Great War Brings It Home*, 87, 90; thoughts of an illuminated politician, 512-13; *Young Winkle*, 91
Harmonious Development of Man, Institute for the, 180-81

Harrer, Karl, 298, 303
Harris, Thomas Lake, 190
Harrison, Jane, 498-99
Harte, Richard, 230-32, 354-55
Hartmann, Eduard von, 62, 349, 352, 378
Hartmann, Franz, 30-31, 36, 41, 46, 59-60, 66-67, 187, 279, 358, 377
Hauer, Jacob Wilhelm, 398-400
Hayakawa, S. I., 504
Heap, Jane, 180, 429
Heard, Gerald, 193, 443, 506, 509
Heimkehr, 40
Heinlein, Robert: *Stranger in a Strange Land*, 502
Heise, Karl, 318
Hellenbach, Baron, 42, 360
Hennings, Emmy, 58, 426
Herrmann, Albert, 316
Hess, Rudolf, 99, 307-8, 311, 319, 325, 493-94
Hesse, Hermann: *The Journey to the East*, 27; 27-28, 55, 58, 431, 443, 497
Heyer, Gustav, 395, 397, 398
Hielscher, Friedrich, 322, 323
Himalayan Masters, 25, 164
Himmler, Heinrich: believer in nature cures and reincarnation, 319; financier and publisher of "Germanic" researches by *SS*, 322; molder of *SS* training as blend of Social Darwinianism and the manipulation of religious symbols, using Catholic and Masonic organizational models, 320; official backer of the Cosmic Ice theory, 325; organizer of *SS* meetings at isolated sanctuaries with exotic guest lecturers, 320-21; theory of *SS* as spearhead of the Nordic bloodline throughout world, 320; wide reader in occult works, 318
Hippius, Zenaida, 155, 156, 165, 175, 196-97
Hitchcock, Ethan Allen, 390, 391
Hitler, Adolf: alleged by Joseph Greiner to be interested in Yoga and Indian fakirs, 300; arrival in Munich *völkisch* circles, 298-99; attitude toward religion, 334-35; backer of Cosmic Ice theory, 330-33; connections between Crowley's Thelema and Hitler's New Order, 493-96; denigrator of impractical aspects of *völkisch* movement, 303, 310; occult remarks, 312-13; private realities compared with those of Steiner, 493-94; probable influence of Schuler's mystic lectures, 302; ties with *völkisch* racism of Liebenfels and Eckart, 282-84, 301; reader of the occult periodical *Ostara*, 302; vegetarianism, 312
Hitler Speaks (Rauschning), 312-13, 494-96
Hitler, Steiner, Schreber (Treher), 493
Hobson, John A., 120-21
Hobson, S. G., 108-9, 110, 126, 193
Hofman, Dr. Albert, 439, 443-44
Hoffman, Abbie, 462-63, 465, 466, 467
Hoffman, Ida, 57-59, 60, 61
Holingshead, Michael, 442
Home, Daniel Dunglas, 159
Hörbiger, Hanns, 313, 325-33, 358
Hörbiger, Hanns Robert, 329
Howard, Ebeneezer, 103-4
Howard, Robert E., 499
Howe, Ellic, 297, 407
Howe, Eric Graham, 476
Hubbard, Al, 444
Hubbard, L. Ron, 504-6
Hübbe-Schleiden, Wilhelm, 30, 36, 66-67, 511
Hudson, Thomson Jay: *The Law of Psychic Phenomena*, 375, 377
Hulme, T. E., 108-9
Hulsenbeck, Richard, 425
Humphreys, Christmas, 435
Huxley, Aldous, 22, 439, 440, 441-42, 444
Huxley, Julian, 88-89
Huxley, T. H., 85, 347

Hypnosis, 352-56
Hypnotism, 353-54

Iliodor. *See* Trufanov, Sergei Mikhailovitch
Illuminated politics: anti-Semitic thread, 128-35; definition of, 13; Hitler's application, 493-96; in Britain, 82, 105-28; in Russia, 173-74; in some sorts of fascism, 420
Illuminati, 242-43
Imagination, 511-14
Imago, 374, 380
Integral life, 152-59
International Buddhist Society, 434
Irrationalism, collective. *See* Flight from reason, 20th century
Irrationalist literature of 20th century, 496-514
Irving, Edward, 29
Issacs, Rufus, 132
Isidore, Metropolitan of Kiev, 163
Isis Unveiled (Blavatsky), 52, 160, 187, 227, 279
Itten, Johannes, 423-24, 425-26
Ivanov, Michael, 186
Ivanov, Vyacheslav, 154, 155, 156, 164, 165, 177, 196

Jackson, Holbrook, 107, 119
Jacolliot, Louis, 306
James, William: anesthetic revelation and, 437, 441; correspondence with Lutoslawski, 189; *The Varieties of Religious Experience*, 438
Jeans, Sir James: *The Mysterious Universe*, 346
Jelikovsky, Vera, 161, 162, 163, 222
Jennings, Hargrave, 380-81, 391, 399
Jesuits, 33, 227-29, 280
Jewish Galicians, 146
Joachim of Flora, 95, 294
John of Kronstadt. *See* Sergiev, Father John
Joly, Maurice, 217, 248

Jones, Ernest, 350, 369, 373, 382
Judge, William Quan, 66, 278
Jung, Carl Gustav: admirer of Gustav Meyrink, 40; analysis of Freud's sexual theory, 379-80; analyst of interwar mood, 348; Biogenetic law, acceptance of, 404; comprehensive reader of occult literature, 38; connection with alchemy, 397-98; connection with Hauer, 398-400; contributor to the "Great Mother" Eranos Conference of 1938, 397; conversion to astrology, 414; culminating point of occult revival, 382; disagreement with Freud, 384-85; explanation of flying saucers, Mons Angels, Fatima, 506; ideas as seedbed for Nazi racism, 400-401; influenced by Gnostic illumination, 386-87, 394, 402, 413; influence on Hog Farm, 450; *Psychology and Alchemy*, 394; *Psychology of the Unconscious*, 385; racial aspects of his psychology, 400-401; *VII Sermones ad Mortuos*, 386; subject to paranormal experiences, 384; theoretician of man liberated from social restraints, 476; user of Freudian methods and occult sources, 385
Jungborn, 56

Kafka, Franz, 497
Kammerling, Brother, 29
Kandinsky, Vasili: friend of Mitrinović, 191; modern artist, 421-22, 424, 425; *On the Spiritual in Art*, 422
Karma, 68, 90, 280, 319, 405
Kassner, Rudolf, 182
Kellner, Karl, 31, 60, 61
Kemmerich, Max, 324, 358
Kemnitz, Mathilde von, 305-7, 309, 367
Kerning, J. B. (born Johann Baptist Krebs), 36-37, 41, 52
Kerouac, Jack, 433-34, 442
Kesey, Ken, 444-46, 450, 455, 471, 482-83, 509-10

Keynes, J. M., 121
Keyserling, Count Hermann, 181-85, 200, 348
Khan, Sufi Inayat, 24, 159
Khlysty, 150
Kierkegaard Søren, 22
Kilner, Walter, 15
Kindred of the Kibbo Kift, 89-99, 118-19, 121-23, 134-35, 404
King, George, 507
Kingsford, Anna, 394, 437
Kingsley, Charles, 124
Kinship in Husbandry, 102
Kipling, Rudyard, 87, 91
Kiss, Edmund, 327, 328
Kitson, Arthur, 121, 131, 133, 193, 512
Klages, Ludwig, 48-52, 54, 181, 282, 332, 397
Klee, Paul, 58, 424
Klein, Joshua, 59
Kleps, Art, 449-50
Klinckowstroem, Count Carl von, 368
Kogutzki, Felix, 62
Korzybsky, Count Alfred, 455, 502-3
Krafft, Karl Ernst, 406-7
Krieger, Wilhelm, 71
Krishna Consciousness, 452-53
Krishnamurti, Jiddu, 25, 67, 73, 348
Kundalini, 27
Künzel, Marthe, 494-95
Künzelmann, Dieter, 469
Kuttner, Henry, 509

Lafferty, R. A. 502
Laing, A. D., 476-78
Lane, Lt. Colonel A. H., 130
Langbehn, Julius, 277, 278, 293, 403
Lang, Edmund, 45, 62
Lang, Marie, 45-46, 62
Lanz, Adolf. *See* Liebenfels, Jörg Lanz von
Lawrence, D. H., 97
Lawson, Alfred William, 429-30, 512
Laurentians, 33, 35
Leadbeater, Bishop C. W., 25, 183

Leary, Timothy, 441-44, 446, 449, 452, 455, 465, 477
Le Bon, Gustave, 11-12, 14-15
Leibniz, Gottfried, 350-51
Leiningen-Billigheim, Carl, Graf zu, 45
Lenin, V. I., 121
Letchworth, 104, 405
Levi, Eliphas, 30, 152, 358
Lewin, Ludwig, 438
Lewis, C. S., 509, 510
Lhotzky, Heinrich, 56, 324, 404
Liberation, 419, 457-72. *See also* Progressive Underground
Liebault, Ambrose, 353, 354
Liebenfels, Jörg Lanz von (Lanz, Adolf), 55, 262, 280-82, 296, 301, 302, 358, 512
Linton-Orman, Rotha, 129
Lipiner, Siegfried, 45, 146, 204
Lipton. Lawrence, 464
List, Guido von, 262, 279-80, 296, 302
Little Eagle, 447
Lloyd George, David, 132
Lodge, Sir Oliver, 24
London Society for Psychical Research, 363-65
London (Theosophical center), 29, 36, 40
Lonecraft (Hargrave), 87
Looking Backward (Bellamy), 103, 509
Lorber, Jacob, 29-30, 32, 36, 277, 281
L'Ordre Nouveau, 194-95
Lorenz, Hermann, 33
Lovecraft, H. P., 500
LSD, 439, 441-47
Luddites, 81
Ludecke, Kurt, 331, 332
Ludendorff, General Erich von, 283, 304-7, 309
Ludovici, Anthony, 124
Lutoslawski, Wincenty, 187-91, 364
Lyman, Mel, 451
Lytton, Edward George Bulwer-: inspiration for Madame Blavatsky, 499; *Rienzi*, 44; *Zanoni*, 497

Index

McDiarmid, Hugh, 126, 128, 193
McDougall, William, 17, 387
MacKay, John Henry, 63-64
McLuhan, Marshall, 463
Macready, John, 317-18
"mad Rechenberg," 58-59
Maeztu, Ramiro de, 108-9, 126, 131, 277
Magic, 15, 17
Magus, 25, 28
Mahler, Gustav, 45
Mailer, Norman: "The White Negro," 432, 434
Maitland, Edward, 43, 394, 437
Malevich, Kasimir, 425
Mammonism, 292
Mann, Charles Holbrook, 389-90
Mann, Kristine, 388-94, 397
Mann, Thomas, 22, 53
Marc, Franz, 422, 475
Marconi scandal, 132
Marcuse, Herbert, 472, 475-76
Maritain, Jacques, 116
Markov, Nicholas Yevgenievich (Markov II), 256, 264-65, 294, 295
Marsden, Victor, 130, 295
Martinism, 168, 242-43, 253-55
Massingham, H. J., 101-2, 105, 116, 127
Master Leonhard (Meyrink), 39-40
Master race. *See* Nazi German regime, *Völkisch* occultism
Materialism, 8, 26-27, 174-78, 202-3
Mathers, S. L. Macgregor, 429
Mayreder, Rosa, 45, 47, 62
Mazdaznan, 32-33, 35, 55, 311
Mein Kampf, 301, 304, 312
Meister Eckhart, 30, 277, 317, 332, 333
Men, Beasts and Gods (Ossendowski), 198-99
Men of the Trees, 101-2
Mental telepathy, 369-75
Merezhkovsky, Dmitri: as writer, 294; influenced by Symbolists, 156; occult influences on, 164, 165; *Peter and Alexis*, 156; political influences on, 196-97; religious consciousness, 158, 164, 179, 266, 315; *The New Way*, 157
Merezhkovskys, the, 156-57, 179
Méry, Gaston, 215-16, 252, 267
Mesmeric movement, 353-56
Mestrović, Ivan, 191
Metteya, Bikkhu Ananda. *See* Bennett, Allan
Meyrink, Gustav (born Gustav Meyer): *The Golem*, 39, 146; 36-41, 146, 221
Miller, Henry, 431-32, 476
Minsky, Nicolai (born N. M. Vilenkin), 155, 164, 165
Mintslova, Alexandra, 165-66
Miracle literature, 497
Mirlees, Hope, 498-99
Mitrinović, Dmitri, 187, 191-95, 435
Modern art, 420-28
Moeller van den Bruck, Arthur: *The Third Reich*, 293-94
Mona Lisa's Mustache (Robsjohn-Gibbings), 420
Mond, Sir Alfred, 130, 291
Mondrian, Piet, 424
Monism, 65-66, 317, 336
Monks, Russian Orthodox, 149, 171
Montenegrins, 167, 168, 252
Montessori, Maria, 403, 405, 406
Monte Verita: Swiss colony with a floating collection of would-be world saviors, revolutionaries, tired intellectuals, magicians, and degenerates, 57-61; influx of Tolstoyans, 174; Baltic mystics, 181; German influx, 277; new phase with Jungian spirit in 1926, 396
Moore, Patrick, 500
Moral Reparmament (MRA), 25-26
Moricand, Conrad, 432
Morris dancing, 95, 101, 114, 119
Morris, William, 105
Morsier, Emilie de, 223, 244, 245, 246-47
Moseley, Oswald, 126-28, 129, 220
Mother Earth (Fordham), 101
Mr. R, 41

Mühle, Feder, 32
Muir, Edwin and Willa, 191, 194
Müller, Gretchen, 33
Müller, Johannes, 56-57, 59, 70, 404
Mumford, Lewis, 105
Munch, Edvard, 422
Munich Cosmics, 47-55, 282
Munitions of War Act of 1915, 110
Mussolini, Benito, 122
Myers, Frederic, 364-65, 366
Mystical anarchism, 196
Mystical logic, 14-15
Mystic Petersburg, 167, 179

Napoleon, defeat of, 9
National Guilds league, 109, 111-12
National Mobilization demonstration, 462
National Socialist German Workers party, 298, 303
Nature's Finer Forces, 37
Nazi German regime: formed in part on illuminated *völkisch* movement, 32-35, 308-9; formed in part on organic life centers and the ignorance-is-bliss understanding of Christianity they taught, 54-61; official newspaper in Munich, 280; the mystic Balt Keyserling its self-proclaimed prophet, 185; transformer of underground to establishment. See also Ahnenerbe; Aryan hero; Central European Irrationalism; Christian sectarianism; Colonies, German; Crowley, Aleister; Dinter, Arthur; Eckart, Dietrich; Feder, Gottfried; *Gottesbund Tanatra*; Häckel, Ernst; Hesse, Hermann; Hess, Rudolf; Himmler, Heinrich; Hitler, Adolf; Hörbiger, Hanns; Jung, Carl Gustav; Keyserling, Count Hermann; Nordic Faith movement; Pietism; Rauschning, Hermann; Rosenberg, Alfred; Scheubner-Richter, Max Erwin von; Secular religion; Strömer von Reichenbach, Freiherr; Swastika; *The Protocols of the Learned Elders of Zion; The Third Reich; Thule Bund;* Treher, Dr. Wolfgang; *Völkisch* occultism
Neill, A. S., 405, 406, 472
Neurasthenic society, 22-23, 47-55, 57-61
Neuroses, sexual basis of, 349
"New Age," 28, 54-61
New Britain movement, 192-94
New Education movement, 403-7
New towns. See Town planning
Nicholas and Alexandra, 167-74, 251, 259-64
Nietzsche, Friedrich Wilhelm, 45, 49, 51, 63, 154, 327
Nihilism, 12
Nikon, Patriarch, 149
Nilus, Sergei, 217, 241-42, 252, 254, 255, 259-60, 294
19th/20th century irrationalism, 490
Noel, Conrad, 113-14, 175
Nordic Faith movement, 399-400
Noyes, John Humphrey, 190

Odic force, 15, 279, 472
Oedenkoven, Henri, 57-61, 67
Olcott, Henry Steele, 24, 43, 65, 160, 224, 244, 278, 353
Old Believers (*Raskolniki*), 149, 153
Oliphant, Laurence, 190
Oliver, Frederick Spencer, 499-500
Olson, Charles, 442
On the Spiritual in Art (Kandinsky), 422
Oppenheimer, George, 53
Optina Monastery, 149
Orage, A. R., 107-8, 119-21, 180, 191-93, 447
Ordens Tempel der Ostens (Order of the Templars of the Orient; also, OTO), 59-61, 67, 68, 319
Order of the New Templars, 280-81
Order of Woodcraft Chivalry, 85-87, 404

Ordre Kabbalistique de la Rose-Croix, 168, 176, 247
Organic life colonies, 54-61
Orlovsky, Peter, 452
Orthodox spirituality. *See* Slav mysticism
Osmond, Humphrey, 439
Ossendowski, Ferdinand: life and ideas of, 198-201, 203-4; *Men, Beasts and Gods*, 198-200
Ouspensky, P. D., 180, 348, 429
Owsley, 444, 445, 446
Ozerova, Helena, 241, 247

Pahnke, Walter, 442
Palmer, Raymond, 508
Papus. *See* Encausse, Dr. Gérard
Paracelsus, 31-32, 317, 319, 512, 513
Parapsychology. *See* psychical research
Pares, Bernard, 156
Parsifal (Wagner), 44, 46
Parsons, Jack, 505-6
Paul, Leslie, 92, 94, 99-100, 118
Paulus, Frau Dr., 59
Pauwels, Louis and Bergier, Jacques (*The Dawn of Magic*), 313
Pearson, Karl, 85
Peddie, J. Taylor, 127
Péladan, Joséphin, 53, 283, 497
Penty, Arthur J., 106-7, 110, 111, 112, 113, 116-17, 119, 126, 128, 178
People-as-divine, 12, 502
Periodicity, 357-61
Philaretes, 188-89
Phillippe, Monsieur, 167-71, 240-43, 248-52
Philosophy of the Unconscious (Hartman), 349
Picasso, Pablo, 428
Pietism, 29
Pike, Bishop James, 448
Polish messianism, 147, 153, 181-82, 189-91
Portsmouth, Lord, 102-3
Pound, Ezra, 108, 117

Prague, 36-41
Prel, Baron Carl du: association with Schrenck, 367; early codifier of opinion on psychical evolution, 17; *Spiritualism*, 318; *The Philosophy of Mysticism*, 349-50
Prem, Sri Krishna, 443
Private realities, 493-96
Progressive underground: as a foundation of English youth movements, 89; as a preparation for the coming new age, 54-61; as opposition to materialism and individualism, 82; embodied in American beat underground, 432-36, 457-68, 484; embodied in English Christian wing of socialism, 105-7, 113-17; embodied in English pagan "natural man" wing of socialism, 117-19; embodied in New Education movement, 403-7; headquartered in England at Letchworth, 104; inclusion, as contemporary elements, 419; incorporation of LSD, 439-41; incorporation of occult art, 422; in form of occult-oriented Eranos Conferences, 395-97; in form of "spiritual evolution" in the educational progress of children, 403-6; Vienna connection, 44-45
Prohaszka, Ottokar, 332-33
Pseudohistory, 499
Psychical research, 364, 393
Psychoanalysis, 349, 352, 371-72
Psychology and Alchemy (Jung), 394
Psychology of the Unconscious (Jung), 385
Purdom, Charles, 104, 193
Pureshkevich, Vladimir Mitrofanovich, 256, 259, 262, 264

Quaker religion, 85-86, 135
Quisling, Vidkun, 366

Râ, Bô Yin (Joseph Schneiderfranken), 32, 35, 41, 297

Index 531

Race-betterment. *See* Eugenics
Ramsay, Professor William, 437
Raskolniki. *See* Old Believers
Rasputin, Grigory, 162, 171-73, 199, 259-61, 264-65, 294
Rasputin, Matriona, 263-65
Ratchkovsky, Pyotr Alexandrovich, 239-42, 245, 248-50, 253-54
Rationalism, 8, 490
Rauschning, Hermann: *Hitler Speaks*, 312-13, 494-96
Rayleigh, Lord, 42
Realpolitik, 12, 276, 430, 457
Reckitt, Maurice, 109, 112, 115
Reich, Wilhelm, 472-74, 475, 506
Reichenbach, Baron, 15, 279, 472
Rejected knowledge: as definition of occultism, 15; influx to West via post-1917 Russian emigrés, 178-85; U. S. versions of, 429; *See also* Flight from reason, 20th century
Relativity, Einstein's general theory of, 346-47
Religion and Art (Wagner), 44
Remizov, Alexey, 164
Renaissance/Reformation outbreak of irrationalism, 490. *See also* Flight from reason, 20th century
Reuss, Theodore, 59-61, 67
Reventlow, Countess Fanny von, 48, 54, 58
Rhine, Dr. J. B., 365-66
Richet, Charles, 161, 244, 364, 367
Richter, Hans, 421, 425, 426, 427
Rienzi (Lytton), 44
Ringbom, Sixten, 421-22
Rittelmeyer, Friedrich, 69, 70
Rivers, Elfrieda, 449
Robsjohn-Gibbings, T. H., 420
Roe, Sir A. V., 127
Rohl, Fritz, 58
Röhm, Captain Ernst, 303, 317
Romney, Hugh, 450
Rosenberg, Alfred: Atlantis speculation, 315-16; Baltic refugee from Bolshevists who brought anti-Semitic ideas to Munich, 283, 284, 293-96; condemnation of Roman Catholicism, 283, 316; definition of German mystic as supreme hero, 317; definition of Jew as creature of the world, 347; intervention with *SS* for Johannes Müller, 57; survivor of transition of Nazis from underground to establishment, as Russian "expert" and ideologist, 304, 309, 313-18, 333; *The Myth of the 20th Century*, an occult racial history, 314-15; the *Weltdienst*, 130
Rosicrucianism, 68-70, 93, 167, 242-43, 497
Rosenburg (Derleth), 54-55
Rothschild, Nathan Meyer, 231-32
Rozanov, Vasily, 155, 157-58, 159, 172, 204, 214, 258, 379
Rubin, Jerry, 461-63, 466
Rural Organization Council, 100
Rural Reconstruction, 98-100
Ruskin, John, 105-6
Russian Orthodox Church, 147-54, 157, 176, 257
Rüttinger, Julius, 310

Sainte-Marie, Buffy, 448
Saint-Yves d'Alveydre, Joseph-Alexandre, 168, 200, 236, 238, 243, 287
Sandoz Corporation, 439, 444
Sanderson, William, 134
Savinkov, Boris: life as terrorist, 196-98; *The Black Horse*, 197; *The Pale Horse*, 197
Scheubner-Richter, Max Erwin von, 283, 296, 309
Schloss Elmau, 56-57
Schloss Mainberg, 56
Schmidt, Anna, 153
Schmitz, Oskar, 54, 397
Schneiderfranken, Joseph. *See* Râ, Bô Yin
Schoenmaekers, M. H. J., 424

School of Wisdom, 184-85
Schrenk-Notzing, Albert Freiherr von, 38, 306, 366-68, 395
Schröer, Karl Julius, 62
Schuler, Alfred, 48-52, 53, 54, 282, 302-3, 332
Schuré, Edouard, 244
Schutz, Hermann, 59
Schwabing, 47-48, 53, 54, 282, 283-84
Science fiction, 496-513
Scientology, 502-6
Scouting for Boys (Baden-Powell), 88
Scultetus, Hans Robert, 328-30
Search for otherness, 509-11
Sebottendorff, Rudolph Freiherr von, 38, 283, 296-97, 310, 512
Sectarianism. *See* Christian sectarianism
Secular religion, 10-12
Seiling, Max, 166, 288-89
Self-realization, 184
Seligman, Kurt, 431
Sergiev, Father John (John of Kronstadt), 147-48, 167, 170, 172, 199, 247, 257
Servile state, 115
Seton, Ernest Thompson, 83-85, 86, 87
VII Sermones ad Mortuos (Jung), 386
Sexual basis of neuroses. *See* Freud
Shapira, Sam, 447
Sharp, Cecil, 95, 114
Shaver, Richard, 508
Shaw, George Bernard, 108
Shestov, Leo (born L. I. Schwarzmann), 178-79
Shiel, M. P., 511
Shirley, Ralph, 220
Shivananda, Swami, 452
Sievers, Wolfram, 322-23
Silberer, Herbert, 380, 391
Silesius, Angelus, 30, 41, 285, 317
Simony, Oscar, 42
Sin Against the Blood (Dinter), 310-11, 318
Sin Against the Spirit (Dinter), 311
Sinnett, A. P., 43, 62, 187

Situationist International, 468-70
Sivers, Marie von, 65, 67, 164-65
Skoptsy, 150
Slade, Henry, 42, 160, 360, 366
Slav mysticism, 145-54, 171, 181, 185
Slavophilism, 153, 168, 186, 283
Snyder, Gary, 433-34, 442, 452, 466
Social Credit: as part of Christian wing of the progressive underground in England, 105; connection to Kibbo Kift, 119-23; connection to fascist and other leading figures, 124-28; connection to Gurdjieff, 180-81; continuation into the 1930s, 117; expression of illuminated politics, 420; proposed by Major C. H. Douglas in *New Age*, 112
Social Darwinianism, 16, 18, 83, 320
Socialism, 12
Social relevance, 117-19, 121-23
Sociological Society, 104
Soddy, Frederick, 121
Sokolov, Nicholas, 264
Solar Men, 124
Soloviev, Boris, 263-65
Soloviev, Mikhail, 156
Soloviev, Vladimir Sergeivitch, 151-54, 159, 161, 177, 260
Soloviev, Vsevolod, 161-62, 223-26, 238, 243, 244-46
Sorel, Georges, 463
Soupault, Philippe, 428
Spaulding ("Dr. Spaulding"), 444
Spengler, Oswald, 18-19, 315, 423
Spiritual development, 15, 17-19, 55
Spiritualism, 14-15, 17, 23-24, 30, 159-64, 347
Springhead, 97-98, 100, 403
Spirit drawing, 392-93
SS, 319-25
Stanley, Augustus Owsley, III. *See* Owsley
Stapledon, Sir George: *The Land, Now and Tomorrow*, 102
Star in the East, 25, 67, 73
Steicher, Julius, 311

Steindamm, Frau, 59
Steiner, Rudolf: Anthroposophy and Rosicrucianism as preached by, 41; Atlantis literature, 315, 499; Bostunitch and, 267; eclecticism of ideas, 68-72, 193; emergence of "Monism and Theosophy" as basic spiritual science lecture, 66; esoteric farming, 103, 146; influence of Goethe on, 62-63, 68, 72; influence on Kandinsky, 422; influence on Russian Symbolist circles, 164-66; leading exponent of occult ideas of education, 404; objective of making the unconscious conscious, 349; origin and personal life, 61-65; political efforts, 286-90, 298; private realities compared to those of Hitler, 493-94; split with Theosophists, 67; transformation from liberal academic to mystical lecturer, 61-65. *See also* Anthroposophy
Stekel, Wilhelm, 368, 372-76, 405
Stepanov, Filip, 239, 241, 242, 254
Stoddart, Miss C. M., 219-20, 236
Storrington Document, 109
Stranger in a Strange Land (Heinlein), 502
Stranniki, 149
Strömer von Reichenbach, Freiherr, 324-25, 358
Struvit (Ulex), 39
Suggestion, 353
Sukhotin, Alexei, 239, 241, 242, 254
Summertime Ends (Hargrave), 122-23
Sun-Wheel, 315, 399
Surrealism, 427-28, 468, 513
Suzuki, D. T., 398, 435
Swastika, 261-64, 280, 282, 297
Swedenborgian New Church, 28-29, 277, 388-94
Swoboda, Dr. Herrmann, 361-63
Symbolic Serpent, 249
Symbolism, 150, 154-59, 164, 421
Symonds, John Addington, 437

Tarnhari, the exalted, 280
Tawney, R. H., 109, 112
Taxil, Léo, 216
Taylor, G. Stirling, 107, 111, 131
Tao, 27
Tchelitchev, Pavel, 431
Templeton, Herbert O., 473
The Book of the Law (Crowley), 494-96
The Confession of the Kibbo Kift (Hargrave), 93, 122
The Dawn of Magic (Pauwels and Bergier), 313
The Electric Kool-Aid Acid Test (Wolfe), 482-83
The Golem (Meyrink), 39, 146
The Great War Brings It Home (Hargrave), 87, 90
The Guildsman, 110, 111, 121
The Hebrew Talisman, 230-33
The Interpretation of Dreams (Freud), 349, 350
The Journey to the East (Hesse), 27
The Key to Theosophy (Blavatsky), 160
The Land, Now and Tomorrow (Stapledon), 102
The Law of Psychic Pheonomena (Hudson), 375
The Lord of the Rings (Tolkien), 510
Thelema, Law of, 495
The Magic Mirror, 37
The Magus (Barrett), 496
The Monist, 187
The Mysterious Universe (Jeans), 346
The Myth of the 20th Century (Rosenberg), 314-15
The New Age, 107-8, 112, 116, 119, 122, 191
The New Era, 405
Theosophical Lodge of the Blue Star, 36-38, 40-41, 43
Theosophical Society: anti-Semitism, 226-27, 229-33, 248; as pillar of 19th-century revival of the occult, 25, 73; establishment in Germany, 30; influence in America, 429; influence in

Germany, 29-31; influence in Holland, 424; influence in New Education movement, 404-6; influence in Prague, 36; influence in Russia, 160-65; propaganda agent in England for Buddhism, 435. *See also* Theosophy; Blavatsky, Madame H. P.

Theosophical Society of Vienna, 37, 41, 43-47

Theosophy: as manifestation of occultism, 15, 17; definition of, 66; doctrine of spiritual development, 17; influence on Eranos Conferences, 396; links to English guild socialism, 108, 113, 116, 180; links to hypnotism, 353-54; links to *völkisch* movement, 277-78; predicted future, 183; promoter of Hindu messiah, 25, 73; transmitter of *The Protocols of the Learned Elders of Zion* to Russia, 219. *See also* Theosophical Society; Blavatsky, H. P.

The Patriot, 129

The Philosophy of Freedom (Steiner), 64

The Philosophy of Mysticism (Prel), 349-50

The Protocols of the Learned Elders of Zion (anonymous): background, character, growth in influence, 213-18; European transmission and influence on imperial Russia, 238-42, 244-45, 247-57, 260; example of liberated imagination gone wrong, 514; read by Rosenberg, 294; use as propaganda in Russian military, 265-66. *See also* Anti-Semitism (English, French, Russian); *The Secret of the Jews*

The Rise of the West (Macready), 317-18

The Secret of the Jews, 233-39, 247-48

The Secret Doctrine, 62, 227, 230, 233, 278, 281-82, 499

The Servile State (Belloc), 115

The Third Reich (Moeller van den Bruck): 293-94

The Tibetan Book of the Dead, 25

The Varieties of Religious Experience (W. James), 438

The War of the Worlds (Wells), 500

"The White Negro" (Mailer), 432, 434

Thousand Year Reich, 18, 33, 454

Thule Bund, 296-98, 307, 310

Time, 16-20

Tolkien, J. R. R.: *The Lord of the Rings*, 510

Tolstoy, Count Leo, 157, 174-75

Tolstoy, Sophie, 152

Town planning, 103-4

Toynbee, Arnold, 190

Treher, Wolfgang: *Hitler, Steiner, Schreber*, 493-94

Trocchi, Alexander, 469

Trufanov, Sergei Mikhailovitch (pseud. Iliodor), 148-49, 257-58, 259

Trevelyan, Katherine, 95

Trützschler, Fritz von, 310

Turgenev, Asya, 165, 166

Tzara, Tristan, 425, 427

Ulex. See Struvit

Unconscious, 347-53, 374

Unger, Carl, 71, 288

Unger, Erich, 426

Ungern-Sternberg, Roman Feodorovich von, 198-204

Union of the Russian People, 254, 256-59

Usury, 115-16

Van Vogt, A. E., 502, 503-4

Vaughan Williams, Ralph, 95

Vedanta, 192

Vegetarianism, 25, 29, 44, 55, 82, 299, 312, 422

Vegetarian socialism, 57-61

Verdin, George, 176

Vienna, 41-47, 75-76

View, 430-32

Villiers, Viscount Serge d'Hotman de, 176

Index   535

Vitalism, 17-19
Vladimir, Metropolitan of Moscow, 257
Vogl, Pastor Carl, 221
Vogüé, Count Melchior de, 152, 174
Voigt, Heinz, 327, 328
Völkisch occultism: academic respectability from the Jung-endorsed Hauer study of the Bhagavad Gita, 400; drift to racial purity and pagan idealism, 51-57, 278; ground-breaker for Nazi rise to power in Germany, 32-35; influence on Weininger, 361-62; leading figures in pre-Nazi Germany, 276-82; snuffed out after Nazi rise to power, 310-11. *See also* Nazi German regime
Völkischer Beobachter, 280, 291
Volynsky, A. L. (born A. L. Flekser), 155
Vyrubova, Anna, 173-74, 263, 265

Wagner, Richard: master of German idealistic Underground, 43-44; *Religion and Art*, 44
Walden, Sophia, 216
Watts, Alan, 434-35, 442-43, 444, 447, 466-67, 476
Watts, L. W., 435
Webster, Nesta, 92, 129, 131-33
Weinfurter, Karel, 37
Weininger, Otto, 361-62
Weissenberger, 33-35, 311
Weissenberg, Joseph, 33-34, 56
Wells, H. G.: *A Modern Utopia*, 92; links with Kibo Kift, as author of utopian literature, 89, 92; *The War of the Worlds*, 500
Welles, Orson, 500
Welwyn, 104, 110
Westlake, Aubrey, 85, 87, 103, 118, 124
Westlake, Ernest, 85-86, 87
Wewelsburg, 320-21
Wheeler, Howard, 452-53
Wilhelm, Richard, 397, 406
Wilkinson, John Garth, 391-93
Williams, Charles, 510

Williamson, Henry, 121
Wilson, Edward Alexander, 193
Winstanley, Gerard, 459
Wirth, Hermann, 316, 321-22, 327, 358
Witte, Count Sergei Yulievich, 159, 238, 239-40, 245, 248, 250, 254, 256, 259
Wolf, Hugo, 45-46
Wolfe, Tom: description of Kesey, 445; *The Electric Kool-Aid Acid Test*, 482-83
Wolfskehl, Karl, 48-50, 58
Wolkonsky, Princess Olga, 152, 244
Woodcraft Chivalry, Order of. *See* Order of Woodcraft Chivalry
Woodcraft Folk, 94
World's Parliament of Religions, 187
Wotan, 400
Wunderapostel Hauser, 39
Wüst, Walter, 322, 323, 324

Yarker, John 59-60
Yeats, William Butler, 18
Yippie movement, 462-67
Young, George, 111, 131-32
Young Winkle (Hargrave), 91
Youth movements, English, 83-99, 117-19, 121-23, 135
Yussupov, Prince Felix, 260-61, 265

Zen, 433-35, 481
Zenithism, 192
Zero A. D. Crisis, the, 490
Zöllner, Professor, 42, 366
Zossimova Hermitage, 149